Neo-Confucian Education

STUDIES ON CHINA

A series of conference volumes sponsored by the Joint Committee on Chinese Studies of the American Council of Learned Societies and the Social Science Research Council.

Neo-Confucian Education: The Formative Stage

EDITED BY

Wm. Theodore de Bary
and
John W. Chaffee

CONTRIBUTORS

Bettine Birge • Peter K. Bol • John W. Chaffee •
Wing-tsit Chan • Ron-Guey Chu • Wm. Theodore de Bary •
Patricia Ebrey • Robert Hymes • M. Theresa Kelleher •
Thomas H. C. Lee • Brian McKnight • Tu Wei-ming •
Monica Übelhör • Linda Walton • Pei-yi Wu • Chün-fang Yü •
Erik Zürcher

UNIVERSITY OF CALIFORNIA PRESS
Berkeley   Los Angeles   London

*This volume was sponsored by the Joint Committee on Chinese
Studies of the American Council of Learned Societies and the Social Science
Research Council, with funds provided by the
National Endowment for the Humanities and the Ford Foundation.*

University of California Press
Berkeley and Los Angeles, California
University of California Press, Ltd.
London, England
© 1989 by
The Regents of the University of California

Library of Congress Cataloging-in-Publication Data

Neo-confucian education: the formative stage / edited by Wm. Theodore
   de Bary and John W. Chaffee; contributors, Bettine Birge . . . [et al.].
   p. cm. — (Studies on China; 9)
   Includes index.
   ISBN 0–520–06393–7 (alk. paper)
   1. Education—China—History—To 1912.   2. Neo-Confucianism.
3. Chu, Hsi, 1130–1200.   I. De Bary, William Theodore, 1918–
II. Chaffee, John W.   III. Birge, Bettine.   IV. Series.
LA1131.8.N46   1989
370'.951—dc19   88–24952
                                                                     CIP

Printed in the United States of America
1 2 3 4 5 6 7 8 9

11-15-89

This volume is dedicated to Wing-tsit Chan in acknowledgment of his leadership of the 1982 conference, in tribute to his many distinguished contributions to the study of Chu Hsi and Neo-Confucianism, and in celebration of his eighty-eighth birthday.

CONTENTS

PREFACE

In the early days of the modernization of East Asia, Neo-Confucianism, as the shared ideology of East Asian countries in the premodern period, was often held responsible for the purported intellectual, political, and social failings of traditional societies in the nineteenth century. Today, as the rapid success at modernization of many East Asians has been compared to the slowness of other underdeveloped countries, analysts have begun pointing to the common culture of China, Japan, Korea, and overseas Chinese communities as a positive, rather than negative, factor in the East Asian peoples' receptivity to new learning, their disciplined industriousness, and their capability for economic and cultural development. Thus, modern East Asia is spoken of as "post-Confucian," signifying that the shared legacy of Confucianism is a defining characteristic of these modernizing nations.

At the same time, some of the East Asian nations most successful in achieving economic miracles, whether they attribute their success to underlying traits of Confucian culture or not, ask themselves if something of great social and moral value in that culture is being eroded by industrialization and social change. This concern is illustrated by Singapore's inviting Chinese-American scholars to serve as consultants on what might be done to restore Confucian ethical teachings in the home and school and by three conferences on Confucianism held on the Mainland between 1981 and 1986.

Yet most traditional ways have been disrupted for at least a century, and Western-educated Chinese (or other East Asians) have often lost touch with the cultures from which they emerged. For them to address the problem of tradition's place in the modern world, with the same assurance they would bring to the solution of professional and technical problems, requires a special effort consciously to reexamine and reevaluate the past. There is no ready-made answer, no packaged prescription, to meet this need.

Among those favorably disposed to a revival of Confucianism today are regimes that, if they are strong enough to provide the security and stability in which economic development can take place, tend to be conservative if not authoritarian. They look to Confucianism as a possible bulwark against unwanted change. Theirs is a one-sided view of tradition, but one shared with many progressives who oppose Confucianism, believing that it does indeed stand for the preservation of the status quo. Tradition is equated with stability and continuity, modernity with rapid change.

Tradition is also thought of as simple—the simple life, uncomplicated times, the old-fashioned virtues. It is what one learned at mother's knee before mother went off to work in an office. Or, among the educated, it is what one finds in the *Analects* of Confucius, which can be interpreted by the liberal-minded to produce a convenient blend of old and new. Yet neither of these simplistic notions takes into account millennia of human experience in East Asia, during which successive generations tried to live by Confucian principles in complex and conflicted situations not wholly unlike our own. What has dropped out of the picture then is the actual dynamic of traditional culture, including the fact that tradition incorporates change and even the experience of earlier attempts to "modernize."

In recent years much progress has been made in the study both of Neo-Confucianism and of the social history of late Imperial China, but so far little has been done to link the two through the systematic study of ideas and institutions in their historical interaction. Now with a better understanding of the continuing vitality of Neo-Confucian thought, and a deeper awareness of how broadly it entered into the educational processes of premodern East Asia, the time has came to reexamine what previously was assumed to be simply rote learning of age-old, and presumably outworn truths.

Past studies of traditional education have too often been based on the twin assumptions of Asian backwardness and Western superiority, and their goal was simply to show how traditional attitudes and methods had come to be replaced by "modern" ones. Now, with "modernization" itself being considered to benefit from the persistence of traditional attitudes, the latter are due for some reassessment. Yet, with the fuller appreciation we now have of both the maturity and complexity of premodern civilizations in East Asia, such a reassessment is recognized to be no simple matter. The basic pattern of Neo-Confucian education may have been common to all, but the social systems and other cultural traditions of China, Japan, Korea, and Vietnam differed significantly. Moreover, in each of these civilizations, marked changes occurred after the initial adoption of Neo-Confucian education. One cannot assume, as was easily done before, that the traditional pattern remained unaltered—an illusion to which many Westerners were prone, predisposed as they were to justify forcible intrusion into established Asian patterns of life on the ground of the latter's stubborn resistance to change. In this view there was no need to study history or the complex inner development of East Asian societies in order to see that the latter had fallen behind in the race for progress, Western style, and had reached an impasse from which only Western arms or revolutionary violence could deliver them.

Today, after the failure of Mao's radical measures, the Great Leap, and the Cultural Revolution, there is more of a disposition to accept the need for gradual reform and greater patience for the kind of painstaking studies required to understand the process. We do not assume that the papers presented here serve as anything more than a first step in a longer-range program of research and scholarly discussion. For us it will be enough if, through a fuller understanding of the formative stage of Neo-Confucian education, we can establish a better baseline from which to proceed, hoping that others may follow up these results with investigations of the East Asian development in its later phases.

No doubt some readers would have preferred it had we directly juxtaposed our findings concerning this formative stage of Neo-Confucian education to the criticisms of it made by modern reformers. Certainly on many points early twentieth-century critiques create a picture of traditional education sharply at variance with the one presented here. Nevertheless such a confrontation, though not without a certain dramatic interest, would, at this stage of our research, still be shadowboxing. Neo-Confucian education underwent a long, complex development between the fourteenth century, where our account ends, and the late nineteenth. Although a common core of ideas and practices persisted in the diverse historical and cultural settings of East Asia, there were also significant discontinuities. No proper assessment of modern reactions can be made except in light of these different perspectives, nor can it be done without taking into better account the traumatic circumstances that produced such modern reactions. For this, much challenging research remains to be done. Although our account tries to be fair to the tradition—both sympathetic and critical—we do not make the revisionist assumption that modern critiques were entirely misbegotten from the start and had nothing to tell us about the limitations and shortcomings of Neo-Confucian education as it evolved into later times.

The studies in this volume were first presented to the Conference on Neo-Confucian Education held in August–September 1984 at the Henry Chauncey Conference Center in Princeton, New Jersey, under the auspices of the Joint Committee on Chinese Studies of the American Council of Learned Societies and the Social Science Research Council, with funds provided by the National Endowment for the Humanities, the Ford Foundation, and the Mellon Foundation.

This conference was an outgrowth of a workshop on "Chu Hsi and Education" led by Wm. Theodore de Bary at the International Conference on Chu Hsi held in Honolulu, Hawaii, in the summer of 1982. In the workshop it became evident that the full significance of Chu Hsi's thought on

education could best be appreciated in the light of other developments in
Sung society and especially of other educational alternatives available,
including Buddhism. As a result the later conference was expanded to
include a variety of specialists outside the Neo-Confucian field, including
scholars in social and institutional history, anthropology, the history of
religious, modern Chinese history, and so on. Here we wish to acknowledge
the participation of several, not represented by papers in this volume, whose
papers or contributions as discussants helped to improve the articles published here: Irene Bloom, Julian Ching, Myron Cohen, Daniel Gardner,
Peter Golas, Marie Guarino, C. T. Hu, Huang Chün-Chieh, James T. C.
Liu, Kwang-ching Liu, John Meskill, James Polachek, Evelyn Rawski,
Conrad Schirokauer, and Deborah Sommer.

ABBREVIATIONS

Abbreviations of Chinese titles and editions are identified at first appearance, except in the case of the following standard works:

SKCS	Ssu-k'u ch'üan-shu
SKCSCP	Ssu-k'u ch'üan-shu chen-pen
SKSC	Sung kao-seng chuan
SPPY	Ssu-pu pei-yao
SPTK	Ssu-pu ts'ung-k'an
TSCC	Ts'ung-shu chi-ch'eng

ONE

Introduction

Wm. Theodore de Bary and John W. Chaffee

The thought of the great twelfth-century scholar and philosopher Chu Hsi loomed large in late traditional Chinese society. As the leading representative of Sung learning whose teachings, supported by the state, influenced the behavior of families and communities and whose commentaries on the Four Books all students committed to memory in preparation for the examinations, Chu Hsi has frequently been credited with (or accused of) providing much of the intellectual mortar that preserved the established order for centuries. However, when viewed in their historical setting and from the perspective of world history, many of Chu's views can be seen as liberal and, indeed, progressive. Nowhere is this more true than in the field of education, to which Chu gave the highest priority in his thought and scholarship. Nor was education for him confined to the elite, for his work on such topics as family ritual, community organization, and public instruction were directed in large part at the nonliterate population. Yet, even though volumes have been devoted to Chu Hsi's philosophy, no sustained or comprehensive study has been directed to Chu as an educator or to the actual manner in which his teachings were propagated throughout East Asia from the thirteenth to the nineteenth century. Lacking such a study, we are poorly equipped to evaluate his actual influence in respect to many of the social and cultural attitudes relevant to the problems of modern society.

In this light we should reexamine the historical role of Neo-Confucianism in fostering a spirit of self-discipline, family solidarity, public morality, and scholarly learning in the premodern era. As a first step we should look at the central importance Chu Hsi attached to general education and consider his views on the aims, scope, method, and priorities of learning. Of particular significance is his emphasis on voluntarism, social reciprocity, collegial inquiry, and discussion. The issues of elitism and egalitarianism, universalism and particularism, are also important in evaluating the success of Neo-Confucianism as it spread· among the diverse peoples of East and

Southeast Asia, replacing Buddhism as the dominant intellectual force in the premodern era.

Because of Chu Hsi's singular and dominant role in the shaping of Neo-Confucian education, normally the term "Neo-Confucian," as used herein, refers to the seminal ideas, texts, and practices identified with him. Although not without their own ambiguities or enigmatic features, nor free from adulteration by later generations, they have a clear derivation from Chu and can be differentiated from earlier Confucianism. For more general purposes the term Neo-Confucian may be applied to that movement of thought that arose in the Sung and later came to be known as *li-hsüeh* or *hsin-hsüeh*, in the broad sense of these terms as used by such historians of Neo-Confucianism as Huang Tsung-hsi, Fung Yu-lan, and Carsun Chang. A distinct subset of Neo-Confucian teachings often more narrowly defined as "orthodox" is the Ch'eng-Chu school, which emerged from the "Learning of the Way" (*Tao-hsüeh*) as identified in the official *Sung History*. This we speak of as "orthodox Neo-Confucianism" to distinguish it from the broader "Neo-Confucian" movement, which stemmed from others than just Chu Hsi among the Sung thinkers. There were, too, different forms of orthodoxy, but in the period treated here it was the local Chinese academies that first established Chu Hsi's teaching as "orthodox" and it was only at the turn of the thirteenth to the fourteenth century that the Yüan dynasty adopted it officially for educational and examination purposes.[1]

Properly to assess the nature and significance of Neo-Confucian education, however, requires us to understand more than just Chu Hsi's philosophy. Volumes have been written about his philosophy that, because they have treated it as an abstract system of ideas supposedly transmitted as pure doctrine from generation to generation, failed to recognize its historical permutations from age to age and country to country. Unrecognized too is the fact that, even as originally expounded by Chu, his teaching was meant to serve the needs of his own times—as a method of learning to be practiced rather than as a doctrine to be imparted or dogma to be imposed.

Chu's teaching was an answer to the problems he encountered in twelfth-century Chinese society. If, at the same time, his views have relevance to later ages, it is because they are concerned with the problems of a mature society and of an age many historians have seen as already, in some ways, modern. Indeed, the revived interest in Confucianism during the Sung period—what evoked the new ideas we label Neo-Confucian—arose from changes so profound in Chinese society as to warrant considering them almost revolutionary. True, in the longer view of Chinese society what may

---

1. For further discussion of these matters see Wm. T. de Bary, *Neo-Confucian Orthodoxy and the Learning of the Mind-and-Heart* (New York: Columbia University Press, 1981), and the introduction to his *The Rise of Neo-Confucianism in Korea* (New York: Columbia University Press, 1984).

at first seem revolutionary often proves to be only change contained within the perduring limits of traditional Chinese society—"change within tradition" as Edward Kracke once put it. Still, these are the developments in the Sung that left their mark on key institutions of late Imperial China and, more particularly, set the conditions and defined systemic patterns in which any kind of serious learning would be carried on.

THE ECONOMIC AND SOCIAL CONTEXT

Among these changes were the substantial growth and diversification of the Chinese economy. As documented in more than a half-century of work by Chinese, Japanese, and Western scholars, major features of this change were, first, the retreat from an earlier T'ang pattern of close state supervision of agriculture and commerce toward a more laissez-faire economy; and second, in consequence of this, the appearance of new problems in the Sung that prompted the reimposition of centralized control or at least provoked new attempts in that direction, whether they succeeded or not.

In the first phase of governmental retrenchment during the late T'ang, following the rebellion of An Lu-shan, the stress on the collection of agricultural revenues rather than on the direct control of production left the upper classes free to accumulate land and promote agriculture, industry, and trade, relatively unimpeded by the central government. The resulting growth from the ninth to the eleventh century took many forms. Technological improvements in hydrology and agriculture stimulated the rapid development of central China and helped push the empire's population over one hundred million for the first time in history. Metallurgical developments, together with the need to defend against the resurgent kingdoms of the steppe, led in the eleventh century to the creation of a major iron and steel industry, the rapid development of Chinese military technology, and the creation of a huge standing army. Agricultural and demographic growth, together with the introduction of paper money in the late eleventh century, brought the commercialization of agriculture in the more advanced regions of China, large-scale urbanization of cities whose functions were primarily economic and not administrative, and the growth of a huge maritime commerce reaching into southeastern and south Asian waters. Finally, the spread of printing, from early use in the propagation of Buddhism to government use in the tenth century and thence to use by the literati and the upperclasses generally, altered access to literacy and the uses of book learning.

During this long process of economic change, the Chinese upper classes underwent two transformations. First, the decentralization of military power in the late T'ang and the ensuing violence and destruction in the Five Dynasties period spelled the effective end of the great families that had dominated the early T'ang and traced their origins back to the Six Dynasties and even the Han.[2] In their place there arose a new elite in the eleventh century whose members came increasingly from southern and central China. Although their political rise was linked initially to the examinations, they were thereafter able to use intermarriage, personal recommendations, and the protection privilege to insure their continued dominance within the bureaucracy. As distinct from their T'ang predecessors, they brought with them into government an optimistic faith in the efficacy of Confucian principles for the ordering of the economy and society, though they often disagreed over how to accomplish this ordering.

The prominence of these families, however, proved as evanescent as it was spectacular. In part because of the bitter factional struggles over the reforms of Wang An-shih and his followers, which made it increasingly difficult for families to maintain access to high office over generations, and in part because of a rapid spread of education and interest in the examinations among the upper classes during the late Northern Sung, this national elite had by the Southern Sung become largely absorbed by a more numerous stratum of local elites active in local affairs, intermarrying mostly within their own prefectures and participating but only sporadically in officialdom, because most literati never made it through the fiercely competitive examinations.[3] Within this large and heterogeneous milieu we place the emergence of an approach to education that can properly be called Neo-Confucian, an approach that was to prove of critical importance to the subsequent history of Korea, Japan, and Vietnam as well as China.

THE RELIGIOUS CONTEXT

Initially, the significance of this new development would no doubt be better seen in contrast to what preceded it, if only we had a more adequate picture of the state of education in pre-Sung China to compare it with. Understandably in the declining years of the T'ang and amid the instability of the Five Dynasties period, public education would have been unlikely to receive much support, whereas private education, where it was still able to serve a declining elite, remained in the restricted custody of families preserving their own traditions of scholarly learning, accessible only to a literate minority.

In these circumstances Buddhism, with greater popular appeal, might be thought a more likely vehicle for the educational uplift of the masses, yet it appears that much of what we think of as education in the secular order was not of great interest to those institutions, whether monastic, eremitical, devotional, or charitable, serving to propagate Buddhism itself. Even with

2. This is argued most persuasively in David Johnson, "The Last Years of a Great Clan: The Li Family of chao-chun in the Late T'ang and Early Sung," *Harvard Journal of Asiatic Studies* 37 (1977):51–59.

3. See Robert M. Hartwell, "Demographic, Political, and Social Transformations of China, 750–1550," *Harvard Journal of Asiatic Studies* 42 (1982):365–442.

the considerable growth of Buddhist studies in recent years, little attention has been drawn to education. It seems not to have been a question that naturally arose in the minds of either T'ang Buddhists or those modern researchers intensively engaged in the study of religious doctrine and praxis as it pertained to the training of monks. Even with the great modern interest in lay Buddhism its role in the more mundane areas of popular instruction does not appear to have aroused much curiosity.

It is our own concern with historical antecedents then, not a manifest Buddhist involvement with education, that brings into focus and sharp relief the dramatic contrast between Buddhism and Neo-Confucianism in this area. One might leap to the thought that the contrast is between an other-worldly religion and a secular humanism or an age of faith yielding to an age of reason. Yet Mahāyāna Buddhism, especially in its Ch'an form, had already accommodated itself to Chinese earthiness and worldliness in a manner congenial to its own spiritual mission, and Neo-Confucianism, for its part, went on to develop religious manifestations of its own. Thus, we must inquire more deeply into the changes actually taking place at this important historical juncture if we are to arrive at a better understanding of its meaning.

In Professor Zürcher's pioneering study of Buddhist education in the late T'ang period, which provides a rough baseline for our study of new developments, we note that although Buddhist evangelism made early use of vernacular literature and printing to reach the masses there is little evidence of Ch'an Buddhist concern with more than a minimum of secular education or cultural studies as distinct from religious conversion and spiritual training. Moreover, in the case of Ch'an, there was a noticeable reluctance to rely on either the spoken or written word as a primary means for the communication of religious truth.

Thus, more of a concession to circumstances than a matter of fundamental conviction led Ch'an Buddhists in the Sung to systematize their teachings and codify their practices in ways little done before and in a manner befitting the more complex society and culture of that age. One could perhaps argue over which of the two teachings, Buddhism or Neo-Confucianism, prompted the other to move in this same direction. More appropriately, however, one could see both as responding to the same historical stimuli, yet in ways characteristic of their different value orientations.

In Chu Hsi's works, and in our chapters here, there are frequent reminders that Ch'an Buddhism represented a formidable challenge to the Neo-Confucians. Whatever one might say about mutual influences between the two, educationally speaking they were competitors, drawing men in different directions. To pursue the Neo-Confucian curriculum, with Chu Hsi's strong insistence on systematic intellectual and moral training and especially with the study of books in both breadth and depth, would be difficult to combine with Ch'an meditative disciplines and koan training.

Chün-fang Yü, who has done much to enlighten our understanding of Chinese Buddhism in the later dynasties, has been prompted by her participation in the present project to investigate Ch'an education in the Sung for the first time. Yet again, the literature so produced was closely linked to a primary concern with monastic training: monastic rules and "lamp records" (*teng-lu*) or "recorded conversations" (*yü-lu*), which preserved the sayings or dialogues of the Ch'an masters. On the level of popular morality and a more devotional religion, vernacular literature conveyed a message more attuned to the religious imagination of ordinary folks. For its part Neo-Confucian education moved into and developed new areas of higher learning that had great significance for the educated class, with its commitment to public service and to assuring the vitality of Chinese social and cultural traditions.

The significance of Northern Sung educational policies should be seen against the background of Zürcher's chapter, which gives a vivid portrait of the size and range of the Buddhist educational effort in the preceding period. Especially intriguing is his description of the ways in which it attempted to serve secular uses, providing laymen at community schools with a basic minimum of Confucian instruction, as well as of Buddhist doctrine, and helping to train significant numbers of literati for government service. This may in part reflect the underdevelopment of state schools and the need of Buddhists to promote greater literacy as a means of propagating their own doctrines. For secular purposes, however, it was a minimal literacy, and by the Northern Sung only traces of this effort remained. As new social and cultural needs appeared, the education of literati quickly became an exclusively Confucian affair.

THE INTELLECTUAL AND POLITICAL CONTEXT

Without the remarkably activist educational policies of the Northern Sung, this Neo-Confucian approach to education would have been almost unthinkable. Support for this assertion comes from Thomas H. C. Lee's contention that education was beset by a number of crises resulting from Northern Sung institutional developments and from the descriptions by Tu Wei-ming and Peter Bol in Part 2 of Chu Hsi's dissatisfaction with education geared to the examinations and concern over "*shih* not acting as *shih*."

Chu's complaint implies that the literati were not fulfilling the leadership functions necessary to the achievement of this ideal. In one sense this calls for the transformation of the social elite into true leaders, whose authority would be exercised to stimulate and guide the "renewal of the people," as Chu Hsi put it. In another sense, however, should the political elite fail to meet this responsibility, it was the higher duty of the literatus to carry on the teaching mission as Confucius himself had, independently of the state. Thus, much as Confucius had liberated the "superior man" or "noble man" (*chün-tzu*) from the ranks of the Chou aristocracy, so might we consider Chu Hsi to have at least potentially unmoored the "literati" from the political order.

From the Confucian standpoint, however, such a condition was less than wholly natural. As Tu Wei-ming explains the Confucian sense of mission, it saw the transmission of culture, service to society, and moral self-transformation as three equally indispensable aims of education. Earlier ambitious efforts at universal schooling, Lee has suggested, proved abortive because too great a preoccupation with institutional arrangements and organizational controls diverted attention from underlying moral issues. Yet the alternative model of education, oriented to the civil service examinations, suffered from too great an emphasis on reproducing information at the expense of moral self-transformation. The latter need, as identified by Tu, was to become the hallmark of the new education projected by Chu Hsi.

Peter Bol's analysis of the intellectual struggles of these times moves in a similar direction. He too sees the crisis of that day, reflected in Chu Hsi's critique of the views of Wang An-shih and Su Shih, as focusing on the literati's sense of mission. "Wang and Su represent the era that asked how the literati ought to relate to the cutural tradition. Chu Hsi introduces the new question of how literati should relate to transcendental principles of morality." In Chinese terms this transition is expressed as a rejection of the centrality of either Su Shih's *wen-hsüeh* (learning based on the cultural tradition) or Wang An-shih's *cheng-shih* (affairs of government) in favor of *tao-hsüeh* (learning of the Way). While acknowledging that the great majority of Chu's literati contemporaries remained committed to *wen-hsüeh* in particular, Bol nevertheless argues that in the long run Chu Hsi succeeded in redefining literati learning, so that "cultivating the moral self" became "the only possible basis for realizing the literati responsibility [both] for maintaining the political order and transmitting the culture."

In "Chu Hsi's Aims in Education," Wm. Theodore de Bary underscores Chu's aim of "learning for the sake of oneself" as the ultimate value in education. This has a twofold significance vis-à-vis alternative claims on human commitment. It affirms the moral and physical reality of the self or person, in contrast to Buddist questioning of the substantiality of the self and—in Ch'an—an unwillingness to predicate anything of it. More than simply reaffirming the moral nature or man's "humanity" as a general principle however, Chu insists here on individual self-respect as the starting point of all education. This then also stands in opposition to the prevalent careerism, that is, study for the sake of passing the civil service examinations. The latter is a shortsighted, expediential view in contrast to Chu's holistic conception of the full human capability.

Pursuing a middle course between Buddhist transcendentalism and utilitarian careerism, Chu pays special attention to what he considers truly practical: schools (as the necessary institutionalization of learning) and curriculum, including the selection and editing of graded texts for use an all levels of education. Establishing the right priorities is crucial to any conception of selfhood as a continuing process of growth and maturation, rather than as an enigma penetrated in a flash of intuition.

These priorities are exemplified by the Four Books, which formed the key texts in Chu Hsi's core curriculum. Chu selected and edited the *Analects* of Confucius, the works of Mencius, the *Great Learning*, and the *Mean* as the central revelatory texts of the Confucian canon, wherein the sincere reader can directly perceive the Way of the sages. Revelation required proper reading, however, and thus Chu developed in great detail a method of reading the texts (*tu-shu fa*), a topic treated by de Bary in his chapter. We should also note that through his prefaces and commentaries on the Four Books, Chu Hsi gives his ideas a practical, methodical, and tangible form such as no other teaching possessed. Hence the continued use of Chu's basic texts in schools throughout East Asia, down into modern times, is not only a credit to the comprehensiveness of Chu's philosophical system but also a tribute to the serious attention Chu gave to the problem of education itself—to "renewal of the people" through schools and not just to philosophical renewal among the scholarly elite.

THE INSTITUTIONAL CONTEXT

In his study of government schools Thomas H. C. Lee has pointed to the almost dialectical relationship between state schools and the civil service examinations in the creation of a new educational order. The early Sung government had no more than a nominal interest in sponsoring schools, and education was largely confined to a small number of famous academies (*shu-yüan*), Buddhist temples, and whatever was provided by wealthy or scholarly families. But its expansion of the examination system under the emperor T'ai-tsung in 977 increased both the demand for education and participation in the examinations, and, thanks largely to the latter, entailed elaborate procedures to insure the system's impartial administration. The educational program of later reformers, from its abortive inauguration in the Ch'ing-li period (1041–1048) to its fruition under Ts'ai Ching (1046–1126) can be viewed in large part as a complex reaction to that expansion. In their attempt to create an empirewide system of schools the reformers responded to both the demands for more schooling and the growing tendency, from the 1020s on, of local officials to establish government schools. However, in their view, even more important was the need to redress an overly mechanistic approach to the selection of men that ignored the evaluation of personal character. In the 1040s Fan Chung-yen (989–1052) proposed a school residency requirement for examination candidates, less anonymous procedures at the prefectural examinations, and a greater emphasis in the curriculum on discussions of the Classics and policy discussions. Wang An-shih

(1021–1086) and Ts'ai Ching argued, more radically, that personal evaluation could best be done through schools, which would not only nurture and train men but also provide the setting for judging those most suitable for government service. Although Wang never attempted to implement this proposal, for a time in the late Northern Sung the government's Three Hall System of schools stretched from county schools to the Imperial University in K'ai-feng and came close to supplanting the examinations themselves.

Yet, as Lee shows in persuasive detail, the reformers' program itself was problem-filled and provoked a sharp reaction. Its enduring legacy was institutional, for the campuses, administration, and methods of financial support pioneered by them became the models for future dynasties. But with this development came the criticism that schools had become burdened by inefficient administration, exposed to favoritism, and geared more than ever to competitive advancement. Moreover, the very success of the Three Hall System in providing schooling to unprecedented numbers of students served to intensify competitiveness. Thus, the emergence of the literati in the Southern Sung as a group whose very size precluded most of its members from serving in government and whose attention was much more centered on local affairs can in good measure be laid at the door of earlier reformers.

By Chu Hsi's day, the educational world had become large, complex, and problematical. Thomas Lee and Pei-yi Wu both note the development of elementary schools and primers and the apparently unprecedented interest in elementary education among Sung writers. Lee goes on to argue that this, together with the development of printing and the growth of government schools, led to a rise in literacy and an attendant sense of crisis, as the very success of education created questions as to its functions and goals. The government schools themselves had become the focal point of literati life in prefectures and counties. Not only did they offer students an opportunity for financial support and formal instruction, but, as Linda Walton shows in her detailed study of Ming-chou, they also served as ritual centers for the officials, degree holders, students, and literati of the locality. It is hardly surprising, therefore, that Chu and other contemporary critics saw the government schools as symptomatic of the literati's problems. Using a highway image that he also applied elsewhere to the Imperial University, Chu Hsi in 1194 criticized conditions at the Fu-chou (Fu-chien) prefectural school: "Teachers and students regard each other indifferently, like men on the highway. Elders are concerned by the daily decline of ancient customs and the disappearance of scholarly spirit, but they are unable to remedy it."[4]

Chu Hsi was not opposed to the government schools per se. As de Bary points out in his chapter, Chu's "Personal Proposal for Schools and Official Recruitment" argued for a universal school system that would fulfill the

---

4. Chu Hsi, *Chu Wen-kung wen-chi* (SPTK ed.) 80:20b. Concerning the university, see his famous critique of schools and examinations, ibid. 60:20b–28b.

functions of the examinations (thus echoing the reform program of the Northern Sung). He also engaged actively in the revival and renovation of government schools throughout his career. But given the realities of the times, Chu seems to have had little faith that pressing educational needs could be solved simply through the government schools. Rather he put his greatest efforts into the academy (*shu-yüan*) and the scholarly retreats (*ching-she*); these were the locus of much of his personal teaching, as discussed in Wing-tsit Chan's chapter. Thus, Chu Hsi as prefect of Nan-k'ang lectured at the prefectural school but also spent much greater time, attention, and even political capital on the revival of the White Deer Grotto Academy.[5] If the academies were his "tools" for working out the "completion of Neo-Confucianism" as Chan suggests, perhaps it was because they allowed for inquiry and learning in a way not possible at the government schools, which were organized on competitive lines and associated closely with the examinations.

In this regard, the White Deer Grotto revival assumes special importance. It was neither unique nor pathbreaking, for by 1180 academies of various sorts were already proliferating. Even the idea of reviving a famous Northern Sung academy with its associations of cultural wholeness and imperial backing had a precedent in the 1167 revival of the Yüeh-lu Academy in Ching-hu-nan.[6] But in the development of Neo-Confucianism, the White Deer Grotto was nevertheless a milestone. Chu Hsi's determination to create an educational retreat where genuine learning could occur, combined with his personal renown and some fear of him at court, made this action controversial. Whether or not John W. Chaffee is correct in viewing objections to the school's revival and Chu Hsi's response to them as an initial skirmish in the battle over "Spurious Learning" (*wei-hsüeh*), the renown of the undertaking and the simultaneous growth in Chu's personal following do seem to mark a new, more public phase in his activities as an educator.

Although Chu Hsi and his followers were not alone in establishing academies, some of his contemporaries whom we could call Neo-Confucian were conspicuously absent from academy-related activities. In his study of why Chu Hsi's great philosophical rival, Lu Chiu-yüan, did not create academies, Robert Hymes offers a provocative answer. He suggests that at the heart of Chu Hsi's interest in voluntary community organizations, such

5. At the actual site of the school there is no natural grotto. The setting is more like what in English would be called a "hollow," and the same is often true at other sites known as *tung*. However, in recent times a local official, noting the incongruous absence of a grotto at the Pai-lu tung, had one artificially constructed, without much pretense even at a naturalistic appearance. Clearly to him *tung* meant "grotto," not just a hollow or ravine. Given the ambiguous use of the term in Chinese, the editors have allowed contributors to exercise their own choice in rendering it as one or the other.

6. See Chaffee's chapter and, for greater detail, his article, "Chu Hsi and the Revival of the White Deer Grotto Academy," *T'oung Pao* 71 (1985):40–62.

as community compacts, community granaries, and of course academies, lay a desire, earlier pointed to by de Bary, to create socially beneficial institutions within a "middle space" or "level" between "the family and the lowest reaches of the state apparatus." Lu's noninvolvement in academies, Hymes then argues, was not because his philosophical idealism made him opposed to book learning (for his interest in education and concern over the effects of the examinations on education are well documented) but rather because the demands and concerns of Lu's huge family organization in Chiang-hsi made him uninterested in working within that middle level.

Whether Hymes's hypothesis will be borne out in studies of other scholar-officials who, like Lu, had absorbing family interests, only time will tell. But it is significant that in Walton's study of Ming-chou, a center of Lu learning, his immediate thirteenth-century followers were, unlike himself, active academy builders.

Nevertheless, the idea of new activity at the "middle level" has great utility for our understanding of Chu Hsi. Monika Übelhör, in her study of the community compact, provides an intriguing comparison between the version of the compact proposed first by Lü Ta-chün in the eleventh century and the one revised by Chu Hsi in the twelfth. Although both versions envision a ritual community promoting harmony and social solidarity, Lü Ta-chün's deemphasis of social hierarchy contrasts with Chu's insistence on the leadership role to be played by the literati (*shih*). This accorded with new social realities for, thanks to the examinations, the literati dominated local society as never before; yet one can also see it as staking out a claim for literati leadership in that institutional space between the family and state.

EDUCATIONAL ANCILLA TO SCHOOLS

Our discussion of Chu Hsi's interest in the "middle level" of society is not meant to suggest a lack of interest in either the state or the family. Indeed, the Sung Neo-Confucians were distinguished by the breadth of their educational vision, reexamining institutions that had always been the foundations of the Confucian social order and probing other areas of life that had hitherto largely been ignored. We should recognize that this process also involved a narrowing of cultural choice, for it was driven in no small part by an antagonism toward those cultures and traditions unassimilated into the Confucian order, most particularly Buddhism. Even as the Neo-Confucians moved philosophically into the realm of metaphysics, which had previously been dominated by the Buddhists and Taoists, so in education they turned their attention to children, family, and community and to the need to educate the public. These were areas that Buddhists and Taoists had long conceded to Confucianism, but in the new Sung situation they could also be seen as potential growth areas—that is, areas that could not but be affected by the new developments stimulating change.

To some extent the need for reform or renewal was felt by all schools of thought in the Sung, not simply the Neo-Confucians. Describing the evidence relating to Sung elementary education, Wu notes a "greater attentiveness toward children displayed by adults," as seen in painting, poetry, and treatises on pediatrics.[7] We might also point to Ssu-ma Kuang's interest in family rituals and Lü Ta-chün's early sponsorship of community compacts as evidence of the wide ranging concerns of Sung scholars. What marked the Neo-Confucians, especially Chu Hsi, was the systematic application of their principles to these diverse areas. Just as learning involved the extension of knowledge, so action involved the extension of that knowledge into every aspect of life.

The domain of the family was of course most central and had always been recognized as such by Confucianists. This is clear in Theresa Kelleher's study of the *Elementary Learning* by Chu Hsi and his disciple Liu Ch'ing-chih. Using an approach that combines educational and moral principles with numerous examples drawn from history, the *Elementary Learning* provides a kind of guide to the early education of a child when that education is entirely within the domain of the family. However, this was hardly a primer, for as Kelleher notes its language is too difficult for a beginning reader. It is also philosophically comprehensive, with its contents organized under the headings of moral education, human relations, and self-cultivation, a fact that may help account for its high reputation in the Neo-Confucian tradition. Nevertheless, the book was indeed concerned with education within the family. The moral principles that it presents can be seen as essential to the educational process within the home, and such a moral formation is a prerequisite for the young student when first immersing himself in the classics. Moreover, in treating the cardinal Confucian relationships, Chu and Liu quite emphatically affirm intrafamily hierarchies, particularly the child's subordination to the parents, the wife's to her husband, youth's to age, and female's to male.

It therefore comes as a revelation in Bettine Birge's study of Chu Hsi and women's education to see him taking flexible positions when writing eulogies of specific women. Although in the *Elementary Learning* and other formal writings where he stressed the "differentiation between men and women" and held women to extremely demanding behavioral codes (such as the nonremarriage of widows), in his tomb inscriptions we see him praising women who exercised great authority in their families, remarried, and in some cases were practicing lay Buddhists. Chu Hsi was also acutely aware of the critical importance of the women's sphere of family life, for they provided

---

7. See also Thomas H. C. Lee's article on the "The Discovery of Childhood: Children's Education in Sung China (960–1279)," in *Kultur: Begriff und Wort in China and Japan*, ed. Sigrid Paul (Berlin: Dietrich Reimer Verlag, 1984).

boys and girls with their earliest—and most critical—education; thus, the importance of the *Elementary Learning*.

This willingness to accommodate social realities, a kind of humanistic realism, is also apparent in Chu Hsi's highly influential writings on family rituals, described in the chapter by Patricia Ebrey. Ebrey's topic is broad, for she analyzes a range of Sung writings on domestic rituals and finds considerable flexibility in the adaptation of classical ritual texts to the Sung context. This allowed for an acceptance of popular customs so long as they were not explicitly Buddhist or Taoist. Her treatment of Chu Hsi is of particular interest, however, for in contrast to Ssu-ma Kuang, whose *Shu-i* was directed specifically at literati (*shih*) and officials (*ta-fu*), and to the government's ritual texts, which were addressed to officials, Chu's *Family Ritual* (*Chia-li*) was easier to use and intended for all people regardless of class.

We can thus see in Chu Hsi a remarkable concern for popular education. Although the Northern Sung reformers also broached the idea of a universal school system, their rationale was elitist: it was to produce the most talent for the service of the state. For Chu, however, the recruitment of talent was secondary to the primary purpose of education, which was to produce moral persons in a moral society. In addition to his *Family Ritual*, he pioneered a new genre of popular education: essays of encouragement and instruction. Described in the chapter by Ron-guey Chu, these were hortatory proclamations issued by Chu Hsi during his varied tenures in local posts. In these efforts at moral suasion, he encouraged schooling, preached the reform of customs and religious practices (vehemently inveighing against the Buddhists), and discouraged litigiousness. How effective these were we do not know, but much as the *Family Ritual* came to be regarded as the standard work on ritual practice so these proclamations became a part of what was expected of model officials in later periods.

In this matter an apparent contradiction should be addressed. If Chu Hsi's educational ideas were truly universal, how do we explain his "elitist" concern for the role of the literati in academy activities and in his version of the community compact? In part this can be explained by the Confucian distinction between "learning" (*hsüeh*) for the elite and "instruction" (*chiao*) for the masses, or, as Ebrey expresses it, between "schooling" and "molding," because the molding properties of proper customs, rituals, and ceremonies were universal and independent of formal learning, which might still be focused on the elite. This, however, could only be a partial answer, for Chu Hsi's interest in universal schooling, seen in the *Elementary Learning* as well as the "Personal Proposal," points to an ideal world in which learning is indeed popular, and in his commentary on the *Great Learning* Chu stresses that true learning must include within its scope the "renewal of the people" (*hsin-min*).

The education thus defined by Chu was clearly humanistic. It combined classical and historical studies for the purposes of intellectual and moral self-cultivation. Yet in *Reflections on Things at Hand*, Chu Hsi, following Ch'eng I, gave favorable notice to the educational model set earlier in the Sung by Hu Yüan, who combined classical studies with technical subjects like governmental institutions, hydraulic engineering, military defense, and mathematics. It would seem then that Chu, while giving priority to basic intellectual and moral disciplines, recognized a need for further specialization at a higher level of social or scholarly engagement.

That one such field of specialization might well be law is suggested by Brian McKnight's chapter on the increasing importance of legal studies for Sung officials. Chu Hsi himself, while decrying too heavy a reliance on law and litigiousness, in keeping with the traditional Confucian preference for "rites" over law as a means of ordering society, often showed himself quite ready, when voluntaristic methods failed, to invoke and strictly enforce Sung laws and regulations. In his expert survey of this area of Sung education, McKnight, an authority on Chinese legal institutions, details the unique curriculum, training, examinations, and career ladder that distinguished Sung legal education from what most literati received and distanced it from the primary concerns of Neo-Confucian thinkers. Yet he also demonstrates how that education remained embedded within the Sung Confucian order. As he says, "with the increasing Confucianization of the content of the law that occurred after Han times, any doubts Confucians might have had about the propriety of being concerned with the law were much reduced. In reading the law, students were in effect reading about the ways in which Chinese values, many of them championed by Confucians, were to be applied in maintaining the desired social order."

The Ch'eng-Chu school was not alone in its concern with current educational conditions or commitment to public service. In the Southern Sung, thinkers like Lu Chiu-yüan and Yeh Shih agreed with Chu Hsi on the corrosive effects that the examinations had upon education but not necessarily with his educational prescriptions. It may be too that Yüan Ts'ai, whose ideas on education in his *Precepts for Social Life* are very pragmatic and family-centered, was far more in tune with prevailing literati ideas than Chu and his followers.[8] Yet that is hardly surprising because this was, after all, the formative phase of Neo-Confucian education. Although some distinctively Neo-Confucian institutions like the academy became popular during the Sung, others like the community compacts and public proclamations apparently did not and only came to fruition in later periods.

Even in the longer perspective, it remains true that Neo-Confucian education, for all its intensive and extensive development in later ages, fell short of achieving Chu Hsi's ideal goal of universal education. Because no other world civilization could boast of much greater success than China

---

8. See Patricia Ebrey, *Family and Property in Sung China: Yuan Ts'ai's Precepts for Social Life* (Princeton: Princeton University Press, 1984).

during the premodern era, there is no universal yardstick by which to judge the overall success or failure of the Neo-Confucian endeavor. Nevertheless, as we explore further the outcome of this effort in post-Sung China, or elsewhere in premodern East Asia, it will remain a question for serious consideration how well the Confucians fulfilled both their leadership role in society and their cultural mission, while meeting Chu Hsi's great challenge that education should provide both a "learning for the sake of oneself" and the basis for a "renewal of the people" at large.

PART ONE

The Background of Neo-Confucian Education

TWO

Buddhism and Education in T'ang Times

Erik Zürcher

THE BUDDHIST IDEAL OF MORAL TRAINING

In the Confucian perspective, education has always meant much more than purely intellectual training and the transfer of certain skills. True education, as defined by Confucian thinkers, cannot be separated from the moral improvement of the individual as a social being; from the earliest times, the terms *hsüeh* "study" and *chiao* "teaching" always have had strong ethical implications. They refer to a total process of acquisition and interiorization of the norms of "the right way of life," to the study and memorization of texts that exemplify those norms, and, at the higher levels of "study," to the creation of an elite whose members—either as local leaders or as administrators—will be qualified to further their application. The nearest Western approximation would be the French *formation*, which, unfortunately, also is untranslatable. I shall not go further into this because Confucian education is not my theme. It is, however, important to note that the Confucian concept of education (in the broad sense of the word) was not exclusively directed toward the formation and selection of an administrative elite. From the beginning that elitist aim was combined with the much more comprehensive ideal of moral training and ideological manipulation of the mass of the people. Thus, Confucianism naturally tended and overtly claimed to monopolize "education" at all levels, and this obviously had important consequences for the extent to which Buddhism was able to realize its own educational ideals and potentialities.

At first sight, the Buddhist claims in this field were as far-reaching as the Confucian ones, in spite of its different orientation. Buddhism not only brought a religious message but also implied a "Buddhist way of life." However, a basic difference lies in the fact that in Buddhism such a basic reorientation of life was, first and foremost, applied to the nuclear group within the system: the *saṅgha*, the community of monks and nuns, novices

19

and postulants, those "who have left the household" (*ch'u-chia*) and thereby have placed themselves outside the world of temporal social relations and obligations. By doing so, they chose another way of life, subject to a very detailed internal code of behavior, the *vinaya* (*lü*). The education received within the *saṅgha* was extensive and exacting; ideally, it implied years of hard learning, total dedication, and strenuous effort. But, here again, what we would call "education" is part of a total *formation*: religious study under a clerical teacher; the acquisition of the countless rules of conduct to be observed toward one's masters, one's fellow monks, other religious persons (such as novices or nuns), and the laity; training in ritual, liturgy, and the techniques of meditation. And all this had a moral dimension, for it had to be combined with a constant struggle to free oneself from sin, desire, and attachment. "Education"—in the narrow sense of literacy, scriptural studies, and intellectual training—merely is one component in this complex.

Apart from what took place within the *saṅgha*, the activities of the Order vis-à-vis the laity also had an educational dimension. The pious layman always has played a double role, as both donor and receiver. As a donor, he creates the material conditions for the existence of the *saṅgha* and thereby forms the support of spiritual life; in return he is entitled to receive religious doctrinal instruction, ritual expertise, and karmic retribution for his good works. The laity may also organize *saṅgha* activities serving a communal cause, such as rituals to pray for rain or the foundation of temples for the salvation of soldiers who died on the battle field. The social stratification of such lay-sponsored activities reaches from grass-roots level to nationwide imperial patronage, but in all cases the *saṅgha*'s response—its part of the bargain—is, in principle, threefold: religious instruction, moral guidance, and the production of "good luck."

Religious instruction directed toward the laity basically consisted of preaching. In medieval times the doctrine was no doubt already spread in writing (scriptures and popular treatises), but this was limited by the low level of literacy and, before the generalization of printing that took place only under the Sung, the rarity and high price of handwritten texts. Preaching took place at all levels, from doctrinal expositions and debates at the court to the popular explication of texts for the common people. Icons and wall paintings in temples no doubt also had a didactic purpose, as they acquainted the public with the enormous Buddhist repertory of themes and forms and thereby enriched their world of religious imagination.

Becoming a Buddhist layman was more than a simple act of faith, in which the believer "takes refuge in the Buddha, the Doctrine and the Order." The practicant solemnly promised to observe "for the rest of his/her lifetime" the Five Rules (abstaining from killing, stealing, illicit sex, lying, and intoxicating drinks). The layman was, moreover, expected to observe certain religious obligations (notably periodic fasting) and to perform good works.[1] Becoming a lay believer was a solemn ceremony; since late T'ang times it was even confirmed by a formal certificate signed by the officiating priest.

However, these rules and obligations were rather general and could therefore easily be integrated in the normal patterns of worldly life. In fact, the remarkable success with which Buddhism was able to find its place in so many completely different cultures was largely based on the summary nature of its rules for the laity: its demands were, on the one hand, so well-defined and recognizable that they could form the base of a certain group solidarity and a sense of relation with the *saṅgha* and, on the other hand, so general that they could function in a traditionally non-Buddhist framework.

But in China, as in other Mahāyāna countries, this simple dichotomous picture of a nuclear *saṅgha* surrounded by a supportive and extraneous laity became less clearcut. Mahāyāna Buddhism tended toward blurring the division between clergy and laity, and in China this tendency toward "upgrading" the layman, the "Boddhisattva who stays in the family" (*tsai chia p'u-sa*) was reinforced by environmental factors. On the part of the *saṅgha*, it led to the formation of an important intermediate category of "postulants" whose position was halfway between the religious and mundane spheres of life; later I shall return to this. On the part of the laity, it led to a more detailed formulation of its "Buddhist way of life." This is most clearly exemplified by the "Boddhisattva vows" (*p'u-sa chieh*), a practice that became popular during the fifth century and that until modern times has remained a basic element in Chinese Buddhism.

The practice is based on a *sūtra* of doubtful authenticity, the translation of which is wrongly attributed to Kumārajīva.[2] The text lists eight "grave" and

1. A detailed description of the entrance ceremonial for the lay believers is found in *Taishō-Tripitaka* (hereafter T) 1488, *Yu-p'o-sai chieh ching* (trans. by Dharmaksema, early fifth century), *chüan* 3, section 14 (*shou chieh p'in*), pp. 1047a–1050b. T refers, as in all following notes, to the *Buddhist Canon of the Taishō Era*, Taishō shinshū daizōkyō, edited under the direction of Takakusu Junjirō, Watanabe Kaigyoku, and Ono Gemyō in 100 vols. (Tokyo: Taishō issaikyō kankōkai, 1924–1935).

The flexibility of the system appears from the fact that a partial acceptance of the Vows also was possible, even down to only one Vow, without losing *upāsaka* status (ibid. p. 1049a). On the other hand, however, the bestowal of a formal certificate proving the acceptance of the vows (both the Five Vows and those of the Bodhisattva, for which see below) lends the ceremonial an official character. Many of such certificates have been found at Tun-huang (e.g., S 330, 347, 532, 2851, 4482, 4844, 4915).

2. T 1484 *Fan-wang ching*, very popular in China into modern times. The terminology certainly is not Kumārajīva's; the text is not mentioned by Seng-yu in his *Ch'u san tsang chi chi* (T2145) of a.d. 515, and in the early Sui catalog *Chung-ching mu-lu*, compiled by Fa-ching and others and completed in 594, it is classed among the "dubious texts" (T 2146, 5:140a). On the other hand, the first references to the Bodhisattva vows being accepted by both monks and laics date from the second half of the fifth century, culminating in the 520s when some forty-eight thousand persons followed the Liang emperor Wu's example and accepted these vows.

forty-eight "light" commandments and prohibitions, some of which are clearly designed for the clergy, whereas others are directed to the laity. But in actual practice the vows are accepted by laymen and clergy alike.[3] The vows subject the practicant to a whole series of obligations that go much farther than the original Five Rules: he or she shall seek instruction in the scriptures; take care of the sick; observe exemplary filial piety toward one's parents; strive to convert one's relatives; liberate animals held in captivity; abstain from obtaining requital even in case of murder of one's relatives; and abstain from meat and from strong-smelling vegetables like garlic and onions. The practicant is not allowed to carry arms, to possess objects used to catch animals, or to associate with soldiers. He vows not to keep a brothel, to interpret dreams, to utter spells, or to make a living as a slave-trader, a seller of animals (for slaughter), or an undertaker. All this is symptomatic of the ongoing tendency toward formulating a more detailed and specific "Buddhist way of life" for the laity, based on the Bodhisattva ideal.

Finally, at the grass-roots level Buddhism no doubt has played a comparable role by propagating the collective performance of "good works," a phenomenon mainly known to us from the many Tun-huang documents pertaining to local clubs and societies. Much has been written about these organizations and their roots in pre-Buddhist Chinese society; however, such fraternities and sororities were hybrid bodies, largely directed toward worldly ends but undoubtedly inspired by Buddhism. At this level, Buddhism has largely contributed to an ongoing process that in later imperial times resulted in the secularized—or rather Confucianized—"community contracts" (hsiang-yüeh) and the charitable and cooperative institutions of lineages. It appears that the Buddhist contribution lies in reinforcing charity: the abandonment of worldly possessions and the ideal of "salvation of all beings" as a means to accumulate karmic merit.

"EDUCATION" MORE STRICTLY DEFINED

What has been said so far may have made clear that the subject, if taken in its larger sense of "Buddhist religious instruction and moral training," is a mer à boire that would virtually embrace the whole complex of lay Buddhism and a considerable part of training within the saṅgha. Because the subject would become unmanageable with such an approach, a rigorous restriction will be necessary. In spite of the larger context, to which I have tried to do justice in the previous section, in this section the theme will therefore be reduced to its most concrete content: education is the systematic transfer of

3. See Hōbōgirin, vol. II, pp. 142–146, S. v. Bosatsukai. For a translation of the rules and a description of the ritual as it was practiced at Foochow in the late nineteenth century, see J. J. M. de Groot, Le Code du Mahāyāna en Chine (Amsterdam: Joh. Müller, 1893). Also see Holmes Welch, The Practice of Chinese Buddhism, 1900–1950 (Cambridge, Mass.: Harvard University Press, 1967), pp. 362–364.

specific skills such as literacy; and, as a result of this transfer, a special group forms whose possession of those skills distinguishes it from the rest of the community.

I shall further distinguish between (1) the training of the monk *within the saṅgha*—a system of education that, at least ideally, makes him a member of an educated elite of a special type—and (2) the educational role of the *saṅgha* vis-à-vis the laity. I must emphasize the facts that the available information largely belongs to the first aspect and that much less is known about external educational activities of the *saṅgha*. This in itself is a remarkable fact, the explanation of which must be sought in the status of the *saṅgha* in medieval China.

The Status of the Saṅgha

The period roughly between A.D. 500 and 850 no doubt constitutes the "Buddhist age" in Chinese history. However, this apogee of Buddhism never led to anything even remotely resembling a "Buddhist state." In all matters related to state and ideology, Buddhism remained marginal. The official political theology was maintained as the legitimation of dynastic rule: the complex of the mandate of heaven and the state cult associated with it hardly absorbed any Buddhist elements. Indian cosmology was not absorbed but in a remarkable way coexisted with the traditional Chinese. The state maintained its exclusive claim as the sole source of political and social order: not the priest but the civil administrator was the focus of authority and prestige. "Higher culture" was still largely the domain of the secular elite—the same elite from which the state recruited its officials and courtiers. The position of the *saṅgha* in T'ang China therefore basically differed from that of the clergy in medieval Western Europe. In the West, the clergy by definition was the carrier of spiritual authority and literacy; the church virtually monopolized education, and the feudal aristocracy largely left the cultural, educational, and administrative sectors for the church to manage. In China the situation was almost the reverse; the *saṅgha* was overshadowed by the existence of an established secular elite that was the focus of power, status, higher education, and literary culture. Even in its heyday the *saṅgha* was never in a position to challenge its monopoly; at best the clergy could expand in complete dependency on that elite and within the limits set by the authorities. Individual devotion, and even imperial patronage, did not change that basic configuration of power.

However, the *saṅgha* by the beginning of the T'ang had already developed into a large and diversified group of literate and sometimes highly cultivated specialists. Within Chinese culture a body of a completely new type had come into being: the *saṅgha* had become a *secondary elite*.

The Saṅgha as a Secondary Elite

The formation of that clerical top level is reasonably well documented, mainly on the basis of about one thousand major biographies of Chinese "eminent monks" in the various *Kao-seng chuan*.[4] The process started in the late third century.[5] In the course of the fourth century two interdependent phenomena occurred: monks of high-class (or at least *literati* background emerged, and Buddhism penetrated the elite, in both the North and the South. However, during the fourth and the fifth century only a handful of monks of high-class origin were active. Between 250 and 400 biographical sources mention only ten cases of high-class background: the elite within the clergy became visible and very active, but it still was very small. In the course of the fifth century, high-class recruitment (sixteen cases) increased but not dramatically. The spectacular upward shift took place in the sixth century (fifty three cases, with thirty eight in the peak period A.D. 525–575) in a time of imperial patronage, both in the Lower Yangtze area (Liang) and in the North (Toba Wei). This sudden outburst of high-class recruitment no doubt also indicates a change of mentality: the *saṅgha* became "respectable"; its status rose to a level at which even very prominent families would allow their children to join the Order and become members of what had grown into a secondary elite of a very special character. I shall later discuss the new and innovative nature of the *saṅgha*; before doing so, I will present more data about this remarkable "upgrading" of the *saṅgha* shortly before and under the Sui.

In a number of cases the texts just mention that a certain monk came from a high-class family, such as Yen-tsung (556–610), whose family "for generations had belonged to the gentry, and was known as the no. 1 lineage (of the region),"[6] or T'an-tsang (566–635) who came from a "family that had been prominent from generation to generation."[7] In many cases the texts indicate a background of Confucian scholarship. Some monks were "students" (*shu-sheng*) at prefectural or commandery level;[8] of Ching-hsüan (568–611) it

---

4. The data are mainly based on the three large collections of monks' biographies: (a) T 2059 *Kao-seng chuan*, 14 *chüan*, by Hui-chiao (497–554), completed ca. 530, containing 257 major and 243 subordinate biographies, from the earliest times until ca. 520; (b) T 2060 *Hsü Kaoseng chuan*, 30 *chüan*, by Tao-hsüan, (596–667), completed ca. 650, containing 331 major and 160 subordinate biographies, from the early sixth century until ca. 645; (c) T 2061 *Sung Kao-seng chuan*, 30 *chüan*, by Tsan-ning (919–1001) and others, completed in 988, containing 533 major and 130 subordinate biographies from early T'ang to early Sung. The *Kao-seng chuan* mainly falls outside the scope of this paper; I have, moreover, for obvious reasons paid no attention to the biographies of non-Chinese missionaries. The data presented here are based upon a total of about one thousand biographies—at first sight an impressive corpus of materials. However, as I have pointed out elsewhere, (*Journal of the Royal Asiatic Society* (1982): 161–176, esp. 9, 164–165), one must always be conscious of its limitations: it shows a propagandistic picture of the highest clerical elite and only occasionally contains information on the mass of the *saṅgha*.

5. Cf. E. Zürcher, *The Buddhist Conquest of China* (Leiden: E. J. Brill, 1959), Vol. 1, pp. 6–9.

6. *Hsü kao-seng chuan* (hereafter HKSC), 2:436b.

7. Ibid., 13:522a.

8. Chih-shun (532–604), HKSC, 17:279c; Ching-ai (533–578), ibid., 23:625c; Shan-fu (d. 660), ibid., 26:602c.

is said more explicitly that he became a student at the commandery school at the age of six and there studied the Classics for three years,[9] which clearly refers to elementary training at an early age. Another monk, Hsüan-ching (died 606), also from a family of *literati*, at the age of fifteen had been selected as a *hsiu-ts'ai*,[10] and Hui-pin (573–645) had been made an assistant teacher at the prefectural school at the age of eighteen, before he joined the Order.[11] The scholarly background of several monks of this generation is mentioned, as in the case of Hui-k'uan (583–653) whose father was the "Erudite of the Five Classics" Yang Wei.[12]

But even more striking is the number of monks who came from families of high official status, often for two or three generations. A few examples suffice. Fa-lang's (506–581) grandfather was the prominent general and regional warlord Chou Feng-shu under the Southern Ch'i;[13] his father Chou Shen-kuei was Extraordinary Cavalier Gentleman-in-Attendance at the Liang court and governor of P'ei, which was also the seat of the family.[14] Hui-heng (514–589) was the grandson of Chou Shao, palace general under the Ch'i;[15] his father Chou Fu was military commander of Ch'ang-shui; he ordered his son to devote himself to Confucian studies.[16] The grandfather and the father of Tao-ch'eng (529–608) had served the Ch'i and the Liang in high civil and military matters.[17]

And, last but not least, for the first time we find monks from families who—rightly or wrongly—claimed an ancient and illustrious pedigree, like those from the genealogies of the great aristocratic families of medieval China, often from lineages that in the early fourth century had migrated to the Yangtze area. There are cases like Chen-hui (568–615), of the illustrious Ch'en clan of Ho-pei, who claimed to descend from the famous general and statesman Ch'en P'ing (died 178 B.C.), one of the founding fathers of the Han dynasty.[18] Seng-min's (A.D. 473–534) first ancestor was the first ruler of Wu, Sun Ch'üan (A.D. 181–252);[19] Seng-feng (ca. 560–640) claimed direct

9. HKSC, 10:502a.
10. Ibid., 17:569b.
11. Ibid., 20:591b.
12. Ibid., 20:600b.
13. Ibid., p. 477b. The biography of Chou Feng-shu is found in the *Nan Chi'i shu* (Peking: Chung-hua shu-chü, 1974) 29:545–547.
14. See note 13.
15. *Tien-chung chiang-chün*. I have been unable to find any other reference to this curious title; I suppose that like so many other "generals" with flowery appellations in the Nan pei ch'ao period it was an honorific post reserved for members of the high aristocracy.
16. Ibid., 9:494a. As was usual in this period, Confucian studies constituted a "family tradition."
17. Ibid., 21:611a.
18. Ibid., 18:574b. The biography of Ch'en P'ing is found in *Shih-chi, chüan* 56, p. 2051 sqq, and in *Han-shu*, ch. 40, p. 2038 and following.
19. HKSC, 5:461c.

descent from the founder of the Liang dynasty; his grandfather Hsiao I was the Prince of Ch'ang-sha, the elder brother of the Liang emperor Wu.[20] Other monks traced their pedigree back to celebrities of the third century.[21]

After A.D. 600 the general rate of high-class recruitment stabilized, with a second peak in the period 650–725 (which covers, among other things, the reign of the fervently pro-Buddhist empress Wu). The general picture remains the same: many monks descending from high officials and scholars, and many cases in which an illustrious pedigree, sometimes reaching back to Han times, is mentioned.[22] Imperial affiliations are not lacking either: Hui-ming (died 673) was a grandson of the Ch'en emperor Hsüan,[23] and our sources mention three eighth- or ninth-century monks who belonged to the imperial Li Clan of the reigning T'ang dynasty.[24] One of these, Kuang-i (died 735), was a son of Li Ch'ung, the Prince of Lang-yeh who in 689 together with his father, the Prince of Yüeh, had made an abortive attempt to dethrone Empress Wu; the infuriated empress had thereupon exterminated his whole family, but Kuang-i had been saved by his wet-nurse.[25]

I have treated this aspect in some detail because sources show that the sixth century witnessed a second breakthrough, as spectacular as the first one of ca. A.D. 300 the sudden influx of high-class elements into the top of the *saṅgha*. It made the *saṅgha*, indeed, a secondary elite, not only because of its religious and scholarly qualifications but also in many cases because of the illustrious social background of many of its monks.

The Saṅgha as a New Phenomenon

It may not be superfluous to stress the unique character of the monastic

20. Ibid., 13:526b. The biography of Hsiao I is found in *Liang shu*, 23:359–360, and *Nan shih*, 51:1265–1266.

21. Hui-yin (538–627) claimed descent from the prominent fourth century scholar-official Kan Pao, known, inter alia, as the author of the *Sou shen chi*; for his biography see *Chin shu*, 82:2149 and following (HKSC, 13:522a). Hui chün (563–630) was a descendant in the eleventh generation of the Marquis of Tu-t'ing, that is, Li Ching (mid-third century), briefly mentioned in *Chin shu, chüan* 46 as the father of the scholar-official Li Chung and as governor of Ch'in-chou (ibid., 14:535a).

22. Hsüan-tsang (602–664) descended from the model magistrate Ch'en Shih (A.D. 104–187) (*HKSC*, 4:446c), and Hui-ch'eng (554–630) even claimed descent from the imperial Liu clan of the Han (*ibid.*, 24:663b). Shen-chieh (fl. ca. 690) was said to have the famous Confucian scholar Kuo T'ai (127–169 A.D.) as his ancestor (*Sung Kao-seng chuan*, hereafter SKSC, 4:630c), and Hsüan-chüeh traced his pedigree back to another late Han worthy, Tai Kun (ibid., 8:758a).

23. SKSC, 8:756b.

24. Ch'i-an (d. 842) descended from an (unnamed) member of the imperial family who had fallen into disgrace and had been banished to the far south (Yüeh) (SKSC, 11:776b); Tao-p'ei (878–955) was a member of the imperial clan, and had been born in the princely quarter of Ch'ang-an (ibid., 17:818c); for Kuang-i see note 25.

25. SKSC, 26:873a. Li Ch'ung and Li Chen, the Prince of Yüeh, respectively were a grandson and a son of Emperor T'ai-tsung. For the biography of Li Ch'ung see *Chiu T'ang shu*, 76:2663–2664.

community when seen in the context of Chinese culture. Pre-Buddhist China of course knew a great variety of religious experts, and the emperor and his representatives in local government themselves had to perform certain religious rites. But the very notion of a clerical body as a corporate entity consisting of individuals who had severed all social ties was unknown. The nature of the *sangha* as a social and political *corpus alienum* led to a whole series of claims that, in a Chinese context, was quite formidable. As a type of organization it was unprecedented; it justified its aims and deviant behavior in metaphysical terms and yet claimed that its existence was advantageous, even most essential, for the world at large, "for the benefit of all beings." In political terms, it claimed to be an autonomous body, free from government supervision and interference, exempt from taxes and corvee, and only subject to its own very elaborate monastic code of discipline. Socially, it confronted Chinese culture with the unprecendented ideal of "leaving the family," a most drastic rejection of family-oriented morality symbolized by the adoption of a religious name. In contrast with class-ridden medieval Chinese society this open organization transcended all class distinctions. It also flouted the even more outspoken Confucian principle of excluding women from ceremonial functions; the female order of nuns, introduced in the fourth century, must have been a startling innovation. The Indian origin of the Doctrine and the notion of a center of spiritual authority outside China defied the prevailing attitude of Sinocentrism.

All these claims and tensions took shape as soon as the *sangha* had come into contact with the elite. They evoked various reactions, both positive and negative, and often resulted in an unstable combination of acceptance and rejection: both recognizing the right of the *sangha* to exist and also constantly checking its growth and controlling its activities. This ambivalent attitude understandably characterized the religious policy of the T'ang. I have shown how, in the decades just preceding the reunification of the realm, the *sangha* had developed into an important secondary elite, the top layer of which was closely interwoven with the secular upper class—an "alternative intelligentsia" with powerful backing. But at the same time the *sangha*'s claims were, in principle and potentially, destructive for state and society, and it consequently had to be controlled.

But T'ang religious policy was not merely repressive. It also aimed at a certain "incapsulation" of the clergy into the Chinese system—a constant attempt to transform the *sangha* from an alien body, standing outside state and society, into a functional group of "religious experts." In the Chinese context this integration naturally took the form of bureaucratization. It can be recognised in a whole set of measures: administrative control, both external and internal; the introduction of clerical titles, insignia, and posthumous names; the creation of semibureaucratic institutions such as the Translation Office; the sale of ordination certificates comparable to the sale of secular ranks and titles; the compilation of the Buddhist Canon under imperial auspices; and the system of clerical examinations with its various "categories," *k'o* no doubt inspired by its secular counterpart. For my subject the last item is most important. The clerical examinations were not only intended to restrict the size of the *saṅgha*, but they were also aimed at "the selection of talent." This Confucian conception had important consequences for education within the *saṅgha*, for, just as in the secular sphere, this "talent" was primarily associated with literacy, the ability to memorize texts, and proficiency in expressing one's ideas in standardized stylistic forms.

TRAINING WITHIN THE SAṄGHA

What I have said so far about the nature, the status, and the functioning of the Buddhist clergy was meant merely as an introduction, somewhat lengthy, but indispensable to place our first subject—the training of the aspirant monk within the *saṅgha*—in its proper perspective. My starting point is the fact that in Sui and T'ang times the clergy must have been one of the most educated (or, more specifically, "literate") groups of the population, even if the monk's literary training was of a very special type.

The highest level of this type of education was the domain of the tiny top of the clerical pyramid: the *magistri*, well-versed in Buddhist scriptural and scholastic literature. But also at a lower level the average monk had to possess a certain degree of literary skill. He had to memorize a considerable amount of text in order to be admitted into the *saṅgha*, and some of his daily activities required a degree of literacy no doubt far above that of the average layman. The importance of texts in the practice of Buddhism also appears from the phenomenon of the monastic library: in the T'ang, before the spread of printing, the libraries in Buddhist monasteries probably constituted the only sizable collections of books outside the capital.

The importance of the *saṅgha* as an educated minority becomes even more evident if we look at its estimated size. Unfortunately there are no clerical census figures for this period; estimates are usually based on the 260,500 monks and nuns secularized during the great repression of Buddhism in A.D. 845. However, this figure certainly does not represent the size of the *saṅgha* as a whole, and it does not agree with certain other data.[26] It may well be that the figure of 260,500 refers to fully ordained monks and nuns, who no doubt constituted a minority. Including the postulants and novices, the real figure would at least have to be doubled; the real size of the *saṅgha* in mid-T'ang times may have been somewhere between six hundred thousand and one million, that is, 1.5 percent to 2 percent of the population.

By setting out to study the "intramural education" within the *saṅgha*, a number of questions arise. In what way, and at what age, was one admitted

26. According to T 2126 (*Seng shih lüeh*) by Tsan-ning (919–1001), 40:247c, in the year 830, when it was decided to grant ordination certificates to all "irregular" monks and nuns, no less than 700,000 applied to be ordained.

to the Order, and what were the most common motivations to do so? What were the disciple's obligations toward his teacher(s)? Was he trained in reading and memorizing Buddhist texts, or was there a preliminary stage of training in "basic literacy"? If so, what elementary texts were used? Which Buddhist texts were most important in training? Which minimal literary skills were required to become ordained?

These questions can only partially be answered. The available information is scattered and scanty; not only are Chinese biographers, religious and secular alike, generally uninterested in the early youth experiences of their personages, apart from stereotyped "wonder child" anecdotes, but also the more significant activities of the "eminent monks" only took place later in their lives. For some answers, I must turn to the invaluable Tun-huang materials, always considering the question of how far Tun-huang is representative. Some information is contained in *Vinaya* passages devoted to novices and to ordination, but these formal rules were probably honored in the breach.

In theory, entrance into the *sangha* was basically a matter of faith and of individual choice. That aspect understandably looms large in the monks' biographies, even in the case of very young children; they contain many anecdotal passages about premature piety and attempts to persuade unwilling parents.[27] In actual fact, poor families may often have sent their children to a monastery out of sheer necessity and probably also because the clerical state offered a chance to acquire a certain degree of literacy. It is, however, important to note that the *Vinaya* expressly forbids accepting any novice without the consent of his or her parents.

Even more important for my subject is the question of the age of entrance; this obviously is related to the nature and level of monastic education. The *Vinaya* rules are clear and strict, but they appear to reflect ideal rather than real practice. According to the *Dharmaguptaka-vinaya*, in principle no person could be admitted below the age of eleven, with the exception of orphans without any remaining relative—they could be taken into the monastery as

---

27. Some examples of parental resistance: SKSC, 4:731a (Seng-yüan, 638–689); ibid., 10:769a (Tao-wu, 760–820, a case of a hunger-strike); ibid., 13:787a (Ch'üan-fu, 881–947); ibid., 16:810a (Chen-chün, 846–924). It is possible that the natural resistance felt by a Chinese family against a son entering the Order form the background of one of the most striking features of the monk's biographies of this period: the great number of reported cases in which the mother during pregnancy or shortly before the conception has a prophetic dream in which the birth of a prominent monk is foretold or symbolically suggested. The content of the dreams shows much variation, although in general the symbolism is obvious enough. In some cases the expectant mother has a vision of monks who convey the message (e.g., SKSC, 4:731a); in other cases she sees a sheen of light or smells incense (ibid., 10:717a, 15:803b); she dreams that she touches sacred objects in a temple (ibid., 7:751a) or that the moon penetrates into her bosom (ibid., 14:790b); she sees an Indian monk enter her home (ibid., 7:751a), she dreams that in front of her a pagoda rises up in heaven (ibid., 12:783b), and so on. Perhaps the theme serves as a kind of legitimation: the child was destined to become a monk so the family could do nothing about it.

"crow chasers" (*ch'ü wu*), that is, to perform the lightest menial tasks.[28] The *Mahāsāṅghika-vinaya* places the normal minimum age at thirteen: "crow chasers" must be at least six years of age.[29] The period of the novice's training ends with his or her full ordination, which has a minimum age-limit of nineteen years.

If the candidate is accepted as a novice, he is placed under the authority of two teachers. One of these, called *ho-shang*, trains him in disciplinary matters such as the observance of the Ten Rules;[30] the other one, usually called *ācārya* (*a-she-li*) is charged with education in a more restricted sense, including the memorization of texts. Apart from the training in texts,[31] in liturgy, and in the countless rules of monastic life, the novice is expected to serve his master in every respect. The disciplinary texts describe such tasks in great detail, down to the way in which the pupil must cleanse his master's bowl and sweep the floor of his cell.[32]

But we should not rely too much upon this ideal image. In China, the practice of monastic life was no doubt less rigid. Thus, in a Sung commentary to the *Dharmaguptaka-vinaya* Yüan-chao distinguishes between real novices (*fa-t'ung sha-mi*, "*śramanera* who conform to the Doctrine") who observe the Ten Rules and formal (*hsing-t'ung sha-mi*) novices who only accept the tonsure.[33] Moreover, already in T'ang times we find the first traces of a category of clerical candidates whose status is still below that of the novices: the (adult) "practicants" (*hsing-che*) who were called "boys" (*t'ung-tzu*) if they were very young. I shall call them "postulants," the term used by Kenneth Ch'en.[34] The postulant stands halfway between the monastery and

28. The rules for the admission of novices are treated in *Dharmaguptaka-vinaya* (T 1428 *Ssu fen lü*), trans. by Buddhayaśas and Chu Fo-nien, late fourth century), 33–34:801b–812c. For the passage on the minimum age for admission, see ibid., p. 810c.

29. T 1425, *Mahāsāṅghika-vinaya* (trans. Buddhabhadra, early fifth century), 29:461b.

30. (1) Not killing; (2) not stealing; (3) no sexual intercourse; (4) not lying; (5) no alcoholic beverages; (6) no comfortable bed; (7) no ornaments; (8) no singing and no dancing; (9) not using or possessing gold or other precious things; (10) not eating beyond the fixed dinnertime.

31. Learning how to recite texts under the ācārya's guidance is explicitly mentioned in all the *Vinaya* as one of the essential parts of the training program. In the *Mahāsāṅghika-vinaya* this part is even mentioned separately, on a par with the whole rest of religious training (T 1425, 29:461a).

32. E.g., the seventy-two rules regarding the right way of speaking with the master, entering his cell, laying out his clothes, preparing his bath, etc., as enumerated in the anonymous, probably fourth century T 1471, *Sha-mi shih chieh-fa ping wei-i*; in the analogous T 1472 *Sha-mi wei-i ching*, trans. Gunavarman, ca. 431, and in Dānapāla's version of ca. 1000, T 1472 *Sha-mi shih chieh i-tse ching*.

33. T 1805 *Ssu-fen lü hsing-shih ch'ao tzu-ch'ih chi* (late eleventh century), III.4:416b.

34. Cf. Kenneth Ch'en, *Buddhism in China* (Princeton: Princeton University Press, 1964), p. 245. Ch'en denotes such postulants with the Chinese term *t'ung-hsing*. However, *t'ung-hsing* is a contracted term combining the first syllables of "boys" (*t'ung-tzu*) and "(adult) practicants" (*hsing-che*). The two categories are clearly distinguished by Tao-ch'eng in his *Shih-shih yao-lan* (A.D. 1019), T 2127, 1:166c: "from the age of seven to fifteen (*sui*) they all are called *t'ung-tzu*," and ibid., p. 167a: "At the age of sixteen (*sui*) and beyond, they have to be called *hsing-che*."

secular life: at his entrance he accepts the layman's Five Rules (not the novice's Ten); he studies Buddhist scriptures and works in the monastery in a subservient position, but he keeps his hair and is not exempted from taxes and corvee labor. After at least one year of service he can be accepted as a novice. This category of "disciples who keep their hair" (*liu fa ti-tzu*) is unknown in Indian Buddhism; its appearance in China is yet another symptom of the blurring of the borderline between clergy and lay believers in later Chinese Buddhism.

However, historical sources show that practice often did not agree with the *Vinaya* prescriptions. For the Sui and T'ang periods in some 160 cases the age of entrance is specified. The average age—eleven years—agrees with the *Vinaya*, but there are many cases of entrance at a younger age, with a clear high at six to eight years (38 cases, e.g., nearly one-quarter) and a number of remarkably young cases: two of five years, and two of four. This is important because it shows that in such cases monastic training (and notably literary education) must have comprised the acquisition of elementary literacy.

The "postulantship" mentioned above was a period of study and training before becoming a novice. This is amply confirmed by biographical sources. Around A.D. 650 the first reference appears to a distinction between the state of novice and that of a postulant; the same passage also makes clear that, in accordance with the T'ang policy of controlling the number of ordinations, the entrance as a novice was subjected to government approval. It relates how the (future) monk Seng-yüan at the age of twelve became a disciple (*ti-tzu*) of Hui-yen in the Hu-ch'iu monastery and how he, twelve years later in 662, "by edict was allowed to shave his head." Only then did he formally become a novice, for the text clearly states that later, under another master, he was fully ordained.[35] The same combination of initial probationary period and government controlled admission to the novitiate appears in the biography of Shen-ch'ing, who around 760 at the age of twelve became a "disciple" and studied the *Lotus sūtra*, the *Vimalakīrti-nirdeśa*, and the *Laṅkāvatāra-sūtra*. "At that time the official regulations were very strict: only those among the house-leavers who were able to recite a thousand leaves (of text) were allowed to be tonsured." Thanks to his thorough scriptural studies Shen-ch'ing passed the test and became a novice in the Ta-li era (766–780).[36] As I shall show, the requirement to know by heart "a thousand pages" is, indeed, extreme; later I will comment upon the quantities of memorized text. The postulant Tao-piao (739–823) also had studied the scriptures in the monastery before passing the exam (757) and becoming a novice; after another eight years (765) he was fully ordained.[37] Even more explicit is the case of Ta-i (691–780), another hard-working student. When in 705 emperor

35. SKSC, 4:731a.
36. Ibid., 6:740c.
37. Ibid., 15:803c.

Chung-tsung restored the T'ang, he permitted, by a special act of grace, that persons could enter the *saṅgha*, and so the local governor Hu Yüan-li held an examination on scriptural exegesis (*k'ao-shih ching-i*). Ta-i came through as number 1 (*ko chung ti-i*: a terminology borrowed from the civil examination system) and became a novice.[38]

The recorded cases become more numerous in the ninth and the tenth century.[39] The introduction of a probationary period before the novitiate sometimes appears to have shortened the latter. Thus, Hsüan-ch'ang, who became a "disciple" as an eight-year-old boy only became a novice in his eighteenth year and received full ordination one year later.[40] The significance of this development for my subject is obvious: in this way, an essential part of scriptural training was shifted to an informal sphere, before the novitiate and halfway between monastery and secular life. Monastic life, formally starting with the novitiate, was expanded to include a group of usually very young postulants, "disciples who kept their hair"; unlike the regular novices, their number was not subjected to official restrictions.

Clerical Examinations and the Test Requirements

The introduction of selective clerical examinations[41] is one of the most characteristic features of T'ang Buddhism. It clearly served two purposes: controlling the size of the *saṅgha* and "upgrading" the clergy as a body of religious specialists. The influence of the civil examination system introduced near the end of the sixth century is evident. Like their secular counterpart, the clerical examinations fell under the Board of Rites; candidates were "recommended" and examined under the supervision of the local authorities; admission to the Order was usually bound to specified quotas, and the terminology was largely borrowed from the civil examinations.

It is probable that when the system was introduced the primary aim was to control the size of the *saṅgha*. As a result of the privileged position of Buddhism under Empress Wu (r. 685–705), the clergy had no doubt increased greatly. After Chung-tsung had restored the T'ang (705), one of his first measures was the institution of clerical examinations in scriptural exegesis for postulants.[42] It is only known that the requirements comprised

38. Ibid., 15:800a.
39. E.g., Hsüan-yüeh (ca. 840), SKSC, 17:746a; Seng-chao (d. 891), ibid., p. 749a; Fu-chang (ca. 910), ibid., p. 751a; Wen hsi (d. 826), ibid., 12:783c; Chen-chün (d. 859), ibid., 16:810a; Hsüan-ch'ang (ca. 810), ibid., 17:818a.
40. SKSC, 17:818a.
41. For a general survey of government policy vis-à-vis the ordination of monks, including the clerical examinations, see Michihata Ryōshū, *Tōdai bukkyōshi no kenkyū* (Kyoto: Hōzōkan, 1967), *chüan* 3, pp. 29–94.
42. *Shih-shih ch'i-ku lu*, by Chüeh-an (1266–1355), T 2037, 3:822. There are some traces of still earlier clerical examinations, held by a committee of prominent monks (fifty *ta-te*) for the selection of 150 postulants, as early as 658; cf. Michihata *Tōdai bukkyōshi no kenkyū*, p. 34. However, probably this *ad hoc* measure was limited to the metropolitan area.

the all-important *Lotus sūtra*: on that occasion the young Ta-i got his grade with highest honors by reciting that scripture.[43] The *Sung kao-seng chuan* (hereafter SKSC) adds that the examination was held under the supervision of the governor.[44]

Fifty years later the empire was again in danger. The grave crisis caused by the revolt of An Lu-shan required drastic measures, also in the sphere of the supernatural. In order magically to reinforce the power of the dynasty, Su-tsung in 758 ordered Buddhist temples to be built at each of the five sacred mountains, the symbols and protectors of the territory. Of course, the effectiveness of his measure wholly depended on the "quality" of the monks, and perhaps that is why on that occasion the emperor also gave new guidelines for the clerical examinations. Prominent monks were instructed to select postulants for the novitiate, and the amount of memorized text was fixed at five hundred pages[45]—a detail that is corroborated by the SKSC.[46] However, this figure apparently refers to a minimum requirement; another SKSC passage speaks of seven hundred pages.[47] And it appears that personal status and influence occasionally could also lead to much lower figures.[48] There is another reason to question the efficacy of the system, for during the same crisis the first attempt was made to refill the depleted treasury by selling ordination certificates—a malpractice that reached enormous proportions under the Sung.

In 773, Emperor Tai-tsung introduced a more diversified program, no doubt based on the civil examinations system. Clerical examinations were divided into three "categories" (*k'o*): Scriptures (*ching*), Discipline *lü*), and Treatises (*lun*), that is, scholastics.[49] This meant an important shift from form, the purely mechanical memorization of texts, to content. The candidate's knowledge and insight were tested by letting him write an essay, although memorization no doubt was also required.

The same devaluation of memorization appears from a measure of the year 825: the authorities involved[50] were ordered by edict to create a clerical

43. *Fo-tsu t'ung-chi*, by Chih-p'an (mid-thirteenth century), T 2035, 30:371b.

44. SKSC, 15:600a.

45. *Shih-shih t'ung-chien*, by Pen-chüeh (Sung), *chüan* 9, quoted by Michihata, *Tōdai bukkyōshi no kenkyū*, p. 35.

46. SKSC, 15:803a, biography of Chen-ch'eng.

47. Ibid., 15:803c, biography of Tao-piao.

48. T 2120 *Piao-chih chi*, a collection of memorials submitted to the authorities by Amogha-vajra (Pu-k'ung, 905–974), collected and published by his collaborator Yüan-chao around 778, in six *chüan*. On p. 835c in a memorial of the year 767 he asks permission for ordination (as novices) on behalf of some postulants, specifying the texts that they have memorized and the number of pages involved. Most texts mentioned here are *dhāraṇī*, in accordance with Amogha-vajra's tantric specialization. In one case the number of pages memorized is not more than 120.

49. SKSC, 16:807a; biography of Shen Ts'ou.

50. The "Commissioners of Merit of the Two Avenues" (*liang chih kung-te shih*), the civil organ that since the late eighth century was responsible for controlling the *saṅgha*; cf. Tsuka-

examination committee charged with testing the postulants' ready knowledge. In this case only 150 pages were demanded from male candidates and
100 from female ones.[51]

Under Wen-tsung (r. 827–841), who again tried to subject the *sangha* to
strict government control, the demands suddenly became excessive: 1,000
pages of memorized texts.[52] But that was a last attempt, and, moreover, one
incompatible with another measure taken in 830 (cf. note 27) that granted
ordination certificates to all illegal monks and nuns. Shortly thereafter the
great persecution of Buddhism took place (842–845); it apparently ended
the old-style clerical examinations. When Hsüan-tsung almost immediately
after his father's death (847) restored the *sangha*, he introduced examinations
of a new type, in which the candidates were not tested on scriptural
knowledge but on "religious quality"; the new three categories were defined
as "disciplinary behavior," "meditation," and "wisdom."[53]

Thus, the general picture is one of an erratic policy, without stable
guidelines and subject to great fluctuations. The amount of memorization
varied from a very reasonable 150 pages (about one-half of the *Lotus sūtra*) to
the extreme demand of 1,000 pages.[54] However, we must assume that the
system did contribute to the intellectual level of the *sangha* as a secondary
elite in T'ang times, at least in terms of literacy.

There is no detailed description of the content of the "required reading,"

moto Zenryū, "Tō chūki irai no chōan no kudokushi," in *Tōhō gakuhō* 4 (1933):368–406. The
"two avenues" refer to the eastern and western halves into which the capital was divided. In 807
the authority of this organ was enlarged to include the task of controlling the Taoist clergy as
well (cf. T 2216 *Seng-shih lüeh*, 2:245c, and T 2035 *Fo-tsu t'ung-chi*, 41:380b).

51. *Ts'e-fu yüan-kuei* (reprint, Chung-hua shu-chü: Peking, 1960), 42:482.

52. SKSC, 6:740c, biography of Shen-ch'ing, where the text also expressly says that at that
time the requirements had been made very severe. Shen-ch'ing was examined under the
supervision of the prefect of Mien-chou (present-day Mien-yang in Ssuchuan), which again
shows that also at a local level the secular authorities controlled the admission to the *sangha*.

53. T 2035 *Fo-tsu t'ung-chi*, 42:388b.

54. These "pages" or "sheets," *chih*, were strips of paper glued together to form a book-roll.
The size of such sheets had at an early age been standardized at a width of ca. 24 cm. (one Han
foot) and a length of 41 to 48.5 cm. The number of columns per sheet was not fixed (the
Tun-huang manuscripts show great variation), neither was the number of characters per
column (in the Tun-huang materials varying from twelve to more than fifty). Cf. Tsien
Tsuen-hsuin, *Written on Bamboo and Silk* (Chicago: University of Chicago Press, 1962) pp.
153–155. On the other hand, the practice of fixing the requirements for the examinations at a
certain round number of "sheets" proves that in these cases *chih* denotes a certain standard unit
of counting. We can perhaps derive that "standard sheet" from the number of *chih* presented in
the last two chapters of the *K'ai-yüan shih-chiao lu* A.D. 730 (T 2124, *chüan* 19–20: *Ju tsang lu*, containing a list of manuscripts recently added to the imperial collection). In this list the size of
Kumārajīva's version of the *Vimalakīrti-nirdeśa* is "61 *chih*" (T 2124, p. 703c). Because the *Lotus
sūtra* contains approximately seventy-eight thousand characters, and the *Vimalakīrti* about
twenty-nine thousand, it follows that of both scriptures the average "sheet" counted about five
hundred characters. Perhaps this was the norm used for fixing the amount of memorized text
for the clerical examinations.

but from scattered pieces of information at least an impression of what was demanded is available. Training centered upon the memorization (*sung, nien*) of considerable amounts of scriptural text, counted in "rolls" (*chüan*), "sheets" (*chih*), or "syllables" (*yen, tzu*). The amounts given in the biographies as having been memorized by individual monks are not representative because they are mentioned as exceptional feats: a daily absorption of "five pages";[55] "a thousand characters";[56] "several thousands"[57] or "eight thousand characters";[58] a total memorization of "more than twenty rolls,"[59] or even "forty rolls."[60]

More significant is the information on the nature of the texts memorized. It confirms the supreme importance of the *Lotus sūtra* (no doubt in Kumārajīva's version), by far the most popular scripture in medieval Chinese Buddhism.[61] Of the forty-one cases in which specific texts are mentioned in relation to the training phase, the *Lotus sūtra* figures sixteen times and the *Vimalakīrti-nirdeśa* and the *Mahāparinirvāna-sūtra* six times each.

The memorization of a long and complicated text like the *Lotus sūtra* or the *Vimalakīrti-nirdeśa* was not an easy job; the gifted Chen-hui (862–935) spent a full year on it.[62] Even if the texts required for the civil examinations were, in general, far more difficult, it cannot be denied that such a program did lead to a fair level of literacy. Another interesting aspect is the fact that in this preliminary stage the texts chosen (or rather "imposed," for they were "given" (*shou*) by the master) practically are limited to well-known scriptures (*sūtra*); the role played by scholastic texts is minimal. The biographical sources clearly show that scholastic study—closely related to the various "schools" of Sui-T'ang Buddhism—took place after full ordination and very often in other centers. That phase of "specialization" did not belong to the curriculum of the postulant or novice.[63]

Elementary Training in Secular Texts in the Monastery

There are unmistakable signs that besides Buddhist *sūtra*s Confucian texts

55. HKSC, 14:537b.

56. Ibid., 16:557a.

57. SKSC, 4:729c.

58. Ibid., 7:746a.

59. Ibid., 7:749c.

60. HKSC, 3:442a.

61. For the all-important place occupied by the *Lotus sūtra* in the Tun-huang materials, see Lionel Giles, *Six Centuries at Tun-huang* (London: The Chinese Society, 1944), p. 7. His observation is fully supported by the historical and bibliographical sources in which the number of significant references to the *Lotus sūtra* (such as recorded cases of study, recital, explanation, the writing of prefaces and commentaries, etc.) is roughly equal to the number of references to all other scriptures taken together.

62. SKSC, 7:748a.

63. In the last phase of the novitiate, or shortly after full ordination, many monks (at least the "eminent" ones of whom we have biographies) enter a period of itinerant travel and

were also studied in the monastery—a practice that can be traced back to the fourth century.[64] Unfortunately, our biographical sources only refer to it in very general terms, such as "at the age of twelve he became a novice, and achieved mastery in both canonical and secular texts."[65] From such statements I cannot infer what non-Buddhist texts were studied; in the next section I shall try to provide some information through indirect evidence.

It is clear that neither the great Mahāyāna scriptures nor the Confucian classics could be used in elementary teaching, and many postulants and novices were young children who needed training in basic literacy. Historical sources are silent about this aspect. However, in order to get a glimpse of it I can turn to a large body of Tun-huang documents, of a type to which so far little attention has been given but which in this perspective becomes very relevant: the writing exercise. Hundreds of such attempts to master the Chinese script have been preserved. In many cases it is evident that they were written under guidance: they often contain corrections and sometimes also large-size model characters more or less successfully copied by the pupil. The nature of the texts provides an impression of these first *gradus ad Parnassum*.

As could be expected, the most commonly used primer is the "Thousand Character Text" (*Ch'ien tzu wen*), the well-known abecedarium created by Chou Hsing-ssu around A.D. 540; because of its unique features (each character occurs only once, and the text can easily be memorized by its rhyme and tetrasyllabic structure), the primer has been used as a mnemonic primer into modern times.

The writing exercises are mostly found on the verso side of book-rolls where the *recto* side carries the main text(s). But they are also found on loose pieces of paper, in the empty space at the end of a text, or even between columns of other writings—apparently paper was too expensive to be wasted. They vary from the most primitive scribbles, obviously the first attempts at writing, to well-developed characters. Combined with the known age of many beginners—five or six years—they move readers by the picture they evoke: tip of the tongue protruding; a tiny hand clutching an unwieldy writing brush.

Many examples show the relation with elementary education. In P 3114

---

study—a way of advanced training and deepening of knowledge and experience that curiously resembles the *Wanderleben* of medieval students in Western Europe. Within the limits of this chapter it is impossible to do justice to that aspect. A study of the phenomenon in its totality—the Indian background of wandering mendicant monkhood; the movement of monks among different centers; their study under various masters, and the way in which this phase of "roaming about" (*yu fang*) influenced their later activities—would constitute an important contribution to knowledge of the practice of Chinese Buddhism of the Sui-T'ang period.

64. Cf. Zürcher, *Buddhist Conquest of China*, Vol. 7, p. 9.

65. Tao-hung, ca. 590, HKSC, 15:547a; analogous remarks on Fa-lin, ca. 635, ibid., 24:636b: I-ching, ca. 640, SKSC, 1:710b; Ta-i, ca. 700, ibid., 15:800a; Shen-yung, ca. 725, ibid., 19:815b.

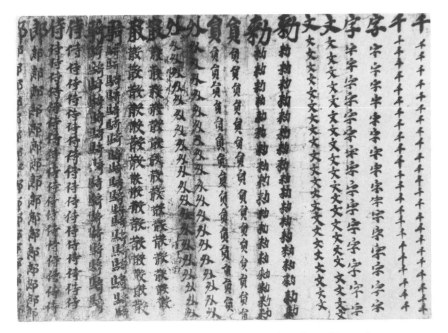

Fig. 2.1. Writing exercise: an advanced student. (P 3114)

(Fig. 2.1) the master has written, in a horizontal line at the tip of the scroll, a series of model characters; a rather advanced pupil has repeated each character many times in vertical columns. The same system, but in a much less developed hand, is found in S 2703 (Fig. 2.2). It contains, in endless repetition, lines 55–66 and 34–48 of the *Ch'ien tzu wen*, with the added remark that this is the fruit of seven day's labor (24–26 and 18–21 of two unspecified months). More advanced are S 5491 (Fig. 2.3) and especially S 5657 (Fig. 2.4), an excellent piece of homework based on *Ch'ien tzu wen*, lines 46–47. But for the real beginners even that primer was too complicated: S 4106 (Fig. 2.5) shows us the desperate attempts of the first hour, limited to some very simple characters. The most advanced pupils could concentrate on writing and memorizing rare characters and variants, sometimes adding the pronunciation (e.g., S 4622; Fig. 2.6).

The next stage probably consisted of copying the moralistic compendiums "Essential Teaching for the Instruction of Young People," *K'ai meng yao hsün*, a short text in rhyming four-syllable lines, composed by Ma Jen-shou. In T'ang times this text was often used as a primer: the Tun-huang materials contain many, mostly fragmentary, writing exercises based on it (e.g., P 3029; Fig. 2.7). The same role was played by another popular textbook, the "Family Teachings of T'ai-kung," *T'ai-kung chia-chiao*. Another type of secular text copied, probably at a still more advanced level, contained practical exercises such as passages from model letters.

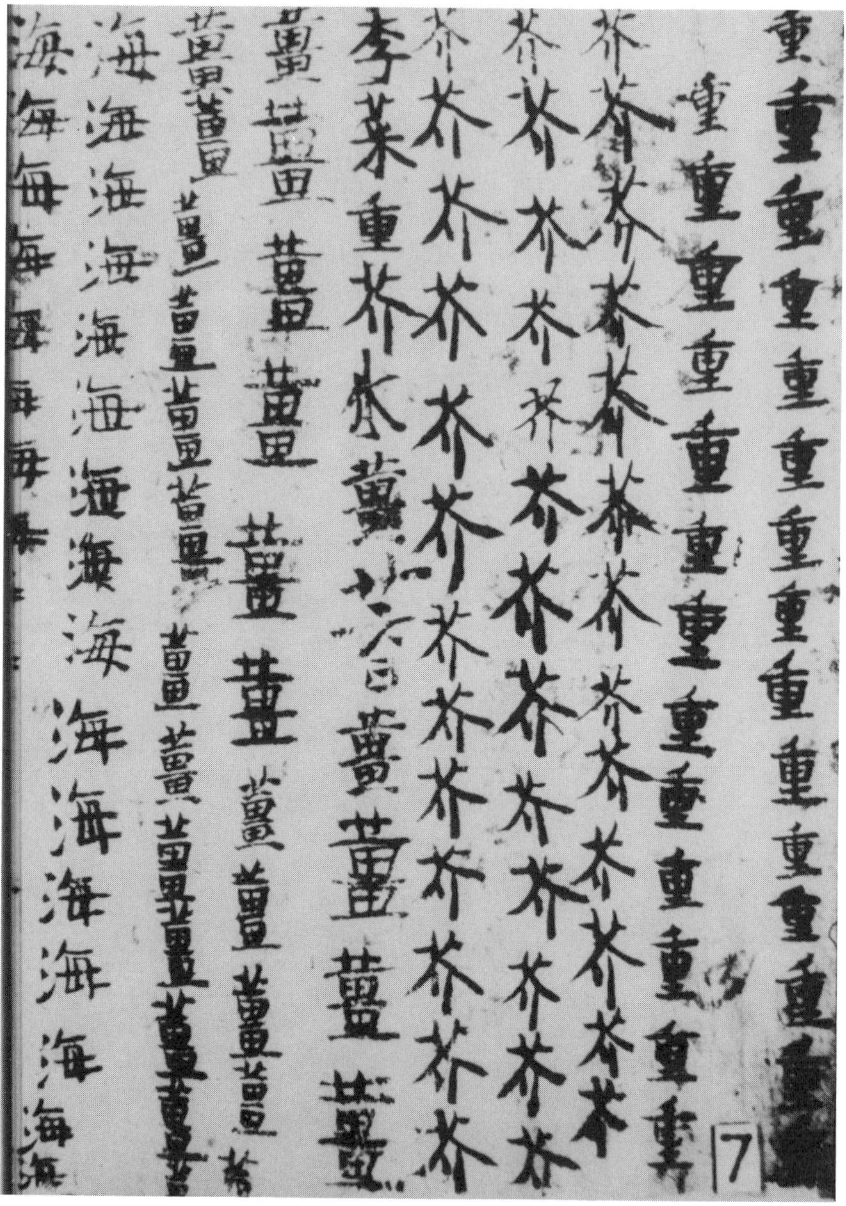

Fig. 2.2. Writing exercise based on *Ch'ien tzu wen*: a less developed hand. (S 2703)

Fig. 2.3. Writing exercise: a more advanced student. (S 5491)

Even though these texts themselves are secular, it is clear that they were produced in a religious context and were associated with Buddhism and monastic life. This is shown by many writing exercises based on Buddhist texts and sometimes even containing a mixture of secular and Buddhist elements. For example, P 3168 (Fig. 2.8) combines seven columns of *Ch'ien tzu wen* with a number of repeated Buddhist terms, and S 5712 (Fig. 2.9) shows a list of rare and variant characters and some Buddhist expressions.

THE ROLE OF THE MONASTERY IN EDUCATING THE LAITY

Thus far I have mainly been dealing with education within the *saṅgha* although I cannot be quite sure in the case of writing exercises in which laymen also may have been involved. Turning to the external educational activities, I must repeat that this aspect is less well-documented than the first. Apart from a number of stray references in secular literature, the main body of evidence suggesting that the monastery played such a role is found in the Tun-huang materials.

I should stress that running schools for the lay public is not one of the well-known social or charitable activities of the Buddhist clergy in T'ang China, as the establishment of dispensaries and orphanages was. As I said before, the role of Buddhism in education was restricted, because of the dominance of Confucianism in this sector of social activity. At the middle and higher levels of education (secondary training in district schools and upward) one must assume that Buddhist institutions played no role, for, if they did, they probably would have been mentioned—and condemned—in secular sources. Monastic activities in the field of external education must therefore be sought at grass-roots level, in the informative sphere of the "community schools" (*hsiang-hsüeh, hsiang-hsü*) relatively free from the regulating influence of the official school system.

Unfortunately, little is known about such village schools in T'ang times, apart from the fact that they existed. There is, of course, abundant informa-

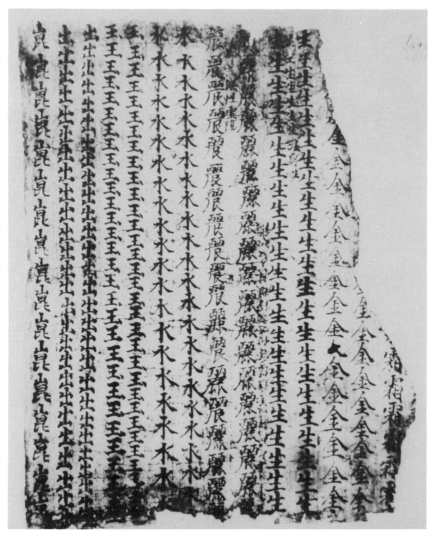

Fig. 2.4. Writing exercise based on *Ch'ien tzu wen*: an especially advanced student.
(S 5657)

tion on the central institutions in the capital: the imperial colleges (*Kuo-tzu hsüeh* and *T'ai-hsüeh*, in principle only accessible to sons of high officials, and the *ssu men hsüeh*, also open to selected commoners and sons of officials of the middle ranks). But that was the top. As usual, the information becomes less specific—and probably more schematized—at the lower levels. There were official schools at prefecture and county levels (*chou-hsüeh*, *hsien-hsüeh*), each divided into several categories according to the relative importance of the

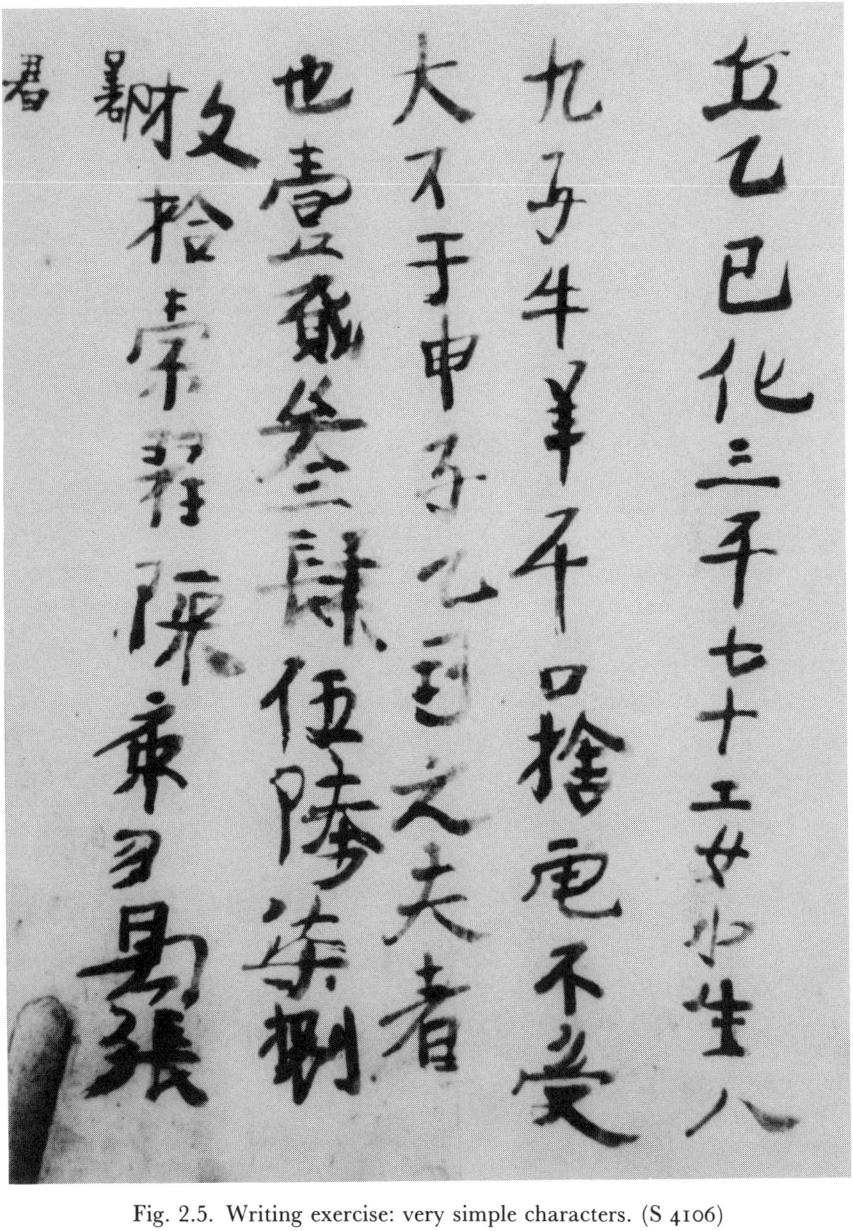

立乙巳化三千七十工女水生八

九弓牛羊不口拾電不受

大不于申子公到之夫者

也壹貳叁肆伍陸柒捌

攵拾宋羅陳乗習易張

君

Fig. 2.5. Writing exercise: very simple characters. (S 4106)

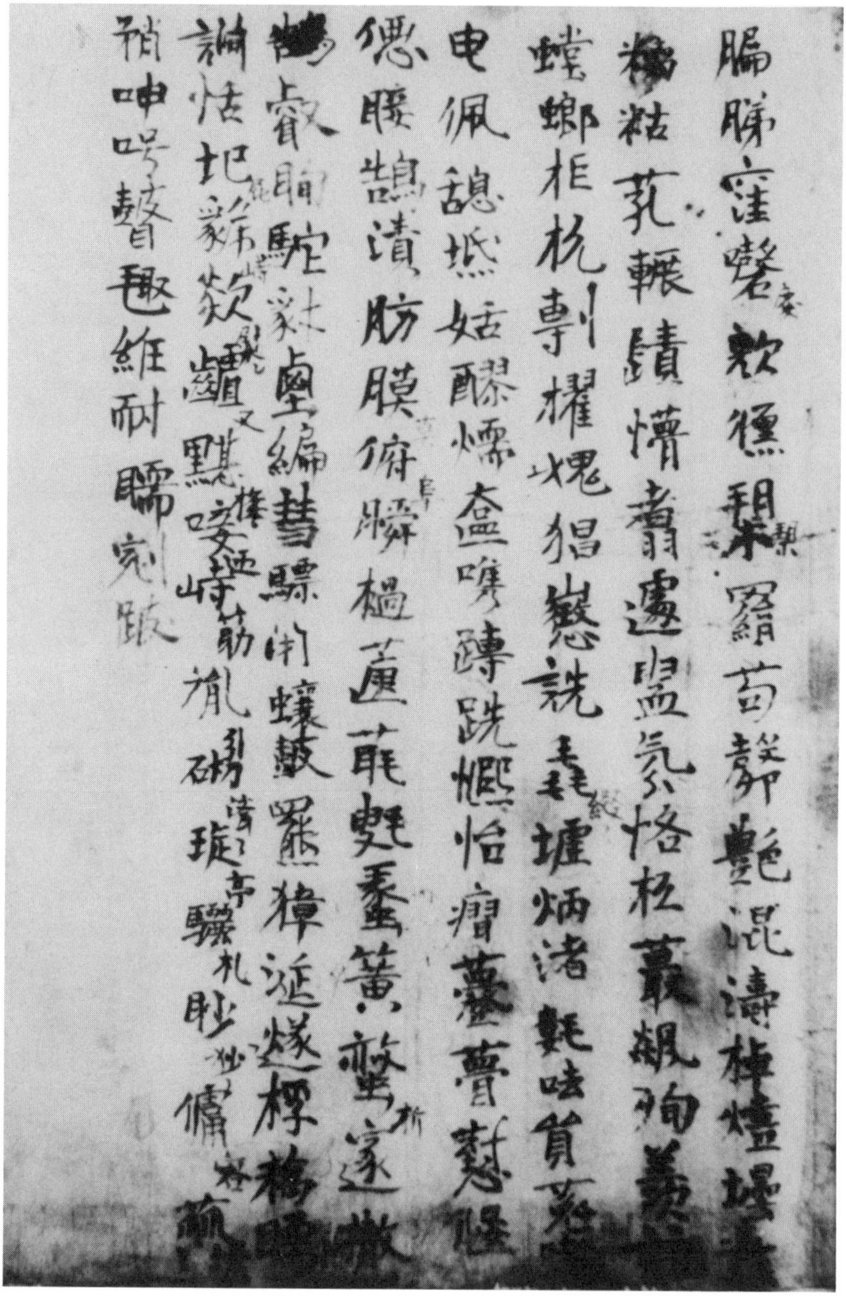

Fig. 2.6. Writing exercise: rare characters and variants. (S 4622)

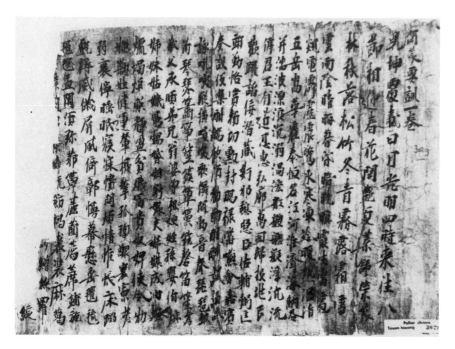

Fig. 2.7. Writing exercise based on *K'ai meng yao hsün*. (P 3029)

administrative unit. But even at the *hsien* level these official schools did not engage in elementary education. Thus, the lowest category of county school, with a modest staff of one "professor of Classics" (*ching-hsüeh po-shih*) and one assistant teacher (*chu-chiao*), admitted students at the age of seventeen to twenty four years, and its curriculum was limited to the Five Classics.[66] However, there also were private schools, probably of a more elementary character, for an edict of 733 specifically allows commoners who have set up such schools to send pupils (probably only the best ones) to the prefectural and district schools for instruction in the Classics.[67] The situation becomes wholly unclear at *hsiang* level, beyond the reach of the official educational system.

However, Buddhist biographical sources occasionally show that such village schools did function, and they, unlike the official schools, were visited by young boys. Thus, the monk Niu-yün (672–735) in his early youth seemed to be stupid. He was sent to the *hsiang-hsüeh* where "after a whole day he still did not know one character"; at the age of eleven his desperate parents finally sent him to a monastery.[68] As a young boy, Ch'ang-chüeh

66. Cf. Yü Shu-lin, *Chung-kuo chiao-yü shih* (Taipei: Taiwan Provincial Normal University, 1961), 5:409–528; for education at the local level see especially pp. 578–585.

67. Cf. ibid., p. 431.

68. HKSC, 21:943b.

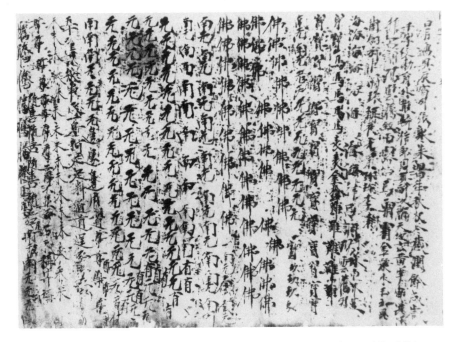

Fig. 2.8. Writing exercise: a combination of *Ch'ien tzu wen* entries and Buddhist terms. (P 3168)

(892–968) in the *hsiang-hsüeh* surpassed all other pupils in "reciting the canonical scriptures."[69] At the *hsiang-hsüeh* the curriculum comprised the "five classics"[70] and the "(writings of) the Hundred Masters."[71] If Buddhist educational activities were directed at all toward the laity, it would be in this world of small and elementary village schools. And in fact, Tun-huang documents do suggest that at the very end of this period (ninth and tenth centuries) such a development had taken place and that lay "students" were somehow attached to Buddhist monasteries.

Many hundreds of Tun-huang texts are provided with colophons of several types, varying from purely religious expressions of faith and of the expected beneficial karmic results of the work of copying to very factual notes specifying the name and status of the copyists and the date of copying. Because in the vast majority of cases the colophons are attached to Buddhist texts, the persons who have either copied the manuscript or ordered its copying mostly refer to themselves by typically Buddhist epithets, such as "the (Buddha's) disciple" lay devotee (*upāsaka, upāsikā*) "disciple having

69. Ibid., 28:996c.
70. Yüan-chen, 704–790; ibid., 20:838c.
71. Tseng-jen, 812–871; ibid., 26:977a.

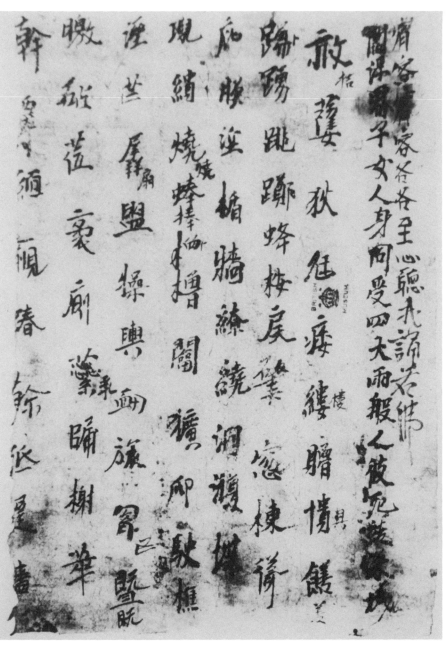

Fig. 2.9. Writing exercise: a combination of rare variant characters and Buddhist terms. (S 5712)

accepted the (Bodhisattva) vows" "donor" or "sūtra copyist." However, we also find a considerable number of colophons signed by persons who call themselves "student" or "young scholar" (*hsüeh-shih-lang*).[72] This appears to be an informal title, somewhat comparable with the popular use of *yüan-wai* to denote an "educated person" in Sung times; it does not figure in any of the official descriptions of the T'ang school system, but it obviously belongs to the sphere of study, education, and scholarship.

Upon looking more closely at this type of colophon, we find that practically none is attached to a Buddhist scripture: the works copied by such "students" almost invariably are secular. This could be explained by assuming that such manuscripts are external materials that somehow found their way into the (basically Buddhist) Tun-huang cache. This, however, is contradicted by the fact that in more than one-half of the cases the *hsüeh-shih-lang* are associated with specific monasteries in the Tun-huang region and that in some of such colophons monks are mentioned beside the "Young Masters." Some examples follow:

S 395   *Text*: "Dialogue between Confucius and (the boy) Hsiang T'o," *K'ung-tzu Hsiang T'o.*
          Colophon, dated 943: "Recorded by Chang Yen-pao, *hsüeh-lang* of the Ching-t'u Monastery."

S 2386 *Text*: "Classic of Filial Piety," *Hsiao-ching.*
          Colophon, dated 943: "Copying recorded by Kao Ch'ing-tzu, *hsüeh-shih-lang* of the Yung-an Monastery."

S 213   *Text*: "Ballad of the Swallow," *Yen-tzu fu.*
          Colophon, dated 924: "Copying recorded by Tu Yu-sui, *hsüeh-shih-lang* of the Yung-an Monastery."

S 3011 *Text*: "The Analects," *Lun-yü* (two chapters with *Cheng-i* Commentary).
          Colophon, " . . . by . . . , *hsüeh-lang* of the Chin-kuang-ming Monastery. . . . In the sixth month of the *mou-yin* year (probably 858) the monk [*sic*] Ma Yung-lung made a copy in his own hand of one roll of the Analects."

S 3386 *Text*: "Verses on the Classic of Filial Piety," *Yung Hsiao-ching.*
          Colophon dated 942: "Copying recorded by Chang Fu-ying, *hsüeh-shih* of the San-chieh Monastery."

72. In his study on religious societies (*she*) in Tun-huang, "Tonkō shutsudo 'sha' bunsho no kenkyū"(*Tōhōgakuhō* 35 (1974):217), Chikusa Masaaki defines the *hsüeh-(shih)-lang* as "student copyists" (*tenaraisei*) attached to a monastery; according to him, they were also the people who wrote, often by way of writing exercises, the many casual notes and documents (like club circulars) and other secular texts found among the Tun-huang materials. His view is shared by Victor Mair, who has listed those materials in his "Lay Students and the Making of Written Vernacular Narrative: An Inventory of Tun-huang Manuscripts." *Chinoperl Papers* no. 10 (1981): 5–96. To my knowledge the only study specially devoted to the *hsüeh-(shih)-lang* is a short paper by Ogawa Kan'ichi. "Tonkō butsuji no gakushirō," *Ryūkoku daigaku ronshū* 400/401 (1973):488–506.

The educational aspect also appears from some *"hsüeh-shih-lang* colophons" attached to elementary textbooks used in schools, notably the *K'ai meng yao-hsün*, which we also have come across in the context of the writing exercises. Thus, P 3189 (Fig. 2.10), containing the last part of the *K'ai meng yao-hsün*, bears a colophon stating that it was copied "by Chang Yen-tsung, *hsüeh-shih-lang* of the San-chieh Monastery."

The association of the name of a *hsüeh-shih-lang* with a monastery is very frequent: out of the sixty-seven colophons of this type assembled by Victor Mair (cf. note 72) in no less than thirty-nine cases such lay students are connected with one of nine monasteries in the Tun-huang area. Because practically all such texts are of a secular nature,[73] this suggests a merger between Buddhist and secular education at the grass-roots level. It appears that this type of education comprised students of different levels. Perhaps the more advanced ones (the *hsüeh-shih-lang?*) also acted as teachers: another manuscript of the *K'ai meng yao-hsün* (S 705, dated 851) bears a colophon stating that it "was copied by An Wen-lu, at the dictation of the student (*hsüeh-sheng*) Sung Wen-hsien." Another interesting fact is that the dated or datable colophons of this type all are concentrated in a rather short and late period, globally between 850 and 990. We must conclude that the role played by Buddhist monasteries in secular elementary education clearly was a late development that took place in the transitional period covering the last decades of the T'ang, the Five Dynasties, and the beginning of the Sung. Such a development would, indeed, fit into the general picture of Buddhism in that period, characterized by strong secularizing tendencies.

Because these colophons point to the existence of a certain type of secular education associated with Buddhist monasteries in the Tun-huang region since the late T'ang, we may venture one step further and study the relative frequency of secular texts in the Tun-huang materials; this may provide a clue to the nature and content of the curriculum. A provisional count, (based on the Stein, Pelliot, and Peking collections and the published part of the Leningrad catalog) yields a result, which, indeed, seems significant. The following texts occupy the ten top places:

1. *Lun-yü* (63 entries)
2. *Ch'un-ch'iu* with *Tso-* and *Ku-liang chüan* (52)
3. Various encyclopedias (*lei-shu*) of modest size (46)
4. *Chi'en-tzu wen* (35)
5. *T'ai-kung chia-chiao* (35)[74]
6. The Mao version of the *Odes* (30)

---

73. The only exception seems to be P 3398 (no. 121 in Mair's inventory), a copy of the *Diamond Sūtra* made by a lay student, dated A.D. 943.

74. The work entitled "Family Teaching of T'ai-kung" is a collection of moralistic utterances expressed in four-syllable verse. In T'ang times, it was used as a primer, together with some other popular elementary textbooks, for which see Meng Hsien-ch'eng and others, *Chung-kuo ku-tai chiao-yü shih tzu-liao* (Peking: Jen-min chiao-yü ch'u-pan she, (1961), pp. 177–179.

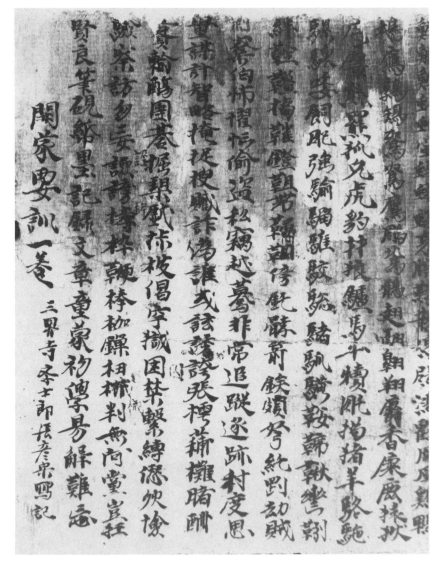

Fig. 2.10. The last part of *K'ai meng yao hsün*. (P 3189)

7. The *Book of Documents* (26)
8. The *Classic of Filial Piety* (25)
9. The *Ch'ieh-yün* and other pronouncing dictionaries (24)
10. Various other dictionaries (*tzu-shu*) (19)

This is, indeed, what we would expect of elementary education: from the basic primer *Ch'ien tzu-wen* the pupil learns basic characters and standard expressions; the primer *T'ai-kung chia-chiao* teaches the pupil moralistic themes in terse and simple language; the Confucian classics clearly emphasize the *Analects* (*Lun-yü* and *Hsiao-ching* also constituted "compulsory memorization" in the official school system); some short encyclopedias and dictionaries are included. The popular and nonofficial character of this type of education is also shown by the fact that these more or less "curricular" texts are embedded in a mass of popular materials: rhapsodies (*fu*); simple poems and doggerels (notably of the Wang Fan-chih type); the apocryphal Li Ling / Su Wu letters, *pien-wen*, model letters, and the like. But what is *not* found in the Tun-huang secular materials is as significant. Apart from the *Wen-hsüan* (the classical anthology that in T'ang times was used as the standard textbook for stylistic training, and this is well-represented with eighteen entries), all the rest of "higher literature" hardly plays a role at this level. The same is true for the dynastic histories that are only marginally represented. This distribution of titles, combined with the emergence of "students" or "young scholars" associated with Buddhist monasteries, at least gives a vague impression of the type of external education that had developed in the late T'ang as a sideline activity of the *saṅgha*, possibly as the result of a merger of the training of semimonastic "postulants" and the community schools (*hsiang-hsüeh*) below the district level.

The fact that in T'ang times, and especially in the latter half of that period, Buddhist monasteries all over China had acquired such an educational role is corroborated by numerous references in secular literature. In a detailed study and a monument of erudition,[75] Yen Keng-wang has listed some two hundred instances in which individuals, many of whom later became prominent as poets, administrators, or generals, in their early years are said to have spent some time, sometimes several years, in Buddhist monasteries. In most cases it is clear that some kind of education or literary training is involved, as appears from the use of terms meaning "to study" or "to receive instruction" (*hsüeh, hsi yeh, ssu yeh*); and, although in general no particulars about the kind of training are given, a few most explicitly state that the education they received in the monastery was not based on Buddhist but on Confucian and secular texts.

Thus, Li Chih who during the 880s served as a courtier and high official, had spent three years in the Hui-shan Monastery at Wu-hsi around 830, during which time he had studied various Confucian classics: *Shih-chi* and *Han-shu*; *Chuang-tzu*; *Han Fei-tzu*, and the *Li-sao*.[76] In the same monastery somewhat earlier, around 800, the future poet Li Shen had studied at the age of fourteen or fifteen; later he returned to the Hui-shan monastery for ten years, living in a monk's cell and copying some five hundred rolls of "classics

---

75. "T'ang-jen hsi yeh shan-lin ssu yüan chih feng-shang," in his *T'ang-chih yen-chiu ts'ung-kao* (Hong Kong, 1971), p. 267–424.

76. *Ch'üan T'ang-wen* (reprint, Taipei: Hui-wen shu chü 1961), 724:11b: "Preface to the Poems on the Hui-shan Monastery," *T'i Hui-shan ssu shih hsü*, dated A.D. 869.

and history."[77] The most informative passage deals with a certain Tuan Wei, who in the second half of the ninth century became a poet of modest renown. In his youth Tuan Wei had been illiterate. He later regretted his lack of literary skill, and when he heard that the Buddhist monastery on Mt. Chung-t'iao (in Shansi)[78] was an important center of study—a "students' lair" (*hsüeh-sheng yüan-sou*)—he went there to be instructed. At first the students despised him and did not want to give him canonical texts to be memorized. However, after he had amazed them with his ability to memorize secular poetry and a rhyming dictionary, they transmitted (*shou*) the *Hsiao-ching* to him. After that he was able to become widely read in the Classics and secular literature within six months. The text explicitly says that only after having completed this crash-course in literary education did he leave the monastery.[79]

The examples given by Yen Keng-wang, and especially the episode about Tuan Wei, are instructive in several ways. First, they show that the external educational activities of monasteries, of which some material remains among the Tun-huang documents, were not limited to the northwestern frontier region; the cases mentioned are spread throughout almost the whole of China. Second, in the case of Tuan Wei no mention is made of studying under a particular "master"; we get the impression of a kind of community of "students," *shu-sheng*, from whom Tuan Wei gets his instruction, which reminds us of the role of the *hsüeh-shih-lang* in the Tun-huang material. Third, the texts clearly show that young people who studied in Buddhist (and, occasionally, also in Taoist) monasteries did so to prepare themselves for the official examinations, and in many instances this informal study is explicitly related to the students' humble background and/or poverty. Finally, it is striking that most examples date from the ninth century, which again agrees with the information from Tun-huang presented above.

Yen Keng-wang suggests a direct link between the practice of studying in monasteries and the rise of Confucian academies (*shu-yüan*) in Sung times. This interesting observation deserves to be followed by further research. However, at this stage the available information is too scanty and too unspecific to regard it as more than a promising but as yet untested working hypothesis. The only form of institutionalization of this type of education explicitly mentioned a few times is called 'charitable schools" (*i-hsüeh*), a term that (like *shu-yüan* itself) strongly suggests a secular origin: an institution based on voluntary contributions and inspired by feelings of "civic duty."[80]

---

77. Ibid., 816:3b–4a: "Note on Our Family Temple in the Hui-shan Monastery" (*Hui-shan ssu chia-shan chi*) by Li Shen's grandson Li Chün, dated 879.

78. Probably the Wan-ku Monastery on Mt. Chung-t'iao, where according to *T'ang chih-yen* (SPPY, 7:1b), the future general Hsü Shang in the early ninth century spent some time.

79. *T'ang chih-yen*, SPPY (Shanghai: Chung-hua shu-chü, 1936), pp. 5b–6a.

80. The term *i-hsüeh* is in itself ambivalent because in context unrelated to any educational institution it occasionally means "(scriptural) exegesis" as a scholastic specialization. Thus,

The Production and Distribution of Written Materials

Finally, we may pose the question: "To what extent has Buddhism contributed to general literacy and reading habits through the production and spread of texts?" It is a vast and complicated subject, and I shall limit myself to a few general remarks on three aspects: (1) the formation, size, and function of monastic libraries; (2) the distribution and circulation of Buddhist texts outside the monastery; and (3) the modest role played by printing in pre-Sung times.

Monastic Libraries constitute another area largely unknown except for the evidence of Tun-huang materials. The large metropolitan monasteries patronized by the court possessed large collections of Buddhist texts. At the center, the mass of available texts was, moreover, constantly enlarged by state-sponsored translation activities and the production of Chinese scholastic works that were offered to the court, with the request that these texts be "entered into the Canon," *ju tsang*. But in this chapter I shall not touch upon that large-scale and well-organized production of new texts. It is a process that, as regards size, level of organization, and degree of state supervision, reached its apogee in the early Sung. For my purpose it is noteworthy that in some cases, especially in early T'ang times, Buddhist texts were consciously distributed from the center throughout the empire. In 648 copies of Hsüan-tsang's voluminous translation of the *Yogācāra-siddhi-śāstra* were sent by imperial edict to a great number of prefectures,[81] and in 689 empress Wu ordered that the *Ta-yün ching* (a text she "promoted" for political reasons) should be spread throughout the realm.[82] Emperor Hsüan-tsung did the

---

HKSC, 25:538c, states that among the disciples of Fa-min (578–645) no less than seventy "monks (specialized in) exegesis," *i-hsüeh sha-men*. In one of the two cases mentioned by Yen Keng-wang *T'ang chih yen-chiu ts'ung-kao*, (p. 374) it seems that the text refers to this kind of *i-hsüeh*: according to *Chiu T'ang-shu* (Peking: Chung-hua shu-chü, 1975), 177:4597, the chief minister P'ei Hsiu (?787–860),when serving as military governor of Feng-hsiang (S. W. Shensi) in 860, often went to the Buddhist monasteries in that region for learned discussions because "there were many *i-hsüeh*; his teachers (all) were monks." Because this took place at the very end of P'ei Hsiu's carreer, when he was in his seventies, it is clear that the term does not refer to any institution of elementary secular education, and I take it that also in this case it simply meant "(scholastic) exegetes." The second example given by Yen Keng-wang is also of questionable relevance: it refers to the fact that as a young man Tsung-mi (780–841) studied in the *i-hsüeh yüan* in Sui-chou (present-day Sui-ning in Ssuchuan), a flourishing center of Confucian studies. There he in A.D. 807 met the Ch'an master Tao-yüan "who in the course of his travels had come to this prefecture." Tsung-mi was deeply impressed by him and immediately became his disciple (*Yüan-chüeh ching ta-shu ch'ao, chüan* 1B, *Zoku-zōkyō* I.14, p. 222b). Because this meeting took place when Tsung-mi was immersing himself in Confucian studies (in fact, according to his biography, SKSC, 6:741c, this encounter precisely brought about his conversion to Buddhism), the "I-hsüeh Hall" at Sui-chou undoubtedly was a Confucian school, and there is no reason to assume that it had any relation with Buddhist monastic institutions.

81. T 2154 *K'ai-yüan shih-chiao lu*, 8:559c; see also T 2053 *Ta Tzu-en ssu san-tsang fa-shih chuan* (biography of Hsüan-tsang, by Hui-li and Yen-ts'ung, ca. 665), 6:256a.

82. T 2126 *Seng-shih lüeh*, 3:248c; T 2035 *Fo-tsu t'ung-chi*, 39:369c: *Chiu T'ang-shu*, 6:121.

same in 736 with the *Diamond Scripture"* (*Vajra-cchedikā, Chin-kang ching*) together with a commentary in his own hand.[83] In one case, the distribution was made for the benefit of the wordly authorities. When in 639 another attempt was made to "sift" (*sha-t'ai*) the *sangha* by secularization of all undesirable elements, emperor T'ai-tsung provided all provincial governors with copies of the *I-chiao ching*, a short text in which the essential duties and norms of behavior of the *sangha* are explained; and consequently it could be used by the authorities as a guideline in dealing with the clergy.[84]

However, as soon as one leaves the center, information on Buddhist collections becomes very scarce. The lacuna is only partially filled by the Tun-huang materials: about fifty lists of titles refer to specific monastic libraries, but none of these contains a complete inventory; most lists are fragmentary, or are "lists of new acquisitions" or "lists of lacking volumes." However, some documents, like S 3624 (Fig. 2.11), a fragment of the inventory of the San-chieh monastery, certainly evoke the picture of large and well-kept libraries. Another document, P 3010, entitled "List of new manuscripts of canonical scriptures, year by year added (to the collection) of the San-chieh Monastery" (*San-chieh ssu li-nien hsin-hsieh tsang-ching mu-lu*), suggests great activity and considerable growth (Fig. 2.12). In many cases the new acquisitions only were *parts* of scriptures. This way of library building probably was a general phenomenon outside the Tun-huang region as well. Handwritten texts were very expensive, and in most cases neither the monasteries themselves nor the donors who ordered the copying of a text as a "good work" could afford to produce complete copies of lengthy texts. Most Tun-huang scriptures are incomplete because piety had its limits; the donors mostly only provided single rolls, or even single sections. In this way, the monasteries had to "scrape their libraries together" by collecting parts of texts; monastic libraries therefore appear to have suffered from both extreme duplication and structural gaps. The several "lists of incomplete scriptures" (*ch'üeh-ching mu, ch'ien tsang-ching mu*) are not the result of neglect or theft but of the method of acquisition itself.

Professional copyists were attached to the monastery; they probably produced manuscripts by order of both the monastery and outside donors. One list of copyists attached to the Chin-kuang-ming Monastery (S 2711, *Chin-kuang-ming ssu hsieh ching jen-ming*) shows a staff of no less than fifty-five persons, both monks and laymen (Fig. 2.13). It is interesting to note that of the twenty-seven lay copyists ten are surnamed Chang—apparently they were members of a family specialized in this trade.

Circulation of Buddhist texts outside the monastery is another topic about which I can speak only in general terms because specific information, at least for T'ang times, is lacking. The spread of at least certain popular texts

---

83. SKSC, 14:795b (biography of Hsüan-yen, 674–742).
84. T 2035 *Fo-tsu t'ung-chi*, 39:365b; cf. also T 2051 *T'ang hu fa shamen Fa-lin pieh-chuan*, 2:204a.

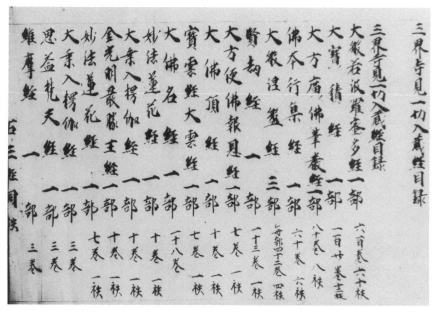

Fig. 2.11 A fragment of the inventory to the San-chieh monastery library. (S 3624)

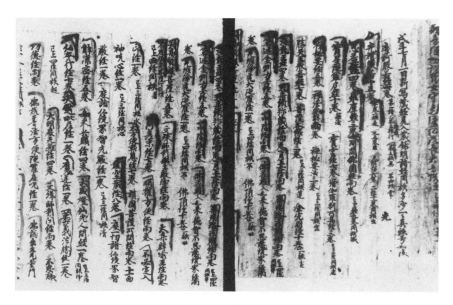

Fig. 2.12 A list of additions to the inventory of the San-chieh monastery library. (P 3010)

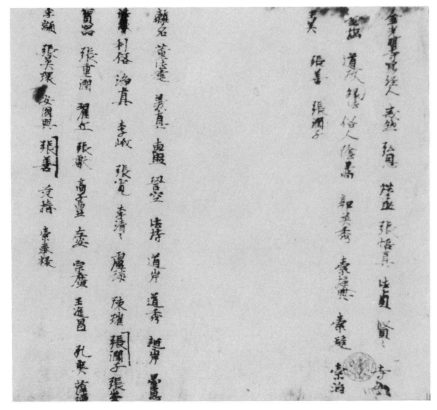

Fig. 2.13 Copyists attached to the Chin-kuang-ming Monastery. (S 2711)

among the lay public must have been stimulated by the common Mahāyāna belief that the pious recital of scriptures is an act of faith with positive karmic consequences. The stereotyped passages, found in many Mahāyāna *sūtras*, list the ways in which a believer can show his piety toward the scripture in question, very often including "reading aloud" (*nien*) and "chanting" (*sung*), and in later times literate lay believers certainly did so, either individually or collectively.

I must, therefore, assume that also in T'ang times Buddhist texts spread outside the monastery and that in this way Buddhism must have contributed to literacy, or rather to the practice of reading. However, the level of literacy was no doubt very low and scriptures did not necessarily have to be read: the text in itself was a sacred object. This "amulet" function is of course even more evident in the innumerable magic formulas (*mantra*), short tracts, and inscribed pictures that were produced in great quantities. Mainly in this sector did the technique of printing have its greatest impact.

The *art of printing*, undoubtedly the most momentous Buddhist contribution to the spread of literacy (and hence, indirectly, to education), primarily allowed mass-production of texts for the lay public. However, it is a remarkable fact that the practice of printing Buddhist texts, in spite of its obvious advantages, spread very slowly. In the Tun-huang cache (closed at the beginning of the eleventh century) the number of printed texts is almost negligible: of the more than eight thousand items in the Stein collection only twenty are printed, and the published part of the catalogue of the Pelliot collection (one thousand items) only mentions two. I must conclude that even after at least a quarter of a millennium the role of the art of printing in the production and spread of Buddhist texts still was absolutely marginal. The extreme scarcity of printed items in the Tun-huang collections—mostly short texts and formulas—shows that the new technique was still in its infant state and that in the period covered by this chapter its influence must have been minimal.

CONCLUSIONS

From my discussion of Buddhism and education, I would draw a number of conclusions. In "Buddhist education" the whole complex of study and teaching was, by definition, aimed at religious instruction; education, as practiced by the *saṅgha*, was subordinated to the religious message. In a certain sense it was thereby limited in its scope. On the other hand, however, it was directed to all people, without distinction of age, class, or sex. Because the message was intended "for the benefit of all beings," the ideal of religious instruction was, in principle, universal.

One central element in religious training was scriptural study and the spread of sacred texts. Countless passages in Mahāyāna *sūtra*s extol the merits of persons, male and female alike (*shan nan-tzu shan nü-jen*, the equivalent of our "brothers and sisters"), who read, recited, studied, and copied the scriptures.

In China, the ideal of scriptural study was reinforced by the influence of the Confucian concept of "recruitment of talent"; its most characteristic expression was the development of clerical examinations under the T'ang. In this way, education within the *saṅgha*, and especially textual memorization and study, came to contain an element of compulsoriness and competition that must have raised the educational level of the *saṅgha* as a whole. In this way, the training of the monk (about nuns almost nothing is known) in China could develop into a religious educational system in its own right.

In the fourth century a small vanguard of "scholar-monks" developed who were the bearers of the great tradition of Chinese Buddhism; in the course of the sixth century this top layer within the clergy developed into a secondary elite, an "alternative intelligentsia." However, it remained a tiny minority within the *saṅgha*. For the average monk, training led to a modest level of literary skill based on the memorization of some popular scriptures, notably the *Lotus sūtra*. In the case of young postulants or novices, this was preceded by training in elementary literacy. But even so, this educational level must have been superior to that of the general population.

Inside the monastery monks also received some training in secular literature, probably because it was considered indispensible in their relations with the outer world. The materials again suggest a very modest program, with emphasis on the most elementary texts.

In late T'ang times, Buddhist monasteries engaged in some kind of external education, at the grass-roots level, probably as the result of a fusion between the semimonastic postulants' training and the local community schools (*hsiang-hsüeh*).

The production and spread of religious texts must also have contributed to the lay public's level of literacy, but owing to the scarcity of information it is unknown to what extent. The process was no doubt much accelerated by the use of printing, but in the tenth century the influence of this technique was still marginal.

Like other universal religions, Buddhism potentially is able to play a dominating role in education; in "Buddhist countries" like Thailand and Burma it has fully developed that potentiality. In medieval China, environmental and cultural factors prevented it from doing so. The main inhibiting factor was the dominance of the Confucian concept of education. In the hypothetical case that Confucian education strictly limited itself to the training of an elite of administrators, it is conceivable that Buddhism would have developed an educational system of its own. But, as I remarked in the beginning, the Confucian ideal of "moral transformation" was by no means limited to the "selection of talent" and the formation of a top layer of scholar-officials. Confucianism had its own brand of moral "education for the masses," in which, in principle, the *sangha* had no role to play. However, materials show that the *sangha* as an alternative intelligentsia with a certain intellectual status and a certain degree of literacy education did manage to play a role through informal channels and at the grass-roots level.

In the late T'ang, even more lay students were attracted to Buddhist monasteries for secular studies. Judging from the number of "*hsüeh-shih-lang* documents" from Tun-huang and considering the fact that probably only a tiny fraction of such materials has been preserved, we must conclude that in early Sung times many thousands of people (all over China, as is shown by the data collected by Yen Keng-wang) had received at least part of their education in monastic surroundings. It is quite possible that in that world of "parochial schools" (as they are called by Victor Mair), where the young students were confronted with both the Confucian and the Buddhist traditions, the study of the Classics was more open, less tradition-bound, and less orthodox than in the official schools where Confucianism was encapsulated, so to speak, within its own universe. In this way, at a social level far below that of the master-minds of Neo-Confucianism, Buddhism may have contributed to breaking down the barriers of Confucian orthodoxy: in its humble and inconspicuous way, it may have created a space in which Neo-Confucianism eventually could operate.

THREE

Ch'an Education in the Sung: Ideals and Procedures

Chün-fang Yü

By the Sung dynasty (960–1280) Ch'an Buddhism already had a history of some two hundred and fifty years from the time of Hui-neng, the Sixth Patriarch (638–713). Generations of charismatic masters had come and gone. The five schools of Ch'an had been firmly established. Patriarchal Ch'an (*tsu-shih ch'an*) had replaced Tathāgata Ch'an (*ju-lai ch'an*) as the essence of the wordless transmission established by Bodhidharma.[1] Ch'an Buddhism identified itself as a "separate teaching outside of scriptures" and took pride in the fact that it did not "establish any words." But, although most Ch'an masters in the T'ang did not engage in literary activities, there was a massive production of Ch'an works in the Sung. If one examines the contents of various collections of the Buddhist canon, Ch'an writings by far outstrip those of other schools.[2]

I would like to thank my refuge master, Sheng-yen, the abbot of Nung-ch'an ssu of Pei-t'ou, Taiwan, and the Ch'an Center of Queens, New York, for his guidance and help in the research and writing of this paper.

1. Tathāgata Ch'an is the highest state of meditation mentioned in the *Lankavatava sūtra*, surpassing that of the non-Buddhist as well as the two vehicles. It is so named because this is the samadhi achieved by the Tathāgata. Tsung-mi stated in his *Ch'an-yüan tu-hsü* that this is the meditation of the highest vehicle (*tsui shang-cheng ch'an*) and is the meditation handed down from Bodhidharma. However, later Ch'an masters contrasted Tathāgata Ch'an with patriarchal Ch'an. The former unfavorably came to stand for nonultimate meditation taught by the *sūtra*s, and the latter was the ultimate meditation taught by the Ch'an patriarchs who carried on the separate teaching outside of scriptures and independent of words. The patriarchal Ch'an is now truly representative of Bodhidharma's transmission. *The Transmission of the Lamp* (*chüan* 2) gives the clear contrast of these two types of meditation when Hsiang-yen was scolded by his master Yung-shen, with "You have achieved Tathāgata Ch'an but not Patriarchal Ch'an." Ting Fu-pao, *Fo-hsüeh ta tzu-tien* (reprint, Taipei: Hua-yen Lien-she, 1961) 2:1088, 1817.

2. Sheng-yen made a page count to illustrate this point. He says, "Among the various schools of Chinese Mahāyāna Buddhism, Ch'an has bequeathed us the most writings. In the section on the schools in the Taishō Daizōkyō Tripitaka, Ch'an classics occupy the first place, running

Despite the irony, the expression "literary Ch'an" (*wen-tzu ch'an*) is appropriate to describe the prolific literary outpourings by Ch'an monks who wrote about other Ch'an monks in the Sung. Aside from the *yü-lu* (recorded sayings), which already appeared in the T'ang and continued to be compiled in the Sung, Ch'an monks in the Sung created a new genre called *teng-lu* (lamp records).[3] They also began to compile monastic codes or "Pure Rules" (*ch'ing-kuei*) as guides to Ch'an monks living the communal life in the public monasteries (*ts'ung-lin*, "thickets and groves").[4] The energetic codification of Ch'an rules paralleled the vigorous compilation of the lamp records. Both reflected an urgently felt need to preserve, rectify, and vitalize the Ch'an tradition. Many Ch'an masters in the Sung lamented the decline of discipline and the neglect of meditation. The Ch'an codes tried to remedy the former and the lamp records to correct the latter. In a way, they served as alternative sources of authority providing the original authority which could come only from the enlightened charismatic masters. For this reason in the golden age of Ch'an, the first two hundred years after Hui-neng, there were

---

1,599 pages while the writings of the T'ien-t'ai school, which is noted for its interest in philosophical doctrines, occupy the second place, running 982 pages. In the section on biographies, Ch'an also heads the list. The biographical writings of the *Transmission of the Lamp of the Ching-te Era* and the *Continuation of the Transmission of the Lamp* alone came to sixty-six *chüan*. When we look at the Zokuzōkyō Tripitaka, in the section containing Chinese works, Ch'an writings came to more than 17 *tse*, running 8,284 pages. Next come Pure Land writings, which occupy less than 4 *tse*, running 1,685 pages and finally T'ien-t'ai which has 1604 pages." *Ch'anmen hsiu-cheng chih-yao* (Taipei: Tung-chu chu-pan she, 1980), p.1.

3. The first such work is the *Ching-te Ch'uan teng lu* compiled by Tao-yüan in 1004. It contains the sayings of 1,701 Ch'an monks. Because it emphasizes their words instead of their acts, the *teng-lu* resembles the *yü-lu* more than biography. The *Chuang teng-lu* was followed by four more similar works: the *T'ien-sheng kuang teng-lu* compiled in 1024 by Li Tsun-hsü, a layman; the *Chien-chung Ch'ing-kuo hsü teng-lu* by Wei-pai in 1103; the *Lien-teng hui-yao* by Wu-ming in 1183; and the *Chia-t'ai p'u-teng lu* by Cheng-shou in 1204. Together the five lamp records were known as the "Five Lamps" (*Wu-teng*). Because each work contains thirty *chüan*, the entire set comes to a huge one hundred fifty *chüan*. They were eventually reduced to twenty *chüan* by P'u-chi at the end of the Sung, and he named it *Wu-teng hui-yüan* (Convergence of the Five Lamps). These records hold a wealth of *kung-an*, *hua-t'ou*, and *chi-feng*; the sharp, quick, and pointed exchanges between masters and disciples provide tantalizingly brief glimpses into the training of Ch'an monks in the Sung. More famous than the lamp records because of its comparative brevity (ten *chüan*) and the frequent use by Ch'an masters of its *kung-an* (one hundred taken from the seventeen hundred found in the *Transmission of the Lamp*), the *Pi-yen lu* (the Blue Cliff Record), compiled in 1125 by Hsüeh-tou Ch'ung-hsien, is perhaps the most representative product of the "literary Ch'an" of the Sung. Even though the term *teng-lu* started with the *Ching-te ch'uan-teng-lu*, this genre actually existed already in the T'ang. The *Pao-lin chuan*, compiled in 801, was the prototype for this kind of literature. The *Tsu-t'ang chi*, compiled in 952, continued this tradition and in turn served as the model for the *Ching-te ch'uan-teng lu*. Yanagida Seizan has devoted his life work to the study of the *Tsu-t'ang chi*. I thank Professor Philip Yampolsky for the information concerning the antecedents of *teng-lu*.

4. Four monastic codes were compiled in the Sung: *Ch'an-yüan ch'ing-kuei* in 1103, *Ju-chung jih-yung ch'ing kuei* in 1209, *Ju-chung hsü-chih* in 1263, and *Ts'ung-lin chiao-ting ch'ing-kuei tsung yao* in 1274. I will use the first, the earliest surviving Ch'an code extensively later in the paper.

neither recorded sayings, pure rules, nor lamp records. Then there was no such need.[5]

But there is another way of looking at the situation. Yanagida suggested that the *yü-lu* and *teng-lu* genres of Ch'an texts should be viewed as teaching devices. He pointed out that the use of the word *yü-lu* as a general name for the literature of Ch'an Buddhism was relatively new and late. It first appeared at the end of the biography of Huang-po Hsi-yün (d. 850) in the *Sung kao-seng chuan*, written by Hui-chiao in early Sung. *Yü-lu* records the acts and words that occurred during a "Ch'an encounter" (*chi-yüan*) between a master and his disciples. He then suggested that the very idea of recording the words of the "Ch'an encounter" most probably started with Ma-tsu and his lineage[6] because of Ma-tsu's vision of truth as imbedded in the concrete behavior and daily activities of the enlightened individual. Truth was neither conveniently contained by a body of scriptures nor linked to a specific course of religious exercise. A person could best be guided by the exemplary model of a master whose every act and every word was a living manifestation of the mind which was the Buddha. In the words of Yanagida:

> Ma-tsu's position is that the ordinary mind is the Tao. This position precludes any attachment to the traditional Buddhist religious practices of meditation and scriptural exegesis. Rather than a pre-conceived course of mental exercises and study, what is needed is some kind of effort directly related to the words and actions of daily life. The student must understand that the day-in and day-out activities of the ordinary mind are the activities of a Buddha. In this quest he is guided by the Ch'an Master, whose behavior exemplifies the functioning of mind as Buddha. In such a milieu, each of the individual actions and utterances of a great teacher constitute an expression of Truth and become considered important models of behavior by his students. This attention to the Master's actions as the models of enlightened behavior led directly to the development of the "recorded sayings" genre. The process was as follows: The greater the number of disciples that surrounded a great teacher became, the smaller each student's opportunities for individual instruction. Hence moments of direct contact with the teacher became prized experiences for the disciples involved, some of whom soon began making secret notes of the events. Eventually certain monks prone to such activity started making anthologies of the teacher's words and actions based on what they heard from other students in addition to their own experiences.[7]

5. I discussed this idea more extensively in a paper, "The Concept of Authority in Ch'an Buddhism," read at the 1977 AAS meeting in Los Angeles. See Chun-fang Yü, "Ta-Hui Tsung-kao and Kung-an Ch'an," *Journal of Chinese Philosophy* 6, no. 2 (1979):218–219.

6. Yanagida Seizan, "The Recorded Sayings Texts of Chinese Ch'an Buddhism," in *Early Ch'an in China and Tibet*, ed. Whalen Lai and Lewis R. Lancaster (Berkeley: Berkeley Buddhist Studies Series, 1983), p. 192. The Japanese original of this article appeared in *Indogaku bukkyōgaku kenkyū* 18; no. 1 (dec. 1969) as "Zenshū goroku no keisei." It was rearranged and translated into English by John R. McRae. I would like to thank John for drawing my attention to this article.

7. Ibid., p. 187.

The "recorded sayings" and later, the "transmission of the lamp" histories received reverence as a result of a new attitude toward Buddhist scriptures. "The attitude which led to this reverence for the oral records of one's predecessor is one which favors individual facts or incidents over abstract generalities. . . . This is fully in accordance with the predisposition toward personalized, 'incidental' expositions of the truth, the concrete rather than the abstract."[8] Because the collective interest of the *yü-lu* and *teng-lu* was in recording the climactic moments of the Ch'an "encounter," which could be expressed either by words or acts, biographical data in the conventional sense are often entirely absent. Despite the wealth of these Ch'an records there is not much information that would give a "texture" to the subject's life. They very rarely mention the early secular life of the subject: When was he born? What was his family's social status? When did he enter the monastery? What kind of education did he receive? What Buddhist texts, if any, did he study? For these questions, one must turn to the biographies of eminent monks. But even among them, very often the kind of information essential for a knowledge of the subject's monastic training was simply left out—a problem I will further discuss later in this chapter.

The Ch'an records are, therefore, of very limited use as source materials for the writing of a conventional history about Ch'an monks in the Sung. But to deplore their limitation is to misunderstand the original intention of their compilers. They were never written to serve as historical documents for future historians. "Encounters" were reverently recorded so that they could become "an important medium of religious teaching and dialogue."[9] New generations of Ch'an practitioners could be, and were, catapulted into enlightenment as a result of timely exposure to and skillful instruction in these materials of great fluidity and vitality.

The primary purpose of Ch'an education is to see into one's nature and to become awakened. At least in theory, if not always in practice, one left the householder's life for the sake of achieving enlightenment. One did not enter the monastery for the sake of learning about Buddhism, acquiring expertise in meditation, or even becoming a moral person, even though all these were greatly emphasized by monastic codes and other inspirational literature (a point I will consider in detail later).

What are some of the teaching methods and devices that had been developed by the Ch'an masters to help their disciples achieve the breakthrough? The *yü-lu* and *teng-lu* are rich sources for such a study. I will discuss some of the uniquely Ch'an teaching methodologies that were fairly standard in the Sung.

---

8. Ibid., p. 189.
9. Ibid., p. 194.

CH'AN PEDAGOGY

All the teaching methods used by later Ch'an masters were found in the Sung, although some aspects of Sung pedagogy have since fallen into disuse. During the last several decades, as a result of the activities of Chinese and Japanese masters, many Americans have come to know the use of *kung-an* (koan) as an unique device used in Ch'an (Zen) training. Most Western books on Ch'an also concentrate on this topic. The use of *kung-an* began in the Sung and became one of the most important methods in Ch'an training. But there were other teaching methods about which less is now known because modern Zen masters no longer use them. Ch'an records of the Sung provide good documentation about the type of *kung-an* most often used, where and when they were used, and, to a much lesser extent, how they were used. Sung monks were well aware of the fact that the use of *kung-an* was a recent phenomenon, and they regarded the compilations of *kung-an* made by Fen-yang Shan-chao (947–1024) and Hsüeh-tou Ch'ung-hsien (980–1052) as the beginning of this trend. Contemporary sources also often betray a sense of ambivalence. Although it was generally agreed that *kung-an* was a powerful device to transform a person's mind, the extensive reliance on the *kung-an* literature as teaching and study material was a cause for alarm and at least in one case, that of Ta-hui Tsung-kao (1089–1163), a justification for outright condemnation. Controversy early surrounded the role of *kung-an* in Ch'an training.

Wan-yen Tao-yen gave a brief history of the rise of *kung-an* anthologies:

> The First Patriarch handed down both the robe and Dharma. But the Sixth Patriarch stopped the transmission of the robe, and he chose those disciples whose practice and understanding had achieved an accord with his to continue the family tradition.... Both Shih-tou and Ma-tsu were his lineage grandsons.... The two masters were full of profound words and wondrous sayings which were circulated in the whole country.... The methods of teaching were many and there was not one special way which students must follow. Five tributaries flowed from the fountainhead of Ts'ao-hsi [Hui-neng]. But although the containers could be either round or square, the water was nevertheless the same in its essence. Each of the five schools had its own fine tradition. Every word and every command uttered in daily life could attract the attentions of learners. It was certainly no accident that the Ch'an public monasteries achieved great fame. After that time, masters began to engage in discussions and exchanges with their students in order to illumine the obscure and elucidate the subtle. In elevating or putting the students down, the masters were only trying to facilitate the transformative power of the Dharma. Their language was tasteless, like gruel made up of boiled wooden shavings or rice composed of cooked iron nails. This then became food for future generations' gestation. Such was the beginning of *nien-ku* ('picking up the words of the men of the past'). Fen-yang was the originator of the tradition, and Hsüeh-tou continued it and made it as boundless as the ocean.[10]

His contemporary, Hsin-wen Yün-fen, however, saw it differently:

The way of the "separate teaching outside of the scriptures" is concise in its
essentials. As first there was nothing to talk about. Former generations simply
practiced it without doubt and kept it without change. In the years of T'ien-hsi
[1017–1021] Hsüeh-tou, who was greatly eloquent in debate, sought something new and different. Fan-yang next created the genre called *sung-ku*
("Praising the men of the past"). Learners of the day were all attracted by it
and the style of Ch'an changed from then on. In the year of Hsüan-ho [1125]
Yüan-wu again used his own ideas and compiled the *Pi-yen lu* (Blue Cliff
Record). At that time some traditionalists such as Tao-ning, Ssu-hsin,
Ling-yüan, and Fo-chien tried to restore the former way. But they could not
alter the trend. Young students treasured the sayings found in it. They recited
it day and night and regarded it as the ultimate of learning. None realized its
shortcoming. The minds of students began to be corrupted. In the early years
of Shao-hsing [1131–1162] Ta-hui went to Fukien and saw that students had
gone astray. So he destroyed the blocks [of the *Pi-yen lu*] and exposed the
heresy. In so doing, Ta-hui dispelled illusion and rescued those who were
drowning. He eliminated the redundancy and corrected excesses, cut down the
heterodoxy and illuminated the orthodoxy. The life of Ch'an was greatly
strengthened. Monks began to know the shortcomings of that custom and
stopped their earlier admiration. If Ta-hui did not correct the mistakes of the
degenerate age by using his farsightedness and the power of his compassion,
the future of the public monasteries would have much to fear.[11]

What Ta-hui vehemently opposed was not the use of *kung-an* as a teaching
device but rather the learners' deplorable tendency to equate knowledge
about *kung-an* with insight into them and thus enlightenment itself. In fact,
under Ta-hui, Lin-chi Ch'an became known as "Kung-an Ch'an," a tradition that saw *kung-an* as an absolutely necessary device in the Ch'an training.
His view contrasted with that of Hung-chih Cheng-chüeh (1091–1157), a
master of the Ts'ao-t'ung school, who was credited with founding the
"*mo-chao* Ch'an" (Ch'an of Silent Illumination), a tradition that saw the
investigation of *kung-an* as less essential than the persistent effort in meditation for the Ch'an enterprise. Ta-hui's faith in *kung-an* was most likely based
on his own personal experiences, about which he left us eloquent accounts.
Ta-hui became a student of Yüan-wu K'o-chin (1063–1135), the compiler of
the *Blue Cliff Record* at the age of thirty-six. He was given the *kung-an* "The
East Mountain walks over the water" (*Tung-shan shuei shang hsing*) to investi-

---

10. Wan-yen Tao-yen's dates were not recorded. His biography is found in *Wu-teng hui-yüan*,
chüan 20, *Wan-tzu Hsü-tsang ching* (Taipei: Hsin-wen-feng Publishing Co., 1977) 138:789–791.
This passage comes from *Ch'an-lin pao-hsün ho-chu, chüan* 3 in *Hsü-tsang ching*, 113:0393.

11. Hsi-wen Yün-fen, like Wan-yen Tao-yen, was a monk belonging to the sixteenth
generation of Nan-yüeh's lineage, but there is no biography about him. This saying is found in
Ch'an-lin pao-hsün ho-chu 4:0404.

gate. He made forty-nine attempts to solve it but was rebuked each time. One day while listening to his master's discussion of this very *kung-an* during a public lecture, he suddenly achieved a breakthrough:

> Master Yüan-wu ascended the high seat in the lecture hall at the request of Madame Chang K'ang-kuo. He said, "One day a monk asked Yün-men this question, 'Where do all the Buddhas come from?' Yün-men answered, 'The East Mountain walks over the water.' But if I were he, I would have given a different answer. 'Where do all the Buddhas come from?' 'As the fragrant breeze comes from the south, a slight coolness naturally stirs in the palace pavilion.' When I heard this, all of a sudden there was no more before and after. Time stopped. I ceased to feel any disturbance in my mind, and remained in a state of utter calmness."[12]

But when he went to the abbot's room for a private interview, Yüan-wu refused to grant him approval. He was then assigned another *kung-an*, "To be and not to be—it is like a wisteria leaning on a tree" (*yu-chü wu-chü, ju t'eng i-shu*). He had to see the master three or four times a day, but as soon as he started to say something, he would be told that it was no good. After working on his *kung-an* for half a year, Ta-hui had another enlightenment experience, once again a result of his hearing the master's response to this very *kung-an*. Ta-hui recalled the event:

> One day while I was having supper in the abbot's quarters, I was so absorbed in the kōan that I just held the chopsticks and forgot to eat. The master remarked to a bystander that my progress in Ch'an was as slow as the growth of the Huang-yang plant [*Buxus mycrophylla*, a plant which allegedly grows only one inch every year]. I then told him by a simile what position I was in. "I am like a dog who stands by a pot of boiling fat: he cannot lick it however badly he wants to, nor can he go away from it though he may wish to quit." The master said, "This is exactly the case. The kōan is really a vajra cage and a seat of thorns to you." I then said to him, "When you were with your teacher, Wu-tsu, you asked him about the same kōan, and what was his answer?" The master at first refused to say anything. But I insisted, saying, "When you asked him about it, you were not alone, but with an assembly. I am sure that there are people who know all about it." The master then said, "I asked him, 'To be and not to be—it is like a wisteria leaning on a tree. What is the meaning of it?' Wu-tsu replied, 'You cannot paint it, you cannot sketch it, however much you try.' I further said, 'What if the tree suddenly breaks down and the wisteria dies?' Wu-tsu said, 'You are following the words.'"[13]

---

12. *Ta-hui Pu-chüeh Ch'an-shih nien-p'u*, compiled by Ta-hui's disciple, Tsu-yung, in *Chung-hua ta-tsang ching* (Taiwan: 1968), second collection, 4, no. 42 under Hsüan-ho seventh year (1125), p. 1696. *Chih-yüeh lu*, compiled by Chu Ju-chi of the Ming, (Taiwan: Hsin-wen-feng Publishing Co., 1976) 31:534–535 supplies some details not found above.

13. *Ta-hui-Pu-chüeh Ch'an-shih nien-p'u*, p. 1696. The translation is in Chün-fang Yü, "Ta-hui-Tsung kao and Kung-an Ch'an," p. 215. See also D. T. Suzuki, *Essays in Zen Buddhism, Second Series* (London: Rider and Company, 1970), pp. 29–31.

Ta-hui said that as soon as he heard this he immediately saw the point of the *kung-an*. Yüan-wu examined him with a few other *kung-an*, and Ta-hui solved them all to the master's satisfaction. Ta-hui was finally recognized as a true heir to the Lin-chi tradition.

Neither of the two *kung-an* Ta-hui struggled with so hard found their way to the *Pi-yen lu* and *Wu-men kuan* (The Gateless Gate), compiled by Wu-men Hui-kai (1183–1260) in 1228, about a century after the compilation of the former. Before the time of Ta-hui, Ch'an masters seemed to favor a number of popular *kung-an* that could be identified. A search of all the available Ch'an records will no doubt yield a larger inventory, but going through the *Wu-teng hui-yüan* (Convergance of the Five Lamp Records), I have come most frequently across the following: "The Tathāgata picks up a flower,"[14] "Po-chang buries the fox,"[15] "The girl comes out of samadhi,"[16] "The National Teacher calls his attendant three times,"[17] "Three *chin* of flax,"[18] "This very mind is the Buddha," "No mind, no Buddha," "Nan-ch'uan kills the cat," "Chao-chou's 'Wu,'" "Chao-chou's 'Wash your bowl,'" and "Chao-chou's 'Oak tree in the courtyard.'"[19] All of these are in the *Wu-men kuan* (and in one instance the *Pi-yen lu*). Some *kung-an*, however, like the ones given to Ta-hui, have become quite obscure, for example, "Hsiang-yen's dragon singing in the withered woods",[20] "The *kung-an* of P'u-hua,"[21] and "Old woman of Mt. Wu-t'ai."[22]

Ta-hui was said to have favored Chao-chou's "Wu" above all other

---

14. Both Shou-shan Sheng-nien (926–993) and Le-tan Yin-ch'ien used it. See *Wu-teng hui-yüan* 11:410 and *Seng-pao cheng hsü chuan*, *chüan* 1, in the biography of Yüan-t'ung Tao-min. *Wan-tzu Hsü tsang ching*, 137:0571. This *kung-an* is No. 6 in *Wu-men kuan*.

15. Lung-ya Chih-t'sai (d. 1138) was questioned by his master Ssu-hsin on the first *kung-an*. He himself used the latter in instructing his disciples. *Wu-teng hui-yüan* 19:0772–0773 and *Nan Sung Yüan Ming Ch'an-lin seng pao chuan*, chüan 1. *Wan-tzu Hsü tsang ching* 137:0634–0635. These two *kung-an* are Nos. 2 and 42 in the *Wu-men kuan*.

16. Ibid., No. 42.

17. Yüan-wu used this *kung-an*, the No. 17 case, in the *Wu-men-kuan*. This was related in the story of Mi-yin An-min. He was a renowned lecturer of *Surangama*. One day he went to Chao-chüeh monastery to visit his friend. He attended Yüan-wu's informal gathering (*hsiao ts'an*). Yüan-wu mentioned this *kung-an* and then said, "Suppose a person practices calligraphy in the dark. Even though the characters are not well formed, the luster is already clear. Tell me where does the luster lie?" An-ming was plunged into great doubt upon hearing this. So on the next day instead of leaving the monastery as he originally planned, he went to see Yüan-wu at the abbot's room. Yüan-wu first asked him about the *Surangama* in order to find out the level of his mind. Ming's answers were all based on his intellectual understanding of doctrinal matters. Yüan-wu said, laughing, "When you enter hell in the future, do not say that this old monk did not warn you." An-ming was greatly surprised and begged to receive instruction. *Wu-teng hui-yüan* 19:0763, *Nan Sung Yüan Ming Ch'an-lin seng-pao chuan*, chüan 5:0668.

18. Jui-yen Ku-yüan used this *kung-an* (No. 18 in *Wu-men kuan*) in teaching Tuan-chiao Miao-lun. *Nan Sung Yüan Ming Ch'an-lin seng pao chuan*, chüan 7:0684.

19. All these *kung-an* were used by Wu-tsu Fa-yen (1024–1104), the teacher of Yüan-wu ko-chin in the *Wu-men kuan*. They are Nos. 30, 33, 14 (*Pi-yu lu*, No. 63), 1, 7, and 37. See *Chih-yüeh lu* 29:514–515.

20. Hsiang-yen Chih-hsien was asked, "What is the Tao?" He answered, "The dragon is

kung-an in training his students. This may be the reason why Wu-men put it at the beginning of his anthology.[23] It also explained why monks after Ta-hui tended to use it more often than other *kung-an*.[24] If a person participates in an

---

singing in the withered woods." Then the monk said, "I don't understand." He answered, "There are eyes in the skull." *Ching-te ch'uan-teng lu* (rpt. Taipei: Hsin-Wen-feng, 1968), 11:8. This *kung-an* was used by Nan-t'ang who enabled Yü-ch'iu Chü-ching to achieve awakening. *Wu-teng hui-yüan* 20:0785.

21. Monk P'u- hua lived his entire life like a *kung-an*. He was full of strange words and outlandish acts. In the 860s before his death he went to town to ask for a monk's robe. Lin-chi heard about it and gave him a coffin. P'u-hua accepted it with delight and told followers that he would go out the east gate the next day to die. But when he went out the east gate followed by a number of townspeople, he declared that this was an unlucky day and he would die outside the south gate the next day. He did not die then either but said that since the west gate was auspicious he would go there the third day. When he repeated the act again, people got tired of him. So on the fourth day he carried his own coffin and went out the north gate. After sounding the bell he entered the coffin and died. It was said that when townspeople rushed out of the gate and opened the coffin they could not find him but heard the sound of a bell far away. *Ching-te chuan-teng lu* 10:187. Hui-yen Mi-kuang used it at a public assembly (*sheng-t'ang*), *Wu-teng hui-yüan* 20:0788.

22. This story is connected with Chao-chou Ts'ung-nien (778–897). A monk went on a pilgrimage to Mt. Wu-t'ai. He asked an old woman the way there. She answered, "Go straight ahead." When the monk was about to leave, she asked, "How would you go there?" Later when the monk reported this conversation to Chao-chou, the latter said, "Wait until I go and expose this old woman." The next day he went and asked her the way to Mt. Wu-t'ai. She made the same reply saying, "Go straight ahead." But when he was leaving again she asked, "How would you go there?" Chao-chou returned to the monastery and told the monk, "I have gone and exposed that old woman," *Ching-te chuan-teng lu* 10:178. Ta-ch'an Liao-ming always used this *kung-an* to test his students during private interviews (*ju-shih*) when he was the abbot at Ching-shan in his old age. *Nan Sung Yüan Ming Ch'an-lin seng pao chuan, chüan* 3:0653.

23. Sheng-yen pointed out that this *kung-an* was not found in the collection of either Fen-yang Shan-chao or that of Hsüeh-tou Ch'ung-hsien, the two earliest *kung-an* anthologies. It first appeared in the *Yu-lu* of Wu-tsu Fa-yen. See *Ch'an-te ti-yen* (Taiwan: Tung-chu, 1980), p. 79.

24. Chien-fu Wu-pen, a disciple of Ta-hui always used 'Wu' in teaching his students. *Wu-teng hui-yüan* 20:0797. Two monks living at the end of southern Sung told us that they achieved awakening by meditation on 'Wu.' Hsüeh-yen Tsu-ch'in (1214–1287) says: 'At the age of eighteen I travelled to the monastery of master Shuang-lin Yüan and practiced meditation there. From morning to night I did not go outside the courtyard. When I returned to the dormitory I would fold my arms in front of my chest. I did not look right or left but restricted my gaze to a spot less than three feet in front of me. At first I watched the word 'Wu.' One day I turned my mind around and tried to observe the origin of this one thought. Suddenly I felt a coolness penetrating clearly through me.' *Ch'an-kuan ts'e-chiu* in *Wan-tzu Hsü tsang-ching* 114:704. Another monk, Meng-shan Te-i told his experience: 'When I was twenty, I knew the existence of this matter [Life and death is a great matter]. When I was thirty-two, I asked seventeen or eighteen elders about how to carry out the work (*tso kung-fu*) but no one could answer my question. Later when I was studying under the elder Yüan-shan, he told me to watch the word 'Wu' day and night. He said, 'You should be like a cat catching mice or a hen hatching eggs. There should be no moment of rest. Before you reach a breakthrough you should imitate the rat's chewing on a coffin. If you go about it with single-mindedness, there assuredly will be a day of total understanding.' After hearing this, I worked diligently day and night. Eighteen days later, when I was having tea, I suddenly understood why Kasyapa smiled when the Buddha held up the flower.' Ibid., p. 703.

intensive meditation session nowadays, the first *kung-an* assigned to him will also very likely be this one. There definitely is a historical connection between Ta-hui's Ch'an pedagogy and that of later Ch'an masters; however, one must be careful not to transpose the modern practice to the Sung too much. Even though the Ch'an records hold voluminous pages of sermons and dialogues between masters and students that usually contain *kung-an*, we know practically nothing about the way in which the *kung-an* was actually used. The compilers used a formulaic convention in recording the appearances of *kung-an*. The master would either *chü* ('raise'), or *t'i* ('pick up'), or *nien* ('choose') such and such a *kung-an*. Sometimes he would also use the compounds *t'i-chü* or *nien-t'i*. The master could do this either at a public assembly (*shang-t'ang*) after he "ascended the high seat" (*sheng-tso*) or during the tension-filled encounters of informal conferences (*hsiao-ts'an*, literally, small assembly) and private interviews (*ju-shih*, literally, entering the abbot's chamber). As far as I can tell, there does not seem to be any reason why some *kung-an* were "raised" at a public assembly while others were raised at private interviews. The records do not say if, in the latter case, the *kung-an* were the ones the master had earlier assigned to the students to work on individually, as one would expect from modern practice. The Ch'an records neither provide information about how often the students had to go to see the master to report on their progress with the *kung-an* nor mention if special intensive meditation sessions, like the modern *sesshin*, were held regularly at the monasteries.

I have devoted considerable space to the discussion of *kung-an*, for I believe that *kung-an*, together with the other Ch'an pedagogical devices I will mention, form the core of the Ch'an curriculum. Frequent criticisms notwithstanding, *kung-an* anthologies such as the *Pi-yen lu* and *Wu-men kuan*, along with the Ch'an *yü-lu* and *teng-lu* literature, were the new Classics for the Ch'an monks of the Sung. They assumed a status comparable to that of canonical *sūtra*s. As I will discuss in the next section, Ch'an monks continued to study *sūtra*s, wrote commentaries and even occasionally referred to them in discussions. But their first love and loyalty was directed toward the Ch'an classics, which they could claim as their own. These were prized because they contained "embodied truth": truth bodily experienced through deafening shouts and physical beatings and truth bodily expressed in "meaningless noises" and "tasteless words." To the uninitiated, which includes both the casual reader and the serious scholar, Ch'an literature is alternatively bewildering and infuriating. It is no wonder that most scholars working in the field of the history of Chinese Buddhism or Chinese intellectual history in general have often been content to keep themselves aloof from this massive body of literature. A true understanding of the *kung-an*, short of a personal enlightenment, is probably beyond the ability of anyone. But with empathy and some knowledge and experience of *kung-an* as used by modern Ch'an teachers, a researcher will not find this literature intellectually opaque or intractable. On the contrary, it represents all the creative elements found in Ch'an Buddhism. This makes Ch'an different from early schools of Buddhism. If one were to draw parallels with the contemporary Neo-Confucian movement, the Ch'an classics would be comparable to the recorded sayings and other writings of the Neo-Confucian masters; the Ch'an public monasteries would be similar to the academies (*shu-yüan*).

I now briefly discuss some other uniquely Ch'an methods of instruction. Ch'an masters used *kung-an* to generate the "sensation of doubt" (*i-ch'ing*) that could stop discursive thought, a fatal flaw of ordinary human consciousness preventing one's ability to see reality as it truly is, and thus create a possible opening for enlightenment.[25] The same purpose could be achieved by a shout or a visual *kung-an* such as holding up a stick, a fly wisk, or, as in Ta-hui's case, a bamboo staff (*chu-p'i*). After achieving enlightenment, Ta-hui always carried the *chu-p'i* when he lectured his students. He would say to them:

> If you call this *chu-p'i* you are wrong. If you don't call this *chu-p'i*, you are wrong also. Don't say anything, but also don't remain silent. You must not think, you must not guess. You are not allowed to get up and leave the room. Nothing you do is appropriate. If you want to grab the *chu-p'i*, go ahead, grab it. I will then use my fist and demand that you make a statement. If you want me to put down my fist, that is all right too. But then I ask you to make a statement about the whole world. Now, can you also take that away?[26]

Other Ch'an masters did not bother to talk so much but simply demanded, "If you call this *chu-p'i* you are wrong. If you don't call it *chu-p'i*, you are wrong also. What would you call it?" while holding it up in the air. Sometimes, as case 43 in the *Wu-men kuan* shows, a spiritually mature student, when being put into this quandary, would grab the bamboo staff immediately and throw it on the ground and, if his action was genuinely spontaneous, receive the teacher's approval.[27]

The use of shouts and blows was already widely practiced by the T'ang masters of the Lin-chi school. As the expression "Te-shan's blows and Lin-chi's shouts" indicates, these two masters were most famous for employing these devices. In the Sung, many Ch'an masters came to use the same

---

25. I discussed the function of *i-ch'ing* created by *kung-an* in the dynamics of spiritual breakthrough in "Ta-hui Tsung-kao and Kung-an Ch'an," pp. 220–224.

26. *Chu-p'i* is "a bamboo staff of office about 3 feet long, the head of which is bound around with wisteria vine. It is also called 'broken bow' because of its shape. It is used by a master when he appears at a Dharma battle," *Two Zen Classics: Mumonkan and Hekiganroku*, trans. Katsuki Sekida (New York and Tokyo: Weatherhill, 1977). Ibid., p. 227; *Ta-hui yü-lu, chüan* 16 T47:899c.

27. Shou-shan Sheng-nien (926–993) liked to use the bamboo staff as a visual *kung-an*. He gave approval to Kuei-sheng when the latter threw the bamboo staff on the ground. *Wu-teng hui-yüan* 11:0415. Another disciple, Kuang-hui Yüan-lien acted the same way when he was challenged by his own teacher. *Ch'an-lin seng-pao chüan* 16:0506.

techniques. In fact, this phrase came to function as a *kung-an*.[28] The "blows" did not always mean actual blows. Nor were "shouts" always actual shouts. This is quite clear from this talk given by Ta-hui:

> Ta-hui asked monks gathered in his chamber, "As soon as monks entered the room, Te-shan would hit them with blows, Lin-chi would shout at them, Yün-feng would say to them, 'What is it?' and Mu-chou would say to them, 'Here is a ready-made *kung-an*: I give you thirty blows.' Do you think that these four old guys have anything to offer us?" One monk answered, "Yes." Ta-hui roared thunderously at him.[29]

Just as teachers would use shouts as a teaching device to guide the student, sometimes students also used them to show their level of attainment. Here is an amusing story about one of Ta-hui's disciples:

> Ta-ch'an Liao-ming of Ching-shan was very tall and had a big stomach. His replies to Ch'an challenges (*chi-feng*) were sharp and to the point and his manner was open and unrestrained. He was outstanding among Master Miao-hsi's [Ta-hui] disciples. When the master was the abbot of A-yü-wang ssu, he prohibited people from uttering shouts when they were in his chamber. But every time Ta-ch'an entered the chamber, he would utter a deafening shout and then withdraw. Miao-hsi put up a placard on which was written "Whoever utters shouts will be fined one string of cash." Ta-ch'an secretly carried 1,000 cash in his sleeves. He entered the master's room, dumped the coins on the ground, uttered several really loud shouts and then went out. Miao-hsi said, "What should I do with this rascal?" So he changed the placard to read, "Whoever utters shouts must pay enough fines to provide offerings for that day." Ta-ch'an went to the treasurer and said that the master wanted ten ounces of gold. Not suspecting anything, the treasurer gave him the amount. He carried the gold in his sleeves and entered the chamber. Again dumping it on the floor, he uttered a loud shout and Miao-hsi was greatly startled.[30]

Lin-chi classified shouts (*ho*) into four types.[31] Later, masters of the Lin-chi

28. "Lung-ya Chih-tsai (d. 1138) was asked about the meaning of 'Te-shan's sticks and Lin-chi's shouts.' He answered, 'So-lu, so-lu [meaningless sounds].' When the monk asked him the meaning of another *kung-an*, 'Why did Bodhidharma come from the West?' Lung-ya again repeated, 'So-lu, so-lu.' So he came to be known as Tsai so-lu." *Wu-teng hui-yüan* 19:0772–0773 and *Nan Sung Yuan Ming Ch'an-liu seng pao chuan* 1:0634–0635. Huo-yen Shih-ti (1107–1179) was also said to have used the "four shouts of Lin-chi" as a *kung-an*, *Wu-teng hui-yüan* 20:0812; *Nan Sung Ming Ch'an-lin seng pao chuan* 1:0642.
29. Biography of Ta-yüan Tsung-p'u, a disciple of Ta-hui. *Wu-teng hui-yüan* 20:0798.
30. *Nan Sung Yüan Ming ch'an lin tseng pao chuan* 3:0653.
31. "One time the shout is like the precious sword of the Vajrarāja. Another time the shout is like a golden-haired lion crouching on the ground. Another time the shout is like the pole and weeds [with which the fisherman brings the fish together in one place]. Finally, there is the roar that is not really a roar." Heinrich Dumoulin, *A History of Zen Buddhism* (Boston: Beacon Press, 1963), p. 120. Many Sung masters would treat Lin-chi's "four shouts" as a *kung-an* and sometimes provide their own "explanations." For instance, Cheng-t'ang Ming-pien, a Ch'an monk in the fifteenth-generation lineage of Nan-Yüeh responded to one question about the

school also classified the blows (*pang*) into eight types.[32] *Pang-ho* (blows and shouts) were skillful devices used in different circumstances and directed at students of various levels of understanding to hasten their awakening.

The Lin-chi school also favored a number of formulas as topics in teaching. Lin-chi himself used the "four attitudes toward subject and object" (*ssu liao-chien*), "fourfold relations of guest and host" (*ssu pin-chu*), "fourfold precedence and subsequence of light and activity" (*ssu chao-yung*), and the "three mysteries and the three essentials" (*san-hsüan san-yao*).[33] Sung masters used all these formulas.[34] Another formula, not connected with Lin-chi, also

---

meaning of the four shouts this way: "Someone asked, 'Why is one shout like the precious sword of the Vajrarāja?' The master said, 'A poisonous snake in an ancient tomb wears horns on its head.' 'Why is another shout like a lion crouching on the ground?' The master, 'The empty space laughs and nods its head.' 'Why is a third shout like the pole and weeds?' The master, 'A stone man claps his hands and bursts into laughing!' 'Why is a roar not really a roar?' The master, 'Pig's head in a cloth bag.'" *Wu-teng hui-yüan* 20:0782. Dumoulin sees the four shouts as characteristics of enlightenment. "The sword might indicate the keenness of enlightenment; the crouching lion, controlled power; the pole and the weeds, the mystery of the homely things of daily life; and the fourth shout, the paradox of experience"; p. 120. Two recent studies suggest other interpretations. Ts'ai Chin-tao in an M.A. thesis, "*Ch'an-tsung ti chiao-yü ssu-hsiang yü shih-shih*" (Taiwan: Chinese Culture College, 1966) quoted the writings of Tsu-yüan (neither the person nor his writings was ever identified, unfortunately) to say that the first two shouts aimed to eliminate illusion and return to truth. Because the sword of the Vajrarāja is the sharpest weapon and the lion is the fiercest animal, they could accomplish this purpose. The third shout, poles and weeds, works like a mirror. The Ch'an master uses this type of shout to find out the learner's ability, sincerity, effort, and understanding. The fourth shout is finally to negate not only all discriminations but also the very shout itself. This final stage can be expediently called "correct enlightenment"; pp. 147–151. Sheng-yen in his book, *Ch'an-men hsiu-cheng chih-yao*, also discusses the four shouts. He quotes from the commentary in a Ch'ing work, *San-shan Lai ch'an-shih Wu-Chia tsung-chih ts'uan-yao*, compiled by Hsing-tung (*Wan-tzu Hsü tsang ching*, vol. 114, pp. 508–518). The main ideas are similar to those offered by the enigmatic Tsu-yüan, p. 94.

32. Blows could be administered either physically or, as more often the case, figuratively (e.g., when the master said, "I give you twenty blows"). The eight types of blows are differentiated into the following: punishing, rewarding, testing, accommodating, blinding, encouraging, "taming the devil," and finally the highest, "the blow that eliminates both the ordinary and the sagely." See Ts'ai, pp. 138–147, and Sheng-yen, pp. 95–96.

33. Dumoulin, *A History of Zen Buddhism*, pp. 120–121. He translates the first formula thus: "Sometimes take away [i.e., negate] the subject and not the object; another time take away the object and not the subject; yet another time take away both subject and object; and finally take away neither subject nor object [therefore affirm both at the same time]." He also tells us that the last formula, "Three mysteries and three essentials," refers to the triad of substance, quality, and activity that are regarded as one and inseparable. The fourfold relation of guest and host is a variation of the first. The dialectic of "light" and "activity" is similarly patterned after the classical "four propositions" *Catushkotika* of Indian *Madhyamika* logic. Light refers to observation and activity means action. In other words, the Ch'an master could either first observe his students and then act, or he could first act and then observe his student's reaction. Alternatively, he could do both or neither. See Ts'ai, pp. 151–160, and Sheng-yen, pp. 94–94.

34. References to these formulas are many in the Ch'an records; for instance, Fen-yang Shan-chao used all of these and added a few more of his own. *Wu-teng hui-yüan* 11:0413–0415. Lin-yin Te-ching used the "fourfold relationship between host and guest." *Wu-teng hui yüan*

came into use: the "three barriers" (*san-kuan*). Although there were different ways of framing it, the most famous formulation was the one made by Huang-lung Hui-nan (1002–1069).[35] He was reported to have used this device in training his disciples.

> Huang-lung used the "three barriers" to test learners. Few monks could get his approval. Someone might venture to say something, but he would just sit straight with eyes closed without making any comment. When he was asked why, he answered, "He who passes the gate goes forward without looking back. If a person has to ask the gate-keeper whether he has passed the gate or not, he is obviously far from doing so."[36]

Another much used formula was the "five ranks of the absolute and the relative" (*wu-wei p'ien-cheng*) and its commentary, the "fivefold relation between the lord and the vassal" (*chün-ch'en*) as developed by the Ts'ao-tung school.[37] References to the use of these pedagogical devices and formulas in the Sung are scattered throughout the Ch'an records. One indication of their popularity was the compilation of the "essentials of the five schools" (*wu-tsung kang-yao*) by Hui-yen Chih-chao in 1188. He entitled his book *Jen-t'ien yen-mu* (Eyes of Men and Heaven) and intended it to serve as a kind of catechism summarizing the key pedagogical tricks of the trade of all five Ch'an schools.

Before I leave the subject of Ch'an methodology, I want also to mention the "Ten Ox-herding Pictures" and the poems eulogizing the pictures, which have become very well known. I have not come across any direct reference to their use by Sung monks. But hypothetically they could be used

---

12:0445, as did Hua-yen P'u-tzu, ibid., 12:0453; Te-shan Tzu-chüan, ibid. 20:0831; and Tz'u-ming, *Ch'an-lin seng-pao chuan* 21:0524. Huang-lung Hui-nan used the "three mysteries and three essentials." *Pu ch'an-lin seng-pao chuan, chüan* 5 in *Wan-tzu Hsü tsang ching*, 137:0602. So did Wu-chun Shih-fan, *Nan Sung Yüan Ming ch'an-lin seng-pao chuan* 7:0681.

35. *Jen-t'ien yen-mu, chüan* 2. Dumoulin translated Huang-lung's version of the "three barriers":

> *Question:* "Everyone has his own native place owing to the casual nexus (Karma). Where is your native place?"
> *Answer:* "Early in the morning I ate white rice gruel; now I feel hungry again."
> *Question:* "In what way do my hands resemble the Buddha's hands?"
> *Answer:* "Playing the lute in the moonlight."
> *Question:* "In what way do my feet resemble the feet of a donkey?"
> *Answer:* "When the heron stands in the snow, its color is not the same."

Dumoulin, *A History of Zen Buddhism*, p. 126. Tou-shüai Ts'ung-yüeh (1044–1091) among others, also set up his own version of the "three barriers." Tseng P'u hsin, *Chung kuo ch'an tsu-shih chuan* (Hua-lien, Taiwan: Hua-huang Bookstore), pp. 258–259.

36. *Ch'an-lin pao-hsün ho-chu* 1:0338.

37. Dumoulin, *A History of Zen Buddhism*, pp. 112–118. Sheng-yen, *Ch'an-men hsiu-cheng chih-yao*, pp. 101–108. Katsuki Sekida, *Zen Training: Methods and Philosophy* (New York & Tokyo: Weatherhill, 1975), pp. 237–249. Whalen W. Lai, "Sinitic Mandalas: The Wu-wei t'u of Ts'ao-shan," in *Early Ch'an in China and Tibet*, pp. 229–257. Lai suggests that five "positions" would be more correct than five "ranks."

as effective teaching aids to illustrate the stages of spiritual cultivation as well as the levels of enlightenment, as indeed they were used later in both China and Japan. Kuo-an Shih-yüan, a Sung monk of unknown date, wrote ten poems to accompany the pictures drawn by a Ch'an monk named Ch'ing-chü. He called it "Ode to the Ten Ox-herding Pictures" (*Shih-nin t'u-sung*).[38] There were other poems of a similar nature and the one by P'u-ming seems to have enjoyed more fame than that of Kuo-an in China, for it received a boost from the advocacy of the Ming monk Chu-hung.[39]

The data on the methodologies, topics, and, to some extent, reading materials employed in Ch'an eduction in the Sung are considerable. But it is very difficult to know the practical details involved in the actual process of Ch'an training. For instance, how often did the abbot ascend to his high seat to talk to his disciples? How often could a disciple enter the abbot's room to have a private talk with the master? When the master gathered his students together, what did he say? When a student entered the abbot's chamber, how and what did he ask the master? Unfortunately, Buddhist chronicles, biographies of eminent monks, and Ch'an lamp records either do not provide answers to these questions or at best provide only limited hints and clues to the actual training process. All one can say for sure is that in most public Ch'an monasteries there was no formal instruction in *sūtra*s or treatises, but there was a library that housed them. Disciples were free to read them, and indeed the abbot might sometimes discuss passages from them in his talks with his students. But there was no *sūtra* lecture. If a Ch'an monk were interested in becoming proficient in either a *sūtra*, a treatise, or *vinaya*, he would go to a master specializing in these matters in a *Chiang* (doctrine) or *Lü* (discipline) monastery for instruction. The themes of the public lectures in a Ch'an monastery would come from the Ch'an classics—the words and acts of former Ch'an masters.

But there is some information about the training of Ch'an monks in the Sung; it is possible to describe the institutional provisions for their training. I can also talk about both the monastic ideals famous abbots in the Sung hoped to instill in their disciples and the negative examples of monastic abuses, which often serve as good sources of current practices, against which they warned their disciples. In the process, some questions I raised in the last paragraph will be answered. I will use two sources for this purpose: first, the *Ch'an-yüan ch'ing-kuei* (The Ch'an-yüan Code), compiled by Tsung-tse in 1103; second, the *Ch'an-lin pao-hsün* (Treasured Instructions of the Ch'an

---

38. Kuo-an told how he came to write the poems in his preface to *Shih-niu t'u-sung*, told by Tz'u-yüan of Sung in *Wan-tzu Hsü tang ching* 113:917. Kuo-an's biography, together with the note that he wrote this work, is found in *Wu-teng hui-yüan* 20:0786–0787. This has been translated into English by M. H. Trevor who used a fifteenth-century Japanese text, *The Ox and His Herdsman* (Tokyo: Hokuseido Press, 1969).

39. Chu-hung wrote a preface in 1609 when P'u-ming's poems together with the pictures were reprinted. By this time, the identity of P'u-ming was lost. Ibid., p. 0924.

Tradition), originally compiled by the famous Ch'an master Ta-hui and his
disciple Chu-yen Shih-kuei but extensively edited and expanded by the later
monk Ching-shan at the beginning of the thirteenth century.[40]

Consider first the procedures governing the interaction between the
master and his students. These were stipulated with great precision in the
Ch'an yüan Code, the oldest surviving code for Ch'an monasteries. It was
widely used in the Sung and served as a model for all subsequent Chinese
and Japanese Zen codes, for it was transmitted to Japan around 1200. In
order to appreciate fully the value of this code, it is necessary to examine
briefly a short essay entitled "Ch'an-men kuei-shih" (Rules of the Ch'an
Tradition), which appears at the end of the entry on Pai-chang in the *Ching-te
ch'uan-teng lu* (Transmission of the Lamp) of 1004. It is "one of the earliest
coherent descriptions of the Ch'an monastic life and rule still extant," and "it
does reveal the basic pattern of Ch'an monastic life that had taken shape
between the T'ang and the northern Sung dynasties."[41] I will summarize the
key points. First, the document makes clear that the Dharma Hall (*fa-t'ang*)
in which the abbot lectured and engaged the community in debate was the
central building. This is significant:

> The rejection of the Buddha Hall, traditionally one of the most prominent
> buildings in Chinese Buddhist monasteries, and one that was eventually
> incorporated into the characteristic Ch'an monastic layout, almost certainly
> derived from fears that the frequent use of a building intended for prayers and
> ceremonial functions would encourage excessive dependence on faith as a
> means to salvation, detract from the energetic practice of meditation, and tie
> the community too closely to secular patrons by providing a setting for the
> frequent performances of memorial services for lay intentions.[42]

40. Ching-shan did not say when he finished compiling the *Ch'an-lin pao-hsün*. But from his
undated preface I can venture the year 1200 as a possible date. He wrote in the preface:
"*Treasured Instructions* was originally compiled by Ming-hsi [Ta-hui] and Chu-yen when they
lived in retirement at Yün-men of Kiang-hsi. I obtained the book from an old monk named
Tsu-an when I stayed at Yün-chu during my travels in the Ch'un-hsi era [1174–1189].
Unfortunately because it was an old copy it had become moth-eaten and, moreover, the
beginning and the end of the book were missing. Later on I sometimes would see quotations
from the book in the recorded sayings and biographies. After ten years, I accumulated only fifty
items or so. Eventually I have compiled about three hundred sayings of masters ranging from
Huang-lung [Huang-lung Hui-han, 1002–1069] to Fo-chao [Fo-chao Cho-yen, 1121–1203], and
Chien-t'ang [Chien-t'ang Hsin-chi]. I came across these sayings at different times, some earlier,
others later. They are not arranged chronologically. The intention [of these sayings] is to make
the reader free himself from the ideas of power, profit, egoism, and others, and strive for
morality, benevolence, and righteousness. The works are easy and natural. There are no strange
or eccentric deeds. They can indeed help one to enter in the Way." *Ch'an-lin pao-hsün ho-chu*, pp.
0309–0310.

41. *Ching-te ch'uan-teng lu*, 6:117. Martin Collcutt translated the essay, less than one page in
the Chinese original. See his "Early Ch'an Monastic Rules: Ching kuei and the Shaping of
Ch'an Community Life," in *Early Ch'an in Chinese and Tibet*, pp. 173–179; this quotation appears
on p. 173.

42. Collcutt, "Early Ch'an Monastic Rules," p. 176.

Second, meditation centering on the orderly and communal life of the Monks' Hall (*seng-t'ang*) was clearly the main pursuit of monks. The Monks' Hall was indeed as important a building as the Dharma Hall. The arrangement and physical set-up of the Monks' Hall were carefully regulated.

> Irrespective of their numbers or of their social status, those who have been permitted to enter the community to study should all reside in the Monks' Hall, arranged strictly according to the number of summers since their ordination. Meditation platforms should be built along the sides of the hall and a stand for each monk to hang his robes and personal belongings on. When resting, monks should lay their headrests at an angle on the lip of the platform and lie down on their right sides with their hands supporting their heads in the posture of the Buddha reclining. They rest only briefly even though meditation sessions have been long. This should not be thought of as sleep but as reclining meditation. Thus [while resting] they still retain [in their spiritual observance] the four proprieties in walking, stopping, sitting and lying down.[43]

Meditation was unmistakably the chief concern of the monks. This was further confirmed by the third point, namely, monks were encouraged to practice on their own initiative. They could have private visits to the abbot's chamber for guidance, and public discussions between the abbot and the members of the community were provided by frequent and regular, apparently daily, assemblies in the Dharma Hall.

> With the exception of regular assemblies and visits by individual monks who enter the Elder's chamber to ask for instructions, the learners should be left to their own diligence in their pursuit of practice and instruction. The community of the whole monastery should gather in the Dharma Hall for the morning and evening discussions. On these occasions the Elder "enters the hall and ascends his seat." The monastery officers as well as the ordinary monks stand in files and listen attentively to the discussion. For some of them to raise questions and for the master to answer, which invigorates and clarifies the essence of Ch'an teachings, is to show how to live in accord with the Dharma.[44]

Many of the lively exchanges and sharp debates recorded in the Ch'an writings probably occurred on these occasions. Because of its extreme brevity, *Ch'an-men kuei-shih* only roughly outlines the Ch'an monastic regime as practiced in the beginning of the Sung. The *Ch'an-yüan Code*, written about a hundred years later, is a much more useful source for picturing life in a Ch'an monastery of the Sung. The Code repeats the general principles governing Ch'an life in a section entitled "Ode to Pai-chang's Rules" (*Pai-chang kuei-sheng sung*). In all, the Code contains more than seventy sections covering a wide range of subjects; it is really a most "comprehensive code regulating almost every conceivable aspect of Ch'an monastic activity."[45] The ideals of the *Ch'an-yüan Code*, just as those stressed in the

43. Ibid.
44. Ibid., pp. 176–177.
45. Martin Collcutt, *Five Mountains: The Rinzai Zen Monastic Institution in Medieval Japan*

legendary *Pure Rules of Pai-chang*,[46] upon which the Code supposedly modeled itself, are meditation, assemblies, and manual labor. Meditation was carried out in the Monks' Hall. The times of meditation were not specified in the Code but by the Southern Sung.

> Communal meditation sessions were held four times daily: from about eight to nine pm, three to four am, nine to ten am, and three to four pm. Each "hour" was measured with a burning stick of incense. The term "four hours' meditation" first appears in Ch'an codes in the *Pei-yung Code* (1311).[47]

The reason why the *Ch'an-yüan Code* did not specify the times for meditation could be, as Collcutt suggested, "that meditation practice was still sufficiently dedicated to need no special regulation."[48] The public assembly

---

(Cambridge, Mass.: Harvard University Press, 1981), p. 141. Collcutt has conveniently summarized the areas covered by the Code on pp. 141–142:

> The proper reception and strict observance of the Buddhist precepts (both Hinayana and Mahāyāna): "The practice of Zen begins with the precepts" (sections 1 and 2).
>
> The monk's costume, equipment, and essential documents. The proper method of packing the bundles of belongings when traveling from monastery to monastery. The correct procedure when requesting to stay overnight at a monastery or when seeking to enroll for a season in a monks hall (sections 3 to 6).
>
> The etiquette to be observed during meals and tea ceremonies (sections 7 and 8). The procedure for requesting the abbot's spiritual guidance and for the private interviews (*ju-shih*) in the abbot's chamber (sections 9 and 10). The forms of regular monastic activities, including the morning and evening assemblies, ceremonies for state and monastic intentions, ceremonies for the opening and closing of the summer retreat, etc. The manner of the regular tours of inspection of the monastery halls by the abbot. The correct procedure for entertaining Buddhist dignitaries and secular officials (sections 11 to 18).
>
> The manner of appoinment and the duties of the two ranks of monastery officers and their assistants. The *Ch'an-yuan Code* mentions ten principal officers: four stewards and six prefects assisted by more than forty subprefects (sections 19 to 40).
>
> The details of special monastery tea ceremonies and feasts (sections 41 to 50). The regulations for the *sūtra* reading. Sound signals. Correct epistolary forms for official monastery correspondence. Procedures to be followed in the case of sickness of an abbot or monk. Personal hygiene and latrine etiquette (sections 51 to 60).
>
> Details of the obsequies for a deceased monk. The monastic and civil procedures for appointing a new abbot. Installation of a the abbot. The proper attitude of mind of the abbot. Formalities upon the retirement from office of an abbot (sections 61 to 68).
>
> Disquisition on the spirit of the Ch'an monastic life and the importance of the abbot and the monastery officers, remembering that they are there for the sake of the community not vice versa (section 69).
>
> The practice of meditation (section 70).
>
> One hundred and twenty questions for monks to test the depth of their religious lives. The detailed form of the ordination ceremony. The training of postulants. The duties of monastery servants. The encouragement of monastery patrons. Rules for lay people in giving feasts for monks. Commentary on the Pai-chang rules (sections 71 to 78).

46. Recently some Japanese scholars, particularly Kondō Ryōichi, have called into question the existence of the so-called *Pai-chang's Pure Rule*. See Collcutt, *Five Mountains*, p. 137. In his article, "The Early Ch'an Monastic Rule," Collcutt has devoted a section, "The puzzle of the Pai-chang ch'ing kuei," to detail Ryōichi's arguments against the existence of such a document. See pp. 171–173.

47. Collcutt, *Five Mountains*, p. 143.

48. Ibid.

(*shang-t'ang*) was held six times a month in the Dharma Hall, on the morning of every fifth day: the first, fifth, tenth, fifteenth, twentieth, and twenty fifth of the month. Evening assemblies (*hsiao-ts'an*), less formal and held in the abbot's chamber, occurred on the third, eighth, thirteenth, eighteenth, twenty-third, and twenty-eighth days of each month. The public assembly was a solemn occasion. The Code stipulates:

> When it is time to attend the assembly, everyone should go with the exception of the attendant of the Monks Hall and that of the dormitory. Those who disobey should be severely punished at the gate. If a person is late on account of unexpected emergency and not because he is lazy or careless, still he should not enter the hall if the abbot has already ascended the high seat. . . . In going to the assembly, monks should not wear hats. The same goes for the abbot. If the person who asks the abbot questions says something funny, one should not laugh aloud or smile broadly. One should be serious and listen to the profound sound with respect.[49]

The public assembly was the time for the abbot to give a formal talk about the essentials of Ch'an. He would refer to a *kung-an* and ask students to respond. The monks could also ask questions or hold public debate with the master. In contrast, the evening assembly was probably less dramatic. The Code describes it as an occasion for family instruction (*chia-hsün*) that holds the monastery in good discipline; it was held during the first watch of the night, from seven to eleven. During the evening assembly, aside from the discussion of *kung-an*, the abbot would talk about matters affecting the monks' daily life or problems in meditation, and he could also offer them general encouragement.[50]

In addition to these assemblies, the monks also had informal interviews with the abbot who could decide when these would be appropriate. The Code calls these interviews "requesting cause and condition" (*ch'ing yin-yüan*) and "entering the abbot's chamber" (*ju-shih*). In the stipulations of the Code concerning how interviews should be carried out, the great stress placed on strict protocol is striking:

> Depending on the individual choice of the abbot, "requesting cause and condition" can take place either after the semi-monthly assembly or after the tea ceremony on the first and second day of the month. Before entering the room, look at the attendant and say to him that you want to request the abbot's instruction. Enter only after the attendant makes the announcement for you. Led by the leader, everyone stands firmly facing north. After each person has a chance to offer incense, the leader representing everyone makes the request to the abbot, saying, "Because Life and Death is a Great Matter and life is impermanent and short, we beg the master to show compassion and give us instruction.[51]

49. For writing this chapter I used the annotated Japanese edition of the Code prepared by Kagamishima, Satō, and Kosaka, *Yakuchū Zen'on Shingi* (Tokyo: Sōtōshu shūmuchō, 1972), p. 75.
50. Ibid., p. 79.
51. Ibid., p. 64.

On "entering the abbot's chamber":

The abbot could decide if this should take place according to rank or the positions in the dormitory. He could also decide if it is to be every other day or on certain fixed days, if in the morning or evening. When the time arrives, the attendant orders the waiter to light the incense and after spreading the mat, he informs the abbot that everything is ready. If there is someone to take charge of the event, he should hang up a placard announcing it. He can either beat on the drum, or the board or the placard to alert everyone. After the abbot takes his seat, the attendant stands outside the room. He stands on the east side with his hands folded in front of him. The monks can either form one line facing east or two lines facing each other. The attendant then enters the abbot's chamber and bows. After that, he turns to the east of the abbot's chair and stands behind the incense altar facing south. He bows once, offers incense with his left hand, and bows again. He bows to the abbot, then bows to everyone. He then returns to the dormitory. In entering the room, each person should walk with hands folded in an orderly fashion. He should not get in front and thereby offend others. He enters from the right side of the threshold. Lifting up the left foot first, he bows to the abbot after entering. He turns and with folded hands bows to the southwest corner of the abbot's chair and takes a stand. After bowing again he tells the abbot either what he has attained in his meditation or what difficulties he is experiencing. He should not talk long. Nor should he speak of worldly things or idle matters lest he takes up the others' time. After talking, he bows and then prostrates. He turns to face east and with folded hands he leaves the room keeping to the left side. He lifts his left foot first so that he will not collide with the person who comes after him.[52]

The minute and detailed prescription for the monks' deportment in all situations is stressed throughout the Code. By molding the monks' ways of walking, talking, eating, and bowing to a fixed standard, the Code hopes to create an orderly and disciplined monastic life conducive to spiritual awakening. The ritualization of behavior in daily life is particularly striking in the training of postulants, "Hsün t'ung-hsing" in the Code. As I shall argue later in the chapter, I believe the rules were created not just for the smooth functioning of the monastery or to teach young postulants good manners. Of course, they might serve these pragmatic purposes, but these were incidental and secondary. The main purpose was the transformation of the young person's very being. Rules changed outward behavior, and it was hoped that *kung-an* and other Ch'an pedagogies would complete the inward transformation and result in the enlightenment experience. Rules of this sort, therefore, form a crucial part of the Ch'an monks' education.

Were the rules always put into practice? In the *Ch'an-lin pao-hsün* (Treasured Instructions of the Ch'an Tradition), which contains advices and instructions given by famous Sung abbots, a number of deviations are obvious. A Ch'ing commentator on the *Treasured Instructions* claimed that the informal assembly was held every evening instead of only six times every month. He also provided other helpful glosses.

52. Ibid., pp. 66–67.

Informal assemblies (*hsiao-ts'an*) are the same as evening assemblies (*wan-ts'an*). Whenever the students are gathered to receive instruction, it is called an assembly (*ts'an*). Teachers of the past wanted the students to consult with them day and night, for they encouraged and promoted the pursuit of the Way at all times. Therefore every evening an assembly was held at the time of the evening meal. But on the occasions when a new abbot was installed, or when officials and other patrons visited the monastery, or when there was a special request, or when instruction was given for the benefit of the dead, or on the four holidays [the days of the beginning and the conclusion of the summer retreat, the winter solstice, and the New Year day], the meeting would be moved to the time when the evening gong was sounded, and it was then called informal assembly. Informal assembly at first had no fixed place. Depending on the number of people attending, it could be held either at the abbot's chamber or the Dharma Hall. In the afternoon the attendant reported to the abbot saying. "There will be an assembly tonight." He reminded the attendant for the dormitory to make the announcement by posting the placard for informal assembly. When the evening gong was sounded, he beat the drum and gathered everybody together. He would then go to welcome the abbot and ask him to take the seat to discuss the essentials of Ch'an.[53]

Not just the frequency of the evening meetings might deviate from the Code. More seriously, correct protocols for conducting the assemblies were also sometimes violated. Several references in the *Treasured Instructions* point to current abuses. First, the "question and answer" and the Dharma debate had at times degenerated into theatrics and melodrama. Wan-yen said:

"In former days, when the past worthy ascended the seat, he would first review the essentials of the great Dharma and then question the assembly. Students would come forward with questions and there was "question and answer." Nowadays, however, someone would compose a poem of four phrases with poor rhyming and this is called "fishing words" (*tiao-hua*). Another person may dart out from the assembly and recite aloud a poem written in former times and this is called "abusing the file" (*ma-chen*). This is truly vulgar. How sad! How unbearable![54]

When a famous master came to the monastery for a visit, the abbot should first take the seat, deliver a speech of welcome, and then ask the distinguished visitor to take the seat and talk about the essentials of the Dharma for the benefit of the community. But "recently the fashion is to ask the visitor to criticize a past *kung-an*, and this is called 'testing him' (*yen-ta*). Wan-yen deplored this custom and declared that "propriety is headed by humility."[55] On the other hand, when a lay visitor came to the monastery, be he the governor, a magistrate, or a literatus, the proper way was for the abbot to see him only if the visitor requested it. After the interview, the abbot

---

53. *Ch'an-lin pao-hsün shun-chu, chüan* 3. Te-yu, in *Wan-tzu Hsü tsang ching* 113:0559.
54. *Ch'an-lin pao-hsün ho-chu* 3:0392.
55. Ibid.

should thank him for protecting Buddhism. If the visitor was well versed in Ch'an, then and only then would the abbot say a few "tasteless words" to inspire respect in their hearts, as Pai-yün Shou-tuan (24–1072) treated Kuo Kung-p'u or Fo-yin Liao-yüan (1031–1098) treated Su Tung-po and Huang Shan-ku. But this, alas, was not the way things were done any more. In the Southern Sung, as soon as an important lay visitor arrived, the guest prefect would immediately get the abbot to go to the Dharma Hall and deliver a lecture for no particular reason.[56]

There was much mechanical formalization in the way the informal interviews were conducted as well. The opportunity of "entering the abbot's chamber" should be regarded as a rare opportunity to solve the great matter of life and death; thus, in former days when the monks saw the placard announcing it, they came forward eagerly to ask questions. But in the Southern Sung, according to Wan-yen, some abbots demanded that everybody, even the old and the sick, pay respect to them by entering their chambers even without something to say. Wan-yen observed wryly, "Musk is naturally fragrant. Why is there need to force people to do something by such coercive measures?"[57]

The *Treasured Instructions* also provided positive models of other abbots who conducted the private interviews with sincerity and vigor. Kao-yen Shan-wu recalled a talk given by Fo-chien Hui-chin (d. 1117) during such a session.

> When I first went to Tsu-shan, I heard Fo-chien talk during an informal assembly. He said, "Greed, ignorance and hatred are more terrible than thieves. You should defend yourselves with wisdom. Wisdom is like water. When unused, it becomes stagnant. When stagnant, it will not flow. Once it stops flowing, wisdom ceases to function. Then what can you do about greed, ignorance and hatred?" Even though I was young at that time, I knew then that he was a good teacher. So I asked to stay at the monastery.[58]

Later on when Kao-yen himself became the abbot of Yün-chü, he would seize the opportunity of private interviews to impress on the monks the necessity of hard work.

> Every time when what the monks answered during private interviews failed to reach Kao-yen's expectations, he would take hold of their sleeves and scold them sternly saying, "Parents nourished your body, teachers and friends furnished your will, you do not suffer the oppression of hunger and cold, nor the toil of corvée labor and military service. Yet you still do not work hard and accomplish your task in the Way. How can you face your parents and teachers in the future?" Among those who heard this, some broke down and cried.[59]

56. Ibid.
57. Ibid.
58. Ibid., 2:0358.
59. Ibid., 2:0360.

DID CH'AN MONKS STUDY SCRIPTURES?

Ch'an monks in the Sung had a large body of Ch'an classics that provided much material for reading and discussion. But what was their relationship with Buddhist scriptures? Did they study them, and, if so, what *sūtra*s and treatises received most attention? What was the Ch'an attitude toward scriptural study? Sung government regulations concerning home-leaving and ordination followed those of the T'ang. The monastic community consisted of male and female postulants, male and female novices, monks and nuns. In leaving home and becoming a postulant a boy had to be at least nineteen and a girl fourteen years of age. A postulant could then be ordained as a novice through examination, by imperial favor, or the purchase of ordination certificates. This ordination was most important, for it granted exemption from tax, corvée labor, and military service to the ordinant. Many remained as novices for life and did not go on to receive the full ordination for monks. The term *seng* could mean novices and monks while *ta-seng* was reserved exclusively for monks. Ordination through examination (*shih-ching tu-seng*) required that a male postulant must be able either to read five hundred sheets or to recite from memory one hundred sheets of the *Lotus sūtra*. For a female postulant, the requirements were three hundred sheets and seventy sheets respectively.[60] The *Lotus sūtra* was chosen because it was used in the T'ang and because, running seven fascicles, it was "neither too simple nor too complicated so that learners did not have to fear either going too far or not far enough in their study and memorization."[61]

According to the ordination regulations, therefore, all members of the *saṅgha*, with the exception of the postulants, were supposed to be literate and to have passed the scriptural test. But the real situation was far more complicated: because of the demand for additional national revenue, the sale of ordination certificates became widespread after 1067 when it was adopted as an official policy.[62] This made mockery of all the regulations, for anyone who could pay the current price for the ordination certificate could be considered a monk. The decline of the moral and intellectual caliber of the *saṅgha*, a fact much deplored by Buddhist leaders in the Sung, was in no small measure due to this lamentable practice. There was another factor. It appeared that the minimum age requirement for home-leaving (becoming postulants) or ordination as novices was never enforced. The age at which a teenager left the householder's life varied widely. Some indeed were reported

60. Takao Giken, *Sōdai Bukkyōshi no kenkyū* (Kyoto: Hyakkaen, 1975), pp. 13–33. *Sung Hui-yao* (Taipei, 1964) 16:7875. *Ching-yüan tiao-fa-shih-lei* (Tokyo, 1958) 50:469. *Fo-tsu t'ung-chi, chüan* 51 in *Chung-kuo fo-chiao shih chuan tsung-kan* (Taipei: Hsin-wen-feng, 1958) 1:452.

61. Kenneth Ch'en, *Buddhism in China: A Historical Survey* (Princeton: Princeton University Press, 1964), pp. 246–248. *To-tsu t'ung-chi, chüan* 47, p. 430.
This was the argument given by Jo-na, the monk secretary of the Left District, in a memorial asking the restoration of the examination system in 1184.

62. Kenneth Ch'en, *Buddhism in China*, p. 391.

to have passed the exam and become novices at the age of nineteen, the minimal legal age for postulants. But this was by no means the norm. I have come across one Chiang-shan Tsan-yüan, a descendent of the famous Ch'an figure Fu Ta-shih, who "left the householder's life at three and became ordained at seven."[63] Although this might be a special case, I have also seen accounts of children who became postulants at seven, nine, eleven, thirteen, and fourteen years old or became ordained at the ages of fifteen, sixteen, and seventeen.

If a child entered the monastery at a very young age, it was highly likely that he did not know how to read. In a rare case, an adult of a lower class, his illiteracy was plainly acknowledged.

> Shi-t'ou Tzu-hui came from a family of hereditary stone cutters. People called him Monk Stone. He was like a blind turtle, not recognizing even one character. He asked people to teach him to chant the *Lotus sūtra*. After he could recite it by heart, he left home and went to stay with Monk Ta-sui.[64]

Tsung-tse, the compiler of the *Ch'an-yüan Code*, did not take the literacy of postulants for granted. In the section regulating the manner of reading *sūtra*s in the Tripitaka Hall (*k'an-ching-tsang*), the Code states clearly that "If a person cannot read, he should be excused."[65] But in its more than seventy sections of regulations, it does not mention anywhere if those members of the *saṅgha* who did not read were taught to read, and if so, what and how.

Assuming that most monks were literate, can something be said about the educational background of the Ch'an monks of the Sung? Unfortunately, the biographies rarely go beyond giving the subject's secular name, the birthplace (but seldom the birthdate), the age of leaving home (but not necessarily the age of receiving ordination), and sometimes the date of death. After laboriously combing all the biographical materials on Ch'an monks of the Sung,[66] I have come up with only forty-nine monks for whom information about their scriptural knowledge was available. The findings are undeniably anecdotal and impressionistic, but they still give us a sense of the extent of their knowledge of Buddhist (and Confucian) scripture and their attitude toward them.

Several Ch'an monks were educated in Confucian classics when they were children. Fo-yin Liao-yüan, abbot of Chin-shan and good friend of Su Tung-po and Huang Shan-ku, came from a Confucian family, even though

63. *Ch'an-lin seng pao chüan* 27:0547.
64. *Ta Ming kao-seng chuan, chüan* 6, in *Chung-kuo fo-chiao shih chuan tsung-kan* 11:922.
65. *Yakuchū Zen'on shingi*, p. 209.
66. I used *Fo-tsu li-tai t'ung-tsai, Ch'an-lin seng-pao chuan, Pu Ch'an-lin seng-pao chuan, Seng-pao cheng hsü chuan, Nan Sung Yüan Ming ch'an-lin seng-pao chuan, Ta Ming seng-pao chuan,* and *Wü teng hui-yüan.* In the retelling of individual cases, I will not indicate the sources because they were composite and drawn from all of the above. In cases where only one of the above supply the information, I will then so indicate.

neither his grandfather nor his father served in the government. He could recite the *Analects* and poems at two years of age. At five he was able to recite three thousand poems, and when a little older he was taught the five classics whose general meanings he could understand. But when he happened to read the *Surangama sūtra* at the Monastery of Bamboo Forest, he loved it so much that he gave up his former studies. Hung-chih Cheng-chüeh, the promoter of the "Ch'an of Silent Illumination" was another child prodigy. He was said to be able to memorize several thousand characters a day and was already well grounded in the five classics at seven. At eighteen he studied Ch'an at Hsiang-shan Monastery, Honan, and when he heard a monk read the passage from the *Lotus sūtra* "With the eyes given to us by our parents, we can see the three thousand worlds all at once,"[67] he achieved enlightenment. His contemporary, Ta-hui, on the other hand, did not begin to study at the prefectural school until he was thirteen. One day while playing with class-mates he hit them with an inkwell that landed on the teacher's hat by mistake. After paying fines he left, saying, "How can learning worldly books be compared to studying the other-worldly Dharma?" He left the househol-der's life. Later when he read the *Ku Yün-men lu* (Ancient Record of Master Yün-men), he felt as if he had known it for a long time. Last, two monks were less famous than the above: Lan-yen Ting-hsü, a Confucian scholar when young, even received a *chin-shih* degree and became renowned as an official. But when he was twenty-five he happened to read the *Fo i-chiao ching* (Sūtra of the Buddha's Last Instructions), and it so moved him that he declared, "I would have been hindered by my Confucian cap [if I did not find this sūtra]." So he gave up his career and became Ta-hui's disciple.[68] Pieh-feng Pao-yin (d. 1190) was also well versed in the "six classics" when very young and exhaustively schooled in the "seven histories." But he suddenly became weary of the world, and after taking the tonsure he listened to the lectures on the *Hua-yen sūtra* and the *Awakening of Faith* and understood everything.[69]

Even though the *Lotus sūtra* was probably the most popular *sūtra* in the Sung, it is clear from the above stories that other Buddhist works often drew their readers to Buddhism. Aside from the ones already referred to, the *Diamond sūtra*, the *Sūtra of Perfect Enlightenment*, the *Sayings of Yüan-wu*, the *Ts'ao-tung kuang-lu* (the Extended Record of Master Ta'so-tung), the *Vimala-kirti sūtra*, and the *"Pao-ching sung"* (Ode to the Precious Mirror[70]) were also mentioned.

Once a person decided to join the *saṅgha*, he had the option of studying in any one of the three types of public monasteries in the Sung: the *Lü*

---

67. Tseng P'u-hsin, *Chung-kuo ch'an tsu-shih chuan*, p. 280. This passage also triggered another monk, Shih-ch'uang Fa-kung, into enlightenment. *Wu-teng hui-yüan* 14:0549.

68. *Ta Ming kao seng chuan* 6:923.

69. Ibid., 6:925.

70. I cannot identify this work. Tung-shan wrote *Pao-ching san-mei*, a classic. Could they be related in any way?

(Discipline), the *Chiang* (Doctrine), and the *Ch'an*. Thus, there are examples of Ch'an monks who had started their training first in *Chiang* monasteries, specializing in the *Lotus sūtra* and related T'ien-t'ai philosophical works, the *Hua-yen sūtra*, the *Awakening of Faith*, the *Pai-fa ming-men lun* (Treatise of the One Hundred Dharmas), and other works of the Wei-shih school. Other Ch'an monks, on the other hand, had earlier studied Vinaya in the *Lü* monasteries before they turned to Ch'an. Although the limited sample gives us a general impression of monks going from one type of monastery to another type quite freely, there are also examples of interschool rivalry. When Ch'an masters met *Chiang* lecturers, they sometimes would show the superiority of Ch'an, taught the latter a deeper understanding of the *sūtra*, or convert the latter to Ch'an. I will cite four examples.

Fa-yün Fa-hsiu left home at nineteen, and at forty he paid a visit to the Ch'an master T'ien-i I-huai (981–1053). I-huai asked at their first meeting, "What *sūtra* do you lecture on?" Fa-hsiu answered, "The *Hua-yen sūtra*." I-huai asked him what was the basis of the *sūtra*, and the answer was the dharmadhatu. When asked what was the basis of dharmadhatu, Fa-hsiu said, "Mind." Then I-huai asked, "What is the basis of mind?" Fa-hsiu could not reply. I-huai finally told him, "With the least divergence in the beginning, the difference will be like heaven from earth in the end. Think carefully and you will come to a discovery." Fa-hsiu started Ch'an practice and after a long time reached enlightenment.[71]

When Chang-shui Tzu-hsü (d. 1030) studied the *Surangama sūtra* at a *Chiang* monastery, he suddenly achieved an insight upon reading the passage "The characteristics of movement and quiescence are from the beginning not produced." He heard about the fame of the Ch'an master Lang-ya Hui-chüeh. So he went to where Hui-chüeh was staying. It happened that the master was holding a public assembly. Tzu-hsü asked, "Purity and clarity are naturally so. Why is it said that mountains, rivers, and earth were suddenly produced?" Instead of answering, Hui-chüeh repeated the question, and Tzu-hsü right away reached enlightenment. The Ch'an master said to him, "Your school [Hsien-shou] has long suffered decline. You should restore it to repay the grace of the Buddha." He followed the advice and later became the abbot of Chang-shui and led a thousand monks. He used the principle of Hua-yen to explain the *Surangama sūtra* and wrote a commentary of ten fascicles.[72]

Huan-t'ang Shou-jen studied *sūtra*s and treatises in the years of Hsüan-ho (1119–1125). He was rather contemptuous of Ch'an teachings. When Yüan-wu was the abbot at T'ien-ning, Ch'an became greatly known, and Ta-hui was only one of several famous disciples under him. Out of curiosity, Shou-jen went there to find out about the situation. He participated at the

---

71. *Chung-kuo ch'an tsu-shih chuan*, p. 225.
72. *Fo-tsu li-tai t'ung-tsai* 18:663.

evening assembly held at the abbot's chamber, thinking to himself that, if what Yüan-wu said deviated from the doctrinal teaching, he would have to refute him. Yüan-wu knew that Shou-jen was in the room, so he called the latter to him and said, "If you explain the teaching according to the *sūtras*, you will be blamed by Buddhas of the three periods. But if you say one word deviating from the *sūtras*, you will be as wrong as Mara. What then would you do?" Before he could make any answer, Yüan-wu quickly hit him with the iron back-scratcher (*t'ieh ju-i*) he was carrying. It knocked out one of his teeth, and, while wiping away the blood with his hand, Shou-jen was suddenly enlightened. After he was converted to Ch'an, he used sticks and blows to train learners. Once he visited a *Chiang* lecturer specializing on the *Sūtra of Perfect Enlightenment*, going there incognito. The lecturer was sitting on the high seat and expounding on the *sūtra* with many quotations from commentaries and scholarly exegesis. Shou-jen listened for a while and laughed. The lecturer, getting off the seat, asked if what he said had deviated from the *sūtra*. Shou-jen answered, "It neither deviated nor conformed." When asked if he himself understood the meaning of the *sūtra*, he answered, "I neither do nor do not understand." The lecturer ended up asking Shou-jen to take the seat to expound the *sūtra*.[73]

The last example involves a *kung-an*-like exchange between Yün-chü Tao-ying and a monk. The monk was heard reciting a *sūtra* in his room. Master Tao-ying asked from outside the window, "Acarya, what *sūtra* are you reciting?" The monk answered, "*The Vimalakirti sūtra*." The master then said, "I am not asking the *Vimalakirti*. But what *sūtra* is the one who recites it?" The monk entered the Way after hearing this.[74]

The last anecdote points to the practice of monks' reading *sūtras* in Ch'an monasteries. *Sūtras* were in fact available for their use. In the Northern Sung, there was a Tripitaka Hall where *sūtras* were stored in every major Ch'an public monastery. In the Southern Sung, the library facility was moved to the Buddha Hall or the dormitory. When that happened, even though *sūtras* were still accessible, the position of the Tripitaka Master (*tsang-chu*) who was originally the third highest officer among the top six in a Ch'an monastery, lost its importance, and the Tripitaka Hall also remained in name only.[75]

The *Ch'an-yüan Code* goes into great length describing the duties of the Tripitaka Master. He was in charge of the Tripitaka Hall, similar to a present day library. Under him there was the attendant of the "*sūtra* reading

---

73. *Nan Sung Yüan Ming ch'an-lin seng pao chuan* 4:0661.

74. *Wu-teng hui-yüan* 13:0481.

75. The commentators of *Yakuchū Zen'on Shingi* pointed out that even in the Northern Sung, *sūtras* could be read either in the *sūtra* reading room of Tripitaka Hall or in the dormitory. In *Chüan* 1, under the section dealing with admittance of monks to the dormitory, it says that according to the ordination seniority, monks should be assigned a *k'an-tu ch'uang* (bed for reading), so there was a facility for reading in the dorm. By the southern Sung, however, *sūtras* were read in the dorm, and the Tripitaka Hall no longer had its original function. See p. 330.

room" (*k'an-ching t'ang*), the equivalent of the reading room in a library. During the Northern Sung when the Code was compiled, the Tripitaka Master was an officer demanding respect, and he was supposed to be well learned in doctrinal matters (*i-chieh*). The Code is detailed in the regulations concerning the correct manner of reading scriptures.

> Before taking up the scripture, one should burn incense and do homage in the Tripitaka Hall. Walking back to one's desk and holding the scripture in one's hands, one should not talk or laugh. One should not pile up writing brushes, ink-well, miscellaneous objects or Ch'an writings on the desk where the scripture is placed. In lighting the lamp, filling it with oil, and extinguishing the lamp, one should be extremely careful so that the sacred teaching would not be damaged or soiled. In the reading room, one may not entertain any visitor. If a friend comes for a visit, he should be ushered to the dormitory. One should not talk with people outside the window of the reading room either, for that would disturb other readers. If the weather is cloudy and damp, if one's hands are still wet after being washed, or if one has been under the sun or working near the fire, then the time is not appropriate for reading *sūtras*. . . . After reading, one has to be careful in putting the scripture back in its covers. If it is tied too tight, the *sūtra* will be damaged. But if it is too loose, it will look untidy. One should not lean on the desk and press down the *sūtra* with one's body weight. One should not hold the *sūtra* ribbon with one's mouth. . . . There is a definite way to open the *sūtra*, untie the ribbon, fold the *sūtra* and retie the ribbon. A person should find it out from the curator of the reading room or those who are familiar with it. Near the *sūtra* desk one should not loosen one's garment to mend clothes or catch lice. If one does not know the word, first consult the "rhyming glossary" (*pien-yün*). You ask someone else only when you are still in doubt. You will disturb others too much if you ask too frequently. Cover the *sūtra* when you have to leave the desk for even a brief moment. But do not put the folded robe on top of the *sūtra*. You must sit up straight when you read the *sūtra*. Do not utter any sound or move your lips.[76]

Individual monks could read *sūtras* for their own edification. From time to time, a patron could ask the monks to chant *sūtras* to generate merit.[77] The Code has a section on "ceremonies for state and monastic intentions" (*nien-sung*) that stipulates that on the "three-eight days"—for example, the third, eighth, thirteenth, eighteenth, twenty-third, and twenty-eighth of the month—ceremonies of chanting the ten Buddhas' names and prayer should be carried out. On the days containing the number three, the monks pray for the prosperity of the state and Buddha Dharma as well as the safety of patrons. On the days containing the number eight, they observe the truth of impermanence and encourage each other to strive hard in their religious efforts.[78] These ceremonies do not contain any *sūtra* chanting. The only other

76. Ibid., pp. 129–131.
77. Ibid., see section 50, "*Sūtra* reading," pp. 206–209.
78. Ibid., section 12, pp. 76–78.

place in the Code where *sūtra* chanting is used to generate merit is found in the section on the "training of postulants"; I will discuss this more in the last part of the chapter. The postulants must chant the *Heart sūtra* three times each at the morning congee and the noon meal in order to "repay the kindness of donors in the ten directions, serving monks as well as humans, animals, and tiny creatures who either labor or lose their lives in supplying food for us."[79]

The reverence shown toward *sūtra*s as prescribed by the Code was a far cry from the popular image of Ch'an practitioners as freewheeling iconoclasts who would tear up *sūtra*s or burn the Buddha's statue for warmth. *Sūtra* reading was an acceptable monastic activity, and the Code does not betray any trace of disapproval toward scriptural study. I would further suggest that the Code itself provides its own materials for study. I have in mind particularly the essay "Rules for Sitting Meditation" (*Tso-ch'an i*) and "One Hundred and Twenty Questions" (*I-pai erh-shih wen*) for monks to test the depth of their religious lives, which form sections 70 and 71 and are contained in *chüan* 8 of the Code. The first essay is a succinct introduction to the correct practice of sitting meditation; Sheng-yen pointed out that Dōgen's essay with the same title was almost verbatim.[80] Since the second, "One Hundred and Twenty Questions," is relatively unknown, I have translated it in full and present it as an appendix. I do not know if this list of questions was intended to be read aloud in an assembly. Like the recitation of the *pratimoksa* at the semimonthly ceremony, such a list could be used in this way. Thus, as each question was asked aloud, the members of the congregation could reflect on their moral purity and spiritual maturity or their lack of the same. But there was no evidence that this was ever done. It probably instead served as a textbook for either classroom instruction or individual study and review, for it is a remarkably comprehensive outline of all the key areas of moral and spiritual cultivation. The list of questions was known to have circulated as an independent book, separate from the *Ch'an-yüan Code*.[81] This was done most likely in order to facilitate its use as a textbook.

The list of 120 questions starts with the most basic Buddhist concept of the "three refuges": No. 1. "Do you respect the Buddha, the Dharma and the Saṅgha?" It ends with the Buddhist summum bonum: No. 120. "Have you realized the great Nirvana?" Between these two questions a wide range of

---

79. Ibid., pp. 325–326.

80. Dōgen's essay, "Fukanzazengi," is found in T 82:1–2. Sheng-yen, *Ch'an-men hsiu-cheng chih-yao*, p. 142.

81. I owe this information to Sheng-yen who claimed that this was the case in the monastic circles both in China and Japan. Tsung-tse seemed to favor the number 120. When he was the abbot of Ch'ang-lu Monastery during 1086–1093, he sent for his mother and took care of her. He persuaded his mother to cut off her hair and recite the name of Amitābha. He composed 120 essays on filial piety discussing it from both worldly and otherworldly perspectives. Ibid., p. 141.

topics are covered. For the convenience of discussion, they can be divided
into five areas: (1) morality common to Confucianism and Buddhism—filial
piety, loyalty, respect, kindness, humility, and other virtues (e.g., Nos.
41–47, 51, 53–57, 71–72, 78–85, 92–97, 99–106); (2) Buddhist precepts
stressed in the Vinaya, particularly that of nonharming (e.g., Nos. 49, 50,
64–70, 73–77, 84–91); (3) Mahāyāna ideals such as the six perfections and
thought for enlightenment (Nos. 3, 107–116); (4) technical knowledge of
Buddhist doctrine and philosophy, heavily T'ien-t'ai and Hua-yen (Nos.
32–40); and (5) Ch'an, primarily knowledge of *kung-an* (Nos. 19–22, 24–27).
The most interesting items are those that do not fall into any category.
Tsung-tse asked the learners to seek out good teachers (No. 2), not to exploit
their disciples (No. 78), not to oppress others because of their position (No.
81), to fear and obey the law of the land (No. 83), to make commitments to
the Buddhist way of life (Nos. 4–6, 8–18), and be diligent in the Buddhist
practice of burning incense, worship, and cultivation (No. 62). The warning
against befriending officials (Nos. 80, 82) and the criticism about the desire
for fame and profit (Nos. 74, 76, 79) were also repeated by Ch'an masters in
the *Treasured Instructions*. They must have been real problems and revealed
real concerns of the Ch'an leadership. Finally, the call to treat barbarians the
same way as Chinese (No. 98), although based in Mahāyāna universalism,
bears the indelible mark of Tsung-tse's forceful and original way of thinking.

Did other Ch'an masters in the Sung share Tsung-tse's approval of
scriptural study? I will now turn to a discussion of the general attitude of
Ch'an masters to scriptural study, and in so doing I offer a hypothesis about
the decline of the importance of the Tripitaka Hall in the Southern Sung.

Treasured Instructions has a number of examples of Ch'an masters who
studied not only Buddhist scriptures but also Confucian classics and history.
Pai-yün Shou-tuan (1025–1072) recalled that "I once studied at the Study
Hall (*shu-t'ang*) of Kuei-tsung Monastery on Mt. Lu and read classics and
history (*Ching-shih*) for more than several hundred volumes. Every time I
opened a book, I would gain some new insight. Indeed, study never fails a
person."[82] Ling-yüan Wei-ch'ing "loved to read Classics and history. He
would not rest from it except to eat and sleep. He stopped only after he could
memorize them." This diligence in study was admired by Huang Shan-ku
who commented, "Brother Ch'ing loved learning just as a hungry and thirsty
person loved food and drink. Yet to him profit and luxury had an evil odor.
This naturally comes from his sincere heart and he is not trying to pretend
anything." His teacher, Hui-t'ang Tsu-hsin (1025–1100), however, scolded
him for it, and Ling-yüan defended himself, saying, "I have heard that he
who exerted himself could achieve results that would go far."[83] Hui-t'ang
himself was reported to be a serious student. He once went to visit

---

82. *Ch'an-lin pao-hsün ho-chu* 1:0317.
83. Ibid., 2:0345.

Hsiao-yüeh Kung-hui, regarded as the foremost *Surangama* scholar in his time. Hui-t'ang was overjoyed by each word and each phrase he heard from the latter's lectures and "cherished them as priceless jewels."[84] Hui-t'ang also greatly admired his own teacher, Huang-lung, for his concentration in study. He said:

> My former teacher spent the summer retreat together with Yün-fang Wen-yüeh at Feng-lin Monastery in Ching-nan. Yüeh loved to debate. One day he became engrossed in debates with monks and they were very boisterous. But my teacher continued to read his scripture and acted as if he did not hear anything. After a while, Yüeh came to my master's desk and, looking at him angrily, accused him of pretending to practice the patience of an eminent monk. My master bowed, thanking him, and continued to read the scripture as before.[85]

How do we explain the two contradictory attitudes of admiration and disapproval? It is not simply a matter of Hui-t'ang's approving the study of Buddhist scriptures but not secular history and Classics. For several masters specifically disapproved even the academic study of Buddhist scriptures. Ling-yüan made this clear to Hui-hung chüeh-fan, the author of *Lin-chien lu* (The Record of the Ch'an Forest) and *Ch'an-lin seng-pao chuan* (Biographies of Monastic Treasures of the Ch'an Forest) and a man renowned for his erudition and ability in debate. Ling-yüan said to him:

> I heard that when you studied the *Surangama sūtra* in Canton, you wrote a commentary on it. This is something I do not wish you to do. For the learning of words (*wen-tzu chih hsüeh*) cannot thoroughly disclose the origin of our nature. It merely obstructs the Buddha's wisdom eye of students of latter days. The mistake is to make them achieve understanding based on the ideas of others but in doing so, they will close the door of their own awakening (*tzu-wu men*).[86]

Scriptures, like *kung-an* anthologies, are not themselves objectionable; the learner's priority and motivation were crucial. If one replaced the search for self-realization with book learning, then one was doomed to failure. However, study, as a discipline of the mind, had a high place for Buddhists, just as it did for Confucians. Two more examples from the *Treasured Instruction* make this argument.

Ta-chüeh Huai-lien (1008–1090) used a familiar analogy from the *Li chi* to compare study with the carving of jade:

> Jade cannot be made into utensil if it is not carved. A person does not know the way if he does not study. The reason why people living at present can know what happened in ancient times or why people who come later can know what happened before their time is because they can model themselves upon the

84. Ibid., 1:0333.
85. Ibid., 1:0335.
86. Ibid., 2:0348.

good and warn themselves about the bad. If you observe those exemplary models who made names for themselve and truly established themselves in their times, none did so without much learning."[87]

Chen-ch'ing Ke-wen (1024–1102) emphasized that study was primarily a way to discipline the mind. Study should be regarded as an aid to self-realization but never compete with it. When the mind is properly attuned through Ch'an training, one can attain awakening as a result of the reading of a secular essay just as much as through any traditional devices in Ch'an pedagogy. Chen-ch'ing's advice was given to Kan-t'ang Wen-chun who had the habit of reading within his mosquito net deep into the night. Chen-ch'ing scolded him:

> In studying you should seek to discipline your mind. If your mind is not disciplined, even if you have much learning, it is of no use. Moreover, the different types of learning of the hundred philosophers are as high as the mountain and as deep as the ocean. If you want to exhaust all these, you are chasing after the trivial by forsaking the fundamental or regarding the base as precious. I am afraid this will obstruct your work in the Way. You must renounce your involvement with all causations and seek only the wondrous enlightenment. When that happens, you will find everything as easy as opening the door or conforming to the groove.

After hearing this, Kan-t'ang gave up his study but concentrated solely on Ch'an practice. One day he heard another monk chanting aloud the essay "Farewell Memorial" (*Ch'u-shih piao*) written by Chu-ko Liang. He suddenly reached a thoroughgoing enlightenment.[88]

Intellectual study, then, be it directed at Buddhist scriptures or Confucian classics, should be a means to spiritual awakening but never an end in itself. But, like the *kung-an* anthologies, scriptures and Classics were also subject to objectification and reification. When that happens, they feed on men's dependence and attachment. The decline of importance of the Tripitaka Hall could perhaps be seen as a conscious effort on the part of Ch'an abbots to discourage too much book learning, something similar to Ta-hui's burning of the printing blocks of *Pi-yen lu*.

THE WAY OF THE ABBOT: MODELS OF CH'AN LEADERSHIP

In the course of this chapter, I have frequently used the *Treasured Instructions* (*Ch'an-lin pao-hsün*) and the *Ch'an-yüan Code* (*Ch'an-yüan ch'ing-kuei*) as primary sources for Sung procedures and practices in the training of Ch'an monks. In this section and the next I will examine these two works more closely for two specific purposes. I will single out the most important qualities of a good

87. Ibid., 1:0317.
88. Ibid., 2:0343.

abbot, the highest member of the Ch'an public monastery, as represented by the words and acts of actual Ch'an masters in the Sung. In the next section, I will look at the education of postulants, the lowest members of the *saṅgha*, and highlight some important areas of concern as stressed by the *Ch'an-yüan Code.*

As I indicated earlier, the *Treasured Instructions* was compiled by Ching-shan late in the Southern Sung. In the preface, he described how he found the original book, compiled by Ta-hui and Shih-kuei, and how, because of its moth-eaten and incomplete state, he had to spend the next ten years to complete the anthology. He eventually came up with a collection of three hundred entries, among which fourteen were the sayings of Ta-hui.[89] Since the Sung, the book has continued to enjoy popularity among monks and lay people alike. It was admitted into the Tripitaka in 1584 and has apparently remained a favorite text among Chinese Buddhists to this day. By the Ch'ing dynasty, it had acquired seven commentaries. According to Sheng-yin, a monk in Taiwan, it was used as a textbook when he studied Buddhism earlier in a Buddhist seminary in mainland China. In 1958 when he started teaching at the Buddhist Seminary in Taichung he decided to lecture on this text, and it lasted six years. His lecture notes resulted in a modern annotated edition.[90] One measure of its fame is the fact that the book has been compared to the *Sung Yüan hsüeh-an* and the *Chin-ssu lu* by its admirers.[91]

What are some of this book's special characteristics that account for its long-lasting attraction? First, the three hundred sayings come from some forty-four Ch'an masters, all of whom lived in the Sung. The book starts with Ch'i-sung (d. 1072) and ends with Lan-yen Tao-hsü (d. 1179). There is no strict chronology, for the Ch'an masters did not necessarily follow each other in the time sequence of their activities. All one can say is that they lived within a span of two hundred years and they knew each other, mostly having a teacher-disciple relationship (*shih-ch'eng*). They were not hoary figures from a mythical past but people who lived within the living memory of Sung readers. Second, although the book is divided into four *chüan*, there are no subject headings to classify the entries. The modern editor, Sheng-yin, divided the three hundred sections into six categories: "advance in virtue" (*chin-te*), "study" (*wei-hsüeh*), "practicing the Way" (*hsing-tao*), "cultivation" (*hsiu-ch'ih*), "right belief" (*hsin-yang*), and "cause and effect" (*yin-yüan*).

Although the categories give the reader a general idea of the coverage, this is really not necessary, for all of the sections deal in one way or another with one central theme: how to be a good person in a morally and spiritually

---

89. Ibid. See note 40 for detail.

90. *Ch'an-lin pao-hsüan chiang-chi* (Taiwan: Taichung, 1969).

91. Nan Huai-chin compared it to the *Sung-Yüan hsüeh-an* in his *Ch'an-tsung ts'ung-lin chih-tu yü Chung-kuo she-hui* (Taiwan: Taipei, 1964), p. 58. Chang Wen-chia, a Ch'ing commentator, compared it to *Chin-ssu lu* in his postscript to *Ch'an-lin pao-hsün ho-chu* in *Wan-tzu Hsü tsang ching* 113:309.

confusing age. I use the words "a good person" instead of "a good Buddhist" advisedly, for the message is remarkably free from sectarian coloration. If one did not know the identity of the speaker, many of the words could have come from the mouth of a Confucian scholar. In fact, the masters used far more quotations from Confucian classics, and sometimes Taoist classics, than Buddhist *sūtra*s to illustrate their point. In a rough count, thirty-four quotations come from the *Changes*, the *Analects*, *Li chi*, *Mencius*, *Shu ching*, *Hsün Tzu*, *Shih chi*, *Lao Tzu*, *Chuang Tzu*, and *Lieh Tzu* in order of frequency. On the other hand, there are only five Buddhist quotations: two from the *Surangama* and one each form the *Nirvana sūtra*, *Sūtra of Perfect Enlightenment*, *Vimalakirti sūtra*, *Lankavatara sūtra* and Vinaya. Only one Ch'an master quoted *kung-an*, but homage was several times paid to Pai-chang and his famous dictum "One day no work, one day no food." Of the T'ang masters, Hui-neng and Ma-tsu were most often singled out for praise and adulation. There are references to Sung thinkers such as Chang Tsai and Ch'eng I-ch'uan (but not Chu Hsi), writers such as Su Tung-po and Huang Shan-ku, scholars such as Hu An-kuo, and statesmen such as Fan Chung-yen and Wang An-shih. But there is no mention of any Neo-Confucian writings.

It is tempting to speculate on the reasons why there should be more references to non-Buddhist works than Buddhist ones. Could the Ch'an masters have wanted to deflect the charge of heterodoxy hurled at them by Neo-Confucians like Chu Hsi and Cheng I whose views, even though not specifically mentioned, could not possibly have been unknown to them? Since the audience also included lay people, could this have been a tactical move: to make the messages more effective by couching them in a language the audience knew best? But more than anything else, this is strong evidence that the Ch'an community of Sung was quite at home with the cultural heritage of the educated Chinese elite. The Ch'an masters were familiar with the symbols and the conceptual framework of their contemporary Confucian peers. They also felt comfortable with their style of intellectual discourse.

The organization of the book may be the third reason for its perennial popularity. Even though the compiler was careful in supplying the source at the end of each selection, the book is not the least pedantic. On the contrary, it is free flowing and lively. After reading the first five selections by Ch'i-sung, the reader comes to the next few selections by Ta-chüeh and so on. The selections were arranged this way only because Ch'i-sung mentioned Ta-chüeh in his last remark. Readers are made to feel as if they are present in a colloquium of like-minded friends, and they shift their attention from one speaker to the next as the speakers shift theirs. The selections, therefore, do not have a formal or logical connection but rather a relationship of free association.

With these introductory observations, I will now turn to a discussion of what could be called the "way of the abbot" (*chu-ch'ih chih tao*): the qualities a good leader of a Ch'an monastery should have. The abbot was clearly seen as the single most important prerequisite for a healthy Ch'an community. He was the concrete manifestation of truth. Not only should he be the embodiment of virtue, but he, like a Bodhisattva, must not be satisfied with his own perfection. He must work to bring others to reach the same perfection. Huang-lung set forth his understanding of the pivotal role of the abbot:

> The duty of an "elder" (chang-lao) is to be a container for virtue. When the former sages established the public monastery, they created rules and set up titles and positions. They chose the monk who had virtue and named him the "elder" so that he could manifest his virtue. Surely it was not an empty name. My former teacher Master Tz'u-ming used to say, "I would rather practice the Way by leading monks in a public monastery than keep the Way for myself by growing old and dying in the remote mountains." If there is no one who can perform the job of the elder well, can the virtue of the Buddha and the patriarchs be preserved?[92]

Kao-yen described the transforming power of the abbot in words reminiscent of the way Mencius described the chün-tzu (superior man):

> None other than virtue, propriety, and righteousness can lead to the greatness of education and transformation (chiao-hua). If the abbot respects virtue, then students will honor politeness. If the abbot practices propriety and righteousness, then students will be ashamed to compete with greed. When the abbot is arrogant, students will resort to exploitation and violence. When the abbot engages in heated argument, students will suffer the disaster of fighting. Former sages knew the importance of prevention so they chose the wise and virtuous and made them head the public monasteries. This way people were made to emulate the examples and become transformed without explicit instruction.[93]

The essentials for the way of the abbot were conveniently summarized in enumerations, perhaps in order to aid the learner's memorization. They are the "two handles," the "three qualities," and the "four times." Wu-tsu Fa-yen (1024–1104) described them in more detail:

> There are two handles held by the abbot: kindness and virtue. The two must be carried out together and neither should be neglected. If there is only kindness but no virtue, people will not be close to you. When you know that kindness can make people feel close to you, you should aid it with virtue, then the kindness you practice can make both those who are above and those who are below you feel safe. It can also attract people from the four directions. When you know that virtue can make people respect you, you should aid it with kindness, then the virtue you cultivate can continue the tradition of former enlightened ones and guide the confused and ignorant. Thus the person who

92. Ch'an-lin pao-hsün ho-chu 1:37.
93. Ibid., 2:0361.

knows the way of abbotship will nurture his virtue and practice kindness. He will propagate kindness and cultivate virtue.[94]

Fu-shan Fa-yüan felt that benevolence, wisdom, and courage constituted the "three qualities" of a model abbot. These three qualities were also emphasized in the *Analects* as characterizing a true superior man:

> There are three qualities an abbot must have, namely, benevolence, wisdom, and courage. Being benevolent, he can practice virtue and make his teaching flourish. He can put everyone at ease, both high and low. He can also gladden people who come and go in his monastery. Being wise, he respects propriety and righteousness, knows the difference between safety and danger, distinguishes the worthy from the stupid, discriminates right from wrong. Being courageous, he is decisive in dealing with matters and has no hesitation. If there are evil and mistakes, he will eliminate them without fail. If an abbot is benevolent but not wise, he is like a farmer who has a rice field but does not till it. If the abbot is wise but not courageous, he is like a farmer who has rice sprouts but does not plant them. If the abbot is courageous but not kind, he is like a farmer who only knows how to weed but does not know how to plant. When the three qualities are all present, then the monastery will prosper. When one is missing, the monastery weakens. When two are missing, it is endangered. When all three are missing, then the way of being an abbot is lost.[95]

The use of Confucian language in the definition of abbotship is certainly most obvious in the "four items." Fo-chih Tuan-yü (d. 1150) gave this speech:

> Four items make up the essence of abbotship: virtue, words and deeds, humanity and righteousness, rites and regulations. The first two form the foundation of teaching while the latter two form the goal. Without a foundation there is no establishment, and without the goal there is no accomplishment. The former sages saw that students could not rule themselves. That was why they established the public monastery system to secure them and set up the abbotship to govern them. . . . A good abbot must first honor virtue and serve as an example in his words and deeds. A good student must first cultivate humanity and righteousness and observe rites and regulations. An abbot cannot stand without students, and students cannot be formed without the abbot. They are like the body and arms or the head and feet. When these two are in harmonious proportion and do not contradict each other, then they can complement each other in their growth. That is why I say: students are protected by the public monastery system which is, in turn, protected by virtue. If the abbot has no virtue, the public monastery will show signs of decay.[96]

94. Ibid., 1:0327.
95. Ibid., 1:0323. According to the annotation supplied by Chang Wen-chia, Ssu-ma Kuang used the same three qualities in his memorial to emperor Jen-tsung.
96. Ibid., 4:0397.

The public monastery (*tsung-lin* or *Ch'an-lin*), over which the abbot presided, was the crucible for Ch'an monks. It was aptly described as a "a place where the ordinary are molded and melt into saints like clay and metal."[97] It was a place where talents were nurtured and cultivated, a place where transformation and education were carried out. The true abbot was the masterful craftsman who effected this task. If this process failed to succeed, one should not blame the students; it was instead the fault of the teacher. Kao-yen said:

> Monks are neither good nor stupid. The key is held by the good teacher. . . . It is like the case of the stone that hides within itself jade. If we throw the stone away, it is simply a stone. But if we polish it, it can emerge as a priceless piece of jade. It is also like the case of the water source. When it is obstructed, it become muddy. But if it is channeled properly, it flows and becomes a river or lake. I feel that in this latter age of the Law, not only are the worthy ignored, but much can be done to improve the way of cultivation and encouragement.[98]

A good teacher relied on powerful allies to carry out his work of transforming his charges. These were Buddhist precepts and the four cardinal virtues of benevolence, righteousness, propriety, and wisdom. Precepts could help monks "to defend the citadel of the heart."[99] The four cardinal virtues could serve as an embankment against flooding by the human heart of profit and desire.[100]

The way of the abbot finally consisted of two aspects: the external and the internal. As a leader, the abbot was always in the public eye and became identified with the monastery he led. But he was also a private practitioner of the Way. The characteristics of exemplary abbots as private practitioners that stand out most prominently are their frugality and lack of desire. Mastery of the mind was achieved through the mastery of all kinds of desires. Thus, concluded Fo-chien, based upon the experiences of a whole life:

> A person who is worthy of being called abbot should be free of desire for anything. Once he is fond of one thing, he will be enslaved by external things. When he has a taste for a particular thing, he will give rise to the mind of greed and desire. When he likes profit and offering, he will want to socialize with patrons; if he likes to agree with others, he will flatter and please; if he likes to win in argument, he will be involved in controversies; if he likes to accumulate wealth, he will stoop to exploitation and cause complaints. To conclude, everything depends on the mind. If the mind is not born, all dharmas are naturally quiescent. All I have gained in life does not go beyond this. Train yourself and teach future disciples with this.[101]

Fo-chien remembered with great admiration the frugal lifestyle of his own

---

97. Ibid., 1:0326. This statement was from Fa-yen.
98. Ibid., 2:0361. This statement was from Kao-yen.
99. Ibid., 1:0325. This was from Fa-yen.
100. Ibid., 2:0358. This was also from Fa-yen.
101. Ibid., 2:0355.

teacher. Even though he had mended the bags for carrying shoes and the begging bowl many times over, he refused to throw them away, for they had accompanied him for fifty years. Once he was given a piece of rare material imported from abroad that was supposed to make one feel warm in winter and cold in summer; he refused it and said, "I can use charcoal for warmth in cold weather and pine breeze for cooling in warm weather. Why should I keep this material?"[102] Hsüeh-t'ang Tao-hsing lived in wealth and nobility but did not show any pride or arrogance. "He was frugal and restrained in his everyday life and was not interested in material things. When he stayed at Mt. Wu-chü, a monk presented him with an iron mirror. Hsüeh-t'ang said, 'The water in the stream is clear and it reflects my hair. What use is there for me to keep this mirror?' So saying he refused it."[103]

> When Cheng-ching was the abbot at Po-ning Monastery in Nanking, Wang An-shih offered fine white silk to the monastery. Chen-ching asked the attending monk what this was, and the latter answered that is was a really fine silk called *fang ssu-lo*. He further asked what this material was good for, and the answer was that it could be used to make monks' robes. Chen-ching pointed to the plain cloth robe he was wearing and said, "I usually wear this kind of robe, and no one seems to be offended by it." He then ordered the silk be sent to the treasurer and had it auctioned off. The money was used to feed the monks.[104]

Frugality and detachment were the foundations of self-cultivation and the essentials for entering the Way. In the midst of material prosperity in the Southern Sung, many monks could not attain this ideal. Ta-hui observed that "monks nowadays would buy blankets when they go to Hunan and silk when they travel through Chekiang."[105] One step further down from this love for material possessions were abbots who curried favor with officials or appropriated monastic funds to buy curious gifts for patrons so that they could be recommended to head large monasteries.[106]

THE EDUCATION OF POSTULANTS

Postulants were the youngest and the least experienced members of the monastic community. Monastic training started with this group. There were specific requirements and procedures in becoming a postulant in the Sung. According to the *Ch'an-yüan Code*,

> In order to become a postulant, the candidate first presented an application to the abbot of a temple, stating his name, age, native district, that he was free from all criminal punishments, and that he had secured parental permission to

102. Ibid., 2:0356.
103. Ibid., 3:0375.
104. Ibid., 1:0342.
105. Ibid., 3:0385.
106. Ibid., 2:0367.

enter the monastery as a postulant. The abbot of a temple, after receiving such an application, then requested an interview with the applicant to determine whether or not he was sincere in joining the order, or whether he was merely seeking to escape from some temporal involvement. Parental permission was absolutely necessary.[107]

Government regulations specified that an applicant must be turned down on any of the following grounds:

a. if a boy was under nineteen and a girl under fourteen years of age;
b. if he had joined once before and then returned to the laity;
c. if he had committed some crime;
d. if he was an escapee from justice;
e. if he did not have in his possession a letter of permission from his parents or grandparents;
f. if there were no adult sons or grandsons in the family.[108]

The *Ch'an-yüan Code* has a section on the training of postulants (*Hsü tung-hsing*) that forms one part of fascicle nine. After describing the procedure for seeking admittance into a monastery, the Code proceeds to discuss the "three chapters" (*san-chang*), listing the principles and particulars in their training. These are "Establishing the Self" (*li-shen*), "Living with Others" (*p'ei-chung*), and "Doing Chores" (*tso-wu*). The first chapter, "Establishing the Self," makes it clear that a postulant was to practice meditation and pursue scriptural study. After stressing the importance of observing the five precepts, the Code says:

Aside from monastic meals, you ought not eat any snacks [i.e., candies, cakes, cookies, congee, drinks, or cooked vegetables]. Unless you are sent to do errands you should not leave the monastic compound. Unless there is something extremely serious, you should not ask for any leave. Those of you who want to work on Ch'an meditation in order to find the Way should concentrate your body and mind so that they are not dissipated or distracted. Those of you who want to chant *sūtras* in order to seek salvation should review your scriptural studies so that you do not become lazy and forgetful. Moreover you should cultivate yourselves in order to repay the kindness of the emperor and officials who protect you, the patrons who provide for you, the parents who bore and reared you, and the teachers who instruct you. If your parents are dead, then you ought to save them from possible evil paths of rebirth by your religious cultivation. If they are alive, then persuade them to take refuge in the Three Treasures and give rise to the mind for enlightenment. Finally, when you eat food and put on clothes, you should always think about their source and ask yourself: If I do not cultivate myself, how can I repay my indebtedness?

From the emphasis on moral and spiritual values, the Code stipulates the correct way to carry oneself in all situations: the proper clothes to wear; the proper way to walk and sit; the proper way to greet a senior monk, lay

107. Kenneth Ch'en, *Buddhism in China*, p. 246.
108. *Ch'ing-yüan t'iao-fa shih-lei*, p. 474.

patrons, and one's own parents; and the proper way to eat and chant *sūtras*. Lofty ideals and the minute regulation of daily activities are juxtaposed. In spiritual training, nothing was unimportant and left outside the scan of attention.

The outer garment ought to be a robe, with a skirt attached to the upper garment. Secular clothes should not be worn. The shoes must be white but not of other colors. You should wear a belt around your waist. Your clothes should always be clean and neat. You should not allow the pants to show under your robe. In winter and summer you should wear leggings. When you attend lectures and informal interviews or when you go to tea ceremonies, you should wear both shoes and socks. In walking you must clasp your hands in front of you and in sitting you should keep your body erect. Do not lean against anything. Do not swing your arms in walking. Do not walk with your arm linked with another person's. When you meet a senior monk, you should bow to him, let him have the right of way, and pay him obeisance as he passes you. If the monk is walking together with an official or a patron, then you should pay respect first to the monk and only after that to the official and the patron. Because you have left the householder's life and you are now wearing monastic clothes, you should not kneel down to any secular person. Even when you see your parents, you should only bow to them. Moreover, do not handle *sūtras* or pure objects [i.e., incense burner, flower vase, utensils for food and drink used by monks] when your hands are dirty. . . . Eat with a correct mind but do not speak. In evening assemblies, when you worship the Buddha in the Buddha Hall, chant with a concentrated mind. Do not think of other matters and follow others' chanting mechanically. After you finish your assigned tasks, those of you who engage in Ch'an meditation should sit in a quiet place to practice meditation, and those of you who read *sūtras* should recite them by your desks. Do not gather to joke and laugh. Do not say frivolous things. Scolding, fighting, and other kinds of disruptive activities are things a person who has left the householder's life does not do. Avoid doing these things by all means.

The second chapter, "Living with Others," emphasizes the importance of harmony and good will. Again the discourses on high principles lie cheek by jowl with instructions on practical matters.

Always remember to be gentle, harmonious, good-natured, and submissive. Do not be selfish, arrogant, and disrespectful. Treat those who are older as elder brothers and those who are younger as younger brothers. Speak slowly and justly but do not broadcast others' shortcomings. If you see two people disagreeing, try to reconcile them. Treat everyone with a compassionate heart. Do not hurt people with bad language. If you oppress and cheat your fellow postulants, or create rumors and discord among them, what is the benefit of leaving the householder's life? Do not use others' money or things without asking their permission. Do not move others' clothes and bedding by yourself. You should not put on clothes standing either on the bed or on the floor. You should not get in bed with your back turned away from the image of Kuan-yin that is housed in the dormitory. Do not write characters, draw graffiti, or in other way deface the walls in the Hall. Do not hang pictures, placards, or other miscellaneous writings on the wall. *Sūtra* desks may not be placed at the foot of the bed. Pillows and screens may not be placed at the head of the bed. Old clothes, shoes, and socks must be placed under the bed. Sheets, quilts, and pillows must be neat and orderly. While you are in the room, you should not talk in loud voice and disturb others, but walk lightly on tiptoe. You ought not sit or lie down to carry on casual conversation except on your own sheet. . . . Do not stir the fire in the burner or make noise by playing with the fire tong. Do not sit by the burner too long in case you inconvenience others. When you hear the knocker for tea or bath, go together with the rest. The dormitory for reading *sūtra*s should be kept clean, and no one should talk there. When you are in the bath room you should not be naked or talk and laugh in a high voice. Do not put on clothes or comb hair while standing on the bed. . . . If you receive money or things from patrons, you should not hide them but must turn them in to the treasurer. You are then given your share.

Finally, these are some regulations from the chapter "Doing Chores":

Upon hearing the knocker for work, immediately go there with the rest. Do not talk at the table where you prepare food. If spittle falls on the food for monks, your sin is not slight. At the place of work, even talking loudly is not allowed, not to mention shouting, laughing, or riotous behavior. You should be quiet and silent so that secular persons can be brought to goodness. Before you serve food, roll up your sleeves and wash your hands clean. In front of the Monks' Hall, do not talk, lean against the pillar casually, or impolitely brandish your hands. Put down utensils gently without making any noise. When you enter the Monks' Hall, do not walk hastily or with big strides. Serve calmly and orderly. Depending on how much each monk wants, you should carry in the appropriate amount but you should not drag in the buckets for salt and vinegar. If you must cough or sneeze while serving, turn your back when you do so. If you have to carry a bucket, hold the free hand in front of the breast but do not hang it by your side.[109]

As I noted earlier in the chapter, ritualized behavior in everyday life was seen as a way to self-transformation. Everything one does can be an occasion to practice mindfulness. Meditation is not separate from daily life. The simplest of actions—be it putting on clothes, taking a bath, or serving food—if carried out with proper mindfulness, can be as conducive to Ch'an enlightenment, as meditation, prayer, or *sūtra* reading.[110]

Ch'an-yüan Code does not say anything about the content of a curriculum for postulants or even if such a curriculum ever existed. A Yüan code, *Ts'un-ssu ch'ing-kuei* (Code for a Village Temple), compiled by Chan-liao Chi-hung in 1341 fortunately provides a good description of such a curriculum. Unlike the *Ch'an-yüan Code* but just like the *Huan-chu-an ch'ing-kuei*

109. *Yakuchū Zen'on shingi*, p. 323–330.
110. Dōgen emphasized the same idea in the monastic code he wrote. Collcutt, *Five Mountains*, p. 148.

compiled by Chung-feng Ming-pen in 1317, this code is brief, intended primarily for smaller monasteries.[111] Even though the code is extant, it has not been very well known.[112] Some books mentioned in the following are no longer identifiable:

> When a postulant is first admitted into the temple, he should first be instructed in the following: the gathas and odes written by patriarchs, the *Treasured Instructions of Monastic Tradition (Tzu-lin pao-hsün)*[113] which has recently been printed, the "Song of Instruction of Postulants" (*Hsün t'ung-hsing ko*) written by the Ch'an master Liao, "Admonitions of Kuei-shan" (*Kuei-shan ching-tse*),[114] "The Song of Realizing the Way" (*Cheng-tao ko*)[115] "The Record of the Monks' Hall" (*Seng-t'ang chi*) written by Yung-an. After these he is next instructed in the "Mantra of Great Compassion" (*Ta-pei chou*), the "Surangama Mantra" (*Leng-yen chou*) and other secret mantras; *Kuan-yin sutra, Sutra of Perfect Enlightenment, Diamond sūtra* and other *sūtra*s. As for the *Analects, Mencius, Doctrine of the Mean*, the *Great Learning, Book of Changes*, and the *Li chi*,he should be taught these with the above as well. But if the books written by patriarchs first enter his heart and lungs, he can turn out to be a good person. For what enters his mind first will become his master. Then even if in the future he should suffer the poison of miscellaneous teachings, they will not damage his correct thought. Moreover, he should be taught not only how to chant and play musical instruments so that he can earn fees at funeral services but also how to recite the sacred mantra called *Kuan-yin ts'ung-ming chou* [Mantra for Gaining Intelligence Taught by Kuan-yin]. Gradually he can become intelligent. Even if he does not become really intelligent, it still can nourish his nature, increase blessing, and eliminate disaster.[116]

CONCLUSION

We do not know much about Ch'an education in the Sung or, for that matter, in any other period except perhaps the twentieth century. No serious study has been done in this area. This chapter is a preliminary attempt to shed some light on a subject that deserves much illumination. Ch'an monasteries were prominent beacons in Sung China, offering spiritual, moral, and intellectual guidance to tens of thousands of people. Unless we know why these people were drawn to the *Ch'an-lin*, how they were trained once there,

111. Imaeda Aishin, *Chūsei zenshū shi no kenkyū* (Tokyo: Tokyo Daigaku Shuppankai, 1970), p. 58. Collcutt, "The Early Ch'an Monastic Rule," p. 169.

112. The content of *Huan-chu Code* is discussed in Chün-fang Yü, "Chung-fen Ming-pen and Ch'an Buddhism in the Yüan," *Yüan Thought*, edited by Hok-lam Chan and Wm. Theodore de Bary (New York: Columbia University Press, 1982), pp. 448–455.

113. There is no other information about this book except that it is extant—one copy printed in Japan in the seventeenth century. *Bussho Kaisetsu Daijiten* 4:269.

114. This work was written by Kuei-shan Ling-yu (d. 853).

115. This work was written by Yung-chia Hsüan-chüeh (665–713).

116. Dōchū, *Zenrin shokisen* (Tokyo: Seishin Shobō, 1909), p. 432.

and what came to be their values at the end of the training process, we cannot fully understand either Ch'an Buddhism or Sung education. I have tried in this chapter to look at four areas of Ch'an education: Ch'an pedagogy, Ch'an monks' knowledge of scriptures, moral ideals exemplified or emphasized by famous abbots, and the training of postulants. My choice of these four areas is dictated by the nature of the available sources. Lamp records and Ch'an works provide material for the first, and the *Ch'an-yüan Code* and the *Treasured Instructions* enabled me to say something about the other three. I have also used the "biographies of eminent monks" literature, but they are by and large disappointing because they do not always contain the kind of data one needs to reconstruct the monks' backgrounds and the contents of their education.

This chapter primarily describes the ideals and procedures of Ch'an education in the Sung. I have provided excerpts from the original sources whenever I felt necessary. Long passages of translations may make plodding reading, but they give an eyewitness flavor synopses cannot.

Because most chapters in this volume deal with Neo-Confucian education in the Sung, it is appropriate to offer some thoughts on the relationship between Ch'an education and that of Neo-Confucianism in the following pages. Ch'an masters in the Sung knew Chu Hsi and Ch'eng I if not firsthand, then definitely by reputation, but they neither identified them as Neo-Confucians nor referred to a Neo-Confucian movement. Like Chu Hsi and Ch'eng I, they liked to quote from the Classics and talk about the ancient sages as exemplary models. I was struck time and again by the Ch'an masters' ecumenical openness toward the classical Confucian and Taoist traditions. The critical competitiveness of the *Chiang* lecturers and *Lü* exegists was entirely absent in their attitude toward Confucius and Mencius. Instead, we can detect the same kind of loving reverence as expressed by the Neo-Confucian masters.

I suggest that both Ch'an and Neo-Confucian masters regarded the classical tradition as their own heritage. Both wanted to revitalize their age by returning to the high standard of moral excellence exalted in the *Four Books*. Two points require emphasis here: First, a universal body of symbols and values originated from the Classics and was shared by Buddhists and Confucians alike. Second, Ch'an masters devoted much of their energy to the criticism of other Buddhist schools and the self-criticism of abuses and deviations in Ch'an itself. This was similar to the Neo-Confucian effort of self-definition by regarding themselves as representing the true *tao-t'ung* and criticizing ordinary Confucian literati as worldlings interested in learning for others instead of learning for oneself. The energy and dynamism of both derived much from this sense of urgency in finding the correct Way. There is, however, a major difference between the two. Although the virulent anti-Buddhist criticisms voiced by Neo-Confucians are well known to students of Chinese thought, there are no corresponding Buddhist attacks on the former.

Is this because the Buddhists were really more tolerant and open-minded? I think not. More likely, perhaps they did not view the Neo-Confucian movement as a threat and therefore did not feel the need to attack. The reverse, of course, cannot be said about the Neo-Confucians. For them, Ch'an was indeed a heresy, which had to be exposed.

There was good reason for them to feel this way. Ch'an Buddhism after all had attracted large numbers of thoughtful Chinese for at least two hundred years when the Neo-Confucian movement began. Even Chu Hsi, despite his general animosity toward Ch'an, would begrudgingly acknowledge that the *Ch'an-lin* tradition had much to offer and contained much to admire. "The Buddhists had a way with the mind. When a good public monastery is headed by a good abbot, monks diligently worked at their mind without any relaxation. That is why they cannot fail but to achieve the goal."[117]

There are a number of striking similarities in the educational principles and ethos of the two traditions. Neo-Confucian education emphasized role models. Neo-Confucian academies had school regulations. Neo-Confucian educators placed special emphasis on the text *Elementary Learning* (*Hsiao-hsüeh*), for they believed that a ritualized way of performing simple tasks like sweeping the floor or bowing to the teacher could inculcate a life-long attitude of seriousness, the prerequisite for self-cultivation in the learner. Did not all these parallel the Ch'an emphasis on learning through modeling, the importance of the Ch'an "Pure Rules," and the ritualization of behavior in daily life reiterated throughout the *Ch'an-yüan Code*? Chu Hsi's *Chin-ssu lu* (Investigation of Things Near at Hand) was composed in 1175, and his "Articles for Learning" was written for the White Deer Grotto Academy in 1180. When a student wanted to write a simple school regulation, Chu Hsi remarked, "If you follow the style of the *Ch'an-yüan Code*, it would be all right."[118] How did all these striking parallels come about? Was the Neo-Confucian academy influenced by the *Ch'an-lin* model? This was a definite possibility. But without knowing much more about the detailed interaction between Neo-Confucians and Ch'an Buddhists, not just giants such as Chu Hsi and Ta-hui but ordinary individual Neo-Confucian scholars and Ch'an monks, scholars cannot go much beyond pointing out the parallels. If there were influences of Ch'an upon Neo-Confucian education, the reverse could have happened as well. For after all, the *Treasured Instruction* did not appear in the T'ang but late in the Sung, either contemporaneous with or twenty some years after the compilation of the *Chin-ssu lu*.

117. *Chu Tzu yü-lei chih-lüeh*, compiled by Chang Po-hsing (Taiwan: Cheng-chung Bookstore, 1969) 7:200. Chu Hsi also admired the single-mindedness of a Ch'an monk, Ku-shan, and felt that Confucian students were inferior to him in their concentration. "The effort of students is often interrupted. Ku-shan once remarked, 'I eat the rice of Ku-shan and excrete the excrement of Ku-shan. All I do is look at the white buffalo.' Learners of today cannot measure up to him." Ibid., p. 204.
118. Chu Hsi's answer to Lu Tzu-ching, *chüan* 7 in *Chu Tzu yü-lei chih-lüeh*. I am grateful to Pei-yi Wu for this reference.

APPENDIX

"One Hundred and Twenty Questions" (Ch'an-yüan Code, chüan 8)

1. Do you respect the Buddha, the Dharma, and the Sangha?
2. Do you try to seek out good teachers?
3. Have you given rise to the thought for enlightenment?
4. Do you have faith that you can enter into Buddhahood?
5. Have you exhausted the feelings for the past and the present?
6. Are you securely settled without relapsing?
7. Can you stand on the edge of a cliff of a thousand feet without flinching?
8. Do you understand clearly the meaning of purifications and prohibitions?
9. Are your body and mind relaxed and tranquil?
10. Do you always delight in sitting meditation?
11. Have you become as pure and clear as the sky?
12. Have you attained the state of "one in all, all in one"?
13. Can you be unmoved in front of any environment?
14. Has *prajna* (wisdom) appeared in front of you?
15. Can you cut off language and words?
16. Can you extinguish activities of the mind?
17. Can you regard any form you see as mind?
18. Can you regard any sound you hear as nature?
19. Can you be like Bodhidharma facing the wall?
20. Can you be like Master Lung-ya hiding his body?[119]
21. Can you be like the Bodhisattva of One Thousand Arms and Eyes?
22. Do you understand the meaning of "Old Buddha communing with the Pillar"?[120]
23. Are you without difficulty with the ultimate Way?
24. Can you raise up the mountain like level ground?[121]
25. "Have you met Bodhidharma without realizing it"?[122]
26. "As a resident within the retreat, can you be oblivious of events happening outside the retreat"?[123]
27. "When clouds gather over the southern hill, will rain fall on the northern mountain"?[124]

119. This is probably a *kung-an*, but I cannot otherwise identify it.
120. This *kung-an* is No. 83 in the *Pi-yen lu* and No. 31 in Hung-chih Cheng-chüeh's *Ts'ung-jung lu.* "Yün-men spoke to his disciples and said, 'The old Buddha communes with the pillar. What level of spiritual activity would that be?' And he himself gave the answer for them, saying, 'Clouds gather over the southern hill, rain falls on the northern mountain." Sekida, *Two Zen Classics* (New York and Tokyo: Weatherhill, 1977), p. 361.
121. Two unidentifiable *kung-an.*
122. Ibid.
123. A *kung-an* used by Sung monks. For instance, a monk asked this *kung-an* when he was with Hsia-t'ang Hui-yüan. *Nan-Sung Yüan Ming ch'an-lin seng-pao chuan* 4:0662.
124. See note 120.

28. Are you fierce and energetic [in meditation] as a lion?
29. Do you teach others with compassion?
30. Can you sacrifice your body in order to protect the Dharma?
31. Is your mind illumined by ancient teachings?
32. Is your spirit calmed by the three observations [of the empty, the mean, and the unreal]?
33. Can you freely go in and out of samadhi?
34. Has the "Universal Door" [Kuan-yin] manifested to you?
35. Have you studied deeply the "six qualities" (*liu-hsiang*)[125]?
36. Have you understood thoroughly the "ten mysteries" (*shih-hsüan*)?[126]
37. Have you harmonized the perfect causations for the "six stages" [of the Bodhisattva career]?[127]
38. Have you attained the ocean of fruition of the "ten bodies" of the Buddha (*shih-shen kuo-hai*)[128]?
39. Do you have the faith of Manjusri?
40. Can you follow the example of Samathabhadra [of returning to work for the sentient beings after his enlightenment]?
41. Is your deportment dignified?
42. Is your speech correct?
43. Does your word accord with your thought?
44. Do you praise yourself but denigrate others?
45. Can you step back to let others advance?
46. Do you make known others' merits?
47. Can you refrain from speaking about others' mistakes?

125. The six qualities refer to generalness, specialness, similarity, diversity, integration, and disintegration. This is a basic Hua-yen concept. Fa-tsang's explanation of the concept in the "Essay on the Golden Lion" can be read in Fung Yu-lan's *History of Chinese Philosophy* trans. Derk Bodde (Princeton: Princeton University Press, 1953), p. 355.

126. Fa-tsang explains another basic Hua-yen concept, the ten mysteries: (1) simultaneous completeness, (2) pure and mixed attributes of various storehouses, (3) mutual compatibility between the dissimilarities between the one and the many, (4) mutual freedom among things, (5) hidden-and-displayed corelation, (6) peaceful compatibility of the minute and abstruse, (7) the realm of Indra's net, (8) relying on phenomenal things in order to elucidate things, (9) the variable formation of the ten ages in sections, and (10) excellent achievement according to the evolutions of mind only. Ibid., pp. 349–351.

127. The six stages of Bodhisattva development, according to the *Hua-yen ching* (the older version). William Soothill and Lewis Hodous, *A Dictionary of Chinese Buddhist Terms* (Taiwan: Buddhist Culture Service, 1962), p. 132.

128. The ten perfect bodies of a Buddha are: (1) Bodhi-body in possession of complete enlightenment, (2) Vow-body, i.e., the vow to be born in and from the Tuṣita Heaven, (3) Nirmanakaya, (4) Buddha who still occupies his relics or what he has left behind on earth and thus upholds the Dharma, (5) Sambhogakaya, (6) Power-body embracing all with his heart of mercy, (7) At will body, appearing according to wish or need, (8) Samadhi-body or body of blessed virtue, (9) Wisdom-body, whose nature embraces all wisdom, and (10) Dharmakaya. Soothill and Hodous, *Dictionary*, p. 226.

48. Can you not show any dislike for difficult questions?
49. Can you be not fond of jests and jokes?
50. Do you always take delight in silence?
51. Can you be without self-deception even in a dark room?
52. Can you be as firm as a mountain in managing the community?
53. Do you always practice humility?
54. Are you peaceful and without argument?
55. Are you fair in handling affairs?
56. Are you glad to hear flattering words?
57. Do you not dislike to hear true words?
58. Can you bear suffering with patience and fortitude?
59. Can you endure harsh scolding?
60. Can you subdue thoughts of pleasure?
61. Can you stop butting into others' affairs?
62. Can you refrain from laziness and neglect in your religious practice?
63. Can you refrain from appropriating public property?
64. Can you refrain from using money and things of others?
65. Can you refrain from keeping gold, silk, and jewels?
66. Can you refrain from hoarding books, paintings, and antiques?
67. Can you refrain from borrowing from others?
68. Do you realize that even though you do not keep silk worms you nevertheless have clothes to wear?
69. Do you realize that even though you do not farm you nevertheless have food to eat?
70. Do you realize that even though you do not fight in war you nevertheless live in safety?
71. Are you satisfied with your upkeep?
72. Can you moderate your eating and drinking?
73. Are you tireless in giving offerings?
74. Can you be without greed in receiving offerings?
75. Are you without extra robes and begging bowls?
76. Do you give dharma talks without thought of profit?
77. Do you not seek others' admiration?
78. Do you not exploit your disciples?
79. Can you be without desire for fame?
80. Can you stay away from royalty and officials?
81. Can you refrain from oppressing others because of your position?
82. Can you refrain from interesting yourself in official affairs?
83. Do you fear and obey the law of the land?
84. Can you refrain from engaging in fortune telling?
85. Can you refrain from becoming intimate with women?
86. Can you refrain from jealousy of the worthy and the able?
87. Can you refrain from envy of those who are superior to you?

88. Can you refrain from despising the poor and lowly?
89. Can you guard against others' mind-senses [and mental activities in general]?
90. Can you refrain from bothering and harming sentient beings?
91. Can you always carry out "releasing life"?
92. Do you always think of protecting the living?
93. Do you respect the old and treat the young with kindness?
94. Do you take care of the sick?
95. Do you feel pity for those who are in prison?
96. Do you help the hungry and the cold?
97. Do you stay away from military battles?
98. Do you regard Chinese and barbarians the same way?
99. Have you repaid the kindness of the sovereign and officials?
100. Have you returned the kindness of your parents who bore you and nourished you?
101. Have you thanked your teachers and friends for their instruction?
102. Do you remember the kindness of patrons who provide your livelihood?
103. Do you cherish the aid your relatives and friends rendered to you?
104. Do you notice the kindness with which the servants work for you?
105. Do you think about the protection provided by nagas and devas?
106. Are you aware of your indebtedness to soldiers who guard the state?
107. Do you feel sorry for the decay of devas?
108. Do you feel pity for the eight distresses[129] found among human beings?
109. Do you feel sad over the fighting among the asuras?
110. Do you lament the loneliness of the hungry ghosts?
111. Do you mourn the ignorance of animals?
112. Do you grieve for the beings in hell?
113. Do you treat the enemy the same way as loved ones?
114. Do you respect everyone as you respect the Buddha?
115. Do you love everyone as you love your parents?
116. Do you vow to save all sentient beings without exception?
117. Do you examine yourself at the three times [morning, noon, and evening]?
118. Have you finished doing what you are born to do?
119. Have you obtained great liberation?
120. Have you realized the great nirvana?

129. They are birth, age, sickness, death, parting with what we love, meeting with what we hate, unattained aims, and all the ills of the five skandhas. Soothill and Hodous, *Dictionary*, p. 39.

FOUR

Sung Schools and Education Before Chu Hsi

Thomas H. C. Lee

In ancient times one studied for the sake of one's self;
now it is for the sake of others.

This famous Confucian dictum[1] about the purpose of education, often cited by Chu Hsi as proposing an alternative to studying for the civil service examinations, reflected his sense of a serious crisis in Chinese education in the eleventh and the twelfth century because of the encroachment of the civil service examinations on the course of educational development. Of course, other problems were looked upon with great anxiety by Chu Hsi's contemporaries and later intellectuals. In this chapter, I shall address myself to these problems in school education in Northern Sung China, describe their social background, and attempt to portray the general educational issues as well as possibilities for reform that lay before the educational thinkers of twelfth-century China.

EDUCATION IN EARLY SUNG CHINA

In his well-known essay on monastic schools in the "mountains and forests" (*shan-lin ssu-yüan*), Yen Keng-wang has described the custom in the late T'ang and early Sung of studying in scenic, as well as secluded, mountain areas, especially where Buddhist or Taoist temples or monasteries were located.[2] Many scholars or officials had fond memories of time spent in such places.[3] Indeed, the Buddhist establishment itself was interested in promot-

---

1. *Analects* 14:25.
2. Yen Keng-wang, "T'ang-jen hsi-yeh shan-lin ssu-yüan chih feng-shang," in his *T'ang-shih yen-chiu ts'ung-kao* (Hong Kong: Hsin-ya yen-chiu so, 1971), pp. 367–424; cited "Shan-lin" hereafter.
3. For examples, see Fang Hao, "Sung-tai fo-chiao tui she-hui chi wen-hua chih kung-hsien," in Chang Man-t'ao, ed., *Chung-kuo fo-chiao shih lun-chi*, vol. 3 (vol. 7 of "Hsien-tai fo-chiao hsüeh-shu ts'ung-k'an"; Taipei: Ta-ch'eng, 1977), pp. 45–140; see pp. 104–106. See, for additional examples, Wu Tseng, *Leng-kai chai man-lu* (Shanghai: Ku-chi, 1979), pp. 528, 557.

ing this practice, as it conformed to the Buddhist predilection for secluded settings in which to conduct religious training. Some elementary schools associated with Buddhist temples evidently were using Confucian primers, along with Buddhist texts, for basic instruction.

Although one should not exaggerate the actual contribution to education of Buddhist monasteries or temples, the popularity of studying in isolated mountain locations certainly originated in the Buddhist *vihara*, or place of spiritual retreat. Many educational gatherings in "mountain groves," although explicitly Confucian institutions, undoubtedly owed something to established Buddhist practice in religious training.

The popularity of Buddhist educational activities reflected both an increased need for education by a larger sector of the population and a decline in the traditional method of classical education often centered around a famous classical scholar. However, with the increased importance of the civil service examinations, which afforded some limited opportunity to commoners who otherwise could not enter service, a greater number of people sought education as preparation for the examinations, and this gradually transformed the way schooling was carried on. After the mid-T'ang, a trend toward private families running their own schools became evident.[4] These private schools could probably concentrate better on preparing young members of the family for the civil service examinations. An outstanding example was a Ch'en clan in the Mt. Lu area, where its members had resided for more than two centuries, who "built a school (*shu-lou*) with several tens of rooms and halls and several thousand scrolls of books." The clan also "put aside 20 *ching* of land to support the school, and bright young clan members were admitted to study in the school."[5] By 939, the clan still had as many as seven hundred people living together and decided to "build (yet another?) school in one of its villas, inviting scholars from outside to study in the school."[6] Other schools were smaller, generally organized either by a teacher who might admit whoever could pay to study[7] or by a wealthy family, which might open it to poorer neighbors.[8]

4. For discussions of the Buddhist contribution to education, as well as the rise of family schools, see Li Hung-ch'i (Thomas H. C. Lee), "Chiang-chang i-feng: Ssu-jen chiang-hsüeh te ch'uan-t'ung," in Lin Ch'ing-chang, ed., *Hao-han te hsüeh-hai* (Taipei: Lien-ching, 1981), pp. 343–410; see especially, pp. 359–374; cited "Ssu-jen chiang-hsüeh" hereafter. Kao Ming-shih, "T'ang-tai ssu-hsüeh te fa-chan," in *Kuo-li T'ai-wan ta-hsüeh wen-shih-che hsüeh-pao*, no. 20 (1971):219–289; cited "Ssu-hsüeh" hereafter. Naba Toshisada, "Tō shōhon Zōsho kō," in his *Tōdai shakai bunka shi kenkyū* (Tokyo: Sōbunkan, 1974), pp. 197–268.

5. Yen Keng-wang, "Shan-lin," pp. 392–393. This school became Tung-chia Academy in the early Sung; see Yeh Hung-li, "Lun Sung-tai shu-yüan chih-tu chih ch'an-sheng chi ch'i ying-hsiang," in Chung-hua ts'ung-shu pien-shen wei-yüan hui, ed., *Sung-shih yen-chiu chi*, 9 (1977):417–473; see, especially, p. 419, cited *SSYCC* hereafter.

6. Yen Keng-wang, "Shan-lin," p. 393. Tung Kao et al., *Ch'üan T'ang-wen* (Taiwan: Ching-wei, 1965), chap. 883, pp. 3a–4a (883:3a–4a).

7. See, for example, the story related by Yeh Meng-te in his *Pi-shu lu-hua*, translated in my "Life in the Schools of Sung China," in *Journal of Asian Studies* 37 (1977):45–60; see pp. 47–48.

But not all wealthy families elected to hire a teacher, especially to teach their children. Instead, they simply sent their children to study in schools run by private teachers. Even the founder of the Sung Dynasty, Chao K'uang-yin, did not have a private tutor. It is said that he was sent by his father to study with a "rustic scholar Ch'en" who happened to run a small school in front of the military camp of his father.[9]

After the Sung unification, it became feasible to build more schools in urban areas. The increase in the number of people seeking education also spurred such construction. This trend is illustrated in the late tenth century by the activities of Ch'i T'ung-wen, whose library was remodeled into a school in 1009. The school was such a success that it became by 1035 as famous as the Ying-t'ien-fu prefectural school and eventually gained renown as an academy in Southern Sung times, when the growth of academies was stimulated by the support received from Chu Hsi's activities and teachings.[10]

There were already visible needs for more schools in the early decades of the Sung, even though at that time the government lacked the financial resources to launch any systematic school building. One reason was that the T'ang system of state education lay largely defunct even as the importance of the civil service examinations started to rise.[11] Another reason was the widespread establishment of printing presses, which significantly reduced the price of books by as much as ten times between the ninth and the eleventh century.[12] The government, aware of these widespread printing activities, started to control the circulation of printed materials, to which it attached great importance throughout the Sung.[13] On the commoners' level,

8. Shao Po-wen, *Ho-nan Shao-shih wen-chien-lu* (reprint of Ming ed.; Shanghai: Shang-wu, 1920) 8:1a, which relates that Fu Pi (1004–1083) was admitted, most likely free, to a family school run by Lü I-chien (997–1042).

9. Ting Ch'uan-ching, *Sung-jen i-shih hui-pien* (Peking: Chung-hua, 1981), p. 2.

10. T'o-t'o, *Sung-shih* (Peking: Chung-hua, 1977), chap. 457, pp. 13418–13419 (457: 13418–13419), cited *SS* hereafter. See also Wang Ying-lin, *Yü-hai* (Yüan ed., Taipei: Hua-lien, 1964) 167:28b–32b; and Li T'ao, *Hsü tzu-chih t'ung-chien ch'ang-pien*, 1881 Chekiang shu-chü ed., now reprinted with supplementary materials and Huang I-chou's *shih-pu* (Taipei: Shih-chieh, 1965) 44:2a, 71:9a, and 117:15a, cited *HCP* hereafter.

11. Both David Johnson and Denis C. Twitchett agree that the decline of the medieval oligarchy was not a direct result of the rise of the civil service examinations. See Johnson, *The Medieval Chinese Oligrachy* (Boulder, Colo.: Westview, 1977), pp. 149–151; and Twitchett, "The Composition of the T'ang Ruling Class," in Arthur F. Wright and Denis Twitchett ed., *Perspectives on the T'ang* (New Haven: Yale University Press, 1973), pp. 47–86, especially, 82–83. See also Thomas H. K. Lee, "K'o-chü: Sui, T'ang chih Ming, Ch'ing te k'ao-shih chih-tu," in Cheng Ch'in-jen, ed., *Li-kuo te hung-kuei* (Taipei: Lien-ching, 1982), pp. 258–315, especially notes 57 and 58 on p. 303.

12. Weng T'ung-wen, "Yin-shua shu tui-yü shu-chi ch'eng-pen te ying-hsiang," in SSYCC 8 (1976); 487–503.

13. The most comprehensive study of this topic is of course Niida Noboru, "*Keigen jōhō jirei* to Sōdai no shuppanho," "*Sōkaiyō* to Sōdai no shuppanhō," in his *Chūgoku hōsei shi kenkyū*, vol. 4 (Tokyo: Tōkyō Daigaku, 1964), chaps. 24 and 25. See also Hok-lam Chan, *Control of Publishing in*

however, the easier access to reading materials provided better opportunities for study, especially study for the civil service examinations, which, within twenty years after the dynasty's founding, were passing hundreds of successful candidates in each test;[14] the examinations were evidently on the way to becoming the most reliable, if still limited, route for young people to rise in the society. Thus, a large number of students evidently took to studying on their own.

At the same time many people, following Ch'i T'ung-wen's example, started running their own private family schools and collecting books for students to study.[15] Generally, one sees that these private institutions were modeled on temple or monastery schools, but they could teach more exclusively Confucian works that now composed the main content of the civil service examinations. By the early Sung, it had become evident that private family schools or private collections of books were equally attractive to people seeking education. One interesting story said that the house close to Sung Min-ch'iu's residence rented more dearly than houses in other neighborhoods because Sung had a very good library.[16]

The Sung government, besides ordering regular civil service examinations and maintaining an elite higher educational institution, the Directorate of Education (*Kuo-tzu chien*), took no part in making education available to its subjects generally, at least in the first few decades.[17] But the examinations alone were to exercise a decisive influence on the direction of Sung education.

THE CIVIL SERVICE EXAMINATION SYSTEM AND ITS EFFECTS ON EDUCATION

Throughout the Sung Dynasty, officials holding a degree from the civil service examinations made up about one-third of the regular bureaucracy, both civil and military.[18] The importance of the examination system therefore was evident to all. In fact, already in the T'ang many critics were commenting on the fact that officials rising through the civil service examina-

---

China, Past and Present (Canberra: Australian National University, 1983), pp. 3–23, and especially note 8 on p. 38 for more bibliographical information.

14. For numbers of degree-holders in the Sung, see Thomas H. C. Lee, *Government Education and Examinations in Sung China* (Hong Kong: Chinese University Press, 1985), Appendices A and B on pp. 279–284; cited *Government Education* hereafter.

15. Yüan T'ung-li, "Sung-tai ssu-chia ts'ang-shu k'ao-lüeh," in *T'u-shu kuan hsüeh chi-k'an* 2, no. 2 (1928):179–187.

16. Chu Pien, *Ch'ü-wei chiu-wen* (TSCC ed.) 4:32.

17. For a general statement on Sung *Kuo-tzu chien* and *T'ai-hsüeh*, see Wang Chien-ch'iu, *Sung-tai t'ai-hsüeh yü t'ai-hsüeh-sheng* (Taipei: Chung-kuo hsüeh-shu chu-sao chiang-chu ch'u-pan wei-yüan hui, 1965); cited *Sung-tai t'ai-hsüeh* hereafter. See also Lee, *Government Education*, pp. 55–103. The lack of resources was the ostensible reason for the neglect of education in the early Sung, but of course this does not address the question of priorities in basic resource allocation.

18. See Lee, *Government Education*, pp. 223–224, and Tables 15 and 16. On average, 32 per cent of the entire bureaucratic force were degree-holders.

tions were overshadowing their aristocratic compatriots. One major difference between the T'ang state education and its Sung counterpart was that
the T'ang government ran its "public" schools primarily to educate the
children of aristocratic families, and the vitality of these schools was still
apparent as late as the ninth century.[19] But a more or less open civil service
examination system could provide a wider spectrum of the population with
chances, however limited, to move up, and many historians of T'ang education consider this the prime factor affecting the nature and direction of
T'ang government education.

But for the civil service examinations to become the most decisive factor in
reshaping a society's routes for social ascent, the system had to prove the
most evident channel for obtaining the largest possible social rewards,
approved by the leadership of the society. The early Sung rulers obviously
had this in mind, especially the emperor Chen-tsung (r. 998–1022), who
often commented on the purpose and nature of the system as the most
reliable and impartial mechanism for the poor to move up.[20]

During the Sung the examination system had three prominent characteristics. First, the system was relied on heavily by the government as the most
effective way to recruit talent into the civil service. Degree-holders enjoyed
unprecedented honor and prestige not only at Court but also in society at
large. Degree-holding status was avidly coveted.[21] Second, because of the
importance of the system and its social significance, the early Sung government found it necessary to employ increasingly strict measures to prevent
cheating in the process. Measures such as pasting over the candidates' names
on the examination scripts, recopying the answers, and making a body-check
of each candidate entering the hall were introduced successively in the early
eleventh century to maintain some degree of fairness, honesty, and
impartiality.[22] Overzealousness in safeguarding this impartiality had its own
serious repercussions later.

And third, the examination content was now definitely Confucian. Unlike
the T'ang system, which had made provision for students to take tests in
non-Confucian subjects, the late eleventh-century limitation of subject mat-

19. Yen Keng-wang, "Shan-lin," pp. 370–377; Ch'en Tung-yüan, *Chung-kuo chiao-yü shih*
(Taipei: Shang-wu, 1976), pp. 202–204; Kao Ming-shih, "Ssu-hsüeh," pp. 269–280. See also
note 11.

20. *HCP* 67:15b and 84:9a; Ma Tuan-lin, *Wen-hsien t'ung-k'ao* (*Wan-yu wen-k'u* ed.; Shanghai:
Shang-wu, 1933) 30:287, cited WHTK hereafter. See also Araki Toshikazu: "Hokusō kajō ni
okeru kanshun no tekitei," *Tōhōgaku* 34 (1967):1–15. See notes 4 to 11 of Thomas H. C. Lee
"The Social Significance of the Quota System in Sung Civil Service Examinations," *Journal of the
Institute of Chinese Studies, The Chinese University of Hong Kong* 13 (1982):287–317; cited "Quota
system" hereafter.

21. Lee, *Government Education*, pp. 227–229.

22. These are listed in Thomas H. C. Lee, *Government Education*, p. 155, and *Sung-tai chiao-yü
san-lun* (Taipei: Tung-seng, 1980), p. 39; cited *San-lun* hereafter.

ter to only the *chin-shih* degree,[23] although effective in evaluating the candidates' classical knowledge and poetic composition, actually meant that familiarity with and comprehension of the Confucian classics was first and certainly most important in preparing for the exams.[24] The introduction of the *ching-i* (exposition of the meaning of the Classics) by Wang An-shih in 1071 was even more significant[25] because this type of test stressed the ability of a candidate to allude profusely to passages in the Classics and juxtapose to them his own sentences in a comprehensible essay dealing with a certain policy or strategy question.[26]

All these characteristics had immense implications for the educational activities of Sung China. First, revived interest in Confucian texts and teaching visibly transformed early Sung education. Although the examinations initially included tests in nonclassical knowledge, many officials seemed to feel the need for more emphasis on testing candidates' knowledge of the Classics. In the beginning, conventional interpretation based on the T'ang commentaries was strictly followed. Indeed, a number of respectable early Sung classical scholars were involved in a comprehensive collation project of the T'ang versions of the five Confucian canons. This was launched in 999 by Emperor Chen-tsung, with Hsing Ping taking charge.[27] The biography of Hsing Ping in the *Sung History* recorded how, in 1002, he was proud to report to the emperor that the printing blocks of the Classics had increased from only four thousand to more than one hundred thousand and that "all families of officials and commoners could have their own copies of the Classics."[28]

The demand for officially printed editions of the Classics was enormous. In fact, even before Emperor Chen-tsung ordered the mass collation and printing project, the government was already receiving requests from various schools, some of the requests going back to as early as 977, when Emperor T'ai-tsung (r. 976–997) agreed to bestow upon the Academy at Pai-lu tung (White Deer Grotto) a set of the *Nine Classics* printed by the Directorate of Education.[29]

The revival of interest in Confucian classics or texts naturally affected the attitude toward Buddhist teachings, and for the first time Buddhist monks

---

23. For a brief account on the reduction of subjects to one (the *chin-shih*), see Chin Chung-shu, "Pei-Sung k'o-chü chih-tu yen-chiu," in *Hsin-ya hsüeh-pao*, Vol. 6 (1964), no. 1, pp. 205–281, especially pp. 211–227, and no. 2, pp. 163–242; cited "Pei-Sung k'o-chü" hereafter.

24. During Wang An-shih's reform, candidates were required to study legal codes and answer questions on them. See Hsü Tao-lin, "Sung-ch'ao te fa-lü k'ao-shih," in his *Chung-kuo fa-chih shih lun-chi* (Taipei: Chih-wen, 1975), pp. 188–229, especially pp. 207–211.

25. HCP 234:6b; Chin Chung-shu, "Pei-Sung k'o-chü," no. 1, pp. 264–268.

26. Ch'en Tung-yüan, *Chung-kuo chiao-yü shih*, pp. 245–251.

27. SS 431:12798.

28. Ibid.; HCP 60:1a.

29. HCP 18:9b.

abandoned their vows and started taking the civil service examinations.[30] Emperor T'ai-tsung issued an order to prevent monks from doing so, on the ground that the civil service examinations were meant to test Confucian scholarship and if a monk could opportunistically give up his vows and change to a course of study for the civil service examinations then his understanding of Confucian scholarship could hardly be "genuine" and would only be "superficial."[31]

Second, civil service examinations increasingly functioned as an effective social institution, turned to by more and more people as a reliable route for social upward mobility. Indeed, with more commoners in the Sung rising into officialdom, the increase in their social prestige and share in social privileges must have created an attractive alternative to what the Buddhist establishment could offer. In any case, a career in governmental service was now more available to commoners; it became especially attractive to them when, in the twelfth century, the government rewarded students of local government schools or candidates who had passed the primary, prefectural examinations with exemptions from labor services.

Third, the demand for education rose; the invention and widespread use of the printing press and the general affluence of Northern Sung China partially accounted for this phenomenon, although the emerging importance of the civil service examinations no doubt remained the greatest single stimulus. The resultant expansion of Sung education constitutes the background for many ideas and practices recommended by Chu Hsi, which can only be understood by comprehending the earlier effort and its ensuing problems. Therefore, I now turn to the development of Sung state schools as the first major factor contributing to the complex interrelationship between the examinations and education in Sung China.

THE DEVELOPMENT AND PROBLEMS OF STATE EDUCATION

By the third decade of the eleventh century, the government was actively encouraging the building of schools by officially awarding to prefectural schools landed endowments, as well as books printed by the Directorate of Education.[32] This was one of the most impressive periods in China's educational history; the government aimed to establish one official school in every

---

30. HCP 24:21b. For a discussion on how Sung government discouraged the study of Buddhism through banning candidates from referring to Buddhist texts, see Araki Toshikazu, *Sōdai kakyo seido kenkyū* (Kyoto: Dōhōsha, 1969), pp. 381–402; cited *Kakyo* hereafter.

31. HCP 24:21b.

32. For statistical indication of the increase in government-built schools, see John Chaffee, "Education and Examinations in Sung Society" (Ph.D. diss., University of Chicago, 1979), Table 12.

prefecture.[33] The government also started to enact regulations on the qualification of teachers and students, setting in motion the trend toward *kuan-hsüeh* (government education).[34] But the most significant development was the awarding of lands to local schools.

In the earlier part of the eleventh century, with the appearance of larger and more or less institutionalized academies, it became evident that some permanent means of support had to be provided. The White Deer Grotto Academy, one of the better organized, had over its history accumulated quite an impressive amount of property, but it was especially lucky to have been endowed with a piece of fertile land by the ruler of the Southern T'ang (923–936).[35] Without such government support, many academies or local schools could not have hoped to survive. Against this background the action undertaken by famous classical scholar Sun Hsieh (962–1033) became significant. While serving at Yen-chou (in present Shantung) in 1022, he decided to apply the income from his personal official land to support the school attached to the local Confucian temple.[36] This action was soon followed by the government's decision in 1023 to endow the Mao-shan Academy with a piece of land.[37] Thereafter, the endowment of landed property by the government became a standard practice as long as the school receiving the endowment was recognized as having a legitimate claim on the government's official attention and concern. This new practice led to the founding of more and more government schools. By the early 1040s, these trends had gathered enough momentum to lead serious thinkers like Fan Chung-yen (989–1052) to ask that the government undertake a comprehensive reform program, and one was in fact launched in 1044. It may be useful briefly to summarize the concerns of the reformers and the measures they recommended.

First, reformers recognized the increasingly important role of examinations in education, and they sought to reassert the supremacy of the Confucian ideal of moral perfection or self-cultivation as the central purpose of school education. They recommended that school residency be required of examination candidates before they were allowed to take the primary, prefectural tests. They also argued for establishing more schools, obviously

---

33. The tendency was for each administrative unit, prefecture or county, to build just one government school in the district. Once such a school had been provided for each district, new construction leveled off. This left room for the opening of private schools if there was enough demand for education among the local people. This was one reason for the rise of academies. See Lee, *Government Education*, pp. 268–273.

34. For a detailed discussion of the varying regulations on the recruitment and qualification of school teachers, see Lee, *Government Education*, Table 6.

35. Sheng Lang-hsi, *Chung-kuo shu-yüan chih-tu* (Taipei: Hua-Shih, 1977), pp. 12–15; Kao Ming-shih, "Wu-tai te chiao-yü," *Ta-lu tsa-chih* 43, no. 6 (1972):22–43.

36. Hsü Sung, comp., *Sung hui-yao chi-kao*, compiled from *Yung-lo ta-tien* (Peking: Pei-p'ing t'u-shu kuan, 1936), *ch'ung-ju* (cj) section 2:3a; cited *SHY* hereafter.

37. *SHY*, cj 2:41b.

hoping that education could be brought to the populace at large. The complicated measures introduced earlier to safeguard the impartiality of the examinations were questioned by reformers who felt that these methods could only be made effective at the expense of the evaluation of the candidate's character, which they argued could better be done during residence at schools.[38] Other recommendations, such as how much stress should be placed on the training of students to write policy essays were more concerned with the conduct of the civil service examinations; I will discuss them in the next section.

The reformers also touched on needs for higher education. They succeeded in getting the government to appropriate more buildings and financial support for the Directorate of Education in the capital. They also recommended the establishment of the Imperial University (*T'ai-hsüeh*), the management of which would be independent and separate from the Directorate School, thus opening it to students of less prominent families who otherwise might not have been admitted to the Directorate School.[39]

Along with the increased attention to the Directorate School and the Imperial University went the widespread building of local government schools. Such progress was not achieved without some cost, as it necessarily meant taking the first step toward closer official control. Actually, many local government schools had been founded on the basis of "officialization" of existing facilities even before the 1044 reform, notably the local academies; the White Deer Grotto, Ying-t'ien fu, and Sung-yang all received government support and official recognition. Many eventually became government schools, though some others, such as White Deer Grotto lost their property and declined.[40] In any case, the number of local government schools significantly increased in the years just before and after the 1044 reform.

Thus, state education received unprecedented attention, and, although markedly affected by the state's purpose of recruiting talented students for service, it was also looked upon as the best way for realizing the educational aims of the Sung government. As more schools developed into official institutions, however, they inevitably impressed people with their increasingly bureaucratic character: whereas discipline in a private institution was merely an aspect of pedagogy, it often appeared in government schools in the form of detailed regulations; whereas private teachers could content them-

38. The educational reform of 1044 has been studied or discussed in various works. see Peter Buriks, "Fan chung-yens Versuch einer Reform des chinesischen beamter Staates, 1043–4," *Oriens Extremus*, no. 3 (1956):57–80, no. 4 (1957):153–184, where a German translation of the memorial is provided. See also Terada Gō, *Sōdai kyōiku shi gaisetsu* (Tokyo: Hakubun sha, 1965), pp. 41–50; cited *Kyōiku shi* hereafter. See also Lee, *Government Education*, pp. 233–239 and passim, and Appendix D where the part of the memorial on education is provided in translation.

39. See Lee, *Government Education*, pp. 62–63, 73–74, and 88–89.

40. See Yeh Hung-li, "Sung-tai shu-yüan," pp. 424–431. See also Liu Tzu-chien, "Lüeh-lun Sung-tai ti-fang kuan-hsüeh yü ssu-hsüeh te hsiao-chang," in SSYCC 4 (1969):189–208.

selves with the informal setting and simple life of a retreat or sanctuary
(*ching-she*), teachers in government schools were salaried officials and rarely
considered education a lifelong vocation.[41] Throughout the Sung, it is sad to
note that few students wrote anything in the way of memoirs that would
testify to warm personal relations with teachers in local government
schools,[42] in contrast to many great teachers who were remembered in quite
personal terms if they met their students in private settings rather than in
government schools.[43] Indicative of the government's more bureaucratic
approach to the matter is a regulation enacted in 1078 that banned meetings
between university students and their professors on private occasions, no
doubt, again, out of the preoccupation with impartiality. Such consequences
of the development of state education were perhaps inevitable, but they
marked one of the more serious problems that Sung thinkers had to face.

In any case, the 1044 reform at least created a precedent for the government's engaging directly and actively in making state-run education available to its subjects, and debates on proper educational policies henceforth
made up an important, nay, the single most important, part of the subsequent reform quarrels. Indeed, zealous concern over the management of
good government schools continued undiminished after 1044. The net result
was the decline of many privately managed schools, such as academies, and
hence of the educational philosophy or conceptual framework that underlay
them.[44]

Politically, the reform in 1044 failed in a very short while, and the newly
independent University reverted to the control of the Directorate of Education. Still, most intellectuals continued to champion the reform ideals in
education: school building activities did not lose their momentum and a
couple of famous teachers, Hu Yüan (993–1059) and Sun Fu (992–1057),
continued to proclaim the reformers' moral ideals in the university.[45] As a

41. There was, of course, some division of labor within the Sung bureaucracy, but teaching
posts in local government schools generally stood low in the hierarchy. For financial expertise
and career prospects of officials specializing in financial matters, see Robert Hartwell, "Financial Expertise, Examinations and the Formulation of Economic Policy in Northern Sung
China", *Journal of Asian Studies* 30 (1971):281–314.

42. See Lee, *Government Education*, pp. 173–180.

43. See HCP 296:15b, 371:20b, 377:20b–21a. These unfortunate developments, repercussions
of the reforms, affected the development of personal ties in government schools. The development, in Ming and Ch'ing, of state schools as part of the examination network did not help to
remedy the situation. As for students' intimate personal accounts from reminiscences about
their teachers, see the records in the *Sung Yüan hsüeh-an*, passim.

44. See Liu Tzu-chien, "Lüeh-lun Sung-tai ti-fang kuan-hsüeh yü ssu-hsüeh te hsiao-
chang," in SSYCC.

45. See Wang Chien-ch'iu, *Sung-tai t'ai-hsüeh*, pp. 8–10; see also Lee, *San-lun*, pp. 52–53,
where the reversion of the University to the control of the Directorate is discussed. The
University evidently regained its independence during Wang's reform and gradually, during the
twelfth century, became indistinguishable from the Directorate in terms of the qualifications for
admission. This reflected the rising importance of civil service examinations more than an
increasing concern for higher education as a prerequisite for government service.

result, the concern over education as the most effective means for training the nation's leaders only intensified. More and more scholar-officials came to believe that schools should be incorporated into a nationwide network, with graduates allowed to receive further education at the Imperial University and from there allowed to enter government service. This feeling was especially strong after the rise of Wang An-shih (1021–1086) who, among various reform measures, recommended the establishment of the "Three Halls method" (*san-she fa*) in 1068, involving ranked levels or grades through which students would advance. The rise of Wang marked the second phase of Northern Sung educational reform movements.

In terms of higher education's relevance to recruitment for government service, Wang's idea was to use rigorous examinations within the University to evaluate the performance of students, with the aim of graduating only those who had progressed all the way from an Outer Hall through an Inner Hall and finally through an Upper Hall, with each smaller and more highly selected than the one below it. The idea was a good one, and at a time when most people looked upon school education as a part of the civil service recruitment process, it was only natural for many of them to feel that the same system should also be introduced to local government schools.[46] Wang An-shih's method continued to appeal to many Sung scholars even after he left the Court, indicating how much the Sung government as a whole accepted the idea of state education as essentially training for office. In 1101, Ts'ai Ching (1047–1126) went even further to extend the system to all local government schools.[47] Thus, he realized the ideal of a comprehensive school hierarchy in which students, starting from the lowest county schools could progress step by step, systematically proceed through the halls and the schools, eventually reach the highest hall of the Imperial University, and then be admitted into officialdom. Ch'eng Hao (1032–1085),[48] the important Neo-Confucian thinker who is normally classified as an antireformer, had advocated this idea as early as 1068. It was also endorsed by people like Tseng Kung (1019–1083) and Chang Tun,[49] although it was left to Ts'ai Ching eventually to enact it.

The introduction of the local Three Halls method by Ts'ai Ching marked the culmination of the Northern Sung search for a viable link between the government's investment in education and its need for qualified officials. Although this reform attempt in the last decades of the Northern Sung eventually failed, its surviving influence was enough to shape the course of

---

46. Terada Gō, *Kyōiku shi*, pp. 166–200; Lee, *Government Education*, pp. 77–78, 126–128, and 256–257; Edward A. Kracke, "The Expansion of Educational Opportunity in the Reign of Hui-tsung of the Sung and Its Implications," in *Sung Studies Newsletter*, no. 13 (1977):6–30.

47. SHY, cj 2:7a–9b; and HCP, *Shih-pu* (SP) 20:6a–7b. Translated as Appendix E in Lee, *Government Education*; cited HCP, SP hereafter.

48. Ch'eng Hao, *Ming-tao wen-chi*, in *Erh-Ch'eng chi* (Peking: Chung-hua, 1981) 1:448–450.

49. For Tseng, see HCP 310:4ab. For Chang, see HCP 301:8ab; SHY, *chih-kuan* (ck) section 29:9b.

education in the Southern Sung and later dynasties. Ts'ai Ching's institutional innovations included the following four developments.

First, the restructuring of the nation's higher educational institutions and the special privilege of "official household" status awarded to upper-hall University students were steps toward recognizing their legitimate position in officialdom.[50] The Three Halls method eventually led to the Southern Sung practice of admitting to the University successful candidates from prefectural examinations (but who were still preparing for the secondary, departmental test, namely, the *te-chieh-jen*) or graduates of local government schools.[51] This led in turn to the Yüan practice of officially recognizing the Directorate student as one category of successful candidate in the civil service examinations.[52]

In a similar manner, the adoption of the Three Halls system expressed the desire to organize the nation's official school structure and so have it supplement or even replace the civil service examinations as a mechanism of recruitment. Indeed Ts'ai Ching had even tried to abolish the examination system itself, but he did not succeed in doing so.[53] The Southern Sung practice of occasionally allowing graduates of local government schools to enter the University for study reflected the persistence of this view of the purpose of government schools.[54] This integration of government schools into the examination system was later to become the institutional basis of the Ming and Ch'ing civil service examination system. To this extent at least, the institutional innovations in the late eleventh and the early twelfth century had long-term significance.

The third important development was the systematization of the ways to finance schools. A decree in 1112 to exempt all school lands from taxes was very important in this regard,[55] but earlier, in 1071, Wang An-shih made it standard that local government schools be endowed with landed estates to become self-sufficient.[56] These measures placed local schools on a par with Buddhist temples or monasteries, although schools still had a long way to go in matching the wealth of Buddhist temples.

One final development was a decree in 1116 to exempt students of prefectural and county schools from various types of labor service and tax burdens.[57] Without going into the details of the exemptions,[58] the spirit of the

---

50. HCP, SP 24:16a.

51. See my study of admission methods in the University during the Southern Sung in Lee, *San-lun*, pp. 116–124. This study is now supplemented with new materials and listed in Table 4 (p. 81) of Lee, *Government Education*. Note that while *chü-jen* was also commonly used to denote the *te-chieh-jen*, because *chü-jen* could also mean simply an examination candidate, to avoid confusion I am using the more technically precise *te-chieh-jen*.

52. Ch'en Tung-yüan, *Chiao-yü shih*, pp. 304–305.

53. Chin Chung-shu, "Pei-Sung k'o-chü," no. 2 pp. 217–230.

54. See note 58 below. See also Lee, *Government Education*, pp. 254–257.

55. SHY, cj 2:18b.

56. HCP 221:5a.

57. HCP, SP 25:3b–4a; SHY, cj 2:30b; SS 157:3663.

decision itself may be seen as significant; some local school students in the Southern Sung perhaps were thus treated as equal to successful candidates of prefectural examinations,[59] and these successful candidates (the *te-chieh-jen*) were exempted from the *ting* (male adult) taxes and from hiring replacements for labor services.[60] They were thus the precursors of the Ming and Ch'ing provincial graduates (*chü-jen*) who enjoyed fairly esteemed social status in late Imperial China. One may then argue that, again, the status of Ming and Ch'ing *chü-jen* as outstanding graduates of local government schools who had passed the *hsiang-shih* (roughly equal to the prefectural examination of the Sung) and the provincial examinations had its origin in the Northern Sung reformers' decision to accord local school students these special privileges.

All told, then, it is evident that Wang An-shih, Ts'ai Ching, and their followers effected a number of important institutional innovations, but their nearly exclusive concern with the institutional aspects of the problem also brought unforeseen difficulties in the actual implementation of their projects. For example, a number of school regulations (*hsüeh-kuei*) were issued, especially in the first two decades of the twelfth century. Of these collections of regulations, only their titles are still extant, such as "Decrees, orders, regulations and forms, and their notes, appendices, indices and comments on the Directorate, the Imperial University, the P'i-yung School and the Elementary School [in the Capital] (168 volumes)"; "New school regulations of the Cheng-ho era (1111–1118), by Cheng Chü-chung (130 volumes)"; "School Regulations on circuit, prefectural and county schools."[61] The legal status, origins, and significance of these "school regulations" merit consideration. Obviously, some derived from the institutional laws (*ling*)[62] and therefore carried a degree of legally binding power. But other promulgations,

---

58. See Lee, *Government Education*, pp. 127–128, for a fuller account. See also Lee, "Quota System," pp. 307–308.

59. Ibid.; briefly speaking, a candidate unsuccessful in the prefectural examinations could apply for admission to study in the university and then go ahead to sit in the departmental examination, once graduated. This method was practiced in 1163 and 1177–1196(?). This is why Chu Hsi criticized the method so vehemently in his famous draft memorial on education, the "Personal Proposal for Schools and Examinations," written in 1187 but never officially submitted. See Chu Hsi, *Chu-tzu ta-ch'üan* (SPPY ed.), 69:18a–26a; cited *Ta-ch'üan* hereafter.

60. See Lee, "Quota system," especially notes 85, 86, and 87. See also Lee, *Government Education*, pp. 127–128.

61. See SS 204:5141–5144 for various promulgations.

62. The first comprehensive compilation was carried out in 1078 by Li Ting. The title was "The Decrees (*ch'ih*), Forms (*shih*) and Orders (*ling*) on the Directorate of Education." He also compiled a collection of 143 "school orders" (*hsüeh-ling*). The legal terms used here were all based on conventional usage and hence enjoyed clear legal status. But once "kuei" (regulation) started to appear, then the legal status became dubious. "Kuei" as a word perhaps was used more in Buddhist circles as, for example, in the famous Ch'an rule, the *Pai-chang ch'ing-kuei*. For Li Ting's compilation, see HCP , 308:8ab; SHY, ck 28:9ab. See also Lee, "Chu Hsi, Academies and the Tradition of Private *Chiang-hsüeh*," in *Chinese Studies* 2 no. 1 (1984): pp. 301–329, for discussion of the Neo-Confucian ideas of "kuei-chü"; cited "Private *Chiang-hsüeh*" hereafter.

under the term of *kuei*, lacked such status and carried little legal force. Still, early twelfth-century reformers appeared rather serious about compilation and publication of these "regulations." This suggests that these regulations must have had more binding power than mere rules designed on an ad hoc basis and applied in limited circumstances. In this sense, then, the issuance of these "regulations" tends to confirm the charge that the reformers were more concerned with legal niceties than with fulfilling the real goals of education.[63]

The idea of "school regulations" arose from the need for discipline and for regulating the progress of school work.[64] In one famous incident at the private school of Hu Yüan (993–1059), it was said that Hu refused to let the prefect of his district lecture from the school platform, and he beat a drum in protest against the man's failure to observe proper regulations.[65] Some Sung educationalists, Ch'eng Hao most notably, were impressed with the decorum and disciplinary order of Zen monks,[66] and perhaps the adoption of such regulations resulted from an awareness of a similar need for discipline in Confucian training. The increase in the number of students naturally also created problems of discipline and academic progress that forced educators to put such regulations into writing.

Furthermore, regulations not only gave detailed application to educational ideals, but they also served as a concise statement of the basic philosophical purposes and commitments of the schools. By the early twelfth century, however, the semilegal type of school regulations, compiled and published uniformly for all schools, had obviously grown beyond the original simple idea of "kuei" as defining limits (a compass for drawing a circle).[67] This may indicate an excessive preoccupation on the part of the reformers with institutional control, rather than a concern over moral issues.

In short, the reformers clearly overburdened themselves with institutional issues. Even while Ts'ai Ching was in power, Ch'en Kuan (1057–1124) and Yang Shih (1053–1135) commented on this zeal over institutional matters as showing a legalistic bent (*fa-chia*), which carried a definite pejorative connotation.[68] The problem was further compounded by the reformers' failure to pay better attention to the moral aspects of either their decisions or even their own behavior. To make matters worse, the reformers entangled themselves in various controversies, ranging from favoring their own disci-

---

63. See note 68 below.
64. See note 67 below and note 62 above. "Hsüeh-kuei" as a term apparently does not appear in any T'ang work.
65. Huang Tsung-hsi, *Sung Yüan hsüeh-an* (SPPY ed.) 1:18a. The same source states that Hu Yüan's school regulations were adopted in 1044, with the approval of Fan Chung-yen, to become the school regulations of the newly independent Imperial University.
66. See Chu Hsi, ed., *Ho-nan Ch'eng-shih wai-shu*, in *Erh-Ch'eng chi* 12:443.
67. See Lee, "Private *chiang-hsüeh*."
68. Chu Hsi, *Ta-ch'üan* 70:6b–13a.

ples to manifesting character defects. Li Ting, a close associate of Wang An-shih during the 1070s, was accused of failing properly to observe filial piety,[69] but Ts'ai Ching was confronted with the most severe accusations of nepotism and extravagance, which did little to help the educational reforms he was promoting.[70] In retrospect, it is difficult to judge whether the accusations were well founded, but the charge that reformers were introducing ideological conformity was serious and may have been well founded. It was based on the oft-repeated dictum of Wang An-shih, found first in his 1067 "Ten-thousand Character Memorial" to Emperor Shen-tsung (r. 1067–1085), that the emperor should seek to "unify morals (*i-tao-te*)."[71] The use of this phrase aroused opposition to the reformers' own efforts, but despite this they invoked it time and again to justify their proposals for reorganizing education.[72] When later this expression of "unifying morals" even appeared in the decree ordering the founding of the School of Painting,[73] it showed how insensitive the reformers were to the complaints of their opponents. Notwithstanding the accusations brought against them for their intolerance of criticism, the reform leaders remained adamant in their refusal to compromise, thus sealing the fate of their cause.

The reaction to this was especially evident at the end of the Northern and the beginning of the Southern Sung, when a desire for reform lingered. The loss of North China to the Jurchens was a shocking experience for the Chinese people. The University students expressed the mood of remorse and the soul searching among officials. This was a trying time for idealistic young people who openly criticized the moral decay of the Ts'ai Ching faction during the last years of the dynasty. Although only a handful of loyal members of the University followed the Court in its move to the South,[74] this group of students, under the leadership of Ch'en Tung, created an uproar in the capital and left to later generations a legacy of uncompromising patriotism.[75] It is significant that these demonstrations, which clearly constituted intellectual protest, should come to be lauded as moral and admirable. The student's wholesale criticism of the government and the university thus came to typify an unyielding demand for absolute perfection, justified by an urgent sense of crisis. When Chu Hsi later discussed education, he undoub-

69. SS 329:10602; HCP 219:5b–6b, 10ab.

70. R. Trauzettel, *Ts'ai Ching als Typus des illegitimen Ministers* (Berlin: K. Urlaub, 1964). See also SS 472:13721–13728.

71. Wang An-shih, *Lin-ch'uan hsien-sheng wen-chi* (Hong Kong: Chung-hua, 1971) 42:450.

72. The phrase must have become widely used, and many authors unwitingly picked it up. Ch'eng Hao was one example, see his memorial cited in note 67. See also, for examples, HCP 229:5a, 243:6b–7a, and *Sung ta-chao-ling chi* (Peking: Chung-hua, 1962) 157:591.

73. SHY, cj 3:1a.

74. Thirty-six, to be exact. See SS 157:3669.

75. For a comprehensive discussion of Ch'en Tung's activities, see Wang Shih-han's *Han-men chui-shih* (*Shang-hui-shu* ed.), and Wang Chien-ch'iu, *Sung-tai t'ai-hsüeh*, pp. 264–289.

tedly had this legacy of the students' righteous protest very much in mind.[76]

The unsettled period of the 1130s, when the Court barely managed to survive in the South, witnessed a continuing enthusiasm for education. There were local officials who, under the most adverse conditions, still felt an imperative need to raise money for schools and often involved themselves in rather complicated schemes to do so. The memorials requesting permission for their unconventional ad hoc arrangements often display the depth of humane concern that only shows itself in the most dire situations;[77] this heightened concern over education became especially evident at a time when the people most suffered from its lack.

To conclude this section, it is clear in the early twelfth century Sung education underwent an important transformation through the widespread establishment of government schools at the county and prefectural levels. This changed the people's way of conceiving the purpose of education, which now came to be considered more as a means preparing for entry into government service than "studying for one's own sake." Many reforms undertaken in the late eleventh and the early twelfth century were primarily institutional changes, centered on improving the link between schools and the government's recruitment process. Nevertheless, such institutional innovations only led to the profusion of school regulations and ever more bureaucratic approaches to disciplinary matters. These could not actually help improve the quality of education; they only mirrored the personality traits of reformers whose steadfast refusal to compromise or cooperate in the face of criticism ultimately brought discredit to their own educational ideals. Still, one must admit that, at least in their institutional reforms, they set a precedent for some of the most significant Ming and Ch'ing developments in education and examinations. Also, their personal failures did not end the continued quest for educational improvement. The quest became even more intense when Southern Sung thinkers, most notably Chu Hsi, seriously articulated their ideas on the purpose and ultimate goals of education.

THE CRISIS IN NORTHERN SUNG
CIVIL SERVICE EXAMINATIONS

The many measures introduced in the early years of the Northern Sung to render the civil service examination system a reliable mechanism for achieving impartial recruitment naturally did not help make it a reliable instrument for either evaluating a candidate's potential as a good official or, even less, testing his moral integrity. At the same time, the system was becoming

76. For neo-Confucian historiography on Sung University students' political activities, see Lee, *Government Education*, pp. 186–187.

77. See, for a couple of useful examples, Lee, *Government Education*, pp. 112–134. See also Li Hsin-ch'uan, *Chien-yen i-lai hsi-nien yao-lu* (1901 Kuang-ya shu-chü ed.; reprint, Taipei: Wen-hai, 1968)109:14b.

an important social institution, exerting an influence that was to reshape the Sung social structure. But there was a serious danger in placing so much weight on an institution that could provide real hope to only a handful of successful candidates; a comprehensive rethinking of the purpose of schooling was neccessary. In a sense then, the crisis created by the civil service examinations led to a serious reevaluation of educational thinking in Sung China. Institutional changes the Sung government had indeed introduced, but Sung intellectuals had to face the issues precipitated by these changes.

Let me begin with a discussion of the institutional value of the civil service examination system as practiced in the Northern Sung, in order to highlight the political issues. First, the many measures introduced in early Northern Sung to prevent candidates from cheating in the civil service examinations could be characterized as exhibiting a concern for maintaining the impartiality of the system.[78] Undoubtedly, early Sung rulers wished to maintain a truly impartial examination system so that the poor but talented could be recruited. But their concern was also of a social nature and not merely with efficiency in conducting the examinations themselves. The problem of a truly fair examination system therefore was how to combine the concern for social equality and geographic distribution with the concern for a truly impartial screening.

A totally blind and impartial selection process might be ideal in that only the best would be recruited. However, this did not make for good politics. Therefore, only thirty years after the Sung unified China (989), an official quota system was introduced on the level of local prefectural examinations so that every district in the empire could be assured of having "right" numbers of successful candidates to compete in the departmental examinations.[79] The introduction of the quota system was not without unfortunate ramifications in the Sung, and it became the source of many disputes in later dynasties.[80] It did, however, have the effect of helping to bring about some degree of balance in local representation and could be used to redress geopolitical imbalances resulting from, say, natural disasters. But the system complicated the social dimension of the civil service examinations: once successful candidates in prefectural examinations were awarded special tax and labor exemptions (during the Southern Sung) or could be directly appointed to offices (as was common in the Ming and Ch'ing), the quota meant in effect that the government was granting official status to a recognized number of privileged people in a given area. As a consequence, quotas often came to be monopolized by candidates from locally wealthy or powerful families.

78. See note 22 above.

79. Geopolitical considerations went back to as early as 1000, causing the fall of the numerical ratio method. See HCP 49:5a; 60:18ab.

80. See Wang Te-chao, *Ch'ing-tai k'o-chü chih-tu yen-chiu* (Hong Kong: Chinese University Press, 1982), pp. 61–71; Shang Yen-liu: *Ch'ing-tai k'o-chü k'ao-shih shu-lu* (Peking: San-lien, 1958), pp. 13–16, 288–352.

The basic consideration behind the quota system was political, but it obviously could affect the direction of the development of Chinese society. Thus, the civil service examination system was left to face a basic dilemma over what it meant to be fair (*kung*), and this became even more serious as the social importance of this institution grew.[81]

During the eleventh century, the problem centered on the question of how the civil service examinations could effectively ascertain the moral qualities and commitment of the candidates. This was reflected in the educational reform of 1044, referred to above. Briefly, the reform consisted of several measures concerning the practice of the examinations. First, the examinations should place more emphasis on policy essays (*lun*) and policy discussion (*ts'e*) questions,[82] that is, on political fitness and practical judgment. Second, the government should require students to fulfill a certain period of school residence (three hundred days), time in which to observe their conduct before they were allowed to register for the prefectural examinations. Third, candidates should prove that they do not have a record of serious crime and that they were not Buddhist or Taoist monks or from contemptible professions.[83]

These measures were justified on the grounds that the examination system as then practiced did not effectively distinguish the morally righteous candidates from the "*pu-hsiao*" (undesirable elements) and that measures were necessary to remedy the situation.[84]

The 1044 reform unfortunately lasted for less than a year, and for various complicated reasons the people most instrumental in the reform were expelled in a very short time.[85] The new measures including the residence requirement were abandoned while the old anonymity method was restored,[86] thus greatly setting back the reform cause and evoking continued concern over the inadequacy of the examination as an effective mechanism for recruiting the best people into service.

When the emperor Shen-tsung ascended the throne in 1068, at the instigation of Wang An-shih a comprehensive reevaluation of educational practices and the examinations was again launched. The emperor concurred and in 1069 ordered a wide spectrum of Court officials to submit their views.[87] At least seven memorials in response to the call exists. The opinions ranged from a total skepticism about Shen-tsung's good will, (Su Shih) arguing that there was nothing wrong with the present system, to the other

81. See Lee, "Quota system," for citations on early Sung decrees or memorials touching on the ideal of "fairness" (*kung*).
82. HCP 147:10ab; see note 38 above.
83. HCP 147:10ab.
84. Ibid.
85. See note 38 above.
86. HCP 153:1ab, 164:3b–5a.
87. SHY, *hsüan-chü* (hc) 3:41b–42a.

extreme of advocating the abandonment of the examination system and replacing it with a process of upward progression through the schools (Ch'eng Hao).[88]

I will summarize these arguments and some experiments attempted in relation to the examinations during the half a century of imbroglio between reformers and their opponents. First, in terms of political association, there were two main factions: one with Wang An-shih (and then Ts'ai Ching) and the other with Ssu-ma Kuang (1019–1086) as leaders. It is nonetheless significant that both factions initially shared a dissatisfaction with the civil service examinations as then practiced. Wang and his followers apparently favored institutional readjustments to build recruitment for government service into the selection process in schools. But they did not deny the importance of selecting the morally outstanding people. This accounts for the *pa-hsing* (eight virtues) examination created by Ts'ai Ching in 1108,[89] with which the government sought to recruit people known for various types of moral accomplishment into officialdom. Ssu-ma Kuang was less sanguine about school education and, in the course of the debates and power struggle, he introduced a couple of alternative examinations to replace the existing *chin-shih* test. His suggestions included the strengthening of sponsorship, restoration of the subject of examination in classical learning and moral integrity (*ching-ming hsing-hsiu*), and even a new type of examination called ten categories (*shih-k'o*) to examine almost exclusively the moral fitness of candidates.[90]

Second, debates also flared up over which Classics and commentaries were most important and should be used more in the examinations. In general, both factions agreed that classical learning could better prepare one to become an upright and useful person and hence good official. This accounts for the easy acceptance of Wang An-shih's introduction of the *ching-i* (exposition of the Classics) type of test into the civil service examinations. However, each faction had its own preference for which Classics to study. The reformers favored more the works dealing with institutions (the *Chou-li*, for example) while the anti-reformers preferred the chronicle *Spring and Autumn Annals*.[91] During the debates, the *Analects* and the *Hsiao-ching* (Book of Filial Piety) emerged as the most widely accepted works.[92] Obviously, the skeptical strain of classical scholarship in the Sung, championing a more liberal and even iconoclastic approach to the standard Classics, be-

88. See Lee, *San-lun*, pp. 58–61.

89. Terada Gō, *Kyōiku shi*, pp. 177–184; Ch'en Tung-yüan, *Chiao-yü shih*, pp. 266–268; Wang Chien-ch'iu, *Sung-tai t'ai-hsüeh*, pp. 35–43.

90. HCP 382:3a–5a; Lee, *Government Education*, p. 244.

91. Robert Hartwell, "Historical Analogism, Public Policy and Social Science in Eleventh and Twelfth Century China," *American Historical Review* 76 (1971):690–727.

92. For a useful account of classical learning in the Sung, see P'i Hsi-jui: *Ching-hsüeh li-shih* (Peking: Chung-hua, 1981), pp. 220–273.

came a factor during this period of intellectual (as well as political) controversy. The T'ang *Five Classics* and their standard commentaries were abandoned in the face of the new criticism. Moreover, continuing in the style of Hu Yün and Sun Fu a more personal approach to classical learning was adopted. Thus, the reformers pressed on and prepared the way for the Southern Sung Neo-Confucian redefinition of the classical canon and the elevation of the *Four Books* over the *Five Classics*.[93]

Third, and most important, mass building of government schools developed on the basis of the local Three Halls method.[94] The immediate achievement was impressive, if only ephemeral. As many as two hundred thousand students were registered in the government schools in 1104.[95] This means that 1 in every 230 Chinese males may have been in school, an impressive figure.[96]

However, precisely because of the mass character of its implementation the reform effort encountered the most severe disagreements over educational purposes and the feasibility of evaluating moral character, central to all earlier debates on policy changes. Obviously, the government was not going to be able to absorb all the graduates from the state schools.[97] Despite these unfavorable odds, to the popular mind school education remained primarily a means for preparing for the civil service examinations, and Ts'ai Ching and his followers could never satisfactorily explain why more schools should be established under such circumstances. In Ts'ai Ching's most important memorial on the comprehensive educational reform, submitted in 1101 the launching of the program, the preface merely stated: "Schools should be made the first business of the day and should be established all over the nation so as to nourish scholars."[98] Clearly the method proposed by Ts'ai Ching and his reformers, who hoped to solve the crisis created by the civil

93. Ibid. See also Chun-chieh Huang: "The Synthesis of Old Pursuits and New Knowledge: Chu Hsi's Interpretation of Mencian Morality," *New Asia Academic Bulletin* 3 (1982):197–222.

94. See note 45 above.

95. See HCP, SP 24:16a. See also K'o Sheng-chung, *Tan-yang chi*, (*Ch'ang-chou hsien-che i-shu* ed., 1986) 1:3a. See the analysis in Lee, *San-lun*, pp. 63–65.

96. The figure for registered population was close to forty-six million. See Lee, *San-lun*, p. 64. Interpreters in general agree that Sung population figures included only (adult) males, although the case is also made that they included both male and female populations. Furthermore, scholars also generally agree that the actual total population in the early twelfth century would have been close to one hundred million. Even so, the Sung achievement still stood out when contrasted with that of the Ming in c. 1450 when a population of sixty-five million supported only thirty-five thousand officially admitted students. For Ming figures, see Ping-ti Ho, *The Ladder of Success in Imperial China* (New York: Columbia University Press, 1962), pp. 173–174.

97. Roughly about one in every fifteen successful candidates of the departmental examinations was approved for official service. The competition in the local prefectural tests could range from one in ten to one in hundreds. I have estimated that a total of 700,000 candidates took part in the examinations in the period between 1101 and 1120; only 4,621 got the *chin-shih* degree. See Lee, *San-lun*, p. 66.

98. See note 46 above.

service examinations, only worsened it, for it did not deal with the question of why people should go to school if the chances for them to move up were so small and there were no other purpose to education.

To many anxious critics this was yet another proof of the reformers' legalistic, if not opportunistic, tendency. Although later Chu Hsi refrained from openly attacking Wang An-shih or his followers in such terms, Chu was clearly aware that institutional reforms would be inadequate to meet the problems created by so many people seeking to enter schools. Indeed, for him it was no partisan matter: whereas many officials in the 1130s would like to see some sort of sponsorship in the line of Ssu-ma Kuang's "Ten Categories" enacted[99] and as late as 1194 the widely respected Chao Ju-yü could still recommend wholesale restoration of the Three-Halls system, Chu Hsi remained dubious about solutions that did not address the value of education per se instead of its mere utility to the government. Reflecting on a proposal by Ch'eng Hao outlining a national school network essentially similar to what Ts'ai Ching had tried to implement, Chu said:

> In ancient times, boys entered primary school at eight and college at fifteen. Those whose talents could be developed were selected and gathered in the college, whereas the inferior ones were returned to the farm, for scholars and farmers did not exchange occupations. Having entered college, one would not work on the farm. Thus scholars and farmers were completely differentiated.
>
> As to support in college, there was no worry about sons of officials. But even sons of commoners, as soon as they entered college, were sure to be supported [by the state]. Scholars in ancient times entered college at fifteen and did not begin to serve in the government until the age of forty. In the intervening twenty-five years, since there was no profit for them to chase after, their purpose was clear. They would necessarily go after the good and in this way their virtue would be perfected. People of later generations have from childhood the intention of chasing after profit. How can they tend toward the good? Therefore the ancients would not allow people to serve in the government until they were forty, for only then were their minds settled. It would do no harm merely to earn a living. But the temptation of wealth from emolument is most harmful. (When support is assured, one's mind will be settled on study).
>
> I do not know on what basis Master Ch'eng said this. In ancient times, in teaching the young, elders in small communities would sit in front of the school and watch them come and leave. They came to school at a definite time. Having finished their lessons, they would withdraw to study at home. When they were promoted [to college], they also went at a definite time. They farmed in the spring and summer and studied the rest of the time. I have never heard that the government had to support them. A family was given a hundred *mou* in the first place. And now more food had to be provided for students! Where did they get all this food?[100]

99. For a general discussion of these matters, see Lee, *Government Education*, pp. 253–257.
100. Chu Hsi and Lü Tsu-ch'ien, *Reflections on Things at Hand*, tr. Wing-tsit Chan (New York: Columbia University Press, 1967), pp. 264–265. The same criticism is also aired in his "Personal proposal," cited in note 59 above.

Although Chu Hsi's comment was directed to a very practical point, the implication was significant; reports that government offices were overburdened with the work of issuing meal coupons to students only showed the weakness of an institutional transformation without a clear sense of direction.[101]

Against this background we can appreciate the comments made by Ts'ai Ching's contemporaries: "If a man chooses not to take the examinations, it is surely all right for him to do so,"[102] or "The ancients practiced at once the cultivation of talents and the recruitment of officials, and let them supplement each other."[103] Chu Hsi himself advised: "A gentleman (*shih*) should be able to distinguish between the examinations and education."[104]

The civil service examination system had thus presented an institutional crisis for school education, and when exclusively institutional measures were employed to remedy it the problem only became more serious. It raised the fundamental issue of what education was really all about.

Having discussed the institutional component of the crisis created by the examination system, I now take up the effect of changes in Chinese society after the civil service examination system had acquired a visible social dimension. The anonymity measures, the closer connection between school education and the examinations, the quota system, the practice of awarding exemptions or privileges to a certain segment of students in local state schools, or to prefectural examination graduates, and, last, the increasing role of the civil service examinations as an effective means for upward social mobility all helped establish the system as the most important factor in the development of Sung society. Families pursuing education with the hope that at least one of their children would obtain a degree became increasingly common.[105] Thus, it was perhaps inevitable that education would become even more oriented toward the advancement and perpetuation of one's family fortunes. Change in the land system in Sung times also helped; free purchase of land was becoming easier as a result of the decline of the big medieval Chinese clans and the greater mobility of tenant farmers.[106] As a result, many *nouveaux riches* found it safer and easier to invest in land than

101. Lu Yu, *Lao-hsüeh an pi-chi*, in his *Lu Fang-weng ch'üan-chi* (Hong Kong: Kuang-chih, no date), vol. 3, 2:14.

102. Yeh Meng-te, *Pi-shu lu-hua* (*Hsüeh-chin t'ao-yüan* ed.) 2:65ab.

103. Huang Shang, *Yen-shan chi* (*SKCSCP* ed.) 18:6ab.

104. Chu Hsi, *Chu-tzu yü-lei chi-lüeh* (TSCC ed.) 3:81.

105. For a fuller discussion, see Lee, "Quota system," pp. 306–310, and *Government Education*, pp. 239–250.

106. Peter Golas, "Rural China in the Song," *Journal of Asian Studies.* 34 (1980):291–325, especially 300–309. See also Liang Keng-yao: *Nan-Sung te nung-ts'un ching-chi* (Taipei: Lien-ching, 1984), pp. 109–129. For recent interpretations on Sung land system, see the annual summaries in *Chung-kuo li-shih nien-chien* (Peking: Jen-min, 1979, 1981, 1982, 1983); see especially, Chang Pang-wei, "Pei-Sung tsu-tien kuan-hsi te fa-chan chi ch'i ying-hsiang," in *Kan-su ta-hsüeh hsüeh-pao* no. 3 (1981), pp. 15–24; no. 4 (1981), pp. 83–90.

before. It is then significant to note that the family (*chia*) should rise as a practical unit of Chinese family organization in the Sung times, as has been demonstrated by Patricia Ebrey.[107]

The development of family organization became involved with the necessity to produce civil service degree-holders. Partly this arose from the administration of the quota system because the award of such privileges as tax and labor exemptions to the successful candidates of prefectural examinations (the *te-chieh-jen*) naturally led to a rise in the status of these people. The status was therefore strongly coveted, and because the examination quotas were assigned on a prefectural basis the influence of these prefectural graduates became intimately related to immediate local politics.[108] The quota device thus helped to create a new type of local elite, made up primarily of prefectural graduates, and in due course affected the configuration of local power structure. The kinship organization, on which elites relied for assertion of influence, naturally had to restructure in response to the changing conditions in which local politics were conducted.

Although the majority of successful candidates, of both prefectural and departmental examinations, came from wealthy or landlord background, the development of the more limited *chia* conception of kinship organization in the Sung, together with the rise in status of the successful candidates of even the prefectural examinations, made it increasingly imperative for the elite to seek to perpetuate their family fortunes through the production of local and central government degree-holders: a wealthy family could easily arbitrate in local affairs over the short term, but for the longer term it needed to produce officials or prefectural examination graduates who could perpetuate its influence over generations. As a consequence, wealthy families became ever more involved in local affairs and educated their family or lineage members so as to enter officialdom or at least to become local literati (*shih-jen*). Indeed, by Chu Hsi's time, the need to involve local literati was so evident that Chu Hsi regularly recommended enlisting their help in local administration.[109] Likewise, kinship orgainzations became directly rooted in their own localities, and the type of lineage seen in later dynasties started to appear. This was a new and significant development.

One result of these developments was the emergence of a stronger community consciousness than before.[110] After the rise in importance of the civil service examinations, it became increasingly difficult for an outsider to register in a place where he sought to settle; the chief reason for such

107. Patricia Ebrey, "Conceptions of the Family in the Sung Dynasty," *Journal of Asian Studies* 43 (1984):219–245.

108. See Lee, "Quota system"; see also Shang Yen-liu, *Ch'ing-tai k'o-chü k'ao-shih shu-lu*, pp. 293–294 and passim., for Ch'ing cases of abusing the quotas.

109. Chu Hsi, *Ta-ch'üan* 18:5a; 99:1a, 18b.

110. See note 108 above; see also Kawahara Yoshirō, *Sōdai shakai keizai shi kenkyū* (Tokyo: Keifu, 1980), pp. 313–338.

difficulty was that he might compete against the natives in the civil service examinations for the prefecture's quota. The difficulty became even more acute in the Southern Sung, when the government had to deal with the serious problem of how to register refugees who had fled to the South.[111] Serious intellectuals had to face this newly risen community consciousness and identity, which, at least partially, was a result of a metamorphosis in the social structure as affected by the civil service examinations. The attempt by Lü Ta-fang to create a "community compact" (*hsiang-yüeh*) was one manifestation of this communal awareness.[112]

Concluding this discussion, the civil service examinations initiated quite a few institutional innovations and a more narrowly defined educational purpose, in contrast to the peripatetic (but more liberal) type of education practiced in the earlier part of the Northern Sung. However, two serious problems remained . How could examinations effectively evaluate the moral standards of a candidate? The ineffectiveness of repeated reforms aimed at solving it led to the conclusion that institutional measures were not adequate. The other problem was sociopolitical. With the building of government schools en masse in the capital and the provinces, reformers began to aim at a broader purpose for education than simply preparing students for civil service because only a handful of candidates could expect to enter officialdom. For all that, the reformers never put forth a satisfactory explanation of the rationale for the mass promotion of state schools.

Further, the emergence of the civil service examinations as an influential social institution necessarily affected the social structure and in particular family organization, then becoming more deeply rooted at the local level. One result was a deeper and more complex involvement of locally wealthy or powerful families in local administration and in the production of successful examination candidates. A sense of local community identity was also on the rise. All these developments were at least partially influenced by the use of the quota system in the examinations. They called for rethinking the importance of family education and how it was related to the local community, as well as for rethinking the moral basis of the community identity. Neo-Confucian thinkers kept these problems very much in mind.

---

111. See Lee, "Quota system," pp. 304–306, for a fuller account.

112. This explains the need felt by Lü Ta-fang and Lü Ta-chün to create a community compact (*hsiang-yüeh*). Liang Ken-yao's interpretation of Sung rural society, although based on Southern Sung materials, brings to mind the kind of community identity at the local level I am trying to explain here. For the *hsiang-yüeh*, see Wm. Theodore de Bary, *The Liberal Tradition in China* (New York: Columbia University Press, 1982), pp. 32–37; and Monika Übelhör's article in this volume. For Liang's argument, see his *Nung-ts'un ching-chi*, pp. 257–320.

LITERACY, POPULAR EDUCATION, AND CRISIS IN PEDAGOGY

Although government schools increased phenomenally in the Northern Sung, private family education on a smaller scale continued,[113] and education at this level, as well as education for general literacy, was perhaps little affected by government policies. But even so, the evolution of education in these areas also presented problems for Chu Hsi.

Despite efforts to broaden educational opportunities for an ever enlarged segment of the Chinese population, a vacuum existed in the area of educational content and pedagogy because the government failed to provide systematic direction. Although education in Imperial China has been always considered one of the most important responsibilities of the Chinese government, in reality, not until the T'ang could one say that state-run elementary schools actually came into existence,[114] and even then they did not develop markedly. Throughout the T'ang, elementary, and especially literacy, education remained largely in private hands.[115] Education for basic literacy and some calculating skills was distinguished from classical learning, which was usually available only to the children of aristrocrats from "private" classical scholars, and this was normally called "private education" (*ssu-hsüeh*).[116]

As long as elementary education for practical purposes was distinct from the aristrocratic type of education and, at least during the T'ang, was generally provided by the Buddhist temples and monasteries, few commoners aspired to more advanced education beyond basic reading and calculating skills. However, with changes in the society at large, this distinction became blurred. First, aristrocratic education went into eclipse as the class declined with the rise in the bureaucracy of civil service examination degree-holders.[117] The records on late T'ang *shan-lin* education, as already mentioned, show that many students were studying on their own, and often this was in preparation for the civil service examinations. Second, there was indeed an increase in the number of people who could afford to educate themselves, as a result of the easier access to books. Again, the progress in printing technology made books cheaper, and many persons were able to build their own private collections of books. Finally, the demand of more

113. Ch'en Tung-yüan, *Chiao-yü shih*, pp. 310–317.

114. For a brief discussion on T'ang elementary school system, see Taga Akigorō, *Tōdai kyōiku shi no kenkyū* (Tokyo: Fumaido, 1953), pp. 225–228. See also Naba's article cited in note 4. Although the term "hsiao-hsüeh" used in institutional terms dated back to A.D. 339, during the Period of Disunion (see Kao Ming-shih, *Chiao-yü ch'üan*, p. 165), only T'ang elementary schools began to admit commoners.

115. Kao Ming-shih, "Ssu-hsüeh."

116. Li Hung-ch'i, "Ssu-jen chiang-hsüeh." For the Han use of the term, see Fan Yeh, *Hou-Han shu* (Peking: Chung-hua, 1973), Chih section 30:3666; and Ssu-ma Ch'ien, *Shih-chi* (Peking: Chung-hua, 1975) 87:2546.

117. See note 11 above.

commoners for a type of education that could be practical in a broader sense than mere literacy and calculating skills went beyond what existing elementary schools were willing or able to provide. All these developments, arising in a new society that was becoming quickly commercialized and more egalitarian,[118] combined to give popular, or elementary, education a new form and direction.

The changing social and economic scene was reflected in the deliberate policy adopted by the early Sung emperors openly to proclaim their wish to recruit more promising persons of humble status into officialdom.[119] The transformation of the aristocratic T'ang society, through the disorders of the tenth century when sheer military strength dominated the day, to a society increasingly dominated by civil bureaucrats consisting of a greater number of commoner degree-holders than before,[120] was also a feature of this general metamorphosis. Gradually these changes in social stratification wiped out the last vestiges of earlier class distinction between aristocrats and commoners. In addition, technological changes, especially in the areas, of agriculture, iron and coal production, and the like,[121] had potential implications for educational content and teaching method.

Traditional literacy education before the Sung, as I have demonstrated elsewhere, usually centered on the clearly defined goal of recognizing Chinese characters for daily practical use.[122] Early primers, such as *Chi-chiu* (Quick to Achieve) and *Ch'ien-tzu wen* (Thousand-character Essay), and those popular in T'ang times, such as *Tsa-ch'ao* (Miscellaneous Notes) or *T'ai-kung chia-chiao* (The Family Teachings of a Grand Old Man), were primarily designed for the learning of characters. Later primers, as well as the *Meng-ch'iu* (Ignorance and Enlightenment), started to include brief historical anecdotes and geographical information, but they were very much of a practical nature. Even the *Pai-chia hsing* (Hundred Surnames), the renowned early Sung primer, exemplified this tradition. The situation began to change, however, in the early decades of the Sung, as seen especially in the

---

118. Robert Hartwell, "Demographic, Political, and Social Transformations of China, 750–1550," *Harvard Journal of Asiatic Studies* 43 (1980):365–442. See also Shiba Yoshinobu, *Commerce and Society in Sung China* (Ann Arbor: Center for Chinese Studies, the University of Michigan, 1970).

119. See note 20 above.

120. Lee, "Quota system," pp. 290–297; Sun Kuo-tung, "T'ang Sung chih chi she-hui men-ti chih hsiao-jung," *Hsin-ya hsüeh-pao* 4, no. 1 (1959):211–304; Miyazaki Ichisada, "Godai shi jō no gunbatsu shihonka," in his *Ajia shi kenkyū*, vol. 3 (Tokyo: Tōyōshi Kenkyūkai, 1963), pp. 105–125.

121. Robert Hartwell, "A Cycle of Economic Change in Imperial China: Coal and Iron in Northeast China, 750–1350," in *Journal of Economic and Social History of the Orient* 10 (1967): 102–159.

122. Thomas H. C. Lee, "Primers, Elementary Texts and Schedule of Daily School Life in T'ang and Sung China" (Paper presented at the Annual Conference of American Historical Association, 1977, Dallas, Texas).

printing projects of the government. Sung rulers seemed to become interested in compiling massive works of a more Confucian nature, and T'ai-tsung (r. 976–997) was particularly enthusiastic about these enterprises, which in earlier dynasties had not been so closely supported by the government.

As a result of the sociopolitical changes already mentioned, many people perceived an urgent need for reconsidering and redetermining the correct pronunication and ways of writing of Chinese characters.[123] Indeed, one may argue that the content of daily vocabulary must have changed enormously from that of the mid-T'ang, limiting the practical usefulness of many conventional primers. The issue of dialects and how properly to distinguish a character or its sound from its dialectical counterpart was a chronic problem for the Chinese language; it became even more acute in the early Sung. Thus, we read about how Wu Hsüan, a *chin-shih* from Hangchow, presented in 983 a revised *Ch'ieh-yun* (a 601 compilation by Lu Fa-yüan, amplified and revised in the T'ang by Sun Mien) to Emperor T'ai-tsung, who then rejected it because Wu had added several thousand unorthodox (*shu*) characters, many of which he had collected from the Wu (Chiangsu) area and given Wu pronunciations.[124]

There was an urgent need for a more reliable dictionary or guidelines for the invention of new characters. In 1007, therefore, a comprehensive revision of the *Ch'ieh-yün* was ordered.[125] The result was the publication of the famous *Kuang-yün*, annotating a total of 26,194 Chinese characters.[126] Even this new revised work, however, built as it was on the existing *Ch'ieh-yün* framework and vocabulary, was obviously not comprehensive enough to reflect the immense variety of new words and the complicated vocabulary of the eleventh century. So a further compilation was ordered in 1037 and completed in 1039.[127] The explicit justification of this new work was that "the [*Kuang-yün*] as compiled by [Chen] P'eng-nien and [Ch'iu] Yung used too many old annotations." It was therefore ordered that "the range of collection should be as wide and comprehensive as possible." The resultant *Chi-yün* now incorporated as many as 53,525 characters,[128] a significant contrast to the earlier *Kuang-yün* in terms of the new characters included. Yet this was not the end of the story. Although the two compilations used here as examples might have been edited with different linguistic principles, the fact that the government felt the need to revise an already carefully compiled dictionary within thirty years tells a lot about the awareness of the enormous changes in the range of vocabulary during the preceding couple of centuries.

123. For the development in linguistic studies in Sung China, see Wang Li, *Han-yü yin-yun hsüeh* (Hong Kong: Chung-hua, 1972), pp. 175–188, 459–478.
124. HCP 24:10a.
125. HCP 30:13b.
126. See Wang Li, *Han-yü yin-yun hsüeh*, p. 183.
127. Ibid., pp. 476–477.
128. Wang Ying-lin, *Yü-hai* 44:29b–30a, 45:29a–30a.

Such changes created problems for elementary teachers who had to determine what constituted a "basic vocabulary."[129]

In this situation it is no wonder that Wang An-shih should venture into philological studies and write his own version of *Tzu-shuo* (On Characters), which as a genre of writing appeared in large quantity in the late eleventh and the early twelfth century.[130] Many of these works on the proper definition and pronunciation of words had importance both for examination candidates and for pupils starting to acquire basic literacy.

New primers and elementary texts started to appear in the twelfth century.[131] But as crises in literacy education generally occur in the aftermath of rapid social change, which necessarily affects commonly held values, these new elementary texts and primers, if they were to be accepted, had to consider society's need for a unified or coherent set of values. As a result, many new primers or elementary texts appeared based on classical works or legal texts.[132] Although generally exhibiting a practical orientation, they also reflected the ways in which elementary education was affected by the development of the civil service examinations. In the era of mass production of books, the importance of compiling good elementary texts was all the more apparent. To face this challenge in literacy education and to bring a society altered by economic and social changes and riven by political strife back to a recognition of timeless values through elementary education was the task of Southern Sung thinkers.

Institutionally, elementary schools remained largely in private hands, although the government was actively involved in building them. One in the capital claimed that it enrolled as many as one thousand pupils in 1114.[133] But as more and more unsuccessful candidates joined the teaching profession, establishing their own schools or being hired by wealthy families to teach their children, literacy education became even more affected by the curriculum of the civil service examinations.

129. See Thomas H. C. Lee, "Functional Literacy, General Literacy and Neo-Confucianism in Sung China" (Paper presented to Association of Asian Studies Annual Conference, 1982, Chicago). It is necessary to point out that the argument presented in this 1982 paper and in this chapter is still speculative, stemming from a research project supported by the Institute of Chinese Studies of the Chinese University of Hong Kong. A preliminary analysis of about two thousand post-Sung technological or popular terms shows that there was a remarkably rapid appearance of such terms in 1051–1100. I interpret this as an index of significant socioeconomic change in the early Northern Sung.

130. Wang An-shih, *Lin-ch'uan chi* 56:608–609; *HCP, SP* 38:9ab. See also Chin Chung-shu, "Pei-Sung k'o-chü," no. 1, pp. 279–280, and Lu Yu, *Lao-hsüeh an pi-chi* 1:4, 2:3.

131. Hsiang An-shih (d. 1208) already mentioned the existence of a *San-tzu hsün* in the mid-twelfth century. It appears that many "san-tzu" type of works were being compiled in the early and mid-Southern Sung. See Ch'en Tung-yüan, *Chiao-yü shih*, pp. 310–314.

132. A simplified and rhymed version of the *Sung hsing-t'ung*, for example, is still extant, suggesting that this type of elementary text had wider usage than merely as examination manual. See Tokikawa Masajirō, *Shina hōsei shi kenkyū* (Tokyo: Yuhikaku, 1940), pp. 221–242.

133. SHY, cj 2:22b.

The influence of "school regulations" also reached down to the level of elementary education. In this connection, it is necessary to add a few words here about the pedagogical significance of the "school regulations" for elementary education. The earliest set of "elementary school regulations" still extant, is dated 1058 and comes from the Ching-chao (present Hsi-an) Elementary School.[134] It may well have been a precursor of the many such regulations that became a new feature of Sung education.[135] Private family schools certainly did not need any written regulations, and monastery-run elementary schools perhaps relied more on rules derived from *sangha* disciplines, but the better organized ones, as well as more advanced schools, needed some kind of written regulations.[136] The Ching-chao Elementary School's regulations combined rules on both behavioral matters and the progress of daily school work; thus, it had a significant pedagogical dimension. Unfortunately the proliferation of many kinds of school regulations in the late Northern Sung, exhibiting strong legalist tendencies, contrasted with the pedagogical usefulness of earlier regulations. Neo-Confucians, and especially Chu Hsi, therefore challenged this concept of "schools regulations" and sought to engender in students a sense of being true to the Confucian ideal of "study for oneself." In short, the general legalistic outlook of the Northern Sung reforms affected the pedagogy of the state schools, and the proliferation of punitive "school regulations" showed a lack of sensitivity to moral values in education, which ought to emphasize voluntarism and spontaneity rather than enforcement. Here then was an unaddressed issue of proper pedagogy.

All told, popular education in the Northern Sung faced problems caused by changes in literacy education and by the rapid increase in demands for elementary education as influenced by the dominant aim of preparing for the civil service examinations. There were also the unresolved issues of discipline versus motivation and careerism versus a genuine humanism. The more traditional idea of popular literacy as knowledge of Chinese characters for practical, daily purposes was not, in this process, superseded by one directed toward preparation for the examinations. Social and economic changes only created a greater need for more serious literacy edcuation—to redefine the elementary vocabulary and compile new primers. The increased availability of books, bringing all sorts of ideas to the attention of a greater number of people, also led to more serious attempts on the part of concerned intellectuals to reconsider how elementary or popular education could fulfill its mission, especially by giving it a more consistent value orientation. Educational goals or ideals had to be put before the students so as to lessen

134. Wang Ch'ang, *Chin-shih ts'ui-pien* (reprint 1805; Taipei: Kuo-feng, 1964) 134:23a–27a. I have translated this into English in my paper cited in note 122 above. Also see Professor Wu's translation of the rules in his article in this volume.

135. See note 62 above.

136. Hence, Chu Hsi talked about the need of "kuei-chü"; Lee, "Private *chiang-hsüeh*."

dependence on "regulations" and their routine enforcement. The collapse of Ts'ai Ching's educational empire served to prove this truth; indeed, despite the grandiosity of his program, his lack of educational vision is indicative of the continuing crisis in Northern Sung education.

CONCLUSION

The one and a half centuries of the Northern Sung was a critical period in the institutional history of Chinese education. It was the first time that the Chinese government had attempted to institute a comprehensive national network or system of government schools and to implement the ancient ideal of recruiting the "talented" (in a Confucian, intellectual, and moral sense) from the educated. Beginning with the third decade of the eleventh century, the mass building of government schools in nearly every prefecture and even county became the new norm, and the government—by appointing private teachers to office, by donating books, and, above all, by endowing landed property to schools—tried to achieve a systematic control over the education of its subjects. Many of these measures became permanent features of Chinese education. But these institutional innovations were much affected by the conduct of the civil service examinations, through which commoners could now hope to move up into officialdom and the government could theoretically seek to recruit the best officials.

The rise in the importance of the civil service examinations established new parameters for the development of state education in the Northern Sung. The government sought to create a reliable and corruption-free system as a guarantee of impartiality, and therefore it designed a number of measures to preserve the anonymity of the candidates. Most of these methods were continued into the Ming and Ch'ing examinations. After the Wang An-shih reform, furthermore, the kind of degrees in the civil service examinations was reduced to only one, that is, the *chin-shih* degree. These changes affected the nature and content of education so that, increasingly, government education subserved the civil service examination system.

However, the more the civil service examination system became a social institution and the greater the attempts to maintain its impartial outlook, the more difficult it became for examiners to achieve the Confucian ideal of selecting only morally qualified candidates. How to design a truly bias- or favor-free examination system that would also judge the moral caliber of a candidate became a critical problem for Northern Sung literati. The idea of promoting graduates from the Imperial University directly to official posts, proposed during Emperor Shen-tsung's reign, and Ts'ai Ching's even more radical idea of establishing a national school network, advancement through which would supersede the civil service examinations, were both institutional answers to this problem. Neither succeeded, although some of the measures adopted in the process were continued into the Southern Sung and afterward.

The problems created by the rising importance of the civil service examinations appeared in two forms: one related to the purpose of education, and the other to the social restructuring that resulted from the examinations· becoming the most attractive route of upward social mobility.

Confusion over the purpose of education not only affected the time-honored tradition of private education administered by classical scholars, but also the popular, literacy education that had often been provided by Buddhist monasteries or temples. Paradoxically, the rise of the idea that education was preparation for the examinations accounted for the mass building of government schools, but it also brought new problems in its train, especially during the Southern Sung. One immediate consequence was the decline of private education. When, however, institutional reform of the state school system in the Northern Sung failed, private schools made a comeback as people had to rely again on family or kinship organizations for education. With the traditional aristocratic type of study under a classical scholar having already lost its social base, a new form was called for that would at once meet the structural constraints of the times and still perpetuate the ideal of "private education." This let to the spread of local academies (*shu-yüan*).

The same held true for literacy education earlier dominated by the practical purpose of learning characters simply for daily use. By Sung times, because of social and economic changes and the influence of the civil service examinations, the design and content of literacy education became more oriented toward the examinations. This development was complicated by the crisis in education for popular literacy; there was confusion among scholars over how to verbalize time-honored values. By the early twelfth century it had become obvious that serious thinkers and teachers would have to take up these issues, ponder the basic values of education, and express them in a new vocabulary.

The social tranformation resulting from the rising importance of the civil service examinations was much shaped by the new power and prestige of successful candidates of the examinations. They grew to become leaders in local affairs and helped to create the village and town patterns of Ming and Ch'ing China. With kinship organizations striving for community cohesion, local communal identity was becoming ever stronger, and later attempts to propagate new educational ideals would have to consider these developments.

Meanwhile, Buddhist education had visibly weakened as the state began to take over educational responsibilities. Nonetheless, in an indirect way, Buddhist temples still assisted the promotion of education in the provinces, and their pedagogy continued to have an influence on Sung education, if often in a disguised or modified manner. This too, then, posed questions as to the basic ideal of education and how to achieve it.

In his challenging study of China's liberal tradition, Wm. Theodore de Bary outlined six important educational issues to which Chu Hsi addressed himself, namely, educational purposes as "learning for the sake of one's self" and as "subduing oneself and returning to decorum," concerns for "elementary learning" and "popular education," and the emphases on "voluntarism and dialogue" and "broad learning"in higher education.[137] Of them, at least four are carefully thought-out answers to the crises and problems discussed in this chapter. If one realizes that there existed in Northern Sung schools a latent crisis over the proper aims of education, one will understand why Chu Hsi should have gone back to the Confucian ideal of "learning for the sake of one's self." Similarly, the pedagogical problem in Northern Sung schools provides a background to Chu Hsi's formulation of his own "school articles or precepts" for the revived White Deer Grotto Academy. Indeed, the very success of the academy movement can be attributed to the combined facts of the revival of the ideal of "private education," the transformation of state schools into preparatory or registration places for the examinations, and above all the reaffirmation of the very value of education itself.

Chu Hsi's concern for children's education and his compilation of the *Elementary Learning (Hsiao-hsüeh)* also reflected the crisis in basic literacy that I have discussed. But, ultimately, for these efforts to succeed, they would have to have a firm basis in the new social structure. In this respect, Chu's stress on popular education and his promotion of both the community compact (*hsiang-yüeh*) and community schools (*she-hsüeh*), as well as local academies, were his response to this need. The wisdom of Chu Hsi lay in his ability both to discover in the changed social structure the means for realizing his educational ideals and to adapt traditional ideals to suit the new conditions of life.

---

137. de Bary, *The Liberal Tradition in China*, pp. 21–36.

PART TWO

Chu Hsi and Neo-Confucian Education

FIVE

The Sung Confucian Idea of Education: A Background Understanding

Tu Wei-ming

Three core ideas in the *Confucian Analects* designate three important areas of concern in Confucian education: *Tao* (the Way), *hsüeh* (learning), and *cheng* (politics). The difficulty in reaching an analytical understanding of Confucian humanism, one of the most complex and influential living traditions in East Asia, mainly lies in the high-level integration of these three areas of concern in Confucius's original insight into the human condition.

Tao, or the Way, addresses the question of the ultimate meaning of human existence. The question is posed at a comparable level of sophistication in symbolic thinking as are questions raised in fundamental theology or theoretical cosmology, even though the point of reference is anthropological, or more appropriately anthropocosmic, in nature. Much misunderstanding of the Confucian project by modern interpreters, especially those under the influence of May 4th (1919) positivism and pragmatism, is due to an insensitivity to or an ignorance of this dimension of Confucian concern. Confucius may have insisted upon the importance of focusing our attention on life rather than death and on humans rather than gods, but to argue, accordingly, that Confucius was exclusively concerned about the living person here and now in the manner of secular humanism is a gross mistake. Confucius was not all preoccupied with the secular world; nor did he simply treat the secular as sacred. In his perception of the Way, as shown in the great tradition of the cultural heroes of his dynasty exemplified by the Duke of Chou, the paradigmatic living example is not a mere creature but is in fact a cocreator of the world in which we live, a guardian of the natural process, and, indeed, a participant of the creative transformation of Heaven and Earth. The question of the ultimate meaning of human existence, in light of

The first part of this chapter was originally prepared for the Conference on the Axial Age and Its Diversity, Bad Homburg, January 4–8, 1983, as a background paper.

the age-old belief that "it is the human that can make the *Way* great and not the *Way* that can make the human great," is thus an anthropocosmic question.

The "transcendental breakthrough," if we dare employ such a loaded expression for comparative purposes, assumes a particular significance in Confucian humanism. It is neither the emergence of the sharp dichotomy of the sacred and the profane nor the breaking away from the magic garden of an archaic religion that marks the distinctive feature of a new epoch. Rather, Confucius's insistence that he loved the ancients and that he was a transmitter rather than a maker symbolizes his conscious attempt to provide a transcendental anchorage for human civilization. To Confucius, what had already been created, notably the "ritual and music" of the human community, was not merely of humans, for it was also sanctioned and sponsored by the Mandate of Heaven. Confucius's implication that "Heaven does not will that *this culture* perish," (*Analects* 9:5) must therefore be taken to mean that his sense of mission, far from being a conservative desire to return to the past, was inspired by his critical self-awareness that "Heaven knows me!" The idea of "this culture" (*ssu-wen*) is thus laden with cosmological significance.

Confucius's concern that the deep meaning of the Chou civilization, the crystallization of the collaborative effort to create a humane society based on ritual and music, be retrieved impelled him to search for the Way in the living person here and now as a point of departure. His mode of questioning, conditioned by the cultural heritage he cherished and the historical moment he recognized, did not permit him to find his answers in revelatory religion or in speculative philosophy. Instead, through an experiential encounter with the highest moral excellence that was thought to have characterized "this culture" in its most brilliant history, he found the Way in the inner resources of the human, anthropocosmically defined.

The focus on the centrality and the fruitfulness of the idea of humanity (*jen*) in the *Analects* was an epoch-making event in the symbolic universe of ancient Chinese thought and clearly indicates that the "breakthrough" is "transcendental" in the sense that humanity, for the first time in Chinese history, was seen as an ultimate value going beyond life and death:

> Confucius said, "A resolute scholar and a man of humanity will never seek to live at the expense of injuring humanity. He would rather sacrifice his life in order to realize humanity." (*Analects* 15:8)

To realize humanity as the ultimate value of human existence eventually became the spiritual self-definition of a Confucian. Even at the time of Confucius, this was widely accepted among his students. Tseng Tzu, a Confucian disciple who can very well be characterized as the knight of humanity, made the following pronouncement:

A knight (*shih*) must be great and strong. His burden is heavy and his course is long. He has taken humanity to be his own burden—is that not heavy? Only with death does his course stop—is that not long? (*Analects* 8:7)

Confucius's faith in the perfectibility of human nature through self-effort, as an answer to the dehumanizing tendencies of the historical moment in which he was inalienably circumscribed, directed his energies to the transformation of the world from within. This focus is predicated on the belief that the ultimate value of human existence is near at hand and that the desire to will humanity entails the availability of the necessary strength for its realization. Mencius's (371–289 B.C.) theory of the moral propensities of all human beings, as an elaboration of the Confucian thesis that men are born upright, provides a transcendental justification for self-cultivation as an essential way of learning to be human. Even Hsün Tzu (fl. 298–238 B.C.), who criticized Mencius's theory of human nature, acknowledged that the cognitive function of the mind is capable of recognizing and thus controlling human desires. This means that self-cultivation is necessary and desirable and that the highest manifestation of humanity in the form of sagehood can be attained. He thus fully subscribed to the Confucian faith in the perfectibility of human nature through self-effort. In theological terms, the Confucian idea of learning to be human suggests an ,authentic possibility for human beings to become "divine" through personal endeavor. This must have been the background assumption when Mencius depicted the six stages of human perfection:

The desirable is called "good."
To have it in oneself is called "true."
To possess it fully in oneself is called "beautiful,"
but to shine forth with this full possession is called "great."
To be great and be transformed by this greatness is called "sage"; to be sage
and to transcend the understanding is called "divine." (7B:25)

The reason that Mencius could suggest, as a matter of course, that we can become not only good, true, beautiful, and great but also sage and divine through personal self-cultivation lies in a fundamental anthropocosmic assumption of his moral metaphysics:

For a man to give full realization to his heart is for him to understand his own nature, and a man who knows his own nature will know Heaven. By retaining his heart and nurturing his nature he is serving Heaven. Whether he is going to die young or live to a ripe old age makes no difference to his steadfastness of purpose. It is through awaiting whatever is to befall him with a perfected character that he stands firm on his proper destiny. (7A:1)

The Confucian "transcendental breakthrough" paradoxically symbolized by the continuity, mutuality, and even organismic unity of Humanity and

Heaven cannot be properly understood in terms of either revelatory theology or theoretical cosmology. Rather, it represents yet another type of symbolic thinking of what Karl Jaspers has called the Axial Age.

If the Confucian reflection on the Way is seen as analogous to fundamental theology, Confucian learning (*hsüeh*), the second area of concern mentioned above, addresses issues comparable to those addressed in systemic theology. It is likely that the Confucian sacred texts, known today as the Five Classics, did not assume their definitive shape until as late as the second century B.C. in the former Han dynasty (206 B.C.–A.D. 8). Indeed, several texts reconstructed after the burning of the books of the Ch'in dynasty (221–206 B.C.) must have undergone significant changes in the hands of the Han editors. However, if the Classics are seen not only as written texts but also as broadly conceived humanistic visions, they can show us the scope in which Confucian learning was conceived in the classical period. As portrayed in the classical period, learning involves five interrelated visions: poetic, political, social, historical, and metaphysical. Together they represent the unfolding of a comprehensive project to retrieve the deep meaning of human civilization in a crisis situation.

The poetic vision that emphasizes the internal resonance of the human community involves the language of the heart. It speaks to the commonality of human feelings and to the sharability of human concerns without resorting to the art of argumentation. A society harmonized by poetry possesses a synchronized rhythm. The interaction among people in such a society is like the natural flow of sympathetic responses to familiar musical tunes and dance forms. This kind of "primitive commune" in which the poetic vision reigned must have become a faint memory by the classical period, but the appeal to the heart remains strong even in the highly sophisticated philosophy of government in the writings of Mencius.

> No man is devoid of a heart sensitive to the suffering of others. Such a sensitive heart was possessed by the Former Kings and this manifested itself in compassionate government. With such a sensitive heart behind compassionate government, it was as easy to rule the Empire as rolling it on the palm of your hand. (2A:6)

The idea of benevolent government underlies the Confucian political vision. The strong belief in the inseparability of morality and politics and in the correlation between the self-cultivation of the ruler and the governability of the people renders it difficult to accept politics as a mechanism of control independent of personal ethics. Indeed, the etymology of the word *cheng* (politics) is "rectification" with a distinctive moral overtone. However, the presumption that the moral persuasion of the elite can easily prevail over the people is based on the considered opinion that a significant role and function of the government is ethical teaching and not on the naive assumption that the masses are simple-minded and thus pliant. The concept of virtue (*te*), which features prominently in Confucian political thought, signifies that because "Heaven sees as the people see and Heaven hears as the people hear" the real guarantee for the well-being of rulership lies in its acceptable performance rather than in its preconceived Mandate. The right of the people to rebel against a tyrannical dynasty, the right of the aristocracy to remove an unjust imperial household, the right of the imperial clansmen to replace an unsuitable king, and the right of the bureaucrats to remonstrate with a negligent ruler are all sanctioned by the deep-rooted conviction that political leadership essentially manifests itself in moral persuasion and that the transformative power of a dynasty depends mainly upon the ethical quality of those who govern.

Society so conceived is never an adversary system but a fiduciary community. The like-minded people, motivated by a sense of participation and bound by a sense of duty, become an integral part of an "organic solidarity" in and through which they realize themselves as fully matured human beings. The rituals that have provided the proper context for self-expression and communication in society are not rules and regulations superimposed by an external authority. Rather, they are vehicles by which one learns to stand, to sit, to walk, to eat, to speak, and to greet in a way desirable to ourselves and pleasing to others. The Confucian six arts—ritual, music, archery, charioteering, calligraphy, and arithmetic—broadly speaking, are all rituals designed to discipline the body and mind so that one can act fittingly in all human situations. Learning to be human, in this sense, can very well be understood as a process of ritualization that involves submitting oneself to routine exercises, deferring to experienced elders, emulating well-established models, and discovering the most appropriate way of interacting with other human beings. Confucius's ability to assume different demeanors in perfect accord with the various occasions that he encountered, as vividly depicted in the tenth chapter of the *Analects*, is a case in point.

The specificity of the depiction of Confucius's attire, facial expressions, gestures, and mannerisms is telling and unequivocally conveys the humanness of the Master. There is little "magic" in the way Confucius walked, spoke, ate, and taught; he was, as he described himself, an untiring learner and teacher. Nor is there anything mysterious about his personality. However, to his students and to those who followed his teachings for centuries to come, the plainness of Confucius's style of life was awe-inspiring. To them, his great strength as an exemplary teacher lay in his everydayness. His conscious choice not to resort to the extraordinary, the powerful, the superhuman, or the transmundane to impress the people was greatly respected as a sign of real inner strength.

The Confucian social vision's emphasis on the ritual of human interaction addresses the way we naturally and inevitably act upon each other in a sharable discourse. Language, as social property, is familiar to all participating members of a community. The Master inspires not because he uses a different language but because his mastery of the one all are supposed to know is so perfect that he often surprises us with delightfully nuanced utterances. We are in awe of him, for he enables us to broaden and deepen our own sense of language and our everyday speech.

The Confucian historical vision, in the same manner, brings new dimensions to the world in which we live here and now. It tells us, often in graphic detail, how the remote past remains relevant to the present lived experience. The idea of collective memory is not an imposition of a radically different perception of reality, but it suggests a more comprehensive way of perceiving what we take to be uniquely ours. History so conceived is a judicious description of why things did not turn out to be what they could have been and not a chronological record of what happened. The so-called "moralized history," however, is not simply an arbitrary application of preconceived standards of praise and blame. Rather, history's function is that of wise counsel with a view toward the future as well as the present, offered as a communal verdict written by an informed impartial observer and not as a private opinion.

The historian so conceived is the conscience of the collective memory shared by all; the historian's responsibility is not only to show what has already been done but also to suggest, whenever appropriate, what other authentic possibilities may have existed and why the failure to realize them has led to disastrous consequences. To write history is therefore a political act committed in the name of the human community as a whole. The sense of dread with which Confucius undertook the task of working on the *Spring and Autumn Annals*, as noted in the *Book of Mencius*, indicates that the very act of doing history presumes an air of prophecy and a dignified posture to set up standards for the future generations. In a tradition where communal participation is highly valued, the judgmental act of writing history is not taken lightly and is always considered tragic. As Mencius pointed out, only when the age of poetry disappeared did the age of history emerge.

A systematic inquiry into the Confucian perception of the human condition cannot be complete without reference to the metaphysical vision. It is commonly assumed that Confucius was neither theistic nor atheistic, but to characterize his attitude toward God as agnostic is misleading. Confucius never claimed any positive knowledge in spiritual matters, and yet, at the same time, he implied that he had acquired a tacit understanding with Heaven. It was a two-way relationship: he reported that he knew the Mandate of Heaven when he became fifty years of age, and he lamented, in extreme adversity, that only Heaven knew him. Although the idea of Heaven is not clearly articulated in the *Analects*, the sense of mutuality between man and Heaven underlay much of the tradition that Confucius inherited. The Confucian metaphysical vision reached fruition in *Mencius*, the *Doctrine of the Mean*, and the *Great Commentary of the Book of Change*. The idea of forming a trinity with Heaven and Earth and taking part in the transformative processes of the cosmos through personal knowledge and self-cultivation later became a defining characteristic of Confucian moral metaphysics. Learning to be human, in this particular connection, not only entails the authentic possibility of going beyond the anthropological realm but also demands continuous effort to transcend anthropocentrism. In this sense true humanity must be sought in the anthropocosmic vision of the unity of man and Heaven.

In our synoptic description of the Confucian project, I have noted the five visions that inform the Confucian perception of the human condition. A human being, in this perspective, is poetic, political, social, historical, and metaphysical. This highly condensed and complex view of the human as a multidimensional being makes it difficult to understand Confucian ideology as *praxis*. The Confucian counterpart to practical theology is often misunderstood as "adjustment to the world." Recent reflections on Max Weber's interpretation of Chinese religion have certainly provided a corrective to the outmoded thesis that a typical Confucian is no more than a well-adjusted man:

> A well-adjusted man, rationalizing his conduct only to the degree requisite for adjustment, does not constitute a systemic unity but rather a complex of useful and particular traits. (*The Religion of China* [New York: Free Press, 1968], p. 235)

However, it is not enough to simply note that there is a functional equivalent of an inner-directed personality in the Confucian tradition. To confront the Weberian mode of questioning, one must take the roundabout way of both historically and philosophically analyzing what the Confucian project is. Thus far, in my preliminary attempt, I have outlined the fundamental thrust of the Confucian Way and the areas of concern that are constitutive of the Confucian perception of the human condition. This provides the necessary background to understand Confucian thought in action.

Confucius's existential decision to retrieve the deep meaning of human civilization as a way of rethinking the human project made it impossible for the Confucians to detach themselves totally from the world. They had to work through the world because their faith in the perfectibility of human nature through self-effort demanded that they do so. Had they been offered a comparable choice of rendering to Caesar what is Caesar's and to God what is God's in which the kings minded political business and the Confucians were allowed to devote themselves wholly to cultural matters, they would have had to reject it. The separation of politics and culture would have seemed to them arbitrary and superficial. However, even though they were in the world, they could not identify themselves with the status quo. To be sure, neither did they appeal exclusively to a transcendent referent as a source for symbolic action, nor did they develop a realm of values totally independent of the political culture of which they were a part. They, nevertheless, had a rich reservoir of symbolic resources at their disposal in which the transcendent referent featured significantly.

The Confucians differed from their counterparts who tapped the symbolic resources of either a revelatory religion or a speculative philosophy in two essential ways. Because they considered themselves guardians of human civilization, they could not in principle sever their relationships with politics, society, and history. As a result, they assigned themselves the task of appealing to common sense, the good reason and genuine feeling of the people, especially of those in power, to reestablish the order of the world. The first difference, then, is the Confucian belief in the ultimate survivability and intrinsic goodness of the human community. The other difference is that having failed in actuality to change the course of history and to bring universal peace in the world, the Confucians created a realm of values within the "system" intersecting the social and political structures, structures basically alien to the Confucian perception of the moral order. Thus, even though they were in the world, they were definitely not of the world. However, unlike the Taoists who chose to become hermits, the Confucians who were alienated from the center of power gained much influence through sophisticated manipulation of the symbolic universe in which political power was defined, legitimized, and exercised. Specifically, they became teachers, advisers, censors, ministers, and bureaucrats.

The Confucians never established a full-fledged priesthood. For them, such an accomplishment would have been, at best, a limited success. Whether by choice or by default, the separation of church and state was never made in Confucian culture. This style of politics developed by Confucians for their intellectual and spiritual self-definition turned out to be a mixed blessing. We witness, on the one hand, the impressive historical record of the ability of the Confucians to moralize politics and to transform a legalist or military society into a moral community. Yet, we cannot fail to recognize also that Confucian moral values have often been politicized to serve an oppressive authoritarian regime. Although the Confucian moralization of politics has become a distinctive feature of Chinese political culture, the politicization of Confucian symbols in the form of an authoritarian ideology of control has been a dominant tradition in Chinese political history.

The full participation of the Confucians in the political life of the state, as exemplified by Confucius's spirit of engagement in the politics of the Spring and Autumn period (722–481 B.C.), made it impossible for them to become either priests or philosophers. However, they could neither adjust themselves to the status quo nor permit themselves to accept the rules of the game defined in narrowly conceived power relationships since their concerted effort to change the world was dictated by a comprehensive vision of the human project. Their concern for rituals, the rules of conduct, the maintenance of a common creed, and grounding human worth on a transcendental basis led them to perform functions in society comparable to those performed by the priests. Their quests for knowledge, wisdom, the dignity of being human, social norms, and the good life impelled them to assume the roles of philosophers.

The priestly function and philosophical role in both the public image and the self-definition of the Confucian scholar compel us to characterize him not only as a "literatus" but also as an "intellectual." The Confucian intellectual was an activist. His practical reasoning urged him to confront the world of *realpolitik* and to transform it from within. His faith in the perfectibility of human nature through self-effort, the intrinsic goodness of the human community, and the authentic possibility of the unity of man and Heaven enabled him to maintain a critical posture toward those who were powerful and influential. Mencius's idea of a "great man" is a case in point. Having pushed aside and characterized the most powerful ministers of the time as docile concubines, he gave an account of the Confucian form of life:

> A man lives in the spacious dwelling, occupies the proper position, and goes along the highway of the Empire. When he achieves his ambition he shares these with the people; when he fails to do so he practices the Way alone. He cannot be led into excesses when wealthy and honoured or deflected from his purpose when poor and obscure, nor can he be made to bow before superior force. This is what I would call a great man. (3B:2)

Note that because Mencius clearly defines humanity as man's peaceful abode and righteousness as his proper path (4A:10), "the spacious dwelling," "the proper position," and "the highway" mentioned above refer to the symbolic resources that the Confucian intellectual could tap in formulating his own distinctive form of life.

Indeed, a significant part of the *Book of Mencius* can be read as a "special pleading" for the worth of the Confucian intellectual who, despite his lack of contribution in productive labor, is an indispensable member of the moral community:

> A gentleman transforms where he passes, and works wonders where he abides. He is in the same stream as Heaven above and Earth below. Can he be said to bring but small benefit? (7A:13)

This critical awareness of the ethico-religious role and function of the Confucian intellectual is particularly pronounced in Mencius's argument against the physiocratic claim that all values are derived from the cultivation of the land. Mencius first presents an analysis of the functional necessity of the division of labor in any complex society. He then elaborates on the mutual dependency of those who labor with their muscles and those who labor with their minds. He concludes with the observation that the management of the people is so demanding and requires so much tender care that the leisure to plow the fields is simply not available to the rulers; "It is not true that Yao and Shun did not have to use their minds to rule the Empire. Only they did not use their minds to plough the fields" (3A:14). By implication, the intellectuals, as members of what may be called the "service sector" of the society, also have more urgent business to attend to, such as cultivating oneself, teaching others to be good, "looking for friends in history" (5B:8), emulating the sages, setting up the cultural norms, interpreting the Mandate of Heaven, transmitting the Way, and transforming the world into a moral community.

The classical Confucian perceptions of Way, Learning, and Politics provide a necessary background for our appreciation of the Sung Confucian idea of education. It is often assumed that a distinctive feature of the rise of Neo-Confucianism in the eleventh century, as a response to the challenge of Buddhism, is social consciousness. The Confucians were engaged in social reform, general education, public work, and indeed nation building. Fan Chung-yen's paradigmatic statement about the sense of mission of the Confucian literatus was a reflection of this new spirit of engagement rather than an idiosyncratic expression of his personal ambition. Li Kou's (1009–1059) political essays with their particular emphasis on ritual and land indicated that the focus of the concerned Confucian statesman in the middle period of the Northern Sung was statecraft. Wang An-shih's New Learning significantly broadened the scope of statecraft and suggested fresh perspectives on politics as a way of realizing a comprehensive vision of society derived from the classics, especially the *Chou Li*. The Li-Wang line of Confucian statecraft was, in a way, a continuation of classical and ritual studies as a basis for maintaining the bureaucratic order in the T'ang.

However, the New Learning, while Confucian in character, provoked strong reactions from those who were instrumental in bringing about an unprecedented Confucian revival, namely the Six Masters of the Northern Sung. The masters who criticized Wang An-shih were later identified as promoters of Tao-hsüeh (Learning of the Way). This designation shows that the primary cause of the dissatisfaction with Wang's reform was that his obsession with wealth and power, which confined politics to administrative considerations, was a significant departure from the Confucian Way. There is certainly a measure of truth in the Marxist interpretation of a class conflict between Wang and his critics, notably Ssu-ma Kuang, one of the Six Masters. If the notion of class is enlarged to include factional, regional, and ideological factors, the conflict between Wang and Ssu-ma was definitely more than a dispute over the proper representation of the Confucian Way. Nevertheless, within the Confucian discourse, it was a matter of grave importance that the statesman who was supposed to enlarge the Confucian gate, to use a prevalent metaphor of the time, actually rearranged the architecture of the Confucian temple. As a result, Confucius, Tzu-ssu, and Mencius were no longer honored but Shen Pu-hai and Han Fei were. Wang

An-shih was not a Legalist in theory or practice, but his preoccupation with achievement (*kung*) and profit (*li*) gave the Confucian masters enough evidence to condemn him as one.

The Confucian masters, in their concerted effort to promote the Way, were charged by their sense of mission to define what their learning was all about. They faced overwhelming odds because their project was comprehensive in scope but with a definite order of priority. Simply put, they wanted to ground their learning in the Confucian Way as they understood it so that the politics that eventually grew out of this moral vision was the Confucian idea of benevolent government. Realistically they knew well the difficulties that they must encounter to bring this about. They did not presume that they could accomplish what Confucius and Mencius had clearly failed to do. Wang, however, strongly believed that his single-minded effort could usher in a new era in human history.

I should mention that one way of broaching the controversy is to contrast Wang's classical idealism with Ssu-ma's historical realism. Yet, the Confucian masters, including Ssu-ma Kuang, were moral idealists whose attempts to moralize politics were dictated by their faith in the perfectibility (and, by implication, the ultimate transformability) of the human community through education. As sophisticated practitioners of the art of bureaucratic living, they had firsthand knowledge of how the society worked at the basic level of governance. Their moral idealism was not predicated on a preconceived political order. They were not armchair philosophers envisioning an ideally perfect social system. On the contrary, they reflected upon things at hand, asked pertinent questions about their time, and offered practicable instructions to their students. Their idealism was a conscious response to what they perceived to be a vacuum in moral education.

In defining their unique approach to education, the early Sung masters were particularly concerned about the authentic transmission of the lost classical vision of learning. Chou Tun-i's straightforward "yes" to the loaded question, "Can one become a sage through learning?" signaled a significant turn in educational emphasis. This shift of emphasis from the acquisition of classical knowledge to the spiritual discipline of self-cultivation—in short, from information to transformation—has far-reaching implications for virtually all aspects of the educational process. Especially noteworthy here is the prominence of the idea of the self as creative transformation. The key concepts, as discussed in Wm. T. de Bary's *The Liberal Tradition in China*, capture the spirit of this new orientation: "learning for the sake of one's self" (*wei-chi chih hsüeh*), "getting it oneself" (*tzu-te*), and "taking responsibility oneself" (*tzu-jen*).

Intent on developing the core curriculum of Confucian education on the basis of self-cultivation, the early Sung Confucian masters redefined all major categories of Confucian concerns in terms of this central vision. Literature is to enrich the life of the mind. But if pursued as an end in itself or, worse, as a frivolous pastime, it becomes an external thing that can harm one's determination to learn to become a sage. Classics are the repositories of sagely wisdom. If classical studies involve no more than textual analysis without any reference to one's personal experience, they are no longer helpful in gaining direct access to the sagely intention. History is the moral drama of the rise and fall of dynasties in the light of Confucius's classical attempt to set standards of evaluation for the future as well as for the past. If understood as the occurrence of events according to the logic of power, history may be full of sound and fury, but it does not signify much for the Confucian devotee. Politics, as rectification, is the institutional framework in which people of different backgrounds, talents, statuses, and so on can work together not only for survival and prosperity but also for self-realization. And society, instead of being an adversary system, is a fiduciary community centering around the primordial form of human-relatedness, the family. If politics becomes no more than a distribution of power or a mechanism of control that benefits only the ruling minority, the Confucians should see to it that this privatized arrangement of the resources of the land be fundamentally changed. Similarly, if society is fragmented by narrowly conceived interest groups, such as undeserving merchants basically motivated by the accumulation of wealth, the Confucians should speak out on behalf of the majority of the working people, that is, the peasants.

Hindsight tells us that the Neo-Confucian educational project may have adversely affected economic and scientific developments in East Asia. Yet, in its formative years, the Sung masters consciously chose to underscore learning for the sake of oneself, a dimension of education thought to have been ignored for centuries. And they chose this attitude toward learning as a corrective to the prevalent trends of putting too much weight on the world outside. The discovery of this dimension of classical Confucian thought put education in a new perspective. Education for the dual purpose of transmission of culture and service to society then had to be integrated with the ultimate concern of moral self-transformation. Understandably the Ch'eng Brothers found Su Shih's conception of culture (*wen*) and Wang An-shih's conception of politics (*cheng*) unacceptable because they both failed to recognize that, without the moral transformation of the self as the linchpin, neither culture nor politics can remain wholesome.

The moral fundamentalism that the early Sung masters advocated may give the impression that they had exaggerated the importance of Confucian "faith" at the expense of the Confucian "cumulative tradition" as a whole. I should also point out, however, that in their effort to chart a course for Confucian learning in the crosscurrents of the pragmatism of the examination system and the escapism of vulgarized Taoist and Buddhist institutions, they in fact created a new tradition for the generations to come.

SIX

Chu Hsi's Redefinition of Literati Learning

Peter K. Bol

THE ISSUE

One of Chu Hsi's examination questions suggests a useful perspective on his enterprise. In it he asks his students, men who thought of themselves as literati or *shih*, to consider the goal of learning and of being a literatus.

> Those who learned in antiquity began by acting as *shih* and ended by acting as sages. That is to say, if they knew how to act as *shih* then they knew how to act as sages. Those who act as *shih* today are many, but I have not yet heard of any who have attained sagehood. Is it perhaps that they do not know how to act as *shih* either? Or is it that sages will definitely not come from among such men? . . . Thus there must be a way [*tao*] by which *shih*, by acting as *shih*, attain sagehood.[1]

In modern life there is a disjunction between the literatus and the sage. The ideal learning enables one to be both a literatus and a seeker of the true goal of learning: sagehood. The task then for Chu is to define the kind of learning that makes this possible. Chu is calling for nothing short of a redefinition of literati values, to be achieved by redefining literati learning. But already some implications of this redefinition are apparent. If the goal of literati learning is sagehood, then in practice literati learning can never cease; it is a lifelong enterprise, continuing past examination success and an official career. If so, it includes everything a literatus does; it is coeval with his life, that which defines the moral life. In implication, at least, Chu intends

I wish to acknowledge the useful comments made on earlier drafts of this paper by Ronald C. Egan, Willard J. Peterson, and the editors.

1. Chu Hsi, *Hui-an hsien-sheng Chu Wen-kung wen chi* (also titled *Chu tzu ta ch'üan*; SPPY ed.) 74:4a.

to redefine learning as something totally inclusive; thus, all aspects of the life of a literatus are transformed into aspects of learning.

When Chu's efforts are placed in the context of Sung history the immensity, difficulty, and loftiness of his task become apparent. First, literati learning had been institutionalized in Sung through an examination system and a growing network of state schools after the 1070s. In a sense the rise of the literati in the early Sung was the result of a successful effort by the first two emperors and their advisers to redefine what it meant to be a *shih* or a member of the national elite. By expanding the examination system to the point that it was the primary means of selecting officials from among the elite—at the time a diverse group consisting of military powerholders, locally powerful families, and bureaucrats—the emperors had gradually made learning the preeminent criterion of office holding and thus elite status. The kind of learning they encouraged was important, for it, more than learning in general, defined what it meant to be a *shih*. The examinations were meant to choose those men thought most likely to uphold the new civil order. The emperors wanted men with civil skills who would be loyal to the idea of civil government. The examinations, by testing for those skills, encouraged men to think of themselves as *shih* because they could demonstrate that they had acquired civil values and talents, not because they came from families with local or military power or impressive pedigrees. The examinations tested what men at the time thought marked the civil man: the ability to compose poetry and prose in good literary style and a knowledge of the great classical, historical, and ritual texts that defined the cultural tradition. The *shih* thus became literati.

To a large extent they remained literati, men who prided themselves on their cultural accomplishments and their grounding in cultural traditions. The examinations remained literary tests as well. There were protests against a system that tended to reduce literati learning to a matter of literary conventions and textual mastery. Wang An-shih (1021–1086) redesigned the test to require that literati study the Classics and consider how their principles could be applied to the present; he also planned to replace the system with a graded school system. Yet opposition eventually led to the compromise that existed in Chu Hsi's times and remained intact through the remainder of Sung: a dual system allowed candidates to choose to be tested either in prose and poetry or in the exegesis of the Classics. The vast majority of literati chose the literary rather than the Classics examination. In Chu's time, for most literati, learning meant literary studies; they read the works of others to learn to compose their own. Moreover, the number of men seeking to establish themselves as literati through this literary examination learning increased dramatically during Southern Sung. In the second half of the twelfth century there were as many as two hundred thousand prefectural candidates, and their number had doubled by the end of the dynasty. Thus, Chu Hsi's potential audience was vast, but in large part it consisted of men who thought they were literati because they engaged in literary studies.[2]

Chu also faced difficulties on a second front. The idea that literati ought to aspire to a higher goal and that learning ought to have a purpose beyond examination success and an official career already had a long and diverse history in Sung. As early as the eleventh century the success of the examinations and the civil order was depriving literary studies of much of the idealism of earlier decades, when the Sung government was still trying to unify the state and deprive the military of power. Literary learning had become a means of getting ahead, an acceptable vehicle for literati self-interest. The desire to persuade literati to take the common interest to heart, to feel moral responsibility for the welfare of society and state, was expressed at first in proposals to redesign the examination system to favor men concerned with saving the world. Fan Chung-yen's reform proposals of the 1040s, Ou-yang Hsiu's promotion of the "ancient style" (*ku wen*) in the 1050s, and the appointment of famous teachers at the new Imperial University in the 1050s were measures intended to instill a concern with ideal values among the literati. For these reformers the goal of literati learning was to understand the ideals of antiquity and realize them in the present, thus to transform society into an integrated social order. They still believed that learning proceeded through the study of literature and that the examinations could be designed to select the truly committed. Wang An-shih's rise to power in the late 1060s represents the political success of this idealistic view. But Wang's "learning" or the "New Learning," as his ideas about how literati could know and realize enduring values came to be known, met considerable political and intellectual opposition. The opposition, however, was divided both by generation and interest. Ssu-ma Kuang (1019–1086), Wang's contemporary, used his historical studies to counter Wang's appeal to the Classics and his particular vision of an integrated order. Like Wang, Ssu-ma sought to understand the proper system of government and defined

2. On the Sung examination system see John Chaffee, "Education and Examinations in Sung Society," (Ph.D. diss., University of Chicago, 1979), and Araki Toshikazu, *Sōdai kakyo seidō kenkyū* (Kyoto: Tōyōshi kenkyūkai, 1969). For the Northern Sung in particular, see Chin Chung-shu, "Pei-sung k'o-chü chih-tu yen-chiu," in *Sung shih yen-chiu chi* (Taipei: Kuo-li pien-i kuan, 1979) 11:1–72, and (1980) 12:31–112. The early Northern Sung dual system, distinguished from the Southern Sung dual system, consisted of a *chin shih* examination, testing the ability to compose in poetry and prose, and the "various fields" (*chu k'o*), testing memorization of various classics, histories, and ritual compendia. See also E. A. Kracke, Jr., *Civil Service in Early Sung China*, (Cambridge: Harvard University Press, 1953), pp. 58–68. For the kinds of objections raised to the examinations see David S. Nivison, "Protest Against Conventions and Conventions of Protest," in *The Confucian Persuasion*, ed. Arthur F. Wright (Stanford: Stanford University Press, 1960), pp. 177–201. The Southern Sung dual system and the rare instances when the two exams were combined are noted in Li Hsin-ch'uan, *Chien-yen i-lai ch'ao yeh tsa chi* (reprint Taipei: Wen-hai, 1981), pp. 377–378 (orig. 13:7a–7b). The reasons for this dual system, the debates over it, and the popularity of the literary track are discussed in Kondō Kazunari, "Nan-sō shuki no Ō An-seki hyoka ni tsuite," *Tōyōshi kenkyū* 38, no. 3 (1979–1980): 40–44. See also Chaffee, p. 217. The figures for prefectural candidates are from Chaffee, p. 59.

the responsibilities of individuals in terms of that system. Once in power (r. 1085–1086) he set about undoing many of the New Policies.

The next generation shifted its attention from state systems to individuals. Both Ch'eng Yi (1033–1107) and Su Shih (1037–1101) asked how literati denied access to political power could maintain their integrity and remain socially responsible. Ch'eng argued that true learning meant to know the Way and become a sage. The "Ch'eng learning" held that the first duty of literati was to transform themselves into moral men, for only morality had a real basis in man's nature. For those who learned in this manner it was not necessary to wait for official success to benefit society; they were helping the world whenever they were acting morally. Ch'eng rejected literary learning on the grounds that it kept literati from devoting themselves to the cultivation of their moral selves. Although Su Shih also treated sagehood as the goal of learning, his sage was not a paragon of strict morality. In the "Su learning" the sage was responsive and creative. His literatus was acting as a sage when, through the two-sided effort of acquiring knowledge and skill and drawing on the inexhaustible source of creation innate to all men, he brought (new) things into being. Thus, Su defended cultural pursuits as one of the most effective ways of learning how to respond appropriately to a changing world.

Except for the brief Yuan-yu period (r. 1086–1093), when opponents of Wang's New Policies controlled the government, political authority to the end of Northern Sung supported the "Wang learning" as the definition of correct literati learning. Proponents of Wang's learning were closely identified with the New Policies and the belief, in which the New Policies were grounded, that ideals were best realized through the "affairs of government" (*cheng shih*). But the "Su learning," with its emphasis on "learning from culture" (*wen hsüeh*), and the "Ch'eng learning," with its stress on "moral conduct" or the "practice of moral virtues" (*te hsing*), continued in spite of official suppression. Su's *wen* continued to appeal, even at court, and Ch'eng's followers continued to spread his teachings. Most of Ssu-ma's followers were forced to choose between Su and Ch'eng. Eventually, largely through the efforts of Chu Hsi, the Ch'eng learning captured the center of literati thought. And even those who objected that this school, which claimed that true literati learning was *tao hsüeh*, or learning from the Way, favored moral cultivation at the expense of political responsibility and cultural accomplishment felt compelled to treat it as the "correct learning" (*cheng hsüeh*). But when Chu began his work of persuading literati that they all ought to believe that sagehood was the only true goal of learning and that there was one correct way of attaining the goal—in short, when he began to redefine literati learning—he still had to sift the alternatives and explain why the Ch'eng learning was correct, whereas the learnings of Wang and Su were wrong.[3]

Chu's indebtedness to the eleventh century is well known, as is the manner in which he drew upon Chou Tun-i, Chang Tsai, Ch'eng Hao, and especially Ch'eng Yi in establishing a coherent philosophical synthesis based on the unity of principle, the relationship between principle and material force, the innate goodness of human nature, and so on.[4] We also have a general understanding of the practical measures Chu used to promote these ideas after the 1060s: the identification of his chosen predecessors as the true possessors of the Way, the writing of a biographical history of their "school," the publication of annotated and critical editions of their writing, the preparation of the famous anthology *Reflections on Things at Hand*, and finally the establishment of the Four Books as seminal Confucian texts and the writing of commentaries on them. If we are to understand the transformation of literati values implied by Chu Hsi's redefinition of learning, it is important to know what Chu rejected as well as what he persuaded literati to adopt. To accomplish this I have looked first at his assertion that a real distinction exists between true learning and examination style learning. An account of the two most important alternatives to Chu's version of true literati learning, the learnings of Wang An-shih and Su Shih, and Chu Hsi's criticism of them follows.

3. For studies of the eleventh-century literati thinkers mentioned here see works by James T. C. Liu, "An Early Sung Reformer: Fan Chung-yen," in *Chinese Thought and Institutions*, ed. John K. Fairbank (Chicago: University of Chicago Press, 1957), pp. 105–131; *Ou-yang Hsiu: An Eleventh-Century Neo-Confucianist* (Stanford: Stanford University Press, 1967); *Reform in Sung China (Cambridge: Harvard University Press*, 1959); and Wm. Theodore de Bary's "A Reappraisal of Neo-Confucianism," in *Studies in Chinese Thought*, ed. Arthur F. Wright (Chicago: University of Chicago Press, 1953), pp. 81–111. On Wang see also Winston Lo, "Wang An-shih and the Confucian Ideal of Inner Sageliness," *Philosophy East and West* 26, no. 1 (1976):41–53. On Ssu-ma Kuang see Anthony Sariti, "Monarchy, Bureaucracy, and Absolutism in the Political Thought of Ssu-ma Kuang," *Journal of Asian Studies* 32, no. 1 (1972):53–76. On Su Shih see George Hatch, "Su Shih," in *Sung Biographies*, ed. Herbert Franke (Wiesbaden: Franz Steiner Verlag, 1967), pp. 900–968. I have discussed some of these issues in "Culture and the Way in Eleventh-Century China" (Ph.D. diss., Princeton University, 1982), especially pp. 79–84, on the Sung usage of "the affairs of government," "learning from culture," and "moral conduct" to denote areas of literati activity and responsibility. In late Northern and Southern Sung it was common to refer to different intellectual orientations in terms of the individuals thought to provide the best models. Thus, for example, "Wang's learning," once men identified with it and him, become the "Wang learning." This does not mean that it was a "school" with leaders and followers and a well-defined doctrine, although the "Ch'eng learning" eventually did become a school. For the willingness of critics to accept Chu's school as defining the "correct learning," see Hoyt Tillman's account of Ch'en Liang and his challenge to Chu Hsi; *Utilitarian Confucianism* (Cambridge: Council on East Asian Studies, 1982), pp. 144, 129; Ch'en Liang, *Lung ch'uan chi* (SPPY ed.) 20:16b.

4. See, for example, Wing-tsit Chan, "Chu Hsi's Completion of Neo-Confucianism," *Études Song*, series II, part 1 (Paris: Mouton, 1973), pp. 59–90; and Chu Hsi and Lü Tsu-ch'ien, *Reflections on Things at Hand*, tr. Wing-tsit Chan (New York: Columbia University Press, 1967).

EXAMINATION LEARNING OR TRUE LEARNING

Why did men learn to act as *shih* without learning to act as sages? In his inscriptions for schools, written from the 1160s through the 1190s and collected in chüan 77–80 of his works, Chu blames the state school system. He recognizes that the current school system, a result of the Sung success in establishing "civil order," far surpasses that of previous dynasties.[5] He recognizes also that this school system is meant to serve the interests of the *shih*: "The court has established schools to nurture the *shih* of the world" and has appointed teachers "to instruct those who act as *shih* among the men" in those places with schools.[6] He points out that schools also serve the purpose of defining "who among the common people are able to act as *shih*," that is, they provide an institutional mechanism in their localities for determining who is a literatus and who is not.[7] This is because "those who are acting as *shih* (*wei shih che*)" differ from both "those who are acting as officials" and "those who are acting as commoners" because the *shih* are engaged in learning.[8] Learning is essential; although literati are those who learn, it is through learning that "those who act as *shih* begin to understand the affairs for which they are *shih*."[9]

The problem, in Chu Hsi's view, is that the schools misinform literati about "the affairs for which they are *shih*." He tells those local officials who brag of their success in increasing the number of *shih* in their locality by instructing students in literary composition and seeing them through the examinations that they really have been missing the point of learning.[10] Theirs is not true learning. It merely teaches men to satisfy social standards and has no bearing on the moral lives of the students. True learning, the way men learned in antiquity, transforms the individual; it shows him how to become a moral man and work toward sagehood.

Chu differentiates true learning from examination learning with a passage from the *Analects*. The first is learning "for oneself" or to "improve oneself" (*wei chi*), and the second is learning "for others" or to "impress others" (*wei jen*).

> [Confucius said,] "Those who learned in antiquity did so to improve themselves; those who learn today do so to impress others." Therefore when the sages and worthies taught men to engage in learning it was not to make them

---

5. Chu Hsi, "Nan-chien chou Yü-ch'i hsien hsüeh chi" (1173) 77:22b, Chu's criticism of customary learning extends beyond the issues discussed here; see Ch'ien Mu, *Chu tzu hsin hsüeh an* (Taipei: Sanmin, 1971) 3:229–292.

6. Chu Hsi, "Yü Li chiao-shou shu" 24:3a–3b.

7. Chu Hsi, "Ch'iung chou hsüeh chi," (1182) 79:4b.

8. Chu Hsi, "Chien-k'ang fu hsüeh Ming-tao hsien-sheng tz'u chi" (1176) 78:1b.

9. Chu Hsi, "Ch'i chou chiao-shou t'ing chi" (1173) 77:20b.

10. Chu Hsi, "Ch'iung chou hsüeh chi" (1182) 79:4a, "Chien-ch'ang chün chin-shih t'i ming chi" (1195) 80:17a.

string together phrases and compose literary pieces, or merely to plan for examination success or rank and salary.[11]

When Chu advises men to "devote themselves to the learning of *wei chi* of the ancients," he is telling them how and why they should learn. It is a purpose and a method that is "lofty; outside of examinations and writing."[12]

This learning is not for impressing others; it is something a literatus does "for himself" in order to make or "form" or "transform himself." Given how he might have previously learned, engaging in the true learning is a transformation, for it implies a shift in values. But, as Chu Hsi describes it, true learning develops what one possesses innately, something real and substantial in the self. From this perspective it is a matter of realizing rather than transforming the self; it does not involve acquiring something one does not have already, such as literary skill, or meeting standards external to himself. "If men have this body they necessarily have this mind; if they have this mind they necessarily have this principle." "All men have it, it is not fused onto us from outside."[13] The good teacher "guides men with what their bodies and minds possess" so that "literati will know that what they learn with is not outside of what their bodies and minds possess."[14] What is learning? "Learning is that through which one (trans)forms oneself."[15] This is a moral enterprise, for men innately possess the four cardinal moral virtues and the principles of the five social relationships.[16]

Unfortunately state schools do not, Chu notes, concern themselves with developing in man those "things which are so by themselves" that "do not depend on writing to be established."[17] Their teachers "have never examined [their students'] basis in moral conduct and the arts of the Way. They choose to transmit only the books of current custom and the enterprise of succeeding. They cause men to see advantage, not righteousness. Those literati committed to (trans)forming themselves are ashamed to discuss these" and find it necessary to go elsewhere.[18]

Because state schools value what is artificial, acquired, and external, they work to the advantage of those with a talent for cultural pursuits and those who, because they are urban and well-to-do, are best situated to nurture such

11. Chu Hsi, "Yü shan chiang i" 74:18a. Citing *Lun yü* 14:24, trans. D. C. Lau, *The Analects* (Harmondsworth: Penguin, 1979), p. 128, modified.
12. Chu Hsi, "Ch'ang chou I-hsing hsien hsüeh chi" (1195) 80:14b. Also see "Nan-chien chou Yü-ch'i hsien-hsüeh chi," 77:21b, and "Hsin chou chou-hsüeh ta-ch'eng tien chi" (1193) 80:13b.
13. Chu Hsi, "E chou chou-hsüeh chi ku ko chi" (1193) 80:9a.
14. Chu Hsi, "Ch'iung chou hsüeh chi" 79:5a.
15. Chu Hsi, "T'ung-an hsien yü hsüeh-che" 74:1b.
16. Chu Hsi, "Nan-chien chou Yü-hsi hsien hsüeh chi" 72:21b.
17. Chu Hsi, "Hui chou Wu-yüan hsien hsüeh tsang shu ko chi" (1176) 78:7b–8a.
18. Chu Hsi, "Heng chou shih ku shu-yüan chi" 79:21b.

a talent. Rural youths and men of moral character are thus ignored.[19] In short, the schools favor what is possible for some rather than what is common to all. Cultural accomplishment (*wen*) is not a fair means of determining who in society has real worth because it is not something all men are innately capable of under all circumstances. Whether a man acts morally or not is such a standard because the foundation and norms of morality are endowed in all men.

> Now cultural accomplishment is of secondary importance to literati. It is not present in fixed proportion in superior men and lesser men. Literati may embrace morality yet be unable in this regard, or, if able, they may be ashamed and think it not worth pursuing. How then [under the present system] will the state be able to employ them?[20]

Chu Hsi tried to do something about the institutional situation on several fronts. He drew up a plan for a better examination and school system, but this remained a "private proposal" and was not adopted.[21] He had greater success adding true learning to the existing curriculum of schools in his jurisdiction and persuading like-minded men to do so in theirs. On occasion such efforts were given tangible recognition in the form of shrines comme-morating the Northern Sung masters as models of true learning.[22] He also encouraged the establishment of academies independent of the state system; the most famous example was his own White Deer Grotto Academy.[23]

If institutional remedies were uncertain, Chu was still free to persuade literati that the choice between accepting state education as a definition of learning and his own vision was a choice between being immoral and moral. To choose the former was to "covet profit and salary" because one "wanted to be a noble man"; to choose with Chu was to "covet the Way and moral principles" because one "wanted to be a good man."[24] In effect Chu demanded that all make the choice he had made in 1158 "to devote myself to this [learning of (trans)forming myself] in order to attain sagehood myself."[25] In Chu's eyes not to share this method and goal was equivalent to lacking a real method and goal. Thus, in the state schools "those who learn lack the means to know wherein their purpose is to be found."[26] And they do not know how to learn: "The Way is not manifest in the world, and literati do not know how to engage in learning."[27]

Chu Hsi was sure that he did know the goal and method of true learning.

19. Chu Hsi, exam question, 74:10a.
20. Chu Hsi, exam question, 74:7a.
21. Chu Hsi, "Hsueh-hsiao kung-chü ssu i" 69:18a.
22. E.g., Ibid., 78:15a, 78:17a, 78:18a, 79:2b.
23. Chu Hsi, "Pai-lu-tung shu-yüan ko shih" 74:16b–17b.
24. Chu Hsi, "Yü yü hsueh-che" 74:23a.
25. Chu Hsi, "Mu chai chi" 77:7b.
26. Chu Hsi, "Hsin chou Ch'ien-shan hsien hsüeh chi" (1179) 78:21b–22a.
27. Chu Hsi, "Shao chou chou-hsüeh Lien-hsi hsien-sheng tz'u chi" (1173) 79:9b.

One of his most cogent summaries of his position, parts of which appear in all his school inscriptions, was written in 1194 for the new emperor, shortly before the official suppression of his teachings as a "spurious learning" (*wei hsüeh*) began.[28]

> The fact that man has this life [means that] Heaven has endowed him with a nature of benevolence, righteousness, decorum, and morality, ordered the relations of ruler and minister and father and son, and instituted the standards that ought to hold for his affairs. But because his physical constitution is imbalanced and his material desires obscure [his understanding] he may mistake his nature and thus confuse his relations and defeat his standards. Yet he will not know he ought to turn back [to seek his nature]. It is necessarily through learning that he opens it up. Only then will he have the means to rectify his mind and cultivate his personal life, thus to become the basis for regulating the family and bringing order to the state. This is why man must learn. But the way in which he learns does not begin from memorization and literary skill, nor does it make a distinction between the sage and stupid or noble and humble.

Thus far Chu has outlined the premises on which true learning rests: we have an innate moral endowment capable of guiding our conduct that is obscured by our physical self, thus leaving us open to immoral conduct. We must engage in a process ("learning") that enables us to recover the innate guides common to all. Chu then explains what this process involves.

> Now it is so that the first priority in the process of engaging in learning is to investigate principle fully. The key to investigating principle is reading books. Nothing is more valuable in the method of reading books than following the sequence [of the text] and concentrating. The basis of concentration in turn lies in residing in seriousness and maintaining commitment. This is an unchanging principle.

For Chu the process of learning has a primary concern, understanding principle, and a means of realizing that concern, reading books. Reading books will be ineffective, however, unless we read in the proper fashion by reading in sequence and concentration. But to read correctly we must have the proper attitude: we must not falter in our belief that these texts ought to be revered; we must be serious and show commitment. Chu then explains why each element is essential; I summarize his explanations in the following paragraphs.

Why should we investigate principles fully? Because there is a principle for each of the five social relationships and for all areas of social conduct at

---

28. Chu Hsi, "(Chia-yen) hsing-kung pien-tien tsou-cha erh" 14:10b–12b. Chu Hsi had been brought to court as the most famous scholar in the land but was being used in a factional struggle. For a description of these events see Conrad Schirokauer, "Chu Hsi's Political Career," in *Confucian Personalities*, ed. Arthur F. Wright and Denis Twitchett (Stanford: Stanford University Press, 1963), pp. 182–183.

home and abroad. By investigation we can understand not only "that by which something is the way it is" (*ch'i so i jan*) but also "the way it ought to be" (*ch'i so tang jan*). Freed from doubt we will be in a state to pursue the good and remove the bad.

Why should we read books? Although the principles of the world under heaven are constant, only the sages of antiquity fully understood them. Thus, their actions and words can also be constant models for us. Whether we are moral, and thus can benefit others, or are immoral, and cannot even save ourselves, depends upon whether we accord with them or not. To understand principle and how we ought to act we must read the Classics. To understand principle as manifested in affairs and to learn about the kinds of situations to which we must be able to respond we must read the histories. Together the Classics and histories contain all principles.

Why should we follow sequence and concentrate? We must read carefully, slowly, and sequentially (and not skip about in the text) so as to "believe deeply and apprehend it for ourselves." In this manner what we are reading will become coherent, and our minds and the principles found through reading will conjoin.

Why should we reside in seriousness and maintain commitment? Concentration depends on the mind, yet the mind is vacuous and unfathomable while it is also the master of the body. It "controls the net of the ten-thousand things." If it takes off after material desires outside the body, then the person loses a master and things lose their coherence, their "net." When this happens we are unable to pay the attention necessary to the words of the sages and historical affairs to seek out their true moral meaning. Thus, if we can keep this mind focused, we will be able to comprehend principles by reading books and realize principles by responding to affairs.

This kind of learning is something "to which literati without official status ought to devote themselves, and even emperors." It enables all men to begin acting like sages, men who fully understand principle. But the correctness of the process is vouchsafed by theory rather than any text. Thus, Chu is sure that if "sages and worthies were to be reborn, the way in which they would instruct men would not go beyond this." This is a universally valid process of learning; it is not one of several acceptable alternatives, but it is the only way. Chu objects to those "among the bureaucrats who, on hearing words of this sort, uniformly point to it as '*tao hsüeh*' [merely learning about the way to be moral] and insist on rejecting it." He does not accept that his learning is partial, that there are other kinds of learning for other areas of life, or that it is one of several holistic understandings of true learning. But when Chu began his career as the spokesman for this learning he faced other kinds of learning, besides examination learning, that were regarded as real alternatives and real contributions to literati life.

DISPUTING THE ALTERNATIVES

Chu Hsi recognized that other "learnings" also claimed to be the true learning for all literati. He traced these alternatives to the eleventh century. One of his examination questions asks his students to sift these for themselves.

> In recent times such [men] as Master Hu [Yüan] of Hai-ling, His Honor Ou-yang [Hsiu] Wen-chung, His Honor Wang [An-shih] Wen, His Honor Ssu-ma [Kuang] Wen-cheng, Rites Compiler Su [Hsün] and his sons [Su Shih and Su Ch'e], and Censor Ch'eng [Hao], the elder brother, and his younger brother [Ch'eng I] have become famous through learning. Their instructions are all extant; you gentlemen have certainly read and recited them. Who among them apprehended the true thread of the doctrine from former sages and worthies?[29]

The correct answer was that the Ch'eng brothers had. To a lesser extent Chu allows Hu Yüan and Ssu-ma Kuang into the fold. But Ou-Yang Hsiu, although he had an inkling, never quite got there. Moreover, he gave rise to Wang An-shih and Su Shih, the principle enemies of the Ch'engs in Chu's view.

> In our dynasty *Ju* learning has flourished more [than before], beginning with Mr. Ou-yang, Mr. Wang and Mr. Su, all of whom held sway at court with their learnings, while Mr. Hu and Messrs. Ch'eng transmitted their learning to scholars [outside the court]. In origin Wang and Su stem from Ou-yang, but there were great dissimilarities in their further development. Mr. Hu and Mr. Sun [Fu] were not accommodated in their time [by the likes of Ou-yang Hsiu] while Messrs. Ch'eng were in even greater disagreement with Wang and Su.[30]

Chu goes on to imply that Wang and Su stood in relation to the Ch'engs as Mo Ti and Yang Chu stood in relation to Mencius; just as Mencius felt compelled to dispute them, so should his students feel compelled to dispute Wang and Su.[31] "I am not fond of disputation," wrote Mencius, "I have no alternative. Whoever can, with words, combat Yang and Mo is a true disciple of the sages."[32]

Chu Hsi found it necessary to dispute Wang and Su because they still had considerable followings and strong political support in twelfth-century Southern Sung. His intellectual dispute was also political, as was usually the case when proponents of a particular kind of learning claimed the right to define values for all areas of literati life. As the number of advocates of the Ch'engs' learning increased, Chu became increasingly embroiled in factional

29. Chu Hsi, "(Chia-yen) hsing-kung pien-tien tsou-cha erh" 74:4b.
30. Chu Hsi, "Pai-lu shu-t'ang ts'e wen" 74:12a.
31. Chu makes this explicit in letters to Wang Ying-chen (Chu Hsi, 30:10b) and Lü Tsu-ch'ien (33:4b).
32. *Mencius* 3B9, trans. D. C. Lau (Harmondsworth: Penguin, 1970), p. 115.

struggles; and, because his allies were usually "out" rather than "in," to support Chu's intellectual claims was also a political statement. To a degree the importance of the Wang and Su learnings involved the willingness of political authority to use them to counter the claims of Chu Hsi and his allies.

Thus, the resurgence of interest in Wang An-shih between 1138 and 1155 had much to do with Kao-tsung's (r. 1127–1162) use of Ch'in Kuei to secure peace with Chin over the opposition of his former ministers. His former ministers had been staunch advocates of Ch'eng learning and virulent opponents of the New Policies regime; they blamed it and Wang learning for the loss of the North. The emperor himself was quite adept at intellectual politics and sought to satisfy all sides. He displayed an interest in history and admired Ssu-ma Kuang; he had literary interests and admired Su Shih, although both had been maligned by later proponents of Wang learning. After Ch'in Kuei's death Kao-tsung merely took the line that there should not be exclusive reliance on either the ideas of Wang or the Ch'engs in the examinations. The court needed the support of officials who had begun their careers during the New Policies era even if it was no longer interested in realizing Wang's ideal of using state institutions to establish an integrated social order. Although Chu's position eventually won, his allies only succeeded in removing Wang from the accessory sacrifices at the Confucian temple and in installing the Ch'engs, Chou Tun-i, and Chang Tsai in 1241.[33]

The Court's post-1155 policy of allowing the competing claims of the Wang and Ch'eng learnings was made more complicated under Hsiao-tsung (r. 1162–1189). This emperor wrote a "Critique of [Han Yü's Essay] 'The Origins of the Way,'" in which he announced that *Ju* learning was merely one of three alternative conceptions of the Way and was, like Buddhism and Taoism, only capable of making a partial contribution to a more complete whole. It certainly had no right to claim special knowledge of the origins of the Way. Criticism led to a change of title. Henceforth the essay, with its advice to "use Buddhism to cultivate the mind, Taoism to nurture life, and Confucianism to order society," was known as "On the Three Teachings."[34]

---

33. The major early account of the struggle to gain official sanction for *tao hsüeh* is Li Hsin-ch'uan's *Tao ming lu* (reprint, Taipei: Wen-hai, 1981). See also his summary account of the "Rises and Falls of *Tao hsüeh*," in *Ch'ao yeh tsa chi*, 1, 6:1a–2b (reprint pp. 211–214). These events are recounted and elaborated in Conrad Schirokauer, "Neo-Confucians Under Attack," in *Crisis and Prosperity in Sung China*, ed. John Winthrop Haeger (Tucson: University of Arizona Press, 1975); see pp. 164–168 in particular. James T. C. Liu has also addressed these issues in "How did a Neo-Confucian School Become the State Orthodoxy?," *Philosophy East and West* 23, no. 4 (1973):483–506. For an understanding of why and how Wang An-shih was important and the modes of conduct adopted by Kao-tsung I am particularly indebted to Kondō Kazunari, "Nan-sō shoki no Ō An-seki hyoka ni tsuite." On the many attempts to remove Wang entirely from the Confucian temple see Ch'eng Yuan-min, "Wang An-shih P'ang fu-tzu heng szu miao-t'ing kao," *Wen shih che hsüeh pao* 27 (1978):115–144.

34. *Ch'ao yeh tsa chi*, 2, 3:8a–8b (reprint, pp. 363–364). Cf. Schirokauer, "Neo-Confucians Under Attack," pp. 180–181.

This imperial eclecticism helps explain, I think, why the emperor was persuaded to support Su Shih, for Su was certainly willing to claim that his ideas could include all three teachings. In 1170 the Court granted Su the extremely honorable posthumous title of Wen-chung (Cultured and Loyal), hitherto bestowed only upon Ou-yang Hsiu and later to be denied Chu Hsi.[35] In 1173 the Court promoted the late Su to Grand Preceptor (rank 1A), and the emperor wrote a preface to Su's literary collection. The documents issued on these occasions make clear that Su was to be seen as a model for all literati.[36] Under Hsiao-tsung in 1169 another effort to replace Wang with the Ch'eng brothers in the Confucian temple was rejected, but in 1177 a proposal to honor Fan Chung-yen, Ssu-ma Kuang, Ou-yang Hsiu, and Su Shih there was nearly carried out.[37] It is clear that Su still had a respectable audience and could serve as a plausible role model.

Chu accused the Court of using the ruler to turn education officials and, through them, the literati against true learning. With dismay and anger he noted the use of examination questions that treated the Ch'eng, Wang, and Su learnings as three partial teachings; they called upon students to explain how the limited contributions of each could together form a more complete whole. Chu could not accept the idea that the learning of Wang or Su could define the true method and goal of learning for all literati. Nor would he allow the second possibility that his learning was an addition, a partial contribution to a whole that included the ideas of Wang and Su. Thus, faced with adherents of Wang and Su and proponents of compromise and synthesis Chu felt compelled to dispute his version of Mencius's Yang and Mo.[38]

The Wang Learning

One consequence of the success of Neo-Confucianism was the demise of Wang An-shih as an intellectual model for literati. But in the twelfth century he still appealed to many. I describe Wang's learning here to show why it was possible for high-minded literati to accept Wang's claim to know the true method and goal of learning and why, for Wang, true learning demanded political action.[39] I will then examine Chu's critique of Wang.

---

35. Li, *Tao ming lu* 8:2a–6a (reprint, pp. 285–292).

36. These documents are included as front material to Su's *Ching chin Tung-p'o wen chi shih lüeh* (Peking: Wen-hsueh ku-chi, 1957).

37. Li, *Tao ming lu* 8:9a–10a (reprint, pp. 299–301).

38. Chu Hsi "Ch'eng chün Cheng-ssu mu piao" (1191) 90:15b.

39. The following account of Wang An-shih's views refers directly to Wang's writings. Many issues in these pieces have been addressed elsewhere. I am particularly indebted to Ts'ai Shang-hsiang, *Wang Ching-kung nien-p'u k'ao* (reprint, Peking: Jen-min, 1973); K'o Ch'ang-i, *Wang An-shih p'ing chuan* (Shanghai: Shangwu, 1933); Hsiao Kung-ch'üan, *Chung-kuo cheng-chih ssu-hsiang shih* (Taipei: Chung-hua wen-hua, 1954), pp. 456–461; Liu, *Reform in Sung China*; and Lo, "Wang An-shih and the Confucian Ideal of Inner Sageliness."

Wang An-shih on Acting as a Sage and the Affairs of Government. When Wang was given political authority under Emperor Shen-tsung (r. 1067–1085) he had already established his reputation as a principled and cultured man committed to using the ideas of the sages, kings of antiquity, to transform Sung into an integrated social order. At the beginning of his career in 1043 Wang had announced his purpose when he wrote "learning to be a sage" gives men a shared identity, for the "speech and conduct of sages are uniform."[40] In 1066 he had not changed. "Learning, learning; it should unify all those who learn." "But those who act as literati today, while they know they should learn, do not know why [and how] to learn . . . . To arrive at the sages' relationship with the Way of Heaven, this is that to which all those who learn ought to devote themselves."[41] Toward the end of his career, when some had come to see Wang as a sage and guide to the modern goal of "unifying morality," he produced his *Explanations of Characters* to aid Heaven in "the revival of Our Culture" by producing "this [book] from which instruction and learning must begin. For those able to know these [explanations] will have nine-tenths of the ideas of morality."[42]

But morality, the sages, and learning did not have the same meaning for Wang and Chu Hsi. Wang uses "the way of the sages" (*sheng jen chih tao*) and "the policies of the former kings" (*hsien wang chih cheng*) interchangeably. His sages and former kings brought order to the world through governing and his vision of true learning reflects this. "Now if it is so that, when one orders the world without employing the means with which the sages ordered the world, [the world] will never be ordered, then to be a literatus but not cultivate the means with which the sages brought about order is not how to be a literatus."[43] Ideally all "the means of ordering the world: community rituals and agriculture, the choosing of worthies and judicature, and the nurturing of both principled and broadly talented men and specialized talents" will originate in learning and schools. For "the world cannot be without government and teaching for a single day." In the ideal school "every thing the literatus hears and sees, day and night, will be the ways with which to order the world and the state."[44]

Literati should learn in order to be like the sages, who created an intergrated social order in antiquity. Civilization began with the sages' spiritual insight into human commonality and the spontaneous processes through which things came into being. On this basis the sages structured institutions that enabled men to continue heaven-and-earth, the way of

40. Ts'ai Shang-hsiang, "T'ung hsüeh i shou pieh Tzu-ku" 2:47.

41. Wang An-shih, *Wang An-shih ch'üan chi* (Shanghai, 1935; reprint, Taipei: Ho-lo), "T'ai-p'ing chou hsüeh chi" (1065).

42. Wang An-shih, "Hsi-ning tzu shuo" 25:149, "Our Culture" (*ssu wen*) is from *Lun yü* 9:57.

43. Wang An-shih, examination question, 24:145.

44. Wang An-shih, "Tz'u-hsi hsien hsüeh chi" 27:166.

heaven, and what was so-by-itself (*tzu jan*).[45] They continued to exercise this special holistic insight into the underlying coherence of things when necessary in later generations. Wang explains:

> Coherent order is the way of heaven. To give coherent order [to things] is the way of man. Heaven decreed sages to give coherent order [to things], but the sages necessarily examined the past and completed themselves and then applied what they had learned to affairs to benefit the world. If it was not the appropriate moment, they did not put the Way into practice without reason.

For Wang, putting the Way into practice implied making changes.[46]

The periodic reform of institutions was necessary, even in antiquity, to reestablish an integrated order. Later sages thus built on the earlier institutions, rather than beginning all over again, and they sought to make them accommodate the changes that had occurred since the previous systematization. Civilization was a cumulative accomplishment. The sages' "method was to apply the four techniques of ritual, music, punishment and policy" to the affairs of their time using their special insight.[47] To act as a sage thus meant to reform and elaborate upon the coherent order of the past to include the new. Wang's Confucius was like this; he "systematized the complete model (*fa*) for the world."[48] Rites and music are examples of how they gave social structure to the inchoate commonality of man and established social harmony.[49]

Learning to act as a sage requires that literati begin by studying the institution and models the sages created in order to understand why their works formed coherent and inclusive systems. Literati should not begin by seeking the holistic intuition of the sages. "If one speaks of the wholeness of the Way then it is present everywhere and it does everything. It is something those who learn cannot rely upon, yet they must keep their minds on it."[50] Wang believes there is a natural integrated order of things, which in theory it is possible to perceive. His writings on human nature, however, clearly show that he did not believe men were endowed with a common set of values or principles that could tell them how to act. Although true order has a real basis, independent of consciousness, men can only know it from the cultural tradition.[51]

The sages' words and deeds are still accessible. Their "teachings on how

45. Wang An-shih, "Ta jen lun" 41:126; "Chih i lun" 41:127; "Lao tzu" 43:142.
46. Wang An-shih, "Chin hung fan piao" (1077) 8:71.
47. Wang An-shih, "Lao tzu" 43:142.
48. Wang An-shih, "San sheng-jen" 39:99; "Fu-tzu hsien yü Yao Shun" 42:130.
49. Wang An-shih, "Li yüeh lun" 41:122, cf. "Ch'ien chou hsüeh chi" 26:155.
50. Wang An-shih, "Han Ch'iu-jen shu" 28:3.
51. See his various discussions of human nature and sentiment: "Yüan hsing" 43:144; "Hsing shuo" 43:145; "Hsing ch'ing" 42:134; "Tsai ta Kung Shen-fu Lun yü Meng-tzu shu" 28:5.

to achieve order and their commands" constitute the beginning of the literary tradition.[52] The Classics, in particular the Rites [*Institutes*] *of Chou*, make it possible to understand the sages' systems and institutions.

> When the Way is present in the affairs of government there are positions for the noble and humble, there is order to the first and last, there are numbers for the many and few, and there are times for the slow and fast. To systematize and employ them depends upon models (*fa*), to extend and practice them depends upon men. No time was better than [the reign of King] Ch'eng of Chou for having men adequate to take responsibility for institutions and institutions adequate for carrying out the models. Those of its models which can be applied to later ages and those of its forms which appeared in records are most complete in the book the *Institutes of Chou*.[53]

Although in antiquity students imitated the sages and held to their forms, this will not work in the present when students try to save the world.[54] Modern learning, the enterprise of realizing the way of sages in the present, requires following the intentions of the sage' institutions rather than their forms. Indeed, true literati learning aims to teach men how to think like sages, that is, to think of how the diverse and complex modern world can be restructured into a coherent, yet dynamic, order.[55] Wang insists that he combines an understanding of the ideas of the Classics with knowledge from later and contemporary sources.[56]

Many have treated Wang's ideas and the political program known as the New Policies as a response to fiscal, military, and social crises. But Chu Hsi, whose world was no less threatened, responded quite differently with a call for moral renewal rather than institutional reform. For Wang, realizing the goal of learning and acting as a sage meant seeking to restructure society through the "affairs of government." He did not believe literati could attain that goal merely through self cultivation. The only reason to "correct oneself," he wrote, was to be able to "correct others,"[57] and the reason for learning "for oneself" (*wei chi*) was to gain the ability to do things "for others" (*wei jen*).[58] Nor could literati work toward this goal through the pursuit of cultural accomplishment, for literature was only justified as a tool for aiding the age.[59]

---

52. Wang An-shih, "Yü Tsu Tse-chih shu" 33:49.
53. Wang An-shih, "Chou li i hsü" 25:147.
54. Wang An-shih, "Yü Ting Yüan-chen shu" 25:32. The intent is laudable, however; see "Ta Sun Chang-ch'ien shu" 32:39.
55. This is, I think, one of the central ideas in Wang's famous ten-thousand word memorial (Wang An-shih 1:1). See also "Shu hung fan chuan hou" 46:168; "Ni shang tien cha-tzu" 3:26.
56. Wang An-shih, "Ch'ü ts'ai" 44:152; "Ta Tseng Tzu-ku" 29:17.
57. Wang An-shih, "Ta Wang Shen-fu shu" 28:7.
58. Wang An-shih, "Yang Mo" 43:141.
59. Wang An-shih, "Shang jen shu" 33:47; "Ch'ü ts'ai" 44:152; "Ta Wu Hsiao-tsung" 30:24.

Chu Hsi on Wang's Learning and the Affairs of Government.   Like Chu Hsi, Wang An-shih believed he had integrated "heaven " and "man." "If one knows heaven but does not know man he will be uncivilized," Wang wrote "If one knows man but does not know heaven he will be false."[60] Unlike Chu Hsi, however, Wang thought this unity was realized through the affairs of government rather than the cultivation of moral conduct.

From the beginning of Southern Sung advocates of Ch'eng learning had attacked Wang and his learning, blaming him first for the loss of the North and then using him to attack Ch'in Kuei and his policies. Chu Hsi claimed to want to end the polarization of politics, and he thought to accomplish that by providing a judgment to which both supporters and critics of Wang would be able to agree.[61] He was critical of Wang's critics; they had not seen Wang's true and fundamental errors and thus had incorrectly judged right and wrong.[62]

Chu redefined the real nature of Wang's error and value in order to show that true learning was applicable to the affairs of government as well. Wang himself had believed this, of course, but many suspected that Chu and those around him had a vision of learning that encouraged literati to abrogate their political responsibility. Chu's own career suggests that such suspicions were not groundless.[63] The title given to the seventh chapter of *Reflections on Things at Hand*, "On Serving or not Serving in Government, Advancing of Withdrawing, and Accepting or Declining Office," indicates that Chu's school did not think good men were obligated to serve in government.[64]

Chu accomplishes this by making three claims. First, he agrees that the New Policies were disastrous in their consequences. Because this was widely accepted, Chu needs only to agree to the proposition in general that they were "the source of all the calamities of the age."[65] However, Chu also contends that there was a crisis in the 1060s that demanded reform in the affairs of government and that, because of the failure of the New Policies, it continues to exist in his own times. The ideal of institutional renewal was and is appropriate.[66] Second, he claims that the ideal goals to which Wang's policies aspired were in fact correct. Third, he asserts that Wang's learning was fundamentally incorrect; thus, Wang was incapable of understanding how to go about realizing those goals in practice since his methods were wrong. This argument allows Chu to conclude that only those who really

---

60. Wang An-shih, "Li lun" 41:121.

61. Chu Hsi, "Ta Chang Yüan-te" 62:3b.

62. Chu Hsi, *Chu tzu yü lei ta-ch'üan* (hereafter cited *Yü lei*). (Kyoto: 1668; reprint, Chung-wen ch'u-pan she) 130:6448; Chu Hsi, "Tu liang Ch'en chien-i i mo" 70:6b–7a,12a–12b.

63. This has been demonstrated by Schirokauer, "Chu Hsi's Political Career."

64. *Chin ssu lu*, tr. Wing-tsit Chan.

65. Chu Hsi, "Tu liang Ch'en" 70:6b–7a, 8a–9a; "Ta Wang shang-shu" 30:7a–7b.

66. Ishida Hajime, "Shu Ki no kinei zengokan," *Gunma daigaku kyōikugakubu kiyō* 30 (1980):67–68. Chu Hsi, "Tu liang Ch'en" 70:9a–9b.

understand the true goal and method of literati learning will be able to accomplish institutional reform without bringing on disasters.

Chu credits Wang with a loftiness of purpose: he aspired to laudable goals. For example, Wang believed in the rectification of names; that is, government should set standards and duties and society should obey.

> Men say that Wang An-shih brought about disaster with his ideas about rectifying names. But Confucius spoke of the rectification of names so how can they say that when Wang An-shih talked about it he was incorrect. If the names had actually been rectified it would have been much better.[67]

Similarly some held that Wang's policies were harmful because he aspired to make morality uniform. Chu rebuts this, too:

> To make morality uniform was the policy of the former kings, it was not a personal idea of Mr. Wang's. Why do you fault it? If you said this to the Duke of Ching [i.e., Wang] he would simply laugh at you and say, "This is precisely because you, Sir, do not understand morality." I fear you would have nothing to say in reply.[68]

Critics who complained that Wang had "changed the ancestral precedents [of the dynasty] and carried out the policies of the Three Eras" had also missed the point. Certainly, Chu replies, changing the ancestral precedents was a necessary task; the Ch'engs and Su had seen this as well.

> As for saying that Wang An-shih took from afar matters from the Three Eras which were unclear and not subject to investigation and forced them into practice, this is not knowing that the policies of the Three Eras were dispersed over wood and bamboo [slips]. Although there are chronological differences the Way is without [differences in] past and present.[69]

Moreover, these ancient policies provide essential knowledge in the necessary organization and priorities of government: "It is up to us to understand and illuminate them. Why should they not be practiced?"[70]

Wang correctly made the Classics the material in literati learning. "Wang Chieh-fu's *Principles of the Three Classics* [*Odes, Documents, Rites of Chou*] certainly were not the ideas of the sages. Nevertheless, he made those who learn know that which integrated them."[71] In fact, Chu hoped to compile a collection of the good points in these commentaries.[72] Chu even defended Wang for elevating the *Rites of Chou* and rejecting the *Spring and Autumn Annals*.[73] Morever, Chu did not accept the criticism that Wang had drawn

---

67. *Yü lei* 128:6388.
68. Chu Hsi, "Tu liang Ch'en" 70:13a.
69. Ibid., 70:8a, 9b.
70. Ibid., 70:10a.
71. *Yü lei* 109:5581.
72. Ibid., 130:6448–6449.
73. Chu Hsi, "Tu liang Ch'en" 70:10b–11b.

heavily on previous commentators, failing to be completely original; "former *Ju*" ought to be used to help men understand the original intention of the sages. Wang's errors were due to his unwillingness to submit to the discipline of learning from the Classics in a true manner; he was unable to "distinguish right and wrong in his ideas."[74] As a consequence,

> What An-shih called the *Rites of Chou* was simply his choice of what agreed with his own ideas. He took advantage of his high reputation to persuade the many. He was not truly interested in antiquity. If he were truly interested in antiquity then the basis of investigating rulership, the task of appealing to worthies, the policies for nurturing the people, the methods for improving customs—all of which antiquity called matters of priority and urgent concern—why did he not give them the slightest attention and instead so concern himself only with resources, wealth, the military and punishments? The greatest basis was not correct. The names were correct, but the content was wrong; the order of priorities was reversed.[75]

The problem, to put it simply, was that "Chieh-fu's learning was incorrect; inadequate for expressing the sages' ideas."[76] Wang lacked the true understanding of the Way necessary to practice true learning.

> I myself hold that knowing the Way is basic. If one knows the Way his learning will be pure. If his learning is pure his mind will be correct. It will appear in his conduct of affairs and be expressed in his words. As for Mr. Wang, when he began learning he apparently wished to surpass Yang [Hsiung] and Han [Yü] and match Yen Hui and Meng [K'o]. He had no deviant intent at first. But because he was unable to know the Way his learning was not pure. When he put his mind to affairs he drifted into deviancy. Moreover, thinking he was right, he relied on gross forced interpretations to conceal [the fact]. This is why he stands accused before the sages.[77]

By not knowing the Way Wang ended up "taking what Lao [Tzu] and Buddha called *tao* to be the Way."[78] He was thus unable to put literati on the right track:

> When Mr. Wang gained political [authority] he understood that not knowing the Way was the problem with the customary learning [of the time]. But not knowing that his learning was inadequate for knowing the Way he then confused the real substance of [the Duke of] Chou and Confucius with the semblance of Buddha and Lao [Tzu]. Although the New Learning promoted [the study of] the principles of the classics and removed poetry [from the examinations] the faults of those engaged in learning instead grew worse.[79]

---

74. Ibid., 70:11b.
75. Ibid., 70:10a. Cf. Ishida Hajime, "Shu ki no kinei zengokan," pp. 73–74.
76. *Yü lei* 109:5581.
77. Chu Hsi, "Ta Wang shang-shu" 30:10a.
78. Chu Hsi, "Yü Tung-lai lun Pai-lu shun-yuan chi" 34:21a.
79. Ibid., 34:22b.

Because Wang did not know the true nature of the Way, he was unable to comprehend the "principles of the way" (*tao li*); thus, all he did was in some way incorrect.[80] As a consequence, he gave too much meaning to phenomena of secondary importance—for example, his concern with institutions[81] and his attempt to discover a system of meaningful principles in the structure of written characters.[82] Because he was unable to "understand principle clearly," he was compelled to force his interpretations onto the Classics, and, being unable to truly understand the Classics, he could never use them to turn back and know their reality in himself.[83] It is not surprising that Wang mistakenly thought that an integrated social order was ultimately based on a mystic intuition of the whole. "He regarded the sayings of Buddha and Lao [Tzu] as the mysterious Way and took ritual and law and changes in affairs as the rough traces. Precisely this was Mr. Wang's most profound error."[84] Wang's learning made it more difficult for men to find the real basis. "He separated inner and outer, he divided mind and phenomena, he caused the constancies of the Way not to be employed in the world." Instead, he offered political programs that contrary to Wang's claims, had no true foundation. "His priorities for ordering the world were all falsehoods drawn from his personal ideas." "Wang An-shih, through errors in his learning, brought defeat to the state and harm to the people."[85]

Yet Wang An-shih was doing what had to be done, and Shen-tsung was the rare ruler who wanted his minister to practice the way of the sages. Although Wang and the emperor were both men of extraordinary ability, the ruler was misled by his minister. If the emperor had let a "true *Ju*" take charge, things would not have turned out badly. Pushed by his students, Chu agrees that "If [Ch'eng Hao] Ming-tao had done it, it certainly would not have resulted in any disorder."[86]

Chu's discussion of Wang An-shih is marked by a contradiction. On one hand Chu lauds Wang's attempt to use state power and institutions to realize the Way in society. But, on the other hand, he contends that if Wang had truly understood the Way, which for Chu involves knowing that men possess moral principles innately, Wang would have given priority to moral cultivation rather than relying on institutions to transform the world. Chu takes both positions because he is using his view of Wang to argue that true learning can include the affairs of government. He aims to persuade literati that self-cultivation, morality, and knowing the Way are basic to successful political action and that only men who share the goals and methods of true

80. *Yü lei* 130:6444–6445.
81. Ibid., 130:6445–6446.
82. Ibid., 130:6449–6450; cf. Chu Hsi, "Tu liang Ch'en" 70:11a.
83. Chu Hsi, "Tu liang Ch'en" 70:11b.
84. Ibid., 70:10b.
85. Ibid., 70:12a.
86. Ishida Hajime, "Shu ki no kinei zengokan," pp. 65–77; cf. *Yü lei* 127:6336–6337, 130:6439–6444; questioned on Ch'eng Hao, 130:6443.

learning can be effective politically. Chu is capturing politics; that is, he wants to establish that his particular definition of literati learning is in fact basic to the political responsibilities of the literati and can, contrary to the claims of those who think self-cultivation turns literati away from service, guide the transformation of society into an integrated social order. Chu cannot accept the synthetic view that treats politics and self-cultivation as activities that are compatible but judged by separate standards.

> Now morality and the innate endowment [*hsing ming*] are related to government and institutions as refined to coarse and root to branch. Although there seems to be a separation [between them] they are the outside and inside [of one thing]. Like the shadow [i.e., government] following a form [morality], they can never be separated. To say now that An-shih's learning only apprehended something in government and institutions while with regard to morality and the innate endownment he did not do enough is not to understand that if he is inadequate in this regard he will not have any place from which to apprehend what is correct [for government].[87]

Chu overlooks the fact that a learning that stresses personal morality will be unlikely to tell men to look for institutional remedies to social problems. Instead, he seeks to demonstrate that his vision of true learning can guide all literati in both managing the affairs of government and maintaining cultural traditions.

The Su Learning

Su Shih was not a moralist. In Chu Hsi's time Su's "learning" had greatest influence in the area of *wen*, literary style and the various forms of composition in prose, poetry, calligraphy, and painting with which literati demonstrated their cultural accomplishment. Lü Tsu-ch'ien, for example, recognized Su (and his father and brother) as a model prose stylist by including him in *The Key to the Ancient Style [in Prose]*. Hu Tzu, author of a major compendium of comments on literature, called him one of the four greatest poets of the T'ang and Sung.[88] Chu was well aware of Su's popularity. Su's works were studied by examination candidates, but they were also admired by some of Chu Hsi's own followers and allies. Lü Tsu-ch'ien and Wang Ying-chen, for example, continued to defend the idea, put forth first in late Northern Sung by literati anxious to unite the opposition to the New Policies, that one could learn *tao* from Ch'eng I and *wen* from Su Shih. Ch'eng Hsün, a disciple of Chu, even argued that Su's understanding of *tao* was fully compatible with true learning.[89]

---

87. Chu Hsi, "Tu liang Ch'en" 70:10b.

88. Hu Tzu, *T'iao-hsi yü-yin shih p'ing ts'ung hua hou chi* (Peking: Jen-min wen-hsueh, 1984), preface.

89. Goyama Kiwamu, "Shu Ki no So-gaku hihan, josetsu," *Chūgoku bungaku ronshū* 3 (1972):29–34, discusses Chu's correspondence with these three men on the Su learning. Ch'en Hsün wrote a *Chronology of the Three Sus* in ten *chüan*. Only its section cited for criticism by Chu Hsi is currently known; see Chu Hsi, "Tu Su shih chi nien" 70:13a–16b.

Chu Hsi recognized that Su learning was not merely a style of cultural accomplishment. His Su also had ideas about literati values and the Way. Su and his followers had claimed this as well.[90] A brief account of Su's understanding of what it meant to learn to "act as a sage" will establish what Chu was trying to dispute.

Su Shih on Acting as a Sage and Learning from Culture. For Su the qualities that gave a man's cultural accomplishment real value—be it in prose, poetry, calligraphy, or painting—were also those qualities that he thought defined the "way of the sages." *Wen* of real value, Su contended in 1059, was the spontaneous composition of men who were "unable not to do it," just as "for the sages of antiquity there were also things which they created when unable to stop themselves."[91] Such works, external expressions of what the individual had accumulated within, were not calculated to satisfy existing standards, yet they had real value and could serve as models for others. However, while Su lauded the individual's ability to bring (new) things into being by evaluating his own and others' works, he also insisted that this had to occur in the context of broad learning and careful analysis of past accomplishments. He charged his disciples with the task of making it possible for others also to see "the great whole of past men."[92]

Believing that sages had composed works that served the common interest because they learned from the past and drew on their own creativity, Su could see his approach to cultural accomplishment as the best way for modern literati to learn how to act as sages themselves. Su wrote extensively on the way of sages and learning. His three essays on the meaning of *Chung yung*, as the idea of centrality and commonality and as a text (*The Doctrine of the Mean*), written for the prestigious decree examination of 1061, claim to reveal the process "to which the Duke of Chou and Confucius adhered in order to become sages."[93] The sage, Su writes, not only knows what tradition

90. Ch'in Kuan, for example, argued that it is wrong to appreciate Su only for his literary work because Su's "way" is "most profound in matters of nature, decree, and self-apprehension." See *Huai hai chi* (SPPY ed.), "Ta Fu Pin-lao chien" 14:1a. Cf. Ch'ao Pu-chih, *Chi le chi* (SPTK ed.), "Chi Tuan-ming Su kung wen" 61:469; and Su Ch'e's biography of Su Shih in *Su Tung-p'o chi* (Kuo-hsueh chi-pen ts'ung-shu), 1.2.0.49–50.

91. *Su Tung-p'o chi* 2.5.24.35, "Nan hsing ch'ien chi hsu."

92. For Su's accounts of his own works as illustrations of this see *Tung-p'o t'i pa* (TSCC ed.), "Tzu p'ing wen" 1:15; *Ching chin Tung-p'o wen chi shih lüeh*, "Ta Chang Chia-wen shu" 47:799; *Su Tung-p'o chi* 3.8.9.18, "T'ai hsi i shou." He also judged the works of others in this light. See *Su Tung-p'o chi* 2.6.30.11, "Ta Chang Wen-ch'ien shu" where he speaks of seeing the "great whole"; *Tung-p'o t'i pa* "Pa Chün-mo fei pai" 4:78, for calligraphy, "Shu Wu Tao-tzu hua hou" 5:95, for painting; *Ching chin Tung-p'o wen chi shih lüeh* "Ta Hsieh Min-shih shu" 46:779–81, for poetry and prose.

93. *Su Tung-p'o chi* 6.18.6.45, "Chung yung lun, shang." The importance of these essays is noted by Su Ch'e, who credits his brother with discovering what earlier men had failed to understand; see 1.20.0.49. The essays have been translated and discussed in relation to Su's

requires, but he also understands that the demands of tradition are fully commensurate with his own sentiments. He is thus able to "delight in" them and practice them without forcing himself.[94] He comes to see that all civilized traditions are outgrowths of human sentiment and circumstances (*jen ch'ing*) because he recognizes that fundamentally men desire not to be one-sided. Ritual and its demands, for example, were the sages' response to the human sentiment that something was needed to balance the human desire for ease that, if taken to an extreme, would result in men "lying naked in bed all day." The development of civilization through history is the cumulative result of attempts to balance a society tending to an extreme.[95] Acting as sages means practicing this approach as a method of keeping the world centered and serving the common good. "Centrality" is a relative state, created by men who go from one pole to the other, thus creating a "center" in between that can define "commonality" for society at that particular moment.[96]

Su elaborates on the implications of this relativistic, pragmatic, and situational way of sages in his other essays from 1061. In politics, where the aim is to unify the world, men should be willing to use either "benevolence and righteousness" or "deceit and strength," depending on the situation and their own capabilities.[97] In morality one should, like Su's Confucius, avoid "making petty theories, thus opening the way to [dogmatic understandings] of right and wrong." To be like Confucius is to "revert to perfect appropriateness."[98] Confucius could be "appropriate" in his responses because he was neither narrow nor exclusive; instead, he took all human experience into account, from the institutions of the former kings to the customs of the barbarians, without becoming confused.[99] Those who learn thus should avoid trying to define moral absolutes and instead seek to understand how what the sages did was anchored in common human sentiment and circumstance.[100]

However, in 1061 Su does claim that his understanding of *Chung yung* has universal validity. It is the key to analyzing all affairs because it accounts for the way things actually take place. "What antiquity meant by *chung yung* was simply to express the pattern (*li*) of the ten-thousand things."[101] He thus

---

approach to culture by Christian Murck, "Su Shih's Reading of the *Chung yung*," in *Theories of the Arts in China*, ed. Susan Bush and Christian Murck (Princeton: Princeton University Press, 1983), pp. 267–292.

94. *Su Tung-p'o chi* 6.18.6.45–46.
95. Ibid., 6.18.6.46–47. Cf. 6.18.7.51–52, "Ch'in shih huang-ti lun."
96. Ibid., 6.18.6.47–48.
97. Ibid., 6.18.10.72, "Chu-ko Liang lun."
98. Ibid., 6.18.8.60, "Tzu Ssu lun."
99. Ibid., 6.18.8.61, "Meng K'o lun."
100. Ibid., 6.18.10.72–73, "Han Yü lun."
101. Ibid., 6.18.1.8, "Ts'e lüeh, ti ssu."

claims that his "learning," which encourages relative judgment and creative response, is the only true learning.

> For fifteen years, since I began to engage in learning until today, I have held that the real problem in learning is to be without self-interest and that the real problem in being without self-interest is to comprehend the patterns of the ten-thousand things. Therefore even if I want to be free of self-interest, it is impossible unless I comprehend the pattern of all things. To consider good whatever I myself like, and to consider bad whatever I myself dislike—to have confidence in myself on this account is to be deluded.
>
> This is why, abiding in darkness and silence, I peruse the transformations of all things. I fully exhaust the patterns [involved when things are acting] by themselves, and I judge them in my mind. Whatever is not in accord with this, even if it was called a theory of wise men in antiquity, will not be accepted.[102]

In claiming the right to judge the value of all other views he is, I think, announcing his intent to be a sage himself.

In the 1070s Su's response to Wang An-shih and the New Policies still reflected these attitudes. In contrast to those who faulted Wang for concerning himself with institutional and social renewal at the expense of following traditional models or encouraging moral cultivation among those with power, Su objected that the New Policies ignored the realities of human circumstance and conduct.[103] In addition he objected strongly to the effects of Wang's learning on literati learning in general. The curriculum Wang created—commentaries on the three Classics and the *Explanations of Characters* and the use of the examinations to test that curriculum—struck Su as an attempt to impose intellectual uniformity at the expense of individuality and creativity.

> When literati are not able to complete themselves the problem lies with customary learning. The problem with customary learning is that it debilitates a man's talents and blocks a man's eyes and ears. He recites the sayings passed on by his teacher [i.e., Wang An-shih] about how characters are constructed and follows the customary style of composition [*wen*]. He thinks that with only a few tens of thousands of words the enterprise of acting as a literatus is fully attained.
>
> Now learning is to illuminate pattern and *wen* is to transmit commitment. Thought is to comprehend what he learns. *Ch'i* is to get his *wen* across. The men of the past directed their eyes and ears and extended what they saw and heard; this was how they learned. They set right their commitment and perfected their *ch'i*; this was how they spoke.
>
> The learning of Mr. Wang is exactly like striking prints: they come out

---

102. *Ching chin Tung-p'o wen chi shih lüeh* "Shang Tseng ch'eng-hsiang shu" 41:723.

103. This attitude permeates his 1071 memorial on the New Policies; *Ching chin Tung-p'o wen chi shih lüeh* 24:369–396, partially translated in Wm. Theodore de Bary et al., *Sources of Chinese Tradition* (New York: Columbia University Press, 1960), pp. 426–431.

according to the block; there is no need to decorate them before they are usable. How could they ever be made into rare and precious instruments.[104]

To his follower Chang Lei, Su wrote:

> There has never beeen such a decline in literature as today. The source of this is really Mr. Wang. Mr. Wang's *wen* is not necessarily not good. The problem is that he likes to make others the same as himself. Ever since Confucius was unable to make others achieve the same benevolence as Yen Hui or the same courage as Tzu-lu, it has not been possible to move others toward each other. Yet with his learning Mr. Wang would make all under heaven the same. The beauty of the soil is the same in bringing things into being; it is not the same in that which is brought into being. Only on barren, brackish soil are there yellow reeds and white rushes as far as the eye can see. This, then, is the "sameness" of Mr. Wang.[105]

To this Su added the criticism that if literati believed that Wang's curriculum alone was sufficient for knowing the Way they would have to suppose that other knowledge had no real value. This, he claimed, had led them to seek validation for the teachings in the realm of the ineffable and mysterious and to turn to Taoism and Buddhism for answers.[106]

In response to Wang's influence over literati learning and in an effort to determine how literati ought to act when, like Su Shih, they were denied access to political authority, Su proposed, in the late 1070s and 1080s, a broader view of the way of sages. He now began to argue that his vision of the way of sages included the realms of both "things" and the mysterious and ineffable. Men could bring into being things of real value if individuals learned how to hold these two realms together. He now claimed that one who learned had to master traditions and understand "things" yet also draw on *tao* as the inexhaustible source of all ideas in the self (parallel to the source of all things in creation).

The mature Su thus supposed there was an ultimate source of values. He could claim that all things were "one" and that each and every thing had value as an aspect of that "one." He could also claim that learning was meant to shift back and forth between the one and the many thus bringing into being in the realm of the many new things, rooted in the intuition of the one inexhaustible source of creativity.

He sought to persuade literati to this view in many ways. His occasional writings from the period often stress the need to detach oneself from things and to avoid becoming entangled by social expectations while maintaining

---

104. Ibid., 4.12.8.43, "Sung jen hsü."
105. Ibid., 2.6.30.11, "Ta Chang Wen-ch'ien shu."
106. *Ching chin Tung-p'o wen chi shih lüeh* "Liu-i chü-shih chi hsü 59:905–906; "Jih yü shuo" 57:931–932; "Yen kuan ta pei ko chi" 54:864.

an interest in and responding to the social world.[107] At the same time he pointed out that men could only transcend social demands if they found something real and transcendent within themselves.[108] There were, he reminded his friends, two sides. One had to accept the demands of both the mysterious and the defined, seeking both ultimate transcendence and mundane knowledge.[109]

Su Shih's commentaries on the *Documents* and *Change* were his most formal and elaborate means of making his views known; his commentary on the *Analects* exists only in remnants. These commentaries also allowed him to claim that his understanding of what it meant to act as a sage applied to the sages of antiquity as well and were fully parallel with the processes of heaven-and-earth. He could claim that he had accommodated both "heaven" and "man." His explanation of the "Great Plan" chapter of the *Documents*, for example, argues that *huang chi* (august correctness) was not merely about the ruler but intended for all men to practice.[110] It means to be totally open and inclusive (*huang*), as a men who is centered within, and exactly appropriate (*chi*), as a man who responds to what is without.[111] The Way will be realized when all those who learn combine internal tranquility with external appropriateness and clear perception with spontaneous response.[112]

Su's commentary on the *Change*, a project begun by his father, makes him more philosophical than he may want to be. He claims that his understanding of this text exposes the "great whole of the Way"[113] but denies that he must show that the particulars of the text always fit the more important "general outline."[114] The true importance of the text is its teaching that men must transcend duality and attain the "one"; only then will they be able to "use duality to aid the people."[115] With attainment of the "one" comes real spontaneity and the ability to let others develop in their own individual ways so that "everything realizes its heavenly principle."[116] From this position he can "use the circle to adapt the square and use spirit to apply knowledge."[117] He can be creative.

107. For examples of this attitude see Ibid., "Chang shih yüan t'ing chi" (1079) 49:816; "Ch'ao-jan t'ai chi" (1074) 50:829; "Shu Liu-i chü-shih chuan hou" 60:992. *Tung-p'o t'i pa*, "Pa chih-hsi shan-chu sung" (1079) 1:9; *Su Tung-p'o chi* 2.6.32.32, "Ssu t'ang chi" (1079).

108. *Ching chin Tung-p'o wen chi shih lüeh*, "Wen yang sheng" 60:986; and "Huang chou An-kuo ssu chi" (1084) 54:872; *Su Tung-p'o chi* 2.6.32.32, "Ssu t'ang chi" (1079); *Tung-p'o t'i pa*, "Pa Ssu-ma Wen-kung pu-ch'in ming hou" 1:12.

109. *Tung-p'o t'i pa*, "Pa ching-hsi wai chi" 1:10, and Su Shih, *Tung-p'o chih lin* (Hsüeh chin t'ao yüan) "Hsüeh t'ang chi wen P'an Pin-lao" 4:6a–10a.

110. Su Shih, *Tung-p'o shu chuan* (Hsüeh chin t'ao yüan) 10:10a.

111. Ibid., 10:7a–7b.

112. Ibid., 7.10:8a–9b.

113. Su Shih, *Su shih i chuan* (TSCC ed.) 8:179.

114. Ibid., 3:60.

115. Ibid., 7:153, 8:180.

116. Ibid., 1:4, 7:155.

117. Ibid., 7:168.

But the "one," the source whence all else arises, should be attained, Su insists, by working "upstream" through what has already been created toward the source. In examining things one must understand the principles (*i*) that explain the pattern (*li*) of the results effected (*te*) when the one source (*tao*) is producing. But, having this knowledge, he must then go beyond it and intuit the "one" as the inexhaustible source of inspiration and creativity within himself. When he then creates something with that inspiration he uses the knowledge acquired from past men, yet he draws more from the source than his predecessors. His work will thus combine the realm of past experience with the realm of the mysterious; it will be composed on the foundation of historical experience, yet it will be a product of *tao* as well.[118]

As I shall show in Chu Hsi's critique, Su holds that there is an ultimate source of values to which men can gain access. This source—*hsing, ming,* or *tao*—can never be reduced to a particular set of values. To be a sage is to be in constant touch with this source, but because the source is inexhaustible one can only be sure that a sage will do things which synthesize past accomplishments while bringing into being the new. Su's understanding of how true learning should proceed makes "learning from culture" or the pursuit of cultural accomplishment a more valuable activity than "moral conduct" or the "affairs of government," although he certainly believes that this process applies to those areas as well. Cultural pursuits offer individuals the best opportunity to be creative while absorbing the lessons of the past. Creative works proves to Su that he is actually in communion with the real source and that whatever he does has true value in spite of what others may say. One of his most famous accounts of his own writing alludes to this.

> My *wen* is like a spring with a ten-thousand-gallon flow. It does not care where, it can come forth any place. On the flatland spreading and rolling, even a thousand miles a day give it no difficulty; when it twists and turns about mountain boulders it takes on the shape of what it encounters. Yet it cannot be predicted. What can be predicted is that it will always travel where it ought to travel and stop where it ought to stop, that is all. Even I am not able to predict the rest.[119]

Chu Hsi did not think this attitude was conducive to true learning.

Chu Hsi on Su Learning and Cultural Accomplishment. Chu Hsi thought Su Shih was dangerous. Su lacked self-discipline; his example encouraged self-indulgence and creativity. Su's writing was clever and insubstantial; his work taught men to value the artful and appealing. Su's ideas were fundamentally incorrect; he led men to misconceive the basis of true learning.[120] In

---

118. Ibid., 9:189–190.
119. *Tung-p'o t'i pa*, "Tzu p'ing wen" 1:15.
120. Chu Hsi's critique of Su Shih has been noted by Ishida Hajime, "Shu Ki no kinei

fact, Chu is rather torn in his attitude toward Su Shih. He attacks him harshly yet admires him grudgingly, just as he at times detests the tendency of literati to enjoy cultural pursuits while finding himself attracted to them as well. Chu criticized state schools for letting literati think that literary accomplishment was proof of achievement in learning, yet he also objected when literati tried to apprehend the Way without working carefully through the appropriate classical texts. He argued that men like Su separated *wen* from *tao*, yet still he claimed that Su's *wen* had the power to infect men's minds and turn them away from moral cultivation. Chu Hsi faced a contradiction not entirely of his own making. Chu saw *wen*, in the sense of the cultural tradition, as necessary to the literati tradition and vital to true learning (it included the Classics, for example); but *wen* was also the greatest threat to the success of true learning, for it provided an alternative definition of what it meant to be a literatus. It is not hard to see in this the tension Chu Hsi experienced in his own life between the pull of cultural pursuits, which he had been raised to appreciate, and his desire to establish himself as the teacher of the Way to the world.[121]

Why was Su Shih so attractive, yet so dangerous? Chu's allies tended to believe that Su had been on the "right side" and thus was necessarily "safe," for he had been an outspoken critic of the New Policies and his work had been proscribed along with Ch'eng I's. Chu objects that Su had supported the New Policies at first and only later contradicted himself. If his Su had become chief minister, the consequences would have been far worse.[122] Su, his students pointed out, had faulted Wang for "wanting to make others the same as himself." Chu saw Su as failing to see that if one were right he ought to want to make others agree.[123] Su's *wen*, some thought, was not incompatible with Ch'eng I's *tao*. But Chu saw Su as an enemy of Ch'eng, a leader of those who had belittled Ch'eng and ridiculed the truth.[124] Of course, given Su's lack of reverence or seriousness, his self-indulgence, and his lack of interest in being completely correct, his hostility toward a man of principled decorum such as Ch'eng I was to be expected.[125]

Chu had an even more difficult time persuading his audience that something was wrong with Su's *wen*, in part because Chu Hsi also admired it. "Tung-p'o's natural character was lofty and clear, his proposals and discus-

---

zengohan," pp. 28–29. His letters to Lü Tsu-ch'ien, Wang Ying-chen and Ch'eng Hsün have been discussed and translated in part by Goyama Kiwamu, "Shu Ki no so gaku hihan, jojetsu," pp. 29–35. In large part Chu's approach to Su is an aspect of his approach to "culture" and literature, a subject discussed by Chang Chien in *Chu Hsi te wen-hsüeh p'i-p'ing yen-chiu* (Taipei: Shang-wu, 1969), and by Ch'ien Mu in *Chu tzu hsin hsüeh an* 5:151–190; cf. 3:602–604 on Su and Wang.

121. Li Chi, "Chu Hsi the Poet," *T'oung Pao* 58 (1972):63–66, 101–102, in particular.

122. *Yü lei* 130:6440, 139:6889–6890, 130:6475.

123. Ibid., 130:6449.

124. Chu Hsi, "I-ch'uan hsien-sheng nien-p'u" 98:21b–22a.

125. *Yü lei* 130:6471, 6474–6477, 6469–6473.

sions have qualities others cannot match. [Works] such as his commentary on the *Analects* also have good points."[126] In various manners Chu Hsi repeatedly allows that Su wrote better than most, frequently had good ideas, and had insight into the classics.[127] Chu himself commits what he usually regarded as an egregious error in others: he treats Su as a model for engaging in *wen* and Ch'eng as the authority for understanding *tao*. "Writing became perspicuous only with Ou-yang, Tseng [Kung] and Su, the principles of the Way only with the two Ch'engs."[128] Chu can read pieces by Su and comment: "You cannot read [them] in terms of the principles of the Way, but these two stele inscriptions have real force."[129]

Chu did not always forget his duty. "The general thrust of Su's *wen* is all right, but his work does not bear up under close reading."[130] Su's writing contains internal contradictions: "a dragon's head with a serpent's tail."[131] His writing is artful and clever when it ought to be substantial and careful; 70 percent substance and 30 percent polish is Chu's advice.[132] In early Sung, Chu contends, writing was good and "customs" were positively influenced. Su departed from that tradition and began the trend, current in Chu's time we are told, of clever writing with its pernicious effects on social mores.[133] Chu writes that "Mr. Su's learning is not correct. His treacherous and disrespectful habits enter deeply into men's minds. I have now become fully aware of their harm." And again:

> Mr. Su's learning uses grandly profound and clever *wen* to encourage the tendency toward riskiness and illusion, thus those who have been poisoned by him are unaware of it even when it has penetrated their flesh and bones. Today we must pull up the root and block the source and unify that to which those who learn listen.[134]

But to root out Su Shih or, as Chu also puts it, to "cut off" the transmission of his learning, it is necessary to persuade literati that they should not appreciate Su's cultural accomplishment.[135] Lü Tsu-ch'ien had written to Chu that there was no need to attack Su Shih as if he were a Yang or Mo, for Su could be taken merely as a literary man and those who engaged in true learning could appreciate his skill while remaining immune to his disease.[136] Chu responds to this defense of synthesis and compromise:

126. Ibid., 130:6478.
127. Ibid., 130:6478–6484, 6492; 139:6894, 6898, 6914.
128. Ibid., 130:6894; cf. Chu Hsi, "Ta Ch'eng Yün-fu shu" 41:12a.
129. *Yü lei* 139:6898; cf. 139:6900.
130. Ibid., 139:6899.
131. Ibid., 139:6900.
132. Ibid., 139:6917; cf. 139:6903–6905.
133. Ibid., 139:6889–6890; cf. 139:6894.
134. Chu Hsi, "Yu Jui Kuo-ch'i" 37:18a, 18b.
135. Chu Hsi, "Ta Ch'eng Yün-fu shu" 41:12a.
136. *Tung-lai hsien-sheng Lü t'ai-shih wen chi, ch'ih tu* (Hsü Chin-hua ts'ung-shu, ed.) 1:7b.

You wrote that Mr. Su cannot be seen as a Yang or Mo in relation to Our Way, but that he is in the stream of T'ang Le and Ching Ch'a [famous poets of ancient Ch'u]. I saw recently that old Mr. Wang [Ying-chen] shares this idea.[137] I think this is an egregious failure to examine principle. Are *wen* and *tao* in fact the same? Or are they different? If there are things outside of *tao* then those who engage in *wen* can think and say whatever they want and there is no harm to *tao*. But if there is no thing outside of *tao* then as soon as there is anything which does not agree with *tao*, then there is harm to *tao*, although this harm may be more or less immediate and more or less deep.

I too once enjoyed the *wen* of Ch'ü [Yuan], Sung [Yü], T'ang, and Ching. Then I reflected that although their language was luxuriant their substance merely had two themes: sorrow and dissolution. By reciting these words everyday I was being transformed by them. Was this not doing great harm to the mind? I then shut them away and did not dare look at them again . . . . If [in Mencius's time] these had circulated among those who learned everywhere, if they had been transmitted within families and men had recited them, as Mr. Su's ideas are today, then could one who acted as a Mencius have desisted [from disputing them]?

How much more so with the learning of Mr. Su. Above he talks about the nature and decree, below he discusses government. His words are not merely [those of] Ch'ü, Sung, T'ang, and Ching. Those who learn begin by wasting a morning because they enjoy his *wen*. But after a time it gradually penetrates their bones and they cannot free themselves. Its destruction of talent and defeat of customs is considerable.[138]

Su also accused Wang Ying-chen of separating *wen* from *tao* because he "only takes the literary composition and does not go on to judge the right and wrong of its principles." If only he would "use *wen* to discuss *tao*, then *wen* and *tao* would both be obtained, and he would thread them on a single strand."[139]

Judging what Su says is more important than appreciating how he says it, Chu writes to Wang, because Su has opinions on issues central to true learning. As a writer Su "moves in and out of being and nonbeing, he ties together moral principles," and "pointing out the advantageous and injurious, he gets at human circumstances." The dangers inherent in Wang An-shih's learning became obvious once the effects of his policies were apparent. But Su never held such power; one must understand through analysis of his words that "if [his learning] had been put into practice at the time and had flourished as had Mr. Wang's, then it would have led to far greater disasters." A careful reader will see that "in discussing *tao hsüeh* (learning that reveals the Way) [Su] missed the great basis, and in discussing affairs he favored opportunism and scheming."[140]

137. Wang had written to Chu that Su's writings were safe as long as one did not use them in seeking the Way; see *Wen ting chi* (SKCS, ed.) 15:7a–7b.
138. Chu Hsi, "Ta Lü Po-kung" 33:4b–5a.
139. Chu Hsi, "Ta Wang shang-shu" (1169) 30:11a.
140. Ibid., 30:7b–8a. In this letter Chu is speaking of both Su Shih and Su Ch'e.

Su's learning is dangerous because "although there seem to be differences between his learning and that of Mr. Wang they are alike in not knowing *tao* yet thinking they are right." Chu can account for all he dislikes about Su on the grounds that Su does not know the Way, for he knows that one who knows *tao* will be pure in learning and correct in mind and all that he says and does will reveal that.[141]

When Su does say something of real value it is the haphazard achievement of the skilled writer who "waits until he is composing *wen* and then searches for a *tao li* (moral principle) to put into it. This is his major failing . . . . He does not first understand *tao li* and then compose *wen*, so the great basis is always off." Su is forced into this position by his inability to see that there is a "single basis" (*tao*) rather than a "dual basis" (both *wen* and *tao*). Had Su understood *tao* he would not have put *wen* first.[142]

Su understands something; otherwise, his values would not threaten true learning. The problem is that what he has at his foundation is not what Chu Hsi knows to be *tao*. Chu uses his critique of Su Shih's commentary on the *Change*, the first of his "Disputations of Adulterated Learnings" from 1166, to show that Su has a fundamentally incorrect understanding of *tao*.[143]

Chu Hsi makes his point by quoting those passages from Su's commentary in which Su puts forth his views on man's innate endowment, *tao*, and their relationship. He does not distort Su, who consistently argues that if a term such as *tao*, *hsing* (the nature), or *ming* (the decree) is used to refer to the one source of all value it cannot be defined by any values that comes from it. Chu responds by pointing out that this source is endowed in us; we can know it fully, and we can use language to talk about it. Thus, for example, Su states that "The 'origin's' [yüan] functions cannot be seen. What can be seen are merely the ten-thousand things, which have drawn on it for their beginning." Chu replies, " 'Origin' is like spring to the four seasons . . . . It is the starting point of Heaven-and-Earth's creating and nurturing . . . . It is always visible, but only one who knows *tao* can recognize it."[144] Similarly Su contends that yin and yang cannot be equated with the things they create, although they cannot be said not to exist merely because we cannot see their semblance. Chu replies that everything is clearly yin and yang, and they can be known.[145] But yin and yang cannot be equated with *tao* (the ultimate source whence things have arisen) because, in Su's view, *tao* as the source of yin and yang must be something greater and farther removed. For Chu this is not so.[146]

141. Ibid., 30:10a.
142. *Yü lei* 139:6915–6916.
143. Chu Hsi, "Tsa hsueh pien" 72:16a–23b. The "Tsa hueh pien" (72:16a–46a) includes critiques of Su Ch'e's *Lao tzu* commentary, Chang Chiu-ch'eng's *Chung yung* commentary, and Lü Pen-chung's *Ta hsueh*, commentary.
144. Ibid., 72:16b–17a.
145. Ibid., 72:19b–20a.
146. Ibid., 72:20a–20b.

Su applies the same argument to human nature. Good, he writes, is an effect of the nature; it is not the same as the nature. One cannot say the nature is good. Similarly benevolence and knowledge are merely names men have given to particular qualities which, like all human abilities, come from the nature, but it is wrong to say that the nature is benevolent or knowing. However, for Chu, the nature defines what is good, and benevolence and knowledge are real and primary qualities innately present in it.[147] Su sees the nature's relation to *tao* as similar to the relation between hearing and sound, a mysterious relation in which it is not clear which comes first or whether they are two or one. But, Chu notes, the nature and *tao* are surely one thing. We can be certain we know our nature, and thus we can be certain we know *tao*.[148]

Chu thinks Su is missing the point entirely when he says either that "to discuss the nature in terms of what is manifest is [to discuss] the semblance of the nature" or that, while all men have the nature and cannot get rid of it, no matter how good or bad they are, it remains ineffable. The nature can be known, Chu objects; it has a source, and it can be spoken of. To fail to see its special qualities is to make man an animal.[149] Su arrives at the conclusion that *ming* (the "decree") is a forced name for the unselfconscious realization of the nature. It cannot be understood as a "decree" that commands one to be a certain way; it is not Heaven's order to man, and it has no fixed content. Chu's *ming* is a decree; it tells man what he ought to be; and men can and should become conscious of it.[150]

Su Shih's supposition that *tao* is something ineffable and inexhaustible does not lend itself easily to the idea that the primary responsibility of a literatus is to cultivate his ability to conduct himself morally. Su was not particularly interested in the problem of moral conduct. But his position can justify cultural pursuits as a way of learning; through them he can draw on *tao* and share his achievements with others. Cultural accomplishment can have real value, and a man can be morally responsible without being a moralist. Chu Hsi remains committed to the existence of a concrete moral endowment which men can aim to know completely and realize in practice. Cultural pursuits are not basic to his enterprise. They can only have real value if they are expressions of true moral cultivation, and only morally committed men can bring about a real culture. He is unwilling to allow the compromise represented by the great "ancient style" writers from Han Yü through Su Shih, in which those who learn combine a mastery of the cultural tradition on its own terms with a sense of moral responsibility for the common good. In the following conversation he insists that *wen* can have value only if it is entirely in service of the Way.

147. Ibid., 72:21a–21b, 22a.
148. Ibid., 72:21b–22a.
149. Ibid., 72:18a–18b.
150. Ibid., 72:18b–19b.

Ch'en said, "[The first sentence in Li Han's preface to Han Yü's works,] '*Wen* is a device for holding the Way together' [to which you are objecting], could we not take it like this: the Six Classics are *wen* and all that is said here is this *tao-li* [of the Classics]?" [Chu Hsi] said, "Not so. That *wen* flows out of *tao*. How could there be *wen* which instead held the *li* of *tao* together? *Wen* is *wen* and *tao* is *tao*. *Wen* is just like something to accompany the rice. If one uses *wen* to hold *tao* together he is taking the root as the branch and the branch as the root. Can it be done? Those who did *wen* after [Han Yü] were all like that." He went on to say that Su's *wen* harmed the true Way more than Lao [Tzu] and Buddha. "For example when the *Change* calls "the advantageous [*li*] the harmony of moral principles" he explains that if moral principles are without profit [*li*] they will not [beget] harmony; therefore [he finds it] necessary to understand the Judgment [of the *ch'ien* hexagram] in terms of profit to make it accord with human sentiments and circumstances.[151] In such cases he not only misses the basic purport of the sages' words, he also obscures their minds." The teacher then put on a straight face and said, "If I had lived then I certainly would have disputed with him." But then he laughed, "And he would not have taken me seriously."[152]

But in the twelfth century Chu Hsi was taken seriously.

CONCLUSIONS: WHAT CAN THIS TELL US ABOUT CHU HSI?

We can use terms from Chu Hsi's critique of Wang and Su to explore three ways in which Chu was redefining literati learning. First, we can see Chu as a middle figure between extremes represented by Wang and Su. Chu's desire to see himself as a modern Mencius, disputing the new Mo Ti and Yang Chu, is suggestive here. His Wang An-shih does remind us of Mo. He wants uniformity and absolutes and is eager to use political power to enforce what is good for everyone. Su Shih is not unlike Yang. He encourages men to be what they want to be and believes the whole world would be better if every man were an individual. Chu Hsi has some of both without the extremes of either. He values Wang's effort to establish uniform standards, but he objects that Wang's basis for defining standards was false. He appreciates Su's unique talent and creativity, but he insists that individuality must have a concrete moral basis. To recognize that Chu's teachings do contain both the universal and holistic and the individual and creative does not mean that Chu was trying to be whole by incorporating the "partial" positions of Su and Wang; rather, it seems to me that this widespread tension in literati thought of the time is also present in Chu's school. The idea of unitary principle and principles for everything is universal and holistic. It allows people to hope that the right and wrong of everything can be defined. Because people can understand principle only through their own personal efforts, which will differ as the qualities of individuals differ, there is room for creativity and individuality.

151. Chu is referring to *Su shih i chuan* 1:5 and 1:4.
152. *Yü lei* 139:6887–6888.

Although part of Chu's success in promoting his true learning was his ability to accommodate such tensions and synthesize both the ideas of his chosen predecessors and the larger trends in literati thought, I am not sure he was as accomodative as he can be made to appear. This is evident when we look at his attitude toward the various fields of literati activity. Chu clearly connects Wang with the idea of using the affairs of government to benefit society and Su with the idea of using learning from culture to cultivate oneself. He understands that politics and culture have their own standards for measuring achievement and that many think it is possible to have great achievements in these areas without being scrupulously moral in one's personal conduct. But Chu, who believes Wang and Su were lacking in personal morality, insists that their lack of moral cultivation means that their achievements are not real. The loss of the North made it easy for Chu to argue this in Wang's case; with Su he must work to persuade people that his writing has evil consequences. Chu's ideal position is unambiguous: only a real commitment to one's own moral cultivation can provide the basis for achievements of true value in politics and culture. Later history suggests that this effectively encouraged the view that the official's first duty was to provide society with a moral model and that the only good literature was that conveying a moral message. Such attitudes were not unknown before the twelfth century, but they do not seem to have been very strong among the elite.

In spite of Chu Hsi's claims to the contrary, he shared a number of similarities with Wang and Su. All claimed to know the Way and thought their ideas about the goal and method of literati learning were anchored in their understanding of the Way. All supposed an ultimate and unitary source of value, believed things could form a harmonious and integrated order, and demanded that those who learn seek to understand the realm of "things." Nevertheless, Chu Hsi's redefinition of literati learning involves a real transformation at the center of literati intellectual life. Again we can use Chu's terms to describe the shift. In a comment on Ou-yang Hsiu's introduction to the "Treatise on Rites and Music" in the *New T'ang History* Chu provides a useful explanation of the difference.[153] He argues that the shift in literati values, which the true learning represents, can be understood as a reintegration of *wen* with *tao*. For the sages, Chu explains, *wen* was merely all the external expressions of their internal substance. But, with the decline of Chou, men gradually shifted their attention to *wen* (external forms) and lost the basis in *tao*; thus, while *wen* flourished with the hundred schools, the Han writers and the post-Han belletrists, *tao* gradually lost all real substance and became separated from *wen*, the mainstream of intellectual endeavor. For

153. Chu Hsi, "Tu T'ang chih" 70:2b–5a; cf. *Yü lei* 139:6915–6916. Ou-yang Hsiu and Sung Ch'i, *Hsin T'ang shu* (Peking: Chung-hua shu-chü, 1975) 11:307.

Chu Hsi true learning reintegrates *wen* and *tao* while Wang and Su learnings leave them separate.

Using these two terms in a somewhat different sense I suggest that, prior to the rise of Chu's school, the cultural tradition had been the source for men who, like Wang and Su, sought to define ideas capable of guiding all literati. With Chu Hsi this changes, and the Way becomes conceived of as something that exists independent of the cultural tradition; its existence is confirmed by the processes of nature rather than the records of culture. In Chu's view the Way, understood most immediately as principles of personal morality innately present in all, must be the basis for understanding and using the cultural tradition to provide models for both the affairs of government (Wang) and personal cultural accomplishment (Su). Cultivating a moral self is the only possible basis for realizing the literati responsibility for maintaining the political order and transmitting the culture; it is also the lens through which Chu Hsi and his school redefined the intellectual history of China from antiquity to the twelfth century. Thus, one might reduce the shift brought about by Chu Hsi's redefinition of literati learning to a change in this central relationship in literati thought. Wang and Su represent the era that asked how literati ought to relate to the cultural tradition; Chu Hsi introduces the new question of how literati should relate to transcendant principles of morality.

Clearly Chu could not countenance either Wang or Su learning, for both failed to make moral cultivation primary; nor could he allow that Wang and Su had made partial contributions that followers of the true learning should incorporate. To do so would have meant that political and cultural achievements could be measured by separate standards, and that would surely have implied that the moral principles of Chu's learning were of value only in the limited sphere of moral conduct and were not universally relevant. Yet Chu Hsi was quick to insist that the primacy of personal morality did not mean that literati who learned correctly could forsake their political and cultural duties. Indeed, the critique of Wang and Su suggests that in some measure Chu's success in redefining literati learning depended upon his ability to explain how men, intent upon "acting as sages," could continue to take responsibility for state and culture.

SEVEN

Chu Hsi's Aims as an Educator

Wm. Theodore de Bary

Chu Hsi thought of himself, like Confucius, as the bearer of tradition rather than as the founder or originator of a new doctrine. Content with the modest role of teacher and transmitter, he was a scholar who devoted himself to editing texts, compiling anthologies, and writing commentaries on the Classics instead of writing treatises to advance his own theories. Indeed, by modern Western standards he would probably have to be put down as the next thing to a "mere translator." Yet, his own modesty notwithstanding, to Chu, as to Confucius earlier must go the credit of instigating a virtual revolution in education.

Confucius, for his part, accomplished this mainly by the force of his personal example as teacher and scholar, reflected in the *Analects* (a book *about* him, not *by* him) and in a personal following that tried to emulate his example. On this score Chu Hsi, too, as a teacher, was hardly less magisterial or commanding in influence. but if I identify him more particularly as an educator, it is because, besides being a great teacher devoted to learning, he was a thinker and an official concerned with the process of education and its institutionalization. For the title of educator in this sense Chu qualifies by virtue of his extraordinary contributions to defining a new Confucian curriculum and a new educational process, seen in both the official schools and private academies that came to prevail throughout East Asia in the second millennium.

Chu's aims in education, which gave that process a clear direction, coherent method, and substantial content, projected a comprehensive vision on his part. To call him visionary would no doubt be overstating or misrepresenting the case, if by this one meant looking into the future and anticipating what its new requirements would be. For Chu it was enough simply to face the present and its compelling needs without speculating on possibilities more remote. As he said, in stressing the need for attending to what was near at hand, "We must only proceed from what we understand in what is near to us and move from there. . . . It is like ascending steps, going from the first to the second, from the second to the third and from the third to the fourth. . . ."[1]

But if Chu did not look to the future to redeem the past, as was often the case in the West, or put his faith in the millennium as the ultimate realization of the human struggle, he nevertheless did expect his step-by-step method to lead upward to some definite goal. This vision he put before his students and readers, offering a comprehensive view of the human reality and, insofar as his reading of past and present would vouchsafe it, a human ideal to be striven for.

In this chapter I shall try to articulate that vision and, where possible, bring out its historical significance in light of the factors that shaped his situation and defined the educational problem for him. Some of these factors Chu himself would have been conscious of, others perhaps not. In any case, before discussing Chu's ideas themselves, I state briefly here what I consider these factors to be. I do so only in summary form because I rely on other chapters in this volume to deal with these developments more fully and more authoritatively than I.

1. The first point to note is that education, both public and private, had become a major issue in Sung politics and thought well before Chu Hsi's time. It was already high on the Neo-Confucian agenda.

2. The new importance of education in the Northern Sung arose in significant part from the expansion of the civil bureaucracy at the inception of the dynasty and from the increased demand this created for persons with requisite learning and skills.

3. Economic development and diversification, as well as rising affluence, although perhaps regionally uneven, and increased leisure for cultural pursuits, provided alternative outlets for the educated. The literati had options other than government service, and they weighed seriously the relative value and priority of the alternatives that the society and culture afforded them. Prime among these was teaching.

4. Expansion of the economy and technological advances created a wider base for the support of education, leading to an increase in the number of schools and academies. Over time the growth of local, semiprivate academies outpaced that of public schools. With this tensions arose, but less from rivalry between public and private endeavors than from either political pressures and literati involvement with them or resistance to state control and the distorting effects of the civil service examinations on education.

5. Schools, especially academies (*shu-yüan*), centered on teachers and

---

1. Li Ching-te, comp., *Chu Tzu yü-lei* (reprint, Kyoto: Chūbun shuppansha, 1979) 49:5a; translation from Wing-tsit Chan, *Reflections on Things at Hand* (New York: Columbia University Press, 1967), p. 94; hereafter cited *Things at Hand*.

collections of books. Hence the spread of printing was bound to have a significant impact on them, as on cultural activity in general. This significance is concisely stated by Carter and Goodrich in reference to the printing of the Classics by Feng Tao in 953:

> The printing of the Classics was one of the forces that restored Confucian literature and teaching to the place in national and popular regard that it had held before the advent of Buddhism, and a classical renaissance followed that can be compared only to the Renaissance that came in Europe after the rediscovery of its classical literature, and that there too was aided by the invention of printing. . . . Another result of the publication of the Classics was an era of large-scale printing, both public and private, that characterized the whole of the Sung dynasty.[2]

A development of such epochal proportions confronted the literati with both new opportunities for the dissemination of knowledge and new problems about how this technological change would affect the learning process. Neo-Confucians became much occupied with the nature and significance of book learning. On a wider scale it became a question of which traditional teachings would take advantage of the new printing technology. Earlier Buddhists had been quick to do so,[3] but Ch'an Buddhism, the dominant form among artists and intellectuals, had declared its independence of the written word (pu li wen-tzu).[4] Two questions emerged: which of these teachings would want to reach a larger public through the use of this medium? And how would they adapt their teaching method to it? Even among Neo-Confucians there was not a single answer, but most found themselves compelled to deal with such issues as the relative importance of reading, lecturing, and discussion. "How to read books" was much discussed in the Ch'eng-Chu school, and Chu Hsi's Reading Method (Tu-shu fa) was widely disseminated. Ch'ien Mu has said that no one contributed more to this development than did Chu Hsi—indeed Chu stands out above all others.[5]

6. Sung Confucians saw Buddhism and Taoism, and especially Ch'an, as still exerting a powerful influence on men's minds. Syncretists minimized the conflict between the Three Teachings by assigning them respective spheres of influence: Confucianism, governance; Taoism, physical culture; Buddhism, mental culture. Neo-Confucians tended to reject such formulae as too facile, on both theoretical and practical grounds. Among the latter was the educational issue: the practical impossibility of mastering three such dispa-

---

2. Thomas Carter and L. C. Goodrich, The Invention of Printing in China and its Spread Westward (New York: Ronald Press, 1955) p. 83.

3. See Carter and Goodrich, Invention of Printing, pp. 26–28, 38–51, 57–58, 63–65.

4. See Wm. Theodore de Bary, ed., The Buddhist Tradition (New York: Modern Library, 1969), p. 208.

5. Ch'ien Mu, Chu Tzu hsin hsüeh-an (Taipei: San min shu-chü, 1971) 1:160–67.

rate systems at once and, given the need to choose among them, the primacy of the moral imperative that claimed priority for humane learning and called for new types of scholarship to meet the increasingly complex problem of secular society.

7. At the same time Buddhist spirituality remained a formidable challenge to Neo-Confucians, who felt a need to provide an alternative compatible with secular goals and lay life. Managing all this in one lifetime was for them clearly a matter of educational priorities.

8. Ch'an Buddhism had its own problems. Its masters worried about the decline of monastic discipline. Having forsworn language as an adequate means of communicating essential truth, in the Sung and Yüan periods they faced a dilemma as in the codification of monastic rules and training. In the end leading monks compromised their own principles by compiling rules, keeping records of dialogues and koans, and publishing them, lest authoritative traditions lapse altogether.[6] Thus, they too accommodated themselves, albeit halfheartedly, to the rising tide of printing and booklearning, yet without ever addressing education as a distinct social and cultural value.

These developments touched Chu Hsi's own life and significantly affected his thought. As the son of a scholar-official, he naturally gravitated toward the same combination of scholarly activity and public service as his father. At the same time Taoism and Ch'an Buddhism appealed to his religious instincts. Thus, as a young man he successfully competed in the civil service examinations while also pursuing and actually experiencing in some vague manner a mystical enlightenment. Thereafter, searching for a way to reconcile the rival claims of scholarship, official service, and the spiritual life, he laid the problem before his teacher Li T'ung.[7]

The answer, which he eventually had to work out for himself, lay in "learning for the sake of oneself." It was a Confucian answer, expressed in the language of the *Analects'* "learning for one's own sake, rather than for others.'" (14:25). "Learning for others," Chu interpreted primarily in terms of the civil service examinations and worldly success, which for him should properly be subordinated to the goal of true self-understanding. Yet the priority he gave to self-understanding in the Confucian sense represented Chu's response also to Buddhism's insistence on giving top priority to the problem of self and no-self, or seeing one's "original face."

In *The Liberal Tradition in China* I have discussed "learning for the sake of oneself" as the underlying theme of Chu Hsi's thought from his early years to

6. See Jan Yun-hua, "Chinese Buddhism in Ta-tu," in *Yüan Thought*, ed. Hok-lam Chan and Wm. Theodore de Bary (New York: Columbia University Press, 1971), p. 388, 397; and Chun-fang Yü, "Chung-fen Ming-pen and Chan," in ibid., 448–449; also "Introduction," pp. 15–22.

7. See Okada Takehiko, "Shu-shi no chichi to shi," in *Chūgoku shisō ni okeru risō to genjitsu* (Tokyo: Mokujisha, 1983), pp. 391–392.

the end of his life as a teacher.[8] In this chapter, however, I wish to distinguish between "learning" in the most general as well as the most personal sense and education as a practical, public, and institutionalized activity. In the mind of Chu Hsi, of course, the two were inseparable: education in the sense of schooling or organized instruction ought also to serve the purpose of "learning for the sake of oneself," but for my purposes here the focus will be on the public aspect.

Chu's basic approach is made clear in the most widely disseminated of his writings—his preface and commentary to the *Great Learning*. Because later tradition followed Chu's recommendation that the *Great Learning* should be studied first among the canonical texts, the gateway and guide to all learning, education in Neo-Confucian schools was almost always premised on the principles so concisely enunciated in the opening pages of that work. Here then I summarize the main points.

First, in his preface, Chu puts forward as the basis of his educational philosophy the central Neo-Confucian doctrine of the moral nature inherent in all men, how it is affected by everyone's physical endowment (i.e., one's actual condition), and by what means the ruler should enable everyone to recover his original good nature and fulfill it.

Among relevant means, schools are most important. Chu believed he had a model for emulation in the schools established by the sage-kings of remote antiquity that reached down to the smallest village and provided education for everyone from the age of eight until maturity. To modern minds the adoption of such a system of universal education might seem an obvious course, but in Chu's time its practicability could not be assumed. Earlier attempts to achieve it in the Sung had failed, and the main factor, later cited by Mary Wright, as militating against schools in nineteenth-century China—that "the sons of peasants could seldom be spared from the fields"[9]—would have applied in the Sung as well. Moreover, if economic realities and the chronic fiscal difficulties of Chinese dynasties could render such a plan unlikely to accomplish, there were other less costly educational means to which he might have had recourse. Well-known measures were hardly uncongenial to a Confucian like Chu: instruction in the home or through clan and community organizations, as well as the whole panoply of rituals by which "moral edification" was supposed to be achieved, especially in rural areas. Indeed, on other occasions Chu himself had used these among the great array of persuasive means by which he would accomplish the people's uplift.

---

8. See Wm. Theodore de Bary, *Liberal Tradition in China* (Hong Kong and New York: Chinese University of Hong Kong and Columbia University Press, 1983), pp. 21–24; hereafter cited *Liberal Tradition*.

9. Mary C. Wright, *The Last Stand of Chinese Conservatism* (Stanford: Stanford University Press, 1957), p. 4.

Nevertheless, in this most central of texts and most considered of arguments, Chu puts the school system up front—not just teaching or tutoring, training in the home, official exhortation, or moral transformation through ritual observance—but quite literally and concretely the "establishment of schools" *(hsüeh-hsiao chih she)* and their operation/administration by the government *(hsüeh-hsiao chih cheng)*.[10] He was not just airing a vague notion or uttering a pious hope; he was making a definite point with regard to the institutionalization of universal schooling and the commitment of resources to that end.

Second, another noteworthy feature of the educational system described in Chu's preface is the combination of universality and particularity in its application. Because all men share the moral nature imparted by Heaven, all have a common need to perfect that nature through education. This was, according to Chu's classical model, to be provided for the children of all under Heaven, from the king and his nobles down to the commonest of people in the smallest lane or alley. Although higher education was not similar for all but only for the more talented, these latter were again to be drawn from all ranks of society.[11]

> Such being the case there was no one without an education in those times, and of those so educated there was none who did not understand what was inherent in his individual nature or what was proper to the performance of his own duties, so that each could exert his energies to the utmost.[12]

Egalitarian though it might be with respect to education, this universalistic approach carries no necessary implication of social leveling. Chu, like Confucius in his time, advocates equal educational opportunity but still accepts the need for a social structure and a hierarchy of authority based on merit. His point is that every individual should have the chance to realize his full human potential, given the limits of his individual endowment, situation in life, or station in society. All possess a common nature, but each has an individualized form, to be perfected by schooling and self-cultivation.

A question may arise, however, about whether this self-cultivation actually aims at an individualized result rather than at conformity to a social norm. It might be argued, for instance, that even though Chu recognizes differences in individual capacity and disposition, the process of self-perfection is meant to bring the individual into line with some ideal type. Insofar as this might be interpreted as an idea or model external to the self to which one should measure up, practically it could mean that self-correction and self-discipline would simply subordinate one's own interest to that of the

---

10. Chu Hsi, *Ta-hsüeh chang-chu*, in *Ssu-shu chi-chu*, (Chung-kuo tzu-hsüeh ming-chu chi-ch'eng ed., Taipei, 1979), preface pp. 1, 2.

11. Ibid., p. 1b.

12. Ibid., p. 2a.

group, expressed in such terms as "subduing self and restoring riteness" *(k'o-chi fu-li)* or overcoming one's own selfishness *(ssu)* and conforming to the common good *(kung)*.

This latter dichotomy, opposing individual selfishness to the common good, was indeed a basic criterion of ethical conduct in Neo-Confucianism, yet it has sometimes been overdrawn, as it was by early Neo-Confucians of a rigoristic bent and later by those who reacted against this ascetic extreme. The former seemed to regard any desires at all as selfish and to call for their total suppression, while the latter, on the same count, attacked Neo-Confucianism as allowing no room for individual self-expression or self-satisfaction. Enough extreme cases can be found to support this view; thus, one cannot dismiss the problem of religious renunciation or even masochism as negligible for Neo-Confucianism.[13] Still most Neo-Confucians remembered well the story of Confucius's scolding Tseng Tzu for carrying filial submission almost to the point of self-immolation: Tseng Tzu had been weeding some melons when he accidentally cut the roots of a plant. Tseng Tzu's father beat him for this, but when Confucius heard about it he said Tseng Tzu should have gotten out of the way rather than submit to his father's stick. "By quietly submitting to a beating like that, you might have caused your father to kill you, and what unfilial conduct could have been worse than that!"

Chu had in mind this reasonable and moderate view: the health and welfare of the person is primary, and human desires are good except insofar as they conflict with others' legitimate needs and wants. Like Confucius in the *Analects* (6:28), he recognized that everyone had ambitions to achieve something for himself, as well as an obligation to respect that ambition in others.[14] The language Chu uses in the passage just cited affirms as the goal of education that all should have outlets for their capacities in accordance with an understanding of both their own individual natures *(hsing-fen)* and their proper roles in society *(chih-fen)*. Here the term *hsing-fen* refers to the concrete, individualized nature *(hsing-chih)*,[15] both moral and psychophysical. Thus, for Chu Hsi's educational purposes, the individual is neither reducible simply to a social role nor wholly definable in relation to some abstract norm of conduct. He leaves room here to pursue "learning for one's own sake" as a larger reality encompassing self and others, uniting the Way within and the Way without.

It is appropriate then to read this passage in light of Chu's more complete guide to self-cultivation, the *Reflections on Things at Hand (Chin-ssu lu)*. There Chu quotes Ch'eng Hao's memorial to the emperor, "The essential training should be the way of choosing the good and cultivating the self until the

---

13. See de Bary, *Liberal Tradition*, pp. 24–27.
14. *Lun-yü chi chu*, in *Ssu-shu chi-chu* 3:19b (p. 216).
15. Morohashi Tetsuji, *Daikanwa jiten* (Tokyo: Taishūkan, 1955) 4:10478–73.

whole world is transformed and brought to perfection, so that all people from the ordinary person on up can become sages."[16] Beyond this one need only look to Chu Hsi's concluding chapter in *Things at Hand*, devoted to the "Dispositions of the Sages and Worthies." These "dispositions" refer to the individual natures of the sages and worthies, as does Chu's language in the preface above, and the portraits presented are those of distinct human personalities, not totally self-effacing copies of a sagely stereotype.[17]

In Chu's preface the final point to be noted is how his explanation of civilization's decline since the early Chou period fits in with his formulation of a remedy. Chu sees the disappearance of the sage-kings and end of virtuous rule as further aggravated by a long lapse in the teaching tradition from Mencius until the Ch'eng brothers in the Sung. This is, of course, a view of history also set forth by Chu in his preface to the Mean *(Chung-yung)*, where he propounds his doctrine of the "succession to the Way" *(tao-t'ung)* and highlights the heroic role of the Ch'eng brothers in rediscovering the true Way.[18] Chu reiterates the myth of the heroic teacher here to underscore the need for true education as the key to systematic reform. In dark contrast to the shining light of the Ch'eng brothers, Chu paints a vivid picture of the corrupting effects of his twin nemeses: Buddhism and Taoism on the one extreme and utilitarianism on the other. The latter corrupted mankind by its pragmatism and opportunism, pursuing power and material gain at the expense of moral principles. Buddhism and Taoism, at the opposite extreme, were too transcendental and not down to earth, indeed Chu acknowledges that for loftiness they exceeded even the *Great Learning* yet lacked its moral solidity and practical method.[19] In this situation only the Ch'eng brothers reaffirmed the inherent goodness of man's nature and recognized the true worth of the *Great Learning* as the Classic par excellence, unequaled for its combination of principle and practicality in the nurturing of man's moral nature.

Throughout Chu's preface and commentary to the *Great Learning* this systematic, concrete, and detailed approach to learning is constantly reiterated. Without specific structures and orderly procedures he believes there can be no effective resistance to the moral erosion of Buddhist "expediency" and Taoist nihilism that have left mankind exposed to the opportunism of power seekers and defenseless against the exploitation of autocrats.

This aim—to combine moral principles with well-defined means of instruction—leads Chu to insist on having a school system and sequential curriculum. Not simply because Chu as a traditionalist reveres the Classics

16. Mao Hung-lai, *Chin-ssu lu chi-chu* (Ssu-ku shan-pen ts'ung-shu, 1st series; Taipei, I-wen yin shu kuan, n.d.) 9:5b. Excerpted and abridged from *Ming-tao hsien-sheng wen-chi* 2:2b–3a in *Ech-Ch'eng ch'uan-shu* 55, (Kinsei kanseki sokan ed.) p. 485; Chan, *Things at Hand*, p. 219.
17. See Chan, *Things at Hand*, chap. 14.
18. Chu Hsi, *Chung-yung chang-chu*, preface in *Ssu-shu chi-chu*, pp. 37–43.
19. Chu Hsi, *Ta-hsüeh chang-chu*, preface 2b (p. 4).

does he find merit in a system such as was spelled out in the *Record of Rites (Li Chi)*; there it says that "according to the system of ancient instruction, for the families of a hamlet there was the village school *(shu)*, for a neighborhood there was the community center *(hsiang)*, for the larger districts there was the institute of retired scholars *(hsü)*, and in the capital there was the college *(hsüeh)*.[20]

Nor simply as a loyal follower of Ch'eng Hao does he appreciate the orderly sequence of priorities embodied in the latter's program of universal education, as quoted in *Reflections on Things as Hand*:

> Master Ming-tao [Ch'eng Hao] said to the emperor: The foundation of government is to make public morals and customs correct and to get virtuous and talented men to serve. Tne first thing to do is politely to order the virtuous scholars among close attendants, and all officers, to search wholeheartedly for those whose moral characters and achievements are adequate as examples and teachers, and then seek out those who are eager to learn and have good ability and fine character. Invite them, appoint them, and have them courteously sent to the capital where they will gather. Let them discuss correct learning with each other from morning to evening. The moral principles to be taught must be based on human relations and must make clear the principles of things. The teaching, from the elementary training of sweeping the floor and answering questions on up, must consist in the cultivation of filial piety, brotherly respect, loyalty, and faithfulness, as well as proper behavior and the qualities derived from ceremonies and music. There must be a proper pace and order in inducing, leading, arousing and gradually shaping the students and in bringing their character to completion. The essential training should be the way of choosing the good and cultivating the self until the whole world is transformed and brought to perfection so that all people from the ordinary person up can become sages. Those whose learning and conduct completely fulfill this standard are people of perfect virtue. Select the students of ability and intelligence, who are capable of advancing toward the good, to study under them every day. Choose graduates of brilliant learning and high virtue to be professors at the Imperial University and send the rest to teach in various parts of the country.
>
> In selecting students, let county schools promote them to prefecture schools, and let prefecture schools present them, as though presenting guests, to the Imperial University. Let them come together and be taught there. Each year the superior graduates will be recommended to the government for service.
>
> All scholars are to be chosen to serve on the basis of their correct and pure character, their filial piety and brotherly respect demonstrated at home, their sense of integrity, shame, propriety, and humility, their intelligence and scholarship, and their understanding of the principles of government.[21]

Both examples speak to Chu's sense of the need to bring order, substance,

---

20. *Li chi*, 36 Hsüeh chi (*Shih-san ching chu-shu fu chiao-k'an chi*), (I-wen yin-shu-kuan reprint of Chia-ch'ing 20 [1815 ed.]), 36:3a (p. 649) trans. adapted from James Legge, *Li chi: Book of Rites* (reprint, New York: University Books, 1967) 2:83.

21. Mao, *Chin-ssu lu chi-chu* 9:4b–6a.

and process into a society seen as shapeless and without moorings, drifting aimlessly between anarchic nihilism and coercive despotism.

In the opening lines of his commentary on the *Great Learning* itself Chu sounds the same keynote when he quotes Ch'eng I to the effect that only owing to the survival of this can one know the successive steps *(tzu-ti)* and procedures by which the ancients pursued learning. Chu then proceeds to explain the three guiding principles *(san kang-ling)* of the *Great Learning*. Here, too, structure and direction are emphasized: *kang* represent the mainstays of a net, and *ling* guidance or direction. The first of these guiding principles is to "clarify or manifest bright virtue." referrring to the moral nature in all men, which is inherently clear and luminous but must be cleansed of obscurations if it is to be made fully manifest. The potential is innate but must be actively developed; the process is one of bringing out from within something that has its own life and luminosity rather than imposing or imprinting on it something from without. This Chu calls the "learning of the great man" *(ta-jen)*, which has the ordinary meaning of "adult" but here suggests the fullness of self-development and the grandeur of the moral nature brought to its perfection.

The second guiding principle is to "renew the people" *(hsin-min)*, that is, to assist others to manifest their moral natures through self-cultivation. Here Chu follows Ch'eng I in substituting the word *hsin* (renew) for *ch'in* (to love, to befriend the people). Chu specifically refers to this as "reforming the old," emphasizing active reform and renovation instead of expressing simple goodwill and generous sentiments. The political implication is that the ruler's self-cultivation necessarily involves him in helping the people renew themselves through education.

Third among the guiding principles is "resting or abiding in the highest good"; this means that, by clarifying bright virtue (manifesting the moral nature) and renewing the people, one should reach the point of ultimate goodness and stay there. "Resting in the highest good," Chu explains, means meeting both the moral requirements of each situation and affair and fulfilling one's capability for moral action. At this point one can rest content. Peace of mind has been achieved by satisfying one's conscience, not by transcending the moral sphere.

If I have discounted earlier any idea that Chu Hsi had millenarian expectations or looked to the future to redeem the present, it was partly in view of these three guiding principles. The impulse to renew and reform is there, but it is enough to achieve what is possible in one's own life situation and within one's own limited capabilities. "To be humane is to accept being human" *(jen-che an jen)* as Confucius said *(Analects* 4:2) However, Chu Hsi's underscoring of these three principles at the outset of his commentary has impressed on later generations the need for active renewal and reform, first with respect to oneself and then out of concern for others.

From there the text and Chu proceed to discuss sequential processses, ends and means, "roots and branches," and priorities in learning. Of these, the best known are the "Eight Steps" (*pa t'iao-mu*: items, specifications), consisting of successive steps in self-cultivation and involving a range of cognitive, moral, and social operations. These are probably the most discussed subjects in Neo-Confucian literature, but I shall confine myself to points that have particular relevance to education, differentiated above from learning in general. Much of the *Great Learning* text is less systematic than Chu Hsi would have liked, and he, like Ch'eng I, was at pains to rearrange it, but his interlinear note explaining this reveals Chu's preoccupation with logical order and step-by-step procedures:

> The text of the commentary [by Tseng Tzu] is drawn at random from classics and commentaries in no particular order. It appears to be unsystematic, but nevertheless there is an underlying thread. It is most precise and detailed as regards its different levels and successive phases. . . .[22]

Chu draws particular attention to the first steps in the process of self-cultivation by adding a special note on *ko-wu chih-chih*, most commonly rendered as "the investigation of things and extension of knowledge." Chu's commentary on these terms, however, should alert us to a possible misunderstanding. He says that *ko* (investigation) means to reach or arrive, and he indicates that in this process principles in the mind are brought into contact with principles in things, that is, made present to each other. Because our word "knowledge" is generally understood in objective terms as things known, it is well to note that in Chinese *chih* makes no distinction between knowing and what is known. Chu Hsi comments: "*chih* is to recognize or be conscious of, to project one's knowing, hoping that one's knowing would be fully employed (literally exhausted).[23] The same passage can be read, translating *chih* as "knowledge" instead of "knowing." But in that case it should not be understood as in "a body of knowledge," for to do so would set an impossible goal for "exhausting" learning: One's knowledge would have to be complete. One would need to know everything, instead of simply developing one's learning capacity to the full.

This is a point of some significance for education because it bears on the questions of book learning and the pursuit of empirical research. To what extent should education, in the form of the reading and discussion of books, be conceived as the assimilation of principles *from* things or as the accumulation of factual knowledge? The issue has been read both ways by later Neo-Confucians, some of whom have stressed objective study and others active experiential learning. Chu seems to have allowed for both in his special note on *ko-wu chih chih*:

> "The extension of knowing lies in the investigation of things" means that if we wish to extend our knowing, it consists in fathoming the principle of

22. Chu Hsi, *Ta-hsüeh chang-chu*, 2b–3a (pp. 10–11).
23. Ibid., 2a (p. 9).

any thing or affair we come into contact with, for the intelligent mind of man always has the capacity to know and the things of this world all have their principles, but if a principle remains unfathomed, one's knowing is not fully exercised. Hence the initial teaching of the Great Learning insists that the learner, as he comes upon the things of this world, must proceed from principles already known and further explore them until he reaches the limit. After exerting himself for a long time, one day he will experience a breakthrough to integral comprehension. Then the qualities of all things, whether internal or external, refined or coarse, will all be apprehended and the mind, in its whole substance and great functioning, will be fully enlightened. This is "things [having been] investigated." This is knowing having reached [its limit].[24]

In this passage I have translated *chih* as "knowing" rather than "knowledge" because, even allowing for the ambiguity of the original Chinese, to render it as knowledge in the sense of something known produces an absurdity and flies in the face of other testimony from Chu. Concerning this text Liu Shu-hsien has recently observed:

> When perfection of knowledge is achieved, does Chu Hsi mean that the mind actually possesses empirical knowledge of all things? This is an absurd position, as Chu Hsi freely admits that there are things even the sage does not know. Hence what Chu Hsi means is that when the mind is pure and clear without the obstructions of selfish desires, it cannot fail to grasp the principles of things and respond freely to things as concrete situations call for, and as the human mind is united with the mind of Heaven, it does not exclude anything from its scope and is in that sense all-inclusive. Moreover, since the principles are none other than manifestations of one single Principle, the realization of the substance and function of this Principle will enable the mind to unfold the rich content of the Principle without any hindrances.[25]

As Liu suggests, Chu Hsi seems to be saying that if one pursues study and reflection long enough one's understanding will be enlarged to the point of overcoming any sense of things or others being foreign to oneself, and the student will have achieved an empathetic insight that is both integral and comprehensive (*kuan-t'ung*). One would have developed a capacity for learning and knowing to its limit and thus would be equally at home with oneself and one's world. At this point "learning for the sake of oneself" would have overcome all distinction between self and others.

THE CONDUCT OF SCHOOLS

From the preceding discussion of Chu Hsi's aims in education three main points emerge: (1) the need for a school system reaching the whole popula-

24. Ibid., 6a–6b (p. 17–18).
25. Liu Shu-hsien, "The Functions of Mind in Chu Hsi's Philosophy," in *Journal of Chinese Philosophy* 5 (1978):204.

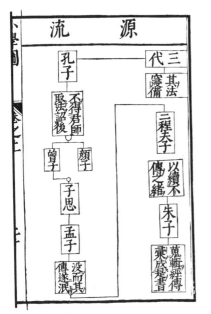 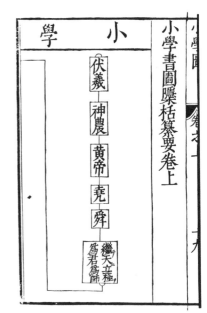

Diagram A. Derivation of Elementary Learning

Fig. 7.1. Illustrations from Japanese Edo period illustrated edition of the *Elementary Learning* (Hsiao-hsüeh) in the Hayashi family collection. (Shōgaku shoto inkatsu sanyō, in *Naikaku bunko kanseki bunrui mokuroku*, p. 298–228). This edition includes pictures and diagrams to illustrate the contents of the *Elementary Learning*. The two diagrams reproduced here sum up the main points of Chu Hsi's preface to the *Great Learning*, linking the two texts and two levels of education. I deal with the same points in the discussion above: The Succession to the Way (tao-t'ung) and the steps by which one takes up learning (ju-hsüeh tz'u-ti) emphasizing a systematic process of education. In Diagram A the lines and commentary illustrate the gap in the transmission of the Way from the time of Mencius to the Ch'eng brothers (i.e., giving the version found in Chu's preface, which leaves out Chou Tun-i and other early Sung figures).

tion, not just individualized instruction for the select few; (2) the need for a well-defined curriculum, adapted at each stage to the student's level of comprehension, maturity, and readiness to take on larger responsibilities; and (3) the importance of having a goal to the educational process and offer the individual a suitable model of the whole person, developing one's potential and exercising one's full capabilities (expressed in the phrase "the whole substance and its great functioning" (ch'üan-t'i ta-yung).

I will now discuss the content and conduct of education as prescribed by Chu Hsi in different institutional settings. Other chapters in this volume do

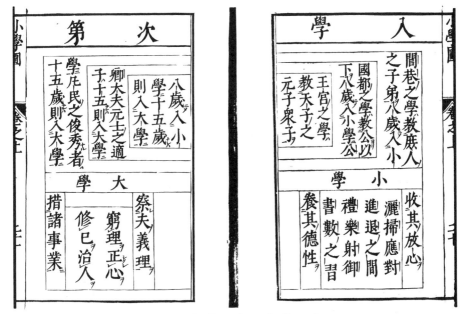

Diagram B. Procedures for Learning

Diagram B consists of two parts, upper and lower. The upper shows the relation of schooling carried on in the villages and feudal capitals to that at the central court, as if in pyramidal form with local schools representing the large base of the common people, state (provincial) schools a higher but less extensive intermediate level, and the school at the capital the apex of the structure; both elementary and higher education is conducted at all three levels. The lower part of the diagram details the content of elementary and higher education; the former emphasizes moral training, ritual observance, and the classic arts, and the latter scholarly and public activities. Overall the impression conveyed is one of a comprehensive, organic process: for the individual, growth from youth to maturity and from lesser roles to greater; for the society, movement from lower to higher forms of organization, and from the periphery to the center. Furthermore, this holistic conception is marked by a notable sense of structure, logical coherence, methodical process, and precision of detail—all characteristics of Chu Hsi's as a whole.

the same in relation to specific schools and academies; here I will try to elicit general principles from those documents most often cited in the later tradition as authoritative guides: Chu's *Reflection on Things at Hand (Chin--ssu lu)*; his "Articles of the White Deer Grotto Academy" *(Pai-lu tung shu-yüan chieh-shih)*; his comments on the "School Rules of Messrs. Ch'eng and Tung" *(Ch'eng Tung erh hsien-sheng hsüeh-tse),* and finally his "Personal Proposals for Schools and Official Recruitment" *(Hsüeh-hsiao kung-chü ssu-i).* Chu Hsi discussed learning, teaching, and schooling on many occasions, a rich body of materials is available for the study of these aspects of his thought. But I believe the texts just cited have been most influential in Neo-Confucian schools of later times.

Reflections on Things at Hand (Chin-ssu lu) centers on the self. It works out from there, through the wider sphere of social activity, toward the goal of learning to become a sage or worthy. In this it follows the basic pattern of Chu Hsi's three guiding principles: from self-cultivation, through social renovation, to attaining and resting in the highest good. Although it has much to say about different aspects of learning, it has surprisingly little to say about schools or how they should be conducted, no doubt because Chu Hsi conceived of schooling essentially in terms of the teacher-student relationship. One can indeed say that the work exudes the atmosphere of the school; much of the text has the quality of teacher-student dialogue and conveys the impression that a scholastic tradition—a disciplined dialogue over the generations—is being perpetuated.

Nevertheless, only the brief chapter 11 is devoted to teaching, and that is almost wholly given to the manner of instruction, not to defining a curriculum or conducting a school. I emphasize the "manner" here, not "methods," because most of what Chu presents in this chapter concerns the example set by the teacher or the nature of the student's response to instruction, rather than specific techniques of pedagogy. For Chu personal inspiration and motivation counted most, with more emphasis on student initiative than on how the teacher would work on or for him. With the depersonalizing and dehumanizing of education in the modern world, it may be refreshing to see how much Chu emphasizes the personal and the human, but it may also leave one wondering about the gap between cultivation of the person and the conduct of the school system Chu Hsi had advocated.

There are, however, two exceptions to this generalization in *Things at Hand*. One refers to the organization of his school by Hu Yüan, the tenth-century master who became much admired for his combination of classical scholarship and practical studies. Supposedly he set up two halls, one for interpreting the Classics and the other for handling practical affairs.[26] This model is also cited in Chu's *Elementary Learning (Hsiao hsüeh)*, another highly influential text.[27] In *Things at Hand* Chu quotes Ch'eng Hao:

> When Hu An-ting (Hu Yüan) was in Hu-chou (in Chekiang province), he set up a hall to study the way of government. When students wanted to understand the way of government, the matter would be discussed here, the discussion including such things as governing the people, managing the army, river conservation and mathematics. He once said that Liu I [1017–1086, a

26. T'o T'o, *Sung shih* (Peking: Chung-hua shu-chü, 1977) 432:12837–12838. Huang Tsung-hsi and Ch'üan Tsu-wang, *Sung-Yuan hsüeh-an*, (Taipei: Ho-lo t'u-shu ch'u-pan she, n.d.) 1:25–26. In the SYHA account there is some question as to whether Liu I may not be attributing his own views to Hu Yüan, but that does not affect the issue here because Chu Hsi and Lu Tsu-ch'ien appear to have accepted both the attribution and the idea.

27. See Theresa Kelleher's chapter in this volume.

student of Hu][28] was an expert in river conservation, repeatedly served in government, and in all cases achieved merit in river conservation.[29]

In the *Collected Commentaries on the Chin-ssu lu (Chin-ssu lu chi-chu)* Chu is quoted in reference to this passage as giving Hu Yüan more credit for his breadth of mind and range of interests than for his precise command of technical subjects.[30] Nevertheless, the citing here, and in the *Elementary Learning* of Hu's program, with its division of studies between the humanities and technical subjects of social relevance, gave such a combination of studies the imprimatur of Chu Hsi. Moreover, the citing of Liu I with approval as a competent technician lent weight and respectability to such studies. In principle such an arrangement was acceptable, even if in practice the same balance was not always maintained and study of the Classics clearly predominated among Neo-Confucians.

The second reference to actual schooling in *Things at Hand* comes in Ch'eng Hao's memorial quoted earlier. Therein one finds specific reference to a school system, a distinction between elementary and advanced education, and a combination of moral and intellectual training. Significantly, however, education is for him closely linked to training officials; witness the inclusion of this memorial in the section of *Things at Hand* dealing with systems and institutions (i.e., basic governmental institutions), not with teaching, as if to emphasize education's political importance.[31] Idealistic as Ch'eng Hao tends to be, he sees the same values and interests as shared by all in human society; it does not occur to him that there might be any incompatibility in the schools' serving both government recruiting and general education. For him, as for most Neo-Confucians of his age, it was simply a question of converting the ruler to sagely wisdom and putting his power to humane uses through education. The idea of a separation of functions or countervailing power as between state and school was hardly thinkable at this time, although Huang Tsung-hsi came close to it in the seventeenth century. There was only the implicit threat, if persuasion failed to gain agreement in principle between ruler and minister, of the Neo-Confucian's scruples demanding his nonparticipation in, or withdrawal from, the process.

In the Yüan period, when the issue of whether the civil service examinations should be resumed was debated at the Mongol court, for the leading Neo-Confucian classicist Wu Ch'eng (1249–1333) the question was, not how the bureaucratic state could be kept out of the schools, but how the schools

28. *Sung shih* 334:10729.
29. Mao Hung-lai, *Chin-ssu-lu chi-chu* 11:4b–5a; quoting *Erh-ch'eng i-shu* 2:7a; trans. Chan, pp. 262–263.
30. Mao Hung-lai, *Chin-ssu lu chi-chu* 11:5a.
31. On the relationship of schools to Ch'eng Hao's political philosophy see Ishida Hajime, "Tei Meidō shōkō —jiseki, shimpō, gakkō kyōiku," in *Rekishi ni okeru minshū to bunka* (Tokyo, 1982).

could prepare and qualify candidates for government service better than the examinations did.[32] At that time Wu cited Hu Yüan, Ch'eng Hao, and Chu Hsi for their views on the school curriculum. Although one cannot be sure of his sources, Wu may well have been prompted by these excerpts about Hu and Ch'eng in *Things at Hand*.[33]

For Chu Hsi's views on the content of education in the schools, I turn first to his "Articles of the Academy of the White Deer Grotto," so often cited as a basic charter by later Neo-Confucian academies. At the risk of repeating what will already be well known to many readers, I cite these articles or precepts for ready reference:

Affection between parent and child;
Righteousness between ruler and subject;
Differentiation between husband and wife;
Precedence between elder and younger;
Trust between friends.

The above are the items of the Five Teachings, that is, the very teachings which Yao and Shun commanded Hsieh reverently to propagate as Minister of Education. For those who engage in learning, these are all they need to learn. As to the proper procedure for study, there are also five items, as follows:
Study extensively, inquire carefully, ponder thoroughly, sift clearly, and practice earnestly.
The above is the proper sequence for the pursuit of learning. Study, inquiry, pondering, and sifting are for fathoming principle to the utmost. As to earnest practice, there are also essential elements at each stage from personal cultivation to the handling of affairs and dealing with people, as separately listed below:
Be faithful and true to your words and firm and sincere in conduct.
Curb your anger and restrain your lust; turn to the good and correct your errors.
The above are the essentials of personal cultivation.
Be true to moral principles and do not scheme for profit; illuminate [exemplify] the Way and do not calculate the advantages [for oneself].
The above are the essentials for handling affairs.
Do not do to others what you would not want them to do to you.
When in your conduct you are unable to succeed, reflect and look [for the cause] within yourself.[34]

32. See Wm. Theodore de Bary, *Neo-Confucian Orthodoxy and the Learning of the Mind-and-Heart* (New York: Columbia University Press, 1981), pp. 59–60.

33. Wu, of course, may also have had access to the original sources from which these excerpts were drawn. See *Wu Wen-ch'eng kung ch'üan-chi* (Ch'ung-jen Wan Huang chiao-k'an pen, 1756), *chüan* shou 34b, suppl. *Chüan* 1:1a–8b; de Bary, *Neo-Confucian Orthodoxy*, p. 59; David Gedalecia, *Wu Ch'eng: A Neo-Confucian of the Yüan* (Ann Arbor: University Microfilms, 1971), pp. 369, 382.

34. Chu Hsi, *Hui-an hsien-sheng Chu Wen-kung wen-chi* (Kyoto: Chūbun shuppansha, 1977) 74:18a (p. 1368); hereafter cited *Wen-chi*. "Pai-lu tung shu-yüan chieh-shih." See also John W. Chaffee, "Chu Hsi and the Revival of the White Deer Grotto Academy, 1179–1181," *T'oung Pao* 61 (1985):40–62.

The significant feature of these rather prosaic articles is their attention to the basic moral and intellectual virtues applicable to one's conduct of personal life, human relations, and public affairs. Considered as the most general aims of the school, they focus on fundamental human values rather than on authority, commandments, or disciplinary rules.

Note, however, the political context of the *locus classicus* cited in the second para, that is, the Five Teachings that Yao and Shun had propagated by the minister of education, which were all one needed to learn. This makes it difficult for Confucians to conceive of an ideal state of affairs in which political and intellectual authority would be separated. To modern minds these precepts may sound quaint, if not archaic, vague, and platitudinous. But Chu, while consciously striving for simplicity to avoid a kind of legalistic overdetermination, had a definite structure in mind, with precise sequences, categories, and numbered sets for ease of retention or recollection by the student. In *The Liberal Tradition of China* I wrote:

> The social functions addressed in the first set of "Articles" give way in the second set to operations that are more intellectual and reflect the particular preoccupations of the Sung scholar. One cannot say that they lack the general human relevance of the moral dicta or would be inappropriate in most human situations, yet the atmosphere of the school prevails; it would be hard to imagine peasants having much opportunity to "study," "inquire," "ponder," and "sift" in the fashion Chu suggests.[35]

For students, however, one could hardly find a more pithy statement of the essential values and procedures governing scholarly inquiry and reflective thought—the critical temper at work in the service of humane studies. Chu believed so deeply, indeed, in having the student develop his own capacity to learn, weigh, and judge for himself, that he encouraged the application of them even to the Classics and the precepts he himself was recommending:

> [I, Chu] have observed that the sages and worthies of antiquity taught people to pursue learning with one intention only, which is to make students understand the meaning of moral principle through discussion, so that they can cultivate their own persons and then extend it to others. The sages and worthies did not wish them merely to engage in memorizing texts or in composing poetry and essays as a means of gaining fame or seeking office. Students today obviously do the contrary [to what the sages and worthies intended]. The methods that the sages and worthies employed in teaching people are all found in the Classics. Dedicated scholars should by all means read them frequently, ponder them deeply and then inquire into them and sift them.[36]

35. de Bary, *Liberal Tradition*, p. 37.
36. Chu Hsi, *Wen-chi* 74:18b (p. 1368).

In *The Liberal Tradition in China* I have also spoken of this approach to learning as a kind of voluntarism that respects the essential autonomy of the self in weighing and sifting whatever is to be learned. This is not, to be sure, a radical autonomy; it does not presuppose a completely free and independent self standing in opposition to all else, but it conceives of it as engaged in a creative interaction with others, in keeping with the humaneness of man's essential nature. Nor, if one is inclined to see this voluntarism as opposed to authoritarianism, should one misconstrue the nature of authority here. Chu shares the traditional Confucian belief in the need of men, and especially the young, for teachers, leaders, and models to serve as edifying examples. To provide the latter kind of valid authority figure, so as not to leave the young without inspirational guidance or cautionary example, is a most serious responsibility for Chu Hsi. Yet he is opposed to the coercive imposition of authority, whether in learning or politics.

This essential spirit is conveyed in the conclusion of the postscript to the "Article" discussed above:

> If you understand the necessity for principles and accept the need to take responsibility oneself for seeing that they are so, then what need will there be to wait for someone else to set up such contrivances as rules and prohibitions for one to follow? In recent ages regulations have been instituted in schools, and students have been treated in a shallow manner. This method of making regulations does not at all conform with the intention of the ancients. Therefore I shall not now try to put them into effect in this lecture hall. Rather I have specifically selected all the essential principles that the sages and the worthies used in teaching people how to pursue learning; I have listed them as above one by one and posted them on the crossbar over the gate. You, sirs, should discuss them with one another, follow them, and take personal responsibility for their observance. Then in whatever a man should be cautious or careful about in thought, word or deed, he will certainly be more demanding of himself than he would be the other way [of complying with regulations]. If you do otherwise or even reject what I have said, then the "regulations" others talk about will have to take over and in no way can they be dispensed with. You, sirs, please think this over.[37]

Chu's disavowal of rules here is clearly not total. It would be best to dispense with prohibitions if the situation can be managed by more constructive means, but resort may well be had to rules if the alternative is disorder and destruction. This is in keeping with Chu's consistent position on the maintenance of order in society: the guidance of rites is preferable to the restraints of law, but the latter must be invoked if rites are not respected.

In Chu Hsi's own lifetime this question arose when he was asked to endorse the "School Rules of Messrs. Ch'eng and Tung" (*Ch'eng-Tung erh Hsien-sheng hsüeh-tse*). These rules, devised by two scholars whom Chu person-

---

37. Ibid., 74:18b–19a.

ally respected,[38] prescribed a school routine and conduct for which the term "rules of decorum" would be more appropriate than any term suggesting a penal code; in fact, the *tse* in the title could just as well be read as "governing principles" or "norms" instead of "rules." Its contents include many dos and don'ts, but there is no mention of punishment stronger than the following:

> Choose [to associate with] those who are diligent and careful, deal with them correctly and treat them with forbearance. If someone errs in small matters, admonish him; if in more serious, make it known to the headmaster. If, when punished, he does not reform, all should ask for the headmaster to dismiss him. No one can be allowed simply to have his own way.[39]

In commenting on these rules of school decorum in 1187 Chu Hsi averred that since time immemorial there had been a need for exemplary models and methods in the education of the young, and especially in village and clan schools. In preparing this text, says Chu, Messrs. Ch'eng and Tung intended the rules for the edification and "renovation" of the children of their fellow villagers. This, he says, fulfills the original intention of the ancients' elementary education and should prove useful to teachers in local schools as a guide for their students. So doing, one might hope to see again in the present, as in antiquity, progress in the accomplishment of learning by the young and fullness of virtue in those of mature years.[40]

Note that Chu Hsi is careful to describe these prescriptions as exemplary models or methods *(fa)* and not as regulations *(kuei)*. Later in 1258 the scholar Jao Lu joined Chu's "Articles of the White Deer Grotto Academy" and the "School Rules of Messrs. Ch'eng and Tung" as complementary manuals—"one to set forth the broad aims of education which human learning should strive to fulfill, and the other to define the constant norms of behavior to be observed in the day-to-day life of the group."[41]

These two guides, says Jao, represent the essential methods for fulfilling the original intent of Great Learning and Elementary Learning. "If the student can carry on in this manner, then root and branch will be mutually supportive, inner and outer will sustain and nourish each other, and the method for entering upon the Way will be complete."[42] Thus, does Jao express his enthusiasm for a total and balanced plan of education, while noting in conclusion that this is to be differentiated from what today are

---

38. Ch'eng Tuan-meng (1143–1191), native of Kiangsi and disciple of Chu Hsi for whom the latter wrote, besides this postscript, several letters and a funerary inscription. See Chu, *Wen-chi* 90:16a (p. 6367); SYHA 69:13 and Pu-i 69:34. Wing-tsit Chan, *Chu Tzu men-jen* (Taipei: Hsüeh-sheng shu-chü, 1982), pp. 245–246; Tung Chu (1152–1214), a disciple of whom Chu Hsi was particularly fond; SYHA 69:14; Pu-i 69:47, Chan, *Chu-Tzu men-jen*, pp. 276–277.

39. Chu Hsi, *Ch'eng-Tung erh hsien-sheng hsüeh-tse* (TSCC ed.), pp. 3–4.

40. Ibid., p. 4.

41. *Ch'eng-Tung erh hsien-sheng hsüeh-tse*, postscript of Jao Lu, p. 5.

42. Ibid., p. 5.

called "regulations" *(kuei)*, which Chu Hsi had refused to enact at the White Deer Grotto Academy.

THE CONTENT OF EDUCATION

Chu Hsi's fullest and most systematic recommendations for the content of education are found in his "Personal Proposals for Schools and Official Recruitment." Here again, as with Ch'eng Hao, the assumption is that there should be one program for all, so that those who serve in government may be drawn in through the same process of education as is made available to others, that is, through the schools and not a separate examination system. Chu introduces the subject, as he had in the preface to the *Great Learning*, by proposing the model of the ancient school system, which gave priority to cultivation in virtuous conduct and moral action rather than to the polite arts (i.e., literary skills), viewing the former as solid and practical learning *(shih-hsüeh)* compared to the emptiness of purely "literary" or aesthetic studies. With one pattern of education and one system of values for all, people would get their proper bearings and set a fixed course to guide their efforts in life and develop their own abilities. Note again the primary value attached here, as in the preface, to individual self-development. This contrasts with the situation in Chu's time when, he says, scholars engage in empty, useless talk and follow one shifting literary fashion after another, leaving the young without a definite goal to which they can direct the cultivation of their talents.[43]

The answer to the prevailing educational confusion is to go back to Ch'eng Hao's proposed system of moral education, abolish the examinations emphasizing literary skills (the composition of *shih* and *fu* forms of poetry), and instate a new curriculum based on the study of the Classics, philosophers, histories, and contemporary problems. Chu also has much to say about abuses in the conduct of the civil service examinations, especially the disparities in local quotas, but I focus here on matters most pertinent to education. If these changes are made, Chu says, "scholars will have a fixed aim rather than be motivated by a competitive spirit: there will be solid practical action instead of empty talk, and solid learning so that no one will lack the means to develop his talents."[44]

The basis for this confident prescription lies in the moral nature inherent in all and the need of all to find the Way in their own mind and hearts, manifest it in their own persons, and carry it out in their own conduct. "The scholar who genuinely knows how to apply himself to this can not only cultivate his own person but extend it to the governance of men and indeed to the state and the world."[45]

43. Chu, *Wen-chi* 69:20–28b (pp. 2269–1273).
44. Ibid., 69:21b.

Obviously Chu's basic assumptions and aims here are the same as in his preface, showing the consistency and continuity in his thinking. Of particular significance in this proposal is the detailed curriculum it offers, and Chu's justification for the extraordinary demands it will make on the student: "The affairs of this world are all things a scholar should know about and their principles are to be found in the Classics, each of which has its own importance and none of which is substitutable for another."[46] Thus, in their different subject matters, the Classics themselves embody a diversity of human experience, all of irreplaceable value. This basic pluralism, moreover, is reinforced by the fact that the classics survive only in mutilated, fragmentary condition, while the passage of time distances our experience from that of the ancients, making interpretation of the Classics problematical and compelling one to supplement them by recourse to other writings. Among these are the works of the masters or philosophers (*tzu*), whose learning, Chu says, "also derives from the sages." Each of these philosophers, of course, has his strong and weak points, from both of which one can learn, emulating their excellences and criticizing their weaknesses. The histories, too, help fill out the picture, dealing with changes from past to present, the rise and fall of dynasties, periods of order and disorder, what is gained and lost in the course of human affairs, and so on. Then, finally the study of contemporary affairs exists as a reflection on the truths of the Classics: rites and music, systems and institutions, astronomy, geography, military planning and strategy, laws and punishments—"these are all necessary in dealing with the contemporary world and cannot be left unstudied."[47]

In *The Liberal Tradition in China* I gave a brief summary of the contents of Chu's curriculum, which may suffice for my purposes here including:

> the *Changes, Documents, and Odes,* as well as four ritual texts (the *Chou li, I li,* and two versions of the *Record of Rites* by the Elder and Younger Tai); the *Spring and Autumn Annals* (*Chun-ch'iu*) with three early commentaries; and the *Great Learning, Analects, Mean,* and *Mencius.* Among the philosophers Chu would include Hsün Tzu, Yang Hsiung, Wang T'ung, Han Yü, Lao Tzu, Chuang Tzu, as well as the principal Sung masters. The next major division of the curriculum would consist of the major histories, to be studied for the light they could shed on the understanding of contemporary problems; these include the *Tso Commentary* (*Tso chuan*), *Conversations from the States* (*Kuo yü*), *Records of the Grand Historian* (*Shih chi*), the histories of the Former and Later Han dynasties, of the Three Kingdoms, the History of Chin, Histories of the Northern and Southern Dynasties, the Old and the New T'ang Histories and the History of the Five Dynasties, and the *General Mirror for Aid in Government* (*Tzu-chih t'ung-chien*) of Ssu-ma Kuang. A similarly copious body of literature (including

45. Ibid., 69:22a.
46. Ibid., 23b.
47. Ibid., 24a.

the encyclopedic *Comprehensive Institutes T'ung tien* of Tu Yu) is cited for those branches of practical learning indicated above (governmental institutions, geography, etc.).[48]

Further, recognizing the difficulties of interpreting the Classics, Chu believes it essential for the student to consult commentaries. "The principles of this world are not beyond the mind-and-heart of man, but the words of the sages are profound, deep and highly refined, beyond what can be reached by mere conjecture."[49] Only after one has weighed the pros and cons of what the different commentators have to say can one reflect on them in one's own mind and judge what is correct. For this purpose then, Chu provides extensive lists of Sung commentators on each of the Classics. Those listed are noteworthy for the diversity of their views, including thinkers usually considered anathema to the Ch'eng-Chu School of the Way: Wang An-shih, cited for his interpretations of no less than four Classics, and Su Tung-po, for instance. Chu is not unmindful of the burden this imposes on the student and the danger of superficiality that extensive coverage always entails; thus, he recommends that the student be responsible for an in-depth knowledge of only one among these interpretations and enough of one other to use it as the basis for a comparative evaluation. Study of each Classic would then involve a careful and thoughtful reading of the original text, the consideration of what different commentaries say, and the drawing of conclusions that are both grounded on evidence and confirmed by what seems right in one's own mind.[50]

Here one can see how Chu applies to the study of the Classics the same procedures he has recommended in the "Articles of the White Deer Grotto Academy": to "study extensively, inquire carefully, ponder thoroughly, sift clearly, and practice earnestly"—all to the end of truly learning for oneself. Having done this, says Chu, "there will be no classics the gentleman has not mastered, no histories he has not studied, and none of these that will not be applicable to his own times."[51] On this last point, although Chu has not referred directly to Hu Yüan's views as he has to Ch'eng Hao's, the former's basic principle of combining classical and contemporary studies, principle and practicality, is incorporated into every phase of Chu's program.

Here then is a conspectus of the learning to be mastered by those Chu Hsi hoped to see in government service. Indeed, he hoped for even more than this—for practical experience of family responsibilities and internship in public office, paralleling the scholarly work described above. Altogether it would serve as the crowning achievement of Chu's educational structure and the full fruit of a rich and varied tradition. Standing on the broad base of a

---

48. Ibid., 69:24a; de Bary, *The Liberal Tradition*, pp. 41–42.
49. Chu, *Wen-chi* 24b.
50. Ibid., 69:25a, 26a.
51. Ibid., 69:24a.

universal school system, it would nurture men's talents and select for higher responsibilities those most capable of meeting them. Elitist in principle, it sought, as Chu said quoting Mencius, "the nobility of Heaven" (true moral and educational worth) and not "the nobility of men" (social rank and privileged position).[52]

Yet this was not what would later become established, in the name of Chu Hsi orthodoxy, as the official curriculum for examinations. I say "in the name of Chu Hsi orthodoxy" advisedly. When a Neo-Confucian curriculum was adopted later as the basis of official instruction under the Mongol ruler Khubilai, the language used by its Neo-Confucian proponents was the very language of the essay just discussed, as were the arguments adduced by them in opposing a resumption of the civil service examinations at that time.[53] It was also to be the language appropriated by other Neo-Confucians later, in 1313–1315, when they successfully established a new examination system based essentially on Chu Hsi's version of the Four Books.[54] Familiar with Chu Hsi's proposals and conscious that they were sacrificing key points in Chu's program in order to adapt to the facts of political life under the Mongols, the Neo-Confucians still paid lip service to the importance of moral training and virtuous conduct, as well as to the role of the schools in developing men of character and practical ability. At the same time they installed a new examination curriculum vastly abridged from Chu's, which could serve as a minimum cultural qualification for the recruitment of officials from Mongol, Central Asian, and Chinese candidates. Still later at the founding of the Ming dynasty, when the new system was confirmed by the Ming founder in all essential respects, the edict promulgating it again drew heavily on Chu's earlier statement of the problem, even while the latter's recommendations were being gutted in favor of a much simpler, functional approach.[55]

In the discussions and pronouncements that accompanied this historic development, effectively fixing examination form and content until 1905, the name of Chu Hsi was hardly mentioned. Neither Khubilai nor Ming T'ai-tsu had much use for Chu Hsi or Neo-Confucian philosophy as such. They were practical men, interested in recruiting competent, dependable officials and not attracted to either the higher reaches of Chu's thought or the niceties of classical scholarship. Despite this, however, their simplified, populist version of the Neo-Confucian curriculum was to become the basis for training and credentialing a new Mandarin elite. Yet perhaps the greatest paradox of all is not that the new system should stand in such sharp contrast to Chu's—so much indeed that it would be liable to most charges he has leveled against

52. Ibid., 69:20b.
53. de Bary, *Neo-Confucian Orthodoxy*, pp. 38–44.
54. Ibid., pp. 53–60.
54. Ibid., pp. 62–63.

the previous system—but that, had it not been for Chu himself, this new development might never have occurred.

The reasons for this are essentially two: first, the impetus Chu Hsi gave to the Neo-Confucian schools provided the principal vehicles for the spread of Neo-Confucian learning; and second, his preparation of the texts would be most suitable for use in those schools and subsequently in the civil service examinations themselves.

Unsuccessful though Chu was in his advocacy of a universal school system, he devoted much of his life to promoting education through academies and local schools. Other contributors, notably Wing-tsit Chan and John Chaffee, deal with Chu's activities in relation to specific academies, and this should suffice to demonstrate Chu's strong commitment in this area. I wish here to emphasize only three key significances of this activity.

First, it demonstrates again Chu's fundamental belief that human action and all hope for social reform must begin at home—in what is near at hand and on the most basic level. If Chu had little hope of prevailing on the court at the highest level, he could at least address the problem in those communities for which he had some direct responsibility as a local magistrate or in which his scholarly reputation gave him some standing.

Second, Chu attached great importance to education rooted in local tradition; it could invoke the authority of historical figures or local personages whose personal achievements grew out of the native soil, met local needs, and helped to share recent, presumably viable, traditions. Chu stressed this emulation of practical examples by his efforts at the commemoration of local worthies and at reviving local schools that had fallen on hard times.[56]

Third, Chu encouraged the building of communities of students and scholars by developing teachers who could also be leaders. This was not new—Neo-Confucians generally had attached great importance to the role of the teacher—but Chu carried on this tradition with great personal devotion. Yet it is significant that he did this primarily by personal example, not by the explicit discussion of teaching methods.

These three factors help explain how Chu, a political failure at Court, was able to exert such a powerful influence at the grass-roots level of scholarship, for there he achieved the success that later compelled the Sung court to give him due recognition and led the Yüan and Ming dynasties to confirm his hold over men's minds. In this way the academies, which grew rapidly and spread greatly in influence after Chu's death in official disgrace, became the prime instruments of Neo-Confucian education. Against the failure of the government schools and the perversions of the examinations, in Chu's terms,

56. This side of Chu's career emerges with particular clarity in Conrad Schirokauer's account of "Chu Hsi as an Administrator," in *Études Song*, series 1, no. 3 (1976):207–236.

the academies served as bearers of the Neo-Confucian message throughout East Asia.

Chu also played a large role in providing the texts and teaching guides for use not only in the schools but even in the examinations themselves. In even the extensive curriculum proposed by Chu numerous works he compiled himself, but more often in collaboration with others, for use on several levels of instruction, do not appear. Several of these are discussed and analyzed more intensively by others in this volume. Here I list some of the more important ones, in rough order of increasing complexity or difficulty.

1. *Elementary Learning (Hsiao hsüeh)*—nominally addressed to the lowest and most basic level of learning; actually a social handbook dealing with a diversity of subjects and not nearly so simple and direct as items 2, 3, or 4.

2. *The Community Compact (hsiang-yüeh)*—as adapted by Chu from that of the Lü family formerly associated with Ch'eng I; contains precepts to be subscribed to by members of local communities for the conduct of basic social relations.

3. Chu's public proclamations—as a local official, establishing guidelines for conduct in several specific fields of human activity.

4. "Articles of the White Deer Grotto Academy"—a basic charter for schools.

5. *The Family Ritual of Master Chu (Chu-tzu chia-li)*—a guide to the conduct of the major ceremonies in the life of the family; represents a radically simplified version of the classic rituals.

6. *Commentaries on the Four Books (Ssu-shu chi-chu)*—a careful and concise commentary on the four basic texts featured by the Ch'eng-chu school.

7. *Memorials and Lectures on the Classics*, for the emperor or heir apparent (*Ching-yen chiang-i*)—although addressed to the ruler, on a high level of importance, often simpler and less scholarly than other instructional works of Chu Hsi but conveying the same essential message.

8. *Reflections on Things at Hand (Chin-ssu-lu)*—sometimes referred to as a gateway to the Four Books; later sometimes so used, but in addressing fundamental philosophical issues often probing questions of great depth and subtlety; perhaps of greatest importance in mapping out the steps to the attainment of sagehood, a lofty ambition but one to which Chu said any country boy could aspire.

9. *The Sources of the Ch'eng-Chu School (I-lo yüan-yüan lu)*—a hagiography of Chu's Neo-Confucian predecessors, near-contemporaries admired as among the sages and worthies.

10. *Outline and Digest of the General Mirror (T'ung-chien kang mu)*—structured synopsis and abridgement of Ssu-ma kuang's *General Mirror for Aid in Government*.

11. Personal Proposals for Schools and Official Recruitment (*Hsüeh-hsiao kung-chu ssu-i*)—a brief document but proposing the most ambitious learning program offered by Chu.

This list, far from exhaustive, may suffice to illustrate the main features of Chu Hsi's educational approach. First, it recognizes the need for an educational process, reaching from youth to maturity and from the common people to the ruler. Second, it accepts the need for a plurality of means to reach different audiences on different levels, although the ultimate aim of all should be attainment of sagehood. This is the educational implication of the interrelated concepts of self-renewal, "renewal of the people," and "resting in the highest good." Third, the path of self-development builds on successive levels of accomplishment; one cannot attain enlightenment in one leap or one instant. Fourth, breadth of learning is to be balanced by concentration and precision, comprehensiveness by selectivity and structure. Fifth, applying these requisites to the classical tradition implies the need for "editing" the Classics—abridging and commenting on them to highlight key principles, focusing on the concrete example or concise formula to make teachings memorable. Sixth, to repossess classical learning it is not enough simply to read the ancient texts; there must also be some continuity with the recent past and some connection with the latest scholarship, if learning is to have some organic relation to a sustained and sustaining life process. Seventh, to accomplish the foregoing aims requires cooperative, collegial scholarship in order to provide a variety of edited, graded materials for the edification of the populace at large. Virtually all the texts cited above are anthologies or reprocessed materials; whatever "original" writing they contain is mostly in the form of preface or commentary.

The results of this process may be seen in the curriculum of the Neo-Confucian academies that followed Chu Hsi's lead in the thirteenth and the fourteenth century. *The Daily Schedule of Study in the Ch'eng Family School* by Ch'eng Tuan-li (1271–1345), often cited as a model curriculum, presents a schedule of readings graded according to the age of the student, with a major division between elementary and advanced education.[57] In the former, from age eight to fifteen, emphasis is placed on reading the original texts of the *Elementary Learning* (*Hsiao hsüeh*), Four Books, Five Classics, and *Classic of Filial Piety* (as edited by Chu Hsi). In the advanced stage, from age fifteen to twenty-two, most of the same texts are read with Chu Hsi's commentary, deleting the *Elementary Learning* and *Classic of Filial Piety* but adding readings from Ssu-ma Kuang's *General Mirror for Aid in Government* (*Tzu-chih t'ung-chien*) and specimens of prose and poetry from Han Yü and Ch'u Yüan.

57. Ch'eng Tuan-li, *Ch'eng-shih chia-shu tu shu fen-nien jih ch'eng* (TSCC ed.) pp. 1–43; hereafter cited *Ch'eng-shih . . . jih ch'eng*. Summarized and excerpted in John Meskill's, *Academies in Ming China: An Historical Essay* (Tucson: Monograph Series of the Association for Asian Studies, University of Arizona Press, 1982) pp. 160–166.

If one compares this list with that in Chu's "Personal Proposals" or the list of materials edited by Chu Hsi above, the educational fare is obviously much more limited. As a practical matter Ch'eng Tuan-li's curriculum is undoubtedly oriented to the new examination system of the Yüan dynasty. Of this John Meskill says,

> Ch'eng Tuan-li devised a complete schedule for the education of a young man from childhood to the year of his examinations. The whole program provided for a very systematic progression through the classical literature and commentaries on it, culminating in diligent practice of the forms required in the examinations.[58]

From the standpoint of Chu's "Personal Proposals" one could question, as I have above, whether the coverage of "classical literature" or the range of interpretation, alternative commentaries, was nearly as broad as Chu himself had wished. Furthermore, there is far more concentration on learning and memorizing forms and models useful for examination purposes and much less on the kind of "inquiring, reflecting, weighing and sifting" that Chu had recommended. An atmosphere of rote learning had prevailed, in contrast to the spirit of voluntarism and critical scholarship encouraged by Chu.

However, the curriculum does exhibit many features of Chu's educational philosophy: the need for selectivity, priorities, graded materials, and a high degree of specificity in study methods. By defining the reading program as he does, Ch'eng clearly thinks of it as a graded core curriculum to be supplemented as time and circumstances allow by further reading works that Chu Hsi had proposed or prepared in much greater variety, as the supplementary notes to this schedule indicate. Indeed, if one were to judge from Ch'eng's intentions alone, one would have to say that he still looked to Chu's curriculum as the standard and expected Chu's basic aims to be served by his own reading program. This is clear from his characterization of the classical core of the new advanced curriculum. Starting at age fifteen, he says, the student should commit himself to the pursuit of learning, "resolving to take the Way for one's aim in learning, and sagehood for one's aim as a man."[59] Then, having completed study of the Four Books and the chosen Classic with its commentaries and having faithfully followed Chu Hsi's reading method[60] with great concentration of mind and intense effort over three or four years,

> all of it without exception substantial learning for the sake of oneself and none of it vitiated by even the slightest idea of selfish gain or ulterior motive, the student will have established himself in reverent seriousness and righteousness,

---

58. Meskill, *Academies*, p. 61. See also Makino Shūji, "Gendai no jugaku kyōiku," in *Tōyōshi kenkyū*, 37, no. 4 (March 1979) 71–74; and Chaffee, "Revival," p. 18.

59. Ch'eng Tuan-li, *Ch'eng-shih . . . jih-ch'eng* 1:9; SYHA 87:62.

60. See the discussion of the Daily Schedule that follows.

strict in his practice of mind preservation and self-examination, and firmly rooted for a lifetime of learning.[61]

As further evidence of Ch'eng's intention fully to adhere to Chu's overall aims, there are numerous writings of Chu Hsi attached to the Reading Schedule, including the "Articles of the White Deer Grotto Academy" and the "Personal Proposals for Schools and Official Recruitment."[62] Ch'eng did not, indeed, think of himself as jettisoning any of Chu's program but only of modifying it for the sake of practical realization. In his preface to the Daily Schedule he spoke in exultant terms of this climactic moment in history when, after centuries of failure to accomplish Confucian goals in education, the time had arrived for Chu Hsi's substantial learning (*shih-hsüeh*) and practical method to overcome the preoccupation with literary composition in both the schools and the civil service examinations. "All fathers and elder brothers have wished their sons and younger brothers to be educated, but only two or three out of them have succeeded." This, he says, is because they did not have a proper understanding of the matter and erred at the start by heading in the wrong direction. The right direction was given in ancient times when the cultivation of virtue was put ahead of literary studies, only to have this order reversed in subsequent dynasties. Of his own time (mid-Yüan period), however, Ch'eng says:

> In the recruitment of scholars virtuous conduct is being put ahead of all else and study of the Classics is being given precedence over literary composition. . . . In the interpretation of the Classics the views of Master Chu are the sole authority, uniting as one the philosophy of principle and study for the civil service examination, to the great advantage of scholars committed to the Way [as distinct from opportunistic candidates]. This is something the Han, T'ang and Sung never achieved, and the greatest blessing that has come to scholars throughout the ages.[63]

Nevertheless, according to Ch'eng, many scholars who study the classics, even if they accept the authority of Chu Hsi's interpretations, still are unaware that one must have a definite reading method, so their study is unsystematic. Hence the need for a guide like the Daily Schedule, which combines Chu's study methods and other relevant writings on the subject, so that "none of the classics will be left unstudied, no principles left unexplained, no aspect of the Way of governance left unmastered, no systems or institutions left unstudied, no age, past or present, left out of one's ken, and no literary form left unmastered. . . ." Yet at the same time, says Ch'eng, having pursued this course of study "to the age of 23, 24 or 25, with this he would be ready to take the examinations."[64]

61. Ch'eng Tuan-li, *Ch'eng-shih . . . jih-ch'eng* 1:14; SYHA 87:65.
62. *Ibid.*, 1:1–2, 3:110–118.
63. *Ibid.*, 1:1–2, preface of Ch'eng Tuan-li.
64. Ibid., 1:1–2, 2:23.

More of this preface dilates on the effectiveness of this method in bringing personal fulfillment to the individual and putting the individual into full accord with the Way while also preparing the way for success in the civil service examinations. For my purposes, however, the foregoing should be enough to suggest how Ch'eng expects the wisdom and practical method of the philosopher to be joined with the process of official recruitment for the transformation of state and society. Written in 1315, the very year the Yüan dynasty initiated the new examinations, his preface exudes the idealism of those who, like Ch'eng went along with Ch'eng Chü-fu (1249–1318) in resurrecting the civil service examination system and installing in it the new "Neo-Confucian" curriculum, in contrast to other Neo-Confucians like Wu Ch'eng (1249–1332) and Liu Yin (1249–1293), who refused to compromise Chu Hsi's basic principles in this way.[65]

Inevitably (and this is a word to be used sparingly), in this unification of power and intellectual authority, the moral and spiritual aspirations of Chu Hsi are compounded with forms of learning routinized for purposes of the examinations, which tend to divert men from the moral and spiritual goals to which Chu Hsi had given the highest priority. Thus, there is more than a touch of irony in the acclaim given to the Daily Schedule several centuries later by Chang Po-hsing (1652–1725), when he reprinted it in his collection of orthodox Neo-Confucian works, the *Cheng-i t'ang ch'üan-shu*. In his own preface to the Daily Schedule, Chang laments the debasement of learning brought on by the examination system:

> In ancient times it was easy to develop one's talents to the full; today it is difficult. In antiquity scholar-officials were chosen for their [moral] substance; today they are chosen for their literary ability. In ancient times the village recommended scholars and the town selected them, so men engaged in substantial learning (*shih-hsüeh*) and outdid each other in the practice of humaneness and rightness, the Way and virtue. At home they were pure scholars; at large they were distinguished officials. Today it is different. Men are chosen for their examination essays. What fathers teach their sons, and elder brothers their younger brothers, is only to compete in the writing of essays. It is not that they fail to read the Five Classics or Four Books, but that they read them only for such use as they have in the writing of the examination essays, and never incorporate them into their own hearts and lives. . . .[66]

It is not difficult to see how the same system could lead to divergent results and even to conflicts within the same individual between the pursuit of worldly success and the quest for moral and spiritual perfection. Thus, a dilemma arose from even the seeming successes of the Chu Hsi school; some of these, from his point of view, could also be seen as miscarriages. For

---

65. de Bary, *Neo-Confucian Orthodoxy*, pp. 52–53, 59–60.

66. Chang Po-hsing, personal preface to the *Ch'eng-shih . . . jih ch'eng, Cheng-i t'ang ch'üan-shu* (Fu-chou cheng-i hsüeh-yüan ed. of T'ung-chih 7 [1868]) 1:1.

instance, successfully making Chu Hsi the centerpiece of the new examinations represented another failure for Chu in the sense of his being misappropriated for questionable purposes. Such success, too, seems to have compromised later efforts to achieve an effective and lasting public school system of the kind he had advocated.

Meanwhile the growth of the academies continued, amidst periodic vicissitudes, to spread Neo-Confucian education in ways Ch'eng Tuan-li would have less cause to regret. For this we have testimony from the *Sung History (Sung shih)*, *Yüan History (Yüan shih)*, and *Case Studies of Sung-Yüan Scholars (Sung-Yüan hsüeh-an)*, describing the fate of the schools of Chu Hsi and Lu Hsiang-shan, starting first with family of Shih Meng-ch'ing (1247–1306):[67]

> The Shih family of Ssu-ming [in Eastern Chekiang, near Ning-po] had all followed the Lu school, but with the advent of Shih Meng-ch'ing it turned to follow Chu Hsi . . . [and] transmitted this to Ch'eng Tuan-li and his brother, who adhered purely to the Chu school.[68]

And from the *Yüan History*:

> At the end of the Sung, the Ch'ing-Yüan area [near Ningpo in Eastern Chekiang], all followed the school of Lu Hsiang-shan and the Chu Hsi school was not carried on. Ch'eng Tuan-li by himself took up with Shih Ching [i.e., Meng-ch'ing] in propagating Chu Hsi's doctrine of "clarifying the substance and applying it in practice" *(ming-t'i shih-yung)*. Scholars came to his gate in great numbers. He wrote the "Working Schedule for Study of Books" *(Tu-shu kung-ch'eng)*, which the Directorate of Education had distributed to officials in the local schools to serve as a model for students.[69]

Note here the process of conversion from Lu Hsiang-shan's teaching to Chu Hsi's, drawing attention to the combination of principle and practice. With the latter concretely embodied in a working schedule of study and the new curriculum, in turn, officially adopted, one can see how these developments in the academies led the way for a new, officially sanctioned, system.

Lastly, I cite the comment of Huang Po-chia (b. 1643), in *Case Studies of Sung-Yüan Scholars*, concerning the underlying philosophical significance of this development:

> In the late Sung the Ch'ing-yüan area was all of the Lu school and the Chu Hsi school was not transmitted there. With Shih Meng-ch'ing, however, there came a change. Following Yang Chien [1140–1125, disciple of Lu] most of the school went into Ch'an and pursued a form of learning without the reading of books. Departing from the source, they drifted apart. Thus, what they transmitted from Master Lu was the very thing that made them lose Master Lu.

67. *Sung shih* 423:12638; SYHA 87:1.
68. SYHA 87:50.
69. Sung lien, et al., *Yüan shih* (Beijing: Chung-hua shu-chü, 1976) 190:4343.

Having studied Ch'eng's Daily Reading Schedule, [I find that] there is nothing missing from root to branch and there is a sequential order in its method, from which one may proceed. . . .[70]

Here Huang suggests a connection between the Lu school's lack of a reading method, reflecting Lu's own depreciation of textual study, the school's getting lost in Ch'an Buddhism, which "did not depend on the written word," and the contrasting growth of the Chu Hsi school linked to its definite method of study and reading program. Since Huang, like his father, was not known for any partiality to the Chu Hsi school, this represents credible testimony to the latter's superior achievement in this respect.

More far-reaching even than the spread of the Chu Hsi school through the academies was its propagation through the development of printing, which carried Neo-Confucian teachings even into homes that could afford little formal education. Whether or not Chu Hsi had any special prescience in anticipating this trend may be arguable, but Wing-tsit Chan's research indicates that Chu was involved in the printing business as a sideline, and it is known that as a local magistrate he used printed handbills to disseminate his proclamations throughout the area of his jurisdiction.[71] In any case, his organization of thought into systematic, easily-grasped structures, his concern for adapting them to different levels of comprehension, his editing and condensing of texts, his attention to the problem of an ordered sequence of readings, the care he took in analyzing and codifying procedures for book learning all took special advantage of the new printing capability. He pronounced with finality in the *Ch'eng Family Schedule*: "For conveying the Way and transmitting it to later generations, the merit of books is great indeed!"[72]

It is no accident that Chu Hsi's recommendations for reading as codified by his followers in what came to be known as his "Reading Method" (*Tu-shu fa*), which addressed the what, when, and how of reading, spread with his other teachings and the publication of his books through East Asia. In its simplest form, this consisted of maxims recommending reverent seriousness and a fixed resolve in the pursuit of learning: a graded sequence and gradual progress in study; intensive reading of text and commentary accompanied by "refined reflection"; reading with an open mind and without reading one's own preconceptions into the text; taking what one reads to heart and making it part of one's own experience; making an all-out effort and keeping strict control.[73] These methods were summarized in a short piece of Chu's entitled "Essentials of Reading," found in his *Collected Writings*. They were also

70. SYHA 87:54.

71. Chu, *Wen-chi* 99:2b (p. 1758). See Wing-tsit Chan, "Chu Tzu ku-ch'iung," in his *Chu-hsüeh lun-chi* (Taipei: Hsüeh-sheng shu-chü, 1982), pp. 205–232.

72. Ch'eng Tuan-li, *Ch'eng-shih . . . jih-ch'eng* 3:45.

73. Ibid., 1:9; 3:120. "Chi-ch'ing lu chiang-tung shu-yüan chiang-i."

discussed in Chu's *Classified Conversations* (*Yü-lei*) and expounded in memorials to the throne. A large portion of the section on methods of self-cultivation in Chu's basic textbook on *Elementary Education* is devoted to the matter of reading methods and how they relate to one's inner self-development.[74] They were further incorporated in the aforementioned "Daily Schedule of the Ch'eng Family School," in the official Ming *Great Compendium of Human Nature and Principle* (*Hsing li-ching-i*) and in numerous reformulations of these methods by Chu Hsi's successors, including the very pointed and detailed discussion by the recent historian Ch'ien Mu.[75] Even the authors of a recent history of Chinese education, though not particularly sympathetic to Chu's philosophy, acknowledge the wide influence of his study and reading methods.[76]

Other Neo-Confucians like Lu Hsiang-shan and Wang Yang-ming may well have been more popular teachers than Chu, who seems to have been comparatively reserved, of a reflective temperament, modest almost to a fault, and not the kind who would wish to promote himself or his own ideas. Other teachings like Buddhism and Taoism, which developed substantial lay followings in these same years, also had more popular appeal than Chu Hsi's refined scholarship. But none of these, for all their charismatic, messianic, or populist features, addressed the problem of secular education the way Chu Hsi did—systematically developing schools, curricula, texts, and study methods. To the extent that the educated elite of East Asia, whatever the differences in their social and political status or functions from country to country, were identified as leaders or officials (*shih-ta-fu*) and as scholars accomplished in book learning (literally "readers of books" *tu-shu jen*), it was Chu Hsi who largely provided the wherewithal for their intellectual and moral formation. Thus, he became the educator par excellence of East Asia into the twentieth century.

74. See Theresa Kelleher's chapter.

75. See Chu, *Wen-chi* (Kyoto: Chūbun) 14:11a–14a (pp. 204–206). *Hsing-kung pien-tien tsou-cha-erh*; 74:25a–26a, "Tu-shu chih yao," *Chu Tzu yü-lei* (reprint Kyoto: Chūbun shuppansha, 1979), chüan 10–11, pp. 255–316; Ch'eng Tuan-li, *Ch'eng-shih . . . jih-ch'eng* (TSCC ed.) 1:9, 3:120; Hu Kuang, *Hsing-li ta-ch'üan* (Kyoto: Chūbun shuppansha, 1981), *Chüan* 53–54, pp. 818–842; Li Kuang-ti, ed., *Hsing-li ching-i* (ed. of Tao-kuang 30, 1850) 8:31b–44b. Ch'ien Mu, *Chu Tzu hsin hsüeh-an*, 4:613–687.

76. Mao Li-jui et al., comps. *Chung-kuo ku-tai chiao-yü-shih* (Peking: Pei-ching shih-fan ta-hsüeh, 1980), pp. 398–400.

EIGHT

Back to Basics: Chu Hsi's *Elementary Learning* (*Hsiao-hsüeh*)

M. Theresa Kelleher

One of the basic Neo-Confucian primers to come out of the Sung was the *Elementary Learning* (*Hsiao-hsüeh*), an anthology of selections from the Classics and other works from the historical period up into the Sung, published by Chu Hsi in 1187. This text became an important part of the Neo-Confucian core curriculum, not just in China but in Korea and Japan as well. Its value lies in the illustrations it provides of Chu Hsi's pedagogical methods and the way it highlights the reforms he thought most important to bring about in family and community life.

Because little has been written about this text in Western languages,[1] in this chapter I propose to discuss the *Elementary Learning* in terms of its purpose, structure, and contents. Because it touches on many different aspects of human life and society, its value and significance for various fields of study is almost unlimited. But aside from drawing attention to the richness of its contents, I will focus here on the text as it reveals Chu's educational approach. Other works of Chu's emphasize individual self-cultivation; the particular interest of the *Elementary Learning* is its greater attention to the social process and how it can contribute to individual self-development.

Chu Hsi gave careful thought to the selection and ordering of his material; it was meant to serve as more than a convenient survey of the Confucian tradition for purposes that were merely conservative or fundamentalist. Rather he sought to organize these materials in such a way as to promote most effectively his own vision of the morally regenerated society, against the alternatives represented by Buddhism and, perhaps even more significantly, by other Confucian reformers. The Sung period was one of rapid social, economic, and political change; the intellectual scene was lively, as the

---

1. There is a French translation of the text by C. deHarlez, *La Siao Hiu ou morale de la jeunesse avec le commentaire de Tschen-siuen.*

traditional Confucian concerns of family and state, ritual and education were
hotly debated in terms of their adaptability to modern life.[2] Chu Hsi, like
Ch'eng I before him in the Northern Sung, took a stance both more
fundamentalist than some others in his insistence on an uncompromising
adherence to classical norms, especially in terms of hierarchical structure in
human relationships, and at the same time more radical in the sense of its
being most influenced by Buddhism in its quest for a deepened spiritual
dimension to Confucianism. What he chose to include in the *Elementary
Learning* reflects his proposed solutions to some major issues of his day, as he
attempted to reform people's values and behavior through education and
ritual.

In his preface to the *Elementary Learning*, Chu Hsi states that his purpose
was to reestablish the learning the "ancients" had developed for young
people. This consisted in specific, concrete modes of behavior that were both
practical and ritualistic, such as sweeping and sprinkling, learning how to
converse with elders, and relating affectively to the human beings around
one—loving parents, respecting elders, and esteeming teachers. Mastery of
these then prepared a person to advance to the next level—pursuit of the
goals of the *Great Learning*: cultivating the self, regulating the family, ruling
the country, and establishing peace in the world. Because many of the texts
Chu Hsi considered worth reading were not easily accessible to Sung
students (and impossible for any one student to read in their entirety
anyway), for him the anthology's value was that it would bring together the
most important passages from these texts for the convenience of the student.[3]

Although Chu Hsi voiced no overt criticism of the present state of
education in his preface, we find repeated expressions elsewhere in his
writings of his great dissatisfaction with the poor preparation of students
coming to study under him.[4] He concluded that so many were unprepared to
undertake "greater" or more advanced learning because they had no secure
foundation on which to build and few skills that would enable them to get a
grip on their studies. He lamented that many students have the idealistic
impulse to practice humaneness and reverence but lack any idea of how to
concretely express these promptings.[5] Chu Hsi was sure that it had been

---

2. The final draft of this chapter has benefited greatly from the discussion at the conference of
papers dealing with related issues during the Sung, such as education, the examination system,
adaptation of classical rituals to Sung life, and the kinship system; the text of the *Hsiao-hsüeh* took
on greater meaning in light of these other papers. This is especially true of Patricia Ebrey's
chapter on ritual and her other work on the kinship system; see "Conceptions of the Family in
the Sung Dynasty," *Journal of Asian Studies* 43, no. 2 (1984):219–245.

3. Preface, *Hsiao-hsüeh chi-chu* (SPPY ed.), 1a. Although my references throughout this
chapter are to the SPPY edition, I was greatly aided by the valuable notes of Uno Seiichi in the
Japanese edition *Shōgaku* (Tokyo: Meiji shoin, 1965).

4. See, for example, Chu Hsi, *Chu Tzu yü-lei* (reprint, Taiwan: Cheng-wen, 1970) 8:211,
14:400, 18:647.

5. *Ibid.*, 14:402.

different in the past, when the ancients had accepted the need for basic preparation on a more elementary level of learning and had disciplined themselves with the ritual rules of proper behavior.

He thus felt compelled to provide a text that would enable people to prepare themselves better for entering the path of advanced intellectual and spiritual development. But what form should it take? He had already written and edited several texts meant to serve educational purposes, the most notable of which was the *Reflections on Things at Hand (Chin-ssu lu)*, which had been published in 1173, almost fifteen years earlier than the *Elementary Learning*. With its planned sequence progressing from self-cultivation to the regulation of the family and governing of the state, the *Reflections* had been envisioned by Chu Hsi as the "ladder" or stepping stone to the study of the Four Books.[6] Although meant as a preparatory text for advanced study of the Classics, it primarily focused on matters of the mind and its cultivation, that is, on Neo-Confucian intellectual and moral formation. With the *Elementary Learning*, Chu Hsi meant to get at something even more basic than the *Reflections*.[7]

In the actual compilation of the text, Chu Hsi relied heavily on Liu Ch'ing-chih (1130–1195), a close friend and associate.[8] Liu, who had attained his *chin-shih* degree in 1157, held a variety of official posts, mostly in the Hupei, Hunan, and Kiangsi areas. His concern for education is illustrated by his construction of two *ching-she*-type academies when he was prefect in Heng-chou (Hunan), and by his books such as *A New Text for Instructing the Young (Hsün-meng hsin-shu)* and *Comprehensive Record of Admonitions to Sons (Chieh-tzu t'ung-lu)*.[9]

This latter text must have impressed Chu Hsi and convinced him that Liu was the man for the job. In eight chapters, the *Chieh-tzu t'ung-lu* includes selections from classical and contemporary Sung sources, especially excerpts from "family instructions" giving good advice to young men. An examination of its contents reveals considerable overlap with the *Elementary Learning*; indeed, the first several passages are actually identical.[10] There are long excerpts from the *Yen Family Instructions (Yen-shih chia-hsün)* of the Sui, the *Liu Family Instructions (Liu-shih chia-hsün)* of the T'ang, and the *Instructions for Those*

6. *Ibid.*, 105:4179.
7. When the *Hsiao-hsüeh* was completed, Chu Hsi compared it to the *Chin-ssu lu* in the following terms: "All the great models (*ta-fa*) for cultivating the self are complete in the *Hsiao-hsüeh*. The pure essence of moral principles is carefully detailed in the *Chin-ssu lu*." *Ibid.*
8. For a description of their relationship, see Wing-tsit Chan, *Chu Tzu men-jen* (Taipei: Hsüeh-sheng shu-chü, 1982), p. 311.
9. See Uno, *Shōgaku*, p. 1; and T'o T'o, *Sung shih* (Peking: Chung-hua shu-chu, 1977), 437:12953.
10. Liu Ch'ing-chih, *Chieh-tzu t'ung-lu* (SKCSCP ed.) 1:1a–3b. This text is not as carefully edited as the *Hsiao-hsüeh*, but it does include both poetry and the Han dynasty female scholar Pan Chao's *Nü-chieh* which the *Hsiao-hsüeh* does not.

Who Are Immature and Ignorant (*T'ung-meng hsün*) by Lü Pen-chung of the Sung, upon which the second half of the *Elementary Learning* draws extensively. According to the Ssu-k'u editors and the Japanese scholar Uno Seiichi, Liu began the project in 1183. Two years later he submitted his draft to Chu Hsi; in 1187 the text was published.[11] From Chu's letters to Liu during this period, some picture of the compilation process emerges. In one letter,[12] Chu Hsi asks Liu if he is finished and says that the earlier he could see the draft the better. He advises Liu not to include too many rules (*fa-chih*) and suggests adding some model sayings and actions of the great figures of the tradition. However, he cautions Liu to be careful about offering as examples persons who may have been immoderate in their feelings or extreme in their actions. Although he admires the pure and loyal spirit of the early poet Ch'ü Yüan, he does not think Ch'ü's *Encountering Sorrows* (*Li Sao*) should be included. He also advises Liu not to take too many selections from *Inquiries of the Young* (*Meng-ch'iu*) because it would present reading difficulties for beginning students.[13] He does, however, approve the inclusion of *yüeh-fu* poems and poems by the T'ang poet Tu Fu.[14]

In two subsequent letters, Chu Hsi continues to prod Liu. He would, he says, consider it most fortunate if the text could be completed soon.[15] When Chu finally does receive the draft, however, he does not forebear from criticizing it. He feels Liu may have rushed things too much and failed to polish it sufficiently. He explains what changes he himself found necessary: he has prefaced each selection with the name of the person or book from which it was taken, thereby identifying each passage more clearly; also, he has added a thematic preface (*t'i-tz'u*) in rhyme at the beginning of the text, so that young people can easily memorize it.[16] In his next letter to Liu, Chu informs him of other editorial changes, namely, that he has put all the stories at the end instead of the beginning of each section, obviously referring to the material in chapters 4 and 6. He wants to place at the beginning material

---

11. See *Ssu-k'u ch'üan-shu tsung-mu t'i-yao* (Shanghai: Commercial Press, 1933), 92:1831; and Uno, *Shōgaku*, p. 1. Wing-tsit Chan informs me that he doubts this chronology; to him it sounds too neat and pat, and he suspects the process continued for a longer period of time.

12. Chu Hsi, *Chu Tzu wen-chi* (SPPY ed. titled *Chu Tzu ta-ch'üan*) 35:17b.

13. The *Meng-ch'iu* is a primer for young people, compiled in the T'ang by Li Han. It is composed of stories, often with moralistic lessons. See both Hayakawa Mitsusaburō, *Mōgyū*, 2 vols. (Tokyo: Meiji shoin, 1973), and Burton Watson, trans., *Meng Ch'iu: Famous Episodes from Chinese History and Legend* (Tokyo and New York: Kodansha, 1979). It is surprising that Chu Hsi should have thought it so difficult when much of the material in the *Hsiao-hsüeh* seems even more so.

14. No poetry at all can be found in the present edition of the text.

15. Chu Hsi, *Chu Tzu wen-chi* 35:19b, 21b.

16. Ibid., 35:22a. The *t'i-tz'u* Chu Hsi mentions here is a short piece that follows the preface and precedes the text proper. It presents in simple, four-character lines, the basic teachings about the cosmic order, human relationships, and human virtue. It laments the fact that most ordinary people have fallen away, lapsed from the way of the sage, and gently beckons the student to take the first step on the way back to this path. *Hsiao-hsüeh chi-chu*, "T'i-tz'u" 1a–2a.

that students can use and apply right away. Selections from the writings of the Neo-Confucian masters like the Ch'eng brothers and Chang Tsai, as well as the matter of the "Community Compact," are consequently also placed later in the text, not at the beginning.[17]

From this, one can see that Chu Hsi had definite ideas in mind for the type of elementary text he wanted in order to fill the great lack in the education of most students of his day. Instead of tackling the job himself, he commissioned one of his colleagues who had already had experience with compiling a similar work. Although Liu did the bulk of the work in terms of assembling material, Chu Hsi took responsibility for the finished product. He rearranged material, deleted what he considered difficult or of no use, and added some annotation to help the reader.

From these remarks of Chu Hsi and from the way, in the first half of the text, he addresses himself variously to *hsiao-tzu*, little ones, and *meng-shih*, young gentlemen, one is led to conclude that the text was meant for children in the elementary phase of their education, which in the Chinese context was from age eight to fifteen. But when one looks at the actual content and language of the *Elementary Learning*, one begins to wonder if it was indeed meant for children. In terms of vocabulary alone, not to mention its length or the sophistication of the issues dealt with in the latter half of the text, the *Elementary Learning* is far more difficult to read than the Four Books for which it was supposedly to serve as preparatory study.[18] Did Chu Hsi intend the learning in this text to be "*hsiao*" in the sense of being for children or in the sense of being primary or fundamental in laying a foundation for the moral life and thus preceding any kind of education at any age? If the latter is the case, which it no doubt is, although the text was not intended exclusively for children, this does not necessarily mean that children were not to constitute its principal audience. Ideally such learning was supposed to begin in childhood, even if its full understanding and implementation might not come until adulthood.[19] In actual fact, there are instances of its use by both children and adults. One can thus conclude that the structure and contents of the *Elementary Learning* were meant to adapt to different levels and various uses.

17. Ibid., 35:23b.

18. Difficulty of language probably is not a good criterion here, for it seems that Chinese children were exposed to the difficulties of their language very early. At least, the language of the primers widely used, in Chu Hsi's day, such as the *Chi-chiu pien* (compiled by Huang Yu of the Han) and the *Ch'ien-tzu wen* (compiled by Chou Ssu-hsing of the Liang), is anything but simple or easy. The most famous of all primers, the *San-tzu-ching* was much simpler in its vocabulary compared to these other primers. It was probably written by the author of the *Yü-hai* encyclopedia, Wang Ying-lin (1223–1296) in the thirteenth century. See the preface to Herbert A. Giles's translation, *San Tzu Ching: Elementary Chinese* (reprint, Taiwan: Ch'eng Wen, 1972), pp. v–vi.

19. The preface to the *Hsiao-hsüeh* speaks of the need for people to practice its teachings while they are still *yu-chih*, young and tender, able to be shaped and not beyond correction.

Testimony as to the actual use of this text in the educational curriculum for children is found in Ma Tuan-lin's (1254–1325) encyclopedic *Wen-hsien t'ung-k'ao* (which prescribes it along with the dictionaries *Erh-ya* and *Shuo-wen chieh-tzu*, the Han primer *Chi-chiu pien*, and the T'ang primer *Meng-ch'iu*),[20] in Ch'eng Tuan-li's (of the Yüan) "Schedule for Daily Learning" (along with the plain texts of the Four Books and Five Classics),[21] in the early Ming Neo-Confucian Wu Yü-pi's "Regulations for Learning,"[22] in the community schools (*she-hsüeh*) of the Ming (along with the *Classic of Filial Piety*, the first Ming emperor's "Great Proclamation," the third Ming emperor's work on filial piety, *Hsiao-shun shih-shih*, and the Four Books).[23]

Just how the text was presented to or made use of by children is another matter. This probably depended on their age and sophistication. In his introductory remarks to chapter 1 of the text, Chu Hsi comments that from his work, "teachers will know what to teach and students will know what to study."[24] This would lead one to assume that it was meant to be used as both a type of syllabus or manual for educators, including parents as well as teachers, and as a textbook for older students. A study on community schools in the Ming states that teachers were advised to *chiang*, or expound, on one or two sections from the text at a time.[25] However, a passage from Wu Yü-pi on how the text should be used puts more responsibility on the student, who is presumably somewhat older:

> As for the *Elementary Learning*, a person cannot but take pains to apply his efforts to it. He should proceed chapter by chapter, passage by passage, carefully digesting it and allowing it to enter his mind. . . . In this way, a person will be able to make some progress. It has long been my humble opinion that the reason the management of affairs by later generations has not been on a par with that of the ancients is that [latter day people] fail to take the *Elementary Learning* as their basis.[26]

As for its adult audience, the most famous case is no doubt that of Hsü Heng (1209–1281), the noted Neo-Confucian adviser to the Mongol court. Upon his "conversion" to Neo-Confucianism, he is said to have thrown away

---

20. Cited in Hayakawa's introduction to the *Mōgyū*, p. 35. Wang Ying-lin, (see footnote 18) has a section on *hsiao-hsüeh*, or elementary learning, in his *K'un-hsüeh chi-wen*, but he does not include Chu Hsi's *Hsiao-hsüeh* among the texts he discuss here. See *Weng-chu k'un -hsüeh chi-wen* (Taipei: Shih-chieh, 1963), pp. 481–502. The *Sung Bibliography* (Hong Kong: Chinese University Press, 1978), ed. Yves Hervouet, incorrectly identified this *hsiao-hsüeh* section with Chu Hsi's text (p. 231).

21. Cited in John Meskill, *Academies in Ming China* (Tucson: University of Arizona Press, 1982), pp. 160–161.

22. Wu Yü-pi, *K'ang-chai chi* (SKCSCP ed.) 8:43a.

23. Wang Lan-yin, "Ming-tai chih she-hsüeh," *Shih-ta yüeh-k'an* 25 (1936):110–113, esp. 112. I am grateful to K. C. Liu for directing me to this reference.

24. Chu Hsi, *Hsiao-hsüeh chi-chu* 1:1a.

25. Wang, "Ming-tai chih she-hsüeh," p. 115.

26. Wu Yü-pi, *K'ang-chai chi* 8:31a.

all his books except this text, and Chu Hsi's commentaries on the Four Books, and dedicated himself to the discipline of its teachings, especially on ritual. He advised his students to do the same. Hsü published his own commentary and abridgement of the text, the *General Significance of the Elementary Learning* (*Hsiao-hsüeh ta-i*), to make it more accessible, especially to the Mongols.[27] In his most famous utterance about the text, he exclaimed, "I have as much faith in the *Elementary Learning* as I do in the spiritual intelligence [of the universe]; I revere it as much as I do my father and mother."[28]

A second example of the text's use by an adult audience comes not from China but from Korea. Michael Kalton, in his study of Yi Dynasty Neo-Confucianism, describes the existence of clubs organized by scholars expressly for the purpose of studying and practicing the teachings of the *Elementary Learning.* "One Kim Koeng-p'il took pride in claiming that he devoted himself exclusively to it until the age of thirty."[29] On the significance of the text in general, Kalton writes, "In its wide and sustained influence upon the fundamental moral instruction and formation of the Confucian elite of China and Korea, probably no other single work has equalled the *Learning for Youth* since it first appeared in 1187 A.D."[30] Although these examples are not exhaustive, they do suggest the variety of uses to which the *Elementary Learning* was put in the years after its publication, both in China and elsewhere in East Asia.

I turn now to the text itself, first to outline its overall structure and then to discuss its contents. As to structure, the text is divided into two major sections: the Inner Chapters (*nei-p'ien*) from 1 to 4, and the Outer Chapters (*wai-p'ien*), 5 and 6. The two sections are roughly equal in length. The 212 selections[31] in the Inner Chapters are primarily from the classical period, and the 172 selections of the Outer Chapters present the "admirable sayings" (*chia-yen*) and "exemplary deeds" (*shan-hsing*) of figures from the Han through the Sung.

Within this structure of Inner and Outer chapters, the material is organized around three basic themes or headings. They are "establishing the educational process" (*li-chiao*), "clarifying the cardinal human relationships" (*ming-lun*), and "reverencing the self" (*ching-shen*).[32] The Inner Chapters

27. Cited in Wm. Theodore de Bary, *Neo-Confucian Orthodoxy and the Learning of the Heart-and-Mind* (New York: Columbia University Press, 1981), pp. 136–137.

28. Quoted in Chu Hsi, *Hsiao-hsüeh chi-chu* 1:1a.

29. Michael Kalton, "The Neo-Confucian World View and Value System of Yi Dynasty Korea" (Ph.D. diss., Harvard University, 1977), p. 69.

30. Ibid., p. 67.

31. The notes in the SPPY edition of the text give the total as 214 items, but I come up with only 212 in my own counting.

32. Alternative translations of the first and third theme titles might include, "establishing the importance of education" or "setting into motion the educational process" for the first, and "reverencing the person" or "being serious about self-cultivation" for the third.

devote the entire first three chapters to each of these, with chapter 4 providing examples of the embodiment of these three in classical history and legend. Outer Chapters 5 and 6 are each discussed under these three headings. Thus, these three headings or themes are treated in four different parts of the book.

The classical quotations Chu Hsi uses in his introductory remarks to each of the first three chapters provide some idea of the rationale behind this threefold thematic structuring of the text. The introduction to chapter 1 quotes the opening lines of the *Doctrine of the Mean*, relating human nature to both the Way and the educational process. "What Heaven imparts to man is called human nature. To follow our nature is called the Way. Cultivating the Way is called education."[33] Here the person with his Heaven-endowed nature is the starting point. But he needs education in order to follow the Way and fulfill his nature. Thus, Chu Hsi here upholds the classical Confucian view that the fundamental and ultimate purpose of education is moral, for the transformation of the person. This function of education gives it a sacred quality such that a person must be committed not just to the content of education but to the process itself and must reverence the means as well as the end.

Chu Hsi then proceeds to relate the moral purpose of education to the realm of human relationships with a quotation from *Mencius* in his introduction to chapter 2. "Establish *hsiang, hsü, hsüeh*, and *hsiao*, [educational institutions on several levels] for the instruction of [the people]. All have as their object to illuminate human relations."[34] Here we have the basic Confucian belief that a person fulfills himself in the midst of, not apart from, other human beings. He does so in relationships that are both particular and hierarchical; the Five Cardinal Relationships include parent-child, ruler-minister, husband-wife, elder-younger brother, and friend-friend. Education is a matter of learning and then carrying out the duties appropriate to each relationship, particularly for those in the lower half of the relationship: child, minister, wife, and younger brother.

Having moved from the person to the educational process to human relationships, Chu Hsi returns full circle to the person in chapter 3, but in such a way that the connection to the human community is not lost. He quotes from the *Record of Ritual* (*Li chi*) to this effect:

> There is nothing the gentleman does not reverence. And reverence for the self
> or person is the greatest of all. He is in his person a branch from his

---

33. *Doctrine of the Mean*, sec. 1. trans. Wing-tsit Chan, in *A Source Book in Chinese Philosophy* (Princeton: Princeton University Press, 1963), p. 98.

34. *Mencius* 3A:3, adaptation of trans. by James Legge, in *The Four Books* (reprint, New York: Paragon Books, 1966), p. 615.

parents;—can any son not have this self-respect? If he is not able to respect his own person, he is wounding his parents."[35]

Cultivation of the self is here situated in the context of human relationships, not as a selfish, individualistic pursuit; one reverences the self out of respect for and gratitude toward one's parents. Cultivation here includes both moral character and what can be regarded as simple good manners. The section is divided into four parts: attitudes of mind (*hsin-shu*), comportment (*wei-i*), dress (*i-fu*), and habits of eating and drinking (*yin-ssu*).

Each of the three themes just discussed—education, human relations, and self-cultivation—are vital to the structure of the whole and to the balance Chu Hsi sought in his program of moral self-reform. But this is not to say they each receive the same amount of attention in the actual text. Table 8.1 presents a numerical breakdown of the selections devoted to each of the three themes over the course of the text, indicating the difference in their treatment.

Most noticeable is how the second theme of clarifying human relationships clearly dominates the other two, and within that, the parent-child relationship. This is particularly evident in the Inner Chapters where 107 items are devoted to this theme in contrast to 13 for education and 45 for cultivation. The parent-child relationship in chapter 2 has 38 items to 20 each for the ruler-minister and the elder-younger relationship, 11 for friend-friend, and only 9 for husband-wife. The numbers alone might be somewhat misleading, of course, if one did not also consider the length of the items. Actually, however, many selections for the other relationships are quite short, making the parent-child relation all the more preponderant.

By giving major emphasis to the moral obligations that attach to human relationships, structuring the text in this way can be taken as a conscious reflection on the lack of such in Buddhist cultivation, as Chu Hsi saw it, where the self is first, the pursuit of enlightenment precedes these obligations, and the demands of human relations are relegated to a lower priority. Here Chu reaffirms the total commitment to the human community, but he differentiates one's responsibilities according to an order of precedence in the claims these relations may make on one. This was meant to counterbalance the tendency of students of his day who aspired to achieve complete spiritual freedom while excusing themselves from the duties of daily life in the Confucian context.

Having described the basic structure of the text, I will now begin a discussion of its contents, but, because of space limitations, I will not be able

35. "Questions of Ai-kung," *Record of Ritual,* adaptation of trans. by James Legge, in *Li Chi: Book of Rites,* ed. by C. C. Chai and Winberg Chai (reprint, New York: University Books, 1967) 2:266.

TABLE 8.1   Breakdown of the Contents of *Elementary Learning*

Topic	Number of Appearances			
	Chap. 1	Chap. 4	Chap. 5	Chap. 6
Education	13	4	14	8
	Chap. 2			
Human Relations				
Parent-Child	38	17	14	10
Ruler-Minister	20	5	10	8
Husband-Wife	9	4	8	5
Elder-Younger	20	3	4	10
Friend-Friend	11	2	3	1
General	9	0	2	11
TOTAL	107	31	41	45
	Chap. 3			
Cultivation				
Mind Cultivation	12	3	16	14
Comportment	21	2	4	7
Dress	6	3	0	1
Food and drink	6	1	3	6
General	0	3	13	0
TOTAL	45	12	36	28
GRAND TOTAL	165	47	81	91

to give due attention to each selection. I will instead try to highlight the main points of each section and then offer a discussion of their significance.

The selections included in the section on "establishing the educational process" at the beginning of the text in chapter 1 situate this process first in the private realm of the family and then in the public realm of the state and community. Within the family, the process begins with prenatal education (*t'ai-chiao*) wherein a woman is advised to conduct herself in such a way that beneficial prenatal influences dispose the child favorably to the development of an upright character. She is told how to sit, sleep, and eat in the proper way and is exhorted to listen to moral teachings in the evening (1:1a–b).[36] Instruction is to continue in the household as small children are taught about numbers, the directions, names, time, as well as obedience to elders. At age

36. References to the passages in the text being discussed will appear parenthetically in the body of my chapter, rather than in footnotes.

ten boys go out of the house for instruction while girls are put under the tutelage of a governess (1:1b–2b).

The next set of selections shifts the locus of education to the public realm and to the responsibility of the government to provide education in some form for the people. After a description of the ancient school system that extended from the village to the capital (1:2b), the sage ruler Shun is praised for seeing to it that among the main organs of his government was a ministry of education (1:3a). Besides the sponsorship of schools, education was to be provided for the community at large by local officials in the form of periodic lectures to the people on morality. One such example is provided from the *Rites of Chou* (*Chou li*; 1:3b).

The remaining sections in chapter 1 focus on the content of the educational curriculum (poetry, history, the rules of propriety, and music—1:3b–4b), the proper attitudes of a student (being deferential and open—1:4a), and finally on its moral purpose (enabling a person better to serve his parents and ruler —1:4b).

The moral purpose of education leads the reader into the next chapter on clarifying human relationships. We have already mentioned that the first one, regarding parent-child, predominates by far over the other four here. It does so because no other relationship is so important in a person's life, as a selection from the *Classic of Filial Piety* (*Hsiao-ching*), included here, makes clear:

> Parents give one life; no bond could be stronger. They watch over their child with utmost care; no love could be greater. Therefore, to love others without first loving one's parents is to act against virtue. To reverence other men without first reverencing one's parents is to act against propriety.[37]

Chu Hsi presents the relationship here in terms of the demands of filial piety that require total commitment on the part of children to their parents. In the form of specific directives taken largely from the "Summary of Ceremonies" (*Ch'ü-li*) and "Domestic Manners" (*Nei-tse*) chapters of the *Record of Ritual*, the text spells out in no uncertain terms what is expected of children (2:1a–5a). They are to be on call from early morning to late at night, ready to respond to any command of their parents. Children dedicate themselves to their parents' every comfort, both physical (dutiful children ensure food, clothing, living space for their parents) and psychological (dutiful children do not worry their parents about their health, swear to die with a friend, or travel to a far off place without telling anyone). Children are never to consider their own comfort or claim any possessions as their own. They try to conform their own personal likes and dislikes to the parents', but in the event the children are unsuccessful, they should always defer to

37. *Hsiao-ching, chüan* 9, trans. Mary Lelia Makra, in *The Classic of Filial Piety* (New York: St. John's University Press, 1961), p. 21.

parental preferences, even if this should mean a son's taking or giving up a wife or concubine against his own wishes—2:4a–b. When parents are sick, the child doubles his attention to them, and when they are dead, offers the appropriate sacrifices in person, maintaining both an inner and outer vigil (2:5b–6b).

There are no preconditions to these prescriptions about filial piety, such as their dependence on the good and generous nature of the parent to become operative. The text concedes that parents are sometimes liable to faults and mistakes, and the child must try to correct them, using however, only the mildest and most indirect of means. If the parent refuses to change ways, or even worse, punishes the child for criticizing, the child is not to feel any anger or resentment, even if beaten until blood flows (2:5a–b). The child can never go so far as to hate the parent.

Just as there are no preconditions, neither are there any exemptions to the demands of filial piety. Even those in the highest positions of power, including the emperor and his top ministers, are subject to the practice of filial piety, as are all down to the lowliest of persons (2:6b–7b).

In the last several selections of this section, the matter of the lack of filial piety is considered. Confucius is quoted as condemning it as the greatest of the ten thousand crimes a person might commit (2:8a). Mencius interprets it as a matter of selfishness in which a person chooses personal indulgence rather than selfless servitude to parents. Among the manifestations of this self-indulgence are laziness, gambling, selfish attachment to a wife and children, and gratification of physical appetites to an excess (2:8a).

The tone of the next section on the ruler-minister relationship is less demanding and intense. Here rules are given governing the correct protocol of a minister in his various dealings with his ruler—for example, when he receives orders from him, when he has an audience with him, when he dines with him (2:8a–b). These alternate with descriptions of how Confucius behaved toward the ruler, always with the utmost of respect and finest of manners. Two different impressions of the way the ruler is to be regarded come through in this section. One sees where Confucius moved his legs only with difficulty (2:8b) and could hardly breathe when in the presence of the ruler at court (2:8b–9a) because of the ruler's awesome dignity. But one also sees the ruler sending Confucius gifts of cooked meat and paying him a personal visit at home when he was sick (2:9a). Here Chu Hsi tries not only to establish the lofty prestige of the ruler in the mind of the reader but also to show the ruler as a personable, kindly person who treats his ministers with respect, thereby affirming the dignity of the minister.

Having so exalted the ruler, the section goes on, in seeming contrast, to deal with the challenge of the minister to deal with the limitations of the ruler, particularly through remostration. To do so, according to Mencius, is "to show respect" for the ruler (2:9b). The ground rules for this require a mutuality in the relationship; that is, "A ruler must treat his ministers with propriety, a minister must serve his ruler with faithfulness" (2:9b). But if the ruler is unresponsive to the remonstrations of the honest minister, the latter's retirement from office is a valid option, though transferring his loyalty to another ruler is not. "A faithful minister does not serve two lords; a chaste woman does not have two husbands" (2:10a).

The third section of this chapter, which deals with the husband-wife relationship, focuses on two matters: the correct protocol for wedding ceremonies and the establishment of proper distinctions between men and women in marriage. As for the former, Chu Hsi wishes to see that the wedding ceremony is taken more seriously and conducted according to the prescriptions from such ritual texts as the *Record of Ritual* and the *Book of Etiquette and Ceremonial (I li)*.[38] The selections here emphasize the importance of the engagement of a matchmaker, public announcement of the event, and the giving of advice by parents to the respective spouses about their duties in marriage (2:10a–b).

As for establishing the proper distinctions between men and women, this was to begin right in the conduct of the wedding ceremony with the groom going forth to fetch the bride, demonstrating that as the man he is to take the lead in all matters (2:10b). After the marriage, the couple is not to freely mix with each other but to observe a certain amount of sexual segregation. To this end, their living space is to be divided into inner (female) and outer (male) quarters, they are not to hand anything to each other directly except during family sacrifices, and they are not to touch each others possessions; at age seventy, they can dispense with some of these rules (2:11a–b).

In the last several selections of this section, the subordinate position of women to men is reiterated in the form of the "three obediences" (*san-ts'ung*), whereby a female is subject to her father as a girl, to her husband as a wife, and to her son as a widow. A man can divorce his wife if she is guilty of any of seven faults.[39] Not only can a woman never divorce her husband, but she may not even remarry after his death. In this, she must be like the loyal minister mentioned above (2:11b–12a).

In the fourth of the cardinal relationships, elder-younger brother, only the first selection deals with it in the literal fraternal sense. The other nineteen items focus on the junior-senior relationship in the broadest sense: the young person's relations with his father's friends, with his teacher, and with the elders of his community. The overall purpose of this section is to encourage a sense of deference to people older than oneself. Seventeen of twenty selections come from the *Record of Ritual* and involve specific dos and don'ts about behavior.

38. See Patricia Ebrey's chapter in this volume for the concern over vulgar marriage practices by Sung intellectuals.
39. These seven include disobedience to his parents, failure to bear a son, promiscuity, jealousy, having an incurable diesease, talking too much, and stealing.

The matters treated include how to converse with elders, how to wait on
them, how to act when one meets them in public, how to conduct oneself in
the classroom with one's teacher. Students are directed to walk with elders
slowly and behind, and they are taught to accept food or wine or gifts offered
to them by elders openly but without appearing too eager (2:12b–14a).
Levels of seniority are distinguished: namely, those twice as old as oneself are
treated as one's father, those ten years older as one's elder brother, and those
five years older or less as somewhere between an elder brother and an equal
(2:12b). The last selection shows the respect Confucius had for the elders of
his community in that when the community drinking ceremony was over, he
always left immediately after the elders did (2:14a).

The last of the cardinal relationships, between friend-friend, is given the
least attention, which is the case throughout the text. Although there are
eleven items (four more than the husband-wife relation), they are all quite
short in length, consisting of no more than several sentences. The first seven
items, taken from the *Analects* and *Mencius*, underscore the moral purpose of
friendship and distinguish between beneficial and harmful types (2:14b).
The last four items, from the *Record of Ritual*, describe the correct ritual
behavior that should inform social interactions between friends (2:14b–15a).

A "general discussion" (*t'ung-lun*) of the five relations follows with nine
items. Here the primary emphasis is on the trinity of male figures (father,
ruler, and teacher), who are seen as having contributed most profoundly to
the life of a young male and to whom he owes the most in service and
devotion (2:15a–16b).

In summarizing this long chapter on human relationships, I note an
overall attempt clearly to establish the authority and prestige of the higher
party to whom the lower party is to submit himself or herself in obedience
and service. Because the book is addressed to the young, it tends to present a
one-sided emphasis on the duties that attach to the roles the young will likely
find themselves in. The various ritual texts, especially the *Record of Ritual*, are
extensively drawn upon to provide specific ways of acting in these relationships. Thus, the various obligations in each relationship are made clear down
to the last detail. This submission of self to another helps eliminate selfishness as the student learns to put others before himself.

Although Chu Hsi wishes the student both to feel high respect for and
display reverence toward those in authority, he does not desire a blind
obedience. Rather, except in the husband-wife relation, he reminds the lower
party of its duty to voice criticism of the one above them when necessary. He
does not introduce this element until he has first built up these authority
figures in the student's mind so that it will not be done lightly.

While chapter 2 views a person's submission to the discipline of human
relations as contributing to the eradication of selfishness, chapter 3 on
"reverencing the self" takes on the matter of selfishness and its opposite
self-discipline even more explicitly. The first subsection on mind cultivation

warns right away against laziness, selfish desires, pride, and insatiable appetites. Reverence and righteousness are two antidotes offered against these (3:1a–b). Also, in selections taken from the *Analects*, the reader is encouraged to cultivate such qualities as honesty, earnestness, moderation, and caution as well (3:1b–2b).

The greater part of chapter 3, however, is not so much interested in mind cultivation but in the more physical aspects of self-cultivation, such as a person's comportment, dress, and habits of eating and drinking. The selections for these topics are primarily concerned with good manners and etiquette: they have the ring of an Emily Post or a Miss Manners to them. But good manners are not the object so much as the practitioner's disciplining of self and the reverencing of others. As in the presentation of the ruler-minister relationship in chapter 2, the material is presented in the form of specific directives from the *Record of Ritual*, alternating with descriptions of Confucius's impeccable manners.

The section devoted to comportment reflects a strong sense of the connection between the physical body and moral character. A person's posture and carriage both reveal his character and influence it. The concern here is that the influence be salutory, and thus the reader is given such injunctions:

> Do not listen with the head inclined on one side, nor answer with a loud, sharp voice, nor look with a dissolute leer, nor keep the body in a slouching position. Do not saunter about with a haughty gait, nor stand with one foot raised. Do not sit with your knees wide apart, nor sleep on your face. (3:2b–3a)[40]

Confucius is also presented as a model, for example, "When he was in the carriage, he did not turn his head quite round, he did not talk hastily, he did not point with his hands" (3:3b).[41]

In line with the sense of the close connection between the body and one's character, the section on dress opens with a description of the capping ceremony, the coming of age ceremony for Confucian males. In this, the young man is told to leave behind childish ways and devote himself to the cultivation of his moral character (3:5a). In the other selections here, the student is advised to be guided by simplicity rather than extravagance in dress (no furs, silks, or the color purple) and also by appropriateness (do not wear a white band on one's hat or clothing while one's parents are alive) (3:5a–b). In eating and drinking, too, one should not be too indulgent but rather should approach these with restraint and good form. The following is a set of table manners meant to achieve this purpose:

> Do not roll the rice into a ball; do not bolt down the various dishes; do not swill down the soup. Do not make a noise in eating; do not crunch bones with the teeth;

---

40. "Summary of Ceremonies," *Record of Ritual*, trans. Legge, in *The Li Chi* 1:76.
41. *Analects* 10.17, trans. Legge, in *The Four Books*, p. 136.

do not put back fish you have been eating; do not throw the bones to the dogs; do not snatch [at what you want]. (3:5b–6a)[42]

Confucius and Mencius are quoted near the end of this section with criticisms of scholars who either are ashamed of inferior quality clothes or food (3:5b) or who concern themselves with food and drink to the neglect of their moral character (3:6b). The message here is that one's bodily needs are to be met in a way that is refined and yet disciplined, not in a selfish manner.

Having thus introduced each of the three themes of education, human relations, and cultivation personal in the first three chapters, Chu Hsi then proceeds in chapter 4 to provide concrete examples from the classical past of persons who have best embodied these themes. He entitled this chapter chi-ku, "examining or studying the ancients," and introduces it with a quotation from Mencius about his anxious desire to become a sage like Shun. The reader is to have that same anxiety and that same aspiration. What follows in the chapter is meant to help him on the road to that goal. The lively character of Chinese narrative style effectively brings the teachings alive to the student in full flesh and blood, and rouses him to action.

The distribution of selections among the three themes here reflects that of the first three chapters; that is, the theme of clarifying human relationships is given the most attention, and the parent-child relation receives primary attention within that section. The sections devoted to the educational process and to reverencing the self are given proportionately less attention than earlier in the text, with only four items for the former and twelve for the latter.

The models for the first theme of establishing the educational process are three of the most famous parents in Chinese history, who took seriously their responsibility for the moral formation of their children at different stages of their lives. The first is T'ai-jen, the mother of King Wen who excelled in prenatal education and thus contributed to the sagely character of her son (4:1a–b). She is followed by the widowed mother of Mencius who wisely sought out a proper environment for the upbringing of her son, moving her residence three times to do so (4:1b). The third parent is a father, Confucius, who is cited as ably directing his son in the study of the Odes and the rules of propriety (4:1b–2a). Absent in this section are any model educators outside the family.

Turning next to the section on human relationships, we find that the one between parent and child remains dominant. The seventeen items devoted to it are greater than the sum total of the other four relations put together—five for ruler-minister, four for husband-wife, three for elder-younger brother, and two for friend-friend—and cover the various dimensions of filial piety articulated in chapter 2.

42. "Summary of Ceremonies," *Record of Ritual*, trans. Legge, in *The Li Chi* 1:80.

The first example is a case of unrequited filial love, the famous one of the sage ruler Shun, who was continually abused by his father and stepmother, despite his unwavering displays of filial piety. The four selections given over to Shun's filiality emphasize that his sorrow was such that not even success at the head of government or the love of two wives could assuage him. And yet he never indulged in the least bit of anger or resentment, continuing to treat both father and stepmother with affection (4:2a–3a).

The cases that follow, less extreme in nature, show various affectionate responses of children to their parents: by attending to their comfort in good and bad health like kings Wen and Wu to their fathers (4:3a–b), by care of their bodies like Tseng Tzu who could proudly display his injuryfree body on his deathbed (4:5a–b), by carrying out the mourning rites in an exemplary way like Kao Tzu Kao whose tears flowed like blood for three years (4:5a), and by sensitivity to the aging process of one's parents like Lao Lai Tzu who at seventy continued to dress and caper about like a child to prevent his parents from dwelling on their old age (4:4a). Models here include the high and mighty as well as the ordinary person, and also men of all age groups. One never ceases from being a child vis-à-vis one's parents, no matter how old or how powerful one becomes.

The ruler-minister relationship in this chapter focuses on the complicated issue of loyalty for ministers from the Shang through the Warring States Period. Like the previous section, it begins with a case of unrequited service, in this case, the situation of three ministers who served under the last evil ruler of the Shang, Chou. When their remonstrations about his cruel and decadent ways went unheeded, they each responded in different ways, illustrating the possible options for a minister. The Viscount of Ch'i feigned madness, Pi-kan continued to attack him directly and met his death by mutilation and the Viscount of Wei retired in protest (4:5b–6a). The next selection considers the case of Po-i and Shu-ch'i, loyalists to the Shang, who though they were not treated cruelly by the new rulers of the Chou, still chose to starve to death rather than go against the principle that a "minister does not serve two lords" (4:6a). The remaining selections deal with the problem of loyalty in the cut-throat Warring State Period (4:6b–7a).

The selections on the husband-wife relation seek to illustrate first the proper degree of formality between the sexes and second the matter of female chastity. As for the former, a certain Ch'üeh of Ch'i is celebrated for respectfully treating his wife like a guest whenever she served his meals in the field where he labored (4:7a), and a certain Chi K'ang Tzu is praised for never overstepping the household boundaries of inner and outer quarters whenever he visited his aunt (4:7b). For examples of the latter, a young widow threatens suicide rather than remarry, and a young wife refuses to leave her husband whom she has just discovered has an incurable disease (4:7b). In their decisions not to remarry but to remain faithful to their husbands, dead or sick, these women find themselves forced to go against their parents' wishes.

The items in the elder-younger brother relationship emphasize the spirit of deference and yielding rather than the assertiveness and competition that might mark this relationship. It begins with another case of unrequited service, here the case of Shun again, whose stepbrother Hsiang repeatedly plotted Shun's death. But Shun continued to show him the most sincere fraternal devotion, without a trace of rancor or ill will (4:7b–8a). The next selection describes the close, deferential relationship between the already mentioned brothers Po-i and Shu-ch'i (7:8a), and the last one deals with two lords fighting over land and how they gave up their contentious ways upon experiencing the spirit of "yielding" (*jang*) that pervaded the kingdom of King Wen (7:8a).

In the friend-friend section, those good at friendship are described as those who maintain a sense of humility and reserve in dealings with friends (7:8a–b).

To sum up this section on human relationships, a variety of models were shown to exemplify the teachings given in chapter 2 about each relationship, namely, filial children, loyal ministers, faithful wives, deferential brothers, and friends. These are the ways they show their dedication and commitment to each other in the relationship. Of special note in the presentation of the models here is Chu Hsi's pedagogical method of beginning three of the five with cases of unrequited service and devotion (and in the case of the husband-wife, of other obstacles, namely, parents). It would seem he wishes to make the point that adherence to duty is not without difficulty. These difficulties pose the most serious test of one's selflessness, that is, whether one can continue to act according to the path of virtue when there is no visible reward in sight but only rejection and suffering.

The third theme of reverencing the self is not given much attention here. All but one of its twelve items are quite short in length. In the first part, models taken from the *Analects* exemplify simplicity and frugality of lifestyle. Among them are Yu who was not ashamed of his tattered robes even when standing next to men in furs (4:9a) and Yen Hui who remained ever cheerful even though he lived in a mean alley with only a meager amount of food and drink (4:9b–10a). In one of the last selections, the only long one, the mother of a high official of the state of Lü continues to weave her own cloth to the dismay of her son who would have her relax and indulge herself. She lectures him soundly about the ruin that results from such behavior and expounds on the efficacy of hard work to keep people honest, virtuous and prosperous (4:9a–b).

At the end of chapter 4, the reader reaches the end of the Inner Chapters, the first half of the text. Here Chu Hsi sounds the basic themes of the text, namely, that the educational process should be situated primarily in the family but also in the state, that a person learns to be selfless by carrying out the appropriate ritual conduct for each of the five cardinal relationship, and that self-cultivation is a matter of refining and restraining various aspects of the self, particularly the physical self. Chu Hsi's approach is to gear learning to the level where behavioral prescriptions and role models most powerfully and effectively inform the character of the student; he is more concerned with evoking action rather than reflection here. I mentioned earlier that he made a conscious editorial decision to put material at the beginning that could be immediately put into practice by the student. Thus, we find a great number of directives for proper behavior from the *Record of Ritual* in this first half. In fact, the Inner Chapters might be called a digest of this text because 92 of the 165 selections in the first three chapters are drawn from it (see Table 8.2). The other major source for the Inner Chapters is the *Analects*, particularly Book 10 which describes Confucius's careful and reverential adherence to proper ritual behavior.

Chu Hsi's method of persuasion here is to present in a simple, straightforward manner the type of behavior that "the ancients" practiced. Although there is a strict, "no nonsense" tone here, still Chu does not indulge in criticisms of young people, tearing them down before building them up again. Nor does he confuse the student with polemics, arguing against alternative ways of doing things. Rather he keeps it simple, focusing on the type of behavior he wishes to encourage. He assumes the tone that this is the most natural and reasonable way to act.

Chu Hsi changes his approach significantly in the second half of the text, the Outer Chapters, even while continuing to deal with the three basic concerns of the first half: education, human relationships, and cultivation (see Table 8.3). Instead of separate introductions to chapters 5 and 6, there is one general introduction to the section as a whole. In this, Chu Hsi quotes from *Mencius*, which in turn is quoting from the *Book of Odes*:

> Heaven in producing mankind,
> Gave them their various faculties and relations with specific laws.
> These are the invariable rules of nature for all to hold,
> And all love this admirable virtue.[43]

The quotation continues: Confucius praises the author of this ode as one who understood human nature; and Mencius reiterates its teachings that every aspect of life and every human relation has a fixed principle and that all should cherish and take seriously the virtuous nature that allows them to understand and follow these principles (5:1a).

Using this quote, Chu Hsi wishes to make two important points so that his purpose in the Outer Chapters might succeed. First, he has to convince the student of the constancy of principle and of human nature, at all times and in all places, operative as much in the present as in the golden age of the past.

---

43. *Mencius* 6A:6, trans. Legge, in *The Four Books*, p. 863.

TABLE 8.2   Major Sources of the Inner Chapters of the *Elementary Learning*
A. Major Sources of Each Chapter

Source	Chap. 1	Chap. 2	Chap. 3	Chap. 4	Total
Record of Ritual	5	65	22	7	99
Analects	3	19	18	11	51
Mencius	1	7	1	4	13
Hsiao-ching	0	6	0	0	6
Tso-chuan	0	1	0	5	6

B. Distribution of Sources Among the Five Relationships: Chapter 2

Relationship	Record of Ritual	Analects	Hsiao-ching	Mencius	Misc. Ritual[a]
Parent-Child	32	2	3	1	1
Ruler-Minister	5	11	1	2	0
Husband-Wife	7	0	0	0	2
Elder-Younger	17	1	0	2	0
Friend-Friend	4	5	0	2	0

C. Distribution of Sources Among the Four Aspects of Cultivation:
Chapter 3

Aspects of Cultivation	Record of Ritual	Analects	Misc. Ritual[a]
Mind cultivation	3	7	1
Comportment	13	7	1
Clothing	2	3	1
Food and Drink	4	1	0

[a] Misc. Ritual includes *Chou-li*, *I-li*, and *Ta-tai-li*.

This calls for valuing the present as worthy of one's serious consideration and commitment. Related to this is the second point that the student should cherish his innate "admirable virtue," for that enables him to discern principle and respond appropriately to the problems of his age. He is thus called upon to take himself and his age seriously.

In the Outer Chapters, Chu Hsi indicates that the material in chapter 5 is meant "to amplify" (*kuang*) and that in chapter 6 "to substantiate" (*shih*) the teachings of the Inner Chapters. But by doing so he does not mean to imply that the second half is merely an embellishment of the first half, that it merely provides examples of how basic principles were applied in historical situations. Rather, he wishes to address himself squarely to the challenge of the application of classical teachings in the modern world. This was a serious concern for Sung Neo-Confucians, and among the texts compiled by Chu Hsi for basic instruction the *Elementary Learning* is perhaps the most striking for its inclusion in roughly equal proportions of both classical and contemporary material to try to deal with this concern. The Outer Chapters reflect Chu

TABLE 8.3   Distribution of Pre-Sung and Sung Sources in the Outer Chapters of *Elementary Learning*

Topic	Chapter 5		Chapter 6	
	Pre-Sung	Sung	Pre-Sung	Sung
Education	4	10	1	7
Human Relations				
Parent-Child	1	13	8	2
Ruler-Minister	0	10	4	4
Husband-Wife	5	3	5	0
Elder-Younger	1	3	8	2
Friend-Friend	0	3	0	1
General	0	2	10	1
TOTAL	7	34	35	10
Cultivation				
Mind	4	12	11	3
Comportment	0	4	1	6
Dress	} 0	} 3	1	0
Food and drink			1	5
General	2	11	0	0
TOTAL	6	30	14	14
GRAND TOTAL	17	74	50	31

Hsi's groping for answers to the pressing issues of his day within the context of the classical past as well as his attempt to rouse students to do the same.

That this task was not an easy one, that no one person had all the answers, is clear from the fact that Chu Hsi casts a wide net for sources in this section (see Table 8.4). He shows a variety of intellectuals from the Han dynasty on grappling with these issues. In contrast to the Inner Chapters where only a few sources dominated (twenty-two in all), here no one text dominates, and there are at least fifty-six different sources. This effectively opened up the tradition beyond the confines of a few canonical authorities and admitted a greater variety of people with something of value to say to contemporary society.

Here Chu Hsi no longer maintains the calm, descriptive tone of the first half. Rather he has included selections that voice outspoken criticism of the current scene, express an urgent need for reform, and offer possible solutions. The gap between ideals and reality is put before the student much more explicitly, calling for him to deal in a more complex way with moral matters. All this gives the Outer Chapters a great sense of immediacy and liveliness, which the Inner Chapters lacked.

TABLE 8.4   Distribution of Major Sources in the Outer Chapters of
Elementary Learning

Source	Chap. 5	Chap. 6
Dynastic histories[a]	9	41
Ch'eng Brothers	25	7
Lü Pen-chung (*T'ung-meng hsün, She-jen chia-lu, Shih-yu ts'a-chih*)	15	9
Ssu-ma Kuang (*Chu-chia ts'a-i, Shu-i, Chia-fan, Chia-i*)	9	8
Chang Tsai	8	0
Yen-shih chia-hsün	6	0
Liu-shih chia-hsün	1	5
Wang T'ung	2	2

[a] Dynastic histories most cited:
  Han shu, 6
  Hou Han shu, 11
  Chin shu, 7
  Wei shu, 3
  San-kuo-chih, 3
  Nan shih, 3
  Old and New T'ang History, 10
  Sung shih, 5

In terms of content, the themes of education and cultivating the self are given more attention in this half than in the first part. Earlier, education had 17 items and cultivation had 57, compared to 138 items for human relations. Here education is given 22 items, most very lengthy, and cultivation 64, compared to 86 items for human relations (Table 8.1). Although the theme of human relations continues to dominate, it does not do so to the same degree. In part, this is because, while human relations remained the perennial concern of Confucianism, education and self-cultivation were areas where much of what was new and creative in Neo-Confucianism found expression.

Besides the quantitative difference in treatment of these three themes, there are different emphases in the content of each theme. This will become clear as I now examine the contents of the Outer Chapters. I will do so by taking each theme and discussing it in terms of its treatment in chapters 5 and 6 together (rather than in two separate discussions). But before I begin some comment is in order about a distinction Chu Hsi seems to have made within the large corpus of material in the Outer Chapters, between those sources that come before the Sung and those that come from the Sung itself.

Except for the theme of education, which draws predominantly upon Sung sources in both chapters 5 and 6, the other two themes tend to draw most of their sources from the Sung in chapter 5 which deals with "admirable words," and most from pre-Sung sources in chapter 6, which deals with "exemplary deeds." Because the Sung saw the resurgence of Confucianism in the form of Neo-Confucianism, it is only natural that it should be a favored period on which to draw for the "admirable words" of the postclassical period. The Han and T'ang were neither particularly creative nor dynamic philosophically and thus lacked material Chu Hsi needed for his purposes. But even if they were somewhat deficient in this respect, they were not lacking in inspirational role models. Of the eighty-one models given in chapter 6, only thirty-one come the Sung; of the fifty pre-Sung models, thirty-nine come before the T'ang.

I turn now to the theme of establishing the educational process in the Outer Chapters, where chapter 5 focuses more on parental responsibility and chapter 6 on institutional reform. The former opens with a selection from a leading Neo-Confucian of the Northern Sung, Chang Tsai (1020–1077), in the form of a critical tirade against the students of his day. To him, they are arrogant, lazy, self-absorbed, and incapable of submitting themselves either to the discipline of the basic rituals, like sweeping and sprinkling, or to the demands of the five relationships (5:1a–b). Chang's words are followed by those of several other Sung thinkers who voice opinions about what is needed in contemporary education—less memorization and more self-cultivation, less essay writing and more reading of the Classics (5:1b–2b).

The bulk of this section, however, is devoted to eight lengthy selections of written advice offered by famous figures to their sons, nephews, or students. These range from the famous general Ma Yüan of the Han and the Three Kingdoms statesman Chu-ko Liang to Neo-Confucians of the Sung such as Shao Yung (1011–1077) and Hu An-kuo (1074–1138). All these written pieces try to point out the common pitfalls of youth—the tendency to criticize others, seek ease, be fascinated with those in power—and offer encouragement in such positive virtues as honesty, frugality, and hard work (5:3a–7a). These eight passages serve a double function here. While young people can benefit from the content, parents are shown the concrete form their involvement in the moral formation of their sons should take, namely, the explicit articulation of what is expected in terms of their moral conduct.

Although this section dwells primarily on the parental role in education, one item here addresses itself to the public official's role in this area. Echoing the lecture included in chapter 1 of the text, an official's retirement speech is given in which he exhorts the people to help each other in distress and warns against the evils of gambling and excessive litigation (5:7a–b).

All the above constitutes for Chu Hsi "admirable words" about education. As for the "exemplary deeds" in this area, we are first presented with two sets of model parents from a prominent Sung family who strictly oversaw the education of their sons and daugthers (6:1a–2a). But the main focus here is on "deeds" in the sense of specific educational reforms offered by several leading Neo-Confucians for the school system of the country at large, namely, Hu Yüan (993–1059), Ch'eng Hao (1032–1085), and Ch'eng I (1033–1107). Although they firmly believed the government should have a role in education, they took issue with the way it was presently filling that role, most particularly, that it was not taking the moral purpose of education as seriously as it should.[44] The selections here focus on Hu Yüan's Two Halls for Learning: Study of the Meaning of the Classics Hall (*ching-i chai*) and Management of Affairs Hall (*chih-shih chai*); Ch'eng Hao's 1086 memorial advocating a comprehensive school system with systematic progression from county schools to the Imperial University; and Ch'eng I's critical remarks on the examination system and its quotas (6:2a–3b).

One last item concerns the adult community at large and its educational needs beyond the school system. Chu Hsi refers to Lü Ta-chün's Community Compact (*hsiang-yüeh*) and its value for instructing people in their moral duties (6:3b–4a).[45]

I now turn to the second theme of clarifying human relationships. Here there is a more even distribution of attention to each of the five relations, except that of friend-friend, than was the case with the Inner Chapters. The parent-child relation still outnumbers the others, but it does so to a lesser degree. There is a sharp increase in the attention given to the relationship between brothers. The tone in chapter 5, given over to the "admirable words" about these relationships, is extremely critical of the way they are presently conducted, except perhaps for the ruler-minister relation. Thirty-four of forty-one items come from Sung sources; the husband-wife relation is the only one wherein most examples come from pre-Sung sources. In contrast, the tone in chapter 6, devoted to "exemplary deeds," is most laudatory of those who go to extremes in their efforts to serve those above them. Most of these come from pre-Sung sources.

Beginning with the parent-child relation, one notes that the treatment of filial piety here is not as broad as it was in chapter 2. Rather it focuses mainly on two matters: obedience and proper rituals due a nonliving parent. On the matter of obedience, the selections exhort students always to seek the guidance of family elders and not initiate actions on their own. They suggest they wear their parents' orders on their belts, the better to reflect upon them and carry them out. If students take issue with their parents over the morality of an order given by them and act according to what they think is right, they are reminded that this does not absolve them from the fact of their disobedience (5:7b–8a).

The other main focus is on the rituals the child is supposed to carry out after the death of parents: the mourning and ancestral sacrifices. Long

44. For a discussion of the sense of crisis in education at this time, see Thomas Lee's chapter in this volume.
45. For a discussion of the community compact, see Monika Übelhör's chapter in this volume.

selections are given from Ch'eng I and one other eminent Confucian intellectual, Ssu-ma Kuang (1019–1086), both of whom decry the way their contemporaries have ceased performing these rites either properly or indeed at all. With respect to the sacrifices to ancestors, Ch'eng I laments that people pay more attention to their immediate living parents than they do to their ancestors. He advocates the erection of an ancestral temple with tablets (not portraits) of the ancestors and also specifies the type of sacrifices that should be offered at certain times of the year. He concludes by commenting on the moral efficacy of having children witness these sacrifices (5:8b).

The passages from Ssu-ma Kuang focus on the duties during the mourning period following the death of a parent. His main complaint is with those who continue to eat meat, drink wine, go to parties, and have relations with the opposite sex during this period. He gives historical examples of people who came to a bad end because they acted thus. He ends by reiterating what the rules are: no meat, wine, fancy food, music, finery in clothing, and sex. Also, no Buddhist monks are allowed to participate in the funeral ceremonies (5:9a–11b).

This section complements the earlier treatment of the parent-child relationship in chapter 2, which, though heavy on specific directives for behavior toward one's parents while alive, included little about ritual duties after their death. The last item forbidding Buddhist monks at funerals is telling. As Patricia Ebrey points out elsewhere in this volume, Neo-Confucians were greatly concerned about reclaiming ceremonies appropriated by Buddhists.[46] This section could thus be taken as an attempt to do so in the area of funeral and mourning rites.[47]

Among the models of filial children Chu Hsi has provided in chapter 6, more cases of spectacular behavior and a more dramatic tone are apparent than in chapter 4. Most of these illustrations are not from the world of the powerful and famous, but rather concern ordinary people who go to great lengths to fulfill their sense of filial affection and obligation. Three such examples follow. In one case, a son offered his life in exchange for his mother's when bandits attacked them as they fled from the chaos of war. The bandits, impressed with this show of filial piety, allowed both to go free. The son spent the rest of his life doing menial labor and suffering other privations in order to provide comforts for his mother (6:4a–b). In the second example a son resigned his official position to rush to his father's sick bed; to help the doctor make his diagnoses, he tasted his father's feces. When he thus discovered that his father had a terminal illness, he wailed every night to

Heaven to take him instead (6:6a). In a third example, a son's stepmother abused him terribly and alienated his natural father from him. Still, the son continued to attend to her comfort, going so far as to seek the fish and fresh fruits she liked even in the dead of winter. His filial piety was so powerful that he could effect "miracles": carp would jump out of the iced pond; fruit would appear on the trees for him (6:5a). This last example is representative of the folklore that grew up about filial piety, which can best be seen in the short collection, "Twenty-four Examples of Filial Piety."[48]

The ruler-minister relationship has a very different tone from the parent-child one in both chapters 5 and 6. Rather than offering criticisms about the relationship, chapter 5 presents bits of advice as to how to be a good official when dealing with colleagues, underlings, and the people, although some of the advice hints at problems. The tone is set by the first selection which advises the official to view his job in familial terms.

> Serve the ruler as one's parents; serve high officials as one's elder brothers; treat colleagues like family members, treat clerks like one's servants; love the common people as one does one's wife, and manage official affairs as one's family affairs. (5:11b)[49]

Other selections encourage him to be diligent about work and pure and upright in character and warn him against unscrupulous scribes and losing his temper (5:12a–6).

As for the models in chapter 6 exemplifying the teachings here, the principal one is Han minister Chi An who served under Han Ching-ti (r. 156–141 B.C.). Chi An would frankly express his opinions to the emperor, as when he told him, "On the surface you seem to practice benevolence and righteousness, but in your heart you have too many desires."[50] Although the emperor tended to react with anger, he took no reprisals against Chi An but rather came to have more respect for him and allowed him many more privileges at court (6:7b–8a). This example contrasts greatly with those in chapter 4 where the perils of remonstrance are shown.

The other models here dispense advice, such as that one owes one's ruler not only frank opinion but also honest personal conduct. Specifically, he should not, in an attempt to take advantage of quotas, register for exams other than in the place of his own residence, he should not indulge in graft or

48. Translated into English by Ivan Chen and published together with his translation of the *Hsiao-ching* in *The Book of Filial Duty* (London: John Murray, 1908). It includes four models from this section.
49. This, along with five other passages in this section, come from the *T'ung-meng hsün* by the Sung official Lü Pen-chung (1084–1145). He compiled this short primer, drawing on the experience and wisdom of three previous generations of famous family members. The *Elementary Learning* takes many of its selections in the Outer Chapters from it. See *Sung Bibliography*, p. 234.
50. Burton Watson, trans., *Records of the Grand Historian of China* (New York: Columbia University Press, 1961) 2:345.

bribery while an official, even if he wishes to spend money on comforts for his parents, and he should not perform his job in a sloppy, hurried manner (6:9a–10a).

One wonders why Chu Hsi chose not to take a more critical view of this relationship in chapter 5 and why he did not present models of extreme self-sacrifice in chapter 6 as he does for the other relationships. Does this reflect a greater concern with the family in the Outer Chapters or a sense of the political arena as greatly different from the other relations?

The treatment of the husband-wife relation is more similar to that of the parent-child in this regard: criticisms of the current scene in chapter 5 and models of self-sacrifice in chapter 6. Having dealt in chapter 2 with the matter of the wedding ceremony itself, the concern in the "admirable words" about this relationship is with the choice of spouses for one's children. Parents are criticized for marrying their children off too young before they can fully understand how to be good parents themselves and for focusing more on questions of wealth than on the moral character of the prospective spouse. Women who marry beneath themselves often tend to be arrogant and disrespectful in their new household; thus, parents should seek for a woman of lower social standing for their sons (5:12b–13b).

Besides the concern about spouses, this section concentrates on the proper behavior for women in marriage. The principle that widows should not remarry, already mentioned in chapter 2, is reiterated, but this time Ch'eng I more chillingly contends that this holds true even if the woman starves to death as a result (5:13b). In the day-to-day running of the household, a woman is to take care only of those matters concerning the provision of food and clothing and the preparation for family rituals. She is not to exercise any power beyond these things, no matter how bright and talented she may be, because that power resides completely in her husband. Women in a certain area of China are criticized for expressing their opinions too directly, socializing too much, seeking office for their sons, and helping their husbands settle their public affairs (5:13b–14a).[51]

The models for the husband-wife relationship are all of self-sacrificing women who have dedicated themselves completely to their husbands and their families, particularly mothers-in-law. One model woman from the late Han refused to remarry even though her husband left her a widow without child at a young age. She insisted on dedicating the rest of her life to the care of her mother-in-law, even though this meant hard work on her part. Upon the death of the mother-in-law, she sold all her possessions to give her a proper funeral and maintain the family sacrifices (6:10a–b). In another case a young widow who lived during the third century A.D., following the Han, progressively mutilated herself—cutting off first her hair, then her ears, and

---

51. Most of the critical remarks about women in the household are taken from the Sui dynasty *Yen-shih chia-hsün*.

finally her nose—to resist a forced remarriage by her parents (6:11a–b). Yet a third woman from the T'ang courageously tried to ward off ten strong bandits from attacking her mother-in-law and was almost beaten to death in the process (6:11b–12a). These women not only act upon their convictions, but they are also able to articulate why they do so. The last two women give almost identical reasons for their actions, namely, that they have a moral sense of benevolence and righteousness; for them not to act as they do would be to throw themselves amidst the ranks of the brute animals who lack such moral sense.

The elder-younger brother relationship contains the same criticism, expressed in the husband-wife section, of women who arrogate too much power to themselves. The opening selection speaks of the natural affection and intimacy shared by brothers, coming as they do from the same flesh. But once they marry, their wives pull them apart with their jealous, wrangling ways (5:14a). A T'ang household head effectively dealt with this problem by lecturing the women about this matter twice a month. Duly chastened, they caused no further trouble (5:14b). Elsewhere, Ch'eng I complains that brothers are not as close to one another as they used to be and blames men for caring more about their own sons than their brothers (5:15a).

The first group of models for the fraternal relationship is chapter 6 deals with those who do not get along with each other: this is blamed in one case on their wives and in the other on conflicts over land. An astute elder brother in one and a wise official in the other skillfully bring the men back together to live in harmony (6:12a–b). The chapter also presents brothers who get along splendidly: one defends his stepbrother against the cruelty of his mother (6:12b–13a); another nurses an elder brother stricken with a contagious disease back to health after everyone else in the family had abandoned him for dead (6:13a); and still another chooses to save the son of his dead brother rather than his own while in flight during the Period of Disunion (6:13a–b). There is also a household in which the elder brother has assumed the role of head after the death of the father and where the younger brothers cheerfully and respectfully observe the proper fraternal hierarchy of power (6:13b–14b). A description of Ssu-ma Kuang's affectionate concern for his elder brother is also included here, providing a contemporary model of this relation (6:14b).

The scant treatment of the friend-friend relationship in the Outer Chapters does not warrant comment, so I will proceed to the "general discussion" sections on human relationships in these two chapters. These are extremely important in that they focus on the household seen as more than the nuclear family. This concern with the management and smooth running of the household is new and significant in the Outer Chapters. It suggests not only that the student is considerably older and more mature than when he studied the comparable material in the Inner Chapters but also that much importance is attached to the preservation of the larger household at a time when it is probably suffering great erosion.

In chapter 5, there are only two items in the "general discussion" section. In the first selection the prominent Sung statesman Fan Chung-yen (989–1052) describes to his sons his motives for establishing his famous charitable estate (5:15b–16a), while in the second Ssu-ma Kuang enumerates the duties of a household head (5:16a). The former selection emphasizes the spirit of generosity and concern for one's larger clan, while the latter stresses the rules of ritual that should govern family life.

Chapter 6 presents the reader with eleven model households, headed by exemplary leaders. Among their virtues deemed worthy of praise are: they are good at correcting sons and grandsons; they live simply; they care for relatives in distress; they have definite rules and rituals for doing everything; and they exercise compassion to keep relations going smoothly in the household (6:15a–19b). One example, which could hardly have been easy for most people to implement, is that of the Ch'en clan of Chiang-chou, who ate all their meals together in perfect decorum—all seven hundred members of them; even their one hundred dogs waited for each other to assemble before commencing to eat (6:19a).

I now take up the third theme of reverencing the self and its treatment in the Outer Chapters. Here the territory is immediately recognizable as Neo-Confucian. The subsection on mind cultivation dominates as the central focus in contrast to the more physical aspects of cultivation in chapter 3. Half the selections here come from the writings of the four masters of the Northern Sung—Chou Tun-i (1017–1073), Chang Tsai, Ch'eng Hao, and Ch'eng I—and most of these selections can also be found in Chu Hsi's other anthology, *Reflections on Things at Hand.*

After four short aphorisms by pre-Sung thinkers, the material proceeds to what Sung Neo-Confucians most prefer to talk about; self-cultivation. Chou Tun-i's famous passage about learning to be a sage, Ch'eng Hao's words on keeping the mind collected and inside the body, and Ch'eng I's "Admonitions on Correct Seeing, Hearing, Speaking, and Acting" are all included (5:16b–17b). The other sections on comportment, dress, and eating habits are modest in comparison and, in fact, are hardly distinguishable from the one on mind cultivation. For instance, the sections on correct dress and eating habits are lumped together as one, and the entries include two *tso-yu-ming* (notes of instruction written on the side of one's seat to keep one alert) by Ch'eng I's disciple Chang I (1081–?) (5:19a–b) and by Fan Tsu-yü's son Fan Ch'ung (5:20a–b). Although both include resolutions about moderation in clothing and eating habits, they seem more concerned with matter appropriately subsumed under the heading of attitudes of mind.

Chapter 5's treatment of "reverencing the self" ends with a "general discussion" section that might be more aptly titled "the relation of reading books to self-cultivation" in that all the items have to do with study and reading books.[52] Presented here are a proposed methodology for reading each of the Four Books, a suggested daily schedule of reading, advice on the proper handling and care of books, and the potential efficacious results of study on one's character (5:21–24a). The section ends with a long passage from Ch'eng Hao about the dangers of heterodoxy, especially Buddhism, and the ill effects of these on true learning. He bids the student to help clear away the insidious weeds of false learning so that true learning might be passed down to the next age (5:24a–b). It is worth noting that this discussion of reading books comes in the section on self-cultivation, not on education. This reflects a deepened awareness in the Sung of the spiritual benefits to be derived from reading, especially the Four Books and Classics, as compared to the harm done by indiscriminate reading.

The models offered in chapter 6 of those who exemplify the teachings on reverencing the self focus on those who have perfected mind cultivation to the point of achieving perfect composure and detachment. These are men who are calm, dignified, and self-disciplined, men who can never be rushed or bribed. One Liu Kuan had such composure that even when his wife had a servant spill hot soup on him to test him he remained unruffled (6:19b–20a). Liu Chung-ying, a T'ang official, was so guided by the dictates of propriety (li) that he exhibited the same formality and seriousness whether at home or at work (6:21b). These examples culminate in that of Fan Chung-yen, whom I have already mentioned in connection with his charitable estate. Here Ssu-ma Kuang praises him for his great sense of moral integrity and self-discipline, and refers to Fan's practice of chanting the motto, "A gentleman (shih) must be the first to worry about the problems of the world and the last to enjoy its pleasures" (6:22b–23a).

In contrast to these positive models, several selections in this section set apart for criticism the men of the Period of Disunion who engaged in "pure talk" and also the literary types of the early T'ang. They are portrayed as superficial, selfish, and not serious about the important tasks of life (6:20b–21a).

The models for comportment stress those able to sit still in a composed manner for long periods of time, without slouching or sprawling the legs. Among these Ch'eng Hao is described as being able to sit all day as if he had been carved from wood; yet still he retained his ability to respond to people with warmth and readiness when necessary (6:23a). Although there is no specific mention here of the practice of meditation called quiet-sitting, which many Neo-Confucians engaged in, certainly the case is made for the type of discipline it bespoke.

The remaining model figures exemplify a great simplicity and frugality in their lifestyles. One understands these items as reflecting Chu Hsi's concern

---

52. For more on this matter, see Wm. Theodore de Bary's chapter in this volume.

for both the problem of affluence and the pressure on officials to adopt a more lavish lifestyle the higher they rise in power. The models presented here refuse to do this, but rather they hold on to their original humble lifestyles no matter how high they rise in officialdom. One of these, an early prime minister of the Sung, Chang Chih-po was criticized for this and was forced to justify himself (6:24a–b). Ssu-ma Kuang describes how his father's generation enjoyed social gatherings for the company they shared, not the food and wine, but now the opposite is the case, as people lie ready to criticize those who fail to entertain lavishly (6:24b–25a). In the next to last item, Ssu-ma Kuang describes his own temperament as one naturally more comfortable with a simple lifestyle, that is he is discomfited by wealth and finery. In fact, at the banquet celebrating his successful passing of the examinations, he refused to wear flowers in his hair, like the other candidates. Upon pressure from the others, he finally compromised and wore a single flower (6:25a).

Having reviewed the contents of the Outer Chapters, we are in a position to compare the differences in emphasis between them and the Inner Chapters in their treatments of the three basic themes. In terms of education, we have seen parents reminded of their continuing responsibility as teachers even when their children have reached young adulthood, as well as the importance of reinforcing parental efforts in the institutional sphere by specific reforms in the educational system sought by Neo-Confucian intellectuals. The theme of human relations focused on the larger extended household, with less attention to the extrafamilial relations of ruler-minister and friend-friend. The concern here was with the potential disruption of the harmony of the larger household by sons who are willful and neglectful of their aging parents, wives who are jealous and unsubmissive, and brothers who wish to go their separate ways. The models dwelt on only the most self-sacrificing of sons, wives, and brothers who dedicated themselves to the good of the household as a whole rather than to their own narrow interests. Also in this section, we saw how adulthood entails more than managing the demands of one or two relationships but rather involves a balancing of the various demands that arise from the complex network of human relationships. In treating the theme of reverencing the self, much more sophisticated forms of self-cultivation were introduced as discipline came to be seen as more a matter of internal motivation than of external pressure or conformity. Rather than an outward show of good manners, the goal was inner composure and serenity.

Having worked through to the end of the *Elementary Learning* text, the student would surely have successfully laid the type of foundation Chu Hsi intended when he compiled this text. The student would have achieved a basic level of self-discipline, a sense of order, a responsiveness to others, and a sense of unselfishness: all these the fundamentals of the moral life. In addition, the student would have developed a certain amount of self-confidence in his ability to interact with others and with that a sense of self-worth.

The text emphasizes that these fundamentals of the moral life are learned in the social sphere, and most particularly, in the most elementary of social spheres, the family. Chu Hsi's vision of the family is thus worth noting here. As a Confucian, Chu Hsi has made it a point, along with other intellectuals of the Sung, to reassert the family as well as the public realm as the field of action for people as opposed to the monastery of the Buddhists. And yet, he does not wish simply to settle for a purely "secular" view of the family as many others of the Sung were doing. He wishes to champion a vision of it that primarily emphasizes its moral and spiritual values rather than its social or economic utility. Thus, he argues for a return to a classical model of the family, yet it is one that could be adopted by all classes of society, and not just the aristocracy as in the Chou period.[53]

It seems to me that Chu Hsi ends up, consciously or unconsciously, trying to imbue the Confucian household with some of the spirit of the monastery. For the monastery offered a model both of community discipline, with its daily regimen and simplicity of lifestyle to which all had to adhere, and personal discipline, with its emphasis on meditation and self-reflection. This adaptation could provide a new ethos for the traditional Confucian family. Its advantage over the monastery for Chu Hsi would be that this is a more natural, well-rounded, and profound way of human development, inasmuch as one would not break away from the primary human relationships as in monastic Buddhism. But it also has an advantage over more secular views of the family; it would activate the individual consciences of family members to serve the larger purposes of the group, and ultimately of Heaven, earth, and all things.

The models of household heads in the last part of the *Elementary Learning* text are extremely crucial to Chu Hsi's purpose here, for they illustrate to the student men who have successfully integrated their various roles as sons, husbands, officials, and brothers, and who thus help to create an environment that influences other family members to do the same. And though the primary field of activity of these men is social, they are not reduced to their social roles but are shown possessing a sense of selfhood that goes beyond these roles. They exhibit great spiritual depth and inner resources, achieved through their efforts at self-cultivation. One might even say that there is an aura of the famous Buddhist layman Vimalakirti about these models, in the particular combination of the secular and the sacred in their lives.

The human person, according to the models Chu Hsi has presented in this text, emerges in a largely social context, starting with one's principal relationship with one's parents but broadening to include a much more

53. For a good discussion of the effort by Chu Hsi and other Sung Neo-Confucians to revive the classical model of the family, see Ebrey's "Conceptions of the Family in the Sung Dynasty," especially pp. 229–232. In the introductory essay to her *Family and Property in Sung China, Yüan Ts'ai's Precepts for Social Life* (Princeton: Princeton University Press, 1984), Ebrey characterizes Chu Hsi's household discipline as "quasi-military" (p. 49).

diversified network. The text makes clear, however, that the person also has needs and dimensions beyond the social that can be considered only with a fully developed sense of *self* based on a deeper integration of the interior life. Education, accordingly, should be based on the primary social relationships, but it should never lose sight of or ignore these deeper dimensions of the self.

The *Elementary Learning* by and large aims to deal with the social development of the person and does not deal with the inner depths of the person to the same extent as the *Reflections on Things at Hand*. Nevertheless, its purpose is to insure that the student will be properly prepared for the next stage in the process of his self-development—learning to take responsibility for himself by first meeting his responsibilities to others. As such, this text fulfills an important function in the total educational program envisaged by Chu Hsi.

NINE

Chu Hsi and Public Instruction

Ron-Guey Chu

In his relatively brief career as a local official,[1] Chu Hsi (1130–1200) became known as an effective administrator. He was also known as a dedicated supporter of education, both in the public and private spheres, and as an incorruptible judge. Perhaps in his efforts to relieve suffering from famine one can see the full extent of his practical success. In 1181, owing to the effectiveness of his policies and to the cooperation and support he got from people of the locality, more than two hundred thousand people, over half the population, were estimated to have been saved from starvation in the drought-stricken area of Nan-k'ang (in present-day Kiangsi).[2] Having won recognition for this, he was soon called upon to deal with disasters on a much larger scale in Chekiang. Although the measures he was in a position to implement were only of a palliative nature and came too late to deal most effectively with the situation, more than two million people in Shao-hsing

I would like to express my heartfelt gratitude to Professors Wing-tsit Chan, Wm. Theodore de Bary, John Meskill, and Conrad Schirokauer. Their guidance and encouragement have made this study possible.

1. For a general account of Chu Hsi's career as a local official, see Conrad Schirokauer, "Chu Hsi as an Administrator," in *Études Song-Sung Studies*, series I, no. 3 (1976), pp. 207–236. Huang Kan (1152–1221), who wrote Chu Hsi's "biographical account" (*hsing-chuang*), said Chu Hsi "in a period of fifty years had served under four reigns. His service outside the court was only nine years, while his attendance at court was only for forty days." *Mien-chai chi* (*Ssu-k'u ch'üan-shu chen-pen*) 36:38b; hereafter cited as *Hsing-chuang*. Works from this collection will be cited as SK edition. According to Wing-tsit Chan, Huang Kan's account is only an approximation in terms of whole numbers; in fact, Chan says, "Chu Hsi attended the court for forty-six days and served as a local official for somewhat more than seven and a half years." *Chu Tzu men-jen* (Taipei: Student Book Co., 1982), p. 11.

2. This figure was reported by Chu Hsi in his memorials on famine relief measures in 1181. The total affected population was 227,883, including 137,607 adults and 90,276 children. Chu Hsi, *Chu Tzu ta-ch'üan* (SPPY ed.) 16:13b; *pieh-chi* 10:20a; hereafter cited as *Wen-chi*.

and Wu-chou alone were said to have been aided by his efforts.[3] From this his fame reached new heights.[4]

Among the many reasons for Chu's success, some political, some personal, it seems that his use of published proclamations (*pang*) played a significant part. Like some of his contemporaries, he took full advantage of this public medium for promulgating laws and policies to achieve administrative purposes. In addition, he brought an educational dimension to its political use. For him *pang* represented more than just edicts or official notices but actually had a suasive, hortatory, and educative function.

A survey of the collected works of major Sung thinkers who were at the same time distinguished local officials, either prior to or contemporaneous with Chu Hsi, indicates that proclamations as a genre do not appear in their collected writings at all. This is true of such notable persons as Fan Chung-yen (989–1052), Ou-yang Hsiu (1007–1072), Chou Tun-i (1017–1073), Ssu-ma Kuang (1019–1086), Chang Tsai (1020–1077), Yang Shih (1053–1135), Yu Tso (1053–1123), Lo Ts'ung-yen (1072–1135), Chang Shih (1133–1180), Lu Chiu-yüan (1139–1193), Yang Chien (1141–1226), and Yeh Shih (1150–1223).[5] It may indeed be that, despite the failure to include such proclamations in their collected writings, these personages did make some use of them. Nevertheless, it is significant that they did not attach the importance to them that Chu did and that the latter had to single out Ch'en Hsiang (1017–1080) as his one predecessor who provided a model and precedent for his own practice in this respect.

In view of the fact that proclamations were essential to the conduct of local government and could not have been dispensed with by anyone who held a significant local post, one wonders why proclamations did not find their way into the collected works of others than Chu Hsi and his followers. No doubt it is because the others regarded the *pang* as no more than routine pronouncements, not of enough inherent substance to warrant their preservation. This stands in contrast to the importance attached to Chu Hsi's proclamations, which attracted much attention in Chu's own time and

3. Shao-hsing prefecture was estimated to have 1.3 million affected people; *Wen-chi* 16:23a. Wu-chou had more than seven hundred thousand people in need of aid; *Ibid.*, 17:18b.
4. The people of Chekiang were so grateful to Chu Hsi that they composed songs in praise of his virtues. *Chu Tzu yü-lei ta-ch'üan* (Kyoto: Chūbun shuppansha) 106:17 (p. 5470); hereafter cited as *Yü-lei*. I will cite the *Yü-lei* by paragraph number in each chapter as well as page number. Lu Chiu-yüan also observed in a letter to Vice Administrator Ch'en Ts'ui in the early autumn of 1182 that the people of Chekiang were regretful over the departure of Chu Hsi. *Hsiang-shan ch'üan-chi* (SPPY) 7:5b.
5. Fan Chung-yen, *Fan Wen-cheng kung chi* (SPTK ed.); On-yang Hsiu, *On-yang Wen-chung kung chi* (SPTK ed.); Chou Tun-i, *Chou Tzu ch'üan-shu* (Kuo-hsüeh chi-pen ts'ung-shu ed.); Ssu-ma Kuang, *Wen-kuo Wen-cheng kung wen-chi* (SPTK ed.); Chang Tsai, *Chang Tsai chi* (Peking: Chung-hua shu-chü, 1978); Yang Shih, *Kuei-shan chi* (SK ed.); Yu Tso, *Yu Chien-shan chi* (SK ed.); Lo Ts'ung-yen, *Lo Yü chang chi* (Kinsei kanseki sōkan, 1st series, 1972); Chang Shih, *Nan-hsüan wen-chi* (SK ed.); Lu Chiu-yüan, *Hsiang-shan ch'üan-chi* (SPPY); Yang Chien, *Tz'u-hu hsien-sheng i-shu* (Ssu-ming ts'ung-shu, 1936); Yeh Shih, *Shui-hsin chi* (SPPY).

thereafter. Many of his followers, when holding local offices, often issued proclamations in the style of their master. Some even printed Chu's proclamations for distribution.[6] Thereafter, proclamations became recognized as a genre of great importance.[7] It is safe to say not only that Chu Hsi brought a new meaning to them but also that, thanks to his proclamations and other educational efforts, popular education attained a prominent and permanent place in the Neo-confucian tradition.

PROCLAMATIONS AS A MEANS OF POPULAR EDUCATION

In what sense can Chu Hsi's proclamations be regarded as a means of popular education? As the discussion below will make clear, in terms of content Chu Hsi issued two kinds of proclamations. One primarily deals with administrative affairs and natural disasters, the other with public morality and social customs. The former can be said to be imformative but not educative. However, some proclamations in this first category do attempt to impart new information to the people. The best examples of this are the proclamations dealing with new farming techniques. Even those concerning famine, which instruct the people on how to behave in such a stressful situation, have a certain educational value.

The educative value of the other kind of proclamation may not be readily apparent. Sometimes identified as *ch'üan-yü wen* (essays of encouragement and instruction), they have a dual nature. As encouragement, they are like moral exhortations, appealing to the people's minds and hearts; as instruction, they sometimes have the character of official directives, implying that failure to comply would expose the offender to punishment. These proclamations often contain exhortations to observe the standard moral values and social practices of Confucian tradition. Some of these moral precepts and prohibitions would be commonly known, certainly to anyone able to read; for instance, everyone should be filial. In this case, proclamations can be regarded as a routine exercise of moral authority and educational responsibility on the part of the government.

Nevertheless, from Chu Hsi's point of view it could by no means be taken for granted that the people were already versed in Confucian morality and had nothing to learn from these proclamations. Chu Hsi's writings often reveal a deep sense of anxiety over the erosive effects of Buddhism and

---

6. Examples of this can be found in Huang Kan (1152–1221) and Wei Liao-weng (1178–1237). See Huang Kan, *Mien-chai chi* 15a–16b, 17a–18a, 21b–22b; Wei Liao-weng, *Ho-shan hsien-sheng ta-ch'üan chi* (SK ed.) 100:12b. Chen Te-hsiu (1178–1235), although not a direct disciple, occupies a central role in Neo-confucian popular education. For his proclamations, see his *Hsi-shan hsien-sheng Chen Wen-chung kung wen-chi* (SPTK ed.), chüan 40.

7. Wang Yang-ming (Wang Shou-jen, 1473–1529), the most eminent Neo-Confucian in the Ming (1368–1644), has bequeathed a rich body of works in proclamations that invite scholarly study. *Yang-ming ch'üan-shu* (SPPY ed.), chaps. 16–17.

popular customs on people's observance of traditional norms of conduct. He clearly felt that the moral precepts in proclamations could serve as part of a cohesive program of ethical teaching, informed perhaps for the first time by his consistent interpretation of the significance of Confucian morality. In this he does not, of course, create a new morality for the people; rather he provides a rational basis for it, especially in the priorities he adopts and selectivity shown in his use of widely known precepts, transforming them into a Neo-Confucian morality that cannot but be identified as uniquely Chu Hsi's. In this respect, the moral teaching he brings to the populace is almost as distinctive as his efforts at popular education.

USES AND AUDIENCES OF PROCLAMATIONS

There are about 115 proclamations, of varying length and differing content, preserved in the collected works of Chu Hsi. Nearly 100 of them were issued in Nan-k'ang from 1179 to 1181, reflecting Chu Hsi's conscientious attention to the affairs of this area and the intensity of his activity there. During his tenure in office, both Nan-k'ang and Che-tung (Chekiang) witnessed great devastation from prolonged drought and mass famine. Consequently, most of his proclamations deal with famine-related problems in one way or another. As such, they instructed people how to handle specific practical matters and could be seen as public instruction in a broader sense.

Perhaps in crises as serious as these nothing was more urgent than providing immediate relief to the affected people. In the proclamations Chu Hsi instructed the populace about where and how they could receive aid. He kept them informed about the extent of the disaster and the status of rescue efforts, so that the desperate peasants would not abandon their land and flee in droves, which, he explained, would only add to and prolong their suffering. He entreated the well-to-do either to sell rice at a normal price or make donations, which would be rewarded later by the imperial court. He also cautioned against rioting or resorting to violence to obtain rice.[8]

In related efforts, Chu Hsi proclaimed the reduction or remission of various taxes, as a further easing of the people's burden.[9] To limit the impact of drought before it occurred and to revitalize the local economy in the aftermath of famine, Chu Hsi paid special attention to agricultural matters as well as the construction of irrigation works. Indeed, his "Proclamation on the Encouragement of Agriculture" (*Ch'üan-nung wen*)[10] drew upon the newest methods of agriculture in his time and thus reflected a significant technological development.[11] The fact that Chu Hsi was interested in disseminating

8. Cf. Chu Hsi, *Wen-chi* 99:9a–11a; *pieh-ch*, (additional collection), chaps. 9–10.
9. Ibid.
10. Two examples of this can be found in Chu Hsi, *Wen-chi* 99:6b–9a, issued in 1179 and 1180.
11. *Shushigaku taikei* (Tokyo: Meitoku shuppansha, 1983), vol. 5, p. 283.

this kind of new and vital information to the public undoubtedly underscores the breadth of his learning and the receptivity he showed with respect to innovation.

To deal with other administrative concerns, Chu Hsi's proclamations addressed the following subjects: the community granary (*she-ts'ang*), draft services (*ch'ai-i*), academies, litigation, local defense, the survey and reclassification of land (*ching-chieh*), and so forth. He also issued prohibitions against dividing family property among brothers, harassing the heads of the community unit (*pao-wu*), and appropriation of the land of the poor, among other things.[12] Many of these proclamations were addressed to the population at large, but others were at times directed to specific segments of society. These specific audiences included scholar-officials, the common people, elders, Buddhists, Taoists, soldiers, government runners, land tenants, dislocated people, passing travelers, upper households, lower households, official households (*kuan-hu*).

However, for purposes of this paper, I will focus on a group of proclamations, fewer in number but no less important, that instruct or admonish the populace in regard to public morality, social customs, ritual observances, and religious practices. With reference to this area of public morality and social edification I speak here of public instruction; while doing so, however, I should like to avoid any implication that Chu Hsi was more given to moralizing than to dealing with practical affairs. Although outside the scope of this paper, Chu Hsi did in fact give much detailed, concrete advice on problem solving and crisis management.

POLITICAL LIFE AND PROCLAMATIONS

As a local official, Chu Hsi was much concerned that people should maintain good human relationships, follow proper decorum, and maintain appropriate ritual observances. These concerns appeared early in his political life. As assistant magistrate (*chu-pu*) of T'ung-an (Fukien),[13] he appealed to his superiors, calling upon them for stiffer enforcement of the marriage ceremony. The document entitled "Petition to Strictly Enforce the Marriage Ceremony" says:

> It is my humble view that among regulations of the rites and the laws, those concerning marriage are of primary importance. They are meant to distinguish male and female [roles], to rectify social customs, and to prevent disaster and disorder at the root. As I have witnessed it myself, I have learned that this prefecture does not have a tradition from the past concerning the practice of the

---

12. Cf. Chu Hsi, *Wen-chi, chüan* 99; *pieh-chi, chüan* 9–10.

13. Chu Hsi's tenure as assistant magistrate was from the seventh month of 1153 to the seventh month of 1156. Wang Mao-hung (1668–1741), *Chu Tzu nien-p'u* (Taipei: Shih-chieh shu-chü, 1973), pp. 9–13; this reprint of the TSCC edition will be cited hereafter as *Nien-p'u*.

marriage ceremony. The common people, because of poverty, cannot afford betrothal gifts. It even occurs that they seduce women to live with them. They call this practice "inviting a companion to become a wife". It is so widely practiced that even the scholar-officials and wealthy families have done it from time to time. People no longer have any shame or fear. The error of this practice goes beyond its violating the rites or the laws of the state. Jealousy and hatred together will bring disastrous fights, and some will fight to the death without even having any regrets. The customs of the people are so indecent and ignorant that I deeply feel sorrow and compassion for them. I beg you, the prefect, to examine the current statutes, make them known, and put an end to this practice. Furthermore, I beg the intendant of the prefecture to select, from the *Five Rites of Cheng-ho*,[14] a marriage ceremony appropriate for scholar-officials and the common people and publicize it so that the people can follow it and the government can enforce it.[15]

Although the petition is not in the standard format of a proclamation and no such proclamation survives from the T'ung-an era,[16] it clearly underscores a major concern of Chu Hsi as an administrator and forecasts the kind of educational work he would sustain throughout his career.

Chu Hsi took up his next administrative post as the prefect of Nan-k'ang some twenty years after his service at T'ung-an.[17] Compared with T'ung-an, Nan-k'ang was considered a culturally superior area, besides being famous for its beautiful scenery. Now with increased duties and authority, Chu Hsi could hope to achieve more than he had before. The very first thing he did as prefect was to issue a comprehensive proclamation[18] which addressed major problems of the locality and set the tone and style of his administration. He seemed to have found this action so beneficial and effective that he thereafter made it his practice to issue a similar proclamation as the first order of business whenever and wherever he assumed a new office.

When Chu Hsi assumed the office of prefect in Chang-shou (Fukien) in 1190, he was immediately faced with such issues as the lax observance of the traditional rites, strong Buddhist influences, decadent customs, and excessive litigation. By effective use of proclamations and other measures, he was credited with bringing about a "great transformation" of local customs. On this point the biographical account of his conduct of life (*hsing-chuang*) says:

14. *Cheng-ho wu-li hsin-i* (its complete title) was compiled by Cheng Chü-chung (1059–1123) and others, under the auspices of Emperor Hui-tsung (r. 1101–1125). Completed in 1113 and promulgated in the same year, it is especially noted for its detailed prescriptions of the rites for the officials and the common people. In his lifelong effort to revise the rites, Chu Hsi drew upon the contents of this work more than once. See *Nien-p'u*, pp. 90–91, 179.

15. *Wen-chi* 20:1b–2a. This petition is undated. It is not certain whether it predates Chu Hsi's regulation on the sacrificial rites in the school.

16. There are several references to the uses of proclamations by Chu Hsi regarding tax collection and school examinations. See *Yü-lei* 106:2, 3 (pp. 5461–5462).

17. Chu Hsi assumed office in the third month of 1179. See *Nien-p'u*, p. 78.

18. *Wen-chi* 99:1a–2b.

As demonstrated by the prevailing customs, the people did not know what the rites were. He, therefore, adopted the rituals of mourning, burial, and wedding of antiquity and proclaimed them to the public. Moreover, he ordered elders to explain and instruct the young. As Buddhist teachings were flourishing in the south, men and women gathered at the residences of monks to convene meetings for the [ostensible purpose of] transmitting the scriptures. There were also unmarried women who set up private nunneries for themselves to reside in. He prohibited every such practice, and, as a result, the customs were greatly reformed.[19]

In Chu's *Life Chronology* (*nien-p'u*), both in the earliest extant edition and the standard authoritative edition, the proclamation about the rituals was spoken of in exactly the same terms,[20] suggesting that both were following the *hsing-chuang*. Chu Hsi's own official biography in the *History of the Sung*, which predates these two accounts, speaks essentially to the same effect.[21] Although the text of the proclamation was lost, there is no reason to believe that Huang Kan (1152–1221), who wrote the *hsing-chuang*, was incorrect. Similarly, another text, *"Li-lüeh"* (Simplified Rituals), was meant to be a manual of rituals. It is said that Chu Hsi compiled it in 1155 on the basis of the *Five Rites of Cheng-ho* and that it was later printed and circulated for the observance of the people.[22] Although no longer extant, one might get some idea of its content and spirit from a proclamation concerning the observance of mourning rites issued on an occasion when Chu Hsi witnessed a *chin-shih* degree holder who had completely discarded proper mourning dress, even though he was supposed to be in mourning for the death of his mother.[23] Ch'en Ch'un (1159–1223), an outstanding pupil of Chu Hsi from that region, reported that it had become a trend among scholar-officials for all to adopt dark dress, rather than white or light colored, as mourning attire and to go on attending social functions as usual, rather than abstain from social intercourse.[24] What is more, Chu Hsi was shocked to learn that even the local elite failed to follow the basic prescriptions of social conduct. This

19. *Hsing-chuang* 36:26b–27a.
20. *Nien-p'u*, p. 171; Yeh Kung-hui (15th century), ed., *Chu Tzu nien-p'u* (*Kinsei kanseki sôkan*, 1st series; Taipei: Kuang-wen shu-chü, 1979), p. 179. Yeh's version of the *nien-p'u* is considered the earliest edition available to date.
21. *Sung shih* (SPTK ed.) 429:12b–13a.
22. The work is called "Simplified Rituals of the Cheng-ho [Five Ceremonials] for the Official and Commoner Compiled in the Reign of Shao-hsing" (*Shao-hsing ts'uan tz'u Cheng-ho min-ch'en li-lüeh*). *Wen-chi* 69:15b–17a. It was a proposal submitted by Chu Hsi as assistant magistrate of T'ung-an, attempting to establish a uniform standard in the observance of rituals for both officials and the common people. Moreover, he proposed to set up a field of study on these rituals in prefectural and county schools so that students could learn the rites through actual practice. Although Yeh Kung-hui asserted that Chu's proposal was adopted, there is no other evidence to substantiate it. Yeh Kung-hui, *Chu Tzu nien-p'u*, pp. 74–75.
23. *Wen-chi* 100:3a–4a.
24. Ch'en Ch'un, *Pei-hsi ta-ch'üan chi* (SK ed.) 28:2a–b.

proclamation, though specific in its purpose, contains many elements typical of Chu Hsi's concern with the rites in general, which I will discuss below. The Buddhist establishment in Chang-chou was a major social force that Confucian officials like Chu Hsi had to contend with. Ch'en Ch'un, a native of that region and a keen observer of the local scene, reported that Buddhist temples were large landholders with holdings amounting to 70 percent of the total property.[25] Often Buddhist prelates took it upon themselves to act as local authorities and prefectural leaders. They frequently mistreated people and offended the appointed officials. Also, they employed loafers as their henchmen who harassed people at will.[26] Thus, at stake were more than just religious issues.

From the Confucian standpoint, Buddhists not only misled people into false beliefs but led to the corruption of customs and conduct.[27] In the "Proclamation of Instruction,"[28] Chu Hsi issued many prohibitions against the following religious activities and questionable moral practices: the setting up of temples or nunneries without official sanction; the holding of meetings, supposedly for the "transmission of scriptures" where men and women gathered day or night; and the pressuring of people to make donations under the pretext that they would serve some beneficial purpose. He also issued a proclamation advising Buddhist nuns to return to lay life.[29] From Ch'en Ch'un we have a report that Chu Hsi prohibited worship at Buddhist pagodas, the celebration of the birthdays of mountain deities, and other reputedly superstitious customs.[30] This report is quoted in Chu's *Life Chronology*,[31] but we have no evidence to indicate what, if anything, was done to actually ban these practices, and there is no extant proclamation to this effect.

The main point of Chu Hsi's proclamations in Chang-chou, however, was not his attack on unorthodox religious practices but, more positively, his efforts to promote proper communal relationships. The "Proclamation of Instructions by Master Ku-ling"[32] was particularly significant in this regard.

---

25. Ibid., 47:7b.

26. Ibid., 8a–b.

27. For a critique of Buddhism on philosophical and social grounds, see *Reflections on Things at Hand*, trans. Wing-tsit Chan (New York: Columbia University Press, 1967), pp. 279–288.

28. For a discussion of this proclamation, see Wm. Theodore de Bary, *The Liberal Tradition in China* (New York: Columbia University Press, 1983), pp. 32–33.

29. *Wen-chi* 100:4a–5b. "Nü-tao" is sometimes incorrectly identified as a Taoist nun. Judging from this proclamation, which makes no mention of Taoist practices, the term actually refers to Buddhist practitioners.

30. *Yü-lei* 106:36 (p. 5493). Other evil customs included licentious plays and worship at "wanton shrines" (*yin-tz'u*). Although his official biography in the *History of the Sung* has reported that Chu Hsi prohibited women from entering Buddhism and Taoism, there is no evidence whatsoever to substantiate this claim. See *Sung shih* 429:1b.

31. *Nien-p'u*, p. 182.

32. *Wen-chi* 100:5a–b.

Ch'en Hsiang, who had been respectfully called Master Ku-ling, was a pioneer in promoting Confucian education on the local level in the early part of the Sung dynasty (960–1279). In addition to this proclamation, Ch'en had to his credit two other proclamations encouraging people to study.[33] No doubt in reissuing Ch'en's proclamation, Chu Hsi was consciously following an honorable precedent of local administration. Later, Chen Te-hsiu (1178–1235), a great admirer of Chu Hsi and himself a noted educator, recalled the illustrious achievements of Ch'en Hsiang in one of his famous proclamations,[34] an act that quite apparently followed the example of Chu Hsi.

One major task in local administration was handling litigation. This judicial duty became even more pressing a responsibility in Chang-chou where people seemed to have been especially litigious.[35] As a consequence, excessive litigation tended to drain the time and energy of the prefect, distracting him from other urgent business and thus becoming an impediment to efficient government. Accordingly, Chu Hsi drew up proclamations to address this issue shortly after he assumed office.

Chu Hsi's last assignment as a prefect was in T'an-chou (Hunan) in 1194. Although his tenure was brief, his policies were basically similar to his previous service in the administration of Nan-k'ang and Chang-chou. Since the proclamations he issued in this period regarding public instruction add little to what he had done before, I now proceed to a topical analysis of his proclamations as a whole.

MAJOR ISSUES IN PROCLAMATIONS

Local Schools

From early on in his career as a local official, Chu Hsi had shown a keen interest in reinvigorating local schools. His biography contains detailed accounts about how vigorously he devoted himself to schools and how he restored discipline and redirected the interests of students.[36] Many commemorative essays (chi) written for local schools and related official documents of his bespeak the same kind of commitment.[37] However, no other source provides us with a better picture of his efforts and activities than do his proclamations. In

---

33. Ch'en Hsiang, Ku-ling chi (SK ed.) 19:1a–3a.

34. Chen Te-hsiu, Hsi-shan hsien-sheng Chen Wen-chung kung wen-chi (SPTK ed.) 40:5b.

35. Ch'en Ch'un, Pei-hsi ta-ch'üan chi 47:1a.

36. Nien-p'u, pp. 9–10 78, 171, 191.

37. Cf. Wen-chi, chüan 20, 74. Chu Hsi wrote seven commemorative essays for seven prefectural or county schools. If one includes the thirteen composed for school libraries and lecture halls and the fourteen for shrines in schools, the total of commemorative essays he did in connection with local schools numbers more than thirty-four, a significant output. See Wen-chi, chüan 77–80. In comparison, Lu Chiu-yüan only wrote five essays; Hsiang-shan ch'üan-chi, chüan 19.

this respect, the Nan-k'ang proclamation is especially worth noting.[38] In the preface Chu states that the primary duty of the prefect is to promote culture and education. This is a theme he emphasized repeatedly in many of his other proclamations and sayings.[39] After recounting the illustrious tradition in education that the region had enjoyed, Chu Hsi lamented that:

> In recent years the scholarly tradition has declined. The prefectural school is supporting only thirty students, and students who take part in the examinations are few. It may be that scholars who devote themselves to explicating the Way and cultivating the self have been unwilling to study at the prefectural school or participate in the examination. But having consulted with personages at large and sought out exceptionally talented men, I have failed to learn of anyone worthy of commendation.[40]

In order to rectify this educational deficiency and restore earlier scholarly tradition, Chu called upon

> senior members of the village and community to select young men who have the ambition to study and send them to school. Their expenses will be provided for and they can become supplemental students of the school and attend lectures and participate in the examinations. In the meantime, the prefecture will take various steps to increase support of the schools. The prefect himself, when free from official duties, will visit the school from time to time and join the teachers in residence in explaining the meaning of the Classics.[41]

This seems to imply that admission of students to the school, at least in principle, is to be based on the "ambition to study" and on merit. Even though social status and other factors might in reality play a determining role, for Chu Hsi to announce in public his intention to admit students on the basis of merit is significant. Similarly, providing for students equally and adequately would probably increase access to education and no doubt, greatly benefit the poor. Indeed, Chu Hsi always demonstrated a keen attention to providing financial assistance to students, in both local schools and academies, so that the disadvantaged would not be excluded. It is impossible to assess what effect, if any, Chu Hsi's measures actually had. Nevertheless, there is no doubt that the aim and intention of his educational efforts were to make education more accessible to the populace as a whole.

Public Morality

For Chu Hsi, one goal of local administration was to achieve and maintain a high level of public morality. He was greatly concerned about it and wherever he assumed office he always addressed this issue in his proclamations.

38. *Wen-chi* 99:1a–2b. For Chu Hsi's other proclamations on schools, see *Wen-chi*, *chüan* 74.
39. Cf. *Yü-lei* 106:22 (p. 5474); *Wen-chi*, 100:3a–4a.
40. *Wen-chi* 99:2a.
41. Ibid., 99:2a–b.

Some instructions in the proclamations concerned prohibitions against social misconduct or unlawful acts. For example, in Chang-chou Chu Hsi gave this admonition:

> People should always be alert to save water, prevent fire, investigate thefts and robberies, and prevent in-fighting. Do not sell salt, or kill plowing oxen. They should not gamble with their properties. Nor should they spread or practice demon religion (*mochiao*). People in the same unit should watch each other. Anyone aware of a crime who fails to report it will share in the punishment.[42]

Some proclamations deal with general moral precepts, such as:

> All members should encourage and remind each other to be filial to parents, respectful to elders, cordial to clansmen and relatives and helpful to neighbors. Each should perform his assigned duty and engage in his primary occupation. None should commit vicious acts or theft, or indulge in drinking or gambling. They should not fight with or sue each other.[43]

Instructions like these probably are not uncommon for any prefect to proclaim in Chu Hsi's time. In fact, the above-mentioned admonitions are almost identical to those contained in the "Amended Community Compact of Mr. Lü" (*Tseng-sun Lü shih hsiang-yüeh*),[44] drawn up by Chu Hsi. They are probably a standard set of public instructions and consequently do not represent ideas that are original with or peculiar to Chu Hsi.

The special contribution Chu Hsi made to the stimulation of a healthy public morality was not that he created a new set of moral standards for the people but rather that he reaffirmed the traditional vision of a just society, with emphasis on certain moral virtues. The "Proclamation of Instructions by Master Ku-ling" that Chu resurrected says:

> The father should be righteous. The elder brother should have brotherly love. The younger brother should be respectful. The son should be filial. Husband and wife should have a sense of obligation to each other. There must be distinction between man and woman. Children should study. The village and hamlet should practice rituals. When dire poverty or hardship is experienced, relatives should come to the aid of one another. Neighbors and the community should help one another on occasions of marriage or death. Do not be lax in efforts in agriculture or sericulture. Do not steal or rob. Do not learn gambling. Do not indulge in hasty litigation. . . . This is to achieve customs in accordance with rites and righteousness.[45]

Here in addition to reasserting these commonplace moral instructions and prohibitions, Chu Hsi emphasized that children should study, that the

42. Ibid., 100:6a.
43. Ibid.
44. Ibid., 74:23a–29b.
45. Ibid., 100:5a–b.

village and hamlet should practice rituals, and that the goal of all these should be to achieve a society dedicated to rites and righteousness. Thus, the local community should serve as an example of what the society as a whole should strive for.

The proclamation entitled "Instruction on Customs" is a special instruction addressed to the common people.[46] The proclamation itself consists of the first five sentences from the chapter on the "Commoner" in the *Classic of Filial Piety*,[47] with Chu Hsi's own commentary inserted. He identified the virtue of filiality as the most fundamental and essential and gave an extended interpretation of filiality that encompassed all areas of human activity.

The *Classic of Filial Piety* says, "One should follow the way of Heaven, utilize the resources of the earth, and be careful about oneself and be frugal about expenses so that one can support one's father and mother. This is the filial piety of the commoner."Chu Hsi commented:

> Even if father and mother are no longer alive, one should practice this so that one can preserve the "estate" [ch'an-yeh] of parents, lest it come to ruin. When parents are alive, if one cannot support them, and when they are dead, if one cannot preserve their "estate" he is unfilial. Such a person Heaven will not tolerate, nor will the earth bear him up. After death, he will be reproached by spiritual beings; while alive, he will be subject to condemnation according to the laws of the state. One cannot but take this warning seriously.[48]

The implication is that filiality for the commoner consists of more than just the physical support of parents during their own life time. It must be extended even to the material legacy of one's parents, including one's bodily person as well as the property bequeathed to one. Therefore, one must continue to be filial even after one's parents are dead. Moreover, the punishment for an unfilial son, Chu Hsi said, is so inescapable that even after death one could expect to meet further punishment from spiritual beings. Chu's reliance on the threat of severe punishment as a deterrent might be seen as a practical recognition of its effect on those with a limited capacity for understanding the arguments addressed to the more educated.

The postscript to the proclamation is also significant. In it Chu says,

> I sincerely advise people to practice and recite this day by day, keep the *Classic [of Filial Piety]* and commentary [on it] in their minds day and night, and diligently follow it. One need no longer recite the Buddha's name or Buddhist sūtras, which are of no use and only waste one's strength.[49]

This indicates that he understood the commoners's need for moral guidance

46. Ibid., 99:5b.
47. In the *Hsiao-ching k'an-wu* Chu Hsi regarded this as a part of the text of the Classic, not as part of the commentary. See ibid., 66:2a.
48. Ibid., 99:5b.
49. Ibid.

and provided suitable instruction for them in keeping with their limited capacity.

In Chu's moral instructions one aspect of human relationships is singled out as having particular importance. In his "Petition to Strictly Enforce the Marriage Ceremony," Chu Hsi affirmed that the marital relationship was of primary and paramount importance among the so-called "five constant relationships." Later in his "Proclamation of Instructions," he reaffirmed the conviction that the marital relationship was unsurpassed in importance by any other human relationship and accordingly that the observance of the marriage ceremony should be strictly upheld.[50] This view is confirmed in another proclamation where he declared that the relationship between husband and wife was the first of the "three bonds," (san-kang) that is, the bond between husband and wife, parent and child, and ruler and minister.[51] Although the priority of one human relationship over another is not absolute and the sequence of the "five constant relationships" listed in the "Articles of the Academy of White Deer Hollow" (*Pai-lu-tung shu-yüan chieh-shih*)[52] may not be intended to fix a strict order of relative importance, there is no question that in his instructions to the people Chu Hsi placed a premium on the marital bond. This may possibly be attributable to the particular local conditions with which he had to deal. Nonetheless, it certainly represents a significant qualification of the view that maintains Neo-Confucianism's tendency is to give express emphasis to the parent-child or ruler-minister relationships over all others.

Chu Hsi's proclamations speak of different methods of moral edification. He appealed to the local leaders to be role models and teachers. He also sought to revive beneficent local customs so that people had the sense of tradition and continuity. Moreover, he offered rational justification for moral conduct.

In the "Proclamation by the Prefect of Nan-k'ang," he entreated the local leaders, elders, and the people to "gather at seasonal festivals so as to instruct and admonish the people and to remind them once more at every opportunity, so that everyone of the younger generation will understand and practice filial piety, brotherly respect, loyalty and faithfulness."[53] In the same proclamation Chu Hsi produced an array of outstanding figures for the people to emulate, worthy example being the quintessential form of Confucian instruction. One might also observe that Chu Hsi showed a particular inclination to dwell on personages of recent times whose legacy might not have completely disappeared. For the same reason, he took it as a principal

50. Ibid., 100:6b.
51. Ibid., 100:4a.
52. Ibid., 74:16a.
53. Ibid., 99:1b–2a.

responsibility of his administration to erect shrines or repair tombs that served as memorials to virtuous men and their good deeds.[54]

In the "Proclamation of Instructions," Chu Hsi provided a basic rationale for moral conduct.

> People should understand that our body originates from our parents and that brothers are from the same source. Therefore, we are endowed by nature with a feeling of obligation to parents and brothers, most profound and grave. What makes us love our parents or respect our elder brothers is not forced but comes from the original mind spontaneously.[55]

Accordingly, the unfilial son and disrespectful brother are acting against Heaven and in violation of principle. Chu Hsi's justification is both naturalistic and rationalistic, as is his philosophy.

The main significance of this form of instruction seems to be that Chu Hsi considered it not enough for officials merely to tell people how they should behave; it was also imperative to help them understand the reasons why they should conduct themselves in a certain manner. The basis of this, according to Chu Hsi, was a shared human nature that was innately good. Because this proclamation was addressed to both the elite and the common people, it implies that even the uneducated should be given an explanation of the basis for social behavior to the extent allowed by their capacity to understand.

Ritual Observances

For Chu Hsi the rituals were vital to meaningful relationships. Without properly performed rituals, the relationships would not be socially recognized, personally observed, or humanly respectable. This concern for and devotion to rituals is most pronounced in many of his proclamations.

His proclamations deal extensively with two kinds of rituals, namely, those concerning marriage and mourning. The "Proclamation of Instructions" warns against elopement and men and women living together without proper ceremony. Because the marital relationship is the first of all human relationships according to Chu Hsi, the proclamation, in speaking of these local practices, states that "no violating of the rites and breaking of the law is more serious."[56] Earlier, in his "Petition to Strictly Enforce the Marriage Ceremony," Chu Hsi expressed the same disapproval. It was understandable, he said, that because of poverty, many common people may not be able to afford the exchange of betrothal gifts; however, he said that it was

---

54. Most notably, Chu Hsi established a shrine to Chou Tun-i in the prefectural school as well as a *"wu-hsien tz'u"* (shrine of the five worthies) that honored T'ao Ch'ien (365–427), Liu Huan (1000–1080), his son Liu Shu (1032–1078), Li Ch'ang (1027–1090), and Ch'en Kuan (1057–1124). *Nien-p'u*, p. 78.

55. *Wen-chi* 100:6a.

56. Ibid., 100:6b.

inexcusable for the scholar-officials and wealthy families to follow decadent local customs. The marriage ceremony is most essential because it serves to "distinguish male and female [roles], to rectify social customs, and to prevent disasters and disorders at the root." Whereas Chu was quite detailed in prescribing the mourning rites, he did not indicate in the proclamations what kind of marriage rite he considered appropriate, other than citing the *Five Rites* of the Cheng-ho period.

With regard to mourning, Chu's "Instruction on the Observance of Mourning and Mourning Clothes in Accordance with the Rites and the Law" addresses both the question of the importance of the rites and the need for specific prescriptions. First, Chu Hsi says that the mourning rites are natural expressions of one's grief when one has lost loved ones. To explain this, he quoted Confucius's saying, "The filial son in mourning the death of parents will not be comfortable if he puts on beautiful clothes. He will not be joyful if he hears music, nor will he feel satisfied if he takes tasty food."[57] Moreover, although the rites were established by the ancients, they had a universal applicability because their original institution was based on inherent human feelings, functioning both to express one's emotions and to channel or restrain them. As to the three-year mourning period, he explained, again quoting Confucius, that it was a natural and reasonable practice because the child was under the total care of his parents for three years and consequently mourning them for three years was correct proportionally as repayment for parents' love and care.[58] Again Chu Hsi's interpretation here is both rationalistic and naturalistic. Because he regarded human nature as the ultimate rationale for the rites and all men as being endowed with the same originally good nature, it was natural for him to believe that everyone should observe the rites. To act otherwise would be unnatural conduct, violating one's own nature, to say nothing of its social and legal disapproval.

The prescriptions Chu Hsi deemed appropriate for mourning would not appear to have been too severe except for the requirement that they be observed for three years.[59] They consisted of wearing dark mourning dress, a bluish dark cap, mourning bands and cloth shoes, and abstaining from liquor, meat, and sex. It is most significant that both elite and common people were to follow the same three-year mourning and abide by the same prohibitions, rather than, as is often supposed, the rites either intended for the upper class alone or different standards of decorum proposed for each class. Although the same requirements might present more of a problem for poorer people, Chu Hsi, like most Confucians, saw the problem rather as

57. Ibid., 100:3a. Original quotation is in *Hsiao-ching* (SPPY ed.) 9:1a.
58. Ibid.
59. In the Sung the observance of the three-year mourning actually continued for only twenty-one months. *Sung hsing-t'ung* (1918 ed.) 1:11a.

restraining the extravagance of both classes, who often became involved in excessive expenditure for nonorthodox rituals. A clearly defined, uniform standard for all would presumably protect the poor from the pressure to spend beyond their means.

In addition to making the rituals known directly to the people, Chu Hsi also petitioned the Board of Rites to revise the sacrificial rites for worshipping Confucius.[60] Chu Hsi's continuing effort to revise the rites and make them available to a wider public began during his early appointment at T'ung-an.[61]

Religious Practices

In his proclamations Chu Hsi pronounced several warnings against local religious practices; some related to Buddhism, others not. His "Proclamation of Instructions" contains the following restrictions: people should not practice or spread demon religion (*mo-chiao*); men and women should not establish hermitages on their own under the pretext of engaging in religious practice; monks and lay people should not hold mixed gatherings of men and women during the day or in the evening under the pretext of worshiping the Buddha or transmitting the *sūtras*; towns and villages should prohibit the collecting of money, or receiving of donations, or the making and parading of images and figurines under the pretext that these will bring good luck or avert bad fortune.[62]

It is not clear what precisely "demon religion" refers to. The expression *mo-chiao* was sometimes used to refer to Manichaeanism, but there is nothing to indicate that Chu Hsi had this specifically in mind. Rather, it probably refers to a type of unorthodox folk religion that includes some kind of demon as an object of worship.[63] If this is the case, the proclamation merely reaffirms what was already prohibited by Sung laws.[64] Setting up a hermitage without official approval also violated the existing laws.[65] In other instances, Chu's proclamations were meant to address misuse or abuse of legitimate religious practices.

Speaking of these actions on the part of Chu Hsi when he was prefect of

---

60. *Nien-p'u*, p. 179.

61. Ibid., pp. 11, 90, 91, 179, 290, 321.

62. *Wen-chi* 100:7a.

63. Manichaeanism has been referred to by such names as *mo-ni chiao, ming-chiao, ch'ih-ts'ai shih-mo chiao*. In another proclamation, "Instruction Advising Buddhist Nuns to Return to Lay Life," Chu Hsi had used the term "*mo-tsung*" (demon sect). *Wen-chi* 100:4b.

64. *Sung shih* 252:16a. Although Sung laws prohibited the practice and spread of unorthodox religions, it probably had little effect on the actual practice of the people in Fukien, known as a hotbed of folk religions.

65. In his "Instruction Advising Buddhist Nuns to Return to Lay Life," Chu says that the establishing of nunneries is in violation of the law. *Wen-chi* 100:4a. Moreover, according to Sung codes, anyone who becomes a Buddhist monk or nun without the proper certificate breaks the law; the punishment for the offender is 100 strokes of a heavy rod. *Sung hsing-t'ung* 12:6b.

Chang-chou, Wing-tsit Chan has noted, "The sole purpose was to wipe out the immoral customs" prevalent at the frontier in that time.[66] In his *Classified Sayings* (*Yü-lei*) Chu says that mixed gatherings for the "transmission of scriptures" should be stopped simply because men and women were congregating in one place without proper separation,[67] implying that the prohibition was not meant to suppress religious beliefs or practices as such. Moreover, in another proclamation, "Instruction Advising Buddhist Nuns to Return to Lay Life," Chu Hsi placed great emphasis on the proper bond between husband and wife and on the unnaturalness of a celibate life.[68] That the proclamation itself was occasioned by a lawsuit against a certain Buddhist nun for having an adulterous relationship in her private nunnery clearly underscores the moral concern. These attacks on Buddhism were mostly indirect—based on practical rather than doctrinal grounds.

Though clearly an antagonist of Buddhism, Chu Hsi was not an unrealistic ideologue. He was fully aware of the limitations the existing situation imposed on his ability to effect the implementation of his ideals and principles. Accordingly, he would not object to modest and selective use of Buddhist or Taoist rituals in funerals.[69] Although he recommended that burials should take place soon after death and coffins stored in temples should be buried within one month,[70] he himself allowed the body of his son to be unburied for more than a year. This was because he believed in geomancy (*feng-shui*) and acted on the advice of a diviner who had so divined. Chu Hsi was firm in asserting the principle of early burial, but he did not rigidly uphold it in actual practice.

Litigation

The handling of litigation was an important and urgent business of local administration. This was even more the case in Chang-chou where people appeared to have been particularly litigious. When Chu Hsi arrived to take office there in 1190, he had to deal with rulings on 243 separate lawsuits that had been handed down by the Office of the Judicial Intendant. The judicial system was clearly overloaded and exploited. To deal with the problem he issued "Proclamation on Litigation in Chang-chou" where he set forth his policies and thoughts on the question of litigation.

Although some lawsuits were legitimate, Chu Hsi observed in the proclamation that:

Many are merely of the nature of incidental quarrels over small amounts of

---

66. Wing-tsit Chan, "Chu Hsi's Religious Life," in *Chu Hsi: Life and Thought* (Hong Kong: Hong Kong University Press, 1987), p. 152.
67. *Yü-lei* 106:25 (p. 5475).
68. *Wen-chi* 100:4a–5b.
69. Wing-tsit Chan, "Chu Hsi's Religious Life," p. 151.
70. *Wen-chi* 100:7b.

money or grain, lands or houses. Such quarrels lead to false accusations by one against the other and to the rousing of hatred. Consequently, there has been a loss of good feeling among neighbors, and restraint in keeping with modesty and shame has disappeared. In the worst cases, some even forget their sense of obligation to their parents and kin. And still worse are those who even disregard the distinction between superior and inferior. . . . Some [lawsuits] have nothing to do with the litigants themselves, but are filed by others on their behalf in order to make personal attacks; and some contain false accusations by fictitious or anonymous litigants.[71]

In another, "Proclamation of Instructions to Lung-yen County," Chu said,

Some [people of Lung-yen county] manipulate litigation and use lawsuits to attack others. There is nothing that they will not do. At first, they use false names to sue others. Later, they try to cover themselves up. When the prefectural or county authorities become aware of this deception and eagerly seek their arrest, they close their front gate, gather a crowd, and take up weapons to resist arrest.[72]

Excessive litigation is not only symptomatic of a lack of social harmony but also an indication, at least in Chang-chou, of a government overrun by powerful local families. Chu Hsi asked the people to retract those false or insignificant lawsuits.

I ask the people to seriously consider whether a lawsuit contains falsifications or the matter involved is of no significance and can be settled in peace, so that litigants may repent early enough and compromise. They should consult with the other party and appear at court for a settlement.[73]

In the meantime, he charged the officials to create a register recording the lawsuits he received so that they could be reviewed and reexamined carefully. "In the future when a judgment is made," he said, "a reason will be given, along with a notice of appeal. Only then will each case be marked 'completed' on the register. If any judgment is not proper, the concerned party can appeal step by step."[74]

However, if a lawsuit were proven false, the punishment was severe. Chu Hsi especially warned "rich land owners and powerful citizens" who disregarded the authority of the government and called upon them to reform. If they failed to do so, Chu said, "The prefect must certainly call on the military commander and county sheriffs to surround, search and arrest the criminals. They will be punished according to the statutes. In no case will the sentence be lenient."[75]

71. Ibid., 100:2a–b.
72. Ibid., 100:12a.
73. Ibid., 100:2b.
74. Ibid.
75. Ibid., 100:12b–13a.

Although Chu favored mediation as a means of settling disputes, he thought that proper litigation had a valuable role to play in achieving a just society. In accordance with this view Chu Hsi in several proclamations reminded the public of its right to appeal and made it possible for the people to do so in legitimate cases by providing detailed procedures for the pursuit of litigation.[76]

CONCLUSION

Unlike Lu Chiu-yüan,[77] Chu Hsi is not known to have given public lectures either in an official capacity or as a private person. The academies he helped restore or renovate, such as the White Deer Hollow and the Yüeh-lu academies, were not intended or used for public lecturing. Thus, Chu's instructions to the public were all disseminated through printed proclamations. In this chapter I have discussed Chu Hsi's public instruction by focusing on several of his proclamations that deal with public morality, social customs, ritual observances, and religious practices. In summary I wish to make several points regarding public instruction and proclamations.

Emphasis on Leadership Role in Popular Education
A study of the proclamations written by Chu Hsi helps provide a basis for judging how he himself adapted his philosophical principles to the needs of public instruction on the level of the common people. He was conscious of the fact that many would receive no formal instruction in school and that their moral education depended to an appreciable extent on what they observed of the educated official's public utterances and conduct of affairs. In his proclamations, Chu Hsi recognized this fact and sought to take advantage of it by encouraging the local leadership to assume an active, responsible part in the reform process.

The Correlation Between the Rites and the Law
Although the practice of the rites is important to the individual, it also pertains to the law and the upholding of government authority. Therefore, on the one hand, Chu Hsi emphasized that the observance of proper rituals was meant to restore good customs in which the individual could develop and thrive as a person while, on the other hand, if the individual failed to act on

76. Cf. Ibid., 100:13b–16a.
77. When Lu returned to his native town of Chin-hsi in 1186, he often gave public lectures in the city and in temples. When he was invited to lecture in the prefectural school, his large audience was said to include both upper and lower classes as well as the young and old. *Hsiang-shan ch'üan-chi* 36:15b, "*nien-p'u*" (life chronology). When in 1192, as prefect of Ching-men (Hupei), he gave a public lecture on a chapter in the *Book of History*, the audience numbered as many as five or six hundred people. Ibid., 36:22b.

what was in his own best interest, Chu felt it necessary to uphold the common interest and insist on punishment for failure to comply. In his proclamations and elsewhere, the rites and the law were often mentioned in tandem—first the observance of rites and failing this the enforcement of law.

> It is hoped that they can thereby [i.e., observing the three-year mourning]repay somewhat the infinite labors of their parents. They should obey the rites and the law, and respectfully receive edification from the Emperor. If one acts otherwise, the law of the state will be enforced as always.[78]

In his more philosophical and educational writings Chu generally emphasized the voluntaristic approach and clearly regarded the enforcing of rules and regulations as a kind of last resort against those who forfeited the right to self-discipline.[79] In the proclamations, however, Chu felt more of a responsibility to uphold the authority of his office and the government; hence the sanctions of the law were more in evidence.

From this perspective one may appreciate how the preservation of Chu's proclamations helps us to see a side of Chu Hsi in action that is less visible in his more scholarly writings. The fact that these proclamations were actually included in his collected writings and made available to educated readers wherever his works were circulated suggests that the educated could likely have known about this side of Chu's character and thought and may well have taken it into account in any estimate of Chu Hsi as a potential role model for scholar-officials.

Adaptation of Rituals to the Changing World

Although observance of the three-year mourning was seen by Chu Hsi as an unchanging principle, the detailed prescriptions for performing it were not. He said in a proclamation:

> In the Middle Period the convention of black mourning dress was practiced, which could not but depart from the intention of the ancient Kings. . . . It is probably not possible for those who mourn the death of their parents to cease all activities in strict observance of ancient rules.[80]

Thus, Chu Hsi acknowledged that through the ages the ways to observe mourning had changed and that they had to be changed to reflect the needs and requirements of different times. In light of his flexible and selective approach to rituals, Chu Hsi strives to arrive at something more practical for his own time, which is suited to local circumstances and tradition and which allows considerable discretion to local authority.

---

78. *Wen-chi* 100:3b–4a.
79. Cf. de Bary, *The Liberal Tradition*, pp. 37–39.
80. *Wen-chi* 100:3a–b.

The Authority of Parents

On one long-standing issue the testimony of the proclamations themselves is clear-cut, that is, the criticism that Neo-Confucians always stressed the authority of parent over child. These proclamations speak to the contrary. The parent-child relationship is one of mutual responsibility. Filiality originates from one's sense of obligation or gratitude. It is a natural response to the parents' love and care for one—a consequence of their initial parental solicitude.[81] Indeed, this kind of reciprocity underlies all human relationships. Thus, although suing one's parents was considered by many an unfilial act, Chu Hsi could find a basis to justify such a lawsuit if the parents had failed in their responsibility to the child.

There was such a case involving a son suing his stepmother who had an adulterous relationship with her husband's cousin and, after her husband was dead, invited him to live with her. Because his uncle recklessly misspent the property of the family, the son filed a lawsuit against his mother. At that time Chu Hsi was the Intendant of the Eastern Chekiang Circuit. Initially he refused to hear the case, but later he accepted it because he thought one had to take into account the respect due to the father, who, though dead, had suffered great injustice.[82] In another lawsuit in which the sons accused their stepmother of abusive treatment, Chu Hsi was of the opinion that the acting judge should not dismiss the suit but should accept it and reprimand the irresponsible mother.[83]

Chu Hsi as a Sympathetic Local Official

Emerging from these proclamations is a picture of Chu Hsi as a man who deeply sympathized with the plight of the common people and had their interests constantly in mind. A case in point is his proclamation on the survey and reclassification of land (*ching-chieh*). In this situation the landed gentry had everything to gain by maintaining the status quo, while many peasants suffered from a double burden as rent-paying tenants who at the same time paid land taxes. In his proclamation, Chu Hsi exposed the devious plans of the gentry as a self-interested group who sought to abort the reform effort.[84] Chu's proclamation amounted to an open attack on their selfishness and greed. In the end, he was overruled by higher authority and the plan failed to materialize. Nevertheless, despite his failure, Chu had reason to console himself that he had done what he knew to be right and had won the minds and hearts of the people whom he sought to protect.

At the same time it must be acknowledged that several remaining questions are difficult to deal with on the basis of sources now available.

81. Cf. de Bary, *The Liberal Tradition*, p. 32.
82. *Yü-lei* 106:21 (p. 5473).
83. Ibid., 106:21 (p. 5472).
84. *Wen-chi* 100:7b–9a.

First, there is the question of the actual impact or effectiveness of these proclamations. Do they perhaps represent no more than a formal exercise of moral authority? It is impossible to know how people at that time perceived and reacted to Chu Hsi's proclamations or what kind of effect they had on the problems he addressed. Related to this is the question of their effectiveness as "essays of encouragement and instruction" (ch'üan-yü wen), that is, as a means of moral persuasion. The efforts Chu makes to provide a rational explanation of moral precepts suggests his awareness of the need to go beyond the mere indoctrination of people; otherwise the content might be much more authoritarian. Recognizing the limits of indoctrination and coercion, he appeals to reason and moral sense. It remains inherently difficult to judge, however, the extent to which Chu Hsi's proclamations had the desired quickening effect on people's motivations.

Second is the question of egalitarianism versus elitism. In his proclamations Chu Hsi prescribes the same rituals for both elite and commoner. Such differentiation as he allows in the observance of the rites is related to the roles and responsibilities of each group or individual. When the elite and the commoner are exhorted to practice the same rituals, as in the case of the three-year mourning, the primary consideration seems to be establishing a uniform, basic standard of ritual. The commoner and the poor are thereby protected from the pressure to spend needlessly on the ritual. Consequently, although they are required to perform rituals, the rituals are simplified to make them affordable. Since the prescriptions for the scholar-officials are no different, the egalitarian consideration is quite evident.

In other cases, Chu calls upon the elite to take the lead in their observance of rituals or in other words to hold themselves to a higher standard than the common people in the strictness, if not in the manner, of their observance. Does this constitute "elitism," or is it simply the kind of elitism that attaches to any leadership group that accepts a greater measure of social responsibility? This question cannot be answered on the evidence of the proclamations alone, but it must be considered in the larger context of Chu Hsi's writings on education and rituals as a whole.

Finally, the full significance of these proclamations will only emerge when they are considered in the light of their use or abuse in later times. A comparative study, for example, of Chu Hsi and Chen Te-hsiu, who also championed local education and made much use of such proclamations himself, would contribute substantially to our understanding of how Confucian values were propagated on the local level in later Imperial China, since Chen had a considerable influence on the formation of Neo-Confucian ideology in the Yüan and early Ming. Whatever the outcome of these further investigations, Chu Hsi's contribution remains significant; he consciously directed his attention to the use of proclamations as important means of public instruction, to such an extent that this genre came to have a prominent place in the collected writings of Chu Hsi and his followers.

PART THREE

Neo-Confucian Education in the Home

Education Through Ritual: Efforts to Formulate Family Rituals During the Sung Period

Patricia Ebrey

I once had a desire to take Mr. Ssu-ma's book [on family rituals, his Shu-i] and add as an addendum corrections, additions, and subtractions, arranged into categories, based on a study of the various authorities' teachings. This would allow the reader to find the main points and from there go to the details, without fear that the steps would be hard to carry out. Even poor and humble people would be able to fulfill the major items of the rituals, skipping the elaborations without missing the basic idea.

Chu Hsi, *Chu Wen-kung Wen-Chi* (SPTK Ed.) 83:15b–16a

Education can be analytically divided into two processes: molding and schooling. Schooling involves teachers, pupils, texts, and progressive stages. The normal method for literary and technical education, schooling always incurs some cost, which must be borne by the pupil, his family, the state, the community, or other unit. Molding (i.e., influencing, socializing) differs in basic ways. Molding is pervasive in all societies; Chinese practice of it, conscious and unconscious, is in no way remarkable. Molding continues throughout life and generally involves little cost. In education through molding, the recipient need not have actively sought to be educated; it is the "teacher," if anyone, who wishes to change or develop the student's attitudes and behavior. Molding that occurs in homes generally is known as "child-rearing," but molding is not confined to homes. Teachers try both to mold and school their pupils; officials and other figures of authority hope to mold those under them.

Chinese scholars were well aware of the importance of molding in the educational process, especially molding through ritual (*li*). To them, ritual included not only ceremonies for special occasions, marked by formality and heightened emotions, but also everyday expressions of deference and respect. In Chinese families, the basic values of filial piety and deference to seniors and males were taught to children primarily by showing them the behavior patterns to practice. Children learned in what circumstance to bow, kneel, sit, speak up, stay quiet, fetch, or wait. Only after the patterns became part of what they took as "natural" might they learn the theoretical moral principle underlying these ritualized ways of acting. Elementary education continued this process. One of the most popular primers of T'ang and Sung times, "The Family Teaching of the Grandfather" (*T'ai kung chia-chiao*), provided in simple verse quick rules for many of these matters. For instance:

> When the father goes out to walk
> The son follows behind.
> If you meet a senior on the road
> Bring your feet together and join your hands.
> In front of a senior
> Do not spit on the ground.
> If a senior offers you wine
> You must receive it with a bow.
> If a senior gives you meat
> Do not give the bones to a dog.
> If a senior gives you fruit,
> Keep the pit in you hand.
> Do not throw it away—
> To do so would be a great offense to ritual.[1]

Teaching ritualized behavior was not only recognized as a good method for educating children, but was also, from early times, seen as a way of civilizing (*hua*) rural folk deemed backward or insufficiently "Chinese." With adults, however, authorities tended to place emphasis on ceremonies, especially the life-cycle rituals conducted by families—coming of age, weddings, funerals, and ancestral rites. Ceremonies were stressed probably because changing the daily etiquette of adults was impractical. But adults could be taught ceremonies—framed, constructed behavior that departs from daily life—and thereby not only absorb the Confucian values expressed in the ceremonies but also gain a greater consciousness of sharing in a common Chinese culture.

Consequently, from the Han through the Ch'ing, local officials took note of irregular marriage and funerary rituals and attempted to reform them as a way of improving the moral fabric of society. Once the populace had learned to perform the outward ceremonies, appropriate ethical relations (*jen-lun*) were expected to follow. For instance, Chu Hsi (1130–1200) once wrote a memorial asking for assistance in teaching appropriate wedding practices. He began by noting that such ceremonies serve to "distinguish male from female, regulate the relations of husbands and wives, rectify customs, and prevent disorder." Lacking such ceremonies, rural commoners who were too poor to pay for engagement gifts often eloped, which they called "taking a companion." The custom had become so entrenched that even *shih* and rich

---

1. Paul Demieville has collated the copies of this text surviving in Tunhuang, providing a Chinese text and a French translation in *l'Oeuvre de Wang Le Zelateur suivie des Instructions Domestiques de L'Aieul, Poèmes Populaire des T'ang* (Paris: Collège de France, 1982). The passage quoted here is from pp. 672–76.

families practiced it. The way to change this deplorable state of affairs, he argued, was to promulgate a form for the ritual based on the imperial compendium issued in the Cheng-ho period (1111–1117).[2]

In this chapter I will examine the efforts of Sung scholars to educate the populace by writing and circulating new formulations of family rituals. Ritual guides differ from most other writing on family matters by their relative lack of concern with motives or values.[3] These manuals tell people what to do, not what to think. This trait made them especially useful in education through molding because those who learned what to do would absorb attitudes and values unconsciously.

Sung Neo-Confucians who wished to promote appropriate family ethics by teaching family rituals faced a major obstacle posed by their commitment to the Classics as a repository of truths. The sumptuary principles in the Classics restricted, explicitly or implicitly, the forms of life-cycle rituals that could be practiced by those without official rank, referred to as commoners (*shu* or *shu-jen*). Indeed, the *Li chi* (Book of Ritual) contains the statement that "Rituals do not go down to the commoners."[4] The bulk of the instructions in the Classics pertain to royalty and nobility, with graded versions that went down to lower officers (*shih*). Not only could these sumptuary principles in the Classics be taken to exclude peasants and artisans, but they could also, quite correctly, be taken to exclude educated men who considered themselves *shih* or *shih-ta-fu* (gentleman and gentleman/official) in the Sung sense of these terms but who did not hold office. In the Classics, *shih* were lower officers, and the T'ang ritual experts who compiled the imperial compendiums of rites equated the *shih* in the *I-li* (Etiquette and Ritual) with the lower ranks of regular officials in their own day.[5]

Sumptuary restrictions were especially severe in regard to ancestral rites. In the Classics commoners were quadruply restricted in the performance of ancestral rites. They were not to have family shrines (*chia miao*) but to use a room of their house for rites; they were not to make sacrifices (*chi*) but only offerings (*ch'ien*); they were not to go back several generations, as the generational depth of rites was based on sumptuary principles, ranked from

---

2. Chu Hsi, *Chu Wen-kung wen-chi* (SPTK ed.) 20:1b–2a. The ways local officials in the Han and Six dynasties used Chinese marriage practices to bring local populations into the sphere of Chinese culture is discussed in Hisayuki Miyakawa, "The Confucianization of South China," in *The Confucian Persuasion*, ed. Arthur F. Wright (Stanford: Stanford University Press, 1960).
3. For a discussion of Sung writings on the values of family life, see Patricia Ebrey, "Conceptions of the Family in the Sung Dynasty," *Journal of Asian Studies* 43 (1984):219–245, and *Family and Property in Sung China: Yüan Ts'ai's Precepts for Social Life* (Princeton: Princeton University Press, 1984).
4. *Li chi*, "Ch'ü-li," (Ssu-pu pei-yao ed.) 1:16a; or see James Legge, trans., *Li Chi, Book of Rites* (1885; reprint, New York: University Books, 1967) 1:90.
5. On the Sung sense of *shih* and *shih-ta-fu*, see pp. 3–5 of Ebrey, *Family and Property in Sung China*. For the equation of the rules for *shih* in the *I-li* with lower ranked officials in the T'ang, see *Ta T'ang K'ai-yüan li*, ed. Hsiao Sung et al. (SKCSCP ed.) 125:18b.

the Son of Heaven down to commoners; and they were only to make four offerings a year, one in each season.[6] In T'ang and Sung sumptuary law the principle that only officials of certain ranks could construct family shrines was reiterated, though the other restrictions are not repeated in legal documents. Commoners did practice ancestral rites, certainly at graves and probably in homes, but such practices were often entangled with Buddhist and Taoist customs and beliefs.[7]

Thus, in promoting Confucian family rituals Neo-Confucians also had to face the well-established popular forms of celebration, mourning, and worship that had not derived from the Confucian classics. Funerals, in particular, had largely become Buddhist affairs, presided over by Buddhist clergy. For weddings, popular practices bore a general resemblance to classical rules: the engagement was confirmed by exchange of gifts; the wedding itself was called "welcoming in person," during which the groom brought the bride from her house to his, where feasting took place. Nevertheless, popular practices followed in weddings diverged from the prescriptions in the Class-

6. The canonical sources for these restrictions are the "Royal Institutions" and the "Rules for Sacrifices" in the *Li chi*, each of which give slightly different schedules. The former states, "The Son of Heaven has seven *miao* (three for *chao* and three for *mu* ancestors, which with the "great ancestor" [the founder of the line] makes seven); the feudal lords have five *miao* (two for *chao* and two for *mu* ancestors, which with the "great ancestor" makes five); great officers have three *miao* (one *chao* and one *mu*, which with their "great ancestor" makes three); *shih* have one *miao*; common people (*shu-jen*) make offerings in their chamber. . . . As for the offerings of great officers and *shih* in their descent line *miao*, if they have land they can sacrifice (*chi*); without it they make offerings (*ch'ien*). Common people in the spring offer (*ch'ien*) scallions. . . ." (Ssu-pu pei-yao ed., 4:8b–9b; Legge, trans., 1:223–226). The "Rules for Sacrifices" states that the seven shrines for a Son of Heaven are for his father, grandfather, great-grandfather, great-great-grandfather, and his "great-ancestor," and two for the tablets of ancestors more remote than great-great-grandfather. At the first five shrines sacrifices were offered once a month and at the remote ones, once a season. Feudal lords did not have the two shrines for remote ancestors and sacrificed monthly only to the three most recent ancestors with seasonal ones for the remainder. Great officers had shrines for their fathers, grandfathers, and great-grandfathers (this contradicts the above passage) and made only seasonal sacrifices at all of them. They could raise temporary altars if they wished to pray to their great-great-grandfather or their "great-ancestor." Higher *shih* (*shih shih*) had shrines to their fathers and grandfathers for seasonal sacrifices only, and could pray to a great-grandfather if they raised a temporary altar. "Official teachers' (*kuan shih*) had one shrine for their fathers but could also sacrifice to their grandfathers there. Earlier ancestors were left as ghosts. "Commoner *shih*" (*shu-shih*) and commoners (*shu-jen*) had no shrines, and their ancestors were left as ghosts. This text then divides *shih* into three levels: those with two shrines, one shrine, and none. (Ssu-pu pei-yao ed. 14:2a–3a; Legge, trans., 2:204–206).

7. For a review of the legislation on *miao*, see Ma Tuan-lin, *Wen-hsien t'ung-k'ao* (reprint, Taipei: Hsin-hsing, 1964) 104:945–948; 105:951–954. On the practice of ancestral rites in the Sung, see Matsumoto Koichi, "Sōrei, sairei ni miru Sōdai shūkyōshi no ichi keikō," *in Sōdai no shakai to bunka*, ed. Sōdaishi kenkyūkai (Tokyo: Kyūko, 1983), and Patricia Ebrey, "The Early Stages of the Development of Descent Group Organization," in *Kinship Organization in Late Imperial China, 1000–1940*, ed. Ebrey and James L. Watson (Berkeley: University of California Press, 1986).

ics in such matters as the use of musicians and songs, negotiation of dowry, use of formal written marriage contracts, and immediate introduction of the bride to the ancestral altar. These customary practices (*su*) had not remained limited to commoners but were regularly copied throughout society; some, in fact most likely originated among the rich.[8]

These obstacles to promoting Confucian family rituals—the sumptuary principles in the Classics and the popularity of Buddhist and Taoist ceremonies and customary practices—were barriers Neo-Confucian theorists recognized and consciously tried to overcome. Two other obstacles frustrated their efforts but were neither fully recognized nor directly addressed. These were the relationship of forms of family rites to the family and kinship system, and the ways differences in ceremonial behavior indicate social status.

Weddings provide a good example of how the elements in a ritual relate to family and kinship institutions. In all societies marriages are marked by ceremonial activities; when compared, certain patterns emerge. Thus, in a stratified patrilineal society, if the families of the bride and groom are of equal social status, property exchanges will be of a different sort than if one or the other is from a higher status group. Even if the Classics, describing an ancient system, prescribed only gifts from the groom's family to the bride's, the very different social relations between affines in the Sung would bar a return to the ancient system. Similarly, weddings often involve more explicit references to sexuality than allowed on any other occasion; the function of these symbolic expressions in facilitating the change in the status of the principal parties usually escaped the notice of Chinese writers, who simply saw the customs as uncanonical and vulgar.

But concern with vulgarity was not simply based on a failure to see the social functions of uncanonical practices. In China, as elsewhere, a person's manners and demeanor were considered a sign of breeding, an indicator of family background and thus of social status. Indeed, because of the relative lack of legal support for social stratification in Sung and later China, manners, ritual, and demeanor may have played an especially large role in the dynamics of social inequality. Much of what marked one as a *shih-ta-fu* was knowing how to act in polite society, what verbal formulas to use in social situations and what ceremonies to follow. Training in etiquette and ritual was therefore a major element in the education of *shih-ta-fu*, and many quides to etiquette were probably written primarily for this purpose.

Given the relationship between etiquette and social standing, the motivation behind a writer's attention to fine points of ritual need not be purely a desire to "improve the popular ethos" or "promote cordiality and honesty in social relations." When a writer addressed his own sons or relatives, such attention often reflected a desire to keep them from becoming vulgar and

8. On wedding practices in the Sung, see Jacques Gernet, *Daily Life in China on the Eve of the Mongol Invasion*, trans. H. M. Wright (Stanford: Stanford University Press, 1962), pp. 158–162.

thus jeopardizing their social standing. And essays written to criticize vulgar practices penetrating the social life of *shih-ta-fu* sometimes seem to reveal the writer's unconscious desire to preserve visible signs of status differences. In theory, the common people should be brought to the level of the upper class, but, were that to happen, members of the upper class would need new ways to distinguish their style. One could label this attitude conventional, rather than orthodox, but conventional ways of thinking often have a stubborn hold because they serve social functions—in this case they helped preserve group prerogatives.

Thus, Chinese efforts in T'ang and Sung times to formulate ritual and etiquette for educational purposes confronted several built-in conflicts. Could one compete with Buddhism and Taoism by offering Confucian rituals if these rituals did not serve the social functions such rituals had to serve? Could one write a standard set of rituals for both the educated and the uneducated and call it "Confucian" when the Classics drew status distinctions? And would upper-class men ever be comfortable if their rites and daily courtesies were not distinct from those of the uneducated classes? But if one drew up separate sets of rituals for gentlemen and commoners, would commoners ever have much enthusiasm for rites that labeled them second class when they could turn to Buddhist versions that drew no such distinctions?

In this chapter, I look at the interplay of these priorities and conflicts in Sung efforts to formulate family rituals for both *shih-ta-fu* and the general public. To narrow my focus, I pay most attention to weddings and ancestral rites and within these areas to ways in which status distinctions and vulgarity were handled. My sources include writings by Ou-yang Hsiu (1007–1072), Ssu-ma Kuang (1019–1086), Ch'eng I (1033–1107), and Chu Hsi (1130–1200) and three manuals of rites (those by Ssu-ma Kuang, Chu Hsi, and the imperially sponsored one completed in 1113). An intellectual historian looking at this material might well concentrate on how the differences among these writers on ritual issues related to their varying philosophical premises. As useful as such a study would be, here I will approach the material differently. First, I will try to see the successive attempts at formulating a new family ritual in the framework of contemporary social life, especially the ways family rites were practiced by *shih-ta-fu* and by the general populace of the time and the social purposes these practices served; and second, I will attempt to discover the reasons why, given this social context, Chu Hsi's *Family Rituals* (*Chia li*) won more favor than the others. I do not doubt that the men whose writings I examine had philosophical reasons for proposing their models and that Chu Hsi's reputation as a philosopher facilitated acceptance of his book. However, the *Family Rituals'* wide use outside the core of Chu Hsi's followers suggests to me that it may have fit actual social life better than the others.

NORTHERN SUNG EFFORTS TO
REFORMULATE FAMILY RITUALS

Early Sung scholars who wished to study the formulation of family rituals could turn to several manuals written during the T'ang. The most authoritative of these was the *K'ai-yüan li*, issued in 732. The bulk of this massive compendium concerned court ritual and the rites performed by the imperial family. Under family rituals, the *K'ai-yüan li* allowed little leeway for popular customs and in no way challenged sumptuary principles. In it there is a graded series of versions of each rite, the lowest for officials rank six and lower. No rules are provided for anyone without official rank, except for grandsons of the highest officials and sons of middle-rank officials.

Besides the *K'ai-yüan li* itself and several digests of it, many etiquette books, *Shu-i* (Etiquette for Letter-Writing and Other Occasions), were written in the T'ang and the Five dynasties. On the whole these etiquette books were tolerant of popular custom and ignored sumptuary principles. Probably addressed to people who considered themselves *shih* even if not serving in office, these books provided a single model for "the general public" (literally the four seas, *ssu-hai*) rather than separate versions for people of varying rank. Four of these books were still in circulation in the eleventh century.[9]

These eighth- and ninth-century etiquette books were designed to help people avoid any possible offense in written communication caused by carelessly using in a letter a term normally reserved for someone of higher, lower, or merely different status. The complexities of status differentiation shown in these guides is so awesome that one can easily understand why any novice in the art of letter writing would feel more secure with a guide. The information on family rituals probably served a similar purpose. Some of it was identical to that found in the Classics but presented in a convenient format; this would be true, for instance, of the division of relatives into mourning grades. In other cases, these texts seem to have presented the practices that had become customary among the leading families in the capital. In the efforts to be correct and avoid looking foolish or rustic, people wanted to know "what is done," not what the Classics prescribed if no one followed those rules any longer.

In the mid-eleventh century leading Neo-Confucian scholars could not accept popular practices in marriages and other family rites as easily as T'ang authorities had. Ou-yang Hsiu (1007–1072), in his famous essay "On Fundamentals," argued that the only way to loosen the hold of Buddhism on the general public was for local officials to promote the practice of Confucian rituals, including weddings, funerals, and ancestral rites. Only because of the

9. Wang Yao-ch'en, ed., *Ch'ung-wen ts'ung-mu* (reprint, Taipei: Jen-jen wen-k'u) 2:79–80. Long parts of several T'ang *Shu-i* survived in Tunhuang. See Ebrey, "T'ang Guides to Verbal Etiquette," *Harvard Journal of Asiatic Studies* 45(1985), 581–613.

decay of these rituals, he argued, had Buddhism found an opening into the daily lives of the common people. Instructing people in these rituals "not only would prevent disorder but also would teach them to distinguish superior and inferior, old and young, and the ethics of social relations."[10]

Ou-yang Hsiu was particularly upset when he found educated men performing rituals that had originated among ordinary people. In a passage in his *Kuei-t'ien lu* he made this sentiment explicit:

Liu Yueh's *Shu-i*, under "wedding rites," contains the ceremonies of the bride sitting on the groom's horse saddle and the parents tying together their locks of hair.[11] I wondered what principle of the classics was involved here, but then noticed that according to Liu Yueh's own preface he had added practices approved by his contemporaries. Thus this is nothing more than a custom current in his age. Yueh lived in the battle-torn Five Dynasties period when rites and music were in decay; he did not have the opportunity to investigate the institutions of the three ancient kings and as an expedient adopted the forms for auspicious and ill-omened rites current in a particular period and gave them some organization. . . . Of all the distortions the most ridiculous is the matter of sitting on a saddle. Today's *shih* families, on the eve of the wedding, take two chairs and put them back to back and place a saddle on them, then order the groom to sit on top and drink three cups. The bride's family sends someone to ask him three times to come down, after which the wedding can proceed. They call it "ascending the high place." All of the relatives of the family celebrating the wedding and all of the male and female guests in the upper and lower rooms stand and watch, considering "the groom ascending the high place" to be a splendid rite. Should anyone fail to perform it, they consider it a breach of etiquette.[12] What distortions and errors!

Today even famous classicists, high officials, and families that have served as officials for ages all act this way. Alas! So many *shih-ta-fu* are ignorant of the principles of rituals and follow the practices of lanes and rustic villages without even knowing they are wrong![13]

Respect for the Classics and the impulse toward "restoration" lay behind Ou-yang Hsiu's condemnation of *shih-ta-fu* following vulgar practices in their wedding ceremonies. Nevertheless, one also senses a snobbish disapproval of anything originating in "lanes and rustic villages." Although Ou-yang Hsiu may have believed in the doctrine of teaching Confucian rituals to commoners, he had very little sympathy for anything actually "common." What most

10. Ou-yang Hsiu, *Ou-yang Hsiu ch'üan chi* (reprint, Taipei: Shih-chieh, 1961), "Chü-shih chi," 17:122.

11. Liu Yüeh wrote his *Shu-i* at imperial command in about 930 because of complaints that the most popular of the earlier *Shu-i* had too many uncanonical practices. See Ou-yang Hsiu, *Hsin Wu-tai shih* (Peking: Chung-hua, 1974) 55:632.

12. Meng Yüan-lao, *Tung-ching meng-hua lu* (reprint, Taipei: Shih-chieh) 5:152, describes a version of this custom.

13. Ou-yang Hsiu, *Kuei t'ien lu* (Peking: Chung-hua shu-chü) 2:34–35.

disturbed him was that educated men did not try hard enough to keep their own practices pure.

Despite Ou-yang Hsiu's belief that *shih-ta-fu* should avoid ceremonial practices not prescribed in the Classics, he found it difficult to live up to his own standards. Unable to manage the sacrifices to his own ancestors because of official duties, he arranged to have Taoist priests in a local temple manage them for him, reportedly encouraged to do so by another leading scholar, Han Ch'i (1008–1075).[14]

Ou-yang Hsiu's younger contemporary Ch'eng I shared his distaste for the prevalence of Buddhist funerals, once saying that only a couple of families in the Loyang area failed to practice them.[15] However, most of his surviving comments on family rites concern promoting Confucian forms of sacrifices to ancestors. That so committed a Neo-Confucian as Ou-yang Hsiu found it impossible to follow the *I-li* in ancestral rites shows the magnitude of the task Ch'eng I set for himself. To promote the practice of Confucian forms of ancestral rites, he allowed several popular practices prohibited in the Classics, including one permitting even commoners to make offerings to four generations of ancestors. In his *Yü-lu* (Recorded conversations) he is reported to have said:

> There are no distinctions in the five grades of mourning garments from the Son of Heaven down to commoners: all of them wear mourning up to their great-great-grandfather. If this is the case with mourning, it should also be the case with sacrificial offerings. Ignoring the details, the principle is this: even those with seven or five shrines (*miao*) only go back to their great-great-grandfather; even great officers and *shih* with three, two, or one shrine, or who make offerings in their chamber, despite their differences, may sacrifice to their great-great-grandfather without harm. If they only sacrifice to their parents, it is like the animals who only know their mothers and not their fathers. To make offerings to parents but not grandparents is not the way of humans.[16]

It need hardly be stated that Ch'eng I was going against centuries of commentaries when he argued that the number of *miao* had no necessary relationship to the number of ancestors worshipped. Elsewhere Ch'eng I allowed some sumptuary differentiation beyond the legal requirement that commoners not have *miao*, saying they should use placards (*p'ai*) instead of tablets (*chu*) for listing their ancestors' names.[17]

In several discussions, Ch'eng I tied promoting ancestral rites to reviving the lesser descent line system (*hsiao tsung*) of antiquity. In this system the first

14. See James T. C. Liu, *Ou-yang Hsiu: An Eleventh-Century Neo-Confucianist* (Stanford: Stanford University Press, 1967), p. 165.
15. Cheng I, and Ch'eng Hao, *Erh Ch'eng chi* (Peking: Chung-hua), p. 114.
16. Ibid., p. 167.
17. Ibid., p. 286.

son of the first son, going back five generations, was called the descent line heir (tsung tzu). He took charge of ancestral rites for all those descended from his great-great-grandfather, some as distant as third cousins.[18] Whereas the Classics present the lesser descent line as developing among the descendants of feudal lords not in the primary lines of descent, Ch'eng I saw it as an institution that could be promoted among the entire population.[19]

Popular practices of Ch'eng I's time included the use of ancestral portraits as objects for sacrifices, sacrifices at graves, the use of solar dates (equinoxes and solstices) for sacrifices, and sacrifices to early ancestors. Ch'eng I objected to the first but accepted in modified form all the others. On portraits he wrote that unless every hair was drawn exactly, one was not actually sacrificing to one's ancestor but to someone else. Consequently, he said that "rich families and scholars" who did not have the requisite political rank to set up shrines (miao) could erect image halls but without the images.[20]

Rites to early and first ancestors Ch'eng I incorporated into his basic schedule of rites. These rites were done not by all those descended from the ancestor, as seems to have become a common practice, but by the same groups that conducted other ancestral rites. Rites at graves, he admitted, were not mentioned in the Classics, but he saw no harm in them as long as they did not lead to neglect of the regular seasonal sacrifices.[21]

Besides Ou-yang Hsiu and Ch'eng I, many other Northern Sung scholars wrote on family rites, especially sacrifices. Tu Yen (978–1057), Han Ch'i (1008–1075), Fan Tsu-yü (1041–1098), Lü Ta-fang (1027–1097), and Chang Tsai (1020–1077) all wrote manuals or treatises on ancestral rites.[22] Later books occasionally refer to Han Ch'i's ideas, such as his acceptance of rites at graves at the spring and fall festivals.[23] A chapter in Chang Tsai's Ching-hsueh li-k'u (Explications of the Classics) on ancestral rites survives and probably expresses some of the same ideas in his other, not extant book. There he wrote that commoners should make sacrifices to more generations than allowed in the Classics, once specifying three generations and another time five. For the case of five generations he said to call the event "eating together."[24]

18. Ibid., p. 179.
19. See Wing-tsit Chan, trans., Reflections on Things at Hand: The Neo-Confucian Anthology Compiled by Chu Hsi and Lü Tsu-ch'ien (New York: Columbia University Press, 1967), pp. 227–232. See also Ebrey, "Conceptions of the Family," pp. 229–232.
20. Ch'eng I, Erh Ch'eng chi, pp. 90, 286.
21. Ibid., pp. 240–241.
22. Ch'en Chen-sun, Chih-chai chu-lu chieh-t'i (TSCC Ed.) 6:180–181.
23. The example is from the added notes in a late Ming annotated edition of the Family Rituals, Hsin-k'o tseng-pu Wen-kung chia li ch'üan t'u, 160a. Another citation is found in Hsing-li ta-ch'üan shu (SKCSCP ed.) 21:24a.
24. Chang Tsai, Chang Tsai chi (Peking: Chung-hua), pp. 292, 295.

SSU-MA KUANG'S *SHU-I*

The one lengthy eleventh-century text on family rituals to survive is Ssu-ma Kuang's *Shu-i*, the same title used by several T'ang etiquette books. This book had considerable influence, especially on Chu Hsi, and deserves detailed analysis. Ssu-ma Kuang, a major historian and classical scholar as well as a leading conservative statesman, had written on family organization and family rituals in a general way in his *Chia fan* (Precepts for family life). His *Shu-i* was written when he was more than sixty years old, living in retirement in Loyang.[25]

The *Shu-i* is a lengthy book, almost sixty thousand characters long. The text is printed in two sizes of type in roughly equal amounts; the larger describes what is to be done, and the smaller comments on it. The first chapter of the *Shu-i* gives forms for official and private letters, and the second describes capping, pinning, and two more technical matters, the arrangement of the room in which rites are conducted and the fabrication of the robes worn. The third and fourth chapters describe wedding ceremonies. At the end of the fourth chapter is a famous essay on principles to follow in managing a family, including such matters as education of sons, supervision of servants, and when and how relatives should bow when meeting each other. The fifth through ninth chapters, half the book, describe funerals and mourning procedures in thirty-nine subsections. Samples of letter-writing phraseology for use by mourners concludes chapter nine. The last chapter prescribes forms for ancestral rites with some general comments and letter forms attached.

Although Ssu-ma Kuang relied heavily on earlier etiquette books in designing his form letters, he does not admit using them in his prescriptions for family ceremonies, probably because he was trying to reform customary practices he considered undesirable. Thus, he turned to the Classics, and his basic source was the *I-li*. For marriage, the "Marriage Ritual for Gentlemen" (*Shih hun li*) in the *I li* was the only classical description suitable for a general set of rules. For funerals and related death rites the *Li chi* contains more details than the *I-li*, and many of Ssu-ma Kuang's notes deal with discrepancies between these two Classics. Ssu-ma Kuang also cites the *Kai-yuan li* over a dozen times, showing that he regularly compared its compromises between the Classics and current practices to his.

Style, Audience, and Customary Practices

In the *Shu-i*, Ssu-ma Kuang saw his audience as *shih-ta-fu* like himself, men who would care what the *I-li* and the *K'ai-yuan li* said. He repeatedly refers to current *shih-ta-fu*; for example, he complains that *shih-ta-fu* wives in

---

25. On Ssu-ma Kuang's *Chia-fan*, see Ebrey, *Family and Property*, pp. 31–42. Niida Noboru, *Shina Mibunhōshi* (1937; reprint, Tokyo: Daian, 1967), p. 607, dates the *Shu-i* to between 1081 and 1084.

the past prepared all sacrificial foods themselves but now disdain to enter the kitchen.[26] His discussions of popular customs or customary practices mostly reflect those common among his social peers. Ou-yang Hsiu had laughed at *shih-ta-fu* who practiced "the groom ascending the high place." Ssu-ma Kuang provides guidance to those *shih-ta-fu* unsure of which popular customs might appear vulgar to men like Ou-yang Hsiu. He did this by integrating some customary practices into a basically classical pattern and explicitly rejecting others. His book might well have been used as a guide in teaching students about ritual, but it was not designed to be read by beginning readers. Its impact on the education of children would have been indirect: families that modeled their daily etiquette and special ceremonies on it would have taught their children principles of social hierarchy, reciprocity, deference, and so on.

To illustrate Ssu-ma Kuang's style, his use of the *I li*, and his efforts to draw the line against popular practices, I have translated the portion of his text for the first of the six rites of marriage, the presentation of the engagement gift (*na-ts'ai*). The main text is in bold face, and the notes in regular type, indented.

Na Ts'ai
the ritual for accepting the selection

The day before the presiding man
I.e., the groom's father or grandfather; in their absence, the senior male of the family at that time. The presiding man of the women's family is the same.
takes incense, wine, and meat
Two or three dishes can be substituted for meat.
and makes a report at the image hall. The presiding man stands facing north, burns incense, offers the wine, prostrates himself, then rises. An altar boy, holding the text, comes forward from the left side of the presiding man and faces east.
Have one of the younger men in the family serve as altar boy, here and later.
The text is the prayer written on paper.
After putting his tablet in his girdle, the altar boy takes the prayer out. Kneeling, he reads it: "A's son B dares to report. . . ." After the altar boy rises, the presiding man bows twice and leaves, closing the door of the image hall. Then he orders the messenger to go to the girl's family.
The "Marriage Ritual of Gentlemen" has no references to the above report at the ancestral shrine (*miao*) but the six rites are all performed in the ancestral shrine of the most recent ancestor. In the *Ch'un-ch'iu* . . . [a historical precedent]. So one can see that all ancient marriages were first reported to the ancestors. Marriages are major events of families and must be reported.
The presiding man of the girl's family also makes a report to his ancestors, saying "My daughter D is soon to marry into the A family," using the same forms as the groom's family. On the appointed day at

---

26. Ssu-ma Kuang, *Ssu-ma shih shu-i* (TSCC ed.) 10:114.

dawn the messenger dresses formally and takes the live goose, its head to the left, decorated with hat strings.

The reason for using a goose for the pledge is that it travels in yin-yang order. If no goose is available, carve one of wood. Decorating it with hat string means to tie it with bright silk ribbons.

He stops outside the gate of the girl's house. The doorman goes in to report. The presiding man of the girl's family, formally dressed, goes out to greet him. With salutes, they yield to each other on entering the gate, and salute and decline precedence in ascending to the hall. The presiding man stands at the top of the stairs facing west. The guest stands on the west stairs slightly to the north, facing east.

In the "Marriage Ritual of Gentleman" the guest ascends the western steps by the main beam and faces east. He goes deep into the hall, showing he is a close relative. Today's homes do not all conform to the ritual; therefore it is enough to be slightly north.

The guest says, "Your honor is kindly giving a wife to B. B's father A, following the ancient rituals, has sent me to ask your acceptance of this engagement gift." The presiding man says, "My child is stupid and we have not been able to teach her. But if his honor orders it, I dare not decline."[27]

The *I-li* has the usher carry these messages back and forth, with phrases about giving orders. Here it is simplified.

Facing north, he bows twice.

This is out of respect for the groom's father; it is not directed at the guest.

The guest gets off the seat and stands, not returning the bow.

A messenger does not dare compete in deference with a senior.

The presiding man and guest both advance to the space between the pillars, and both stand facing south. The guest presents the goose and the master accepts it, then passes it to an attendant. They then exchange documents.

The documents record the phrases used in giving the engagement gifts and "asking the name."[28] Record only the year, month, and day, and the bride's father's rank and name. The guest and presiding man each take one. After the presentation of the goose the documents are exchanged. The groom's family's document is kept by the bride's family and vice versa. This practice can be used as a substitute for the popular practice of "draft documents" (*hsing shu*).

Taking it, they withdraw. Each passes the document to his attendant. The guest descends and goes out the gate facing east.[29]

This text is several times longer than the relevant portion of the *I-li*. Without its notes, it is slightly more than half the length of the *K'ai-yuan li*'s rules for the lowest officials. Although it largely follows the format of these two texts, it

27. These phrases are taken directly from the *I-li*, "Shih hun li." See John Steele, trans., *The I-li* (London: Probsthain, 1917), p. 36.

28. "Asking the name" (*wen-ming*) is the next of the classical six rites of marriage.

29. Ssu-ma Kuang, *Shu-i* 3:30–31.

is not a compromise between them. Ssu-ma Kuang wanted to preserve as much as possible of the form and spirit of the *I-li* but sensed that many "customary practices" could not be completely prohibited if he wished anyone to use his book. Some of Ssu-ma Kuang's changes are trivial modernizations; clothes, food, or gifts were changed to those available in his day. Others involve repeated reports to the ancestors that he believed implied but unstated in the *I-li*. Ssu-ma Kuang also reduced the distinctions between eldest sons and other sons, reflecting the changes in family structure since the classical period. In the passage quoted above, the main divergences between Ssu-ma Kuang's text and the *I-li* were the reports to the ancestors in the image hall; decorating the goose; having the guest and presiding man address each other directly; and exchange of marriage documents.

The exchange of marriage documents in the passage above was explicitly described as an accommodation to customary practice (*su*). Documents of this sort seem to have been used since the Later Han at the latest.[30] According to the description in the *Tung-ching meng-hua lu* (Dreams of the splendor of the eastern capital), the exchange of draft documents was the first step in engagements in Northern Sung Kaifeng.[31] Ssu-ma Kuang's accommodation involved limiting what would be written on the documents. Sample documents found in Sung and Yuan encyclopedias show also mother's name, ancestors back three generations, and dowry in land and goods, all of which Ssu-ma Kuang deleted.[32] Ssu-ma Kuang wanted the other parts eliminated because he disapproved of treating marriages like "sales."[33] Because dowry was often substantial among Sung upper-class families, one can easily see why it became customary to put the amount on paper, and Ssu-ma Kuang's objections most likely had little effect on his contemporaries' practices.[34]

Elsewhere in Ssu-ma Kuang's prescriptions for the marriage ritual he rejected as foolish very early engagements and the ceremony of joining locks of hair. However, he found ways to accept parts of eight other customary practices, including "laying out the bedclothes," whereby the bride's family delivered the dowry the day before the wedding. He said it was acceptable to set out the objects of daily use such as blankets, canopies, and screens but not objects of clothing, which should be left in their cases. "The current custom

30. Tu Yu, *T'ung-tien* (reprint Taipei: Hsin-hsing) 58:336c.

31. Meng Yüan-lao, *Tung-ching meng-hua lu*, 5:151.

32. See, for instance, *Hsin-pien shih-wen lei-yao ch'i-cha ch'ing-ch'ien* (1324; reprint, Taipei: Ta-hua), pp. 489–492.

33. Ssu-ma Kuang, *Shu-i* 3:33.

34. On dowry in the Sung, see Ebrey, "Women in the Kinship Structure of the Southern Song Upper Class," *Historical Reflections* 8 (1981):113–128. One effect of Ssu-ma Kuang's objections may have been less explicit expression of the exchange aspects of weddings. Liu Ying-li, in compiling an encyclopedia in the early fourteenth century, put contracts at the very end of his eighteen chapters on marriage, alluding to Ssu-ma Kuang's comment that they were barbaric but noting that they were still customary. See *Hsin-pien shih-wen lei-ch'ü han-mo ta-chüan* (1307 ed.), *i*, 18:16b–17a.

is to display them all, in a desire to boast of their quantity and value. This is a maidservant's attitude, unworthy of consideration."[35] In the case of the groom adorning himself with a crown of flowers, well-attested elsewhere, Ssu-ma Kuang thought it seemed very unmasculine, but he allowed that one or two flowers could be stuck in the groom's hair.[36] (The wedding rituals involve several reversals of male and female roles, the symbolism of which seems to have escaped Ssu-ma Kuang.) Similarly he frowned on the new practice of brides riding in sedan chairs but said it would be acceptable if the bride suffered from motion sickness in carriages. Another custom described in other Sung sources is a ceremony of the bride and groom bowing to each other on their first encounter; Ssu-ma Kuang believed that this showed respect and should be practiced.[37] He also was willing to have the bride introduced to her husband's ancestors on the day of the wedding rather than wait the three months the *I-li* had required.[38] A three-month waiting period was probably not feasible in the Sung, seeming to assume a "returnability" of brides ill-suited to the creation of strong ties between marrying families.

Although Ssu-ma Kuang made these accommodations to popular custom, perhaps sometimes following earlier etiquette books, he by no means merely codified contemporary practices. This can be seen most easily by a comparison of his instructions to the description of marriage practices in the *Tung-ching meng-hua lu*. Among the noncanonical practices this text describes are use of musicians, numerous exchanges of gifts, some of mostly symbolic value, an inspection of the bride by someone in the groom's family, symbolic resistance to several of the steps in the ceremony that could only be overcome by token bribes, and tossing of grains as symbols of fertility.[39]

Besides making accommodations to popular customs, another way Ssu-ma Kuang tried to make his ritual prescriptions more practical for his day was to consider the expense of various requirements. Occasionally he added notes on how poor families could reduce costs. For instance, again on marriage, he noted that the traditional red silk given as a marriage present had no practical use and was therefore a burden for poor families; he suggested they substitute five lengths of mixed colors tied into a bundle.[40] Reference to expense, however, comes up more frequently in his discussions of mourning and burial, where the classical prescriptions seem to assume that expense was no object. For instance, in discussing the dressing of the corpse, Ssu-ma Kuang described the use of clothing in the ancient rituals, which had required even the lowest grade (*shih*) to use fifty-two pieces altogether. "This is something the poor cannot manage. Now we will

35. Ssu-ma Kuang, *Shu-i* 3:33.
36. Ibid., 3:34.
37. Ibid., 3:36.
38. Ibid., 3:35.
39. Meng Yüan-lao, *Tung-ching meng-hua-lu* 5:151–153.
40. Ssu-ma Kuang, *Shu-i* 3:32.

simplify and for the preparatory stage use one piece and for the first and
second laying out use as many as are available from the deceased's own
clothes or mourning gifts provided by friends and relatives."[41] Despite his
references to poverty, Ssu-ma Kuang's revisions for the sake of economy
seem aimed at practices expensive even for ordinary *shih-ta-fu* families. By
taking such poverty into consideration, however, he was able to make a set of
rules for the performance of family rituals that all *shih-ta-fu* could follow;
differentiation by wealth would not involve the procedures followed, only the
size or quality of items employed.

Ancestral Rites and Sumptuary Principles

In one of his writings, Ssu-ma Kuang described the evolution of the
system of ancestral shrines (*chia miao*) since ancient times. He noted that
whereas high officials in T'ang times made use of the permission given them
to erect shrines, during the Five Dynasties period the practice fell into disuse.
"During Jen-tsung's reign (1023–1063), the highest officials made offerings to
their recent ancestors in their chambers, just like commoners." Even when
detailed rules on family shrines were drawn up in 1050, only Wen Yen-po
(1006–1097) erected a shrine.[42] Because officials had not taken to conducting
rites any differently from commoners, in his *Shu-i* Ssu-ma Kuang put all of his
instructions in terms of an image hall (*ying-t'ang*), a type of ancestral altar
anyone could use.[43]

The term "image hall" does not appear in the classics, but there are a few
references to image halls in the writings of other eleventh-century men,
including Ch'eng I, suggesting that it was a common term at the time.
Ssu-ma Kuang referred to the images in the image hall, apparently the type
of ancestor portrait Ch'eng I also mentioned, housed there in addition to
offering placards (*tz'u-pan*).[44]

On the whole, Ssu-ma Kuang did not go far beyond the Classics in his
instructions on ancestral rites. He allowed sacrifices (*chi*) only four times a
year, in the middle month of each season, each time to three generations (i.e.,
great-grandfather, grandfather, and father). If Ssu-ma Kuang saw his audience as the equivalent of the ancient great officers (*ta-fu*) instead of the
ancient *shih*, he may well have considered his instructions within classical
restrictions. He based his ancestral rites largely on the *I li* chapter that
describes the rites to be performed by great officers ("The Lesser Set of
Sacrificial Beasts") not that to be followed by *shih* ("The Single Sacrificial
Beast"); in the case of marriage, the *I li* had only one version. If Ssu-ma
Kuang's rules are compared to those in the *K'ai-yuan li*, they are closest to
those for middle-rank officials; the lowest officials by contrast could only

41. Ibid., 5:58.
42. Ssu-ma Kuang, *Ssu-ma Wen-cheng kung ch'uan-chia chi* (Wan-yu wen-k'u ed.) 79:793–794.
43. Ssu-ma Kuang, *Shu-i*, 10:113.
44. Ibid., 10:121.

make offerings to two generations. The major difference between the two formulations is that Ssu-ma Kuang used fewer assistants than the *K'ai-yuan li* used.

Where Ssu-ma Kuang diverged from the Classics, he may well have been following earlier etiquette books. Concerning the day to be used in sacrifices, Ssu-ma Kuang noted various theories. The *I li* referred to the day *ting-hai*, and some said any *hai* day would be acceptable. An early T'ang book on ancestral rites said to use the equinoxes and solstices. Either system might lead to days inconvenient for officials, who Ssu-ma Kuang proposed could therefore chose a convenient day and divine to check its acceptability.[45]

Ssu-ma Kuang's *Shu-i* was used as a manual for the practice of family rites by at least a few families.[46] It certainly had advantages over trying to use the *I-li* as a guide. Nevertheless, probably because it was aimed at the relatively small audience of *shih-ta-fu* who might have considered trying to use the *I-li*, it seems neither to have gained a large audience, even among the educated, nor later to have provided much competition to the *Family Rituals*. Chu Hsi described the problems even educated men had with it:

> When the reader sees the detail of the steps and procedures [in Ssu-ma Kuang's book], he will think that what cannot be easily comprehended often cannot be easily practiced, and be afraid even to try. Also some, on seeing the size of the rooms, the numbers of attendants, and the cost of the utensils will conclude that they do not have adequate resources [for the rites]. Consequently, although the book is in circulation, those who have copies merely store them in their trunks. No one has been able to put its instructions into practice.[47]

THE COURT-SPONSORED RITUAL OF THE CHENG-HO PERIOD

Carrying on the tradition of the T'ang dynasty, the Sung government issued several ritual manuals. In the early Sung the government issued the *K'ai-pao t'ung-li*, based closely on the *K'ai-yüan li*. In the Chia-yu period (1056–1063), Ou-yang Hsiu supervised a compendium of revisions, the *T'ai-ch'ang yin-ko li*, in 100 *chüan*, but this book dealt only with imperial family rituals. A full revision, more comprehensive in scope, was done between 1107 and 1113. It resulted in the 220 *chüan Cheng-ho wu-li hsin-i* (New forms for the five categories of rites of the Cheng-ho period), called *Wu-li* here for short. The compilers were apparently more interested than any of their predecessors in the educational goal of shaping the rituals for commoners.

This compendium was produced by creating a temporary bureau, the

---

45. Ibid., 10:113.
46. T'o-t'o et al., *Sung shih* (Peking: Chung-hua, 1977) 434:12877; Lou Yüeh, *Kung k'uei chi* (TSCC ed.) 105:1484.
47. Chu Hsi, *Chu Wen-kung wen-chi* 83:15a–b.

bureau for deliberating on ritual (*i li chü*), under the Department or Ministries (*shang-shu sheng*). Two deliberators and five examiners were assigned to consider all aspects of the ritual institutions and submit their recommendation for imperial approval.[48] A long series or memorials and imperial responses resulting from their efforts has been preserved in the prefatory chapter of the *Wu-li*. From the beginning, the intention seems to have been to bring ritual to ordinary people. An edict of 1107 stated, "The way to guard against the people's (*min*) taking customary practices as their model lies in the five categories of rites."[49]

The number of generations of ancestors to which officials and nonofficials could make offerings was one of the first issues debated. In 1108 an examiner, Yü Su, asked guidance in formulating rules for ancestral rites, noting that "No ritual is more important than sacrifices (*chi*), which are the means to extend support and filial service."[50] The imperial response stressed the importance of keeping the essentials of the ancient systems, but said the officials could make adjustments appropriate to current conditions with regard to the number of generations honored, the items used for offerings, the differentiation by rank, and the ways of accommodating absences from home or lack of wealth.[51] The subsequent proposal made in 1110 noted that in the ancient period feudal lords had made offerings to their four ascendant ancestors plus their "great ancestor" (*t'ai-tsu*) for a total of five, great officers (*ta-fu*) had made offerings to two ascendant ancestors plus their "great ancestor" for a total of three, and appointed officers (*ming shih*) had made them only to their fathers and grandfathers. After further discussion of classical precedent, the officials came to current custom:

> Nowadays ranked officials *p'in-kuan*) do not go as far as commoners (*shu-jen*); both make offerings for three generations, drawing no distinctions either by the rank [of the one making the offering] or the extent of the favor [received from the ancestor]. These vulgar practices are by now well entrenched. At present we wish to model ourselves on the Chou system; those in high positions can be compared to the ancient feudal lords and should make sacrifices to five generations; those below can be compared to the ancient great officers and should make offerings to three generations. If the next level is compared to the ancient "appointed officers" and made to sacrifice to two generations, it would violate people's filial feelings and desires to honor the departed. If this principle were enforced, it would evoke deep uneasiness, thwarting the intention of the former kings in instituting rituals to continue affection. We request that officials of the rank of executive (*ch'ih cheng*) and up make sacrifices to their ancestors from great-great-grandfather down, and everyone else to three generations.[52]

---

48. Pi Yüan, ed., *Hsü tzu-chih t'ung-chien* (Peking: Chung-hua, 1957) 89:2301.
49. Cheng Chü-chung, ed., *Cheng-ho wu-li hsin-i* (SKCSCP ed.), *shou*, 6a.
50. Ibid., *shou,*, 7b.
51. Ibid., 8a.
52. Hsü Sung, ed., *Sung-hui yao chi-pen* (reprint Taipei: Shih-chieh 1964), *li*, 12:2b.

The emperor rejected the proposal to allow everyone to make sacrifices to three generations, noting that gradations in ritual distinguish the honored and lowly, and the ranking of emperor seven, feudal lords five, great officers three, and *shih* two was an unchanging moral principle. "To allow subordinate officials (*shih ts'ung kuan*) down to *shih* and commoners to all make offerings to three generation without gradation or distinctions of numbers—how can this be the idea of the ritual!"[53]

Although the proposal to provide rules for ancestral rites performed by commoners was disapproved, the *Wu-li* did incorporate rules for commoners for the other family rites—coming of age, weddings, and funerals—something the *K'ai-yuan li* had lacked. Overall, the rules for "ranked officials" were modeled on the *I li* and *K'ai-yuan li*, perhaps via the *K'ai-pao li*, but the rules for *shu-jen* conform more closely to common customs. In the case of weddings, the rules for commoners differed from those for ranked officials in these regards: the "six rites" were condensed into four; lamb, chicken, or duck could be substituted for goose as a "calling" gift; the matchmaker/ intermediary acted as messenger throughout the engagement process; and marriage documents were exchanged. Ssu-ma Kuang's prescriptions for weddings do not seem to have particularly influenced these formulations. If his prescriptions are compared to those in the *Wu-li* text, his are closer to those for officials, but at the same time include several customary practices that the *Wu-li* did not allow even commoners.

Among the accommodations to popular custom, probably the most significant is the use of a matchmaker/intermediary (*mei-shih*) to carry messages between the two families. The classical model, which had a representative of the groom's family call on the bride's family directly, did not fit as well with the Sung situation where brides and grooms usually came from families of nearly equal rank. An intermediary (often the matchmaker, so familiar from fiction) served to avoid the direct confrontation of the two families and could be interpreted as serving the interests of both. Because the *I-li*'s rules had never been intended for commoners, no canonical principles were violated when the *Wu-li* had intermediaries carry out the early exchanges in the marriages of commoners.

When these new ritual rules were finally issued in 1113, people were expected to put them into practice. According to the treatise on ritual of the *Sung shih*,

> An officer of ritual correctness was created, and it was permitted that gentlemen and commoners ask him about the new forms of etiquette. The governor of Kaifeng, Wang Ko, was ordered to edit a classified version for common use and print it for general dissemination. This would make it possible for everyone to know the ideas of the rituals, and those who did not carry them out could be charged with wrong-doing.[54]

53. Ibid.
54. T'o-t'o, *Sung-shih* 98:2423.

In less than a decade, however, this ambitious scheme was abandoned as too bothersome.[55] Nevertheless, in the 1150s when Chu Hsi was registrar of T'ung-an county in Fukien, the *Cheng-ho wu-li hsin-i* was still the standard work for local officials to use in instructing the populace in ritual matters. Chu Hsi criticized the book because the clerks who looked after legal and ritual matters found it difficult to understand; most times they followed prior practice and only consulted it hurriedly when faced with a special event, making it even harder to follow. Moreover, the required antique clothes and utensils were impractical for local officials, and, because the *Wu-li* was put together by a committee, there were internal contradictions. Chu Hsi did, however, concur with the intention of making a standard manual widely available:

> The best course would be to take those practices actually used by officials and commoners in prefectures and counties, compare them to recent formulations and edit a manual titled "A brief reformulation of the Cheng-ho rituals for commoners and officials, of the Shao-hsing period." It should be printed and three copies distributed to each county and prefecture (one for the governor, one the school, and one a famous mountain temple).[56]

CHU HSI'S FAMILY RITUALS

After its publication in the early thirteenth century, Chu Hsi's *Family Rituals* quickly became the standard reference work on the proper way to perform family rituals, not merely displacing earlier books such as Ssu-ma Kuang's but largely eliminating the need to write any more such books. In later centuries the *Family Rituals* was quoted and excerpted in a wide range of books, from genealogies and gazetteers to popular reference books and the legal codes.[57] Of all the writings attributed to Chu Hsi, this may be the one

55. Ibid.
56. Chu Hsi, *Chu Wen-kung wen-chi* 69:17a–18b. The temples referred to included both Buddhist and Taoist ones.
57. Most "popular encyclopedias" from late Sung on cite the *Family Rituals*, often under each rite separately. Some examples from the Sung and Yuan include *Shih-lin kuang-chi*, ed. Ch'en Yüan-ching (reprint, Peking: Chung-hua); *Chü-chia pi-yung shih-lei ch'üan chi* (reprint, Kyoto: Chumon); *Hsin-pien shih-wen lei-yao ch'i-cha ch'ing-ch'ien*. Genealogies often cite it, either to say that the descent group followed it, or to explain how they diverged from it. For instance, the *Hsiao-shan Lai-shih chia-p'u* (1900 ed.) 1:4a, says "The rituals for *shih-ta-fu* managing their families must be based on Master Chu's *Family Rituals*. Even if one cannot completely copy what the *Family Rituals* says, one cannot set aside those aspects of it which can be practiced." The author then justifies why his group did not stop at four generations in its ancestral rites. Gazetteers often referred to the *Family Rituals* in sections on popular customs, either to praise the populace for following its provisions or pointing out where they diverged. On references to the *Family Rituals* in law codes, see Niida, *Mibunhōshi*, p. 599. J. J. M. de Groot, a scholar who made a close study of religious life around Amoy in the late nineteenth century, referred to the *Family Rituals* as the "chief vademecum of the people in their domestic rites." See his *The Religious Systems of China* (reprint, Taipei: Ch'eng-wen, 1972), III, 832.

most often consulted by people with little formal education.[58]

Chu Hsi lived three generations after Ssu-ma Kuang and Ch'eng I and two generations after the compilers of the *Wu-li*. Many changes had occurred during this period, in both the intellectual issues attracting the philosophers, and their social milieu. Chu Hsi's *Family Rituals* would not have been written the way it was except for the earlier works already discussed, not only because large parts are directly copied or paraphrased but also because these earlier efforts clarified the key issues: How far could one go in following the *I-li*? How could one revive ancestral rites as a Confucian ceremony? Where should one simplify to reach a wider audience? Chu Hsi thought neither Ssu-ma Kuang nor the *Wu-li* had gone far enough in simplifying for a broad audience. For Chu Hsi the educational goal of teaching the commoners Confucian rituals came first and outweighed reforming the practices of *shih-ta-fu* to avoid vulgarity and preserving classical hierarchical principles.[59]

The *Family Rituals* begins with a preface, also preserved in Chu Hsi's *Collected Works*, that explains the principles underlying the work's compilation.[60] First, a distinction is drawn between the fundamental features of

58. Chu Hsi's role in creating the *Family Rituals* was questioned by Ch'ing scholars; however, recent research is reversing this view. Ch'ien Mu and Ueyama Shumpei both argue strongly for accepting the *Family Rituals* as a work of Chu Hsi. They cite Chu Hsi's repeated references to working on family rituals and point to the quick acceptance of the book in the early thirteenth century when many of Chu Hsi's close disciples were still alive. As in other books accepted as Chu Hsi's products, such as the *Chin ssu-lu* and *Hsiao hsüeh*, it is likely that colleagues or disciples did a significant part of the compilation. And, as Huang Kan noted in publishing the book in 1216, the text in circulation did not represent Chu Hsi's final opinion on all points; he had ideas for changes, but he never had time to incorporate them. Thus, some discrepancies between what Chu Hsi wrote elsewhere and what is found in the *Family Rituals* are only to be expected. As Ueyama notes, some arguments against Chu Hsi's authorship are easily answered by admitting that the work was edited more than composed and never reached truly final form. See Ch'ien Mu, *Chu Tzu hsin hsüeh-an* (Taipei: San-min, 1971) 4:165–173; Ueyama Shumpei, "Shushi no 'Karei' to 'Gireikyō dentōkai,'" *Tōhō gakuhō* 54 (1982): 173–256. Because in this chapter I am not focusing on Chu Hsi's philosophy but on formulations of family rites, it makes little difference how many words in this text Chu Hsi wrote and how many were supplied by disciples or editors; for convenience, I will credit Chu Hsi with all of them.

59. It is not known exactly when Chu Hsi wrote or edited the *Family Rituals*, and most likely he worked on it sporadically over a period of decades, beginning as a young man. He is reported to have said, "My father died when I was fourteen, and at sixteen I was finished with the mourning for him. During that interval all that we had to follow for the sacrificial offerings were the old rituals of our family. Although the text of these rituals was incomplete, it was very well arranged, and my late mother managed the sacrifices with great reverence. Not until I was seventeen or eighteen did I examine the family rituals of various authorities to fill in partially the text of our rituals." Chu Hsi, *Chu Tzu yü-lei* (1473; reprint, Taipei: Cheng-chung, 1970) 90:23b–24a. In 1173 he entrusted to a student the task of collecting the writings of authorities on forms for sacrificing. Yet in an 1190s postscript to a friend's book on family rituals based on three earlier works, Chu Hsi said he had never finished the revision of Ssu-ma Kuang's book he had once planned. On the date of the *Family Rituals*, see Ueyama, "Shushi no 'Karei,'" pp. 215–225.

60. The *Family Rituals* of Chu Hsi survives in two transmissions,—a five-*chüan*, version, and

family etiquette expressed every day, such as seniority, love, and respect, and ceremonies practiced only occasionally, such as coming of age, weddings, funerals, and sacrifices. The preface also notes that many physical elements of the ancient rituals—buildings, utensils, clothes—were no longer in common use, but scholars disagreed on where to change and where to make a major effort to preserve ancient forms, leading some to concentrate on less essential features and others to propose costly procedures. Quite likely Chu Hsi had Ssu-ma Kuang in mind as someone who tended to get bogged down in the details of ceremonies.

In coverage, the *Family Rituals* is narrower than the *Shu-i*, excluding forms for general correspondence included in the first chapter of Ssu-ma Kuang's work. The material is also organized differently; each of the four family rituals has only one chapter, even the funeral chapter which is longer than the other three together; and a chapter on "general principles" is added at the beginning. This introductory chapter begins with a discussion of the room for ancestral rites, followed by the fabrication of the ritual robes and Ssu-ma Kuang's essay on managing families.[61] In addition, two sections are copied verbatim from the *Shu-i*, one attributed and one not; in many other places the *Family Rituals* paraphrases Ssu-ma Kuang.

Style, Audience, and Popular Customs

One of the most important differences between the *Shu-i* and the *Family Rituals* is in style. The *The Family Rituals* sticks less closely to the format of the *I-li* and presents its material in almost outline form. The key steps of each ritual are readily apparent in large type. Much more of the detail, including words to be spoken, descriptions of objects to be used, and so on, is in indented sections of small characters where it can easily be skipped. Moreover, considerably less detail is given. From my calculations, Chu Hsi kept his descriptions of the rites about 40 per cent shorter than Ssu-ma Kuang's, in both cases counting the notes. Chu Hsi's notes are not nearly as scholarly as Ssu-ma Kuang's. The only authorities Chu Hsi cites frequently are Ssu-ma Kuang and Ch'eng I; Ssu-ma Kuang is cited over twenty times, many of the passages a page or more in length, usually from Ssu-ma Kuang's discussions of the flaws in popular customs. Given these passages, Ssu-ma Kuang's "voice" comes through more clearly in the text than does Chu Hsi's. Ch'eng I is also cited nine or ten times, but the quotes tend to be quite short. There are only five or six citations to the Classics in the entire book.

---

an eight. Scholarly opinion now holds that the five-*chüan* version is closer to Chu Hsi's original text; here my references to the *Family Rituals* will be to a Ch'ing five-*chüan* version of the Pao kao t'ang.

61. Chu Hsi referred to his rearrangement of the material in the *Shu-i* in the notes. For instance, after the section, "Specifications for the Long Robe," he noted: "This section originally was at the end of the Capping Ritual. Here it comes in the earlier chapter because although an embellishment these are clothes worn on a daily basis." (*Chia li* 1:8a.)

To illustrate this stylistic difference I will translate the portion of the *Family Rituals* that overlaps with the portion of the *Shu-i* given above. It does not correspond perfectly because it represents a combination of the first two of the classical six rites, with the second, "asking the name," coming at the very beginning; to match exactly, the extract from Ssu-ma Kuang would have to be about one-third longer.

Presenting the Engagement Gift
(*Na ts'ai*)—the ritual for accepting the selection, known today, in the vernacular, as the engagement.
The presiding man prepares the document.
The presiding man is the presiding man of the marriage. For the document use the type of formal stationery in common use. If the groom is the son of someone in a secondary descent line, his father fills out the document and informs the descent line heir.
At dawn he takes it to make a report at the offering hall.
The procedure is the same as in the report in the capping ceremony. The prayer board begins the same way, then says, "B's son A (or B's such-type relative C's son A), of so-many years, is full grown but does not have a mate. We have now made plans to take in marriage the daughter of X, of _____ office, _____ prefecture. Today we present the engagement gift. Unable to overcome our filial feelings, earnestly. . . ." If the descent line heir is the one being married, he makes the report in person.
Next the presiding man sends a son or younger brother to serve as messenger to go to the girl's family. The presiding man of the girl's family comes out to meet the messenger.
The messenger is formally dressed when he goes to the girl's family. For the girl's family, it is also the descent line heir who serves as presiding man. He meets the messenger formally dressed. Except when the girl is the descent line heir's daughter, her father sits to the right of the presiding man. If he is of a senior generation, then he sits forward a little; if of a lower one, then he sits slightly behind. After tea has been served, the messenger stands up and says, "Your honor is kindly giving a wife to A. My (such-type relative) B, of _____ office, following the ancestral rituals, has sent me to ask your acceptance of the engagement gift." His attendant brings him the document, which he gives to the presiding man. The presiding man answers, "My child (or younger sister, niece, grandchild) is stupid and we have not been able to teach her. But if his honor orders it, I dare not decline." He turns north and bows twice. The messenger steps aside and does not return the bow. He asks permission to leave, and on receiving it takes his appropriate place to wait. If the engaged girl is an aunt or elder sister of the presiding man, then he should not say she is stupid and untaught, but the other phrases should be the same.
Next the presiding man of the girl's family takes the document and reports its content at the offering hall.
The procedure is the one followed at the groom's family. The prayer board

62. See note 27.

begins the same, then has "X's number so-many daughter (or such-type relative Y's number so-many daughter) has grown up and is now promised in marriage to the son of B, of _____ office, _____ prefecture (or such-type relative C's son). Today we have had the presentation of the engagement gift. Unable to overcome our filial feelings, earnestly. . . ."

He goes out and gives the messenger the document of reply. Then he entertains him.

When the presiding man goes out, he invites the messenger to come up into the hall, where he gives him the document of reply. The messenger takes it and asks permission to leave. The presiding man invites him to stay as a guest and then brings wine and food to serve to him. From this point on, the messenger exchanges bows and salutes with the presiding man, as in everyday guest-host etiquette. The attendants also are entertained, but in a separate room. They are given gratuities.

The messenger returns with the reply. The presiding man of the groom's family makes another report at the offering hall.

No prayer is used on this occasion.

Besides reducing detail, Chu Hsi made several changes in the rite itself. He combined some of the classical "six rites" of marriage, perhaps following the *Wu-li*, which had also reduced the number of steps for commoners but not for officials. Chu Hsi did not copy the imperial plan exactly, combining rites one with two and three and four with five while the *Wu-li* had combined rites two with three and four with five. Yet the spirit is much the same, probably in both cases reflecting common practice.

Another change Chu Hsi made was full acceptance of "marriage documents." Although he quotes Ssu-ma Kuang's objections to negotiating the value of dowries, he leaves that under the discussion of "displaying the bedclothes" and does not use it as a reason to resist the customary use of marriage letters. In the ritual these letters seem to take the place of the classical goose, unmentioned by Chu Hsi.

Chu Hsi was not without his own principles, however, and found places where he strongly resisted "customary practice." For example, Ssu-ma Kuang had allowed introducing the bride to the ancestral altar on the day of the wedding, but Chu Hsi argued that it was not right to accept her fully into the family before she was introduced to her parents-in-law on the second day. Chu Hsi's compromise, making token use of the "three," was to introduce the bride on the third day.[63]

A more fundamental change from Ssu-ma Kuang and the *I-li* is Chu Hsi's overlay of the lesser descent line system. Given Chu Hsi's wish to write a practical manual and, in most other regards, to accommodate popular custom, the centrality he gave to descent line heirs is perplexing. Ch'eng I had argued for reviving the descent line system and having descent line heirs preside over ancestral rites, but in surviving writings he neither drew out all the implica-

63. *Chia li* 3:11a.

tions Chu Hsi did nor suggested that descent line heirs would officiate at weddings or cappings. In the *Family Rituals* the presiding men (*chu*) of a wedding were not to be bride's and groom's fathers or grandfathers, as they were in the *Shu-i* but whenever possible the great-great-grandfather's descent line heir, a relative possibly as distant as a third cousin; next choice was the great-grandfather's descent line heir, and so on.[64] This scheme had no connection with Sung custom and never gained any widespread acceptance, undoubtedly because marriage involved property and the *chia*, the family as a property-owning unit, was too thoroughly established in the social, legal, and economic order of the time for any wider unit to take over even symbolic control of marriage. It is true that other forms of extended agnatic kinship organization developed in this period, forms differing fundamentally from the descent line system while adopting some of its terminology. Although these descent groups and lineages took on rites to common ancestors, they did not normally interfere with household level ritual activities such as marriages.

Ancestral Rites and Sumptuary Principles

As Wing-tsit Chan has shown, in his personal life Chu Hsi took quite seriously religious rites to ancestors and other spirits.[65] In his formulation of ancestral rites in the *Family Rituals*, he largely followed the principles Ch'eng I had outlined. He made no use of portraits and did not even use the term image hall. He allowed rites to four generations within the "lesser descent line" system, and more often than only once a season. Perhaps most important , he explicitly stated that commoners (*shu*) could do all these forms of the rites.

> The ancient ancestral temple (*miao*) system does not appear in the classics.
> Moreover, today's *shih* and commoners of low rank are not able to do parts of it
> [because of sumptuary laws]. Therefore, I have purposely named the ancestral
> hall "offering hall" (*tz'u-t'ang*) and have extensively adopted customary rituals
> (*su li*) in making rules for it.[66]

Presumably Chu Hsi abandoned the term image hall because, like Ch'eng I, he disapproved of the use of ancestral portraits. In a letter Chu Hsi argued that housing both images and spirit tablets in image halls was uncanonical

---

64. *Chia li* 3:1b, 2:1b.

65. Wing-tsit Chan, "Chu Hsi's Religious Life," International Symposium on Chinese-Western Cultural Interchange in Commemoration of the 400th Anniversary of the Arrival of Matteo Ricci, S.J., in China, Taipei, September 11–16, 1983. Chu Hsi believed that patrilineal descendants shared some of a deceased man's *ch'i*; therefore, it could not be said to have fully dispersed. Through descendants' sacrifices, responsive communication was possible. *Chu Tzu yü-lei* 3:117.

66. *Chia li* 1:1a–b. Chu Hsi was exaggerating when he said the *miao* system did not appear in the Classics; see note 6.

and violated the principle that the spirits of the ancestors should be concentrated in a single place.[67] Yet, like Ssu-ma Kuang, he could not use the canonical term *miao* because such structures were limited by sumptuary legislation to higher officials. The term that he chose—*tz'u-t'ang*—was not new, but he was using it in a new way. The term had been used in the Han for buildings erected at graves, intended as the place offerings would be made to the person buried in the grave. During the Sung the term was widely used for halls erected as sites for making offerings to great scholars, successful officials, or groups of worthy men. These halls, as places people other than relatives could pay their respects, were outside the ancestral cult.

Chu Hsi not only gave a new meaning to the term offering hall, but he made it the center of his *Family Rituals*, the first thing discussed in the first chapter. Moreover, he increased the occasions on which reports to ancestors were made in other rites, a tendency Ssu-ma Kuang had earlier manifested.[68] Following popular custom and Ch'eng I, he also prescribed forms for ancestral rites at graves, on anniversaries, and to early ancestors.

Chu Hsi discussed the sumptuary principles underlying ancestral rites several times with his friends and students. In a letter to an official named Wang he explicitly criticized the rules in the *Wu-li*.

> As for the Cheng-ho system, although it was based on an examination of ancient systems, often it got the number right at the expense of losing the idea. ... If we examine it according to the sayings of Master Ch'eng, then since the great-great-grandfather is one for whom one wears mourning garments, one must also sacrifice to him.[69]

Chu Hsi also followed Ch'eng I's interpretation that the canonical restriction of the number of *miao* allowed people of different rank was unrelated to the number of generations of ancestors they could worship. "Even those with seven or five *miao* stop at great-great-grandfather; and those with three or one *miao* must reach great-great-grandfather. It is just that the elaborations are not the same."[70] The *Yü-lei* records a further comment:

> Wen-chi said, "Today both *shih* and *shu* families make offerings to three generations. Is this a violation of ritual?" [Chu Hsi] said, "Although one makes offerings to three generations, if there is no shrine (*miao*), one cannot say it is usurping [the privileges of superiors]. What the ancients called shrines were large in size with gates and chambers, like a residence, not like the single rooms people use today."[71]

Thus, Chu Hsi ignored the imperial ruling of the Cheng-ho period that

67. Chu Hsi, *Chu Wen-kung wen-chi* 40:3b–4a.
68. Ueyama, "Shushi no 'Karei'" pp. 226–28.
69. Chu Hsi, *Chu Wen-kung wen-chi* 30:15a, 16b.
70. Ibid., 30:16b.
71. Chu Hsi, *Chu Tzu yü-lei* 90:25a.

low officials and commoners were not to make offerings back even three generations; to the contrary, in the *Family Rituals* he advocates four generations as the norm. Nevertheless, Chu Hsi did not envision each household setting up an altar with tablets for four generations of ancestors, for he tied his plan to the lesser descent line system that Ch'eng I and Chang Tsai had advocated reviving. Whereas Ssu-ma Kuang had each family head conduct rites, Chu Hsi had each descent line heir do it in his home.[72] Ch'eng I had argued that as everyone wore mourning for a great-great-grandfather, everyone should be able to make sacrifices to him, but Chu Hsi, following the logic of the descent line system, allowed only the descent line heirs. Others could, of course, attend as worshippers, but this would not always work out. What if they lived far away? Or the one who held the genealogical position of heir was uneducated or uninterested in rites?[73]

Although organizing ancestral rites on the basis of the descent line rather than the family might sound like a step in the direction of descent group rites, so important in later periods, it should be recognized that it was at best a small step. Even the largest unit, the descent line of the great-great-grandfather, did not hold group rites for their collective ancestors. The descent line heir only presided over rites to his own direct ancestors; he did not have the tablets for his grandfather's brothers and cousins and so on. These men's descendants might attend the rites he conducted to be present at the offerings to their common great-great-grandfather, but they would have to go elsewhere for sacrifices to their great-grandfather and grandfather.

The descent line system is the least practical of anything in the *Family Rituals*, and it is therefore not surprising that it was effectively eliminated in the versions most people used in later periods. This was accomplished in several ways. Many versions of the *Family Rituals* copied into other books are "large type" only.[74] As Chu Hsi had intended, the large type can stand on its own as a quick guide to the essential steps of each rite; nowhere in the large type does the term descent line heir appear.[75] At the beginning of the Ming, the government decreed that the *Family Rituals* was to be followed by commoners in marriages, yet the official summary in the *Ta Ming hui tien* does not define the presiding mans as a descent line heir and has the bride's and groom's fathers issue the instructions.[76] The *Ta Ming chi li*, which cites the

72. *Chia li* 1:2a–b. On Chu Hsi's use of the descent line system, see also Makino Tatsumi, *Kinsei Chūgoku sōzoku no kenkyū* (Tokyo: Nikko, 1949), pp. 11–27.

73. These sorts of issues were often discussed by philosophers and commentators, but their frequency suggests that a relatively rare situation in classical times, had become in the Sung a fairly common occurence.

74. "Large type only" passages from the *Family Rituals* appear in all the encyclopedias mentioned in note 57.

75. Because the textual history of the *Family Rituals* is obscure and students at times seem to have been set to work on it, possibly the overlay of the descent line system was done as an academic exercise, a feature Chu Hsi might have changed had he had time to revise the text.

76. Li Tung-yang et al., *Ta Ming hui-tien* (1587; reprint, Taipei: Hua-wen) 71:7a–12a.

influence of the *Family Rituals*, has all officials set up offering halls, whether or not they were descent line heirs.[77] Then, from mid-Ming on, a revised and commented edition of the *Family Rituals* prepared by Ch'iu Chün (1418–1495) gained greater popularlity than the original text; Ch'iu's book also eliminated use of the descent line heir in capping and marriage and downplayed it in ancestral rites.[78]

CONCLUSIONS

At the beginning of this paper I argued that to use family rituals as a means of educating people Neo-Confucians had to confront four obstacles: The sumptuary principles of the Classics, the popularity of non-Confucian and noncanonical practices, the need for rituals to work in the current family and kinship system, and the significance of ceremonial activities as markers of social status. By way of conclusion, I will consider how well the three books I discussed here dealt with these problems.

Ssu-ma Kuang's *Shu-i* set aside the problem of sumptuary restrictions and status markers by addressing only *shih-ta-fu* and positing that they were the equivalent of the classical *shih* and *ta-fu*. Nevertheless, he never explicitly excluded *shu* and *min* from performing the rites he described. His book could not be used to teach rituals to the uneducated or attract them away from Buddhism, but, if used in *shih-ta-fu* homes, it would shape the values of children and adults there.

Ssu-ma Kuang did make efforts to see that his rituals would work. He only eliminated categorically Buddhist and Taoist practices and ones he saw as crass, revealing a "maidservant's attitude." Could *shih-ta-fu* practice his rituals? Of course, any individual who set his mind to it could just as he could follow the *I-li*. The difficulty I see in the practices' broader adoption is that adequate substitutes were not always provided for the customary practices eliminated. For instance, Ssu-ma Kuang curtailed use of marriage documents and disapproved of the practice of witnessing the full dowry but did not provide alternative ways to express or handle the exchange aspects of marriage; he disapproved of treating marriage as a transaction and thought it could be changed if people tried. Likewise, he eliminated Buddhist or Taoist clergy as experts in funeral and ancestral rites without offering a practical substitute. He needed about twenty-five thousand characters to describe funeral and mourning procedures. Very few individuals, excepts those who made a hobby of ritual texts, would feel competent to manage their own parents' funerals by the "cook book" method using the *Shu-i*. If funerals had to be so complicated, most educated men would still feel the

77. *Ming chi li* (SKCSCP ed.) 6:13a. The influence of the *Family Rituals* is cited, but the presiding man is not a descent line heir under either cappings or weddings (28:23a–34b).
78. Ch'iu Chün, *Chia-li i-chieh* (1617 ed.).

need to bring in a ritual expert to handle the ceremonies. Ssu-ma Kuang's book would provide a good guide for a Confucian funeral specialist, but such men seem to have been rare in Sung China, and Ssu-ma Kuang had no power to create them.

The *Cheng-ho wu-li hsin-i* was addressed to a wider audience, providing separate rules for officials and nonofficials. Drawing a sumptuary line between officials and commoners was unobjectionable in a legal sense: officials had many privileges, and the right to conduct family rites on a grander scale, more closely modeled on the Classics, seems in this context a minor privilege. But family rites are also family occasions, and not all family members had the same political status. What if the son or the younger brother outranked his father or elder brother? Should political status intrude on family matters? Such conflicts were relatively rare in classical times, and in the Classics could be treated as exceptions; but they were commonplace by the twelfth century. Moreover, educated men who considered themselves *shih* but did not hold office (not excluded by Ssu-ma Kuang) were now explicitly classed with "commoners" (*shu-jen*) and told that it would be offensive to conduct rites above their rank. The compilers of the *Wu-li* argued to the emperor that telling such people they could only make offerings to their fathers would go against long-established custom and evoke resistance; most likely such men simply ignored it, as Chu Hsi did. In the case of marriage, well-to-do educated families probably would seek some intermediate form between that of uneducated commoners and officials, not content merely to have a more splendid version of a rite that could be easily identified as a commoner's by its steps or procedures. Indeed, the less legal status such a family had, the more important it was to avoid looking vulgar.

The *Family Rituals* differs from the *Shu-i* in attempting to address a larger audience—not only *shih-ta-fu* who would use it themselves but also local officials who would instruct commoners in its provisions. In this it was comparable to the *Wu-li*. However, unlike the *Wu-li*, it provides a single model for everyone, and in the crucial area of ancestral rites this model opens to all what had once been the privilege only of feudal lords. Therefore, the *Family Rituals* goes the farthest in combating the prevalence of Buddhist and Taoist customs at the local level by providing a guide that does not make commoners second class.

Were enough of the social functions of the rites preserved? With some notable exceptions, most of Ssu-ma Kuang's accommodations to popular customs were accepted, and Chu Hsi added a few of his own. The overlay of the descent line system was not practical and was soon abandoned or ignored. The relative sketchiness of the *Family Rituals* might have been an asset in making it more workable; wherever the *Family Rituals* did not explicitly exclude a popular custom, people may have felt free to add it as an embellishment, so long as it did not go counter to the basic structure of the rite.

Equally important , the *Family Rituals* made a dent in the need for a liturgy specialist. Certainly the steps for coming of age ceremonies and weddings were simple enough that a literate family head with a copy of the book could conduct them himself. Just as Ssu-ma Kuang used fewer assistants (ushers, celebrants, etc.) than the *I-li* or *K'ai-yuan li*, Chu Hsi used fewer than Ssu-ma Kuang. For funerals , although Chu Hsi's text is significantly shorter than Ssu-ma Kuang's, with most of its bulk in the "small type," it would still be an exaggeration to say that conducting funerals according to it would be easy or that any literate man could organize his parents' funerals. But it would be easier than using the *Shu-i*. In later periods, when descent groups flourished, they often patterned their ancestral rites on the *Family Rituals*; sometimes they may have had a member or two who mastered the steps for funerals in this text and who could serve as a master of ceremonies for kinsmen's funerals.

What about the need upper-class men felt to keep their own polite behavior distinct from lower-ranking groups? Here again the sketchiness of the *Family Rituals* may have been useful. Because the *Family Rituals* provides fewer specifics about a ceremony's appearance, I think it would be possible for higher status families to conduct the ceremonies on a grander scale, perhaps with more attention to classical flourishes, and poorer or lower-ranking families to follow the same procedures on a simpler scale. Ssu-ma Kuang had discussed such variation in terms of the relative wealth of his audience, seeming to assume they were all *shih-ta-fu*. Chu Hsi expands this gradation beyond the *shih-ta-fu* so that the entire populace follows the same set of rules, varying by degree but not by kind. This, I think, was probably adequate to allow higher-ranking families to maintain clear behavioral markers of their social status while lower-ranking families would not see themselves as arbitrarily excluded. It also fits better with the social stratification of Sung and later China in which legal differences in status were relatively minor.

Finally, let me raise a question for future research. Did Sung scholars achieve their educational goals in writing updated guides to family rituals? Did their texts contribute to the standardization or Confucianization of the family values and family behavior of peasants and other commoners? I suspect that they did but neither directly nor automatically. The texts, especially Chu Hsi's *Family Rituals*, provided the necessary textual basis for agreement in the basic outlines of the rites to be conducted at different social levels. Yet elite-commoner interaction in ritual situations was also needed for this knowledge to spread. This interaction was probably achieved most often through descent groups, a form of social organization that became more and more prevalent in later centuries. In descent groups commoners participated in ancestral rites and other ceremonies modeled on the *Family Rituals* under the supervision of elite members. To explore this process of cultural transmission will require close examination of the use of the *Family Rituals* by descent groups.

ELEVEN

Education of Children in the Sung

Pei-yi Wu

Notwithstanding all the emphasis Sung Neo-Confucians placed on education of the young, they wrote very little on how children were actually reared and trained. There was much reiteration of the ideal regimen stipulated in canonical classics such as the *Li Chi*, but we know almost nothing about the Neo-Confucians' own childhood in general or their primary education in particular. Nor are the historians more helpful. The scarcity of information regarding elementary education contrasts with the abundant records on private academies, the Imperial University, and the examination system. The paradox appears all the greater if one believes, as so much circumstantial evidence suggests, that education of children proliferated during the Sung as never before.

Historical records yield no quantitative information on primary schools, but the available figures pertaining to higher education give some idea as to the probable number of elementary students. If the candidates who participated in the capital examination or the applicants for the Imperial University represent only a fraction of those who had gone to school as children—the happy few who had survived various hurdles in the long selection process—then from the magnitude of this top section of the pyramid one can extrapolate the breadth of the base. The number of examination candidates during the Northern Sung seldom fell below 10,000, while in the year 1202 more than 37,000 traveled to Hangchow to take the entrance examination for the Imperial University.[1] Assuming that only one out of every 200 who had begun elementary education had the stamina, motivation,

The research for this paper was made possible by a grant (CC'80) from the American Council of Learned Societies. A PSC-CUNY research award enabled me to use the libraries in Taiwan.

1. Teng Ssu-yu, *Chung-kuo k'ao-shih chih-tu shih* (Taipei: Taiwan hsüeh-sheng shu-chü, 1967), p. 140. Sung Hsi, *Sung-shih yen-chiu lun-ts'ung* (Taipei: Chung-kuo wen-hua yen-chiu-so, 1962), p. 145.

aptitude, luck, and financial resources to finish the long years of preparation and to pass all the successive tests in order to qualify for the Imperial University examination, then it is probably safe to estimate that, in any given year during Chu Hsi's prime in southern China, as many as 740,000 children had their first taste of memorizing incomprehensible texts and copying complex characters.

There are other reasons for believing that education of children was widespread during the Sung. First, with the opening up of opportunities for nearly everyone regardless of family status and the attractive prospects of upward mobility through the avenue of successive examinations, parents, whatever their occupation, must have been eager to have their sons educated. The rewards of education were certainly greater than ever in view of the generous emoluments received by government employees, the genial and lenient treatment of civilian officials by all Sung emperors, and the greatly inflated size of the bureaucracy. The situation is aptly summarized by Su Ch'e (1039–1112) in a memorial submitted to the throne in 1069:

> Nowadays the procedure for the selection of government officials is such that none who memorizes texts and does literary exercises can be denied the opportunity of becoming a civil servant. The entrance is not difficult while the rewards are gratifying. Therefore huge crowds flock to this enterprise. There are very few peasant, artisan, or merchant families that fail to have a son or two who abandon the family line and attempt to join the ranks of scholar-officials.[2]

Su Ch'e's observation may not have applied to the lower echelons of nongentry families, but bright children of humble origins were not always excluded from the competition. Some clans provided free school for the children of impoverished members. Sometimes, branches of a poor family would pool their resources to enable the brightest boy of the family to be educated at least to the first hurdle. Given the nature of Sung society and such conspicuous incentive, matching initiative would not have been long wanting.

Second, the nature of commercial practice and the money economy during the Sung was such that even a casual examination leads to the inescapable conclusion that a sizable portion of the populace must have received at least a rudimentary education. Widespread use of credit mechanisms, the nationwide circulation of private notes and commodity bills, the ever-expanding remittance system, and the vast amount of bookkeeping resultant from heightened commercial activities are all predicated on a minimal necessary level of general literacy and knowledge of arithmetic. Athough almost nothing is known about the education of the class of children who were not expected to join the scholar-official world, one is compelled to assume that in Sung China there must have been informal schools, however limited in scope

2. Su Ch'e, *Luan-ch'eng chi* (SPPY ed.) 21:4b.

and scale, in which some child-apprentices learned reading, writing, book-keeping, and basic calculation. In urban centers and towns—China was more urbanized at the end of the Sung than near the end of the nineteenth century[3]—children of merchant or artisan households could probably receive rudimentary education from their elders or older apprentices. In rural areas, schools were perhaps necessary for those children whose illiterate elders were eager to see the next generation partake in the growing rural prosperity. A modest level of rural literacy, I suppose, was the prerequisite to the transformation of Sung peasantry into what Mark Elvin calls "a class of adaptable, rational, profit-oriented, petty entrepreneurs."[4]

Institutional historians and other members of the literati are silent on just how this putative rural literacy was acquired. One brief glimpse into this forgotten grove is provided by the poet Lu Yu, who occasionally reports on events of his rural sojourn.

> The whole neighborhood resounded with the noise made by children of the winter school.
> The uncouth schoolmaster at the desk takes good care of himself.
> After he finishes his lessons with "village texts" he closes the door and goes to sleep.
> At no time does he have to show his face to the world.[5]

Lu's own explanatory notes to the poem are just as tantalizingly short. "In the tenth month, farmers send their sons to school, which is called the 'winter school.' The texts they study, such as *Miscellaneous Characters* (*Tsa-tzu*) and *The Hundred Family Names* (*Pai-chia hsing*) are called 'village texts.'"[6]

Although the *Tsa-tzu* is presumably used here by Lu Yu to denote a particular book, the term often stands for a genre of primer. A *tsa-tzu* is usually nothing more than a list of words, divided into lines of four or six characters with a loose rhyme scheme. The list often breaks into sections, each with a specific theme or topic. The purpose of a *tsa-tzu* is to acquaint the reader with the necessary vocabulary, either as a foundation of basic literacy or for a particular trade or vocation. Judging from the extant fragments of an early specimen, the genre may have begun before the sixth century. The *Pai-chia hsing* is a list of common Chinese surnames. Like most versions of the *tsa-tzu*, the list is arranged in a ditty style, with four characters to each line and a rhyme scheme. The usefulness of this primer is indisputable: the small number of Chinese surnames—not quite five hundred—has made the mastery of the list both feasible and necessary for anything above rudimentary social or business activities.

---

3. Mark Elvin, *The Pattern of the Chinese Past* (Stanford: Stanford University Press, 1973), pp. 177–178.
4. Ibid., p. 167.
5. Lu Yu, *Chien-nan shih-kao* (SPPY ed.) 25:3b.
6. Ibid., 25:3b–4a.

In another poem on village children Lu mentions that they studied with a scholar during the winter. When spring came the boys returned to work in the field with their elders:

They learn just enough to do corvée and pay taxes.
There is no need to envy and toil for glory and high offices.[7]

It is clear from this verse that the purpose of educating the rural children was not to provide them with the first crosspiece on a ladder leading to fame and power in the Confucian officialdom. Education's humble but useful function must have been to provide the poor rural children, who during all other seasons were probably fully occupied with helping their elders in farm labor, just the sort of minimum indispensable for any future farmer eager to participate profitably in the expanding market economy so as to take advantage of the transformation described by Elvin. The two textbooks constituted the most practical primers for those children who would soon be called upon to keep books and handle transactions with creditors. With the advancement of printing during the Sung those two primers were undoubtedly omnipresent throughout China, rendering elementary education, at least in a rudimentary form, more accessible than ever before.

Another trend that suggests an increasing interest in elementary education is the greater attentiveness toward children displayed by adults during the Sung. Children now appear in paintings much more frequently than before. The plethora of toys and games recreated by painters hints at the indulgent attitude of adults, perhaps indulgent and affectionate to the point of spoiling their sons and daughters.[8] The Sung period also saw a profusion of treatises on pediatrics. Poets wrote about their children more frequently and with greater specificity than previously. The intense grief expressed by mourning writers over the death of their children contrasts with the more stoical attitude of previous dynasties. If all these signs point to a shift in sensibility that was to culminate in the seventeeth century, the trend most probably also extended to the field of educating the young.

The most concrete and discernible factor in the shaping of education of children during the Sung was government policy. During the reign of the emperor Jen-tsung (1023–1056) many schools were established by the state, not only in the capital but also in the prefectures, subprefectures, and even counties. In 1071 the title elementary school master (*hsiao-hsüeh chiao-shou*) was first created, and in 1102 every county was ordered to establish an

7. Ibid., 1:17b.
8. For a cogent discussion of the representation of children in Sung paintings and the proliferation of treatises on pediatrics see Thomas H. C. Lee, "The Discovery of Childhood: Children Education in Sung China (960–1269)," in *Kultur: Begriff und Wort in China und Japan*, ed. Sigrid Paul (Berlin: Dietrich Reimer Verlag, 1984), pp. 165–168. I did not know Professor Lee's work until he kindly gave me an offprint at the conference. In revising this chapter I have attempted to avoid elaborating the points so admirably developed in his article.

elementary school.[9] Historians, however, do not go beyond the barest of facts: there are no descriptions of such schools nor is there quantitative information on the number or size of the elementary schools. Fortunately, the charter of one prefectural elementary school is extant,and it may fill somewhat the lacuna of history.

The prefecture in question is Ching-chao, the capital of which coincides more or less with the modern city of Sian. Probably because of its historical and strategic importance, Ching-chao was allowed by the emperor to open a prefectural school in 1034, a rather early date. In 1054 a prefectural elementary school was established on the premises of the local Confucian temple. The school charter, inscribed on a stone tablet that survived at least into the nineteenth century,[10] follows in translation.

> *Item.* Before any student is admitted into the elementary school, he must first have an interview with a teacher, bringing along an account of his family (*chia-chuang*) and an affidavit from the head of his family. The affidavit must declare the family head's wish to have the child attend the school. It must further state that as long as the child is in school he will observe all the school regulations. The affidavit with the school officer's signature affixed will be kept in the school file.

> *Item.* Two to four proctors will be selected among the students. The proctors will be responsible for transmitting lessons to other students and reporting on their misdeeds.

> *Item.* Each day the teachers will expound on two to three pages from the Classics, explain the pronunciation and meaning of the passages assigned to the students for memorization, provide calligraphical examples for the students to copy, choose topics for practice in prosody and rhymed-prose (*fu*) writing, decide on phrases for matching exercises, and select narratives to be committed to memory.

> *Item.* The students are divided into three forms in terms of curriculum:

> *The Top Form.* Each student will be daily questioned on three passages chosen at random from the Classics that have already been expounded by the teacher; the student will memorize passages running to more than one hundred characters, practice calligraphy for ten lines, and compose a poem in the style of ancient or regulated verse, with five or seven characters to each line. Every third day he will write a rhymed-prose piece with four stanzas, study a specimen of the same genre, and read three to five pages of history or biography, which must contain three anecdotes to be committed to memory.

> *The Middle Form.* Each student will daily memorize a prose passage consisting of about one hundred characters, practice calligraphy for ten lines, compose one poem of four lines, match one phrase in a parallelism exercise, memorize two stanzas of rhymed-prose, and commit one anecdote to memory.

---

9. Ma Tuan-lin, *Wen-hsien t'ung-k'ao*, Shih-t'ung ed. (Taipei: Hsin-hsing shu-chü, 1959), p. 432.

10. The text is collected in *Chin-shih ts'ui-pien*, comp. Wang Ch'ang (1805 ed.) 234:23a–25a.

The Lower Form. Each student will daily memorize a prose passage consisting of about sixty characters, practice calligraphy for ten lines, commit to memory one poem.

Item. When students misbehave they will be punished in accordance with the magnitude of their offenses. Those under fifteen will be flogged while those over fifteen will pay a cash fine that will go into the general fund of the school. In all cases the proctor will make a note in the school record and the school officer or the teacher will endorse the entry. The students are forbidden to steal, gamble, fight, or initiate litigations; leave or return to the school premises without reporting; damage or throw away books or documents; write graffiti on windows or walls; destroy school property; exchange information at tests; fail to finish exercises or examinations; or indulge in rowdiness or make loud noises.

Item. Students will be granted, in accordance with regulations of the prefectural school, a fixed number of holidays and days of leave. If a student requests leave under false pretexts or fails to return from leave on time, he will be punished in accordance with the established practice. The head of his family will be so notified.

Valuable as the charter is, it leaves much unsaid. For instance, there is no discussion of the students' age range; apparently some were older than fifteen. Strictly speaking, *hsiao-hsüeh* is not equivalent to Western elementary school because nothing in traditional China compares to a modern middle or high school. The records from the earliest times down to the Sung indicate no intermediate stage or institution between the *hsiao-hsüeh* and *ta-hsüeh* (university). Most treatises on education written before modern times agree on the age at which students begin the two schools respectively. The ideal system, if not the actual practice, of classical China is summarized in the *shih-huo chih* section of the *Han-shu.* Students were supposed to

enter the *hsiao* at the age of eight. They study the calendrical characters, geography, writing, and arithmetic; they begin to understand family etiquette. At the age fifteen they enter the *ta-hsüeh*, where they study the ceremonial and musical teachings handed down from the Sages. Now they understand the court and governmental protocol.[11]

From the modern point of view the curriculum of the Ching-chao Elementary School appears simple and narrow; it must have been designed for those students whose goal was promotion to the prefectural school and success at various levels of future examinations. This concern is demonstrated by the emphasis on prosody and rhymed-prose writing; these two, while serving no practical purposes—Chu Hsi, no mean poet himself, wanted to have them removed from the list of subjects examined at the *chin-shih* level so the students would concentrate on more useful things[12]—could not be ignored by any Sung candidate. They constituted part of the required courses in the

11. Quoted in *Wen-hsien t'ung-k'ao*, p. 430.
12. Teng, *Chung-kuo k'ao-shih chih-tu shih*, p. 164.

Imperial University throughout the dynasty except for the short period when Wang An-shih, who had more in common with Chu Hsi than is usually acknowledged by today's progressive writers, exerted influence on court decisions. Because parallelism is an indispensible rhetorical device in both prosody and rhymed prose, it is understandable that matching exercises were part of the daily regimen in the Middle Form.

Given the prominence of the Ching-chao prefecture and the fact that one signatory of the charter was Wen Yen-po (1006–1097), a highly respected statesman and scholar who was then the military governor of the region, there is reason to believe that the document may have served as a model for other local governments considering the addition of an elementary school. Standard histories, however, make no reference to this charter. During the Yüan-feng period (r. 1078–1085), an elementary school was established for the first time in the national capital, and the charter, no longer extant, of that school was distributed in 1106 by the central government to the localities as an example to be followed.[13] At the beginning the Capital Elementary School had only two dormitories. By 1114, as the enrollment grew to almost 1,000, eight more dormitories were added. Teachers received an increase in salary but were forbidden to accept cash gifts. The ages of the students ranged from eight to twelve. Similar to the Ching-chao Elementary School, students here were also enrolled in three levels. Promotion to an upper level was based on knowledge of characters and Classics.[14]

In the accounts of the Sung elementary school I have seen, nothing is said about the place of mathematics in the curriculum. However, other sources, lead me to surmise that mathematics must have been taught to some children during the Sung. First, there was a faculty of mathematics in the Directorate of Education (*Kuo-tzu chien*), and during the early years of the twelfth century there were as many as 260 students in that faculty.[15] Prior to admission to the faculty, the students must have had some training in the subject. Some presumably may have been noticed for their talent or interest even in childhood and thus would have begun their career fairly early in life. Some graduates of the faculty could in turn provide mathematical instruction for the young, because only a few would succeed in winning loftier niches in the government.

Another indication that mathematics was taught at a very elementary level is provided by surviving fragments of Sung mathematics primers. One such specimen is the *Jih-yung suan-fa* (Arithmetic for Daily Use) published in 1262. The purpose of the primer is stated clearly in the preface.

> The *Nine Chapters* of the Yellow Emperor is the fountainhead of mathematics. I once annotated it in detail because I noticed that its principles were

13. Quoted in *Wen-hsien t'ung-k'ao*, pp. 329, 300.
14. Ibid., p. 329.
15. Li Yen, *Chung-suan-shih lun-ts'ung* (Shanghai: Shang-wu yin-shu-kuan, 1947) 4:273.

profound yet the methods simple. A friend of mine commented that the book could not serve as a primer or provide solutions for everyday matters. And beginners found it troublesome. The present book first introduces methods of multiplication, division, addition, and subtraction. Next are problems involving measurements of all sorts. Included are also thirteen ditties and sixty-six diagrams. For every method a complete history of its development is given, and all problems are meant for practical application. I hope that this book in two volumes will be of some slight value for daily use and contribute to elementary education.[16]

The book, judging from the extant fragments of it, appears to have fulfilled what the author promised. The following sample problem is fairly representative of the level and simplicity of the content.

Suppose a catty (*chin*) of certain goods was bought for 6,800 cash. How much would an ounce (*liang*) cost? Answer: 425 cash.[17]

Yang Hui, the author of this primer, was one of the most gifted mathematicians of the Southern Sung. His surviving works testify to his great talent, but almost nothing is known about his life. In this he was not unlike other great Sung mathematicians, who, in the words of Joseph Needham, "were mostly wandering plebians or minor officials." Their "attention was devoted less to calendrical calculations, and more to practical problems in which common people and technicians were likely to be interested."[18] This practical approach was probably responsible for the appearance of four books on the abacus between 1078 and 1162.[19] The use of this instrument in China may have begun much earlier, but its plebian and practical association probably prevented its mention in pre-Sung literature. The publication of these books must have benefited the training of young apprentices in shops or factories. Thoroughly trained, even a young child could perform extraordinary feats with the abacus.

Today gifted children are of course discovered and encouraged everywhere, but in Sung China only literary precociousness received much attention. Children with such gifts, regardless of amount of schooling or domicile, could bypass regular channels and request a special examination at the Court. This preferential treatment of exceptional children had a long history in China, but the zeal of Sung emperors is not matched either before or after. Honors and gifts were lavished at court audiences on toddlers who could recite passages from the Classics or extemporize in prosody. The more

16. Quoted in Li Yen, *Shih-san shih-ssu shih-chi Chung-kuo min-chien shu-hsüeh* (Peking: K'o-hsüeh ch'u-pan-she, 1957), pp. 4–5.

17. Quoted in Li Yen, *Chung-suan-shih lun-ts'ung* (Shanghai: Shang-wu yin-shu-kuan, 1935) 2:107.

18. Joseph Needham, *Science and Civilisation in China* (Cambridge: Cambridge University Press, 1959) 3:42.

19. Ibid., 3:78.

appealing prodigies were kept in the palace as "study-companions" of the imperial children. One such marvel was Lü Ssu-hsing who during the reign of Emperor Hsiao-tsung (1163–1189) demonstrated his talents at court. Only four years of age, he was able to "recite texts, understand the phoneti- cal representation of characters, distinguish the tones, and draw the Eight Diagrams." The emperor, greatly impressed, gave the child a government post as well as cash and ordered him to be a study-companion of the duke of Jung-kuo, the imperial grandson.[20] The court's enthusiasm for child prodi- gies went to such lengths that sometimes old barriers and precedents could be set aside in the face of nature's wonders. In 1174 a female child by the name of Lin Yu-yü requested to be tested, and the government granted her wish. After she demonstrated her prodigious memory the emperor awarded the girl the title of dame (*Ju-jen*).[21]

Generally speaking, the Sung court's appreciation of the literary and mnemonic accomplishments of the very young must have had salutary effects. The education of imperial children, never neglected throughout the Sung, could not but be strengthened by the future ruler's exposure to talented boys from families of commoners. This may have been one reason that Sung emperors tended to feel comfortable with civilian officials, in contrast with the Ming, when the Confucian-literati as a group were looked upon as enemies or at best strangers. Sung rulers almost never sought confidants among eunuchs, servants, or adventurers from the outside world. Childhood camaraderie was to have far-reaching consequences.

The success story of these prodigies probably impressed the populace much more than the gentry. Egalitarian and upwardly mobile Sung society, alert to any incentive and eager to jump at any opportunity, could not have ignored the swift and direct avenue to fame and wealth accessible to every child. Many talented children from families without a scholarly tradition, who otherwise would not have received much of an education, must have been the beneficiaries of such calculations on the part of their ambitious parents. The trickle-down effect, far-reaching but not always conducive to the welfare of the children, can be gauged from examining the case of Jao-chou, a prefecture in northern Kiangsi. The following account comes from Yeh Meng-te (1077–1148):

> Ever since Chu Tien-hsi was granted an official title for being a child prodigy toward the end of the Yüan-feng reign [1078–1085], the common and uncouth natives of Jao Prefecture, greatly impressed, vied in attempting a repetition of the coup. As soon as a child reached five or six and could read a little, he was, whatever his aptitude, taught the five Classics in succession. The child was placed in a bamboo basket which was raised to the top branch of a tall tree. This was to cut him off from all distractions. At the onset the teacher and the

20. *Wen-hsien t'ung-k'ao*, p. 330.
21. Ibid.

parents would agree on the price of the successful completion of each Classic, and the money was not handed over until each task was finished. Consequently the helpless children were harassed day and night. For quite some time the court suspended the special examination for prodigies, but after the Cheng-ho reign [1111–1117] the practice was revived. Since then a few boys of the prefecture have made the grade, which gave rise to the folklore that Jao-chou was the home of prodigies. But those happy few are smaller in number than the children who, deficient in aptitude, were harassed to the point of death.[22]

Yeh's sympathetic understanding of children's travails distinguishes him from most Sung writers, who in numerous "family instructions" and "family models" make exacting demands on the conduct of the junior members of their clans without any concern for the effectiveness of endless admonitions and prescriptions. There is little evidence of understanding the nature of the young. Knowledge of child psychology, very much a product of the modern world, of course cannot be expected of any educational theorist living before this century. It is then all the more remarkable that Neo-Confucian philosopher Chang Tsai should have anticipated educational principles that are commonplace today when he discussed the rearing of children in *Chang tzu ch'üan shu*.

> Do not think that young children have no memory. They do not forget any experience. This is the reason that he who is good at rearing children always begins educating them when they are still infants. Thus they will gain all the benefits. They will then remain pleasant in their disposition: when they grow up, their nature will be amiable. Children should be taught by showing them, with consistency, what is good and what is bad. It is very much like the case of not wanting a dog to go into the hall. If you do not want that, hit the dog whenever it tries to go into the hall. But if you hit the dog when it tries to go into the hall and then go on to feed it in the hall, the dog would never know what to do. After that you would never be able to prevent it from going into the hall even if you beat the dog everyday.(SPPY ed. 6:7a).

Very few of the gifted children from any prefecture were known to have grown into prominent adults, and none ever wrote about his early triumphs or subsequent disappointments. In fact, Sung Chinese were almost universally reticent about their own early education. I have so far found only two autobiographical accounts of childhood schooling. Su Shih (1037–1101) remarks that "when I was eight I went to elementary school where I was taught by a Taoist priest by the name of Chang I-chien. Among the several hundred children in the school the teacher thought highly only of Ch'en T'ai-ch'u and me."[23] That Su Hsün (1009–1066), already sufficiently educated

22. Yeh Meng-te, *Pi-shu-lu-hua* (TSCC ed.), p. 37.

23. Quoted in Wang Pao-chen, *Tseng-pu Su Tung-p'o nien-p'u hui-cheng* (Taipei: Taiwan University, 1969), p. 11.

and on his way to a measure of scholarly fame, should have sent his son to be educated by a Taoist priest seems, at first glance, rather unusual. Such a practice, however, may have been more widespread than the scanty records suggest. During the T'ang both Buddhist and Taoist temples are known to have offered secular education to boys of humble origins, and it was not uncommon for Buddhist temples during the Ming to operate free elementary schools (*i-hsüeh*) where a secular curriculum was offered. Even though I have yet to find a duplication of Su Shih's experience, in the syncretic climate of the Sung other learned clerics must have run elementary schools or taught in them. There was, at any rate, no shortage of well-educated members among the Taoist and Buddhist clergy, judging by the massive literary output and their prolific prosodic exchanges with the Confucian literati. Su Shih himself, like many among his peers, maintained lifelong associations with members of religious orders.

Like Su Shih, another member of the literati, Yeh Meng-te, was also taught as a boy by a private teacher from Szechuan. A prototype of what was to become a frequent comical figure in popular literature, Yeh's teacher deserves attention and even sympathy.

Mr. Lo, born in the Pa Gorge, was a native of Ta-chou. He did not associate much with the people of central China. His appearance was extremely rustic and plain, but his learning broad, pure, and thorough. My late father liked him and thought so highly of him that I was sent to him as a disciple. That to this day I can still remember a little from the Six Classics is due to his instructions. He was quite poor but he did not bother with improving his condition. He had a wife, two sons, and a lame maidservant. He lived in a small cottage with a thatched roof in the western part of the town. There were only three rooms; he housed his disciples in two of them, while his wife and sons occupied the remaining one. Open and direct, Mr. Lo laughed and joked a great deal. Nobody ever saw him lose his temper. One day, noon had passed but no meal had yet been served. His wife sent the lame maidservant to tell him that the rice was used up. Mr. Lo replied: "Let's bear with it. Soon a gift of rice will come." Upon hearing it, the wife, overcome by anger, leaped out from behind the screen. She grabbed a bamboo plate from the desk and hit him in the head. Dishevelled and running from her, the teacher stumbled and fell outside the cottage. The children gathered around him and reveled. Finally they helped him to his feet. It just happened that in a little while a bag of rice, which my father had sent him as a gift, arrived. Mr. Lo calmly told his wife: "I didn't deceive you, did I? I am starved. Hurry up and cook!" This scene, having taken place almost fifty years ago, is to me still as vivid as yesterday. Every morning after the teacher got up he would give each child his particular assignment from the Classics. In doing so he had to recite several hundred passages, but that did not tire him. After that he would stroll in his slippers while chanting away, with deliberate speed and varying pitch. I once followed him stealthily, and what he chanted turned out to be morally uplifting passages. The boys sometimes made fun of him by mimicking his chanting, but he never got angry. He loved to write poems, and there were several hundred of them.[24]

Since the good-natured but impecunious Mr. Lo anticipates so well the stock character of the impractical schoolteacher in fiction and drama, it is possible that he may have represented a type not at all rare during the Sung. Perhaps the humble and cramped schoolhouse so dear to Yeh's memory was more representative of Sung elementary education than the state schools at county seats or prefectural capitals.

Many other Sung children were not sent to school but were taught at home by their parents or family tutors. The mother often played an important role in the education of the children, especially if the husband was frequently away or had died young. The case of Chou Pi-ta (1126–1204), Chu Hsi's patron at court, may have been typical. His mother, a young widow versed in history and the Confucian classics, taught her two sons herself until they were old enough for the family tutor, whom she personally selected.[25]

The life of another well-educated woman and exemplary mother is recorded by Lu Yu in *Wei-nan wen-chi*.[26] When Madam Yang's husband died in 1124 she was left a young widow with two infant sons.

> As soon as the two boys were able to speak the mother began to teach them herself, using the *Classic on Filial Piety*, the *Analects*, the *Mao shih* and the *Kuo feng*. In her philological explanations and parsing she displayed a superb mastery of pedagogy. The two sons never went to private schools yet they became fully versed in all elementary subjects.[27]

That so many mothers were literate suggests that during the Sung the education of female children, at least among the gentry, was quite widespread, even though history does not provide much information on this important issue. Support for this contention is found in Ssu-ma Kuang's *Chia fan*, his admonishments to his family.

> No human being should be without education, and in this regard can there be any difference between male and female? Therefore, every girl must, before she leaves her parents' household, study the *Classic on Filial Piety*, the *Analects*, the *Book of Poetry* and the *Book of Rites*. She should acquire some understanding of the great principles.[28]

Another indication of the education of Sung women is the quantity and

24. Yeh Meng-te, *Pi-shu lu-hua*, pp. 81–82.
25. Chou Pi-ta, *Erh-lao-t'ang tsa-chih* (TSCC ed.), p. 77.
26. Lu Yu, *Wei-nan wen-chi* (SPPY ed.) 34:6b–7b.
27. Ibid., 34:7a.
28. Ssu-ma Kuang, *Wen-kung chia-fan* in *Chu-wen-tuan-kung shih-san chung* (Nan-ch'ang, 1897) 9:6:2b.

variety of their writings. In addition to the great woman poet Li Ch'ing-chao there were at least fifty-five other women known to have written a considerable amount.[29] This naturally raises the question of who taught such girls. Ssu-ma Kuang does not specify. In view of the strict segregation of the sexes during the Sung, it is unlikely that girls were taught by anyone other than their close relatives.

For the boys from families of means, private tutors were never in short supply. Because only a small number among the candidates could pass the successive examinations and enter into civil service, the vast majority sooner or later had to find other means of livelihood. For them teaching was one of the least distasteful alternatives to an official career. The oversupply of available teachers probably made elementary education affordable even to families of moderate means. Although there is no information on the percentage of unsuccessful candidates who found consolation in teaching children, in one city, Chia-hsing in the lower Yangtze Valley, the seekers of such opportunities were so numerous that a gregarious friend of the poet Lu Yu was pressed into running an informal employment agency for prospective private tutors.[30]

The private tutor, *men k'e* or *kuang k'e*, because of his unofficial and ambiguous role in the social hierarchy and organization, was denied a place in Chinese institutional history. In contrast, the schoolteacher enjoyed much more respect. He might have had to contend with poverty and unruly pupils, but his was always an honorable profession. He could always point to Confucius as the most illustrious member of the calling, but the same cannot be said of the family tutor. His very mode of eking a living violated the Confucian code of etiquette, for the *Ch'ü li* chapter of the Confucian classic *Li chi* clearly stated that "it is proper to have students to come to the teacher for instruction; it has never been heard that a teacher would go to his student."[31] This canonical injunction was cited by self-respecting scholars during Han times when they resisted the importunate beckoning of imperious parents.[32] Such a lofty stance could not be always maintained by later impoverished scholars. As expanded opportunities for education swelled the ranks of scholars, many of whom came from modest families, the Sung saw not a few struggling candidates swallowing their pride and moving into prosperous households as resident tutors. Room and board as well as a small stipend were the usual reward for their services. Once a scholar entered the household of his employer, he was both by name and *de facto* just another family retainer, one of that nebulous group of men whose long history of

---

29. See Hu Wen-k'ai, "Sung-tai kuei-hsiu i-wen k'ao-lüeh," in *Sung-shih yen-chiu chi* (Taipei: Taiwan shu-tien, 1964) 2:67–84.

30. Lu Yu, *Lao-hsüeh-an pi-chi* (TSCC ed.), p. 5.

31. Quoted in Yü Cheng-hsieh *Kuei-ssu ts'un-kao* (TSCC ed.), p. 113.

32. Ibid.

complex roles stretched from the celebrated assassins of classical China to the nineteenth-century *mu-yu* (private secretary). In the eyes of some social critics he could sink even lower. One of the Sung descriptive books on Hangchow grouped the family tutor together with such *demimondain* figures as the gambler, the scribbler, the guide, the messenger, the storyteller, the falconer, the boxer, the cockfighter, and the go-between in all forms of commerce.[33]

The family tutor did not fare much better in popular literature. In one of the Yüan plays he appears as a lovelorn pretender, totally negligent of his duties. For our purposes the most interesting section of the play is the following dialogue between his two equally comical disciples, Wang and Ma.

> *Wang*: I am the child of Mayor Wang, and my name is Wang Cheng. This is Ma Ch'iu, the child of Judge Ma. A month ago my father hired a tutor by the name of Han Fei-ch'ing to teach us at home. This year I am fifteen years old. I began to study at six and up to now I have been at it for nine years. I have thoroughly memorized one book, the *Hundred Family Names*, and I can recite it backwards and forwards at will. But my father still says that I am empty-minded.
>
> *Ma*: I am Ma Ch'iu, fourteen years old this year. I have studied for eight years. Except for five pages, I have committed to heart one book, the *Meng ch'iu*. Today I am again sent to your house to study. Since I started school a month ago this family teacher of yours has not taught me a single word. Every day he just sighs and moans. I don't know why.[34]

The author of the play, Ch'iao Chi (1280–1345), was born only a year after the fall of the Southern Sung and lived most of his adult life in the old capital Hangchow. He had, then, ample opportunity to observe a way of life still very reminiscent of the heyday of the Sung. Given the robust realism of Yüan comedies, it is possible that Ch'iao drew his characters and scenes, especially the minor ones, from life. The underachievement of the two schoolboys was probably exaggerated for comic effect, but other details of the dialogue may very well reflect the contemporary practice. The age—six *sui* (five by Western reckoning)—at which Wang and Ma began their schooling seems somewhat low compared with the stipulations in canonical Confucian texts. Children were not supposed to enter elementary school (*hsiao-hsüeh*) until they reached eight *sui*. The discrepancy can be accounted for by the supposition that home instruction preceded formal schooling both in classical China and during the Sung and Yüan. This is the case with the curriculum for children designed by Ch'eng Tuan-li (1271–1345), a contemporary of the playwright. Ch'eng's pupils entered into the clan school (*chia shu*) at eight *sui*, but before that the children were required to study a primer. Ch'eng does not specify

---

33. Wu Tzu-mu, *Meng-liang lu* (TSCC ed.), p. 181.

34. Ch'iao Chi, *Li T'ai-po p'i-p'ei chin-ch'ien chi* in *Chin-Yüan tsa-chü* (Taipei: Shih-chieh shu-chü, 1962) 2:3:15–16.

the exact age at which children received their first lesson, but judging by the extremely difficult content of the first textbook used in the clan school, the *Hsiao hsüeh* by Chu Hsi, the children of his clan may have very well spent more than a year to prepare themselves for this demanding curriculum.[35]

That the two schoolboys in the play were required to memorize what meager texts they had is another familiar feature of childhood education during the Sung-Yüan period. In fact, the emphasis on memorization obtained throughout the premodern world. In China the practice of committing all learning materials to memory began from time immemorial and persists to this day. This practice, perhaps more than anything else, determined the style and format of textbooks for children. The Sung scholar Hsiang An-shih (d. 1208) clearly stated this fact: "In teaching children, the ancients often used rhymed materials similar to the modern primers such as the *Meng ch'iu, Ch'ien tzu wen, T'ai-kung chia-chiao*, and *San tzu hsün*."[36]

Hsiang is almost unique among Sung-Yüan scholars in that he comments on popular primers without disdain. Lu Yu, as I mentioned earlier, refers to them derogatorily as "village texts," while others like Chu Hsi and Ch'eng Tuan-li attempted to supplant them with more didactic and difficult reading texts. Nevertheless the popular primers, whose date and authorship in nearly all cases remain to this day matters of dispute, displayed a vitality and tenacity unmatched by the products of well-meaning but impractical Neo-Confucian leaders. Three of the popular primers, outlasting their humble brethren and high-born rivals, survived into the twentieth century. Even by the time of late Ming the three had already gained full recognition by the Neo-Confucians as the staples for elementary education. Lü K'un (1536–1618) in his proposal for a *she-hsüeh* (community school) suggests these texts:

---

35. Ch'eng Tuan-li, *Ch'eng-shih chia-shu tu-shu feng-nien jih-ch'eng* (TSCC ed.), p. 1.

36. Hsiang An-shih, *Hsiang-shih chia-shuo* (TSCC ed.), p. 83. Here *San tzu hsün* is apparently an alternate name for *San tzu ching*; these two titles were still used interchangeably in the eighteenth century, as indicated by the reference to the book in a poem quoted in the entry on *San tzu ching* in the *Tz'u hai* (Shanghai: Chung-hua shu chü, 1948), p. 18. Poet Shao Chin-han (1743–1796) stated: "I have just read Liang Chen's *San tzu hsün*," but in his footnote to that line he explained that the book in question was "the *San tzu ching* edited by Liang Chen of Nan-hai." Professor James T. C. Liu in "Pi *San tzu ching* keng tsao te Nan-Sung ch'i-meng-shu," *Wen shih*, no. 21, p. 134, suggests that the *San tzu ching* may have had several different versions during the Southern Sung. He has discovered one such variant in the "Chi'i-meng ch'u sung" by Ch'en Ch'un (1153–1217). If the *San tzu hsün* cited by Hsiang An-shih (d. 1208) was as well known as the other three popular primers mentioned in the same breath by Hsiang, it may well have been known to Ch'en and even served as a model for his "Ch'i-meng ch'u sung." This conjecture would account for the similarity in format and content between Ch'en's primer and the *San tzu ching* that we know today. See also James T. C. Liu, "The Classical Chinese Primer: Its Three-Character Style and Authorship," *Journal of the American Oriental Society* 105, no. 2 (April–June 1985): 191–196.

Those who are under eight years of age should first study the *San tzu ching* so as to broaden their knowledge; the *Pai chia hsing* for daily use; and the *Ch'ien tzu wen* which also makes good sense.[37]

The long-lived popularity of these three works made them convenient targets during various upheavals in twentieth-century China. Both the May Fourth reformers and the Cultural Revolutionaries saw symbolic value in attacking what to them represented all the wrongs they found in traditional China, however, the three have not been entirely without defenders. Chang Chih-kung, writing in the 1950s, pointed out the simple truth that the three combined to form a complete and self-sufficient set of reading primers: they supply the beginner with about two thousand basic characters, which, when mastered, constitute primary literacy. Furthermore, these primers are written in simple and clear language, their content is never arcane or tedious, very few characters in them are too obscure or rare, and the texts are easy to memorize. These, Chang maintains, are the reasons that the three survived for almost a thousand years and outlasted their numerous rivals.[38]

The primer that received the bitterest attack during the anti-Confucian campaign of the mid 1970s was the *San tzu ching*. Its notoriety was, in a sense, to be expected, for this book, more than any other primer, contained much of what modern critics would readily recognize as ideology. The values and ideals formulated in the *San tzu ching* are all consistent with the basic tenets of Confucianism, even though Confucians for one reason or another might find this or that section of the book unsatisfactory. The greatest importance of the book lies in its clearly stated, repeatedly voiced, and well-illustrated central message: education is for everyone, and everyone needs education. Such a loud and persistent message, absorbed and memorized by countless children over the centuries, must have had enormous consequences. Before we attempt to gauge the impact of the *San tzu ching* we must consider its content.

Echoing Mencius, the book begins on an optimistic note. "Men, one and all, in infancy are virtuous at heart."[39] The egalitarian implication is continued in the next line: "Their moral tendencies the same, the practice wide apart."[40] It follows that education is of utmost importance: "Without Instruction's friendly aid our instinct grew less pure;/ But application only can proficiency ensure."[41] The book cites examples from ancient lore, showing the efficacy of education. Then, more exhortation:

37. Quoted in Chang Chih-kung, *Ch'uan-t'ung yü-wen chiao-yü ch'u-t'an* (Shanghai: Shanghai chiao-yü ch'u-pan-she, 1962), p. 25.

38. Ibid., p. 26.

39. Herbert A. Giles, trans., *The San Tzu Ching or Three Character Classic and the Ch'ien Tzu Wen or Thousand Character Essay* (Shanghai: A. H. de Carvalho, 1873), p. 1. The translation is sometimes rather free, but its Victorian didacticism retains the flavor of the original better than any modern attempt at a more literal rendering.

40. Ibid.

41. Ibid.

To feed the body, not the mind—fathers, on you the blame!
Instruction without discipline, the idle teacher's shame.
Study alone directs the course of youthful minds aright:
How, with a youth of idleness, can age escape the blight?
Each shapeless mass of jade must by the artisan be wrought,
And man by constant study moral rectitude be taught.
Be wise in time, nor idly spend youth's fleeting days and nights:
Love tutor, friend, and practice oft Decorum's sacred rights.[42]

Next the book provides knowledge of the most elementary nature, such as
the seasons, the five agents, the basic human relations, even the names of
grains and domestic animals. In its didactic formulation of the norms of
human relations the book never advocates total obedience or blind loyalty.
Contrary to all the calumnies heaped on it from the twentieth century, the
book goes further than most premodern opinions in suggesting at least a
measure of reciprocity.

Father and son should live in love, in peace the married pair:
Kindness the elder brother's and respect the younger's care.
Let deference due to age be paid, comrades feel friendship's glow,
Princes treat well their minister—*they* loyalty should show.
These moral duties binding are on all men here below.[43]

Neither the father nor the sovereign is granted any divine rights or prerogatives. The belief in the universality of the moral laws is so strong that no
distinction is made of persons or status. In contrast to the post-Sung
insistence on absolute loyalty that contributed to despotism, the social
relations formulated in the *San tzu ching* are all founded on reciprocity.
Whatever the responsibility of Confucianism in the fostering of repression
and injustice in China, our primer is innocent of most charges brought
against it from the 1920s to the 1970s.

After a long recitation of Chinese history the primer returns to its main
theme, the importance of education. A great diversity of cases is given to
demonstrate anew the universality of education. The impoverished, late
bloomers, women, and prodigies all prevailed alike. Before the primer closes
with one more exhortation, "Waste not the flying moments in unprofitable
play:/ Strive, O ye youths, with might and main these precepts to obey!"[44]
there is the smug and almost prophetic declaration of the proud author:

Men's hearts rejoice to leave their children wealth and golden store!
I give my sons this little book and give them nothing more.[45]

Perhaps the anonymous author would have been even more complacent if
he had been able to anticipate the extent that scholars in the 1980s have

42. Ibid., p. 2.
43. Ibid., p. 4.
44. Ibid., p. 12.
45. Ibid.

attributed the economic successes of the newly industrialized countries in East Asia to what is called the "post-Confucian ethic" or "bourgeois Confucianism." Precisely the kind of world view and moral values expounded in the primer *San tzu ching*— optimism, egalitarianism, freedom from fatalism, belief in the basic goodness of man, affirmation of this world, trust in the apparent order of things, and approval of advancement and success—are believed to have provided the cultural component necessary for a great economic and industrial revolution. This little red book may have played as crucial a role in the economic transformation of Sung China as post-Confucian ethics is playing in the remolding of late twentieth-century East Asia.

TWELVE

Chu Hsi and Women's Education

Bettine Birge

INTRODUCTION

Chinese society is known for the subordination of women up to modern times. More specifically, it is often alleged that a decline in women's status occurred during the Sung dynasty. The question of how and when this ostensible decline occurred cannot be addressed here; however, it can be noted that after the Sung, in the Ming period, a more severe form of subjugation is evident than is seen earlier. In contrast to the pre-Sung T'ang dynasty, in Ming times, foot binding was widely practiced, laws on inheritance and adoption discriminated against women and affinal kin, and social rules bolstered by tax privileges militated against the remarriage of widows.

To explain this change, people have often pointed to the new doctrine of Neo-Confucianism and especially to the scholar who systematized it, Chu Hsi.[1] Nevertheless, there has been little study of Chu Hsi's own writing on women. Assumptions about the formative stage of Neo-Confucianism have been derived in some cases from later developments in chinese history.

In this chapter I will explore Chu Hsi's ideas about women's education and the role he assigned to women in society. In particular, it will contrast the harsh standard of behavior dictated by Chu Hsi's prescriptive texts with accounts of women's virtuous activity seen in Chu Hsi's other writing. Chu

I would like to thank Professors Wm. Theodore de Bary, Wing-tsit Chan, Pei-yi Wu, and Robert P. Hymes for their advice during the preparation of this paper. I also thank Peter Lee, Suzanne Bogas, and Pamela Oline for their help and encouragement.
    1. Throughout the twentieth century, Chinese intellectuals and politicians have blamed Confucianism for the oppression of women. History books, in Chinese and in English, have supported the claim that Sung Neo-Confucianism caused a decline in the status of women. See for instance Ch'en Tung-yüan, *Chung-kuo fu-nü sheng-huo shih* (Peking: Commercial Press, 1937), pp. 130–140; and Esther Lee Yao, *Chinese Women: Past and Present* (Mesquite, Tex.: Ide House, 1983), pp. 75ff.: hereafter cited as *Chinese Women*.

Hsi's published work shows that he condoned a wide range of activity and responsibility for women that affected life both inside and outside the home. A picture emerges of women not just as victims of ideology and social custom but as active participants in a system that they helped to structure.

The task of determining Chu Hsi's thoughts on women's education is hindered by the limits of the original Chinese sources. If one looks through his *Collected Works* (*Wen-chi*), there are no items about women's education. Nor is there any heading about women in the *Classified Conversations (Yü-lei)* or in Ch'ien Mu's *New Anthology of Chu Hsi (Chu-tzu hsin hsüeh-an)*. Even the *Reflections on Things at Hand (Chin-ssu lu)* has no section on women. Nevertheless, women were not left out of Chu Hsi's vision of a morally rejuvenated society.

We know that Chu Hsi was concerned about moral instruction for women. In a letter to his disciple Liu Ch'ing-chih (1130–1195) he complained of the inadequacy of existing texts for women, such as the *Precepts for Women (Nü-chieh)* by Pan Chao of the Han. Moreover, he put forth a tentative list of chapter headings for his own book.[2] Chu Hsi evidently hoped that Liu Ch'ing-chih would help compile the text along the lines of the *Elementary Learning* (Hsiao-hsüeh) that Liu completed in 1187 under Chu Hsi's direction. But nothing was done before Liu's death in 1195, and Chu Hsi did not have the means to produce the work himself. Thus, we must piece together Chu Hsi's thoughts on the subject as they are revealed in other works not written for women per se.

Chu Hsi's other writing that discussed women directly or indirectly was of two different genres. The first comprised the prescriptive, educational texts, where he quoted from the Confucian classics and later historical writings to prescribe ideal life-cycle roles of daughter, wife, and mother. Presumably, his own book for women would have been along this line. These works did not portray women as individual people but presented a normative pattern for women's behavior. The text that referred most to women was the *Elementary Learning* which drew largely from the ritual classic *Record of Rites* (*Li chi*), especially the chapter on "Rules for Domestic Life" (*Nei-tse*). The *Reflections on Things at Hand* also made occasional reference to women.

---

2. The eight headings were: Propriety (*cheng-ching*), Subordination (*pei-jo*), Filiality (*hsiao-ai*), Harmony (*ho-mu*), Diligence (*ch'in-chin*), Frugality (*chien-chih*), Generosity (*k'uan-hui*), and Learning (*chiang-hsüeh*). *Hui-an hsien-sheng Chu Wen-kung wen-chi* (*Collected Works of Chu Hsi*) 100 chüan; *Hsü-chi* 11 chüan; *Pieh-chi* 10 chüan (Ssu-pu ts'ung-k'an ed. Shanghai: Commercial Press, 1929) 35:29b. Hereafter cited as *Wen-chi*. Wing-tsit Chan has provided me with this reference discussed in his book on Chu Hsi (Taipei 1987). In that work, he comments that the item on Learning seems unprecedented but states that we cannot tell to what extent Chu Hsi was being innovative. I am also indebted to James McMullen of St. Anthony's College, Oxford University, for pointing out a reference to Chu Hsi's intended work in the Japanese sources: Kumazawa Banzan (1619–1691), *Banzan zenshū* 2:359. Banzan cites only seven of the eight chapter headings, leaving out Diligence.

The second genre of writing in which Chu Hsi addressed the topic of women dealt with them directly and as individuals. This writing comprised short biographies of women in the form of funerary inscriptions (*mu-chih-ming*). Although these were also meant to promote ideals, they were descriptive rather than prescriptive texts that ostensibly portrayed actual contemporary women whom Chu Hsi considered models of Confucian virtue. Chu Hsi's inscriptions for women, augmented by statements from texts like the *Elementary Learning*, form the basis of this essay.

Chu Hsi wrote seventeen funerary inscriptions for women, which survive among more than one thousand for women in the Sung dynasty as a whole. Many more and longer inscriptions were written for men, but the existence of funerary inscriptions for women in itself demonstrates that women were the subjects of formal recognition and remembrance by Chu Hsi and other literati.

In order to interpret these documents, it is important to understand the nature and origin of *mu-chih-ming*. A *mu-chih-ming* was carved onto two square pieces of stone, usually the *chih* on one and the *ming* on the other. These were fitted together and placed inside the tomb, where they would last longer than a surface marker. In addition, a copy of the essay was preserved with the works of the author. Men of letters wrote funerary inscriptions for their family members and friends. But many elite (*shih-ta-fu*) families sought to hire for this purpose famous scholars, who were strangers, to lend prestige to the documents. Chu Hsi denounced literati who took money to write eulogies for people whom they did not know. Nevertheless, Chu Hsi himself, because of his renown, was often approached to write inscriptions. Except for three he wrote for his own family, his inscriptions were for the mothers of his associates, women whom he had never met. Moreover, although he did not write for money, the sources suggest that he usually received an honorarium for his trouble.[3]

Funerary inscriptions were written in a standard format. The first part, the *chih*, was a biography that stressed a woman's praiseworthy deeds. The second part, the *ming*, was a eulogistic poem. Set phrases extolling Confucian virtues appear in inscriptions of many authors in different dynasties. Yet within this framework, those of Chu Hsi, like those of other authors, emphasize certain points that he personally singled out for praise. They represent a model of Confucian behavior as Chu Hsi defined it. Moreover,

---

3. In a letter to his student Lin Che-chih, Chu Hsi refers to money received for writing something, probably a funerary inscription; *Wen-chi*, pieh-chi 6:6a–b. The relevant passages are quoted by Wing-tsit Chan in his article on Chu Hsi's poverty, "Chu-tzu ku-ch'iung," in *Shu-mu chi-k'an* 15, no. 2 (1981):13. This article is reprinted in Chan's *Chu-hsüeh lun-chi* (Taipei: Hsüeh-sheng, 1982), pp. 205–232.

Also, in return for writing someone's biography, Chu Hsi was given a copy of the *Han shu* which he donated to the White Deer Hollow Academy; *Wen-chi* 81:25b. I thank Chan for this information.

each inscription is unique and can include touching details and anecdotes that presumably did reflect actual historic events in a woman's life. Thus, within each, one not only finds statements of laudable ideals, but one can also ascertain Chu Hsi's understanding of how women should apply these ideals to their own lives.

From internal evidence we know that Chu Hsi relied on three major sources of information for these biographies. These were the personal letter requesting that Chu Hsi write the inscription, Chu Hsi's own knowledge of the subject, and, most important, the *hsing-chuang* or "biographical account" that would have been written previously by someone close to the subject. Chu Hsi sometimes quoted extensively from a *hsing-chuang* or letter. For instance, in his inscription for Mme. Yü, who died in 1132, he wrote:

> Her eldest son, Ming, . . . had his halfbrother, Ssu, [son of a concubine] take a letter and the *hsing-chuang* written by Mr. Chia Ying of the same hamlet, rank *Ch'eng-i lang*, and come to me to ask me to write her funerary inscription. My family is in Chien-yang, Ch'ung-an county, not more than 100 *li* from where Mme. Yü lived. Very early, I was able to associate with her two sons. Therefore I was able to hear them speak of her deeds, and I dared to admire her highly. I only regret that I was not able to pay obeisance to her in her lifetime. However, after her death, today I have been fortunate to have been asked to write her inscription and to set up a tablet to proclaim her deeds to later generations. How could I dare refuse?[4]

In giving the details of Mme. Yü's life, Chu hsi is evidently quoting directly from the *hsing-chuang* of Mr. Chia, for at the end of the long inscription he writes: "According to what Mr. Chia recorded, Mme. Yü's deeds were like this. For the most part, they accord with what I myself had heard."[5] Then he goes on to add his own words of high praise and admiration.

In this case, Chu Hsi both knew the woman from her sons and was supplied with the *hsing-chuang* from which he quoted liberally. In other cases, his association was more distant, like that of Mme. Yü who died in 1132 when Chu Hsi was only two years old:

> The year after she died, she was buried in Shao-wu county on the plain of Shih-ch'i. Her husband ordered the gentleman of T'ai-chou [her second son] to write her biographical account [*hsing-chuang*]. But there was not yet anyone to whom he could entrust the tomb inscription. Forty-six years later [1178] the gentleman of the Tuan-ming palace ordered me, [Chu] Hsi [to write the inscription] based on the *hsing-chuang*. His words are with the inscription for her husband and do not appear here. I only rely on the *hsing-chuang* to select the important things about her and write the [following] inscription.[6]

4. *Wen-chi* 92:12b–13a.
5. Ibid., 92:14a.
6. Ibid., 91:19a.

In other inscriptions, Chu Hsi quotes verbatim from letters about the woman.[7]

Even though Chu Hsi based his inscriptions on writings by other people, it is clear that he made conscious choices about what to include in his essays. He used his own criteria in deciding what was praiseworthy in these women, and whatever appeared in the inscriptions were points he thought should be emulated by others. They provide a reliable and authentic source for Chu Hsi's ideas about women.

This point notwithstanding, Chu Hsi's ideas were naturally colored by the society in which he lived. Before analyzing his contribution to women's education, it is important to review the historic background to his remarks.

China, like many other societies, had a long tradition of subordination of women. From earliest times, the principle of *yin* and *yang* equated men with *yang*, Heaven, the sun, light, strength, and activity; women corresponded to *yin*, Earth, the moon, darkness, weakness, and passivity.[8] Ancient legends and stories made women into objects of fear and mistrust and blamed them for misfortune, as in the stories of Eve or Pandora's Box in Western culture. The *Book of Songs*, a Confucian classic, contained admonitions like, "A wise man builds up a city, but a wise woman overthrows it. . . . Disorder does not come from Heaven, it is produced by a woman."[9] The *Book of Songs* also referred to the tradition in which boy babies enjoyed a bed and fine robes while girl babies were placed on the floor and wrapped in swaddling cloth to emphasize their subservience.[10] Pan Chao of the Later Han reiterated this tradition in her *Precepts for Women.*[11] Confucius himself showed no empathy for women:

> The Master said, "Women and people of low birth are very hard to deal with. If you are friendly with them, they get out of hand, and if you keep your distance, they resent it."[12]

In Sung times, discrimination against women was part of the fabric of society. By law and custom, no schools or academies trained women. Women

7. See, for instance, *Wen-chi* 92:29b, "Funerary Inscription of the Wife of Mr. P'an," translated in full in the appendix.

8. This equation is made in the earliest extant commentaries of the *Book of Changes (I-ching)*. For further remarks, see Richard Guisso, "Thunder Over the Lake: the Five Classics and the Perception of Women in Early China," in *Women in China*, ed. Richard Guisso and Stanley Johannesen (Youngstown, N. Y.: Philo Press, 1981), p. 49ff.

9. *Shih ching*, Mao no. 264; adapted from James Legge, trans., *The She King, The Chinese Classics*, Vol. 4 (1871; reprint, Hong Kong: Hong Kong University Press, 1961), Pt. 3, Bk. 3, Ode 10, p. 561. (This poem is not translated by Waley.)

10. Mao no. 189; Ibid., Pt. 2, Bk. 4, Ode 5, p. 307. Also translated, poem 257, by Arthur Waley, *The Book of Songs* (New York: Grove Press, 1960), pp. 283–284.

11. Nancy Lee Swann, *Pan Chao: Foremost Woman Scholar of China* (New York: Century, 1932), p. 83.

12. *Analects* 17:25; Arthur Waley, trans., *The Analects of Confucius* (New York: Vintage Books, 1938), p. 217.

could neither sit for the civil service examinations nor hold office and participate in government legitimately. In the Confucian temples, no one venerated statues of female sages. A contemporary of Chu Hsi, Yüan Ts'ai, who was not a part of the *tao-hsüeh* movement, spoke of women as lacking fundamental ethical and moral qualities. He asserted that women caused discord in the family because they "lacked a sense of the common interest or of fairness."[13] He further described wives and daughters as, "often petty, quick-tempered, quarrelsome, obstinate, cruel, oppressive, and ignorant of the ancient and recent moral truths."[14] He blamed wives for passing damaging gossip and for being susceptible to the lies of maids.[15]

Sung Neo-Confucians perpetuated these prejudices. Chou Tun-i (1017–1073) reasserted the cosmology of gender inequality in his *T'ai-chi t'u-shuo*, associating men with Heaven (*ch'ien*) and women with Earth (*k'un*).[16] Like Yüan Ts'ai, he attributed problems in the family to women, and Chu Hsi underscored this attitude by including his words in *Reflections on Things at Hand* (*Chin-ssu lu*): "If members of the family are separated, the cause surely lies with women. . . . 'When two women live together, their wills move in different directions.'"[17] The philosopher Liu K'ai (947–1000) is quoted by Chu Hsi in the *Elementary Learning* as saying that differences between wives caused calamity equal to an attack by robbers.[18]

---

13. Yüan Ts'ai, *Yüan-shih shih-fan* 1.35, as translated by Patricia Buckley Ebrey in *Family and Property in Sung China, Yüan Ts'ai's Precepts for Social Living* (Princeton: Princeton University Press, 1984), p. 206; hereafter cited Ebrey, *Family and Property*, or, following references to *Yüan-shih shih-fan*, simply as "Ebrey trans."

14. Ibid., 3.30; Ebrey trans., p. 290.

15. Ibid., 1.36; Ebrey trans., p. 207.

16. *T'ai-chi t'u-shuo shu-chieh*, ed. Ts'ao Tuan (1376–1434) (SKCSCP ed. Taipei: Commercial Press, 1976), p. 1b, first diagram, and p. 4a. See also Ch'en Tung-yüan, *Chung-kuo fu-nü sheng-huo shih*, pp. 135–36. Note that Chou Tun-i used the *k'un:ch'ien* and *yin:yang* equations to assert the *complementarity* of the genders; neither was complete in itself.

17. Wing-tsit Chan, trans., *Reflections on Things at Hand, the Neo-Confucian Anthology Compiled by Chu Hsi and Lü Tsu-ch'ien* (New York: Columbia University Press, 1967), p. 202; hereafter cited *Things at Hand*, or, following references to *Chin-ssu lu*, simply as "Chan trans." This passage is also quoted in Ch'en Tung-yüan, *Chung-kuo fu-nü sheng-huo shih*, p. 137. Chou Tun-i is quoting from the *I-ching* commentary on hexagram 38, *k'uei*; cf. James Legge, trans; *Yi King, The Sacred Books of the East*, Vol. 16 (Oxford: Clarendon Press, 1882), p. 243.

18. *Hsiao-hsüeh chi-chieh*, ed. Chang Po-hsing (1651–1725) (Kuo-hsüeh chi-pen ts'ung-shu ed.; reprint, Taipei: Commercial Press, 1968), p. 119; hereafter cited *Hsiao-hsüeh*. Ebrey, in *Family and Property*, agrees with scholars like Ch'en Tung-yüan in concluding that philosophers such as Liu K'ai and Chu Hsi had greater prejudice against women than did men like Yüan Ts'ai, pp. 85–86; I do not think the evidence warrants such a statement. Prescriptive texts like the *Elementary Learning* were meant to admonish the reader in strong and convincing terms. Thus, they employed images like "an attack by robbers," in contrast to Yüan Ts'ai's more literal descriptions of household problems. In many ways, Chu Hsi gave women more credit and responsibility for managing a household than did Yüan Ts'ai who considered them helpless and qualified only to raise children; Ebrey, *Family and Property*, p. 84.

The great Neo-Confucian Ch'eng I (1033–1107) also maintained that women were inferior to men. In a funerary inscription to his niece, who died at the age of twenty-four, he says, *"Even though* you were a girl, you were an extraordinary person."[19] Chu Hsi quotes him in *Reflections on Things at Hand* to reiterate the inequality between the genders. This passage has the interesting suggestion that gender differences had to be learned:

> Between man and woman, there is an order of superiority and inferiority, and between husband and wife, there is the principle of who leads and who follows. This is a constant principle. If people are influenced by feelings, give free rein to desires, and act because of pleasure, a man will be driven by desires and lose his character of strength, and a woman will be accustomed to pleasure and forget her duty of obedience. Consequently, there will be misfortune and neither will be benefited.[20]

Chu Hsi's writings must be understood within this long history of attitudes toward women. Like his contemporaries, he believed that women possessed human qualities different from those of men and that these determined a woman's station in life.

Chu Hsi did not believe that women had the same intellectual capabilities as men. Women could not understand the higher metaphysical principles he himself promoted. He praised the literary talent of Li Ch'ing-chao (1084–1147), but when he saw poems of hers that discussed Confucian principles in history, he exclaimed, "How could a woman have written such words!"[21] He further insisted that a woman's humaneness, the highest human virtue for Chu Hsi, flowed from her ability to love. Thus, he implied that women had only an emotional response to virtue rather than an intellectual appreciation of it.[22]

Chu Hsi may not have created the tradition of subordination, but he did revive and strengthen certain gender distinctions found in the classical teachings. The basis of his doctrine on women was the principle of the "Differentiation [of Function] between Husband and Wife" (*fu fu chih pieh*). This was one of the Five Moral Relations of Mencius, which together formed the bedrock of Chu Hsi's Neo-Confucian ethics. He reiterated these principles over and over, and some consider this relation between husband and wife to have been the most important of the five relations.[23] Men and women, in accordance with their different capabilities and natural dispositions, engaged in two separate spheres of activity. Women could not undertake men's responsibilities, and men could not perform women's tasks.[24]

19. *I-ch'uan wen-chi* in *Erh-Ch'eng ch'üan-shu* (SPPY ed.) 7:8a; italics mine.
20. *Chin-ssu lu, chüan* 12, sec. 12; Chan trans., p. 272.
21. *Chu-tzu yü-lei* 2 vols. (Kyoto: Chūbun shuppansha, 1979) 140:5352.
22. Ibid., 4:91.
23. See for instance in his texts like "Pai-lu tung shu-yüan chieh-shih," in *Chu-tzu ta-ch'üan* (Chung-hua shu-chü ed.) *chüan* 74, pp. 16b–23a; and the *Hsiao-hsüeh.*
24. This idea, common in other societies as well, has been explored in works of women's

The differentiation of function between men and women began with spatial restrictions. Women were to stay in the interior of the house while men occupied the outer quarters and concerned themselves with the world at large. Chu Hsi found a strong statement of this principle in the *Record of Rites* (*Li chi*):

> The observances of propriety commenced with a careful attention to the relations between husband and wife. They built the mansion and its apartments, distinguishing between exterior and interior parts. The men occupied the exterior; the women the interior. The mansion was deep, and the doors were strong, guarded by porter and gateman. The men did not enter the interior; the women did not come out into the exterior.[25]

The spatial separation extended to a prohibition on men and women handing things to each other and interacting casually in any way:

> The men should not speak of what belongs to the inside of the house, nor the women of what belongs to the outside. Except at sacrifices and funeral rites, they should not hand vessels to one another. In all other cases when they have occasion to give and receive anything, the woman should receive it in a basket. If she has no basket, they should put the thing on the ground, and she should then take it up. Outside or inside, they should not go to the same well, nor to the same bathing-house. They should not share the same mat lying down; they should not ask to borrow anything from one another; they should not wear similar upper or lower garments.[26]

Ssu-ma Kuang, whom Chu Hsi greatly admired and quoted, upheld this strict practice of separation. In his *Precepts for Family Life* (*Chia fan*), he quoted from this *Li chi* passage, recommending that men and women never sit together, speak together, pass things directly to each other, and so on.[27] One wonders how these admonitions were enforced.

The confinement of women to the home became a standard feature of upper-class Chinese society. Chinese terms for wife, like *nei-jen*, literally "person inside," or *nei-chu*, "domestic helper," reflected this restriction of women within the house.

Chang Po-hsing (1651–1725), in his comments on Ch'eng I's injunction to pick a daughter-in-law carefully, remarked:

> Male persons are usually outside the home. Their character can easily be seen

---

studies. For a current theory and critique, see Ivan Illich, *Gender* (New York: Pantheon Books, 1982), and "Symposium: Beyond the Backlash: A Feminist Critique of Ivan Illich's Theory of Gender," *Feminist Issues* 3 no. 1 (1983): 3–43.

25. *Hsiao-hsüeh* pp. 33–34; adapted from James Legge, trans., *The Li Ki*, vol. 3 of *The Sacred Books of China* (1885; reprint London: Oxford University Press, 1926) Part I, pp. 470–471.

26. *Hsiao-hsüeh*, p. 34; Legge trans., *Li Ki, Pt.* 1 p. 454. Cf. *Mencius* 4:17.1.

27. *Chia fan* (Taipei: Chung-hua tzu-hsüeh ming-chu chi-ch'eng, chen pen, 1978), *chüan* 1, pp. 464–467. Ebrey refers to these rules in *Family and Property*, p. 48.

in their speech and their dealing with others. Female persons confine themselves to their own private quarters. It is difficult to know their character.[28]

Even in the twentieth century, elite Chinese women were praised for never being seen outside the house, and in Korea and Japan, after Neo-Confucianism took hold, upper-class households always had separate quarters for men and women.

According to Chu Hsi, differentiation between men and women produced the appropriate affection between husband and wife. Such affection was the natural beginning of love for children, filial piety, righteousness, and the performance of rites. The *Elementary Learning* stated:

> When there is differentiation between men and women, only then is there affection between parent and child. When there is this affection, only then does righteousness come forth. When righteousness comes forth, only then are the rites performed. When the rites are performed only then is there tranquillity for all living things. The absence of such distinction and righteousness is the way of beasts.[29]

Although Chu Hsi endorsed the concepts of separation and differentiation, he did see the interrelationship between the spheres of men's and women's activities. Each depended on the other, and over a lifetime the two spheres could overlap. In particular, boys were raised together with girls in the women's sphere until the age of eight when they left and entered the men's world.[30] Women had to be educated to perform their special tasks in the household. They also had to be able to train both their sons and daughters to undertake their separate functions in the world.

In the rest of this chapter I will focus on four aspects of women and education. The first section will consider the goal of women's education, namely the code of behavior that embodied Chu Hsi's conception of womanhood. I will discuss both the ideal form of this code, as seen in prescriptive texts like the *Elementary Learning*, and the actual practice of it, as typified by the model individuals for whom Chu Hsi wrote funerary inscriptions. The second section will examine the importance of mothers in promoting primary education, both moral cultivation and book learning, for boys as well as girls. The third part of the chapter provides information on female literacy and suggests that women were not excluded from the literate culture of Chinese civilization. The fourth explores Chu Hsi's attitudes toward women practic-

28. Quoted in Chan, *Things at Hand*, pp. 173–174.

29. *Hsiao-hsüeh*, p. 33; see also Uno Seiichi, *Shōgaku* (Tokyo: Meiji shōin, 1965), p. 95; hereafter cited *Shōgaku*. My own translation, adapted from Legge trans., *Li Ki*, Pt. 1, Bk. 9, "Chiao t'e sheng," p. 440.

30. The *Great Learning* and other Neo-Confucian texts say that boys left the women's quarters and began formal education at age eight. The *Li chi* puts the separation at age ten, and it is quoted that way in the *Elementary Learning*; see *Hsiao-hsüeh*, p. 3, and *Shōgaku*, pp. 19–20; Legge, trans., *Li Ki*, Pt. 1, p. 478.

ing Buddhism and how he reconciled their practice with Confucian principles. An appendix provides translations of some funerary inscriptions that
Chu Hsi wrote for women.

THE GOAL AND CONTENT OF
WOMEN'S EDUCATION

The Chinese words used for education, *hsüeh* (learning) or *chiao* (instruction),
can be understood in two different senses. The first is book learning, *tu-shu*,
which includes instruction in letters and schooling for boys outside the home.
Chu Hsi's program of "broad learning," *po-hsüeh*, referred to this kind of
education and applied exclusively to men of the elite class.[31]

Book learning, however, was not an end in itself for Chu Hsi. It was meant
to contribute to the second, more important aspect of education—moral
cultivation. The content of moral cultivation was derived ultimately from the
Classics that revealed the Way of Heaven (*t'ien chih tao*) as described by the
sages. Those who discovered and interpreted these truths were literate men
like Chu Hsi. But moral cultivation began even before literacy, and it applied
to all classes of society and to both men and women. It included a religious
and ritual aspect of life that had to be taught independently of written texts.
As set forth in the *Great Learning* and reiterated in the *Elementary Learning*,
children's tasks like "sprinkling and sweeping" formed the basis of instruction.[32] The Way of Heaven was "not outside of human life and daily
activity."[33] It was initially found not in books but in self-cultivation and
"returning to one's original nature" (*fu ch'i hsing*).[34] The *Doctrine of the Mean*
opens with this definition of instruction: "The Nature is that which is
endowed by Heaven; to adhere to the Nature is called the Way; to cultivate
the Way is called instruction (*chiao*)."[35]

In this sense of education women were expected to be both students and
teachers. The focus on women highlights the ritual and spiritual aspects of
education. In contrast to the philosophical, secular side of Neo-Confucianism

---

31. Chu Hsi's program of "broad learning" included reading the Classics as well as
historical and literary writing from later periods. See his "Pai-lu tung shu-yüan chieh-shih," and
Wm. Theodore de Bary's discussion in *The Liberal Tradition in China* (New York: Columbia
University Press, 1983), pp. 40–42, and in his chapter in this volume.

32. *Hsiao-hsüeh*, introduction, p. 1; also explained beautifully by Hsü Heng (1209–1281) in
"Hsiao-hsüeh ta-i," *Shushigaku taikei*, vol. 10 (Tokyo: Meitoku shuppansha, 1976), p. 475.

33. Ch'en Ch'un (1153–1217), "Yen-ling chiang-i" in *Pei-hsi tzu-i* (Ts'ung-shu chi-ch'eng ed.
Shanghai: Commercial Press, 1937), p. 77.

34. Chu Hsi, "Ta-hsüeh chang-chü hsü in *Ssu-shu chi-chu* (Taipei: Chung-kuo tzu-hsüeh
ming-chu chi-ch'eng, chen pen, 1978), p. 1.

35. First line of the *Elementary Learning*, quoting the first line of the *Doctrine of the Mean*; also
quoted in Hsü Heng, "Hsiao-hsüeh ta-i," p. 476a.

dominated by elite men of letters, one glimpses the daily life practices that could be undertaken by all people.

The first principle of moral cultivation for women was the same as that for men—filial piety. The relationship between parent and child was the first of Mencius's Five Moral Relations, "the object of education,"[36] and filial piety was the subject of the first and longest subsection of the *Elementary Learning*. The Neo-Confucians restored the *Classic of Filial Piety (Hsiao-ching)* to a prominence it had not enjoyed since the Han, and when asked about texts that applied to the education of women Chu Hsi agreed that this text and the *Analects* were the most important.[37] Ssu-ma Kuang thought girls should memorize these two texts from the age of seven.[38]

In the Confucian world order, children were to learn filial piety as a natural response to the love they experienced from their parents.[39] But for women, this natural process presented complications. In Chinese society, where marriage was patrilocal and the family patrilineal, a young woman moved into her husband's family and was considered a member of his clan or patrilineal descent group. A woman's filial piety had to be directed toward her parents-in-law to whom she had no childhood bonds. She was to "serve her father- and mother-in-law just as she had served her own father and mother."[40] Although filial piety was just as important for men as for women, the task of serving elder parents fell into the woman's sphere of the home; a woman fulfilled a man's Confucian obligation to his parents, by waiting on them hand and foot.

For Chu Hsi, this filial piety toward a previously unknown mother- or father-in-law was also supposed to derive from the natural love between parents and children. In funerary inscriptions, Chu Hsi linked the willingness of a daughter-in-law to serve her in-laws with the love that existed between her and her parents-in-law, although a daughter-in-law's service had to come first:

> When Mme. Wang resided at home, she served her parents and was filial to them; her parents loved her. When she was nineteen years old, she got married, and she transferred her filial service to her father- and mother-in-law; her father- and mother-in-law also loved her.[41]

---

36. *Mencius* 3A:3.10.

37. *Chu-tzu yü-lei*, chüan 7, p. 204.

38. Cited in Ch'en Tung-yüan, *Chung-kuo fu-nü sheng-huo shih*, p. 133; Yao, *Chinese Women*, p. 87.

39. For instance, *Analects* 2:6; the three years mourning for parents corresponded to the three years of infancy spent in the loving arms of the parents, *Analects* 17:21. See also de Bary, *Liberal Tradition*, pp. 30–32, 36.

40. *Hsiao-hsüeh*, p. 11. Kay Ann Johnson, as well as others, has pointed to the miseries that such a "patriarchal-patrilineal-patrilocal configuration" could cause; see *Women, the Family and Peasant Revolution in China* (Chicago: University of Chicago Press, 1983), p. 9.

41. *Wen-chi* 92:29b.

Or,

> She served her mother-in-law, Lady Luo, with filial respect and attention. Lady Luo loved her like her own daughter.[42]

Parents-in-law were described as weeping as much as the husband when a wife died.[43]

These passages suggest that the sanctified relation between mother- and daughter-in-law produced love and filial service. Other writers of the Sung, who agreed that a wife must always serve her in-laws, described the situation less optimistically. Yüan Ts'ai, a contemporary of Chu Hsi warned:

> When a woman addresses members of the household as "father-in-law," "mother-in-law," "elder brother," "younger brother," . . . she is using arbitrarily fixed terms, not ones derived from natural relations. Therefore she can lightly forget favors and easily nurture resentment.[44]

He says elsewhere, that if she is disliked by her in-laws, she "simply must put up with it" and continue to obey them singlemindedly in the hope that they will eventually realize their mistake.[45]

Chu Hsi also insisted that a girl must serve her mother- and father-in-law unfailingly, whether or not she loved or was loved by them. This lesson was driven home in the *Elementary Learning* with numerous gruesome stories taken from historical writings about women who protected their mothers- or fathers-in-law from harm at the risk or cost of their own lives.[46] Such stories of sacrifice seem exaggerated, but Chu Hsi makes them real by claiming that a woman he knew had acted in the same way:

> The Madame happened to incur a serious illness. In the still of the night, Miss Luo [her daughter-in-law] went out into the dew and burned incense to pray that her own life be shortened in exchange for her mother-in-law's years. Accordingly, in a few months the Madame's illness dissipated and one morning, three years later, Miss Luo suddenly died. [She was thirty six *sui*.][47]

Chu Hsi commented at the end:

> Miss Luo went to the point of giving up her body and dying in place of her mother-in-law. She adhered to Decorum [li] to the point of ending her life. Her worthiness far surpasses that of others. How could I not make a record of it?[48]

42. Ibid., 90:15a.
43. *Wen-chi* 92:29b, 90:15b. The Ch'ing novelist Ts'ao Hsüeh-ch'in satarized this point when he described the excessive and improper grief of Cousin Zhen over the death of his lovely daughter-in-law. See David Hawkes, trans., *The Story of the Stone: A Chinese Novel by Cao Xueqin*, Vol. 1 (Harmondsworth: Penguin Books, 1982), p. 259ff.
44. *Yüan-shih shih-fan* 1.35; Ebrey, *Family and Property*, p. 206.
45. *Yüan-shih shih-fan* 1.21; Ebrey, *Family and Property*, pp. 195–196.
46. Uno, *Shōgaku*, pp. 418–425.
47. *Wen-chi* 90:15a–b.
48. Ibid., 90:16a.

A modern reader may think that it was only by an unfortunate coincidence that Miss Luo died three years after her mother-in-law's illness, but Chu Hsi firmly believed that she had died in answer to her own prayers. Here is evidence of the powerful religious and mystical elements of Neo-Confucianism. Heaven (*t'ien*) is listening to the prayers and agrees to exchange one life for another. The concept of Decorum (*li*) went beyond a mere ideology of social hierarchy.

Chu Hsi approved of a woman giving up her life for her mother-in-law. Thus, filiality for women did not extend to preserving the body intact as it did for men.[49] Chu Hsi never advocated self-mutilation, but in later dynasties the theme was taken to great lengths. It was most often done by young women who cut off their own flesh for medicine to cure their in-laws of disease.[50]

Although Chu Hsi did not condone flesh cutting, service to in-laws could include considerable hardship. His funerary inscriptions frequently described the miseries caused by harsh mothers-in-law. He praised women for enduring extreme demands without complaints. In some of his inscriptions, these demands were described in a tone that bordered on the ridiculous:

> Her father- and mother-in-law were both very advanced in years. The rules of Decorum were strictly enforced, and few of the daughters-in-law of the household were able to fulfill the intentions of the parents. Only Mme. Yü attended to them by their side, and never disobeyed them in matters of Decorum. . . . She exerted herself to be quick and diligent, so that she could fulfill the slightest desire of her parents-in-law. After offering food, she would withdraw and stand on the side in a posture of respectful readiness to listen [for further instructions]. She only worried that in some small way she would not live up to their standard to the point where sometimes she secretly hoarded additional provisions to be prepared for further demands. Even in the midst of civil disorder and extreme hardship, she had to seek and obtain things in many ways so that the smallest wish was not left unsatisfied.[51]

Another mother-in-law is described as not allowing her daughters-in-law to sit down in her presence during twenty years of service.[52] Speaking of his own mother, whom Chu Hsi could observe firsthand, he says:

49. *Analects* 8:3.

50. The Ch'ing encyclopedia *Ku-chin t'u-shu chi-ch'eng*, compiled in 1725, gives examples of exaggerated filial piety, including flesh cutting, often by women, in different ages. Compiled by Ch'en Meng-lei et al. (Peking: Chung-hua shu-chü, 1934) *li-hsüeh p'ien, hsüeh-hsing tien*, Vol. 611–612, chüan 179–189. I thank Wing-tsit Chan for this reference. In his translation of Wang Yang-ming's *Ch'uan-hsi lu*, Chan also notes that the earliest reference to flesh cutting out of filial piety is in *Hsin T'ang shu* 196:4b; Wing-tsit Chan, *Instructions for Practical Living and other Neo-Confucian Writings by Wang Yang-ming* (New York: Columbia University Press, 1967), p. 107, n. 44. Wang Yang-ming himself questioned the validity of the practice; *Ch'uan-hsi lu*, chüan 139; Chan, *Instructions*, pp. 107–110.

51. *Wen-chi* 92:13a–b.

52. Ibid., 91:14a.

She served her father- and mother-in-law with filiality and respect, and she was diligent to the point that she was able to do things that other people would find difficult.[53]

Chu Hsi used similar words to describe his sister's careful attention to the needs of her father-in-law.[54]

A woman had to remain filial to her in-laws even after they had died by performing sacrifices to them. Chu Hsi praises one woman for performing this duty unfailingly even when she was very sick and weak[55] and another for mourning in-laws whom she had never met:

> When she was married, she did not even get to meet her father and mother-in-law (before they died). But every year, she performed the winter sacrifices to them. She had to conduct the rites with her own hands, and when they were over, she would always sob and weep for her parents-in-law.[56]

Filiality and service to one's in-laws was closely related to the Neo-Confucian emphasis on the ritual patrilineal descent line or *tsung*.[57] Sung Neo-Confucians sought to revive the classical ideal of an extended clan structure where descendants for five generations shared property and ritual obligations. In Sung law and society in general, a woman had strong ties to her natal family, and the interests of the nuclear family, or patriline, were nearly always upheld over the interest of the larger clan.[58] But in Chu Hsi's classical revival, a woman was not to promote either her natal family's interests or those of her husband's immediate patriline. Rather she was to dedicate herself to protecting her husband's clan or *tsung*. This meant that loyalty to the clan elders, namely her in-laws, was more important than loyalty to her husband, and that the sons of her husband's brothers were as important as her own sons.[59]

This principle was the basis for the Neo-Confucian prohibition against the remarriage of widows. Such an injunction was stated in the *Li-chi*,[60] but the Ch'eng-Chu school elevated it to a new importance. A woman not only had

53. Ibid., 94:25b.
54. Ibid., 91:26b.
55. Ibid., 92:3b.
56. Ibid., 93:25a.
57. Ebrey nicely summarizes this concept and shows how it influenced or did not influence, Chinese society; "Conceptions of the Family in the Sung Dynasty," *Journal of Asian Studies* 43 (February 1984): 219–246.
58. See ibid. and also Patricia Ebrey, "Women in the Kinship System of the Southern Song Upper Class," in *Women in China*, ed. Guisso and Johannesen.
59. The *Elementary Learning* has examples of women sacrificing their own sons to save the sons of their husbands' brothers. Such stories came from the *Lieh-nü chuan* of Liu Hsiang (80?–7? B.C.). See S.F. Balfour, "Fragments from the Gallery of Chinese Women, or Lieh Nü Chuan Written by Liu Hsiang," *T'ien Hsia Monthly* 10, no. 3 (March 1940): 267ff. They were also repeated in Ssu-ma Kuang's *Chia fan*, see chüan 7, pp. 646–650.
60. Legge trans. *Li Ki* 1, chap. 27, p. 439.

to guard her chastity and be faithful to her husband even after his death, but, more important, she had to continue to serve her husband's clan no matter how many of its members survived.

The *Elementary Learning* illustrated the prohibition on widow remarriage in the harshest terms. A widow's duty to be chaste took precedence over filial piety to her natal parents, and again, the Confucian respect for the body did not apply to women. One story, from the Three Kingdoms period,[61] recounts how a girl was widowed at a young age without any children, but continued to live with her husband's family, being supported by his elder brother. She cut off her hair to show her sincerity and then cut off her ears to prevent her family from marrying her to someone else. Later, her husband's family was completely exterminated, and her uncle took her back to her parents who had the intention of arranging a remarriage. When the girl discovered their intentions, she slipped into the bedroom and cut off her nose. The blood flowed all over the mats, and her parents were horrified. No one who saw her could keep from crying. When asked why she was staying chaste after her husband's clan had been completely exterminated, she answered:

> "I have heard that humane (*jen*) people do not change their behavior on account of prosperity or decline, and righteous (*i*) people do not let their hearts be influenced by life or death. Previously, the Ts'ao clan [her husband's] prospered, and I wanted to protect it to the end. Just because today it has perished, why suddenly abandon it? That would be the way of beasts; how could I do such a thing?"[62]

The most famous statement that a widow must not remarry comes from Ch'eng I, as quoted in *Reflections on Things at Hand*:

> *Question*: According to principle, it seems that one should not marry a widow. What do you think?
> *Answer*: Correct. Marriage is a match. If one takes someone who has lost her integrity to be his own match, it means he himself has lost his integrity.
> *Further question*: In some cases a widow is alone, poor and with no one to depend on. May she remarry?
> *Answer*: This theory has come about only because people of later generations are afraid of starving to death. But to starve to death is a very small matter. To lose one's integrity, however, is a very serious matter.[63]

This injunction was radical for Sung times and even later. Chang Po-hsing (1651–1725), the great Neo-Confucian commentator, actually deleted this passage from his *Collected Commentaries on the Reflections on Things at Hand*

---

61. The story is recorded in the commentary by P'ei Sung-chih (372–451) of the *Wei Shu* by Ch'en Shou (233–297) (*San-kuo chih*, Vol. 1, Peking: Chung-hua shu-chü, 1973), chüan 9, p. 293. P'ei Sung-chih took the story from the *Lieh-nü chüan* of Huang Fu-miao (215–282).

62. As quoted in *Hsiao-hsüeh*, pp. 162–163; Uno, *Shōgaku*, pp. 422–424.

63. *Ho-nan Ch'eng-shih i-shu*, in *Erh Ch'eng ch'üan-shu* (Ssu-pu pei-yao ed.) 22B:3a; translated in Chan, *Things at Hand*, p. 177.

(Chin-ssu lu chi-chieh);[64] perhaps he found it extreme and doubted its authenticity.

Indeed, the harshness of these words is tempered by comparing Neo-Confucian theory with the actual practice of its adherents. Ch'eng I's own father, when confronted with a parallel situation, acted quite differently. Ch'eng I considered his action praiseworthy enough to be included in a funerary inscription that he wrote for his father:

> Later, when my cousin's own daughter also became a widow, fearing that my cousin was deeply grieved, he took the widowed daughter home and gave her in marriage.[65]

Chu Hsi's *Classified Conversations* recorded:

> Someone asked, "Taking the widowed grand-niece home and giving her in marriage seems to contradict the teaching that a widow should not remarry. How about it?" Chu Hsi answered, "Generally speaking, that should be the case. But people cannot follow that absolutely."[66]

From this passage one sees that Chu Hsi was conscious of the distinction between sagely ideals and practical living. Remarriage of widows was extremely common in the Sung dynasty. Yüan Ts'ai took it for granted in his *Precepts for Social Living*.[67] Fan Chung-yen (989–1052) even alloted money from his charitable estate to help widows remarry.[68] Chu Hsi basically accepted the Sung practice without complaint; however, he did wish to posit a new standard of behavior for those who aspired to be sages. In a letter to his friend Ch'en Shih-chung, he urges him not to let his widowed sister remarry:

> Previously, Ch'eng I commented on this matter, saying that to starve to death was a small matter, but to lose one's integrity was a large matter. If you look at it from the point of view of social custom, it truly seems impracticable, but if you look at it from the point of view of one who knows the Classics and understands principle [*li*], then you must know that one cannot deviate from this [precept]."[69]

---

64. Chan, *Things at Hand*, p. 177, n. 21.

65. As quoted in *Chin-ssu lu* 6:3b; Chan, *Things at Hand*, p. 179.

66. *Chu-tzu yü-lei* 96:11a, p. 3928; translated in Chan, *Things at Hand*, p. 179.

67. *Yüan-shih shih-fan* 1.21, 1.48, 1.50, 1.51; translated by Ebrey in *Family and Property*, pp. 195, 217–219. In some cases, women even took their husband's property with them when they remarried, cf. *Yüan-shih shih-fan* 1.26; Ebrey, *Family and Property*, p. 200; and Hung Mai (1123–1202), *I-chien chih* (Beijing: Chung-hua shu-chü, 1981), vol. 1, *chia chih*, chüan 2, p. 16. For general information on the remarriage of widows in the Sung, see Ebrey, "Women in the Kinship System;" and Ebrey, *Family and Property*, p. 99. See also texts like the *Ming-kung shu-p'an ch'ing-ming chi* (Tokyo: Koten Kenkyūkai, 1964), a collection of legal decisions concerning family disputes in the Sung. This text is discussed by Ian Burns in "Private Law in Traditional China (Sung Dynasty)" (Ph.D. diss. Oxford University, 1973).

68. Ch'en Tung-yüan, *Chung-kuo fu-nü sheng-huo shih*, p. 132. Esther Yao also mentions this in *Chinese Women*, p. 76, but she mistakes funds from the charitable estate for government funds.

69. *Wen-chi* 26:29a; also quoted in Ch'en *Chung-kuo fu-nü sheng-huo shih*, p. 139.

Chu Hsi applied different standards according to the circumstances. None of his funerary inscriptions mentions that a woman suffered any hardship or took drastic action not to remarry. He describes the difficulties of his own mother's widowhood but does not suggest that she had to resist any temptation to remarry. The opportunity probably did not arise:

> When my father died, I [Chu] Hsi was only fourteen years old. My mother toiled to take care of me. . . . We lived in poverty and sickness in acute distress that no one would be able to endure. But my mother managed it all happily.[70]

The doctrine of filial piety and loyalty to the husband's clan, was supported by Chu Hsi's affirmation that a woman must obey her husband. This was a traditional Confucian rule reminiscent of the ancient belief that women were the weaker sex. Nearly all Chinese writers promoted such obedience, especially in the Sung.[71] The *Elementary Learning* quoted the famous lines of Confucius found in the *Rites of the Elder Mr. Tai*:

> Confucius said, "The wife is one who bends to the will of another and so her rectitude lies in not following her own will. Her moral principle is that of the Three Obediences: at home she follows her father; when married, she follows her husband; when he dies she follows her son. She never ventures to act according to her own will."[72]

Another part of the *Elementary Learning*, quoting the *Record of Rites*, compared a woman's subservience to the idea that "regulates the relation between the strong and the weak, . . . heaven and earth, ruler and subject."[73] As shown above, Ch'eng I considered it a "constant principle" that the husband lead and the wife follow. In a funerary inscription for his father, Ch'eng I claims that these precepts were followed in his household: "Mother conducted herself with humility and obedience. Even in small matters, she never made decisions alone, but always asked father before she did anything."[74]

Chu Hsi's inscriptions, like those of many other writers in the Sung, abound with adjectives that indicate obedience, such as tranquil (*ching*),

---

70. *Wen-chi* 94:25b.

71. The theme of obedience appears in the funerary inscriptions of nearly every writer in the Sung. Thus, it is seen with almost equal frequency in the works of Fan Tsu-yü, Su Shih, or Yeh Ts'ai. The theme appears in T'ang inscriptions as well, although apparently it was not quite as common.

72. *Hsiao-hsüeh*, pp. 35–36; Uno, *Shōgaku*, p. 102. Uno Seiichi points out that the *Ta Tai li-chi* does not actually attribute these words to Confucius. Instead, they are attributed to him only in *K'ung-tzu chia-yü*; trans. by R. P. Kramers, *K'ung Tzu Chia Yü, the School Sayings of Confucius* (Leiden: E. J. Brill, 1950) with questionable authenticity. Chu Hsi evidently adopted the words "Confucius said" and added them to the *Ta Tai li-chi* quote. Uno Seiichi personally questions whether these were indeed the words of Confucius, but he admits that Chu Hsi believed that they were and that this passage has since had a profound influence on women in China; *Shōgaku*, p. 104.

73. *Hsiao-hsüeh*, p. 33; Legge, trans., *Li Ki* Pt. 1, p. 322.

74. As quoted in *Chin-ssu lu* 6:17; Chan, *Things at Hand*, p. 179.

complaisant (*wan*), gentle (*jou*), respectful (*kung*), and diligent (*ch'in*). However, these could be combined with less passive terms, such as firm (*chien*) and correct (*cheng*), and Chu Hsi often referred to women as wise (*hui*) and clever (*min*).[75] Anecdotes in the inscriptions reveal how the strict rules of obedience found in the ritual texts were practiced in a modified form and how Chu Hsi approved of these modifications. An intelligent Mme. Yü is praised for influencing her husband Mr. Chiang:

> Mr. Chiang's nature was unyielding and upright. . . . When other people committed errors, he would go and confront them to their face and upbraid them. When Mme. Yü noticed that perhaps he was too excessive, she would always gently hint and explain to him. Mr. Chiang respected her in these matters.[76]

Chu Hsi is illustrating how a woman might temper her husband's behavior and even alter it to accord more with her own will rather than his, all within the boundaries of Confucian obedience.

These principles of filiality, loyalty, and obedience were supposed to be enforced by the threat of divorce. The *Elementary Learning* listed the seven reasons for divorcing a wife, quoted as the words of Confucius:[77]

> disobedience to a husband's father and mother
> being unable to produce children
> being licentious
> being jealous
> having an incurable disease
> talking too much
> stealing.[78]

These rules reflected the Neo-Confucian emphasis on the viability of the clan or *tsung* and the continuation of the family line. The first three crimes threatened the blood line and the clan authority. It was a woman's duty to produce offspring and to serve her parents-in-law. The last four items were threats to family harmony and to the law of obedience. Such behavior violated the decorum (*li*) of family relations and could lead to even greater problems in society. There were no grounds for a woman to divorce her husband. However, three reasons were given for a man not to divorce his wife. These included the condition that she had been filial to his parents by mourning them for more than three years; such a rule reinforced filial piety in its ritual as well as material aspects.[79]

A comment by Ssu-ma Kuang shows that these rules for divorce were not often practiced in the Sung and were censured by public opinion. In his *Precepts for Family Life* he lamented:

75. See for instance *Wen-chi* 91:14b, 92:29b, 92:3a, 93:17b, 93:25a.

76. Ibid., 92:13b.

77. See Uno, *Shōgaku*, p. 104; and note 72 above.

78. *Hsiao-hsüeh*, p. 35; Uno, *Shōgaku*, pp. 102–103.

79. Ibid. The other two reasons were if she had no home to return to, and if her husband's house had been poor when she married and subsequently became rich.

Husbands and wives are joined by morality [i]. If morality is violated, they separate. Yet when today's gentlemen dismiss their wives, the crowd condemns them, considering it misbehavior. Therefore gentlemen seldom do it. But according to the ritual texts there are seven grounds for repudiating a wife; one should find out on what grounds a repudiation was made. If the wife has indeed violated ritual, expelling her is a moral duty. In antiquity, the family of Confucius expelled wives in three generations, and many other worthy scholars also expelled their wives for reasons of moral duty. How can this be a blemish to one's behavior?[80]

Chu Hsi may have reiterated that women must obey their husbands, but the separation of the two worlds—inside and outside the home—left women to act largely on their own initiative. Within the home, women carried out the dictates of Confucian living as managers of the family.

"Managing the Family" was intermediate between "Cultivating the Self" and "Ruling the Country," in the stages of personal and social cultivation as given in the *Great Learning*.[81] One's own family had to be in order, after personal cultivation, before it was possible to turn one's attention to the larger community.

Yet while men worried about self-cultivation and the society at large and contemplated metaphysical issues, a woman was to take care of the daily affairs of the household, as Chu Hsi described in funerary inscriptions. As with filial piety, women were responsible for carrying out the most basic of Confucian principles within the home.

Chu Hsi was not the only writer to recognize the important role of women within the home. Many Sung writers described the need for a principal wife to manage household affairs; this was often cited as a reason for a man to remarry after being widowed.[82] But it has not often been acknowledged that Chu Hsi advocated such an independent and essential function for women.

Unlike Ssu-ma Kuang, who wanted men to keep close track of all household affairs and to make all the decisions, Chu Hsi praised men for staying away from the mundane world of the household and leaving it to their competent wives.[83] It was not considered bad for a man to ignore the household, even the education of his sons:

> Mr. Chou's conduct was genial and easy going, and he did not engage himself with matters of the family or property in his conduct of affairs. Great Lady

80. Ssu-ma Kuang, *Chia fan*, chüan 7, p. 657; translated in Ebrey, "Conceptions of the Family," p. 225.
81. See, for instance, *Ssu-shu chi-chu*, p. 8 and "Articles of the White Deer Grotto Academy," among other works.
82. See Ebrey, *Family and Property*, p. 98, citing Yüan Ts'ai; and Hung Mai, *I-chien chih*, vol. 1, *chia-chih*, chüan 2, p. 11, and chüan 16, p. 143. The *Li chi* stated that the eldest son, no matter how old, had to have a wife to carry out the funeral sacrifices. But if there were no such eldest son, a wife was not needed for the ceremony; see Legge, trans. *Li Ki*, Pt. 1, p. 316.
83. Ebrey comments on this difference; see *Family and Property*, pp. 46–50.

Ch'en assisted him with diligence and earnestness, and [herself] managed the family affairs frugally and methodically. She instructed her children very strictly.[84]

Household management had several aspects. The side stressed most in the *Elementary Learning* included the manual tasks of spinning and weaving to provide clothing for the household and the preparation of food and sacrifices. These tasks were always referred to as woman's work (*nü-kung*). The *Elementary Learning* set forth a course of study for girls in the home to learn these skills and obedience from age ten. In contrast, boys at this age were to go out to schools for lessons in etiquette and letters:

> A girl at age ten did not go out. Her governess taught her to be complaisant and agreeable, and to obey, to handle hemp fibers and manage silk cocoons, to weave silks and spin threads, to learn women's work in order to furnish garments.[85]

Chu Hsi echoed the ritual texts when he routinely praised women for being good at "women's work" or for performing the tasks it included:

> With regard to women's work, she was not the least bit remiss, and she did not practice wasteful extravagance on ribbons and embroidery. Therefore, she did not dislike humble circumstances, and she was at peace with impoverishment that other people would find difficult [to live with].[86]

> Her ability to handle silk and hemp and to stitch fine threads surpassed that of others.[87]

The first passage shows the relation between women's work and another Confucian virtue, living frugally. Chu Hsi thought it honorable to live economically without any pursuit of selfish gain, but the woman had to cope with straightened circumstances and make ends meet. Women were praised for their ingenuity when the family did not have much money. Chu Hsi commended his own mother for "managing happily" even though the family lived in "poverty and sickness, acute distress that no one would be able to endure" because Chu Hsi did not have a government appointment.[88]

A third aspect of household management, together with virtues of complaisance and sincerity, was keeping harmony among its members, especially the women. In large extended families, wives and sisters of the various sons

84. *Wen-chi* 93:25a. In another example, 90:19b–20a, a woman took care of the household so her husband could pursue duties of office and other goals.

85. *Hsiao-hsüeh*, p. 4; Uno, *Shōgaku*, p. 22. This passage is taken from the Nei-tse chapter of the *Li-chi*, (Legge, trans., *Li Ki*, Pt. 1, pp. 478–479) and is also quoted by Ssu-ma Kuang in *Chia fan*, chüan 6, pp. 591–592.

86. *Wen-chi* 92:29b.

87. Ibid., 92:28a.

88. Ibid., 94:25b. Chu Hsi also promoted frugality (*chien-chih*) in his prospective work on women; see note 2.

shared living quarters and interacted daily with the servants. A perennial problem in Chinese society was fighting among those who stayed inside the home. When a woman was young she had to be good natured and able to get along with her sisters-in-law. When she became mistress of the house, she had to keep harmony among all the family members and manage the servants:

> When she lived among her sisters-in-law, both older and younger, she was reverential and never spoke words of blame. She treated the servants generously but with discipline.[89]

Being kind to other relatives and neighbors was also praised over and over.[90] Ch'eng I described how his mother was appreciated for her kindness and obedience in managing the household:

> Mother and father treated each other with full respect as guests are treated. Grateful for her help at home, father treated her with even greater reverence. But mother conducted herself with humility and obedience. . . . She was skillful in ruling the family [*chih chia*]. She was not stern, but correct. She did not like to beat the servants, but, instead, looked upon little servants as her own children. . . . Whenever father got angry, she always gently explained the matter to him. But if we children were wrong, she would not cover up. She often said, "Children become unworthy because a mother covers up their wrongdoings so the father is unaware of them."[91]

This idyllic image of gentle management of the family and servants contrasts with a warning from Yüan Ts'ai that women, because of their petty natures, will beat and abuse servants.[92]

Chu Hsi put less stress on gentleness and complaisance in household management. In contrast to Ch'eng I who said that his mother was "not stern," Chu Hsi often described women as managing the household "sternly and methodically" (*yen erh yu fa*)[93] or "frugally and with method" (*hsien erh yu fa*).[94]

The women in Chu Hsi's funerary inscriptions stand out for their initiative and strength.[95] Women were often left to support the whole family or even the clan when widowed. One woman, née Lu, had to care for her siblings at a young age when her mother died; then after she was married when her husband and father-in-law died, she had to manage all the affairs of the estate and support not only herself and her own sons but also her

89. Ibid., 92:29b.
90. See, for instance, ibid., 93:25a.
91. *I-ch'uan wen-chi* 8:6a; quoted in Chan, *Things at Hand*, p. 180.
92. *Yüan-shih shih-fan* 3.30; Ebrey, *Family and Property*, p. 290.
93. *Wen-chi* 92:3a.
94. Ibid., 93:25a.
95. See, for instance, ibid., 90:12a, 90:19a, 91:26b, 92:3b, 93:25a.

husband's mother and young siblings. She is said to have kept track of every penny.[96]

Another remarkable example, that of Mme. Yü, well known to Chu Hsi, illustrates many of these aspects of household responsibility. It is worth recounting her story in detail.

Born with the surname Liu, she was adopted into the family of her father's sister and took their surname Yü. She married into the Chiang clan and endured considerable hardship serving her parents-in-law until they passed away. When she was just forty *sui*, her husband died, and she seems to have taken over all the affairs of the Chiang clan as well as those of the remaining Yü family. Chu Hsi gives her full credit as head of the household: "She used decorum [*li*] and regulation [*fa*] to bear herself up and to manage and maintain the household."[97] "Maintaining the household" included instructing her sons and performing yearly sacrifices. Moreover, Mme. Yü demonstrated her commitment to the larger clan by giving all of her husband's lands to his brothers and transferring the land deeds to them. She acted in her husband's name saying, "This was the intention of my late husband."[98]

When her adoptive father Mr. Yü was aging, she went home and cared for him in his last years. When he died, she made all the funeral arrangements and went into full mourning for three years. She would have inherited his property because he had no other children;[99] but instead "she selected on his behalf a son from his clan to ensure proper sacrifices, and she returned the property to this [adopted] son."[100] In addition to choosing an heir on behalf of her stepfather, she welcomed home her poor and widowed elder sister-in-law. Mme. Yü supported this other widow for sixteen years and arranged the marriage of her son.[101]

Within a description of feminine virtue. Chu Hsi leaves no doubt as to who was the boss in the household:

> In daily living and management of affairs, she paid attention to the finest details. When she spoke with people she always adhered to filial piety, brotherly respect, loyalty and trustworthiness. Her words were simple, but the principle had nothing lacking. Relatives in both her and her husband's family praised her actions highly and were persuaded by her words. If anyone had misgivings, they would always go to her and consult about the matter. When there was a problem that was difficult to resolve, and all the mouths [in the

96. Ibid., 93:8b–9a.
97. Ibid., 92:13b.
98. Ibid.
99. Since Mme. Yü was married, a portion of her stepfather's property might have gone to the state. For a discussion of female inheritance in the Sung, see Ebrey, "Women in the Kinship System," and Ebrey, *Family and Property*, especially introduction, pp. 116–120.
100. *Wen-chi* 92:13b. This passage also shows that Chu Hsi approved of women having the power to adopt an heir, a privilege they lost in the Ming.
101. *Wen-chi* 92:13b.

community] were clamoring without stopping, if someone reported, "Mme. Yü's words are like this," the matter would always be settled harmoniously.[102]

Mme. Yü must have wielded considerable power. She had the wherewithal to support her family even after giving away her husband's property and her own family inheritance. Corresponding to Chu Hsi's ideal of womanhood, she diligently served her in-laws, kept harmony with her sisters-in-law, and lived frugally. She managed everything within the home, which gave her far-reaching responsibilities, and her authority seems to have reached even beyond the family. Chu Hsi further commended her for being highly literate and well versed in both the Confucian and Buddhist classics. She was skilled at medicine and divination practices and may have offered her services to others.[103]

The Neo-Confucian ideal of the ritual patrilineal descent line, or *tsung*, theoretically cut off a woman from her natal family. But in this exemplary case chosen by Chu Hsi, as in others, a woman's family ties remained strong and deeply influenced later decisions. Mme. Yü actually took responsibility for people of three different surnames. As dictated by Neo-Confucian ideals, she renounced her husband's patrimony and gave it to his brothers in a selfless act to aid the Chiang clan. Later, she was called on to care for her stepfather, and to reestablish *his* patriline. Strictly speaking, this was a job for a male (or female?) member of his own Yü clan. In the case of her sister-in-law, Mme. Yü acted on behalf of a third, unnamed clan. According to a literal reading of the precepts in the *Elementary Learning*, this other widow would have stayed in her husband's family to sacrifice to his ancestors and to serve any remaining members. Her son's affairs would have been handled by her husband's relatives, no matter how distant. These relatives were probably deceased or too poor (Chu Hsi says that the woman had married an old and impoverished man), and the responsibility fell to Mme. Yü who had become the acting head of the widow's natal household. She even arranged the son's marriage.

Another inscription reveals that, contrary to the *tsung* ideal, even the women who held Chu Hsi's esteem continued to own private valuables not merged with the clan property. Chu Hsi glorifies a woman for donating what must have been her dowry to her husband's family:

> When her father-in-law passed away, her husband [Mr. Huang] was very poor. The elder and younger brothers all looked at each other and planned to sell some fields to pay for the funeral. Mme. Yü said, "Do not destroy the livelihood of your ancestors." She then withdrew and sold her own private possessions to meet [the expenses of] the occasion. Because of this, Mr. Huang was able to take care of [the funeral] without troubling the rest of the family.[104]

102. Ibid., 92:14a.
103. Ibid., 92:13a–14b.
104. Ibid., 91:14a.

Chu Hsi's picture of Mme. Yü planning funerals, dividing land, arranging marriages, and settling disputes is highly reminiscent of Ts'ao Hsueh-ch'in's detailed account of a fictional woman's household duties in the Ch'ing dynasty. Wang Hsi-feng is called on to substitute for Cousin Chen's wife as the "female head of household" in the great novel *Story of the Stone*. Many pages tell of her strenuous duties, and the author summarizes:

> Indeed, so multifarious had her activities become that it would be impossible to list them all. As a consequence she was far too busy to pay much attention to eating and drinking and could hardly sit or lie down for a moment in peace .... Yet although she was so busy, a passion to succeed and a dread of being criticized enabled her to summon up reserves of energy, and she managed to plan everything with such exemplary thoroughness that every member of the clan was loud in her praises.[105]

This imaginative account six hundred years later than the life of the actual Mme. Yü surely describes a situation close to what she experienced. Chu Hsi knew that an elite Sung household needed a strong female head, just as the fictitious Ch'ing household needed one. He appreciated the competence and strength of Mme. Yü and hoped that other women would take on such heavy and far-reaching responsibilities.

WOMEN AS EDUCATORS WITHIN THE HOME

Chu Hsi was deeply concerned with moral education in the family and the community in order to bring about a peaceful, self-governing society. He was aware of the formative influence mothers have on their children, and thus it was crucial that a mother have the virtue of being able properly to teach her children.

Chu Hsi's compilation of the *Elementary Learning* (*Hsiao hsüeh*) shows his concern with early, preliterate education. The first passage quoted after the introduction is from the former Han dynasty *Biographies of Women* (*Lieh-nü chuan*) by Liu Hsiang (80?–7? B.C.). It describes education to be a process of moral nurturance that begins even before birth as part of the process of creation. Women as mothers are the earliest cultivators of the Way of Heaven in a child:

> In ancient times, a woman with child did not lie on her side as she slept; neither would she sit sidewise nor stand on one foot. She would not eat dishes having harmful flavors; "if the food was cut awry, she would not eat it" [Analects 18:3]; "if the mat was not placed straight, she would not sit on it" [Analects 21]. She did not let her eyes gaze on lewd sights nor her ears listen to depraved sounds. At night she ordered the blind musicians to chant poetry. She used right reason to adjust affairs, and thus gave birth to children of correct physical form who excelled others in talent and virtue.[106]

---

105. David Hawkes, trans., *The Story of the Stone*, Vol. 1, pp. 282–283.

106. *Hsiao-hsüeh*, p. 2. Cf. Albert Richard O'Hara, *The Position of Women in Early China According to the Lieh Nü Chuan, "The Biographies of Chinese Women"* (Taipei: Mei Ya Publications, 1971).

This passage has a religious tone and emphasizes ritual conduct. Chu Hsi used similar words in a funerary inscription, praising a woman for being aware of her role in prenatal moral education:

> When [Mme. Yu] was pregnant, she resided properly and quietly. She burned incense and read Confucian and Buddhist texts. She did not utter hasty words nor give angry looks, saying, "This is the way that the ancients instructed the child in the womb." Thus her children were all born worthy and talented, and the way in which she instructed them was excellent.[107]

In the case cited here Mme. Yu is literate, and her own training came from a female relative who taught her wifely virtue as well as letters. As described by Chu Hsi:

> A cousin of her father, Madame Juan, on account of her virtue, was a teacher for girls [nü shih]. When Mme. Yu was young, she studied from her. She was taught the *Precepts for Women* of Pan Chao and she understood the general meaning. When it came to the arts of needlework and writing, she did not practice them with particular attention, yet she quickly surpassed others in ability.[108]

Much of this passage by Chu Hsi echoes the words of Pan Chao (A.D. 45?–120?) whose *Precepts for Women* Chu praised highly, recommending that women study them.[109] Pan Chao herself describes being taught by her mother:

> I, the unworthy writer, am unsophisticated, unenlightened, and by nature unintelligent, but I am fortunate both to have received not a little favor from my scholarly father and to have had a [cultured] mother and instructresses upon whom to rely for a literary education as well as for training in good manners.[110]

One sees here and in Chu Hsi's funerary inscriptions that education in the home, both in wifely virtues and in letters, came from women. The *Elementary Learning* states this explicitly with regard to moral education, though not literacy:

> In all cases when a child was born, they sought to select from among the various aunts one who was generous, loving, virtuous, reverential and careful of her words, to be the child's teacher.[111]

This education in etiquette and letters that was passed down by mothers did

---

107. *Wen-chi* 91:14b.
108. Ibid., 91:14a.
109. *Chu-tzu yü-lei,* chüan 7, p. 204. Chu Hsi made repeated efforts to get the *Precepts for Women* republished. See *Wen-chi* 25:12a, 33:21b, and pieh-chi 13:14b–15a. I thank Wing-tsit Chan for this information taken from a draft of his book on Chu Hsi (Taipei 1987).
110. Swann, *Pan Chao,* p. 82.
111. *Hsiao-hsüeh,* p. 2; Uno, *Shōgaku,* p. 18: translation adapted from Legge, *Li Ki,* Pt. 1, p. 473.

not only apply to girls. In some cases the woman is described as "helping the father" with the education of the sons:

> She helped Mr. Chang instruct their sons, and they all attained scholarly achievements. The oldest, Yang-ch'ing, subsequently passed the *chin-shih* examination.[112]

In other cases, the woman had to take over the instruction of the children along with other household duties when her husband died:

> When Mr. Chiang died, her children were all still young, and Mme. Yü was only forty years old. . . . She instructed her children herself and taught them the Classics and precepts.[113]

However, in most cases the woman appears to have had the first responsibility for the education of the children, especially the sons, whether or not her husband was alive. It was her duty to see that her sons were properly instructed and established in successful careers. Of Mme. Yu, mentioned above for her prenatal education and her knowledge of Pan Chao's *Precepts for Women*, Chu Hsi further commends her children's education:

> When they were barely able to speak she took them on her lap and taught them the *Book of Poetry* and the *Book of History*. When they were a little older, she immediately welcomed teachers and selected friends for them. She taught them repeatedly and encouraged them fully.[114]

Another example shows that a woman could plan the upbringing of her sons even as she died and that responsibility was transferred from one woman to another:

> [Mme. Hsü] was married for eight years when she died. She gave birth to a daughter, but lost her. She gave birth to a son named Shih. He was only two years old when Mme. Hsü fell ill. Thinking that she was about to die, she indicated that her son should belong to her mother-in-law, saying, "Your daughter-in-law is about to die. I would like to take this son and entrust him to you. When you teach him, you must be strict. Do not think that because he has no mother you should be generous with your kindness. If by good fortune he is able to become established, it will be as though your daughter-in-law did not die." In the end, Shih grew up and studied at the Imperial University. He gained a fine reputation, subsequently passed the *chin-shih* examination in the first class, and returned home. Within and without the family, the older people only then began to recount to each other Mme. Hsü's dying words, and they sighed at how far sighted her understanding had been.[115]

Mme. Hsü is given credit for her son's achievements years after her death. Chu Hsi praises her for "teaching her son without love" (i.e., without being

112. *Wen-chi* 91:26a; another example is in *Wen-chi* 90:12b–13a.
113. *Wen-chi* 92:13b.
114. Ibid., 91:14b.
115. Ibid., 92:28b.

indulgent),[116] a theme often repeated. Many women are said to have taught their sons "very strictly"; this resulted in their later scholastic and moral achievements.[117] Ch'eng I writes of his mother:

> Mother had six sons. Only two are still living. Her love and affection for us were of the highest degree. But in teaching us she would not give in a bit. When we were only several years old, sometimes we stumbled when we walked. People in the family would rush forward to hold us, for fear we might cry. Mother would always scold us with a loud voice and say, "If you had walked gently, would you have stumbled?"[118]

It was important to teach children with both love and discipline. Chu Hsi's sister is said to have "cared for and instructed her children lovingly but with discipline."[119]

In his seventeen inscriptions for women, nearly every woman is praised for the instruction she gave to her sons, and in particular the moral foundation that was necessary for their later achievements. Chu Hsi describes his own mother saying, "she toiled to take care of me and to teach me so that I was able to know what direction to take."[120] Other women taught their sons "how to learn" and thereby gain scholarly achievements.[121] There are many examples. A moral foundation for learning was stressed, but, as shown above, more specific knowledge of letters and behavior was also included. This would be different for boys and for girls. One woman, Miss Ting, taught her sons with the help of a strict husband to prepare them for higher learning, and she taught her daughters details such as performing the ancestral sacrifices, how to treat guests, how not to go out at night, and how not to talk too much. Chu Hsi described all this in the vocabulary of the *Elementary Learning*.[122] He concluded: "Therefore her sons were all known for their scholastic achievements, and her daughters after they were married were able to serve their families."[123]

Women lived in a separate world within the home, but they influenced the other world of men in this role as teacher. Boys were raised within the world of women, and there they received cultural values and basic literacy training. At the age of eight, they graduated into the world of men but their primary Confucian "formation" was already complete.[124]

116. Ibid., 92:29b.
117. Ibid., 92:4a, 93:25a.
118. *I-ch'uan wen-chi* 8:6a; also quoted in *Chin-ssu lu* 6:17, Chan, trans., *Things at Hand*, p. 180.
119. *Wen-chi* 91:26b; Yüan Ts'ai warned that mothers were likely to indulge their sons and that fathers must not listen to them regarding the conduct of their sons, see Ebrey, *Family and Property*, p. 190.
120. *Wen-chi* 94:25b.
121. Ibid., 92:9a.
122. Ibid., 93:27a; cf. *Hsiao-hsüeh*, p. 11ff.
123. *Wen-chi* 93:27a.
124. Chang Po-hsing's introduction to the *Hsiao-hsüeh* repeats the maxim that boys enter "elementary education" (*hsiao-hsüeh*) at age eight, taken from the Great Learning and works of

As evident in these examples, women were given credit when their children were successful; their formative influence did not go unappreciated. A common phrase was something like: "This [achievement] was also something that was accomplished because of the instruction of Madame Wang [his mother]."[125] Or another comment was : "The worthiness of the mother was enough to perfect the son. The worthiness of the son is enough to bring prominence to the parents."[126] Except for the funerary inscriptions Chu Hsi wrote for the women in his own family, his inscriptions were all in response to requests from men who wanted to credit their mothers for their achievements. On the one hand, this satisfied the Confucian obligation of filial piety to a man's mother; on the other, it showed that Chu Hsi granted women an important role in the early education of children for which they should be given credit. On the model of Mencius's mother and on that of T'ai Jen, mother of Wen Wang of Chou, a woman was to take responsibility for the proper upbringing of her sons and daughters.[127] The real life examples in the Sung show that this upbringing not only comprehended moral preparation to show children "the direction in which to go"[128] but could also include actual instruction in the Classics and poetry. Therefore, a woman's role, in both the classical and the moral instruction of her children, was crucial to the success of Neo-Confucian education and to Chu Hsi's moral society as a whole.

Evidence from the Yüan dynasty, when Neo-Confucian education was taking hold, also confirms that women in scholarly families taught their sons to be literate. A study by the Japanese scholar Makino Shūji shows that, although nominally fathers had overall responsibility for the education of their sons, in a high percentage of the cases cited, preschool instruction was received at the hands of the individual's mother, grandmother, or aunt. Moreover, the education extended specifically to the study of texts.[129] Clearly, women had an important part in transmitting Chinese literati culture.

THE QUESTION OF LITERACY

The evidence that women trained their children in letters as well as morals indicates that many women in gentry households in the Sung dynasty were

---

Chu Hsi and Ch'eng I. Nevertheless, the *Elementary Learning* quotes the *Li chi*, saying that boys stay in the home until age ten (see note 30). Ssu-ma Kuang in his *Chia fan* also quotes the *Li chi*, chüan 1, p. 468; see Legge, trans., *Li Ki*, Pt. 1, p. 478.

125. *Wen-chi* 90:20a.

126. *Wen-chi* 93:25a; in other examples, women were given credit for their sons passing the *chin-shih* exam; see *Wen-chi* 91:9a, 91:15a, 93:27b.

127. See Albert Richard O'Hara, *The Position of Women in Early China*, which includes the stories of T'ai Jen and Mencius's mother.

128. Cf. *Wen-chi* 94:25b; Chu Hsi is talking about his mother.

129. Makino Shūji, "Gendai no jugaku kyōiku," *Tōyōshikenkyū* 37 (1978–1979):542–545.

literate. Other data from the Sung make this conclusion indisputable.

It is widely acknowledged that women in wealthy households through the Ch'ing must have acquired a modicum of literacy in order to manage the large domestic organizations for which they were often responsible.[130] The women in the Ch'ing novel *Story of the Stone* are nearly all highly literate. Lin Dai-yü read the Four Books and other classics, and the young women all wrote poetry.[131] At the end of the Ming, even those who advocated that women not be literate argued that they learn only enough to keep household accounts.[132]

In the Sung dynasty, no one suggested that women should be excluded from learning to read and write. Chu Hsi even included (book) learning (*chiang-hsüeh*) among the eight headings of his prospective book for women. However, the existing prescriptive texts did not explicitly advocate women's literacy. The *Elementary Learning* of Chu Hsi says only that girls should be taught basic numbers and the calendar in the early years while they are together with boys:

> At six years they were taught the numbers and the names of the cardinal points; at the age of seven, boys and girls did not occupy the same mat nor eat together; . . . at nine they were taught to number the days (i.e., the Chinese cyclical calendar).[133]

The text continues, quoting the *Record of Rites*, to say that after age ten a boy left the women's quarters to be tutored in writing and arithmetic; it is silent about literacy for girls. Instead, they were taught to be obedient, furnish garments, supply sacrifices, and the like.[134]

The basic education prescribed in this passage was probably enough to manage a household as described in many funerary inscriptions in the Sung. The Southern Sung commentator Yüan Ts'ai warned that, if widows could not read and do arithmetic to manage family accounts, "the usual result is the ruin of the family."[135]

Beyond the level of reading accounts, Chu Hsi's forerunner Ssu-ma

---

130. See, for instance, Evelyn Sakakida Rawski, *Education and Popular Literacy in Ch'ing China* (Ann Arbor: University of Michigan Press, 1979), p. 7. For discussions of female literacy in the Ming and Ch'ing, see Joanna Handlin, "Lü K'un's New Audience: The Influence of Women's Literacy on Sixteenth-Century Thought," and Mary Backus Rankin, "The Emergence of Women in China at the End of the Ch'ing: the Case of Ch'iu Chin," in *Women in Chinese Society*, ed. Margery Wolf and Roxanne Witke (Stanford: Stanford University Press, 1975).

131. See Hawkes, trans., *The Story of the Stone*, vol. 1, pp. 82, 100, 118, 271–272, 351, 366–367. Even Li Wan whose father did not think girls should be educated was able to write poetry when called upon to do so; ibid., pp. 108, 366.

132. Ch'en Tung-yüan, *Chung-kuo fu-nü sheng-huo shih*, pp. 187–188; Yao, *Chinese Women*, p. 88.

133. *Hsiao-hsüeh*, p. 2; Uno, *Shōgaku*, p. 18; Legge, trans., *Li Ki*, Pt. 1, p. 478.

134. *Hsiao-hsüeh*, pp. 3–4; Uno, *Shōgaku*, pp. 19–20; Legge, trans., *Li Ki*, Pt. 1, pp. 478–479.

135. *Yüan-shih shih-fan*, 1.53; Ebrey, trans., *Family and Property*, p. 221.

Kuang strongly advocated the reading of texts, saying that women's education was as important as men's. He recommended that girls memorize the *Analects* and the *Classic of Filial Piety* at age seven. At age nine they should be able to explain these texts and go on to the *Biographies of Women* of Liu Hsiang and the *Precepts for Women* of Pan Chao, both of the Han dynasty. Ssu-ma Kuang further lamented that women no longer learned history and moral texts but instead practiced music and poetry, occupations he thought inappropriate for proper ladies.[136]

Chu Hsi echoed Ssu-ma Kuang's suggestions:

> *Question:* Given that girls should also have instruction [*chiao*], in addition to teaching them the *Classic of Filial Piety*, how would it be to teach them just the passages of the *Analects* that are immediately comprehensible?
> *Answer:* That would be alright. Pan Chao's *Precepts for Women* and Ssu-ma Kuang's *Precepts for Family Life* would also be good.[137]

These passages seem to take it for granted that elite women were literate, but fragments from funerary inscriptions show that some girls learned only ideas and not texts. Of his own daughter Chu Hsi wrote: "Though you were unschooled you understood my ideas."[138] Another woman is said to have understood principles of correct Confucian behavior even though she "did not study [texts]."[139] Ch'eng I in a touching eulogy for his unmarried niece also wrote: "We didn't teach her to read books [*tu-shu*] but she herself understood the meanings [of texts]."[140]

Despite the fact that not all women learned to read, there is ample evidence that many women did. Many passages in the sources describe upper-class women to be entirely literate. The texts that they read were both Confucian and Buddhist and included history, Classics, and poetry. Chu Hsi explains of one woman, Mme. Yü, who died in 1182 at the age of eighty:

> By nature she liked to look at books. She read the *Book of Changes* and the *Analects* and understood their general meaning. On the lower level, she understood everything about Taoist cultivation, medicine, divination and various techniques [like astrology and geomancy].[141]

Chu Hsi praises her deep knowledge of Buddhism to which she turned later in life.[142] To this intriguing example is added Mme. Yu, mentioned above,

---

136. Ch'en Tung-yüan, *Chung-kuo fu-nü sheng-huo shih*, p. 133; parts of this opinion are in *Chia fan*, chüan 6, pp. 594–596. Yao, in *Chinese Women*, p. 87, says that Ssu-ma Kuang objected to poetry because it was associated with prostitution, but I do not find those exact words in *Chia fan*.

137. *Chu-tzu yü-lei*, chüan 7, p. 204; also excerpted in Ch'ien Mu, *Chu-tzu hsin hsüeh-an*, 5 vols. (Taipei: San-min shu-tien, 1971), p. 176.

138. *Wen-chi* 93:1a.

139. Ibid., 92:9a (from a statement by the woman herself).

140. *I-ch'uan wen-chi* 7:8a.

141. *Wen-chi* 92:14a–b.

142. Ibid.

who read Confucian and Buddhist texts while pregnant; she also "daily recited the *Precepts for Women* and other classical texts in order to admonish herself," and she taught her sons poetry on her lap.[143] Another Mme. Wang, "liked to read the *Analects*, *Great Learning*, *Doctrine of the Mean*, and *Mencius*, and she understood the general meaning."[144] Of a Mme. Huang, Chu Hsi wrote, "from an early age she liked Buddhist books. She read and recited them and did obeisance all day long."[145]

One of the most noteworthy examples of all is Ch'eng I's mother, Mme. Hou. She was highly literate, as described in funerary inscriptions for her and her husband, all by Ch'eng I:

> When [my mother] was young, her intelligence surpassed that of others. As for the matter of women's work, there was nothing that she was not able to do. She loved to read books, and she had a broad knowledge of history, both ancient and modern. Her father loved her more than his sons. He often asked her advice on affairs of state, and followed her ideas. He always sighed, "How I regret that you were not a boy!" . . . She loved literature but she did not compose flowery essays. She considered it vastly wrong for present-day women to pass around literary compositions, notes, and letters. The poetry that she composed in her life did not exceed two or three pieces, and none of it survives.[146]

The last point reflects the opinion of Ssu-ma Kuang that women should not concentrate on poetry and literature but should study historical and didactic texts.

These examples of Chu Hsi and Ch'eng I do not stand alone. Many authors whose works survive from the Sung also refer to women's literacy in funerary inscriptions. These writers include scholars of the Northern and Southern Sung dynasties who both were and were not associated with the Neo-Confucian school. None of them discriminates against poetry, often cited as a woman's forte. I cite only a few of many examples.

The Confucian Fan Tsu-yü (1041–1098) writes in an inscription:

> [Mme. Ts'ao] liked to read Confucian books, and she composed more than one hundred pieces of poetry in five and seven character metered verse. People recited them a lot. Her literary compositions were also ingenious. Her father used to say, "This girl should become the spouse of a worthy gentleman."[147]

He describes another woman saying, "By nature she enjoyed poetry and

143. Ibid., 91:14a–b.
144. Ibid., 92:29b.
145. Ibid., 93:28a.
146. *I-ch'uan wen-chi* 8:6a; parts of these passages are included in *Chin-ssu lu* 6:17, Chan, trans., *Things at Hand*, pp. 180–181.
147. *Fan t'ai-shih chi* 51:13a–b; the young woman eventually married into the imperial Chao clan.

literature, and she also liked to compose essays."[148] Another Northern Sung writer, Lu Tien (1042–1102), praises several women in similar terms: "She liked to read books, and she was good at composing poetry";[149] and, "she worked strenuously on reading books."[150]

A contemporary of Chu Hsi, Yang Wan-Li (1127–1206), gives the curriculum of a Mme. Liu, who "was taught the *Classic of Filial Piety*, the 'Rules for Domestic Life' [from the *Record of Rites*] and the *Biographies of Women* by Liu Hsiang. When she had finished reading them once, she could recite them, and people were surprised."[151] Another contemporary, Liu Tsai (1166–1239) elaborated on a similar course of study for a Mme. Hsiang but added a wide selection of T'ang and Sung poets:

> From the age of six, her elementary teacher taught her the "Rules for Domestic Life" [from *Record of Rites*], the *Precepts for Women* [by Pan Chao], and the *Biographies of Women* [by Liu Hsiang], as well as the poetry and essays of Han Yü, Liu Tsung-yüan, Ou-yang Hsiu, Su Shih and others.[152]

Thus, throughout Chinese history, there were literate wealthy women. In the six Dynasties period, women in both the North and the South were famous for their learning. This included expertise in Confucian texts as well as Buddhist and Taoist *sūtras*, and there is evidence that aristocratic men sought to marry learned women.[153] As noted above, in Yüan times, women were teaching boys to read, and the education of elite women extended to the study of texts.[154]

Criticisms of female literacy began in the late Ming, possibly in response to the increase in women's schooling. A fierce debate ensued over whether women should be literate and allowed into schools.[155] By Ch'ing times, the side of this debate represented by the maxim "only the virtuous man is talented, only the untalented (illiterate) woman is virtuous" had gained credence, and female literacy in scholarly families may thereafter have declined.[156] Nevertheless, it is wrong to attribute this attitude to Sung Neo-

---

148. Ibid., 50:6b.
149. Lu Tien, *T'ao-shan chi*, 36 chüan (Taipei: Commercial Press, 1979) 15:174.
150. Ibid., 15:175.
151. Yang Wan-li, *Ch'eng-chai chi*, 133 chüan (SPTK ed. Shanghai: Commercial Press, 1929) 132:6b.
152. Liu Tsai, *Man-t'ang wen-chi*, 36 chüan (Taipei: Commercial Press, 1979) 30:26a.
153. Beatrice Spade, "The Education of Women in China During the Southern Dynasties," *Journal of Asian History* 13, no. 1 (1979):15–41.
154. See note 129.
155. Handlin, "Lü K'un's New Audience," pp. 16, 29ff.
156. Ch'en Tung-yüan, *Chung-kuo fu-nü sheng-huo shih*, pp. 188–202; Yao, *Chinese Women*, p. 88. See also Ying-shih Yü, "The Rise of Confucian Intellectualism," *Tsing Hua Journal* n.s. 11, nos. 1–2 (December 1975):105–146, esp. 141 (I thank Ari Borrell for leading me to this article); Handlin, "Lü K'un's New Audience," pp. 29–38; and Rankin, "The Emergence of Women in China," pp. 40–43. There is very little evidence about female literacy rates at any time in Chinese history, and these scholars do not agree with each other.

Confucians. Although the educational process in the Sung was primarily oriented toward the male members of the family, book learning was not restricted to them. On the contrary, whenever family circumstances allowed, young women must have shared to some degree in the learning. Even though Chu Hsi emphasized "differentiation [of function] between men and women," with males active in the public world of other educated men, women could not have performed their own crucial function within the home had they not taken part in the higher culture the family system strove to maintain. Chu Hsi not only accepted this fact but also strongly affirmed it.

WOMEN AND BUDDHISM

The Sung dynasty is strongly associated with the Confucian revival that this volume discusses; yet Buddhism was widely practiced, and even staunch Confucians, like Wang An-shih, converted to Buddhism in their old age. Buddhism was especially popular among women of all classes. The "feminization" of Buddhism is represented by the extraordinary sex change of the principal god Kuan Yin—from male to female. She became Sung-tzu Kuan Yin, the Goddess of Mercy who bestowed sons, and the patron saint of women and childbirth.

The extent to which elite women practiced Buddhism is evident in Chu Hsi's funerary inscriptions. Chu Hsi was a bitter critic of Buddhism, and much has been made of his severe remarks in the *Classified Conversations* (*Yü-lei*), his commentaries, and in other texts. Nevertheless, his objections to Buddhist practice were confined to men and did not extend to women. Chu Hsi tolerated women practicing Buddhism, and he even praised them for their pious deeds. In the earlier discussion of literacy the books women read often included Buddhist *sūtra*s.

Chu Hsi not only praised women for their ability or inclination to read Buddhist books, but he also approved of transmitting such education to children, at least while they were in the womb. As quoted above, he had high praise for Mme. Yü, who studied Buddhist *sūtra*s while pregnant.[157] She presents an interesting departure from the original ideal of instruction in the womb (*t'ai-chiao*), practiced in the Confucian tradition.[158] In Chu Hsi's record, her death also reflected her religious conviction. When she was about to die, she saw her husband weeping over her, and she said to him: "Meeting and parting, life and death are [inevitable] like night and day. Why are you so distressed?"[159]

Chu Hsi praised women for their literacy and teaching of Buddhism, and

157. *Wen-chi* 91:14b.
158. Instruction in the womb (*t'ai-chiao*) was lauded in the opening passage of the *Elementary Learning (Hsiao-hsüeh*, p. 1) where Chu Hsi quoted from the *Lieh-nü chuan* by the Han Confucian Liu Hsiang. Liu Hsiang in turn is making reference to the *Analects* 10:8–9.
159. *Wen-chi* 91:14b.

he most of all approved of the ascetic practices their devotion generated. He admired the discipline of Buddhist monks and wished to emulate it in the Confucian academies, but in the case of women he specifically commended them for being Buddhist—approbation he would never have applied to men. Great Lady Ch'en was praised for managing the household affairs while her husband ignored the family, but when she was older Chu Hsi approved of her withdrawing from the family:

> In her later years, she liked Buddhism, and she understood the general points of it. Thereafter, she no longer tended to the affairs of the household. So with poor clothing and a meagre diet she passed over twenty years. She grieved over the sorrows of others and relieved their destitution and sickness. Even though she exhausted her strength, she did not tire [of helping others].
> ... Great Lady Ch'en, because of the illustriousness of her family line had bestowed on her the current title [of Great Lady]. The people of the community glorified her, but Great Lady Ch'en's [ascetic] attitude with which she managed herself was not any different from the days before.[160]

Chu Hsi praised her asceticism and concern for others, and he strongly implied that these derived from her practice of Buddhism.

In another example Chu Hsi described a woman's sudden Buddhist enlightenment:

> Later in life she studied Buddhism. Suddenly one morning, she appeared enlightened as though she had gained understanding in her heart. Thereupon, she cast aside her hair pins and ear ornaments, she rejected wine and meat, and she wore simple clothes and ate coarse vegetarian food until the end of her life.[161]

Later, this woman, Mme. Yü, was due to receive a noble title on the occasion of an imperial birthday. But she refused to let her sons present the civil authorities with a record of her deeds. She told them:

> I have already rejected the world of mortals. Why bother with this [title]? Moreover, if I were granted the title and did not acknowledge it, this would be deceiving the sovereign. How would I dare to be at ease?[162]

Her religious commitment then eased her death, as Chu Hsi relates:

> In the ninth year of *jen-yen* [1182] Mme. Yü was eighty years old. One day she said to her sons, "I am about to leave." Her sons were alarmed and agitated. They called in doctors and brought forth medicines. [But] she directed them all to leave and said, "Do not trouble yourselves over me." Thereupon she fell into a sweet sleep for six days, and died. It was the fifteenth day of the third month.[163]

160. Ibid., 93:25a.
161. Ibid., 92:14a.
162. Ibid.
163. Ibid.

Chu Hsi even hinted that Mme. Yü was better known for her accomplishments as a lay Buddhist than for her conduct as a Confucian. His words show that lay Buddhist practices closely resembled the ascetic values of Neo-Confucianism. Nevertheless, Chu Hsi wished to emphasize that women like Mme. Yü were more rightly to be praised as Confucians. At the end of the inscription, while idolizing Mme Yü as an outstanding model of Confucian virtue, he lamented: "But the world sometimes praises her for her Buddhist learning. Such words make light of her indeed!"[164]

In contrast to Chu Hsi's praise of Buddhist adherents among women in the home, he was opposed to women becoming nuns. It was acceptable for women to believe as long as they did not opt out of their social and sexual obligations. If women established families, served their parents-in-law, raised children, and thus fulfilled their duty to society in Chu Hsi's Confucian terms, then lay Buddhist ascetic practices were acceptable and even praiseworthy. But nuns, who had rejected family life, threatened the Confucian order, which placed the family at the center of social control. In the face of the Buddhist challenge to the family, Chu Hsi could tolerate no deviation from full participation in the family system. While he was an assistant magistrate of T'ung-an in Fukien between 1154 and 1157, he demonstrated his conviction by prohibiting women from becoming Taoist or Buddhist nuns. Furthermore, in 1190 as magistrate of Chang-chou, Fukien, he banned nunneries.[165]

His philosophy of women's crucial place in the society and family is revealed in the prohibition order that gave the reasons for the banning. In his order, Chu Hsi argued that women should be "matched up" or mated to men and that they belonged inside the home. Women had their lot (*fen*) in life just as men did, and theirs was to be married; only then could the Way of the ancient kings be carried out. He added that, if women and men did not marry, in a hundred years there would be no more people in the world.[166]

The extensive practice of Buddhism by married women in the Sung was tolerated by Chu Hsi and even encouraged. Indeed, the demands of lay practice overlapped considerably with those of religious Confucianism. But when Buddhist devotion disrupted the family or interfered with traditional Confucian values, it had to be stopped.

---

164. Ibid., 92:14b.

165. The banning order is printed in *Wen-chi* 100:4a–5a and is discussed in Wing-tsit Chan's biography of Chu Hsi, in *Sung Biographies*, ed. Herbert Franke (Wiesbaden: Franz Steiner Verlag GMBH, 1976), pp. 282, 287. It is interesting to speculate whether there may have been a shortage of wives in the area, for female infanticide is thought by some scholars to have been widespread in Fukien at that time; see Yao, *Chinese Women*, p. 92.

166. *Wen-chi* 100:4b.

CONCLUSION

In twelfth-century China, it was universally believed that women were born with human qualities different from those of men. Writers of all persuasions, Chu Hsi among them, concluded that women should be subservient to men and that wives should obey husbands. Chu Hsi was no exception, for his ideology of female subordination reiterated the ancient Confucian doctrine that prescribed a woman's function and place in society.

In its ideal form, as seen in texts like the *Elementary Learning*, this doctrine was severe. It reinforced the principle of the "differentiation between men and women," including both a distinction of function and a spatial separation between the sexes. Women were to stay inside the home and occupy themselves with the domestic sphere while men concerned themselves with the world outside. Women had to serve their husbands' parents unfailingly and obey their husbands absolutely. They learned to conduct the sacrifices to their husbands' ancestors and to keep harmony within the extended family. The texts dictated that when her husband died a woman was to stay loyal to him and his clan by never remarrying, no matter what her age. These virtues reflected the Neo-Confucian emphasis on preserving the ritual patriline or *tsung*. The prescriptive texts illustrated these principles with stories of women's self-sacrifice, hardship, and even death.

These texts, used for primary education, were meant to posit an ideal. They presented the highest goal to which one aspired—the virtue of a sage. But at the same time, Chu Hsi understood that "one cannot always practice this [ideal] absolutely."[167] He accepted the need for a certain graded application of these ideals in daily life. His funerary inscriptions for women revealed his interpretation of such practical accommodation as it applied to the lives of actual Sung women.

In these short biographies, Chu Hsi sanctioned a wide range of behavior and responsibility for women. A woman's obedience to her husband could include gentle remonstrance. Her household duties went well beyond "woman's work" of cooking and sewing to encompass supervising servants, arranging marriages, and managing land transactions. If she were widowed, a woman might be responsible for the overall support of an extended family.

Chu Hsi also assigned women the task of providing primary education to children. Mothers had to give their children a correct moral foundation and teach them Confucian decorum. Moreover, many women taught their children to read and recite Confucian classics. As Chu Hsi and others indicate, these women of the elite class must have been literate. Chu Hsi never stated that literacy was imperative for women as for men, nor did he provide any detailed curriculum for women's schooling at home; however, he commended women for their book learning, and he endorsed its benefits to their

167. *Chu-tzu yü-lei* 96:11a, p. 3928; Chan, trans., *Things at Hand*, p. 179; see note 66.

children. Furthermore, he gave mothers credit for the literary success of their sons.

Women had a crucial function to fulfill within the home. According to Chu Hsi, the Way of Heaven was close at hand to be practiced in every activity, no matter how routine or insignificant. Within the domain of the home, women had to be educated to shoulder their responsibilities and carry out the Confucian Way. They provided an integral link in the preservation and transmission of Confucian culture. Chu Hsi praised women for their independent initiative in this regard and for their ability to make decisions, even as he admonished them to be obedient. He could not tolerate women who abandoned their duty to the family and society; thus, he opposed women becoming nuns. However, Buddhist lay practice was accepted and even commended if it did not interfere with Confucian obligations. A woman's function complemented that of a man, and without a woman in the home a harmonious principled order could not be realized. The object of Neo-Confucian education for women was to teach them their role and their duties in a moral society and prepare them to teach these duties to others.

Chu Hsi assigned to women a new moral imperative just as he did to men. Chu Hsi's ideal virtues for women did not differ from those of classical Confucianism, but a woman's conduct within the home was given greater significance by Chu Hsi. Later followers saw this and turned their attention to the curriculum of women's education that Chu Hsi had not specified in detail. At the same time, the ideal of feminine behavior that was posited in the prescriptive texts was emphasized more and more to women. It is possible that, as with men's education, the later orthodoxy for female conduct that grew out of this ideal lost some of the voluntarism and accommodation that Chu Hsi applied in his own time.

APPENDIX: FUNERARY INSCRIPTIONS FOR WOMEN WRITTEN BY CHU HSI

Burial Inscription for
Daughter Named Ssu (Chu Hsi's daughter) [168]

Daughter of the Chu's
You were born on the day *kuei-ssu.*
From this your name was taken
And you were styled Shu [second child]. [169]
Your father was myself Hui-weng [Chu Hsi]
Your mother was Miss Liu.

---

168. *Wen-chi* 93:1a. This inscription contains only the verse section (*ming*) of a usual funerary inscription, i.e., it has no prose introduction (*chih*). It is written entirely in three character phrases, giving it a touching, childish effect. I have translated it into verse to preserve some of this quality.

169. Her given name (*ming*) is Ssu, and her style name (*tzu*) is Shu (second child).

When you were four years old
You wailed the loss of your mother.
When you were fifteen,
You received the hairpin and the earring.
You were betrothed to the Chao's
But suddenly you died.
Alas! You were born
Complaisant and wise.
Though you were unschooled
You understood my ideas
Your words on the brink of death
Were of filial piety and sibling affection.
You were buried with your mother
According to your own wish.
I, your father, write this epitaph.
Your mother watches over you.
If you have consciousness,
    you will not be afraid.
In the Sung, the reign of *Ch'un-hsi*,
In the year of *ting-wei* [1187],
In the eleventh lunar month,
On the day of *jen-yen*
I made this record.

Tomb Inscription for Miss Chu, Wife of Mister Chu, Vice Minister of Personnel (Chu Hsi's mother)[170]

My deceased mother, the honorable Miss Chu, was from She county in Hui prefecture [Anhui province]. Her ancestors were of a great clan in that prefecture. Her father was named Ch'üeh. He was the first in his family to be a scholar by profession, and he had a high standard of conduct. He married Miss Yü of the same commandery, and in the third year of *Yüan-fu* [A.D. 1100], in the eleventh month, on the day *keng-wu*, she gave birth to my mother.

My mother's nature was humane, generous, proper and virtuous. When she was eighteen years old she was married to my late father. His name was Sung, his courtesy name was Ch'iao-nien, and his surname was Chu. At that time she served her father and mother-in-law with filiality and respect, and she was diligent to the point that she was able to do things that other people would find difficult.

Because my father was a collator at the Imperial library, she was bestowed with the title of Ju-jen. When my father died, I, Chu Hsi, was only fourteen years old. My mother toiled to take care of me and to teach me so that I was able to know what direction to take. Unfortunately, when I grew

170. *Wen-chi* 94:25b.

up I was stupid, and I did not meet the requirements for government appointment. We lived in poverty and sickness in acute distress that no one would be able to endure. But my mother managed it all happily.

She died on the day *wu-wu*, in the ninth month of the fifth year of *Ch'ien-tao* (1169). She was seventy years old.

She had three sons. The oldest and middle son both died young. I, Chu Hsi, was her youngest. I held the classification title of Left *Ti-kung-lang* [Rank 9b] with a commission as compiler in the Bureau of Military Affairs. She had one daughter who married Liu Tzu-hsiang, the registrar of Ch'ang-t'ing county [in Fukien] with the classification title of Right *Ti-kung-lang* [Rank 9b]. She had three grandsons, Shu, Yeh and Tsai, and two grand-daughters, Sun and Tui. They are all young.

In the next year in the first month, on the day of *kuei-yu*, she was buried in Chien-ning prefecture, Chien-yang county [in Fukien], on the North side of T'ien-hu lake, a distance of one hundred *li* to the northeast away from my father's grave near white water cliff.

I, the unfilial son, Hsi, wail my longing for her and weep over my separation from her. I have ventured to record on her tomb stone like this the vastness of her love. Alas! How painful it is!

Funerary Inscription of the Wife of Mr. P'an[171]

P'an Yu-kung, of Chin-hua county [in Chekiang] newly appointed Sheriff of Hai-men, sent me this letter:

When I, Yu-kung, was young, I took to wife Madame Wang of Ku-shu [in Honan]. It has now been fifteen years [since that time].

Together with her I followed my father and went to the commandery of Nan-hai [in Kuangtung], but unfortunately, she fell ill and died. My two parents wept for her, and grieved for a long time. I, Yu-kung, also could not control my grief.

When Lady Wang resided at home, she served her parents and was filial to them; her parents loved her. When she was nineteen years old she got married, and she transferred her filial service to her father- and mother-in-law. Her father- and mother-in-law also loved her.

When she lived among her sisters-in-law, both older and younger, she was reverential and never spoke words of blame. She treated the servants generously but with discipline. In her conduct she was modest, serious, frugal and sincere. With regard to women's work, she was not the least bit remiss, but she did not practice wasteful extravagance on fancy ribbons and embroidery. Therefore, she did not dislike humble circumstances, and she was at peace with impoverishment that other people would find difficult [to live with].

She liked to read the *Analects*, the *Great Learning*, the *Doctrine of the Mean*, and

---

171. *Wen-chi* 92:29b. P'an Yu-kung (*tzu* Kung-shu) was a student of Chu Hsi along with his brother Yu-tuan. Moreover, his father, P'an Chih (1126–1189), was a close associate of Chu Hsi for whom Chu Hsi wrote a long funerary inscription; see *Wen-chi* 94:1a.

Mencius, and she understood the general meaning. She often said to people, 'I examine myself all day long. In my service to those above and my treatment of those below, if I am blessed to find no errors, only then will I let myself withdraw and rest. But I feel only a little satisfied that I have [fulfilled] this intention, and every day I renew [my efforts] and there is no end.'

She died on a certain day of a certain month in the year *ping-wu* of the reign period *Ch'un-hsi*, [1186], when she was only thirty-three years old. Now, we are about to take her coffin back to bury it at Mt. Hsü in Shang-yü county of Hui-ji circuit [in Chekiang]. I hope that you Sir will feel grief for her and write a funerary inscription for her, for then it will suffice to comfort me a little.

Madame Wang's great grandfather was Wang Sheng, titled *Kuang-lu ta-fu* [Rank 2b]; her grandfather was Ling-chu, titled *Ch'ao-i ta-fu* [Rank 6a]; her father was Wang Tsung, titled Feng-i lang [Rank 8a]. Her mother was Madame P'an.

When Madame Wang married me, Yu-kung, she bore a son named Lü-sun. By means of a memorial from my father, he was given the title of *Chiang-shih-lang*. He is now thirteen years old.

I [Chu Hsi] had occasion in the past to be associated with Yu-kung's venerable father, the gentleman of Hunan, and I saw that the way he applied himself to office resulted in good government. Yu-kung and his brother both came to study with me, and I saw that the way they cultivated themselves was strict. Lü-sun, at the age of seven, was in attendance at the side of his grandfather, and I saw that he looked and listened with undivided attention and he advanced and withdrew in an appropriate manner.

Today, I read Yu-kung's letter and use it to substantiate the fact that we know his wife's worthiness cannot be doubted. Because of this I underscore his words and write an epitaph for her.

Funerary Tablet Inscription for Madame Hsü[172]

Madame Hsü's ancestors were the descendants of T'ai Yüeh [a minister of Emperor Yao (r. 2356–2254 B.C.)]. During the Three Dynasties they were of the Chiang surname,[173] and their feudal state was between that of Ch'en and Cheng. Those of their later descendants who lived in Kao-yang [in Shantung] were a prominent clan. In middle antiquity they moved to Tan-yang [in Anhui] and again moved to Yung-chia [in Chekiang]. In the T'ang Sung period, there was an ancestor named Hsü Ling-kuei who held office in the eastern Yangtze area and who was an academician in the Imperial Library.[174] He was demoted to administrator of Shan-yang, where he lived in exile in Chien-chou prefecture, Kuan-li garrison [in Fukien]. As a result, the

172. Ibid., 92:18a.

173. It states in the *Records of the Historian* of Ssu-ma Ch'ien that the descendants of Minister T'ai Yüeh were of the Chiang surname; *Shih-chi*, 130 chüan (Beijing: Chung-hua shu-chü, 1982), vol. 5, *chüan* 6, "Shih-chia," p. 1577. Chu Hsi is thus making reference to the *Shih-chi*.

174. It is clear from the context and other passages that he was an official in the capital of the Southern T'ang (Nan T'ang) dynasty (A.D. 937–975) in the Five Dynasties period.

family settled in the place called Wu-t'ung village. Today, Kuan-li has become Cheng-ho county, and the Hsü's of Wu-t'ung have especially flourished. Those of them who have scattered in the four directions without a doubt comprise over a hundred branch families. Moreover, even today, the geneology of the T'ien-yu and Pao-ta[175] reign periods has been handed down from generation to generation, and the line of descent can still be verified.

Madame Hsü's father was named Tieh. He married Miss Ch'iu of the same commandery. Miss Ch'iu was also from a scholar household and an eminent clan. Therefore, when Madame Hsü was born she was modest and virtuous. Her ability to handle silk and hemp and to stitch fine threads surpassed that of others. When she was nineteen years old, she married a gentleman of the district named Mr. Huang Ch'ao-tso. She was married for eight years when she died. She gave birth to a daughter but lost her. She gave birth again to a son named Shih. He was only two years old when Madame Hsü fell ill. Thinking that she was about to die, she indicated that her son should belong to her mother-in-law, saying "Your daughter-in-law is about to die. I would like to take this son and entrust him to you. When you teach him, you must be strict. Do not think that because he has no mother you should be generous with your kindness. If by good fortune he is able to become established, it will be as though your daughter-in-law did not die." In the end, Shih grew up and studied at the Imperial University. He gained a fine reputation, subsequently passed the *chin-shih* examination in the first class, and returned home. Within and without the family, the older people only then began to recount to each other Miss Hsü's dying words, and they sighed at how far sighted her understanding had been.

At the beginning, Madame Hsü was buried on the east side of Wu Mountain. But there were civil disturbances, and the tomb could not be protected. Thus, her remains were moved to a certain hamlet of a certain district in the neighborhood of the Yen-fu Buddhist monastery.

Madame Hsü's son taught at the school of a certain prefecture and then also taught at the *Tun-tsung yuan*[176] school in Shang-wu, Shao-hsing county [in Chekiang]. When he was of a certain age, because of a serious illness, he retired from government service. He was specially promoted from *Ts'ung-cheng lang* [Rank 8b] to *T'ung-chih lang* [Rank 6b], and he was bestowed [by the emperor] with the purple silk clothes and silver fish ornament to return to his home town.

One day, I visited him in his illness. Even though he had wasted away, his spirit had not declined. He brought out a document that had been written by the former professor in O prefecture, Mr. Wu Chün-te, that described the

175. Pao-ta was a Southern T'ang reign period (A.D. 943–957). T'ien-yu has several possibilities, the most likely being a reign period of the state of Wu, in the Five Dynasties era (A.D. 904–919). It could also refer to the T'ang reign period (A.D. 904–907).

176. This school is mentioned in other biographical sources for her son Huang Shih (1110–1175). See Ch'ang Pi-te, Wang Te-i et al., *Sung-jen chuan-chi tzu-liao so-yin* (Taipei: Ting-wen shu-chü, 1977), p. 2837.

geneology and life events of Madame Hsü. He said to me in tears, "Unfortunately, in my life, I, Shih, was not able to know my mother, and there has been no way for me to resolve my life long sorrow. Still, I hope that my conduct will not disgrace her and I will be able to manifest my mother's [goodness] without end. Today, my illness is such that I fear I will not be able to fulfill my determination. Moreover, even the tablet with her funerary inscription has not yet been set up. You sir, have reason to pity me. . . ." Before he could finish his words, he was again overcome with sorrow, and sobbing, many tears streamed down. I was also so grief-stricken that I could not look up. I quickly promised to undertake the writing, and left. I could not bear to provide nothing to comfort his [aching] heart. Thus I wrote this introduction to the inscription, and the inscription says:

> Madame Hsü's family came from Kao-yang.
> Their geneology survived past the T'ang.
> Looking at death, she was not afraid and her voice rattled,
> "Teach my son without love and afterwards he'll prosper."
> How worthy! How filial! For years he never forgot.
> I underscore her deeds and venerate this hillside plot.

Funerary Inscription for Great Lady Ch'en[177]

Great Lady Ch'en was from Chien-yang county, San-kuei hamlet [in Fukien]. Her father was Ch'en An-shih, a superior scholar of broad learning. He founded a charitable school in the south part of the county seat, and those who followed and studied with him were very numerous. He married Miss Ho, and she bore Great Lady Ch'en. When Great Lady Ch'en was seventeen she married Mr. Chou of the same hamlet. Mr. Chou's conduct was genial and easygoing, and he did not engage himself with matters of the family or property in his conduct of affairs. Great Lady Ch'en assisted him with diligence and earnestness, and [herself] managed the family affairs frugally and methodically. She instructed her children very strictly. When it came to her treatment of her relatives and her behavior toward the neighbors in her village, she always had kind intentions.

When she was young, she lost her parents, and she was unremitting in her grief and longing. When she was married, she also did not get to meet her father and mother-in-law [before they died]. But every year, she performed the winter sacrifices to them. She had to conduct the rites with her own hands, and when they were over she would always sob and weep for them.

In her later years, she liked Buddhism, and she understood the general points of it. Thereafter, she no longer tended to the affairs of the household. So with poor clothing and a meager diet she passed over twenty years. She grieved over the sorrows of others and relieved their destitution and sickness. Even though she exhausted her strength, she did not tire [of helping others].

177. *Wen-chi* 93:25a.

Her middle son obtained the *chin-shih* degree and rose to be a high official. He twice met with imperial favor. Mr. Chou [her husband] was therefore able to receive the title of *Ch'eng-feng lang* [Rank 8b] and retired from official life. Afterwards Great Lady Ch'en, because of the illustriousness of her family line had bestowed on her the current title [of Great Lady]. The people of the community glorified her, but Great Lady Ch'en's [ascetic] attitude with which she managed herself was not any different from the days before.

On a certain day of the third month of the third year of *Chao-hsi* [1190] she died of sickness at home. At the time of her death, her mind was clear and bright and not disorderly, and she had enjoyed sixty-eight years of life. Mr. Chou, whose private name was I, and whose style name was Chao-chia, had died five years earlier. He was posthumously promoted to *T'ung-chih lang* [Rank 6b]. Her three male children were Ming-tso, Ming-chung, and Ming-tso. Ming-chung obtained the title of *Ch'eng-i lang* [Rank 7b] with a commission as the administrator of Kuang-tse county in Shao-wu military prefecture. In his studies and his managing of affairs he was skillful and diligent and surpassed others beyond measure. She had five daughters. Her sons-in-law were: Ch'en Tun, Hsiao Ssu-chi, Ch'eng Pi-hsien, and Ch'en Liu. Her youngest daughter is not yet married. She has two grandsons, Sun-heng and Chen-heng, and three granddaughters who are all still young.

In the next year on a certain day of a certain month, her various sons buried Great Lady Ch'en in the western part of the county on the south side of T'ien-hu mountain in the Hsin mountain range. To the East only a few hundred steps was the tomb of Mr. Chou on Kuang-p'ing mountain.

Ming-chung [her son] came to me, asking me to write a funerary inscription. Since he is a friend of mine, I could not refuse. The inscription says:

The worthiness of the mother was enough to perfect her son.
The worthiness of the son is enough to bring prominence to the parents.
The luxuriant foliage of the Western mountain range renews itself for countless
    generations.
I write about it to foretell the future of Great Lady Ch'en's descendants.

PART FOUR

Neo-Confucian Education Beyond the Family

The Community Compact (*Hsiang-yüeh*) of the Sung and Its Educational Significance

Monika Übelhör

In his commentary on the *I-ching* line, "A gelded boar's teeth—good fortune," the eminent Sung Confucian Ch'eng I (1033–1107) explained:

As the boar is an unyielding and easily provoked animal, his teeth cut savagely sharp. If one tries to control his teeth by force one will have to work hard and still not be able to stop his ferocity. Even if one were to bind him in his ferocity, this still would not make him change. But if, by gelding him, one takes away his strength, although his teeth remain, his fierceness will stop of its own. . . . The superior man follows the principle of taking away the force behind the boar's teeth. He knows that the evil of the world cannot be suppressed by force. Therefore he examines its activating force, gets hold of its essential element, and stops up its source. Consequently, although he does not rely on the severity of punishment, the evil will stop of itself. This can be compared to stopping robbery. People have hearts full of desires. If one does not understand how to instruct them and they are pressed by hunger and cold, even if punishments and executions should be administered daily, how could this overcome the millions of hearts bent on gain! The sage, however, knows the ways to stop those desires. He does not think highly of intimidation and punishment, but promotes governmental measures and education [*cheng-chiao*]. He induces the people to embrace agriculture and sericulture and to understand the principles of integrity and shame. Then even if you rewarded them for it, they would not steal.[1]

By this approach, says Ch'eng I in the opening passage of his commentary, the sage exerts no effort, and yet the empire is governed.[2] Chu Hsi included this passage in the chapter on "The Principles of Governing the

---

1. *Ch'eng I-ch'uan I chuan* (SPPY ed.) 2:41a–b.
2. See Wing-tsit Chan, *Reflections on Things at Hand, The Neo-Confucian Anthology Compiled by Chu Hsi and Lü Tsu-ch'ien*, (New York: Columbia University Press, 1967), p. 208. Ch'eng I's text is quoted there in a slightly abridged version.

State and Bringing Peace to the World" in the *Chin-ssu-lu*, his summation of Sung learning. This text forcefully reminds us that the Confucian notion of education has a twofold purpose: first, as the transmission of a body of learning aimed at cultivating moral insight in those who would qualify for social leadership, it served to train an elite; and second, it served as an appropriate device to make the populace behave in a way deemed necessary to arrive at a well-ordered society.

The community compacts (*hsiang-yüeh*)—locally organized associations aiming at mutual encouragement to practice socially desirable behavior—are seen as such attempts to influence the general populace. These compacts began to appear in Northern Sung times, and from then until the time of the Republic the formation of such associations was encouraged at intervals by Confucians concerned with upholding the tenet that education at large forms an integral part of good government and that social order is brought about not by laws and regulations but by educational means.[3]

The first known *hsiang-yüeh* is the "Lu Family Community Compact" (*Lü-shih hsiang-yüeh*).[4] It was installed in Lan-t'ien (Shensi) in 1077 by Lü Ta-chün (1031–1082), member of a family of both local and national prominence.[5] This covenant became famous in Chu Hsi's version, the *Tseng-sun Lü-shih hsiang-yüeh* (Lü family community compact, with additions

3. For an attempt at reviving the community compacts in Republican days, see Guy Alitto, *The Last Confucian, Liang Shu-ming and the Chinese Dilemma of Modernity* (Berkeley: University of California Press, 1979), pp. 42, 207.

4. The Lü compact is partly—under the heading of "Community precepts of the Lü family"—translated in John Meskill, *Academies in Ming China* (Tuscon: University of Arizona Press 1982), pp. 164–166. The earliest edition of the Lü compact I could find is that in the *Lan-t'ien hsien-chih* of 1571, 1:22b–27b. It also carries a postscript by Chu Hsi included in *Ching-chia ting-pen Sui-an hsü-shih ts'ung-shu hsü-pien*, from which I quote, (hereafter cited LSHY) *The Sung-Yüan hsüeh-an*, (reprint; Taipei: Shih-chieh shu-chü, 1963) 31:630–633, mistakenly cites Injunctions 1 to 4 of Chu Hsi's version as the text of the LSHY, an error that probably stems from the fact that, without access to the Lü version, Chu Hsi's remark on his treatment of the text might be taken to mean that he took over Injunctions 1 to 4 verbatim from Lü's text, adding only the prescriptions concerning the monthly meetings of the compact, cf. *Hui-an hsien-sheng Chu Wen-kung wen-chi* (SPPY ed.) 74:28b (hereafter cited CWKWC). This mistaken attribution often has been repeated. Thus, in the appendix to Wada Sei, *Shina chihō jichi hattatsushi* (Tokyo, 1939), pp. 224–226, is an abridged version of Chu Hsi's text under the heading of "The Community Compact System of Lü Ta-lin." Ta-lin was Lü Ta-chün's younger brother, to whom the authorship of the LSHY has sometimes been ascribed. Wada's blending of the two texts was a consequential oversight, because several modern scholars after him based their evaluations on the materials Wada presented in his book.

5. Lü Ta-chün, *chin-shih* of 1057, after short service as an official, retired to his native place to enact the ideas of his teacher Chang Tsai. The authorship of Lü's compact has frequently been ascribed to Lü Ta-fang (1027–1097), Lü Ta-chün's prominent elder brother who from 1088 to 1094 served as prime minister, or to his eldest brother Lü Ta-chung. As Chu Hsi pointed out in a postscript to the Lü compact and to extracts of correspondence connected with it, this is an error; cf. LSHY 14a–b. The biographies of the three brothers, as well as of their brother Lü Ta-lin, a renowned Confucian scholar and to whom the compact is sometimes ascribed, are

and deletions by Chu Hsi). In this piece Chu Hsi included the full text of the Lü compact, with only a few changes, but he added regulations that doubled the length of the original version and also somewhat changed the character of the compact. Thus, the two versions represent two different approaches. To make this clear, I shall present the two texts separately.

The Lü compact was designed as a voluntary association of unspecified members of a local community, presumably the size of a village (*li*).[6] It centered on four types of injunctions: the first two concerned proper personal conduct; the second two consisted of provisions for the exchange of gifts on the occasion of marriages and funerals and provisions for mutual help in times of need.

Desirable behavior, specified in the injunctions in some detail, was to be furthered by publicly acknowledging laudable acts, exposing infractions and, if necessary, fining those who violated the terms of the agreement. Praise and blame were to be administered during monthly assemblies of the compact members and recorded in respective registers.[7]

The assembly also was to elect one or two orderly, upright, and incorruptible persons to act as heads of the compact who would be responsible for conducting a fair discussion about appropriate rewards or punishments. In addition, one person from among the compact members was to take care of current affairs in monthly terms.[8]

The four general injunctions are:

1. Admonish each other to virtuous behavior and the undertaking of virtuous activities.
2. Correct each other's wrong actions.
3. Associate with one another according to the rules of decorum and customs (*li su*).
4. Offer assistance to each other in cases of illness and calamities.

In Injunction No. 1, "Admonish each other to virtuous behavior and the undertaking of virtuous activities,"[9] virtue is defined in stereotypical Confucian wording, that is, the ability to regulate oneself and one's family,

found in T'o T'o, *Sung-shih*, (Peking: Chung-hua shu-chü, 1976) 340:10839–10868. The Lü brothers also found an entry in the *I-lo yüan-yüan lu* (TSCC ed.) 8:629–638, the *Sung-Yüan hsüeh-an* 31:629–638, and the *Sung-Yüan hsüeh-an pu-i* (Taipei: Shih-chieh shu-chü, 1962) 31:1b–20b, 35b. Biographies of Lü Ta-fang and Lü Ta-lin are included in Herbert Franke, ed., *Sung Biographies* (Wiesbaden: Franz Steiner, 1976), pp. 735–741.

6. Lü Ta-chün, in his postface to the LSHY (p. 8b), writes that he is offering the text to all the noble-minded (*chün-tzu*) of his native community (*wu li*). Therefore, we may surmise that *hsiang* in the context of the LSHY is not to be understood as pointing to the administrative unit *hsiang* that in Sung times comprised more than 500 households. Cf. Brian McKnight, *Village and Bureaucracy in Southern Sung China* (Chicago: University of Chicago Press, 1971), p. 75.

7. LSHY, pp. 7a–b.
8. LSHY, p. 8a.
9. LSHY, pp. 1a–2a.

including one's servants, to serve one's elders and instruct one's sons and younger brothers, to live in harmony with relatives and friends, and to understand the need for selecting good company. But virtue is also said to mean the capability to generously extend charity, to help in cases of need, to take over responsibilities, to accomplish something for the good of the whole community, and to settle disputes—all general social virtues.

Worthy activities, the second component of this injunction, included the practical enactment of the enumerated virtues. In addition, scholarly pursuits, keeping one's fields in order, managing the family property, and engaging in charitable enterprises as well as devotion to the "six arts"[10] also count as worthy activities.

In Injunction No. 2, "correct each other's wrong actions,"[11] wrong behavior is classified in three categories: (1) acts contrary to good conduct (fan-i); (2) offenses violating the community covenant; and (3) violations of the task to perfect oneself morally. The first group encompasses transgressions such as getting drunk, gambling for money, quarreling to the extent of engaging in physical combat or using abusive language, instigating lawsuits, denouncing others, transgressing the rules of decorum, disregarding the laws, being rude to old and worthy persons, pointing to other person's shortcomings, not correcting one's own shortcomings upon being made aware of them, giving insincere advice, betraying agreements, misleading others by spreading rumors, gossiping about the former misdeeds of others, talking about other people's private affairs and blunders, and slandering others by all kinds of means including anonymous writings and satirical poems. Cheating and egoistically working for one's own profit in commercial transactions also fall in this group.

The second group of offences mentions in a general way negligence of the task to admonish, to correct, and to help each other, whereas the third group again is quite specific in enumerating wrongful acts, such as: not selecting the right persons as friends, idly roaming about, making fun of people, more specifically teasing others with the intent to insult, galloping on horseback,[12] playing polo without regard for damaging other people's property, not keeping clean, being rash and boorish in one's actions, being irreverent, speaking when one ought not to speak and saying nothing when one ought to speak, dressing stylishly or not dressing correctly. Not discharging one's tasks faithfully, in one's lifestyle not taking into account the financial situation of one's family, and not being able to put up with poor circum-

---

10. I.e., decorum, music, archery, charioteering, calligraphy, mathematics.

11. LSHY, pp. 2a–3b.

12. Causing harm by galloping recklessly seems to have been a recurrent occasion for rifts in a community. During his service as a local official, Chu Hsi had to deal with a fatality brought about by the son of an official who, riding his horse, had killed the child of a commoner. Differing from his colleagues, who pleaded for sparing the son of the official, Chu Hsi did not allow lenient treatment of the offender; cf. *Chu-tzu yü-lei* (reprint, Taipei: Cheng-chung shu-chü, 1962) 106:2b.

stances but pursuing financial gain by improper means also fall into this group. The last admonition has a positive counterpart in Injunction No. 4's stipulation that if a member, although living in dire poverty, is content with his lot, the covenant members should provide him with a loan that would enable him to establish a means of livelihood out of which he would be able to repay the loan on a monthly or yearly basis.[13]

Injunction No. 3, "Associate with one another according to the rules of decorum (*li*) and customs (*su*)"[14] regulates how to behave toward a compact member whose family celebrates a marriage or mourns a deceased. If letters are to be sent on these occasions the community members are to discuss it and decide on one model all will use. Also, a sliding scale is envisaged for contributions, taking into account the different economic situations of the various members, as well as the different degrees of intimacy with the family in question. Those who can not afford to give money are told to help out with utensils or able-bodied assistance.

Injunction No. 4, "Offer assistance to each other in cases of illness and calamities,"[15] not only covers such things as help in case of fire, danger of flood, danger of robbers, illness, and death, but it also provides for cases in which a member is brought to court because of wrong accusations. It is stated that, if a compact member is wrongly sued, the association should see to it that in the trial the real facts are brought to light,[16] and, if this proves impossible (admitting that this could happen), the compact should help the family of anyone wrongly indicted. Also, the compact should appoint trustees for orphans and arrange their marriages. In case the orphans are well-to-do, they should take care of their property until they are grown up; in case they are poor, the covenant should see to it that they are not cheated out of their dwelling places. This injunction also contains the provision mentioned above that the members of the compact should assist the honest poor by making a loan with which they might establish a better means of living.

All in all, the most salient feature of the Lü covenant is a very practical concern to ease the social, emotional, and economic stresses in a given community. Lü Ta-chün's community compact aimed at the promotion of very down-to-earth virtues that could bring about a harmonious community life based on mutual interdependence and a feeling of solidarity.

To sum up, the Lü covenant offers a vision of a community wherein people behave well in the sense that they dress properly, do not indulge in drinking and gambling, and do not create hatred or resentment by gossip or worse

---

13. LSHY, p. 6a.

14. LSHY, pp. 3b–5b.

15. LSHY, pp. 5b–6b.

16. For an illustration of how important such support could be, see Miyazaki Ichisada, "The Administration of Justice During the Sung Dynasty," in Jerome Cohen et al., eds., *Essays on Chinese Legal Tradition* (Princeton: Princeton University Press, 1980), p. 74 n. 31.

forms of personal attack. More important, it is a community in which the trustworthy shouldering of public responsibilities is encouraged, abuse of powerful position is castigated, and the danger of dire impoverishment—be it from illness, natural catastrophe, lawsuits, or suffering from the abuse of social position and privileges by others—is reduced. In terms of ideology the compact is based on the Confucian respect for both seniority and care and consideration for either those in hierarchically lower positions or those lacking the support of their immediate family. Less in tune with Confucian thinking is the occasional threat of recourse to the Legalist means of meting out punishment and reward. But this was a phenomenon often encountered when Confucian principles were adapted to everyday life. In the early Sung it was an acknowledged fact. Thus, Lü Ta-chün's contemporary, the famous statesman Ou-yang Hsiu, did not hesitate to assert that in the conduct of governmental affairs the Confucian and the Legalist approach often complemented each other.[17]

Turning to Chu Hsi's version of the community compact,[18] one finds he introduced some alterations of solely an editorial nature. However, Chu Hsi also changed some provisions of the Lü text, and in two places he added long sections. Thus, whereas in the Lü text Injunction No. 3, "Associate with one another according to the rules of decorum and customs," the only concern is with the conventions to be followed in cases of felicitous and infelicitous events in family life, in Chu's version the following three items are added: (1) observance of rank and seniority; (2) occasions for visiting and modes of salutation; and (3) formal social gatherings, and the welcoming and bidding of farewell on the occasion of long journeys.

In the first paragraph of his amendments Chu Hsi provides a minutely elaborated system to structure the compact members according to five age groups:

> the venerated [*tsun-che*]—those thirty years or more older than oneself and of the age group of one's father,
> the senior [*chang-che*]—those ten years or more older and in the age group of one's elder brothers,
> the peers [*ti-che*]—those less than ten years older or younger than oneself,
> the junior [*shao-che*]—those ten years or more younger, and
> the young [*yu-che*]—those were twenty and more years younger than oneself.

Moreover, the peer group was to be subdivided into those who were somewhat older [*shao-chang*] and those who were somewhat younger [*shao-yu*].[19]

The next two paragraphs of Chu Hsi's amendments to Injunction No. 3 of the Lü compact hold detailed prescriptions concerning the way one should

---

17. Cf. James T. C. Liu, *Ou-yang Hsiu: An Eleventh Century Neo-Confucianist* (Stanford: Stanford University Press, 1967), p. 129.

18. Chu Hsi's version of the community compact is found in CWKWC 74:23a–29b.

19. CWKWC 74:25a. The footnote to this paragraph says that one text puts the age difference of those to be venerated at twenty years older than oneself.

greet a fellow compact member in the street, at what times of the year one should make calls on fellow compact members, how to invite them, how to conduct banquets, what dress to wear, what name cards to use, at which place to descend and alight from a horse when paying a visit, and so on. These prescriptions, based on the Classics of ritual,[20] are written out in full detail for all thinkable variations; the prescriptions for salutation and behavior change according to the age differences among those who meet and visit.

The second substantial addition appears at the end of the whole text, where Chu Hsi has appended another long paragraph with regulations for the monthly meetings of the compact. In the Lü text the regulation for the monthly compact meetings had read as follows:

> Every month there shall be a meeting, where a meal is provided. Once every three months there shall be a gathering where wine and a meal is served. The person in charge [each month] shall be responsible for raising the money to cover the expenses. At these meetings the good and bad deeds shall be entered in the registers and rewards and punishments shall be administered. Any difficulty troubling the covenant should be remedied after a general discussion (kung-i).[21]

Chu, in his regulations for the monthly meetings, elaborates, in the same minute detail as in his amendments to Injunction No. 3, the order in which the various age groups should enter the assembly hall, how they are to proceed once inside, where they have to take up their positions, who should greet whom with what kind of bow, in which way the greeting is to be answered, and so forth.

Moreover, according to Chu Hsi's text, these monthly meetings not only serve for administering praise and blame or punishment, but there is also the provision that, after the communal meal, the members are to reconvene and spend the afternoon listening to story telling (shuo-shu), practicing archery, or holding leisurely discussions on a limited set of topics, political matters being excluded. Lü's provision that the monthly assemblies should also deal with any problems troubling the compact is dropped in Chu Hsi's version.[22]

Chu Hsi did not eliminate the very down-to-earth paragraphs of Lü Ta-chün's text. In fact, he added the item "to pay one's taxes" to the enumeration of praiseworthy activities in Injunction No. 1, thus touching on one of the most crucial issues of the time, when tax evasion by powerful families had become rampant.[23] But it is important to note that, although

---

20. I.e., chaps. 3 and 4 of the *I-li*, and of *Li-chi* chüan 61 (45), "On the significance of the drinking ceremony in the *hsiang*"; chap. 42 in Séraphim Couvreur, *Memoires sur les bienséances et les ceremonies* (Paris, 1950).

21. LSHY, p. 7b.

22. CWKWC 74:29b.

23. CWKWC 74:23b–24a; for the problem in question, see McKnight, *Village and Bureaucracy*, p. 58.

Chu Hsi's text contains these provisions, his amendments to Injunction No. 3 and those concerning the monthly assemblies bring in yet another dimension. These additions not only double the length of the Lü text, but they also change the covenant qualitatively by providing a different focus.

In order to grasp this, one may compare the paragraphs concerning the rules of decorum (*li*) in the two texts. In a general sense, rules of decorum in Confucianism can be said to provide the appropriate outer expression for the right inner attitude. They can also be looked upon as a means by which, through training in a certain way of behavior, people are led to internalize certain moral norms or, at least, to conform to them. Now, comparing the two texts, one finds that Injunction No. 3, in both versions headed "Associate with one another according to the rules of decorum (*li*) and customs (*su*)," in Lü's version simply contains provisions on how to share in other people's feelings of joy or sorrow. Chu Hsi, however, expanded this injunction with detailed prescriptions for polite social intercourse. In matters of rules of decorum the gist of his amendments lies in making manifest hierarchical distinctions or, more precisely, in getting the community to pay attention to such distinctions. He principally achieved this through his regulations for both banquets and compact meetings which, although not including the community drinking ceremony (*hsiang-yin-chiu*), nevertheless were shaped after the choreography that the ritual Classics, the *Li-chi* and the *I-li*, provided for such occasions.

Whereas Lü Ta-chün's community compact seems to be a device for smoothing daily life in the local community, Chu Hsi's version seems to be more of a device to regulate the social life of the educated elite. If one can see Lü Ta-chün's community compact as a convention of all household heads in a given community aimed at creating an atmosphere conducive to the generally satisfactory management of communal affairs, it is hard to imagine that the common members of a community had the money and the leisure to comply with the provisions Chu Hsi added to Injunction No. 3—let alone the fact that most dress he prescribed was dress of the educated elite.[24]

This does not mean that commoners were altogether excluded from Chu Hsi's compact. In fact, the very detailed instructions of his version, which were to be read aloud and explained during the monthly assemblies, would also teach members of humble family background how to comply with the rules of decorum. Chu Hsi himself stated that he undertook his revision of ceremonial texts with this aim in view.[25] Still, in respect to the overall

---

24. Thus, of the seven different forms of dress which Chu Hsi in his amendments to Injunction 3 prescribes (i.e., the *liang-shan, pei-tzu, lan-shan, tao-fu, shen-i, tsao-shan, kung-fu*) all except the *shen-i* are the dress of officials or degree-holders. Likewise noteworthy is the footnote Chu Hsi added to Injunction 3 in regard to congratulatory gifts. He specified occasions for offering such gifts: capping ceremony, birth of a son, and making ready as recipient of a recommendation, having passed the state examinations, accepting an office. CWKWC 74:27a.

25. See his letter to Lü Tsu-ch'ien, CWKWC 33:27a.

direction of the compact a couple of new phrases and alterations in wording that Chu Hsi introduced into the Lü text, despite their brevity, should not be overlooked. Thus, there is the provision that being seated according to seniority does not apply to those who are not members of the elite (*shih*);[26] commoners were plainly relegated to the rear. Moreover, Chu Hsi undertook some slight but telling changes in the provisions regarding the leadership of the compact. In Lü's version the paragraph in question reads:

> [The community compact is regulated by] one or two persons. All the members of the compact should elect an *orderly, upright, and incorruptible* person to serve [as head of the compact]. . . . [Beside] there is to be one person on monthly duty. Each month one member of the compact, *regardless of his social standing*, shall, in accordance with age, in turn carry out this function.[27]

Chu Hsi's provisions read:

> All the members are to select a person senior in *age and virtue* to act as compact head. Two persons of *learning* and character should assist him. From amongst the covenant members one person is to be on monthly duty.[28]

Not only are commoners relegated to the rear, but learning as a qualification for leadership is also stressed. In view of Chu Hsi's preoccupation with the niceties of social intercourse, it appears that the weight of the practical concerns of the community compact may have been correspondingly diminished.[29] It is also noteworthy that Chu Hsi's compact seems to be planned to cover a much larger area than the immediate local community; his text holds the provision that members living far away could join the compact meetings only at the sessions of the first, fourth, seventh, and tenth month, and for those living even further away it was permissible to come only once or twice a year.[30] In an area larger than a local community it is, however, hardly possible to join in a communal effort at moral improvement aimed at eliminating causes of conflict in daily life—an endeavor which, to my understanding, was the main purpose of Lü Ta-chün's covenant.

In evaluating the possible significance of the two compacts the following specific feature of local administration in Imperial China should be taken into account: the central government of that time was unable to extend its control over low-level administrative units. Only officials down to the level of the county (*hsien*) were appointed by the central government. Below this, the management of important administrative tasks was left to the local com-

26. CWKWC 74:26b.
27. LSHY, p. 8a.
28. CWKWC 74:23b.
29. Telling in this regard is another seemingly minor alteration of Lü Ta-chün's text that Chu Hsi undertook. In Injunction 3 he dropped the provision that, if letters were to be sent on the occasion of social events, the compact members should decide on a model all would see (LSHY, p. 4a).
30. CWKWC 74:28b.

munity or rather to its leading families. These tasks were: tax allocation and collection, the organization of communal works and social welfare, arbitration, and the upholding of public order by security as well as educational measures.[31] It is obvious that the social behavior the community compacts sought to promote and regulate corresponds to this list of administrative tasks.

If one asks about the possible motives behind the forming of community compacts in the last third of the eleventh century, one must keep in mind that the early Sung period, socially speaking, seems to have been relatively open and fluid. By then, the gradual weakening of the influence that the so-called great families of old held in central and local government had finally ended, whereas the literati elite that was to succeed it in centuries to come had not yet established itself. For some time membership in the non-official segment, of the ruling class, it seems, was mainly determined by wealth.[32] Given the fact that low-level administrative tasks were handled by the local communities themselves, without doubt the absence of a well-defined local elite complicated matters. Therefore, various schemes to organize communal administration were tried out in the Sung period.[33] Significantly, just when the Lü compact was devised, two important innovations in the field of sub-*hsien* administration were being tried out: in 1055 the attempt was made to substitute government-paid clerks (*li* for the system of village elders (*ch'i-chang*); and from 1070 to 1075, under the chancellorship of Wang An-shih, recourse was had to the *pao-chia* system.[34] Needless to say, both moves, besides attempting to cope with low-level administrative tasks, were also aimed at enhancing central government control over local affairs. Of Lü Ta-chün we know that his family were partisans of the so-called Conservative party (*Chiu-fa-tang*), the political opponents of Wang An-shih.[35] This makes it all the more understandable that Lü should rely on local initiative in settling matters of communal life, trying in this way to keep central government agencies at a distance.

As regards possible precedents—albeit with the reservation that the community compacts were "voluntary," locally initiated, and not centrally prescribed associations—the *Rites of Chou* (*Chou-li*) is usually considered the main source of inspiration for the formation of the community compacts.[36] In

---

31. McKnight, *Village and Bureaucracy*, pp. 24, 38.

32. Ibid., p. 6.

33. Ibid., chaps. 2 and 3, pp. 81ff., 159ff., 167ff.

34. Cf. Yanagida Setsuko, "Gōsonsei no tenkai," in *Sekai rekishi* (Tokyo: Iwanami, 1970) 9:319.

35. Cf. T'o T'o, *Sung shih* 340:10843; see also Franke, *Sung Biographies* 2:736. Within the Conservative party, however, the Lü brothers seem to have belonged to the moderate wing.

36. See Kung-ch'uan Hsiao, *Rural China: Imperial Control in the Nineteenth Century* (Seattle: University of Washington Press, 1967) p. 201. The prescriptions of the *Chou-li* to which the community compacts are said to refer are cited and commented on in the *Ku-chin t'u-shu chi-ch'eng, ming-lun hui-pien* (Taipei: Wen-hsing shu-tien, 1964) 42:246–250.

fact, in the *Ti-Kuan, Ta-szu-t'u* section of the Rites of Chou, where the population of the realm is divided into a set of hierarchically arranged administrative units, those units were assigned several tasks: providing mutual protection, helping each other in cases of economic difficulties, assisting one another in conducting funerals, coming to help in times of natural catastrophes, assisting each other in ceremonial matters, and communally honoring their worthy members.[37] These responsibilities correspond with many items of the Lü compact, but there are also differences. Thus, it is noteworthy that the last task listed in the *Rites of Chou*, "honoring the worthy," according to the classical texts, was to be performed in the solemn setting of the community wine drinking (*hsiang-yin-chiu*) ceremony and not just over a simple meal or by awarding praise and blame in the very blunt way described by the Lü text. It is also to be noted that emphasis on the effort of individual members to work for improvement in their daily conduct—one of the most salient features of the Lü compact—is absent in the *Rites of Chou*. For the attitudes that needed special attention in this effort, Lü took many points from the *T'ai-kung chia-chiao* (The family teachings of the ancestor), a primer in use for the education of the young.[38]

No doubt, there existed a long tradition of devices for mutual help, more or less in line with the stipulations of the *Rites of Chou*. But there seem to have been yet other models at hand. As Japanese scholars have pointed out from the documents found at Tun-huang, Buddhist lay associations flourishing there in the late T'ang show remarkable resemblances to the community compacts in both organization and goals. Differing from earlier Buddhist religious associations, these late T'ang clubs were not concerned with the accumulation of religious merit. Rather, like the community compacts of the Sung, these lay associations aimed at improving social manners and at providing help in times of need; likewise, their statutes stipulated regular meetings at which food or wine were served and fines for the violation of rules were to be paid.[39] Naba, the first scholar to point out the similarities between the community compact and these clubs,[40] did not maintain that the community compacts were modeled after these Buddhist organizational forms.

37. This text is translated by Paul Demieville, *L'oeuvre de Wang le Zélateur suivie des Instructions Domestiques de l'Aïeul, Poèmes Populaires des Tang* (Paris: College de France, 1982).

38. For the notions that good acts are to be praised and bad must be corrected as soon as one is aware of them, see ibid., pp. 657–685; that in case of calamities neighbors have to help each other (p. 665), that one must not meddle in other people's affairs or talk about the shortcomings of others (pp. 657 and 757), and that one has to mediate in case of quarrels (p. 665).

39. A short mention of these religious clubs and the absorption of nonreligious goals is found in Jacques Gernet, *Les aspects économique du bouddhisme dans la société chinoise du Ve au Xe siècle* (Saigon: Ecole Française d'Extrême Orient, 1956), p. 253; and in Kenneth K. S. Ch'en, *The Chinese Transformation of Buddhism* (Princeton: Princeton University Press 1973), pp. 295.

40. Naba Toshisada, "Tōdai no shayū ni tsuite," *Shirin*, 23 no. 4 (1938):78, mistakenly ascribes the text to Lü Ta-chung and gives as date of completion 1182.

In fact, the shift in orientation of Buddhist lay associations in the late T'ang
may be taken as evidence of a propensity to work out devices for ordering
earthly life—a specific trait, so it seems, of Chinese religious life—which, in
the course of time, also led Buddhists to model themselves after long-
established Chinese forms for cultivating social contacts and exerting educational influence. A long list of forms of organization, for both mutual help
and admonishment, coming from various sources of Chinese religious conviction can be cited,[41] whereby the device of grading good or bad behavior with
an eye toward reward or punishment seems to have been part of religious
practice in China.[42]

So far I have not come across explicit evidence that the same clubs
mentioned in the Tun-huang documents also existed in the inner provinces of
the Chinese realm. Fortunately, however, we do possess a few letters by Lü
Ta-chün in which he discusses problems that arose during his attempt to put
his plans for a community compact into practice.[43] In these letters we read
that his *hsiang-yüeh* were by no means created in an organizational vacuum;
quite to the contrary, the common people (*hsiao min*) of his native region
already were used to forming organizations on their own initiative in order
to cope with difficulties ensuing from flood, fire, robbers, funeral expenses,
disease, and false accusation. As leaders of such associations they used to
elect so-called *shen-t'ou* or *hang-lao*.[44] Thus, it seems that Lü Ta-chün, by his
hsiang-yüeh device, attempted to assert Confucian leadership in local communities, an attempt well in tune with one major trend of his time; the
Northern Sung passed as an epoch in which a decidedly Confucian elite with
new élan set out to take the lead in all walks of life and to wrest from other
social forces the influence which they had held for centuries in Chinese
society.[45]

The impression that Lü Ta-chün set out to promote Confucian ways in an
environment in which other ways prevailed is reinforced by information
found in the *Community Etiquette* (*Hsiang-i*), another text compiled by Lü

41. See the list of examples in Shimizu Morimitsu, *Chūgoku gōson shaki ron* (Tokyo 1941), pp.
283–304; cf. also Naba, "Tōdai no shayū ni tsuite," *Shirin* 23, no. 2 (1938):2:234 seq.; 22, no. 3
(1938):516.

42. For a demonstration of this in the case of the "Ledgers of merit and demerit" (*kung-kuo
ko*) see Richard Hon-chun Shek, "Religion and Society in Late Ming: Sectarianism and Popular
Thought in Sixteenth and Seventeenth Century China" (Ph.D. diss., University of California,
Berkeley, 1980), p. 131.

43. These letters are appended to the text of the Lü compact; LSHY, pp. 9a–14a.

44. LSHY, p. 10a.

45. Thus, in regard to institutions of public welfare, Arthur Wright, *Buddhism in Chinese
History* (Stanford: Stanford University Press, 1979), p. 93, points out that, whereas during the
T'ang period so-called charitable works (care for the aged, infirm, orphaned, etc.) were largely
in the hands of pious families or of temples and religious organizations, in the Sung corresponding measures were undertaken by the government.

Ta-chün.[46] The *Community Etiquette* holds provisions covering four fields: etiquette in regard to guests (*p'in-i*), ceremony concerning matters of good fortune (*chi-i*), etiquette on occasions for congratulations (*chia-i*), and etiquette on sorrowful occasions (*hsiung-i*).

Item 1 deals with the same matters that make up Chu Hsi's amendments—that is, occasions for paying visits, cases that allow exceptions to paying visits, age gradation and correct behavior in line with it, exceptions to precedence of seniority, how to invite guests, how to respond to invitations, how to dress when visiting, proper use of name cards, proper demeanor while visiting, how to conduct banquets, how to greet when meeting in the streets, and the welcoming and farewell to villagers who return from or leave for a long journey.[47]

Item 3 relates to the proper etiquette for betrothals and the capping ceremony. In regard to the former Lü Ta-chün deplores the chaotic and vulgar manner in which betrothals were conducted, disregarding the six rules of decorum (*liu-li*);[48] in regard to the capping ceremony—which, too, seems to have been neglected in Lü's time—he stresses the need clearly to mark the different stages in life as a means of learning to obey those in hierarchically higher positions.[49] And in item 4, again deploring the disregard for the rules of old, Lü Ta-chün provides detailed instructions on which way and in what garb to pay the various visits of condolence.[50]

If these paragraphs already include complaints that people were being taken in by non-Confucian ways of life, item 2, "Ceremony concerning matters of good fortune," bears even stronger evidence of Lü Ta-chün's effort to stem this tide. This paragraph covers sacrifices to ancestors and to the various spirits of the mountains and rivers, as well as prayers offered at times of flood or drought. The regulations concerning ancestor worship were explicitly meant to extinguish improper ritual (*fei-li*),[51] and in regard to sacrifices to the various spirits the point is driven home that such sacrifices

---

46. This text is appended to the Lü compact in the LSHY edition cited in note 4 above, pp. 15a–39. In his postscript to the *Hsiang-i*, Chu Hsi writes that this text, under the heading of *Su-shih hsiang-i*, had been *wrongly* attributed to Su Ping and his brothers. According to the collection of Lü Ta-chün's writings, which Chu Hsi used, this text was Lü's work; only the preface was written by Su Ping; cf. LSHY, pp. 39a–b. For Su, a man of humble origins and a student of Chang Tsai and the Ch'eng brothers who was politically patronized by the eldest of the Lü brothers, Lü Ta-chung, see *I-lo yüan-yüan lu* 9:87; cf. also *Sung-Yüan hsüeh-an* 31:638–639, and *Sung-shih* 428:12733.

47. LSHY, pp. 15b–28b.

48. I.e., sending presents to the bride's home, asking the name, finding an auspicious day, sending the betrothal presents, fixing the date, going in person to receive the bride.

49. LSHY, pp. 31b–32a.

50. LSHY, pp. 32b–37a.

51. LSHY, p. 29b.

are to be performed by the state (*kuo-chia*). Nothing good would come if, as seems to have been the custom in Lü's times, all kinds of sacrifices and prayers were addressed to the spirits by private individuals. As to steps taken in times of flood or drought, the *Hsiang-i* allows for libations at the village altar (*li-she*). But, again, it contains the admonition that it is unfitting for the elite (*shih-chün*) to partake in sacrifices to the mountains and rivers or in popular performances with all their clamor and dancing.[52]

Differing from the Lü compact, the *Community Etiquette* does not contain provisions for material assistance, for instance as a means of expressing condolence. It centers mainly on appropriate ceremonies and matters of etiquette, providing a code of conduct at the local elite. It is noteworthy that Lü Ta-chün dealt with these concerns separately from his community compact, whereas Chu Hsi, who knew of this text,[53] included these aspects in his version of the compact.

Before trying to further assess the difference between the two I would like to point out that Chu Hsi did not simply take over the text of the *Community Etiquette*, but he reformulated the regulations, introducing a much more elaborate system of hierarchical grading than Lü Ta-chün had used. For example, Chu Hsi provided a scale of five age grades (see earlier discussion), plus two subgroupings, whereas the Lü text simply reads:

> Senior [*chang-che*] are those who are ten or more years older than oneself. (Friends of the father and relatives [including those] for whom one does not mourn but who are of the father's generation, as well as officials of elevated rank [*i-chüeh*], all fall into the same category.)
>
> Peers [*ti-che*] are those who are less than ten years older or younger than oneself.
>
> Junior [*shao-che*] are those who are more than ten years younger than oneself.[54]

Moreover, with respect to hierarchical grading I note that, much as Lü Ta-chün stressed the necessity of respect for elders and attention to proper sequence in the family hierarchy,[55] and although he did provide prescriptions for seating order at meetings,[56] provisions for anything like a communal drinking ceremony or other devices to emphasize the precedence of rank and seniority—for instance, in Chu Hsi's prescriptions for conducting the monthly assemblies—are conspicuously absent, not only in Lü's plan for a community compact but also in his *Community Etiquette*. Clear hierarchical grading seems to have been a particular concern of Chu Hsi, and I cannot say that his version of the community compact constitutes just a blending together of Lü Ta-chün's texts.

52. LSHY, pp. 30a–b.
53. See note 46.
54. LSHY, pp. 15b–16a.
55. See Lü's remarks in connection with the capping ceremony, LSHY, pp. 31b–32a.
56. LSHY, pp. 22b–23a.

There is little information about what hopes and intentions Chu Hsi might have entertained in connection with the community compact. His life chronology does not contain any notice of when he drafted the text, but apparently he worked on the Lü compact and *Community Etiquette* (*Hsiang-i*) from 1173 to 1175, although he might not have finished his own version at this time.[57] But it is known that Chu Hsi, when actually serving as a local official in 1190–91, paid much attention to promoting a ten-point program for neighborhoods (*pao*) of which the first six items are virtually identical with the contents of the Lü compact but not with his own version of the *hsiang-yüeh*.[58]

To clarify the difference between the Lü compact and Chu Hsi's version a short recapitulation of the Confucian tenets on government by educational means might be of help. To begin with, I think one precondition, which Mencius had driven home with particular emphasis, was generally accepted, that is, in order to effectuate such a way of governing the fundamental needs of the populace at large had to be provided for.[59] Only on the condition that a regular livelihood was secured for the people would the basic assumptions work on which the Confucian order rested: obedience by those in hierarchically lower positions to those above them, an obedience to be matched by loving consideration on the part of those in high position for the well-being of those below.

The two main inducements to enact such a system were: first, the high social prestige attached to the display of concern for the well-being of the community as a whole encouraged the well-to-do and those harboring ambitions to local leadership to spend part of their wealth for this purpose; and second, devices clearly distinguished between high and low and also expressed attitudes of deference and restraint upon ostentatiousness.

According to notions formulated in the Classical and the early Imperial periods, the latter point—making clear distinctions—was to be served by institutions like the community drinking ceremony (*hsiang-yin-chiu*) and the archery ceremony. The declared purpose of these ceremonies was to make

57. At 44 *sui* (1173) Chu Hsi completed the *I-lo yüan-yüan lu*, in which he also presented the Lü brothers (Wang Mou-kung; comp., *Chu-tzu nien-p'u*, TSCC 1:54); and, as stated in the *Chu-tzu nien-p'u k'ao-i*, TSCC 1:274, in 1174 he compiled *chia-li* and other ritual texts of various eras, a *Lü-shih chia-chi li* being one of the works specified. Chu Hsi's postscripts to both the Lü compact and Lü's *Hsiang-i* date from the next year. There also exists an 1175 letter to Lü Tsu-ch'ien, in which Chu Hsi writes that he wanted to produce a revised version of the Lü compact but had not yet found the leisure to complete his plan; see CWKWC 33:27a; cf. Wing-tsit Chan, "Chu Hsi's Religious Life," paper presented at International Symposium on Chinese-Western Cultural Interchange (Taipei, Sept. 11–16, 1983), p. 59.

58. For the ten-point programme see Conrad Schirokauer, "Chu Hsi as an Administrator," in Françoise Aubin, ed., *Etudes Song—In Mémoriam Etienne Balazs*, Series I, no. 3 (Paris: Mouton, 1976), p. 218.

59. See e.g., *Mencius* Ia: 7.21–23.

manifest the precedence of age[60] and to train people in the essentials of polite social intercourse. The good effects of these exercises are related in the *Li-chi*:

> Paying homage, displaying deference, holding banquets with a pure heart, and showing respect—these are the means by which noble men [*chün-tzu*] meet each other. If noble men pay each other homage and are deferential, they will not contend with one another. Holding banquets with a pure heart and treating each other respectfully, they will not be neglectful [of social manners]. Not being neglectful and not contending with one another, they will keep away from quarreling and disagreement. . . . This is the means by which the noble escape from man-made disaster.[61]

Regarding the archery ceremony, a ritual that Chu Hsi included in his provisions for the monthly assemblies, one should note its several purposes: proving the well-balanced state of mind of the archer; training the archer that whenever he missed his aim, be it in actual shooting or more figuratively, to look for the causes of failure first in himself and not in others and to exert himself to make sure that his own ways were absolutely correct.[62]

Both the drinking and the archery ceremonies were elaborate settings for expressing respect and modesty. The explanation that the *Li-chi* offers for this standing on ceremony is most interesting: it served to show that one accorded the rules of decorum (*li*) precedence over riches. And, as remarks the *Li-chi*: "If you put decorum in the first place and relegate wealth to the second, then the people will practice respect (*ching*) and deference (*jang*) and there will be no contest."[63]

Government by education, as we also read, does not mean that the exemplary man (*chün-tzu*) daily visits each of the various families to exert an educational influence upon them. Instead, he assembles the families together and, by celebrating these ceremonies with them, provides for their instruction.[64]

When assessing the two covenants against these essentials of the Confucian way of government, it is noteworthy first that neither text provides for any drastic measures of enforcement as the text quoted at the beginning of this essay might have led us to expect. Also, in contrast to the community compacts of later times, no particular emphasis is placed on submissive attitudes.[65] Neither Lü Ta-chün's nor Chu Hsi's compacts represent blunt attempts at indoctrination; rather, they aim at bringing to life the moral potential of the compact members. In this respect each version relies mainly

60. Cf. *Li-chi cheng-i*, SPPY 61:9b, 12a; 62:1a; Couvreur, *Bienséances* 2:658, 663, 668.
61. *Li-chi cheng-i* 61:7b; Couvreur, *Bienséances* 2:653–654.
62. *Li-chi cheng-i* 62:7b; Couvreur, *Bienséances* 2:678–679.
63. *Li-chi cheng-i* 61:9a; Couvreur, *Bienséances* 2:658–659.
64. *Li-chi cheng-i* 61:9b–10a; Couvreur, *Bienséances* 2:660–668.
65. See f.i. the *hsiang-yüeh* lecture system of the Ch'ing, Hsiao, *Rural China*, p. 185. For the stress on submissive attitudes, note especially p. 617, n. 22.

on one of the above delineated voluntary means of bringing about a harmonious social order. The Lü compact appeals to the prestige that accrues from publicly acknowledged acts of virtue and, conversely, relies on the fear of suffering public opprobrium, trusting the individual members to recognize their interdependence with all members of the community. Being focused on mutual help and considerate behavior, the compact's main aim seems to have been to diminish the material and emotional causes of conflict, thereby providing a given community with a sense of cohesion and security. This was to be brought about by direct appeal to the goodwill and common sense of all members but especially to the sense of responsibility of those in socially strong positions.

At the same time, Chu Hsi's version seems to have been inspired by a strong sense of the need for a hierarchical structuring of society and a belief in the gentle but irresistible force of ritually conducted communal ceremonies. In the end, Chu Hsi's compact was directed at the same practical results as the Lü version, that is, harmoniously ordered communities that provided for the needs of all its members. As I have shown, Chu Hsi did not cut down on the very down-to-earth contents of the directives concerning praiseworthy and blameworthy acts. But in his text Chu Hsi pursued this aim using a more indirect approach, addressing himself mainly to the leading families and providing them with a platform from which to create a sense of cohesion among them as well as to provide a model for their conduct. Here one must take into account that, in the Confucian understanding, clarifying hierarchical distinctions was not an end in itself. Rather it was the means of impressing on those in hierarchically higher positions their duty to lead exemplary lives and to shoulder the responsibilities of moral leadership at all levels of society. Thus, attending to the rules of decorum would serve as a means both for the pursuit of moral self-perfection and for extending extending moral influence. In view of this leadership function Chu Hsi added two more noteworthy items to the catalog of virtues in Injunction No. 1, that is, "the ability to straighten out governmental measures and educational means" and "the ability to lead the people to do good."[66] Such an approach was based on convictions that found expression in various dicta, for example: "Self-disciplined and ever turning to the demands of the rules of decorum (*li*)—everyone in the world will respond to his humanity (*jen*)" and "The moral force (*te*) of the noble man (*chün-tzu*) is like the wind, that of the inferior man (*hsiao jen*) like grass—when the wind passes over it, the grass must bend."[67] This approach upheld the idea that the people at large would become good if only their leaders led exemplary lives.

This idea was one tenet of the movements that, from Sung times on, were

66. CWKWC 74:23b.

67. *Lun-yü* 12:1 and 12:19; for an exposition of this notion of the power of *li* see Herbert Fingarette, *Confucius—the Secular as the Sacred* (New York: Harper & Row, 1972).

promoted in the academies (*shu-yüan*) as centers of Confucian learning and cells for reforming society from the grass roots. In fact, I find that in the rules for the famous *Pai-lu tung* Academy issued in the early sixteenth century, the Lü compact was mentioned among other articles and precepts.[68] Taking the community compact as an association of mutual admonishment and help in matters of daily life, as it appears in Lü Ta-chün's version, the inclusion of this text in a set of regulations for life in the academies may seem out of place. But this is less surprising, given the particular focus of Chu Hsi's version of the compact that served to promote and often passed under the name of the Lü compact.[69] Indeed, it indicates how the function of the community compact had come to be understood and accepted.

68. See Meskill, *Academies in Ming China*, p. 97.

69. In the beginning of the Ming dynasty, Chieh Chin (1369–1415), in a memorial to the throne, proposed the introduction of the LSHY; cf. Hsü Fu-yüan et al., *Huang-Ming ching-shih wen-pien* (reprint, Taipei: Kuo-fan ch'u-pan-she, 1964) 3:281–300. However, one of the reasons Chieh gives for introducing this device (p. 294) is the prevailing neglect of polite exchanges of salutation; in his time, he must have had Chu Hsi's version of the compact in mind.

FOURTEEN

Chu Hsi and the Academies

Wing-tsit Chan

I intend this chapter as a report on Chu Hsi's (1130–1200) actions in connection with the academies. Before proceeding, however, I must first clarify the relationship between the *ching-she* and the academy.

The term *ching-she* comes from the *Kuan Tzu*, where it is said, "When calm is achieved in the mind . . . that can be an abode of refinement (*ching-she*)."[1] From the very start, *ching* means refinement and not "wonder" or "essence." The *Kuan Tzu* is traditionally ascribed to Kuan Chung (d. 645 B.C.), but most scholars believe with Chu Hsi that it is a compilation from various sources in the Warring States period (403–222 B.C.).[2] It is recorded in the *Hou-Han shu* (*History of Eastern Han,* A.D. 25–220) that Pao Hsien, a specialist on the *Analects,* established a *ching-she* to lecture and teach.[3] A number of other Confucianists of this period had their own *ching-she*.[4] The term originally meant, therefore, a place where a Confucian scholar lectured and taught. Before long, however, the Taoists began to use it as a place to refine their cultivation of life. It is recorded in the biography of Sun Ts'e (175–200) that a Taoist priest established a *ching-she* where he burned incense and read Taoist books.[5] By the fourth century, the Buddhists were using the term to translate *vihāra,* a Buddhist retreat.[6] When Lu Hsiang-shan's (Lu Chiu-yüan, 1139–1193) pupils built a cottage for him to live in on a

---

1. *Kuan Tzu* (SPTK ed.) 16:2a.
2. Chu Hsi, *Chu Tzu yü-lei,* ch. 137, sec. 4–5, (Taipei: Cheng chung Book Co., 1970), p. 5221.
3. *Hou-Han shu* (SPTK ed.) 69B:2b.
4. Ibid., chüan 83, biography of Chiang Kung, and chüan 97, biographies of Liu Shu and T'an Fu.
5. *Wu chih* (SPTK ed.) 1:4b–5a, annotation.
6. For example, in Kumārajīva's (344–413) translation of the *Treatise on the Perfect Wisdom Scripture* (Prājñāparamitā). See the *Shuo-lüeh* (Chin-ling ts'ung-shu ed.) 20:7b–8a, for the use of *ching-she* by Buddhists, Confucianists, and Taoists.

mountain where he was invited to lecture in 1187, he liked the mountain and built a *ching-she*. In a letter to a pupil he said that the term came from the biography of Pao Hsien, originally meant a Confucian place for lectures and discussions, and therefore was quite satisfactory for the purpose.[7] Thus, the original Confucian term, appropriated by the Taoists and Buddhists, was not in common use by the Confucianists in the twelfth century.

However, Chu Hsi had built a cottage by the side of his mother's grave in Chien-yang County, Fukien, about twelve kilometers from Chien-yang City, in 1170 and called it Han-ch'üan Ching-she (Cold spring study). Lü Tsu-ch'ien (1137–1181) stayed there during his visit in 1175, and together they compiled the *Chin-ssu lu* (Reflections on Things at Hand), the first Neo-Confucian anthology.[8] Chu Hsi had attracted pupils when he, at age twenty-four, was keeper of records (magistrate) at T'ung-an, Fukien (1153–1156). His first pupil was probably Hsü Sheng, who became a pupil at age thirteen,[9] and there were many others.[10] By the 1170s, he felt the need of a place for his visiting pupils to stay, and there are records of pupils visiting him at the Han-ch'üan Ching-she.[11] The earliest record of Chu Hsi's conversations were made there in 1173.[12] But when I wanted to visit the site of the *ching-she* in 1983, people in Chien-yang told me they could not even locate the site.

In 1183, Chu Hsi built the Wu-i Ching-she in scenic Wu-i Mountain in northern Fukien. It became a very busy place, attracting many scholars and pupils.[13] When Wang Juan went to see Chang Shih (1133–1180) for instruction, Chang told him that "At the present time, the Way is in Wu-i. Why don't you go there?"[14] Because Wu-i was an intellectual center of the time, a full description of the *ching-she* is in order. Attracted by its scenery, Chu Hsi had been going to the mountain for forty years. During his lifetime, he wrote many poems on the scenery.[15] The *ching-she* was situated in a large area of several *mou*[16] between two slopes of a high cliff at the fifth of the nine turns of the Wu-i River. The main building had three units. The main unit was called Jen-chih (humanity and wisdom) Hall of which Chu once called himself its master.[17] The chamber on the left of the main hall was his living area, and

---

7. *Hsiang-shan ch'üan-chi* (SPPY ed.) 2:5a, 36:15b.

8. *Reflections on Things at Hand*, trans., Wing-tsit Chan (New York: Columbia University Press, 1967), p. 1.

9. For him, see the *Sung-Yüan hsüeh-an pu-i* (Taipei: World Book Co., 1962) 69:102a–103a; and Wing-tsit chan, *Chu Tzu men-jen* (Taipei: Student Book, 1982), pp. 200–201.

10. See the *Chu Tzu wen-chi* (SPPY ed., *Chu Tzu ta-ch'üan*) 87:14b; hereafter cited *Wen-chi*.

11. See Chan, *Chu Tzu men-jen*, pp. 84, 93.

12. See the list of recorders at the beginning of the *Chu Tzu yü-lei*.

13. See Chan, *Chu Tzu men-jen*, pp. 62, 81, 142, 149, 153, 190, 320, 327, 356.

14. Ibid., p. 62, and T'o T'o, *Sung shih* (SPTK ed.) 395:9a.

15. *Wen-chi* 1:8a, 14a; 3:2b–3a; 4:9b; 6:23a–b; 9:3b–6a.

16. A *mou* is one-sixth of an acre.

17. See Wing-tsit Chan, "Chu Tzu tzu-ch'eng," *Chinese Cultural Renaissance Monthly* 15, no. 5 (May 1982): 2.

that on the right was reserved for guests. Beyond the right slope and behind a stone gate was the building for pupils, and further south was a building for Taoist priests. There were a number of pavilions and a natural rock stove around which eight or nine people could sit to enjoy tea. Many pupils built cottages along the river. The *ching-she* area could be reached only by boat. Chu Hsi believed there were immortals and spiritual beings in the mountain, and "it was a heaven outside of the human world."[18] Once he found an image of the legendary sage Fu-hsi and wanted to install it in the *ching-she*. According to Chinese tradition, Fu-hsi was the originator of the Eight Trigrams, the foundation of Chinese metaphysics.[19]

In one poem, Chu Hsi said, "Let guests be entertained by the scenery. There is no need for chicken and fine grains for dinner." He was then the superintendent of the Taoist Ch'ung-yu Temple in the mountain several miles from the *ching-she*, a sinecure involving no duties or residence but permitting him to teach and write full time. Because his income was meager, the *ching-she* was a very simple structure, using local lumber and bamboo. Once Hu Hung (1163 *chin-shih*) visited him there and felt greatly offended because Chu Hsi did not treat him with chicken and wine; later, in 1196, when Hu Hung was an investigating censor and the Court was attacking Chu Hsi's learning as *wei-hsüeh* (false learning), he prepared a memorial to impeach Chu Hsi for ten crimes, a memorial that led to Chu Hsi's dismissal as lecturer-in-waiting and the termination of his political life.[20]

It is not clear when the *ching-she* was renamed *shu-yüan*. As a *shu-yüan*, it underwent a number of reconstructions and expansions over the years. In 1448 when it was ravaged by troops, Chu Hsi's eighth generation descendant rebuilt the whole compound as the Chu Wen Kung Temple. Before the Cultural Revolution in the 1960s, the *ching-she* and the temple proper, rebuilt in 1717, were still intact, together with wooden tablets of pupils on both sides of the image of Chu Hsi. When I visited the compound in 1983, however, only part of the two walls of the *ching-she,* separated by about five and a half meters, and their wooden windows remained. The temple proper next to it, rebuilt as an auditorium, is now used as a sanitarium. The Wu-i administration said they will rebuild the compound and recreate as many original Sung features as possible. Further up in the mountain but within walking distance, a stone arch commemorating the Shu-kuei Ching-she is understood to have been built in 1115 by Chiang Chih whose courtesy name was Shu-kuei. Chiang retired from the government and built the structure as a retreat. It was probably named Shu-kuei Ching-she after his death to commemorate him, for he would not think of naming the place after himself.

The third *ching-she* built by Chu Hsi was the Chu-lin (bamboo grove)

18. *Wen-chi* 9:2b–6b.
19. Ibid., separate collection, 6:19b.
20. Yeh Shao-weng (c. 1175–1230), *Ssu-ch'ao wen-chien lu*, fourth collection, "Biography of Hu Hung."

Ching-she in Chien-yang, Fukien, about eighty kilometers south of Wu-i Mountain. In 1192, he moved from Wu-fu-li in Ch'ung-an county to K'ao-t'ing in Chien-yang, for he had always admired the scenery there. Because his father had once considered moving there for its scenery, Chu Hsi built a small house and called it K'ao-t'ing Shu-t'ang (Hall of books with thoughts of one's father). Later in 1194, when the number of pupils greatly increased, he built the Chu-lin Ching-she east of his residence. All the chronological biographies assert that in 1194 the Chu-lin Ching-she was built later and its name was changed to Ts'ang-chou Ching-she (Blue Waterside Study).[21] In his *Chu Tzu shih-chi* (True Records of Master Chu), Tai Hsien (1496 *chin-shih*), specifically explained that the new name was adopted because the place was surrounded by water. Popular tradition has been that the new name was given because it means a place for a hermit, and Chu Hsi took the literary name Tun-weng (Old Man in Retirement) in 1195 after he was dismissed from his lectureship-in-waiting and retired to Chien-yang. But no one has ever specified when the name was changed.

I have published an article to dispute this tradition. I found that several months before Chu Hsi died in 1200 no one ever used Ts'ang-chou but always Chu-lin. If Chu Hsi changed the name, he should have done so when he took the literary name Tun-weng in 1195. But I found that the name did not appear until after Chu Hsi's death, and, because he had used the literary name Tun-weng, people began to use the term *ts'ang-chou* to conform to the meaning of *tun-weng*, especially because Chu Hsi had used the literary name of Ts'ang-chou Ping-sou (Sick Old Man of Blue Waterside). But he used this name only a month before he died, and it was most unlikely that when he was seriously ill he took trouble to change the name of the study. I therefore concluded that because Chu Hsi had used the names Tun-weng and Ts'ang-chou Ping-sou, people after his death began to use this term to call the *ching-she* and eventually it became better known than Chu-lin.[22] It is also possible that later followers of Chu Hsi thought the name, originally popu-larly used in Buddhism, was too Buddhistic for their comfort. It should be pointed out that when the term *K'ao-t'ing ching-she* is used, as, for example, in the chronological biography in the *Chu Tzu shih-chi* under the year 1195, it does not mean another *ching-she* but the Chu-lin Ching-she in K'ao-t'ing.

Of the three *ching-she*, the most important is the Chu-lin because most of his famous pupils attended him there and most of the recorded conversations took place there. In 1225, the Chien-yang magistrate built a temple to offer sacrifice to Master Chu. In 1244 an imperial order turned the *ching-she* into the K'ao-t'ing Shu-yüan. Over the centuries, ruin and reconstruction suc-ceeded each other a number of times, with the academy changing sites. According to Mr. Hsü Kuan-hsing of the Institute of Culture of the Chien-

---

21. For example, Wang Mao-hung, *Chu Tzu nien-p'u*, 3rd ed. (Taipei: World Book Co., 1973), p. 214.

22. "Ts'ang-chou ching-she pien," *Hua-hsüeh yüeh-k'an*, no. 104 (August 1983):1–2.

yang government who accompanied me on my visit in 1983, the area of the academy compound was 200 meters long by 50 meters wide. The academy originally had a three-story Confucian temple.the Master Chu Temple was on its side. It had a stone statue of the Master, accompanied by wooden tablets of three direct pupils, namely, Huang Kan (1152–1221), Ts'ai Yüan-ting (1135–1198), and Liu Yüeh (1144–1216), and one indirect pupil, Chen Te-hsiu (1178–1235). There were also many stone tablets of calligraphy in the temple. However, both buildings were in ruin for a long time, and by 1964, practically nothing was left. Only the foundation of a wall and the stone arch remain; the area is now a vegetable garden. The area along the four sides had from the very beginning been rice fields.

The four large characters "K'ao T'ing Shu Yüan" written by Emperor Li-tsung (r. 1225–1264) are carved horizontally on top of the arch. On the right of the plaque is the date of the fourth month of 1531 and on the left the name and title of the governor who reerected the arch. On top of the plaque are carved four characters written by Emperor K'ang-hsi (r. 1662–1722). These inscriptions appear on both sides of the arch. When I visited the place, the arch was standing near the edge of the river with the entrance road covered by water. Because a water pump station had been built upstream and the water level has been rising, the Institute of Culture has moved the arch to the side of the hill across the river. The Institute has a blueprint ready for the whole compound, its intention is to restore it in all its genuine aspects.

For one person to have built three *ching-she* must be quite unique at that time. May I say that Chu Hsi purposely recaptured the institution from the Buddhists and Taoists and thus reasserted the Confucian heritage? This is an interesting thought. It is all the more interesting because Lu Hsiang-sha had to justify the use of the term *ching-she* in 1187.

It may be argued that the term *ching-she* had been used by Confucianists before Chu Hsi's time. Earlier I mentioned the Shu-kuei Ching-she built in 1115. In the chronological biography compiled by the sixteenth generation descendant Chu Yü, it is said that Chu Hsi's father died in the Huan-hsi Ching-she (Surrounding Stream Study). In both cases, I believe a later name was used. As I have said, Shu-kuei would not think of using his own name for the *ching-she*, and all other chronological biographers say that Chu Hsi's father died in his host's residence.

What is the relationship between the *ching-she* and the *shu-yüan*? Originally the *shu-yüan* was an enclosure (*yüan*) to preserve and compile books (*shu*) whereas the *ching-she* was a retreat. Gradually both evolved to be a place for study and teaching. Because of this common function, the *ching-she* was also called *shu-yüan*. Although Chu Hsi's *ching-she* were not called *shu-yüan*, they were referred to as such.[23] A clear case is the opening religious ceremony of

---

23. See *Wen-chi* 35:23b, 50:31b.

WING-TSIT CHAN

the new academy in 1194. The place is referred to as *ching-she* in the *Chu Tzu wen chi* (Collection of literary works of Master Chu) but as *shu-yüan* in the *Chu Tzu yü-lei* (Classified conversations of Master Chu).[24] And Chu Hsi himself referred to a *shu-yüan* as a *ching-she*.[25] Writers have regarded the *ching-she* as *shu-yüan*.[26] But, as it has been pointed out, the two institutions were quite different. The *ching-she* was used earlier by the Confucianists and later by the Taoists and Buddhists also, but while the Confucianists used the term *ching-she* for the *shu-yüan*, the Buddhists and Taoists have never used *shu-yüan* for their *ching-she*.[27] I venture to add that by Chu Hsi's time, the *shu-yüan* could be both private and public but the *ching-she* was strictly private. Moreover, the *shu-yüan* had a formal organization, with a director, an endowment, and so forth, whereas the *ching-she* was simply identified with a scholar. In such a case, when the *ching-she* is referred to as *shu-yüan*, it means the central hall where books were stored and formal lectures and discussions took place. I believe this was the case with the Chu-lin Ching-she. In describing in detail Chu Hsi's activities in the last several days of his life, Ts'ai Ch'en (1167–1230) said these activities took place in the *shu-yüan* on the lower floor.[28] In the record of daily religious ceremony in the Chu-lin Ching-she, the *shu-yüan* mentioned there probably refers to this central hall.[29]

Chu Hsi has briefly but clearly explained the transition from the *ching-she* to the *shu-yüan*. He said that the *ching-she* was originally a place for scholars living together to study and discuss; later, with official encouragement and sponsorship, they became such *shu-yüan* as the Yüeh-lu (Mountain slope) and the Pai-lu-tung (White Deer Hollow). Between 1041 and 1077, government schools spread over the country, and the private huts of lay scholars came into disuse. Their sites are now in ruin and full of weeds.[30] The case of the White Deer Hollow was even worse.

The White Deer Hollow Academy was one of the leading academies in the Northern Sung (960–1126), but by the Southern Sung (1127–1179) it, along with others, had passed into oblivion. Chu Hsi was appointed prefect of Nan-k'ang Prefecture in 1178.[31] When he took office the next year, one of the first things he did was to revive the White Deer Hollow Academy. According to his petition to the government for the restoration, the Pai-lu-

---

24. Ibid., 86:12a; and *Chu Tzu yü-lei*, chüan 90, sec. 30, p. 3641.
25. *Wen-chi* 83:15a.
26. For example, Sheng Lang-hsi, *Chung-kuo shu-yüan chih-tu* (Shanghai: Chung-hua Book Co., 1934), p. 40.
27. Ch'en Yüan-hui et al., *Chung-kuo ku-tai ti shu-yüan chih-tu* (Shanghai: Educational Press, 1981), pp. 9–12.
28. *Ts'ai-shih chiu-ju shu* 6:19b. Also in Wang Mao-hung, *Chu Tzu nien-p'u*, p. 227.
29. *Chu Tzu Yü-lei*, chüan 107 sec. 54 (p. 4252).
30. *Wen-chi* 79:21b, "An account of the Stone Drum Academy in Heng-chou."
31. The capital was in present Hsing-tzu county, Kiangsi.

tung is in Lu-shan, ten or more li[32] from Nan-k'ang City. It was the place where Li Po[33] of the T'ang dynasty (618–907) lived in retirement. A *shu-yüan* was built there to commemorate him during the Southern T'ang dynasty (937–975). It was a national school with land endowment. At the beginning of Sung, students still numbered several hundred. With the advent of the prefectural school, however, the academy disappeared. Even its site could not be known and was found only after a search. The scenery in the mountain was the best in the southeast. There were close to one hundred Buddhist and Taoist edifices, but this single Confucian *ching-she* no longer existed. It was his responsibility as a government official, he said, to restore it.[34] It should be added that Li Po kept a white deer and was prefect of the area in about 826. The place is called *tung* not because it is a cave but a large area of many square miles surrounded by mountains, thus making it look like a hollow.

Within a month after Chu Hsi arrived at office in Nan-k'ang, in the fourth month of 1179, he instructed the prefectural school instructor to inquire about the forgotten site.[35] With historical data supplied by Liu Ch'ing-chih (1139–1189) and with information of a lumberman, the site was found.[36] It was in Hsing-tzu country,[37] a very scenic spot[38] twenty *li* east of the Wu-lao (Five Old Men) Peak.[39] He immediately petitioned to rebuild the academy.[40] Hsing-tzu magistrate Wang Chung-chieh and prefectural school instructor Yang Ta-fa were commissioned for the project.[41] Probably Wang was chiefly responsible because Chu Hsi mentioned his name only and wanted him mentioned in Lü Tsu-ch'ien's account of the academy.[42] At first, they planned to build twenty small buildings, but to economize only five were built.[43] The work was begun in the tenth month of the sixth year (1179) of the Ch'un'hsi period and was finished in the third month of the following year.[44] Upon completion, religious sacrifices were performed, and lectures

---

32. A *li* is one-third of a mile. Specifically the place was fifteen *li* from the capital. See *Wen-chi*, 7:11b, 86:3b.

33. Not to be confused with the famous poet, Li Po (701?–762).

34. *Wen-chi* 20:8b–9a, "Petition to Rebuild the White Deer Hollow Academy." Greater details are found in his "Dispatch on Pai-lu-tung," *Wen-chi* 99:4b–5a.

35. *Wen-chi* 99:4a–b, "Dispatch on Pai-lu-tung," and 16:17b, "Report upon the expiration of term of office."

36. Ibid., 1:2a, "Prose poem on Pai-lu-tung."

37. Ibid., 16:17b, "Report upon the expiration of term of office."

38. Ibid., 99:5a, "Dispatch on Pai-lu-tung."

39. *Pai-lu Shu-yüan chih* (1622 ed.) 1:3a.

40. *Wen-chi* 20:8b–9a, "Petition to rebuild the White Deer Hollow Academy."

41. Lü Tsu-ch'ien, *Tung-lai chi* (Hsü Chin-hua ts'ung-shu ed.) 6:4a, "Account of the White Deer Hollow Academy"; *Chu Tzu nien-p'u*, p. 81.

42. *Wen-chi* 34:19a, 79th letter in reply to Lü Po-kung (Lü Tsu-ch'ien).

43. Ibid., 16:18a, "Report," and 26:11a, "A separate note to the chief councilor."

44. *Chu Tzu nien-p'u*, p. 81.

began.[45] He told Ts'ai Yüan-ting that the academy was on high ground, far superior to Wu-i Ching-she, and could accommodate many people.[46]

First, he requested the emperor to bestow a plaque for the academy. The response was slow, and he had to appeal in a memorial in 1181 before he succeeded. Evidently the court was cool to the idea of reestablishing the academy. As Chu Hsi understood it, the court must have felt that, given the prefectural and county schools, there was no need to spend money for the project.[47] But he had his own reasons for reestablishing the academy, as I shall explain. To make sure the academy stood on a firm foundation, he donated 487 *mou* of land as endowment for the academy,[48] and he was much concerned with the academy acquiring more land.[49] He requested an appointment from the chief councilor to be the *tung-chu* (Master of the Academy) with a nominal salary as in the case of a superintendent of a temple[50] so he could devote his whole time to writing and teaching. He did not receive the appointment because, before his term as prefect was up, he was appointed to another government post, however; he called himself *tung-chu* in his prose poem on the academy.[51] For actual administration of the academy, he recommended Yang Jih-hsin in the ninth month of 1180 to be the *t'ang-chang* (Head of the academy).[52]

In early Northern Sung the academy performed three functions, namely, teaching, preserving books, and sacrificing to Confucius and worthies. The function of the White Deer Hollow Academy conceived by Chu Hsi, however, was more extensive; in fact, it included six aspects: instruction, "Articles for Learning," curriculum, lectures, religious sacrifices, and library.

Instruction. I do not know how many students the academy had at Chu Hsi's time. At first, it was planned to have about twenty students,[53] but it is not known how many students actually enrolled. However, at least sixteen of Chu Hsi's pupils studied with him there, including famous ones like Lin Yung-chung, Hu Yung, Ts'ao Yen-yüeh (1152–1228), and Ts'ai Nien-ch'eng.[54] An innovative program inaugurated by Chu Hsi was to invite twenty-eight successful civil service examination candidates to come to the academy during vacation time while the students were away, with free room

45. *Wen-chi*, separate collection, 6:14b, "Letter to Huang Shang-po."

46. Ibid., supplementary collection, 2:20a, "Eighty-ninth letter to Ts'ai Yüan-ting."

47. Ibid., separate collection, 9:2a, "Posted notice concerning the Hollow Academy"; 16:11b and 18b, "Report"; 13:19a–b, 7th memorial of 1181.

48. *Pai-lu Shu-yüan chih* 16:1a.

49. Letters to friends in *Wen-chi*, separate collection, 6:18b, 21b, 22a; supplementary collection, 2:19a.

50. Ibid., 26:11a–12a, "Letter to the chief councilor"; also 7:4b.

51. Ibid., 1:1b.

52. Ibid., separate collection, 9:1b, "Request for the head of the Hollow Academy."

53. Ibid., 16:18a, "Report."

54. See Chan, *Chu Tzu men-jen*, pp. 88, 102, 135, 136, 142, 146, 169, 194, 195, 196, 288, 314, 334.

and board. He frankly told these scholars that literary composition required for the civil service examination was no way to cultivate the self, and a quiet place at the academy should be an inducement to intellectual progress.[55] It is doubtful if such a plan for "scholars-in-residence" had ever been offered before.

"Articles for Learning."   According to him, the real purpose of education is to enable the student to understand moral principles so he can cultivate himself and extend them in dealing with others. To this end, he composed the *chieh-shih*, literally "posted notice," and had it posted on the lintel. The *chieh-shih* is usually called "Articles for Learning" (*hsüeh-kuei*), but it must be understood that they do not mean compulsory rules but moral precepts. The text of the *chieh-shih* is as follows:

> Between father and son, there should be affection.
> Between ruler and minister, there should be righteousness.
> Between husband and wife, there should be attention to their separate functions.
> Between old and young, there should be a proper order.
> And between friends, there should be faithfulness [*Book of Mencius* 3A:4].
> The above are the items of the Five Teachings.

> Study it extensively, inquire into it accurately, think over it carefully, sift it clearly, and practice it earnestly [*Doctrine of the Mean,* chap. 20].
> The above is the order of study.

> Let one's words be sincere and truthful, and one's deeds be earnest and reverential [*Analects* 15:5]. Restrain one's wrath and repress one's desires. Move toward the good and correct one's mistakes [*Book of Changes,* hexagrams 41 and 42].
> The above are essentials for self-cultivation.

> Rectify moral principle and do not seek profit. Illuminate the Way and do not calculate on results [Tung Chung-shu, 176–104 B.C., in the *Han shu,* or History of the Han dynasty, SPTK 56:12b].
> The above are essentials for handling affairs.

> Do not do to others what you do not want them to do to you [*Analects* 15:23]. If you do not succeed in your conduct, turn inward and seek for its cause there [*Book of Mencius* 4A:4].
> The above are essentials for dealing with others.[56]

These "Articles for Learning" must have been posted after the academy was completed in the third month of 1180. In a postcript, Chu Hsi explained

---

55. *Wen-chi,* separate collection, 9:3b–4a, "Soliciting recommended persons to the White Deer Academy"; 6:17a, "Letter to Huang Shang-po."
56. Ibid., 74:16b–17b.

that these precepts are concerned with fundamentals. He said that in the past school rules imposed detailed regulations on the student's behavior. In his opinion, such a system showed that the school had a low opinion of the students. What he wanted was to offer some basic moral guidelines for students to make their own decisions. It is interesting to note that, in addition to the quotations from ancient Confucian classics, there is one from Tung Chung-shu who has never been considered in the direct line of transmission of the Confucian doctrine. There is no doubt that Chu Hsi wanted to emphasize motivation.

Although the "Articles for Learning" consist only of quotations, there is no better summary of Confucian morality in such a succinct form either before or after Chu Hsi's time. It is a logical document. It starts with the Five Human Relations and then goes on to the order of study. By study is meant learning how to cultivate the person, how to handle things, and how to deal with others.

His pupils, Ch'eng Tuan-meng (1143–1191) and Tung Chu (1152–1214), together wrote in 1187 the "school rules" (*hsüeh-tse*), specifying what to wear and how to sit. On the surface, such rigid requirements would be contrary to Chu Hsi's "Articles for Learning." However, these rules were not for the academy but for elementary education. In a postscript, Chu Hsi said that Ch'eng and Tung wrote these for "the youngsters of their community," and as such they were beneficial. In 1258, Jao Lu (fl. 1256) grouped these rules and Chu Hsi's "Articles for Learning" together and posted them, saying that while one gives the fundamental principles of learning so the student knows how to direct his effort the other prescribes daily decorum so he knows what to adhere to; these are the ways of higher education and elementary education of the ancients.[57] Ever since, the two have often been mentioned together.

The influence of Chu Hsi's "Articles for Learning" cannot be exaggerated. Many academies, including the Yüeh-lu Academy, adopted them as their own. They have inspired a long series of similar "regulations." Perhaps the most famous are the "School regulations" of Hu Chu-jen (1434–1484), an outstanding Neo-Confucianist of the Ming period and the "Assembly compact" (*hui-yüeh*) of the Tung-lin School by Ku Hsien-ch'eng (1550–1612). Hu simply listed six fundamental principles—setting up one's purpose, preserving one's mind, extending one's knowledge, handling affairs, perfecting oneself, and perfecting others—and quoted sayings from ancient sages and worthies to support each point.[58] Following Chu Hsi's "Articles for Learning," Ku headed the compact with them and said he merely elaborated

---

57. The rules are found in the *Hsüeh-kuei lei-pien* 1:2b–5b, Chu Hsi's postscript in 1:5b, and Jao Lu's remarks in 1:6a.

58. For a series of these regulations for learning, see ibid., ch. 1–3, and the *Pai-lu Shu-yüan chih*, chüan 6–8.

on these articles without presuming to add anything. He listed the "four essentials"—knowing the root, setting up one's purpose, honoring the Classics, and examining the incipient activating force—"two delusions," "nine increases (advantages)" and "nine decreases (disadvantages," and commented on them at length.[59] It is generally agreed that Chu Hsi's "Articles for Learning" have exerted a tremendous influence throughout Chinese history.[60] They have not only unified the moral guidelines in academies but have also influenced government schools. The *Daikanwa jiten* (The Great Chinese-Japanese dictionary) lists eight books on Chu Hsi's "Articles for Learning." Six of these are by Japanese Neo-Confucianists, including such eminent Neo-Confucianists as Yamazaki Ansai (1618–1682) and Satō Issai (1772–1859). This is a measure of its influence in Japan.[61]

Scholars have maintained that Chu Hsi's "Articles for Learning" were influenced by Buddhist monastic regulations, especially the *Pai-chang ch'ing-kuei* (The Clear Regulations of Ch'an Patriarch Huai-hai, 720–814).[62] I doubt very much that this was the case. Huai-hai's monastic rules were mostly lost by Chu Hsi's times; as reconstructed later, it consists of eight chapters including Buddhist chants and verses. It deals with the organization of the monastery, detailed ceremonies, and so on. If it were the model for Chu Hsi, his articles should have been much more complex. I believe he did not have to have a model. After all, he was innovative in many respects. If he had to have a model, the one that readily comes to mind is the "Community Compact" of Lü Ta-chün (1030–1081); it is under the four headings of "mutual encouragement in moral undertaking," "mutual advice on mistakes," "mutual associations according to customs," and "mutual assistance in misfortune."[63] Chu Hsi was much attracted to it and supplemented it.[64]

Curriculum. We have no record of what was taught in the academy or what texts were used. We only know that the *Book of Mencius* and the *Kuan Tzu* were daily lessons,[65] although that may be after Chu Hsi's time. From the essays preserved in chapter 74 of the *Chu Tzu wen-chi* between "Questions at the White Deer Academy" and "'Articles for Learning' at the White Deer Hollow Academy," it is clear that a great emphasis was on the *Analects* and

59. *Tung-lin hui-yüeh* in the *Ku Tuan-wen Kung i-shu* (1877 ed.), pp. 4b–17a.

60. See Sheng Lang-hsi, *Chung-kuo shu-yüan chih-tu*, pp. 56, and Ch'en Yüan-hui, et al., *Chung-kuo ku-tai ti shu-yüan chih-tu*, pp. 37–38.

61. *Daikanwa jiten* 8:40.

62. Sheng Lang-hsi, *Chung-kuo shu-yüan chih-tu*, p. 21; Ch'en Yüan-hui et al., *Chung-kuo ku-tai ti shu-yüan chih-tu*, pp. 138–139. The *Pai-Chang ch'ing-kuei* can be found in the *Taishō shinshū daizōkyō*, no. 2025.

63. The compact can be found in the *Sung-Yüan hsüeh-an*, chüan 31.

64. *Wen-chi* 74:23a–29b.

65. Ibid., 81:24a, "A colophon on the *Han shu* preserved at the White Deer Hollow Academy."

the *Book of Mencius*. Besides emphasis in "The Essentials of Book Reading," there is a special essay on each of these Classics. Compared with the instructions and questions at the county school in T'ung-an where Chu Hsi was keeper of records (magistrate) from 1153 to 1156, it can readily be seen that, whereas previously all Confucian classics were stressed, only selected ones were now emphasized. He grouped the *Great Learning*, the *Analects*, the *Book of Mencius*, and the *Doctrine of the Mean* as the Four Books in 1190, which came to dominate Chinese thought for the ensuing centuries. May one assume that at the White Deer Academy a transition from the general Classics to the Four Books was taught?

Lectures. Besides his own occasional lectures there whenever official duties permitted, he invited Lu Hsiang-shan to lecture at the academy in the second month of 1181. Lu had come with some pupils to request Chu Hsi to write his brother's tomb inscription which Lü Tsu-ch'ien had composed. At Chu Hsi's invitation to lecture, Lu chose to speak on *Analects* 4:16: "The superior man understands righteousness; the inferior man understands profit." He moved his listeners to tears, and Chu Hsi asked Lu to write down his lecture and later had it inscribed on stone.[66]

Students have suggested that this lecture was the forerunner of the lecture assemblies in the Ming period (1368–1644),[67] especially in the academies. I should think that the lecture by Lu may at most be considered as setting an example for later lectures that eventually evolved to be lecture assemblies. These assemblies with banquets, and so forth, were highly organized and often involved more than one lecturer in discussions. Chu Hsi did open the door of the White Deer Grotto Academy to a visiting lecturer, a lecturer of the opposite persuasion to boot. This radical move inevitably led to debates in the Ming period. The number of famous lecturers at the White Deer Hollow Academy over the centuries is legend; many were his own pupils.

Religious sacrifices. When the academy was completed in the third month of 1180, Chu Hsi led his pupils to perform sacrifice before the tablet of Confucius (551–479 B.C.), Confucius's pupil Yen Tzu (521–490 B.C.?), and Mencius (c.372–c.289 B.C.).[68] When he was succeeded in his Nan-k'ang post in 1181 by Ch'ien Wen-shih (Ch'ien Tzu-yen), he had wanted a temple for Confucius without an image. He preferred a tablet that would be put in place at the time of the sacrifice. Ch'ien, however, argued for an image. Chu Hsi said that if there had to be an image, it should be one sitting on the ground so as to avoid the impression of Confucius stooping for food. This would conform to the practice he had seen elsewhere. But much to Chu Hsi's regret,

66. For the lecture, see *Hsiang-shan ch'üan-chi* 23:1a–2a, and for Chu Hsi's postscript on the lecture, see *Wen-chi* 81:25a.
67. Ch'en Yüan-hui, *Chung-kuo ku-tsi ti shu-yüan chih-tu*, pp. 141–145.
68. *Wen-chi* 86:3b–4a.

Ch'ien rejected his proposal and erected a standing image. Later, he wrote a treatise on worshipping before a seated image, in which he recalled his acquiescing to Ch'ien but wanted his essay to be posted in front of the Confucian temple.[69] In a conversation recorded in 1192, he considered a standing image as contrary to moral principle.[70] As late as 1195, in a letter to a friend he still recalled this incidence with regret.[71]

Chu Hsi did not start the practice of sacrificing to Confucius in schools. Nevertheless, because he reported to Confucius in a religious ceremony at the opening of the reestablished academy and began his daily program with sacrifice to Confucius in his *ching-she,* he underlined the importance of religious sacrifices in education. Gradually the practice assumed an enhanced position in the academies. Special altars or temples were established for Northern Sung Neo-Confucianists, especially Chou Tun-i (1017–1073), Ch'eng Hao (1032–1085), and Ch'eng I (1033–1107), and Chu Hsi himself. Eventually some of the temples for Chu Hsi became academies, and some academies were turned into temples for Chu Hsi. Of course, a number of academies had temples for local worthies or Neo-Confucianists of their own school, but by and large temples in academies were dedicated to the Neo-Confucianists of the Chu Hsi school. In other words, religious sacrifices in the academies were closely tied up with the Neo-Confucianism of the Chu Hsi tradition.

Library. When the academy was opened, there were no books. Thereupon he wrote to several officials to solicit donations. In response, he received several copies.[72] He himself donated a set of *Han shu* that he had been given as honorarium for writing a biography for someone.[73] He petitioned the Court to bestow copies of the Classics hand-written by the emperor's father, printed copies of the commentaries on the Nine Classics, the *Analects,* the *Book of Mencius,* and so on.[74] But even when he left Nan-k'ang, they had not arrived, and he had to petition the Court again in a memorial in 1181, after which they finally arrived.[75] Besides searching for books, he also ordered the inscription on stone of writings by Shao Yung (1011–1077), Ch'eng I, and

69. Ibid., 68:1a–4b, "A treatise on worshipping before a seated image."

70. *Chu Tzu yü-lei,* chüan 3, sec. 74 (p. 83).

71. *Wen-chi* 46:7b, "Letter in reply to Tsang Chih-hsü."

72. Ibid., separate collection, 6:15a, "Letter to Huang Shang-po."

73. Ibid., 81:24a, "A colophon on the *Han shu* preserved at the White Deer Hollow Academy."

74. The Nine Classics in Sung times were the *Book of Changes,* the *Book of History,* the *Book of Odes,* the *Spring and Autumn Annals,* the *Tso chuan,* the *Book of Rites,* the *Rites of Chou,* the *Classic of Filial Piety,* the *Analects,* and the *Book of Mencius.*

75. *Wen-chi* 16:11b, 18b, "Report", 13:19a–b, 7th memorial of 1181;90:7b, "Tomb Inscription for Ts'ao Li-chih"; Wang Ying-lin, *Yü-hai,* (SKCS ed., reprint, Taipei: Commerical Press, 1983) 167:35b; Yeh Kung-hui, *Chu Tzu nien-p'u,* (1431 ed.) under the 6th year of Ch'un-hsi, (1179); Tai Hsien, *Chu Tzu shih-chi* (1151 ed.; reprint, Taipei: Kuang-wen shih-chü, 1979) under the same year; Wang Mao-hung, *Chu Tzu nien-p'u,* p. 287.

others.[76] Interestingly enough, in the library holdings of early seventeenth
century, there was neither the *Hsiao-hsüeh* (Elementary Education) compiled
by his pupils under his direction nor the *Chin-ssu lu* compiled by him in
collaboration with Lü Tsu-ch'ien.[77]

To make certain that the record of the reestablishment of the academy
would be preserved for posterity, Chu Hsi asked Lü Tsu-ch'ien to write an
account to be inscribed on stone. He took the matter so seriously that he
discussed Lü's first draft paragraph by paragraph.[78] When the final draft
came, he sent copies to two friends[79] and asked another friend to write in seal
style for the stone inscription.[80] The final draft[81] is much shorter than the
original and focuses on three points: namely, catching up with Buddhists and
Taoists, strengthening the educational system, and the promotion of the
learning of the sage. As noted in Lü's account, all Buddhist and Taoist
temples ruined by war were being repaired, but the academy existed only in
weeds. Chu Hsi was more specific. As he recalled, there were more than a
hundred Buddhist and Taoist temples in Lu-shan, but there were only three
schools in the whole prefecture.[82] For the whole country, Buddhist and
Taoist temples numbered more than a thousand in each prefecture and
several dozens in each county whereas there was only one school in each
prefecture or county.[83] This implies that the learning of the Confucian school
was in danger of being overtaken by heterodoxical teachings.

Lü's account also laments the Court's failure to adopt the school system
recommended by Ch'eng Hao due to opposition by Wang An-shih
(1021–1086). Ch'eng Hao had recommended an educational system to the
emperor; in that, promotion from county through prefectural schools to the
national university would be on the basis of the understanding of the
teachings of the Confucian classics as well as moral conduct, and appointment to government positions would depend on such understanding and
ability. Wang, the chief councilor, was enforcing radical reforms that the
Ch'eng brothers were bitterly opposed. Wang, who wanted quick results,
saw no merit in Ch'eng Hao's recommendation. One result was the growth of
literary compositions in civil service examinations and in school education.[84]
Both the Ch'eng brothers and Chu Hsi saw such literary exercise as superficial and incapable of learning the true teaching of the sages. To Chu Hsi, as

76. Ibid., 81:21a, 22a; 82:18b; 83:15a; separate collection, 7:10a–b.

77. *Pai-lu Shu-yüan chih* 15:3a–8a.

78. *Wen-chi* 34:21a–23a, eightieth letter to Lü on his account of the White Deer Hollow
Academy.

79. Ibid., separate collection, 6:15b, "Letter to Huang Shang-po."

80. Ibid., 34:23a, eighty-first letter to Lü Po-kung.

81. *Tung-lai chi* 6:42–5a.

82. *Wen-chi* 16:18a, "Report."

83. Ibid., 13:20a, seventh memorial in 1811.

84. Ibid., 34:21a–22b, letter to Lü on his account of the academy.

to the Ch'eng brothers, true learning means learning to be a sage. The central objective of such training is best summed up in a sentence from his prose poem on the White Deer Hollow Academy: "Let enlightenment and sincerity advance together and establish seriousness (or reverence) and righteousness simultaneously."[85] The ideas of enlightenment and sincerity come from the *Doctrine of the Mean*, chapter 21, but Chang Tsai (1020–1077) elaborated on the concepts and coupled them with morality and knowledge. In the sixth chapter of his *Cheng-meng* (Correcting Youthful Ignorance), "Ch'eng-ming" (Sincerity and Enlightenment), Chang said that if one can transform one's impure or unbalanced physical endowment of material force, which leads to selfish human desires, one can return to the Principle of Heaven with which one is originally endowed. Such transformation can be achieved only with knowledge attained by moral nature and not with bits of information gained through seeing and hearing.[86]

The doctrines of seriousness and righteousness are, of course, taught in the *Analects* and the *Book of Mencius*. Coupling the two, however, was the special contribution of the Ch'eng brothers.[87] These basic tenets in the Confucian School were neglected in favor of literary compositions in government schools. As Lü's account has emphasized, the reestablishment of the academy was to promote the Chang-Ch'eng doctrines, a point stressed by Chu Hsi in his discussion with Lü.[88] The reestablishment may not have been a deliberate attempt to replace the government school system and to change the direction of education, but conceivably the people at Court may have regarded it as a challenge if not a threat. That explains the reluctance and long delay in granting the plaque and books.

When Chu Hsi left the academy, students gave him a farewell banquet.[89] He was much concerned about the future of the academy, but he was later able to write to the officials of the academy expressing pleasure over both repair of the academy damaged by rain and a gift of some books and inquiring about the number of students.[90] He also wrote a friend to say that his sojourn at the academy was like a dream.[91] After he left, students erected a shrine west of the lecture hall to offer sacrifice to him, but at his request the shrine was demolished. After his death, a temple was built in the compound to honor him and other Neo-Confucianists.[92]

85. Ibid., 1:2b.
86. For a translation of this chapter, see Wing-tsit Chan, *Source Book in Chinese Philosophy* (Princeton, N.J.: Princeton University Press, 1963), pp. 507–514.
87. *I-shu* 5:2b, and 18:19a. The idea is derived from the *Book of Changes*, commentary on the second hexagram.
88. *Tung-lai chi* 6:4b; and *Wen-chi* 34:21a, 22b.
89. *Chu Tzu yü-lei*, chüan 106, sec. 7, p. 4196.
90. *Wen-chi* 52:46a, "Letter in reply to the officials of the White Deer Hollow Academy."
91. Ibid., separate collection, 6:20b, "Letter to Yang Po-ch'i."
92. *Pai-lu Shu-yüan chih* 2:4a–b.

The future of the academy was assured when two of his pupils, Li Fan (1190 *chin-shih*) and Chang Hsia (1161–1237) sucessively became head and Huang Kan and Ch'en Mi (d. 1226) lectured there.[93] They were followed later such outstanding Neo-Confucianists as Hu Chu-jen and Ts'ai Tsung-yen, a leading pupil of Wang Yang-ming (Wang Shou-jen, 1472–1529), as head of the academy. Wang Yang-ming himself donated land, and his leading pupil Tsou Shou-i (1491–1562) wrote an acount of Chou Tun-i, Chu Hsi, Lu Hsiang-shan, and Wang Yang-ming for the instruction of the students of the academy.[94] Thus, many prominent Neo-Confucianists were identified with the academy. However, when Ch'en Hsien-chang (Ch'en Pai-sha, 1482–1500) was invited to become head at age fifty-four, he declined. He preferred to stay in Kwangtung.[95]

Learned scholars were not the only ones identified with the academy. Common folks in the Lu-shan area identified themselves with it in the belief of a story handed down from generation to generation. They believed that Chu Hsi lived at the mountain all his life, had superhuman power, and was buried there after his death. According to the legend, a fox-fairy in the likeness of a young woman came to live with him and serve him; she brought a pearl of great value and persuaded Chu Hsi to swallow it, which became the fountain of his great wisdom. Later, a frog-fairy, also in the likeness of a young woman, came to live with him, too. One day the two women quarreled and were missing the next day. A dead fox and a dead frog were found under the old bridge below the academy. Chu Hsi buried them with due ceremony in the academy grove.[96]

In the Wu-i Mountain I came across a similar legend. According to it, a young woman by the name of Li-niang (beautiful maiden) came to study and live with Chu Hsi. After a while, an old couple warned him that the young woman was a fox spirit who came to steal the jade bowl he inherited. When Chu Hsi seemed incredulous, they whispered into his ear a secret. Thereupon, Chu Hsi stayed up night after night. The young maiden accompanied him all the time but eventually fell asleep. Two jade chopsticks protruded from her nostrils but finally dropped to the ground and created the shadow of a fox. When she woke up, she confessed that she was the spirit of a fox who had been cultivating her spiritual ability in the mountain for a thousand years. The old couple were actually two turtles being trained by her, she said. Without the chopsticks, she added, she had to leave. Then she suddenly disappeared. In great sorrow, Chu Hsi picked up a brush to write in front of a window, but the brush flew away like an arrow. When hit by the arrow, the

93. Ibid., 5:7a–9a.
94. Ibid., 5:10b–23a, 6:17a.
95. Ibid., 5:17b.
96. This story is told in "The White Deer Hollow University" chapter in *Sacred Places in China* by Carl F. Kupfer (Cincinnati: Western Methodist Book Co., 1911), p. 74. I am grateful to John Chaffee of the State University of New York at Binghamton for the material.

old couple immediately turned into their original being, namely, a pair of turtles. One day when Chu Hsi walked by a bush of flowers, he found a dead fox in it. He reverently buried it. The turtles were condemned to be rocks that still lie on the bank of the eighth turn of the Wu-i River like stone turtles.[97] This may be the source of the Lu-shan legend, for Wu-i Mountain was a hotbed of myths.

Whether people in the Lu-shan area still believe in the story is not clear, but it is certainly an enduring part of the White Deer Hollow Academy heritage. The more concrete heritage is the compound and the buildings. When I visited the academy in August 1983, I found it in a very good condition and well taken care of. This is remarkable after so many destructions and reconstructions over the centuries. At the entrance there is a bulletin board with a diagram of the academy's layout. One enters by going through the Wu-ch'ien-men (Gate of the Creative Element and High Noon). It consists of six stone columns with three plaques on top, on which there are artistic patterns but no inscription. The gate, about four and a half meters high and nine meters wide, was erected in the Ming dynasty. Proceeding from the gate, one finds lotus pools on both sides with lotus flowers blooming, where, it is believed, Chu Hsi planted lotus. About four meters further is the Li-sheng-men (Gate to Pay Homage to the Sage), on which are carved four large characters "Pai Lu Shu Yüan." This gate, with a double roof, looks more like a building than a mere passage. On its right is the Yü-shu-ko (Chamber for Imperial Books) that used to house the Nine Classics bestowed by a Sung emperor but is now used for other purposes.

Proceeding from the Li-sheng-men for about four meters one reaches the Li-sheng-tien (Hall to Pay Homage to the Sage), popularly called the Confucian Temple. It was rebuilt three times during the Ch'ing dynasty (1644–1912) and completely destroyed during the Cultural Revolution in the 1960s. Rebuilt the year before my visit, it houses no image of the Sage but has a stone carving of Confucius drawn by Wu Tao Tzu (d. 792). On the right of Li-sheng-tien is Ming-lun-t'ang (Hall of the Clarification of Human Relations), a building erected in 1436. It has been well preserved, although the couplets on the two pillars at the entrance ascribed to Chu Hsi contain a mistaken character. Behind this hall in an embankment below another building is a small cave in which a white stone deer stands on four legs. It is said to be a Ming dynasty sculpture. In the garden to the left of Li-sheng-tien, there used to be many stone tablets of calligraphy. Some were destroyed during the Cultural Revolution. Since then, the government has built three walls to place the 130-odd tablets, mostly of Ming and Ch'ing vintage, including a stone tablet of calligraphy by Tsou Shou-i. The most significant are Chu Hsi's "Prose Poem on the White Deer Hollow," Lu Hsiang-shan's

---

97. For the whole story, see the *Wu-i-shan min-chien ch'uan-shuo* (Foochow: Fulien People's Press, 1982), pp. 28–29, "Chu Hsi and Li-niang."

lecture, and the "Academy Instructions of the Two Worthies." The two refer to Ch'eng Tuan-meng and Tung Chu whose "School Rules" are completely inscribed on one of the tablets. In the garden there is a red cinnamon tree said to have been planted by Chu Hsi; this is questionable but by no means impossible. Of certain authenticity are the four huge characters "Feng-ch'üan yün-ho" (Spring of Wind and Galley of Clouds) carved on the cliff and two even larger characters (about eighteen inches square) "chen-liu" (Using Currents as a Pillow) in the middle of a stream. It is not known if Chu Hsi actually rested his head on this rock, but he must have enjoyed with many friends the cliffs, stream, and many pavilions.

The second academy reconstructed by Chu Hsi was the equally famous Yüeh-lu Shu-yüan. He visited Chang Shih in Ch'ang-sha in 1167 when Chang Shih was lecturing there. Chu Hsi had learned from his teacher Li T'ung (1093–1163) the doctrine of sitting silently to purify the mind, thus emphasizing self-cultivation, and was not satisfied with it. He heard that Chang Shih had learned from his teacher Hu Hung (1106–1161), the doctrine of putting self-examination before self-cultivation and wanted to go to Chang Shih to inquire about it. In the eighth month of 1167 he took two pupils with him to go to Ch'ang-sha. According to one of them, for three days and three nights the two scholars discussed the ideas of the *Doctrine of the Mean*—the concept of equilibrium before the emotions are aroused and that of harmony after they are aroused[98]—and could not agree.[99] They stayed at Ch'ang-sha for two months and then toured Heng-shan. During the excursion, the two scholars and a pupil of Chu's exchanged 149 poems and parted on the twenty-third day of the eleventh month.[100]

Wang Mao-hung (1668–1741) said that there is no record of their discussions,[101] but, according to the *Yüeh-lu chih* (Accounts of the Yüeh-lu Academy), they discussed the ideas of the *Doctrine of the Mean* for a month.[102] The *Yüeh-lu Academy Bulletin* also said that he lectured there and wrote the four large characters "chung hsiao lien ch'ih" (loyalty, filial piety, integrity, and the sense of shame), which are still preserved on stone in the academy today. He also named and wrote the plaques for several terraces and pavilions in the academy compound.[103] Although there is no record of his giving any lecture, it is perfectly reasonable to assume that he did.

Twenty-six years later, in 1193, Chu Hsi was appointed pacification commissioner of the Ching-hu area based at Ch'ang-sha. He arrived in the fifth month of the following year. He found the academy not in the best of repairs, and immediately set out to reconstruct the place. Within two months

---

98. *Doctrine of the Mean*, chüan 1.
99. Wang Mao-hung, *Chu Tzu nien-p'u*, p. 29.
100. Ibid.
101. Ibid., p. 257.
102. *Yüeh-lu chih* (7th ed., 1932), pp. 4a–b.
103. *Yüeh-lu Shu-yü4an t'ung-hsün*, no. 1 (1982):3.

of his arrival, he began to renovate the academy. First, he increased enrollment and faculty. He recruited ten more students with daily provision of rice
and money, and he appointed successful civil service examination candidate
Li [Kuei-ch'en] of Li-ling to be an instructor as well as the administrator[104]
and candidate and education officer Cheng [I-chih][105] to work with him.[106]
He posted the White Deer Hollow Academy "Articles for Learning" as
guidelines for the conduct of Yüeh-lu students.[107]

Second, he rebuilt the academy. According to the earliest extant chronological biography of 1431, he "rebuilt the academy on open, high, and dry
ground."[108] In a letter to Ts'ai Yüan-ting, he discussed with Ts'ai the site in
detail, telling him that T'ing-lao had drawn a plan, that Yen-chung had
objected to it but preferred another site, that he had asked T'ing-lao to draw
another plan, and that he was afraid that his successor, an opponent of the
Ch'eng-Chu School, might sabotage it.[109] There is no record of what buildings were erected after Chu Hsi left, but records indicate that work had
begun.[110] Wang Mao-hung, who had not seen the earlier chronological
biographies, rejected similar accounts in later chronological biographies. His
arguments are that in Chu Hsi's dispatch about the academy, Chu did not
mention the rebuilding and that there was no record of a final decision on the
site.[111] However, Chu Hsi's dispatch was concerned only with enrollment
and faculty and need not have discussed the rebuilding. As to the final site,
the need to redraw the plan does not preclude its final adoption and
execution. At any rate, the rebuilding had been accepted without question
both before and after Wang objected.

Wang also raised doubts about the Hsiang-hsi Ching-she on the west
bank of the Hsiang River. Chu Hsi had written to a friend and told him that
T'ing-lao had completed the plan for the *ching-she*.[112] He wrote his successor
asking him for a kind word to complete the *ching-she*[113] and later told him that

104. He was Chu Hsi's pupil. For him, see *Sung-Yüan hsüeh-an* 69:30b, and Chan, *Chu Tzu men-jen*, p. 348. Li-ling is a county in Hunan Province.

105. His courtesy name was Chung-lü. At first he studied with Chang Shih, but later he went to Chu Hsi. For him, see Chan, *Chu Tzu men-jen*, p. 341, and the *Yüeh-lu Shu-yüan t'ung-hsün*, no. 1 (1982):27.

106. *Wen-chi* 100:13a–b, "An official dispatch on appointing instructors to administer the Yüeh-lu Academy."

107. *Yüeh-lu Shu-yüan t'ung-hsün*, no. 1 (1982): 25.

108. Yeh Kung-hui, *Chu Tzu nien-p'u*, under year 1194. This is followed by Tai Hsien, *Chu Tzu shih-chi*, chüan 7, "Chronological biography," under year 1194.

109. *Wen-chi* 44:8b–9a, 7th letter to Ts'ai Yüan-ting. T'inglao was the courtesy name of Jao Kan, Chu Hsi's pupil, was the magistrate of Ch'ang-sha county. For him, see the *Sung-Yüan hsüeh-an* 69:28a. Yen-chung was the courtesy name of Ch'en Shih-chih, also Chu Hsi's pupil. For him, see the *Sung-Yüan hsüeh-an pu-i* 69:203b.

110. *Wen-chi* 29:12a, "Letter to Commissioner Wang Ch'ien-chung."

111. Wang Mao-hung, *Chu Tzu nien-p'u*, p. 326.

112. *Wen-chi*, separate collection, 2:8a, "Letter to Liu Chih-fu."

113. Ibid., 29:12a, "Letter to Commissioner Wang Ch'ien-chung."

T'ing-lao had shown him the imperial plaque for the *ching-she*.[114] Wang argued that the plaque could not have been meant for the academy because there had never been a case where an academy changed its name. He suspected that the academy was never rebuilt but T'ing-lao had erected another building, although he was not sure.[115] Had Wang seen the *Yüeh-lu chih*, it would have dispelled his doubts, for it is recorded there that the Hsiang-hsi Ching-she, possibly a dormitory, was built by the river.[116]

Third, Chu Hsi himself lectured at the academy and attracted many scholars. According to the earliest chronological biography, a great number of scholars from neighboring prefectures gathered in Ch'ang-sha. Chu Hsi, although tired with official administration, discussed ideas with them in the evenings, and he affected them greatly.[117] According to the *Academy Bulletin*, there were a thousand students at the academy and not enough water in the pool for their horses.[118] If this is an exaggeration, there are records of his lectures at the government study and the academy. But it is recorded in the *Chu Tzu yü-lei* that on the third day of the eighth month of 1194, more than seventy scholars gathered in his official study in the evening. The discussion centered around the subject of deep pondering in reading; his main point was to read carefully and not to interpret deep pondering in any special way.[119] Although the meeting took place in his official study, it is unreasonable to assume that only the prefectural school students attended. Some, if not most, of the participants must have been academy students.

There is also the record of his lecturing at the academy. Once he went there, and two students were selected by drawing lots to speak on the *Great Learning*. Because their presentations were unsatisfactory, he stopped them and said the academy was not established just to train people for the civil service examination. He regretted that, because of official duties and the separation of the academy and the prefectural office by a river, he was not able to come as often as he would like. He said he would discuss regulations for both schools with instructors and administrators the next day. Then he spoke on the beginning sentences of the *Great Learning* about manifesting the clear character of one's nature.[120] The regulations he had in mind were probably the "Articles for Learning" of the White Deer Hollow Academy that he finally adopted for the academy in Ch'ang-sha. According to all chronological biographies, although he was extremely busy with administra-

---

114. Ibid., supplementary collection, 7:4b, "Letter to Commissioner Wang."
115. Wang Mao-hung, *Chu Tzu nien-p'u*, p. 326.
116. *Yüeh-lu chih*, p. 3a.
117. Yeh Kung-hui, *Chu Tzu nien-p'u*, under year 1194. A similar account is found in Tai Hsien, *Chu Tzu shih-chi*, and Wang's *Chu Tzu nien-p'u*.
118. *Yüeh-lu Shu-yüan t'ung-hsün*, no. 1 (1982):26.
119. *Chu Tzu yü-lei*, chüan 116, sec. 15, p. 4447.
120. Ibid., chüan 106, sec. 41, p. 4220.

tion and tired in the three months he was in Ch'ang-sha, he lectured and discussed with students in the evenings.

There is no trace of the Hsiang-hsi Ching-she today, but the academy is in excellent condition. Outstanding Neo-Confucianists like Chang Shih and Wu Ch'eng (1249–1333) have written about its glorious past. Throughout the centuries, it has been destroyed, rebuilt, and expanded. Some damage was done during the Cultural Revolution, but the buildings built in the Ming and Ch'ing periods have been well maintained or repaired. The reconstruction effort is more vigorous and has achieved far greater results than in any other educational institution. After being used for various schools in the twentieth century, it was made the first college of Hunan University in 1924. In 1982, the government of the People's Republic declared Ch'ang-sha a cultural historic city and the academy an important cultural relic. When I visited the academy in 1983, I was led by Professor Yang Shen-ch'u, director of the Yüeh-lu Academy Research Institute, and several Institute members as well as officers of the Hunan Academy of Social Sciences. Before we entered the main gate, we came to the Ho-hsi-t'ai (Pavilion of Bright Sunlight). When Chu Hsi gave it its name in 1167, it was on top of the Yüeh Mountain behind the academy in a strategic location to watch the sun. In time it disappeared. In 1789 the head of the academy built a pavilion in the present location, and in 1821 the pavilion was given the name He-hsi-t'ai as a memorial of Chu Hsi. It was freshly remodeled and painted just before my arrival, and my hosts told me that special attention had been given to this pavilion because it symbolizes the prominence of Chu Hsi in the history of the academy. On the walls are two large characters *fu* (blessing) and *shou* (longevity), said to have been written by a Taoist priest with a broom and yellow mud. Some even believed that the Taoist priest became an immortal. Since the characters are now black, they must have been repainted in recent times.

About a *li* to the right of the pavilion is the pool where horses are believed to have exhausted its water when Chu Hsi lectured. A small pavilion stands on it. About three *li* to the right is another pool on which stands one more pavilion, built in 1789 by the head of the academy.

About a *li* ahead from He-hsi-t'ai stands the main gate, built in 1868. It is about twenty-four feet high with two square stone columns and twelve steps. On top the stone plaque reads "Yüeh-lu Shu-yüan" in gold color reproduced in 1980 from a Ming dynasty carving; it is believed to be the calligraphy of Emperor Chen-tsung (*r.* 998–1022). The couplet on the columns, whose author and writer are unknown, were reproduced on wood from a photograph in 1980. Between the main gate and the lecture hall there had been a second gate, destroyed during the war with Japan in the 1930s and reerected early in 1984.

Two *li* ahead of the main gate lies the lecture hall, the center of the academy. Rebuilt in the early eighteenth century and renovated in 1868, it is a large unit, ninety square feet, with courtyards and side rooms. The walls of the central hall are full of wooden plaques, couplets, and stone tablets, and more stone tablets are preserved in special rooms. Of these, the most important and famous are the four large characters *chung hsiao lien ch'ih* written by Chu Hsi. Each tablet is about 4.7 feet by 7 feet, and each character is about 4 by 5.5 feet. Undoubtedly these are the largest extant examples of Chu Hsi's calligraphy. The tablets were installed here in 1827 by the head of the academy. Because of the tablets, the hall has been called the Chung-hsiao-lien-ch'ih Hall. Of special interest are the four tablets on which are inscribed Chu Hsi's farewell poems for Chang Shih when they parted in 1167. Although all four were lost during the war with Japan, two have recently been discovered. One is broken, but the characters on both are still quite clear. There are several tablets of "regulations" modeled after Chu Hsi's "Articles for Learning."

Both left and right, between the main gate and the lecture hall, about thirty studies face north and south. Rebuilt after the war with Japan, they are now used for offices and classrooms. The Reconstruction Committee plans to rebuild fifty two rooms as they were in Sung times. On the right of the lecture hall, there had been eight scenic spots, making the area most beautiful. Also ruined during the Sino-Japanese war, the sites still await restoration. On the left is the Confucian Temple rebuilt after the war, as was the gate to the temple compound. The present stone steps, stone lion, stone wall, and so on of the compound are legacies from the Ch'ing dynasty. The Reconstruction Committee told me that before long the whole temple compound, rebuilt and renovated, will be used for cultural exchange activities.

Going further for half a *li*, we reached the site of a former building destroyed in the war. About half a *li* further is the former library to preserve imperial books; it was also destroyed during the war but has been replaced with a modern office building. They plan to rebuild the library in the Sung style with its original name. Several Ming dynasty structures in this area were used for sacrifices to Chou Tun-i, the Ch'eng brothers, Chu Hsi, Chang Shih, and some heads of the academy. They are in fairly good condition and have been used as offices and dormitories. Compared with all educational institutions, the Yüeh-lu Academy is the most well preserved, the best restored, the most scenic, and the most saturated with dynamic activity.[121]

Other than the two famous academies rebuilt by Chu Hsi, he is said to have founded the T'ung-wen (of the same language) Academy in Chien-yang, about sixty kilometers southwest of the Chu-lin Ching-she. The tradition is that he stored books there. I was told in Chien-yang that even the site is no longer known. I believe that Chu Hsi may have stored books there

---

121. For the history of the academy, plans and actual work of restoration, texts of accounts and tablets, and certain pictures, see the *Yüeh-lu Shu-yüan t'ung-hsün*.

for some special reason, but the place was turned into an academy some time after his death as a memorial to him. In fact, there is evidence that the academy was built decades after Chu Hsi's death.[122] It is also claimed that when Chu Hsi was keeper of records at T'ung-an, he established the Yen-nan Shu-yüan in Yen-nan Mountain in Chin-men Island, within the jurisdiction of T'ung-an.[123] It is unlikely that in his twenties even before he founded a *ching-she* he established an academy and it is doubtful if he ever visited the outlying island. Certainly not one of his pupils came from there.

This does not mean that Chu Hsi's relation with the academy is limited to the Han-ch'üan, Wu-i, Chu-lin, and Hsiang-hsi Ching-she and the White Deer Hollow and the Yüeh-lu academies. He lectured at least in six others,[124] and he wrote accounts for three and a postscript for a poem on another.[125] He stayed in one for a considerable period[126] and wrote plaques for at least nine academies, all of which were different from the ones I just described.[127] Eliminating duplicates, he was personally involved in twenty-four academies, including three *ching-she*. Some categories must have overlapped. For example, he must have lectured in some of those academies for which he wrote plaques. And many others must have gone unrecorded or still hidden in local gazeteers. Many temples were built to offer sacrifice to him, and others were built to commemorate his visit. A great number of these later became academies. Writing in 1506, Tai Hsien listed twenty-eight of them.[128] And writing in 1888 on academies in Hunan alone, Wang Hsien-ch'ien (1842–1917), the renowned Hunan scholar, listed ten academies. All except one were related to Chu Hsi in one way or another.[129] At least eight of his pupils founded academies, and one's father and another's grandson did.[130] At least seven served as head of academies.[131] And at least six lectured or taught in seven academies, including one with several hundred

122. In the *Chien-yang hsien-chih* (1929 ed.), p. 36a, there is an essay on "raising the beam of T'ung-wen Academy" by Hsiung Ho (fl. 1270). Traditionally, the first thing to do in constructing a building was to raise a beam to be the central piece of the roof.

123. Kuo Yao-ling, *Chu Hsi yü Chin-men* (Chin-men: Chin-men county Cultural Records Committee, 1969), pp. 5–6.

124. See Chan, *Chu Tzu men-jen*, pp. 65, 85, 326; Wang Hsien-ch'ien, *Hu-nan ch'üan-sheng chang-ku pei-k'ao* (1888 ed.) 13:3b; Yang Chin-hsin manuscript on Hunan academies in the Sung period, pp. 3, 7.

125. Chan, *Chu Tzu men-jen*, p. 183; *Wen-chi* 79:21a–22a 81:2a–b; Wang Hsien-ch'ien, *Hu-nan ch'üan-sheng, chang-ku pei-k'ao*, 13:7a.

126. Chan, *Chu Tzu men-jen, p.* 205.

127. Chu Yü, *Chu Tzu wen-chi ta-ch'üan lei-p'ien* (1721 ed.), ch'e 8, 21:1a–2b.

128. *Chu Tzu shih-chi,* chüan 7.

129. Wang Hsien-ch'ien, *Hu-nan ch'üan-sheng chang-ku pei-k'ao*, ch. 13.

130. Chan, *Chu Tzu men-jen*, pp. 156, 216, 297, 300, 302, 326, 355; *Yüeh-lu Shu-yüan t'ung-hsün*, no. 1 (1982) 27; Wang Hsien-ch'ien, *Hu-nan ch'üan-sheng chang-ku pei-k'ao*, 13:8b; Yang, manuscript on Hunan academies in the sung period, pp. 3–5, including an indirect pupil.

131. Chan, *Chu Tzu men-jen*, pp. 96, 129, 156, 192, 260, 335, 336, 345.

followers.[132] At least three were known to promote the "Articles for Learning" of the White Deer Hollow Academy.[133] There is no question that Chu Hsi and his pupils were more active than any other group in the Sung period in promoting the institution of the academy.

One more academy activity must be recounted, although it does not have a direct relationship with Chu Hsi—academy publication of books. To this day, academy editions are considered among the best. I was surprised to read that Chu Hsi engaged in printing business because no writer anywhere had ever mentioned it. After some research, I discussed it, perhaps for the first time in print, and concluded that he did it partly because poverty compelled him to seek some side income and partly because he wanted to publish books on Neo-Confucianism to promote the Neo-Confucian cause.[134] Because he printed the *Hsiao-hsüeh* as a Wu-i Ching-she publication,[135] one can safely assume that his intensive activity of printing at a famous publication center of the time, Chien-yang, had close connection with the Chu-lin Ching-she. We can also assume that his printing enterprise must have inspired later efforts in the academies to publish Neo-Confucian works.

Given these facts, perhaps one may ask some interesting questions and draw a general conclusion. Suppose Chu Hsi and his pupils had not done anything for the academies, would the numerous Buddhist institutions eventually replace Chinese schools and thus turn China into a Buddhistic country like Japan? Even if government schools could stem the tide of Buddhism, would government education not end up in literary composition for the purpose of civil service examination? And even if Neo-Confucianism occupied a place in government schools, would it be the variety of the Ch'eng-Chu School, the "new laws" of Wang An-shih, or the historical school of Lü Tsu-ch'ien? It is not fantastic to suggest that the historical schools might come to dominate. As a youngster, I was taught Lü Tsu-ch'ien's *Tung-lai po-i* (Extensive Discussions by Lü Tsu-ch'ien) in a country school. This shows how influential Lü was in popular education. In short, if Chu Hsi had kept aloof from the academy, would there still be the Neo-Confucianism of the Ch'eng-Chu School? Without it, China might be better or worse; it certainly would be different.

Scholars have often suggested that the Ch'eng-Chu Neo-Confucianism came to prevail in Chinese history and became the orthodoxy because of government promotion in making Chu Hsi's commentaries on the Confucian classics and other Neo-Confucian works the official basis for civil service examination in 1313 and in ordering by imperial command the compilation

132. Ibid., pp. 68, 168, 216, 219, 261. See above, n. 93, and *Sung-Yüan hsüeh-an pu-i* 69:154b.
133. Ibid., pp. 216, 279, 320.
134. See Wing-tsit Chan, *Chu-hsüeh lun-chi* (Taipei: Student Book Co., 1982), pp. 220–222.
135. *Wen-chi*, supplementary collection, 2:25b.

of the *Hsing-li ta-ch'üan* (The Great Collection of Neo-Confucianism) in 1415 and the compilation of the *Hsing-li ching-i* (Essential Ideas of the Ch'eng-Chu School of Nature and Principle) in 1715. Surely government influence was tremendous. One wonders, if there were no movement of private academies, would the *Hsing-li ta-ch'üan* and the *Hsing-li ching-i* have come into being at all. The emperors concerned may have wanted to use Neo-Confucianism to support their authority, but without the private academies would there have been the Ch'eng-Chu Neo-Confucianism to start with?

Elsewhere I have suggested that Chu Hsi "completed" Neo-Confucianism by determining its direction, clarifying the relation between principle (*li*) and material force (*ch'i*), developing the concept of the Great Ultimate (*T'ai-chi*), culminating the concept of *jen* (humanity), establishing the Tradition of the Way (*Tao-t'ung*), and grouping the *Analects*, the *Great Learning*, the *Book of Mencius*, and the *Doctrine of the Mean* as the Four Books.[136] I shall now add that the *ching-she* and the *shu-yüan* were his tools to implement them.[137]

---

136. "Chu Hsi's Completion of Neo-Confucianism," in *Etudes Song-Sung Studies*, ed. Francoise Aubin, ser. 2 no. 1, 1973, pp. 59–90. Chinese translation in Chan, *Chu Tzu men-jen*, pp. 1–35.

137. For an illuminating discussion on the evolution and relation of the *ching-she* and the *shu-yüan* and Chu Hsi's role in promoting the tradition of private *Chiang-hsüeh* (discussion for learning), see Thomas Hong-chi Lee, "Chu Hsi, Academies and the Tradition of Private *Chiang-hsüeh*," *Han-hsüeh chi-k'an* 2, no. 1 (Summer 1984), pp. 8–13, 21–27.

FIFTEEN

Chu Hsi in Nan-K'ang:
Tao-hsüeh and the Politics of Education

John W. Chaffee

For two years from early 1179 to early 1181, Chu Hsi served as prefect of Nan-k'ang in the Southern Sung circuit of Chiang-nan-tung. Aged fifty (Chinese style) on his arrival at that rural backwater in central China, Chu was already known as both a prolific scholar and an eminent philosopher of the day. He was also famed for his reluctance to serve; this was only his second active post, as distinguished from sinecures, in some thirty-one years as an official, and he came to it only after the strong and repeated urgings of the Chief Councilor Shih Hao (1106–1194) and his friends Lü Tsu-ch'ien (1137–1181) and Chang Shih (1133–1180).[1] He proved, however, a vigorous prefect, devoting extraordinary efforts to alleviating a famine that was devastating the prefecture, regularly lecturing at the prefectural school, and undertaking antiquarian research into the residential remains of renowned natives from earlier periods.[2] Most notably, Chu also revived the long defunct White Deer Grotto Academy (Pai-lu-tung Shu-yüan) that in the tenth and early eleventh centuries had flourished on the slopes of the scenic Mount Lu some five miles north of the prefectural capital.[3]

Studies of Chu Hsi's life and thought have tended to pass rather quickly over these years in Nan-k'ang. His revival of the White Deer Grotto Academy has been accorded a prominent place in Chinese educational

1. For biographical details, I have relied primarily upon Wang Mou-hung, *Chu-Tzu nien-p'u*, 4 chüan (SKCS ed.); Conrad Schirokauer, "The Political Thought and Behavior of Chu Hsi," (Ph.D. diss., Stanford University, 1960); and Goto Shunzui, *Shushi* (Tokyo, 1943); hereafter the *nien-p'u* cited *Nien-p'u*.

2. On the last, see especially boto, *Shushi*, pp. 48–49.

3. For detailed studies of the revival, see Ch'en Tung-yüan, "Lu-shan Pai-lu-tung shu-yüan yen-ko k'ao," Pt. 1, *Min-tuo tsa-chih* 7, no. 1 (1937):1–32; and John W. Chaffee, "Chu Hsi and the Revival of the White Deer Grotto Academy, 1179–81," *T'oung Pao* 71 (1985):40–62.

history, as a model for subsequent Neo-Confucian academies and source of the influential "Articles" Chu wrote for it. Famous, too, was the visit in the spring of 1181 of Chu's great rival, Lu Chiu-yüan (1139–1193), and his lecture at the academy on the subject of righteousness and profit, a lecture Chu praised highly. But with these exceptions, the greater importance of his subsequent posts—he went from Nan-k'ang to serve as the intendant for the Ever Normal Granaries, Tea and Salt in Liang-che-tung—and the rising tide of attacks in the 1180s and 1190s upon Chu Hsi and his followers, who were accused of "spurious learning" (wei-hsüeh), have tended to overshadow the Nan-k'ang years. They were, it would seem, the lull before the storm.

It is my contention in this chapter that such perceptions are misleading. Chu Hsi's educational activities in Nan-k'ang were in fact full of controversy as were his relations at the time with the Court. In this the revival was far from unique, for at secluded country locales throughout the empire, but especially in the central Yangtze valley, Fu-chien, and southern Liang-che, educators critical of the kinds of learning found in the government schools were establishing academies, more than two hundred and fifty in the Southern Sung all told.[4] The White Deer Grotto revival did not initiate this movement, but it occupied a prominent place within it, because of both the fame of its Northern Sung antecedent and the personal involvement of Chu Hsi.

In part, too, the controversy was caused by the rapid growth of Chu's literati following. The late twelfth century was a period of exceptional literati activity and prominence, thanks largely to the unprecedented popularity of the examinations. Competition in the triennial prefectural examinations, on the order of one prefectural graduate in ten candidates in the eleventh century, had escalated to one in a hundred or worse in the late twelfth.[5] As a result the literati milieu became larger and more heterogeneous than ever before, encompassing scholars, artists, poets, teachers, and book collectors as well as literati turned merchant or monk, book printers, and wandering scholars who either lived off their connections or by their wits. Within this society those who sought moral or philosophical instruction, often in reaction against the single-minded pursuit of examination success, constituted a small minority, but their numbers too were growing; and they were highly visible, for they usually attached themselves to famous scholars.

Of those scholars, none was more popular than Chu Hsi, whose following eclipsed those of others, at least from his Nan-k'ang period on. To many in a Court acutely conscious of its need for literati support, the very size of Chu's following and the fervor of his followers appeared threatening. Although

4. See Chaffee, "Chu Hsi and the Revival," pp. 46–47.

5. For an analysis of this change and its consequences, see John W. Chaffee, The Thorny Gates of Learning in Sung China: A Social History of Examinations (Cambridge: Cambridge University Press, 1985).

most of them not officials, opponents labeled them a faction—thereby
extending the meaning of that term—and eventually had them banned from
the examinations in 1195, an extreme sanction for literati. But neither the
short-term success nor the long-term failure of the proscription of *tao-hsüeh*
(the School of the Way, as Chu and his followers were called) should obscure
the remarkable role that these provincial literati played in Chu's movement
for moral and educational reform.

THE REVIVAL UNDER FIRE

The revival of the White Deer Grotto Academy had its inception in a visit
Chu Hsi paid to Mt. Lu in 1179. When he and his companions came across
the old academy's ruins on the eastern slope of the mountain, he recounted
its origins as the residence of a T'ang official and its flourishing as a school in
the Southern T'ang and early Sung, when the emperor T'ai-tsung (r.
976–997) presented it with a set of the Classics, an event recorded in the
dynastic annals.[6] He bemoaned its demise in the early Southern Sung,
particularly since Buddhist institutions had continued to flourish on the
mountain, and resolved to rebuild it.[7] The restoration, completed by the
third month of 1180, was a considerable undertaking involving both public
and private resources. The rebuilding was supervised by two local officials,
the Hsing-tzu county magistrate Wang Chung-chieh and the prefectural
school preceptor Yang Ta-fa, financed by donations from the local elite, and
used corvée labor.[8] From the local government it received fields in neighboring Chien-ch'ang county for educational support.[9] Finally, thanks to a
solicitation by Chu to prefectures throughout Chiang-hsi, the academy also
received books from officials and local families.[10]

Although these facts tagether with descriptions of the teaching there by
Chu, Lu Chiu-yüan, and other have often been recounted, the standard
treatments of the revival make no mention of the controversy that surrounded it. Yet when one carefully examines Chu's reports and letters to the
Court concerning the revival—unfortunately there are no corroborating
documents by others who were involved—a picture emerges of a rather
beleaguered Chu Hsi reacting indignantly to sharp attacks both on the
manner of the academy's revival and on its educational activities.[11]

6. For the record in the annals, which Chu considered very important, see Li Tao, *Hsü
tzu-chih t'ung-chien ch'ang-p'ien*, 520 chüan (1622 plus later addenda; Ch'ing edition) 2:6b;
hereafter cited PLSYC.
7. Lü Tsu-ch'ien, "Pai-lu-tung shu-yüan chi," in *Nien-p'u* 2:24a–b.
8. Ibid., 2:23b, 24b.
9. PLSYC 3:14a.
10. Ibid., 2:25b; *Nien-p'u* 2:2b and Chu Hsi, *Hui-an hsien-sheng Chu wen-kung wen-chi*, 100
chüan (SPTK ed.) 11:25b–26a; hereafter cited *Wen-chi*.
11. Most relevant documents may be found in PLSYC 24b–10a. as well as in scattered
locations in the *Wen-chi*.

The primary issue of contention concerned the educational functions of the academy. Like other prefectures, Nan-k'ang had its own government school, and Chu Hsi, known for his interest in education, had from his arrival taken an active role there, not only teaching frequently but also aiding in its renovation in 1180.[12] With the revival of the White Deer Grotto Academy, the question naturally arose, why another school for the elite? In his initial reports to the Court, Chu Hsi played down the academy's educational functions. His petition to the Minister of Rites requesting permission for the revival justified it solely in terms of its cultural symbolism, emphasizing the Academy's eminent history and its place in the dynastic annals.[13] He was even more emphatic in a postscript to the petition, stating that the academy would have only three to five rooms, would not supplant the government school, would not require much in the way of official funds, and was meant to maintain the traces of antiquity.[14]

In fact, the restored academy proved to be a major educational center. The academy history recounts that in 1180 students increased daily,[15] and the names of some seven disciples who studied with Chu Hsi there are known.[16] In addition to Lu Chiu-yüan's letters (mentioned above), there remain study questions that Chu Hsi preserved for students there,[17] and one is told that Chu visited the academy every holiday and spent his time instructing and walking with the students.[18] Perhaps most interesting, in the fall of 1180 Chu invited the twenty-eight *chü-jen* and nominees for the university entrance examination to come and study at the academy before setting off for the capital.[19]

Reports on this activity were making their way independently to the capital, for in Chu's next communication with the court on the subject, a letter from 1180 to the Minister of Rites, he defended himself from attacks by "rustic and insulting individuals." He began, "The insignificant Hsi has already made his supplication in full in an earlier scroll, and will not test himself by suddenly requesting that limits be exceeded. Forgetting his crimes, he dares to speak selfishly of this," and then proceeded to make his case again for the academy. After describing the great beauty of Mount Lu, he recounted his discovery of the academy's ruins on the luxuriant but wild mountainside and his realization of its significance:

> He [Chu Hsi] considered that although [the place] was distant and rustic, it had in fact received the attention of the first [Sung] emperors and should not be

---

12. *Nien-p'u* 2:20b, 30b–31a.
13. "Shen hsiu Pai-lu-tung Shu-yüan chuang," *Wen-chi* 20:9a–10a; PLSYC 2:3b–4a.
14. "Hsiao t'ieh-tzu," *Wen-chi* 20:10a; PLSYC 2:4b.
15. PLSYC 3:2a, 14a.
16. See note 54 below. Eleven others who were said to have studied with Chu in Nan-k'ang undoubtedly studied at the academy as well.
17. "Chiang-t'ang ts'e-wen," PLSYC 2:13b–14b.
18. *Nien-p'u* 2:23b.
19. "Chao chü-jen ju shu-yüan chuang," PLSYC 2:10b–11a.

lying in ruins. On arriving at this conclusion, he had rebuilt upon the site small buildings of seven frames (i.e., the distance between beams) and five rooms in size, for he foolishly thought that the court might wish to restore this ruined office in order to demonstrate the imperial ancestors' teachings of reverence for Confucians and esteem of learning. Although unfilial himself, he therefore asks to be able to complete the preparations.

Having admitted that the academy was larger than he had originally reported, Chu went on to acknowledge its educational function, though he took pains to minimize it: "Within the academy the headmaster would, with one or two students, read books and discuss the Way, so that the superior might be aided in understanding commands and the inferior might follow their life goals." Out of compassion for the students, grain allowances would also be provided.[20]

If Chu Hsi thought that this would settle things, he quickly learned otherwise, for next he wrote to Chief Councilor Chao Hsiung (1129–1193) in response to a sharp request for information about the academy's revival. Denying any guilt or misconduct, Chu declined to answer Chao's questions or accusations specifically, saying that had been done in his earlier letter to the minister. Instead he said that if his protestations of innocence were not accepted, either he should be removed from his post or the position of headmaster (*tung-chu*) of the White Deer Grotto Academy should be revived and he be named to it according to the provisions for temple guardianships (i.e., sinecures).[21] This challenge apparently went unanswered, for although he was shortly to leave his prefectureship, it was after a promotion to an intendancy in Chiang-hsi, which was changed to Liang-che-tung before his departure.

In the third month of 1181, shortly before leaving Nan-k'ang, Chu Hsi approached the court with a final request for the academy.[22] Citing the imperial gifts of Sung T'ai-tsung and Chen-tsung to the academy and their subsequent loss, Chu asked that the Court donate a tablet bearing the academy's name, a printing of the Classics from a handwritten copy by the emperor Kao-tsung, and printed commentaries on the Nine Classics. Referring to the critics who complained of the inadequacies of the revival, he said that they dealt with just one part in ten thousand. The academy was a school, he acknowledged, with small buildings of twelve rooms and only ten or twenty students—his numbers continued to grow—but rather than seeing it as a threat to the government schools, Chu argued that it should be viewed against the threat of an ubiquitous Buddhism:

20. "Yü Shang-shu cha-tzu," ibid., 2:4b–5b; *Wen-chi* 26:11b–12a. The letter does not make clear that it was addressed to the Minister of Rites and not another minister, but because his initial petition went to the Ministry of Rites, we can assume that this did, too.

21. "Yü Ch'eng-hsiang cha-tzu," ibid., 2:5b–6a; *Wen-chi* 26:12b–13a.

22. "Ch'i tz'u Pai-lu-ting Shu-yüan ch'ih-e," ibid., 2:6a–8a.

Although the prefecture already has a prefectural school which is sufficient for nourishing the literati, the flourishing of the Grotto [Academy] is so venerable as to transmit the accumulated sageliness of past dynasties. If we regard with tenderness the profundity of its bright and favored virtue, then on principle we cannot let it fail. How much more so [is this the case] when in the vicinity is found the sounds of bells and drums of temples, the destruction of human relationships, and talk of emptiness and magic? . . . Yet the halls for the rites and music of the Former Kings which form the basis of cultivating the people and teaching customs are, on the contrary, scattered and separated. In the prefectures and countries [of Nan-k'ang] there are only three [schools]. Thus we renovated this Grotto.[23]

This request met with little success, however, for some six months later in his last official communication concerning the academy, another plea for the tablet and Classics that he wrote on the occasion of his imperial audience at the Yen-ho Palace, Chu professed his disquiet (*pu-an*) at the Court's lack of action.[24] He complained that men in both Court and countryside had been spreading rumors and ridiculing the academy as a "strange venture." After recounting one last time the academy's history, he returned to his attack on Buddhism and, secondarily, Taoism in answering the question of why academies should be built when there are already government schools. They were subversive in their denial of ruler and father, he charged, in contrast to the Confucian affirmation of the three bonds (ruler-subject, father-son, and husband-wife) and five norms (humaneness, righteousness, propriety, knowledge, and faithfulness). And their popularity made them a threat. Their temples often numbered in the thousands in cities and even small towns had several score, whereas schools were limited to one for each county and prefecture and in many places even these had disappeared.[25]

This, finally, appears to have prodded the Court into action. In the eleventh month of 1181 classics from the Directorate of Education were given to the academy,[26] although the academy records themselves are silent on the reception, use, and later history of the books.[27] There also appears in the annals a brief reference to the revival, to my knowledge the only reference in the twelfth-century annalistic literature to the academy. It states that "the revival of the White Deer Grotto Academy followed the memorial of Chu

23. Ibid., 2:6b–7a.

24. "Yen-ho-tien tsou-shih," ibid., 2:8a–9b; *Wen-chi* 13:8a–10b.

25. PLSYC 2:9a.

26. Wang Ying-lin, *Yü-hai*, 200 chüan (Taipei: Hua-wen shu-chü, 1967), 167:20a. See also *Wen-chi* 90:7b. This evidence, kindly provided by Wing-tsit Chan, disproves my assertion to the contrary in, Chaffee, "Chu Hsi and the Revival," p. 44.

27. Although one would expect such an imperial gift to have been received with great fanfare and housed in a specially constructed library, there is no reference to that in the PLSYC, unless in fact a *Li-sheng-tien* ("Hall of Homage to the Sages") built in late 1182 was used for that purpose. PLSYC 3:14a. There are also no later references to the plaque or books in either the PLSYC or Ch'en Tung-yüan's history of the academy.

Hsi" and then provides an account of the academy's history, but it says nothing about the revival or the court's reaction to it.[28] It would thus appear that the academy had finally received the recognition, however grudging, that Chu Hsi had so stubbornly been seeking, and likely it was related to the fact that Chao Hsiung, Chu's most visible critic during his Nan-k'ang years, had in the eighth month of 1181 been replaced as chief councilor by Wang Huai (1129–1193), who was at this time more sympathetic to Chu.[29] But the success undoubtedly had its costs, both in terms of the efforts Chu was forced to expend and the animosities the revival aroused.

THE CRITICS AND THE ISSUES

One of the most interesting features of the White Deer Grotto revival controversy is that it was controversial at all. As far as I can tell, no one questioned the authenticity of the site, the history of the academy, or the academy as a symbol of early Sung culture. There were, moreover, ample precedents for establishing academies. As I have described elsewhere, academies were growing in numbers in the decades prior to 1179, and the White Deer Grotto revival might better be seen as an important milestone in the academy movement rather than as its beginning.[30] Most of these academies were modest and informal establishments, but in 1160 the Yüeh-lu Academy of Southern T'ang and Northern Sung fame was revived amid considerable fanfare and no apparent controversy. What then was the dispute about, and who were the critics?

To take the latter question first, it is clear from Chu Hsi's writings that he was under attack both in Nan-k'ang and at the court. Exactly who his accusers were I cannot say because Chu named no names. He may not have known, for he was not furnished with copies of their accusations. On one occasion he chided them for not daring to make public accusations, and on another he stated: "I do not know what they have said."[31] He did suggest more than once that the accusations were coming from officials,[32] and this would certainly make sense given the access they evidently had to the highest levels of government.

The most likely critic in Nan-k'ang was the prefectural school preceptor, Yang Ta-fa, a Wu-chou native who received his *chin-shih* degree in 1175 and who, as a general censor in 1195, was a petitioner for the edict against

---

28. Liu Cheng, *Huang Sung chung-hsing liang-ch'ao sheng-cheng*, 64 chüan (Taipei: Wen-hai ch'u-pan-she, 1967) 59:2228; hereafter cited *Liang-ch'ao sheng-cheng*.

29. See T'o T'o et al., *Sung-shih*, 495 chüan (Taipei: I-wen yin-shu kuan, 1962) 112:25–26a for the change from Chao to Wang and 396:7b on Wang's attitude towards Chu Hsi in 1181.

30. See Chaffee, "Chu Hsi and the Revival."

31. PLSYC 2:5b, 9a.

32. Ibid., 2:7a, 8b, 9a.

wei-hsüeh.[33] Chu Hsi, by first teaching in the prefectural school and then reviving the academy and enlisting Yang's assistance was clearly encroaching on Yang's educational domain. It would hardly be surprising if this made Yang resentful, especially since Yang had to deal with not only Chu but also his very numerous and quite possibly rather irritating followers. Yet even if Yang were writing accusatory reports, one need not assume he was acting alone. Both active and retired officials throughout Chiang-hsi were all aware of the revival, thanks in part to Chu's solicitation of books, so there were plenty of people around who might have resented his actions.

Chu Hsi's standing at the Court in 1180 and 1181 was problematical. The emperor Hsiao-tsung had held him in high regard since his accession in 1162 and generally viewed Chu's repeated refusals to serve with tolerance, even while others were growing increasingly critical. Thus, in 1173 the emperor actually praised Chu for being "content with poverty and happy in the Way."[34] But Hsiao-tsung could be infuriated by Chu's memorials. When in the fourth month of 1180 Chu responded to a request for memorials by submitting a blistering denunciation of the ministers about Hsiao-tsung who had "seduced the emperor's resolve and made him disbelieve in the great Way of the former kings,"[35] Hsiao-tsung was enraged and remarked, "He takes me for a fool!" He was deterred from dismissing Chu from his post only by Chief Councillor Chao Hsiung, who argued against making a martyr of him.[36]

Ironically Chao Hsiung, the recipient of Chu's second letter concerning the academy, appears to have been Chu's chief antagonist at Court in this period. In 1178 Shih Hao had initially wanted to give Chu a capital post, but Chao had successfully argued that Chu should be given a provincial post and be made to demonstrate his "utmost sincerity."[37] Moreover, only after Chao's demotion in 1181 did the Court give Chu the Liang-che-tung intendency and grant the academy official recognition.

The primary charge made by Chu's critics appears to have been that the academy was usurping the prefectural school's role.[38] During the Northern Sung the government had instituted a system of government schools in counties (*hsien-hsüeh*) leading to the Imperial University (*T'ai-hsüeh*) at the capital, and under the emperor Hui-tsung (r. 1101–1126) these had taken

33. Conrad Schirokauer, Biography of Yang Ta-fa in *Sung Biographies*, ed. Herbert Franke, 5 vols. (Wiesbaden: Franz Steiner Verlag GMBH, 1976) 3:1230.

34. Li Hsin-ch'uan, "Hui-an hsien-sheng fei su yin," *Chien-yen i-lai Ch'ao-yeh tsa-chi*, 40 chüan (TSCC ed.) 2.8:445 (i.e., Pt. 2, chüan 8, p. 445); hereafter cited CYTC

35. *Liang-ch'ao sheng-cheng* 58:2185.

36. CYTC 2.8:446. The argument about martyrdom is from Schirokauer, "The Political Thought and Behavior of Chu Hsi," pp. 102–103. The CYTC says only that Chao made "pretended excuses" for Chu.

37. CYTC 2.8:445.

38. See especially PLSYC 2:8a–9b and *Wen-chi* 13:8a–10b, 20:10a.

over a large part of selection functions of the examination system. Since the loss of the North, the schools had ceased to function as a system, and in places they had fallen into disrepair; but in much of the empire they continued to thrive, preparing students for the examinations and supported by local elites and officials.[39] There were other kinds of schools, to be sure: small schools established by families, lineages, and communities for their sons and academies created by noted scholars for students who came seeking their instruction. But these generally did not rival the government schools as highly visible and prestigious institutions. The White Deer Grotto Academy, however, did.

Chu Hsi responded to criticisms of rivalry in two ways: he minimized the educational importance of the academy and appealed to the threat of Buddhism. Concerning the former, he appears to have been less than completely candid, for he first described the academy as a three- to five-room building without any teaching, then said that it had five to seven rooms and one or two students, and finally talked of twelve rooms with ten to twenty students. I should point out, in fairness to Chu, that formal pedagogy was not something that could be simply distinguished from other functions of the academy, nor was it its only educational function. The academy was a center for rites, a visible symbol of Confucian culture standing amidst a Buddhist forest, and it was at times a gathering place for literati of all ages and stations.[40] Because these aided in the spread of culture and the realization of the Way, they could also be considered educational. But that the academy was attracting students and had become a flourishing center of teaching is clearly indicated by the evidence,[41] and one can only conclude that Chu was trying to minimize this fact in the face of criticism.

The same cannot be said of Chu Hsi's invocation of the dangers of Buddhism and Taoism. Ever since his early infatuation with Buddhism, Chu had been one of its outspoken critics. Aware of the intellectual seductiveness of Ch'an and alarmed by the omnipresence of Buddhist and Taoist temples, Chu was undoubtedly speaking from the heart when pleading for a more visible Confucian presence in the countryside, a presence epitomized by the academy at Mt. Lu. Nor was he alone in his portrayal of a beleaguered Confucianism, for others were using the same argument to support the construction of government schools.[42] Yet one wonders if this religious argument satisfied Chu's critics and, furthermore, how central it really was to the revival of the Academy. The great visibility of temples bespoke the popularity of Buddhism and Taoism within society at large. Although this

---

39. See Thomas Lee's chapter in this volume. For statistics on government schools in different periods of the Sung, see Chaffee, *The Thorny Gates of Learning*, chap. 4.

40. See Linda Walton's chapter in this volume.

41. On the growth of student numbers in 1181, see PLSYC 3:2a, 14a.

42. See, for example, Yüan Chüeh, *Yen-yu Ssu-ming chih*, 20 *chüan* (Sung Yüan Ssu-ming liu chih ed.) 15:5b.

surely concerned Chu, who elsewhere had devoted considerable energy to popular education and the reform of public morality,[43] in Nan-k'ang he was primarily concerned with the literati and the inadequacies of their Confucian education.[44]

In a letter that Chu Hsi wrote to Lü Tsu-ch'ien on the subject of the academy's revival, he contrasted the early Sung when customs were admirable with the present day, when literati (*shih*)

> consider learning [*hsüeh*] to be no more than paragraphs, sentences and the meaning of passages. They also suffer from vileness and confusion. Thus the literati of today who are conscious of the past are frequently distressed by their still inadequate understanding of the great Way of the Former Kings and discuss how it might be renewed.[45]

This concern for the education of literati was particularly evident in his Articles of the White Deer Grotto Academy, about which he wrote:

> In recent ages, regulations have been instituted in schools and students have been treated in a shallow manner. This method of making regulations does not at all conform with the intention of the ancients. Therefore, I shall not now try to put them into effect in this lecture hall. Rather I have specifically selected all the essential principles that the sages and the worthies used in teaching peoples how to pursue learning; I have listed them as above one by one and posted them on the crossbar over the gate.[46]

Chu's "selected principles" numbered five: the List of the Five Teachings that prescribed the attitudes underlying the five Confucian relationships; the Order of Study that prescribed one's approach to study; Essentials of Self-Cultivation; Essentials of Managing Affairs; and Essentials of Getting Along With Others.[47] In other words, Chu viewed self-education and moral self-cultivation as essential to political and social activity, yet this was precisely what most schools, especially the government schools, tended to ignore.

At the heart of this neglect loomed the civil service examinations, for such were their rewards that they encouraged study that was both formalistic and motivated by profit. Chu was not opposed to the examinations as such—

43. See Wm. Theodore de Bary, *The Liberal Tradition in China* (Hong Kong: Hong Kong University Press, 1982), pp. 32–33.

44. It is, of course, possible that Chu was concerned by the challenge of Ch'an education, which as Chün-fang Yü has pointed, had both a literati following and pedagogical similarities with Neo-Confucian education. But, if so, it is not evident in his Nan-K'ang writings on Buddhism; they treat it as a moral and religious system, not as a competing form of education.

45. "Yü Lü Po-kung lun Shu-yüan chi shu," PLSYC 2:16a.

46. Ch'eng Tuan-li, *Ch'eng-shih chia-shu tu-shu fen-nien jih-ch'eng*, 3 chüan (Pai-pu ts'ung-k'an ed.), Outline of Principles 2a; and *Nien-p'u* 2:24a. The translation follows that of de Bary in *The Liberal Tradition in China*, pp. 37–38.

47. Ch'eng Tuan-li, *Ch'eng-shih chia-shu*, Outline 1a–2a; *Nien-p'u* 2:23b–24a.

although he was later to write a famous critique of them advocating substantial reforms[48]—but he was mindful of their limitations and critical of the kind of study they engendered. In his invitation to Nan-k'ang *chü-jen* to come and study at the academy he wrote:

> The country uses examinations to select literati. Now in cultivating the ancient rules of past dynasties, such things as the meanings of the Classics, poetry, discussions and policy questions are inadequate for the utmost obtainment of the world's literati. Rather one must select those literati who attend their superiors through the discussion of learning and the cultivation of character.[49]

Later in the invitation he also pointed out that the pastoral environment of the academy was conducive to solitary study and reflection.[50]

Was it this antipathy of Chu Hsi's too examination-oriented education that exercised his critics in Nan-k'ang and made them fear the White Deer Grotto Academy as a threat to the commandary school? Yes, it seems, at least in part. It is noteworthy that, while Chu's criticisms of contemporary education are much in evidence in his writings for an academy audience and his Nan-k'ang poetry, there is no hint of them in his petitions and letters to the court.[51] Such criticisms, it would appear, were politically sensitive. But even so it is unlikely that his criticisms would have stirred up much opposition had he not attempted to realize his educational ideals at the academy and had he not had scores of devoted followers with him in Nan-k'ang trying to practice what he preached. The emergence of a literati movement dedicated to the practice and propagation of Chu's teachings, I would submit, most alarmed his critics both in Nan-k'ang and at the capital.

CHU HSI'S DISCIPLES

Since Huang Tsung-hsi's pathbreaking seventeenth-century study of the Confucian scholars of the Sung and Yüan,[52] it has been widely recognized that the contributions of Sung learning were not only philosophical but also social. Both the numbers of those involved in Confucian studies and their social visibility were unprecedented. Of all Sung thinkers, moreover, none could compare with Chu Hsi in terms of the size of their followings. According to recent meticulously researched studies of Chu Hsi's disciples by Tanaka Kenji and Wing-tsit Chan, Chu by the time of his death had attracted almost five hundred disciples who can definitely be identified as

---

48. "Chu Tzu hsüeh-hsiao kung-chü ssu-i," in Ch'eng Tuan-li, *Ch'eng-shih chia-shu* 3:40b–50b.
49. "Chao chü-jen ju shu-yüan chuang," PLSYC 2:10b.
50. Ibid., 2:11a.
51. See Chaffee, "Chu Hsi and the Revival," for a discussion of this discrepancy.
52. *Sung Yüan hsüeh-an,* 100 chüan.

such.[53] The greatest numbers were from Chu's home circuit of Fu-chien, but he had large followings from Liang-che and Chiang-nan and smaller followings from Ching-hu-nan and -pei and Kuang-nan-tung as well.[54]

Wing-tsit Chan, in his analysis of the data assembled in his book on Chu's disciples, points out the importance of Chu's travels to different parts of the empire for attracting disciples from those regions. Thus, his visits to Wu-yüan county (in Chiang-nan-tung) in 1176, to Ching-hu-nan in 1167 and especially 1194, to Nan-k'ang in 1179–1181, and to Liang-che-tung in 1182 all resulted in men seeking him out as their teacher.[55] If one, using Chan's data, analyzes the chronology of the growth of Chu's following, it becomes clear that his time in Nan-k'ang marked the beginning of his great popularity as a teacher.[56] Chu had had disciples before. Lin Yung-chung, described in one source as his "oldest follower," had been with him since 1167 and his leading disciple Huang Kan since 1176.[57] He had also gained three important disciples during his visit to his ancestral graves in Wu-yüan in 1176: Ch'eng Tuan-meng, Ch'eng Hsün, and T'eng Lin.[58] In contrast to this handful, there were larger groups of enumerated followers: some seven disciples studied with Chu at the White Deer Grotto Academy;[59] eleven are recorded as having studied with him in Nan-k'ang;[60] nine were Nan-k'ang natives although whether they studied under him there is not known;[61] and seventeen from outside of Nan-k'ang are recorded as having been with him

53. Tanaka Kenji, "Shumon deshi shiji nenko," Tōhōgakuhō, Pt. 1:44 (February 1973): 147–218; Pt. 2:48 (December 1975):261–357. Wing-tsit Chan, Chu-tzu men-jen (Taipei: Hsüeh-sheng shu-chü, 1982); hereafter cited Men-jen.

54. For a geographical analysis, see "Chu-men chih t'e-se chi ch'i i-i," in Men-jen, pp. 1–27. This same article is also found in Wing-tsit Chan, Chu-hsüeh lun-chi (Taipei: Hsüeh-sheng shu-chü, 1982), pp. 299–329.

55. Men-jen, pp. 11–13.

56. Hoyt Tillman has noted this difference in his observation that Chu Hsi and Ch'en Liang both began attracting large numbers of students in the early 1180 Utilitarian Confucianism: Ch'en Liang's Challenge to Chu Hsi (Cambridge: Harvard University Press, 1982), p. 183.

57. Men-jen, pp. 145–146, 261–262.

58. Ibid., pp. 245–246, 243–244, 325.

59. The page numbers in this and 60, 61, 62 all refer to Men-jen. These were Hsiung Chao (288–289) Hu Yung (169), Liu Pen (314), Lu Yen (102), Ts'ai Nien-ch'eng (334–335), Ts'ao Yen-ch'un (195–196), and Ts'ao Yen-yüeh (195). Except for Ts'ai, from neighboring Chiang-chou, all were Nan-k'ang natives.

60. Chin Ch'ü-wei (160–161), Chou Fang (135), Chou Heng-chung (136), Chou Mo (141–142), Huang Hao (265–226), Li Hui (125–126), P'eng Fang (233), P'eng Hsün (233–234), P'eng Li (236), Ts'ao Chien (194–195) and Yü Chieh (88). In addition, Fu Meng-ch'üan (232), a student of Lu Chiu-yüan's, studied with Chu in Nan-k'ang, but because he thereafter returned to Lu he has not been counted. All these men were Nan-k'ang natives.

61. Chou Te-chih (138), Fei Han-ying (249), Feng I (252–253), Fu Hsü (198), Li Fan (129), Li Shen-tzu (mentioned with Yeh Yung-ch'ing and also in PLSYC 2:22a–23a), Yang Yu-chih (267), Yeh Yung-ch'ing (278), and Yü Sung-chieh (87–88).

there.[62] In addition to these forty-four disciples, Chan records some twenty-three friends and acquaintances who were associated with him there. Most of these disciples were commoners. Only a few like Huang Kan and Wan Jen-chieh already had official rank, and only ten (23 percent) were officials at any time in their lives.[63] Indeed, several like Chin Ch'ü-wei, Ts'ai Nien-ch'eng, and Lin Yung-chung somewhat earlier publicly turned their backs on the examinations and were content to seek the *Tao* in retirement.[64]

The literati who flocked to Chu and the White Deer Grotto Academy must have made a strong impression on the officials and local elite of Nan-k'ang. For those upset about the academy and its educational activities the disciples with their moral fervor and dedication to self-cultivation must have seemed objectionable, especially since, as James T. C. Liu has pointed out, the *Tao-hsüeh* adherents set themselves off from their contemporaries in dress and behavior:

> Though times had changed, they searched among Northern Sung portraits and earlier records to recover the bygone styles and dressed accordingly. Among other features, they chose to wear a tall hat with a pointed top, a beretlike gear for casual wear, a roomy gown with broad sleeves, and a fine white-gauze shirt underneath. Their mannerism was strict: they sat squarely with their back erect, walked in measured steps looking straight ahead, bowed slowly and deeply to express sincere propriety, spoke in a dignified way with few gestures and carefully made at that. Many people looked upon their lofty air as strange, stupid, snobbish, arrogant, or more like a Taoist than a Confucianist.[65]

Writing in 1811, Ch'en Liang cast the activities of Chu's disciples in Liang-che-tung in the guise of a heterodox sect:

> Because their own eyes are only occasionally open, they believe they have a secret art of learning. In small cliques of twos and threes, they whisper into each other's ears as though they are passing along secret information. They demark and establish boundaries between themselves and others like ties at the sacrificial altar of a secret society. They completely exclude a generation of men as outside of their school.[66]

Similar criticisms were leveled in Nan-k'ang, for Chu in his letter to the chief councilor denied the charge that he and his followers used incense in

---

62. Chang Yang-ch'ing (192–193), Chang Yen-hsien (191), Chao Tzu-ming (289–290), Ch'en Shih-chih (207), Ch'en Tsu-yung (218), Ch'eng Tuan-meng (245–246), Chou I (141), Fang Mo (mentioned under Liu Chin, 315), Hsü Tzu-ch'un (199–200) Huang Kan (261–262), Kuo Chih (206), Lin Yung-chung (145–146),Teng T'ao (345), Wan Jen-chieh (248–249), Wang Ch'ao (65), Wang Yüan (mentioned under Chang Yang-ch'ing, 193), and Yü Yü (88).

63. This is close to Chan's figure of 28 for the disciples as a whole. *Men-jen*, p. 15.

64. Ibid., pp. 160–161, 145–146, 334–335.

65. James T. C. Liu, "How Did a Neo-Confucian School Become the State Orthodoxy?" *Philosophy East and West* 23 (1973):497.

66. Quoted in Hoyt Tillman, *Utilitarian Confucianism*, p. 183.

their worship and heterodox teachings and insisted that they used literature, learning, rites, and righteousness to develop themselves into officials.[67] When Chu petitioned the Court for the donation of Classics and tablet, moreover, he took care to point out that such a "display of the Confucian spirit" would benefit not only his own disciples but in fact the "myriad generations of the world."[68]

Despite such cautionary protestations, Chu Hsi clearly had a sense of leading an educational and moral movement. In a letter to his disciple Ch'eng Tuan-meng (1143–1191), Chu stated that as a result of the White Deer Grotto revival, friends in Chiang[-nan] and [Liang-]che were assembling together.[69] Because Ch'eng himself had just recently been expelled from the university in Lin-an because of his advocacy of Tao-hsüeh, it does not seem unreasonable to read into Chu's letter a sense of estrangement from, if not opposition to, the prevailing authorities.[70] It is also noteworthy that the regions mentioned by Chu together with his native Fu-chien accounted for most Southern Sung academies, many of which were founded by Chu or his followers.[71]

I should stress that neither large student followings nor gatherings in academies were unique to Chu Hsi and his followers, even though they were most prominent on both counts. I need only mention Lu Chiu-yüan in Hsin-chou, Ch'en Liang in Wen-chou, and Lü Tsu-ch'ien in Wu-chou, and Yang Chien in Ming-chou; all attracted numerous disciples and taught in private schools called academies (shu-yüan or ching-she), although such names were often additions by later followers. In a general way this activity reflected the explosive growth of literati numbers in the twelfth century, a growth which created extreme competition in the examinations and engendered a sense of cynicism and alienation among many who participated. To turn from a life of examinations to one of philosophical inquiry and moral renewal was therefore an attractive option and one increasingly chosen in the last decades of the twelfth century.

67. PLSYC 2:6a.
68. Ibid., 2:7b.
69. Ibid., 2:23a.
70. A native of Jao-chou who had become a disciple of Chu's at Wu-yüan in 1176, Ch'eng had entered the university in Lin-an in 1180 and developed a following among his fellow students. In conversations with them, in a memorial to the throne, and in the policy question of the university's annual examination that asked about the learning of Wang An-shih, the Ch'eng brothers, and Su Shih, he argued for the primacy of principle (li) in government and for the proposition that the Tao of the Former Kings had been transmitted through the Ch'engs. As a result of this "unorthodox" answer, he was failed from the university, and his hopes for an official career were dashed. Ch'eng must have gone directly from Lin-an to Nan-k'ang because he is recorded as having been there with Chu. For the last decade of his life he taught in his home community and gained some fame for the Neo-Confucian educational text, Ch'eng Tung erh hsien-sheng hsüeh-tse, which he coauthored with his student Tung Chu. CWKWC 82:14a, 90:16a–17b; Men-jen, pp. 245–246.
71. See Figure 2 in Chaffee, "Chu Hsi and the Revival."

What distinguished Chu Hsi from his contemporaries was not just the size of his following or his intellectual preeminence but also his political visibility. Although he had never held a post in the Court or capital, his repeated refusals of office and his uncompromising memorials to the throne had made him a figure of controversy within the Court, especially since his memorials emphasized time and again the importance of personnel selection and the failings of current leaders. His 1180 memorial that so enraged Hsiao-tsung dealth at length with the idea of "compassion for the people" as the great priority of government and with the need for reforming the military, but its central thesis was that the public principles (*chi-kang*) of the empire must be the "fair and upright policies of the ruler's mind" and avoid the "private [interest] of prejudiced factions and the rebellious."[72] The oppressiveness of the current leadership was such, he argued, that upright literati did not wish to serve and were afraid to speak up, and the harm being done was not limited to the regulations but extended to the people, finances, military affairs, and even the imperial temples.[73] In a similar manner, Chu memorialized a year later that "when your highness began your reign you generally selected and established heroes to govern affairs, but unfortunately among those chosen, you were unable to completely obtain [virtuous] men."[74]

Chu Hsi's opponents at Court found him a formidable antagonist and a somewhat elusive target. They were unable to take issue with the substance of what he and other *Tao-hsüeh* adherents preached because so much of that came from the Classics themselves.[75] They could, of course, accuse Chu of not living up to the lofty ideals that he preached or, worse, of misconduct and immorality, and in fact the strongest critiques of him in the 1190s were primarily ad hominem.[76] But many of the attacks were directed against Chu's teaching and his followers. The censor Ch'en Chia, in his famous memorial on "spurious learning" in 1183, charged that *Tao-shüeh* adherents were hypocritical and false, interested only in wealth while mouthing the words of the Former Kings. They traveled about like men of the market, exalting their minuscule goodness and talking loftily of retirement.[77] Although Chu and his disciples were not named by Ch'en, there is little doubt that he had them in mind.[78] Later attacks were more explicit. Thus Investigating Censor Shen Chi-tsu wrote of Chu in 1198:

72. *Liang-ch'ao sheng-cheng* 58:2184.

73. Ibid., 58:2185–2186.

74. Ibid., 59:2225.

75. See, for example, Liu Kuang-tsu's 1190 defense of *Tao-hsüeh* in which he argues that it did not consist of the personal teachings of the Ch'engs but rather came from the *Great Learning* (*Ta-hsüeh*). Li Hsin-ch'uan, *Tao-ming lu*, 10 chüan (TSCC ed.) 6:53; hereafter cited TML.

76. See especially Shen Chi-tsu's bitter attack on Chu in 1198. TML 7A:67–68.

77. Ibid., 5:43–44.

78. The memorial was written in response to Chu's impeachment of T'ang Chung-yu, an act that cost him the critical support of Wang Huai. See Conrad Schirokauer, "Neo-Confucians

He has collected together immoral disciples to benefit and enlarge his faction. Together they eat coarse and tasteless food and [wear] large-sleeved robes with broad belts [i.e., those of ancient scholars]. He has gathered disciples at the Goose Lake Temple in Kuang-hsin and presented himself at the Ching-chien Hall in Ch'ang-sha. He hides his form and footsteps like a ghost or goblin. Those literati and officials who buy reputations, delight in profit, and want his help [for those endeavors], also follow him with praise and recommendations.[79]

Most extreme of all was the charge made by Right Policy Monitor Shih K'ang-nien in 1200, just after Chu's death, that Chu and his disciples met at night like demon worshippers and engaged in Taoist-like chanting and Buddhist sitting.[80]

Shen Chi-tsu's use of the term "faction" (*tang*) in the above quotation is intriguing. Of course, by the time he was writing, the net to snare the heterodox had been cast very widely. It had caught not only such high ministers as Chao Ju-yü, Liu Cheng, and Chou Pi-ta[81] but also many of Chu's philosophical rivals, labeling them all as a faction and banning them and their followers from the examinations.[82] Yet by including Chu's largely commoner disciples in his faction, Shen was significantly extending the traditional meaning of faction of a group of officials acting in concert towards some political or private end.[83]

But why be concerned about mere literati? One reason was precautionary. In 1168 Hsiao-tsung responded to a discussion of the examination curriculum by historian Li T'ao with this comment:

> In examination essays, Lao Tzu, Chuang Tzu and Buddhist sayings may not be used. If [students] prepare themselves in the mountains and forests, what harm will result? If they enter the examination halls, then the governence of affairs will certainly be harmed.[84]

Similarly Ch'en Chia in his memorial warned that the *Tao-hsüeh* adherents were a faction in the making, developing ties with each other that would prove disastrous for the empire should they ever come to power.[85] But

---

Under Attack: The Condemnation of *Wei-hsüeh*," in *Crisis and Prosperity in Sung China*, ed. John Haeger (Tucson: University of Arizona Press, 1975), p. 169.

79. TML 7A:67. This description of clothing suggests yet another way in which Chu's disciples set themselves apart from their fellow literati.

80. Schirokauer, Biography of Shih K'ang-nien, *Sung Biographies* 2:870–871.

81. See the listing by rank of the *Wei-hsüeh* faction in TML 7B:81–82.

82. For the heterogeneous character of the *Wei-hsüeh* faction, see Schirokauer, "Neo-Confucianism Under Attack," pp. 184–196.

83. For a discussion of the concept of factionalism in the Northern Sung, the period that supplied most examples for discussions of the subject in Hsiao-tsung's court, see James T. C. Liu, *Ou-yang Hsiu: An Eleventh Century Confucianist* (Stanford: Stanford University Press, 1967), pp. 52–67.

84. *Liang-ch'ao sheng-cheng* 47:1746.

85. TML 5:44.

beyond considerations of prudence one can discern a chronic concern about the customs and opinions of the literati. Thus, "literati spirit" (*shih-feng*) was a frequent topic of discussion and complaint in the Southern Sung court.[86] Even more to the point, a memorial in 1180 by Imperial Librarian Chao Yen-chung attacking the Ch'eng brothers was framed by a discussion of the "literati spirit," a spirit that, according to Chao, was being harmed by the fleeting and insubstantial talk of nature and principle by followers of the Ch'engs.[87]

There was, of course, a contrary perspective to this subject of literati spirit. Writing in the early twelfth century, Li Hsin-ch'uan argued that because followers of Ch'in Kuei, the dictatorial chief councilor of Kao-tsung's reign (1127–1162), continued to hold power under Hsiao-tsung, the discussion of national issues had yet to attain correctness. Only those "literati of the mountains and forests" (*shan-lin chih shih*) who did not burden themselves with concerns of "glory and shame, the noble and base" had the ability to make things right.[88] Tu Wei-ming has described the twelfth-century Neo-Confucians as a fellowship of self-identified Confucians, a core group dedicated to educating the larger literati community and converting the ruling minority. "Fellowship" in fact seems a more accurate description in English of Chu Hsi and his followers than "faction," for in advocating the reform of morality, customs, and government, his strategy consisted not only of appeals for the emperor's support but also of educating literati, an activity that went beyond the traditional bounds of politics.

This was an audacious course of Chu to pursue, given his lack of ministerial supporters prior to the later 1180s and also considering that the combined followings of him and his *Tao-hsüeh* rivals were never more than a small fraction of the several hundreds thousand literati regularly taking the examinations.[89] For a time it was also remarkably successful; Chu and his disciples proved excellent propagandists, pursuing their cause through memorials, letters, teaching, writing, and even the printing of their books.[90] But it proved a dangerous course as well. Many were alienated by the fervor and what they perceived as the pretensions of the *Tao-hsüeh* adherents; indeed, Hu Hung, the reputed author of Shen Chi-tsu's famous memorial, turned against Chu after a visit to his home in Chien-an during which he felt disrespectfully treated.[91] More important, the state's control of the examinations proved a very effective weapon when used against the *Tao-hsüeh* movement. The prohibition on students of "spurious learning" taking the examinations resulted in many literati denying any connection with the movement, claim-

86. See, for example,the topic index of *Liang-ch'ao sheng-cheng*.
87. *Liang-ch'ao sheng-cheng* 58:2194–2195.
88. TML 5:41–42.
89. See Chaffee, *The Thorny Gates of Learning*, pp. 35–41, for an analysis of literati numbers.
90. On their use of printing, see *Men-jen*, p. 12.
91. Ibid., p. 170.

ing other teachers, and changing their distinctive form of dress.[92] Although many ignored the prohibition and courageously maintained their commitments to *Tao-hsüeh*, in the years immediately following Chu's death in 1200 the *Tao-hsüeh* movement appeared moribund. Thus, Li Hsin-ch'uan's short history of the movement in 1202 was entitled "the rise and fall of *Tao-hsüeh*."[93]

But such a requiem was premature, and the reascendence of *Tao-hsüeh*, specifically of Chu Hsi's thought, to an eventual position of state orthodoxy seen thereafter became apparent.[94] But this lay in the distant future when Chu was in Nan-k'ang. In no sense were the tumultuous events that followed determined by what happened there. Still, Nan-k'ang can be seen as a beginning in several ways. Educationally the revival of the White Deer Grotto Academy provided a Neo-Confucian focus to the proliferating academies of the twelfth and thirteenth centuries, and in the long run it helped create a tradition of academy education distinct from that which prepared one for the examinations. For Chu Hsi himself, Nan-k'ang marked the end of his long period of retirement and writing and a return to the active role of the Confucian scholar-official, which was monitored closely and with suspicion by his enemies in court. Finally, while Chu Hsi and the renovated academy attracted disciples in growing numbers, the *Tao-hsüeh* movement began to take shape, as did the controversy that attended it during the ensuing twenty years. Although none could have known it then or for some time to come, a sea change had begun, and the political and intellectual culture of both the literati and the state would never be the same.

92. TML 7B:74–75.
93. "Tao-hsüeh hsing-fei," CYTC 1.6:79–80.
94. See James T. C. Liu, "State Orthodoxy?" pp. 483–505.

SIXTEEN

Lu Chiu-yüan, Academies, and the Problem of the Local Community

Robert Hymes

It is well known that the teaching of Lu Chiu-yüan (Hsiang-shan; 1139–1192), though in some ways a formidable rival to that of Chu Hsi while Lu lived, began to decline in influence soon after Lu's death.[1] By the early years of the Yüan dynasty its line of transmission seems to have been effectively cut off.[2] Yet a visitor to Lu's home prefecture of Fu-chou (Chiang-hsi) as late as the mid-thirteenth century would have found Lu's teachings still honored or propagated at a number of local institutions. At three different shrines in the prefectural city and in the seat of Lu's home county, Chin-ch'i Hsien, local officials offered regular sacrifices to Lu and to his two brothers and fellow teachers, Chiu-ling and Chiu-shao.[3] More significantly, Lu's thought formed the central teaching of two local academies (*shu-yüan*) in the Fu-chou area. The Hsiang-shan Academy in nearby Kuei-ch'i Hsien, Hsin-chou, had been founded in 1231 by Yüan Fu, son of one of Lu's two most prominent disciples, Yüan Hsieh (1144–1224). Its first instructor was Ch'ien Shih, a student of Lu's other major disciple, Yang Chien (1141–1226).[4] Closer to home, a second Hsiang-shan Academy had stood in the Chin-ch'i county seat since 1233. Its founder, the county administrator

---

1. An important factor in the decline of Lu's influence was the decision of many of his students after his death to go and study with Chu Hsi. See for example the case of Pao Yang in Huang Tsung-hsi, *Sung Yüan hsüeh-an* (SPPY ed.) 77:12a.

2. The notion of a direct line of philosophical transmission from Lu to Wang Yang-ming has surely by now been generally discarded. On this subject, and on the real origins of the Ming School of the Mind, see Wing-tsit Chan, "The Ch'eng-Chu School of Early Ming," in *Self and Society in Ming Thought*, ed. Wm. Theodore de Bary (New York: Columbia University Press, 1970), pp. 29–51, especially pp. 42–45.

3. Robert Hymes, *Statesmen and Gentlemen: The Elite of Fu-chou, Chiang-hsi, in Northern and Southern Sung* (Cambridge: Cambridge University Press, 1986), p. 314. See also Lu Chiu-yüan, *Hsiang-shan ch'üan chi* (SPPY ed.) 36:26a–b, 36a–39a; hereafter cited as HSCC.

4. HSCC 36:31b–32a, 33a–b.

(whose philosophical affiliations, if any, are not recorded), installed Lu's own student, Fu Tzu-yün, as the Academy's first head instructor.⁵ At these two sites Lu's teaching found continued expression, at least for a time, through one of the prototypical institutions of Southern Sung Neo-Confucianism, the local academy.⁶

Most interesting about these two academies is that Lu Chiu-yüan himself had had, except in the most indirect way, nothing to do with either one. Their founding followed his death by some forty years. Yüan Fu had clearly wished the academy in Kuei-ch'i to be seen as a direct continuation or restoration of the "hall of repose" (*ching-she*) at Elephant Mountain (Hsiang-shan, whence the soubriquet), where Lu himself had taught between 1187 and 1191. The connection, however, was tenuous. No teaching seems to have been going on at the old hall of repose for some time when Yüan acted. Yüan had judged even the site of the older hall too difficult for access and so established his academy at a new location, "not far" from Elephant Mountain. Among the academies of the Fu-chou region—and these were many⁷—no direct institutional legacy from Lu Chin-yüan survived.

The lack was not an accident. Lu seems to have had little interest in leaving an institutional legacy of this kind; indeed he seems to have had, for a Southern Sung Neo-Confucian, remarkably little interest in academies. The nearest thing to a counterexample, clearly, is the Elephant Mountain hall of repose itself; but Lu seems to have been a rather casual participant in its founding. Invited to the mountain by his student P'eng Shih-ch'ang, who had discovered the site and built a house there to accommodate his teacher, Lu constructed a hall himself—the hall of repose—and brought his nephew with him to the site the following spring to study (*tu-shu*) there. In time more and more of his students joined him, building dwellings and studies for themselves at the site. When Lu's term in his current sinecure as nominal head of a Taoist temple expired and he was without salary, his students at the hall of repose began providing him with fees.⁸ As finally constituted, the hall did approach in function a rather informally structured academy, and Lu offered instruction and conversation there for the next several years. But he made only passing references to it in his works; he made no formal record

5. HSCC 36:34a.
6. On academies and their upsurge in Southern Sung, see Terada Gō, *Sōdai kyōiku shi gaisetsu* (Tokyo, 1965), pp. 265–271, 296–299 306–310; John Meskill, *Academies in Ming China: A Historical Essay* (Tucson: University of Arizona Press, 1982), pp. 13–16.
7. The gazetteers for Fu-chou and the collected works of Fu-chou men preserve some record of fourteen institutions called *shu-yüan* founded by Fu-chou locals during Southern Sung; eight of these were founded before or during Lu's lifetime. For almost all there is clear evidence that they were places of instruction rather than simple libraries.
8. For the founding and later history of the hall, see especially also the apposite sections of Lu's *nien-p'u* in HSCC 36:15b–21b; see also the references in a letter to Chu Hsi, HSCC 36:5a, and a letter to Lu's grandnephew, 36:8b. See also Terada, *Sōdai kyōiku shi gaisetsu*, p. 279.

of its founding or of the construction of any of its buildings. He produced no rules or regulations for its students—not even a set of simple admonitions along the lines of Chu Hsi's rules for the White Deer Grotto Academy. Lu came to the hall rather late in his career; there is not the slightest indication that he saw it as a model for other educational or academic institutions, nor any that he had set out with the clear and deliberate intention of founding an academy. He founded no others, in either his home region or office. The latter omission is particularly interesting: as we shall see, Lu's term of office in Ching-men prefecture, which immediately followed his years at Elephant Mountain, revealed him as a highly activist local administrator, yet he made no effort to replicate the model of his hall, or to follow the example of many other local officials of his time, by founding an academy or hall of repose for Ching-men scholars. If there was an "academy movement" in Southern Sung—and the term does not seem to me too strong—Lu was in no real sense a part of it.

Lu's relative disinterest in academies is particularly striking when one considers the performance of his contemporary and rival, Chu Hsi. Chu's interest in and promotion of local academies is well known.[9] In his own home region of Fu-chien he founded at least seven;[10] and in office he committed himself to the restoration or rehabilitation of two others: the Yüeh-lu Academy in T'an-chou (Hu-nan) and, most famous of all, the White Deer Grotto Academy in Nan-k'ang prefecture (Chiang-hsi). The innovativeness of Chu's activity in this field may sometimes have been exaggerated: as John Chaffee has pointed out, the rise of the local academy in Southern Sung was well under way before Chu entered the scene. Yet as Chaffee also argues, the influence of both Chu's rules for the White Deer Grotto and his affirmation of the academy's function as an alternative to the examination-centered education of the official schools was enormous and lasting. That the academy as an institution held an important place in Chu's notions of the proper role and conduct of education in society is clear.

Lu Chiu-yüan's lack of interest, at least active interest, in an educational institution that so deeply interested Chu Hsi is in some respects strange. The private local academy, again, was a commonplace on the Fu-chou institutional landscape by the time Lu began to gain prominence as a teacher.[11] Lu was certainly far from unacquainted with Chu Hsi's own efforts: his visit in 1180, at Chu's invitation, to the White Deer Grotto Academy, where he delivered a moving lecture on righteousness and profit as understood by the true gentleman and the small man, did much to draw attention to his

9. Citations could be very numerous; but see for instance Terada, *Sōdai kyōiku shi gaisetsu*, pp. 267–271, 296–299. A recent reevaluation of Chu Hsi's contribution to the academy movement is John Chaffee, "Chu Hsi and the Revival of the White Deer Grotto Academy, 1179–1181 A.D.," *T'oung Pao* 61 (1985):40–62.
10. I follow Chaffee, p. 49.
11. See note 7 above.

teaching.[12] Chu's attempt to secure a proper place for the sort of education that placed value on study for itself rather than as a route to examination success should, one might think, have won Lu's sympathies: his own views on the proper goal of study and on the destructiveness of exam-centered education were not very different from Chu's. Finally, his inattention to establishing, within his home region and elsewhere, the institutional foundation for the promulgation of his thought may have played some part in the later decline in his influence. In this respect the efforts of his intellectual descendants to establish academies for his teachings in the 1230s may be read as belated attempts to save the day by supplying what their master had omitted. In the attempt, they gave his doctrines an institutional dress inspired by his rival.

This, then, is my problem. Why did Lu, in contrast to Chu Hsi, take so little part in the promotion and spread of academy education? Why, to put the question in a broader light, was his contribution in the institutional sphere to the development of Neo-Confucian education in the Southern Sung virtually nonexistent, and Chu Hsi's so great? The question is perhaps small. It may even seem, to one familiar with Lu's deemphasis of book learning and his stress on the self-sufficiency of the individual mind, to answer itself. I will attempt to argue here, however, that these familiar aspects of Lu's thought cannot wholly explain his neglect of the academy as a vehicle for his thought. Light may be shed on the problem from quite a different angle, I will argue, if one sees the local academy in a broader social and institutional perspective. The view I will offer of Lu Chiu-yüan's position should be taken as a tentative suggestion, the more so as it will involve positing strands in his thinking that he never explicitly articulated. These strands were, however, articulated in Lu's own time, in particular by his brother Lu Chiu-shao. My argument, then, is in many respects speculative; but as I will show, it finds at least implicit support in other recent work on the intellectual and cultural history of the Sung.

I begin with, I hope, a straw man. One may cite certain passages from the works of Lu Chiu-yüan seeming to commit him to a view of the mind and of self-cultivation that would find little use for academies, schools, or indeed any regular structure of education. Lu's famous claim that "If in study we know the fundamental, then the Six Classics are all my footnotes"[13] does seem to push book learning far into the background. Along similar lines, one may cite a point Lu had hoped to argue with Chu Hsi in their famous encounter at Goose Lake Temple—"Before Yao and Shun, what books could one read?"[14] His brother Chiu-ling restrained him, thinking perhaps that he

12. HSCC 23:1a–2a, 36:10b.
13. HSCC 34:1b.
14. HSCC 36:9b.

was going too far. The implication, of course, was that if the founding sages Yao and Shun could attain their wisdom with no books to inform them, so too could the student of the present day.

Other passages might seem to call the enterprise of teaching itself into question:

> There is only one mind. My mind, my friends' mind, the mind of sages thousands of years ago, and the mind of sages thousands of years to come are all the same. The substance of the mind is infinite. If one can completely develop his mind, he will become identified with Heaven. To acquire learning is to appreciate this fact. This is what is meant by the saying, "Sincerity means the completion of the self, and the Way is self-directing." *When is it necessary to depend on words?*[15]

> *Principle is endowed in me by Heaven, not drilled into me from the outside.* If one understands that principle is the same as master and really makes it his master, one cannot be influenced by external things nor fooled by perverse doctrines.[16]

> Establish yourself in life and respect yourself. *Don't follow other people's footsteps or repeat their words.*[17] [Emphasis mine throughout.]

To take such passages, amounting almost to slogans, too literally, however, would be to distort Lu's real position, particularly as represented in his educational practice. In the first place, as Wing-tsit Chan has pointed out, Lu rejected not the study of books itself but what he saw, in the practice of those around him, as too niggling a concentration on books, on quantity of reading rather than on quality of understanding, and particularly on commentaries rather than on the original.[18] Often his remarks clearly presuppose that the classic texts themselves, as well as other books, will be read and attended to in the proper way.

> When I read, I merely look at ancient annotations, and the words of the sages are clear of themselves. Take the saying "Young men should be filial at home and respectul to their elders when away from home." This clearly means that when at home you are to be filial and when away from home you are to be respectful. What is the need for commentaries? Students have exhausted their energies in them and therefore their burden has become ever heavier. When they come to me, I simply reduce the burden for them.[19]

> In reading, one certainly cannot do without understanding the [literal] meaning of the text. But to take merely understanding the [literal] meaning of the

15. HSCC 35:10a. The translation follows Wing-tsit Chan, *A Source Book in Chinese Philosophy* (Princeton: Princeton University Press, 1963), p. 585.
16. HSCC 1:3a; Chan, *Source Book*, p. 574.
17. HSCC 35:22a; Chan, *Source Book*, p. 586.
18. Chan, *Source Book*, p. 581.
19. HSCC 35:8a; Chan, *Source Book*, p. 584.

text as correct is merely the learning of a boy. One must look at where the *intent* lies.[20] [Emphasis mine.]

Reading need not be exhaustive [of the sense]. Read calmly and easily; remember what you can remember; with time it will become clear of itself. Do not be ashamed of not knowing.[21]

When one reads the histories one must look to the reasons why [a man] succeeds and why he fails; to the ways in which he is right and to the ways in which he is wrong. If a passage is outstanding, swim and soak in it; after a time it will gain in force of itself. If one can read three or five chapters in this way, it is better than [merely] scanning thirty thousand chapters.[22]

When one who studies reads books, let him first immerse himself in the passages that are easy to understand. If he thinks these over deeply and repeatedly and in a way that has bearing on himself, then the others that are hard to understand will dissolve into clarity in a rush. If he looks first at the passages that are hard to understand, he will never get there.[23]

Lu Chiu-yüan is not discouraging reading. Far from it; he is positively enjoining reading but reading of a particular kind. But let him speak in his own defense:

Men say that I do not teach people to read books. Now when [Li] Min-ch'iu, for example, once came to ask me for my starting-points, I instructed him to read the *Hounds of Lü* and *T'ai Chia* [chapters from the *Book of Documents*], the "Trees of Mt. Niu" from the Kao Tzu [section of the *Mencius*], and so on. When have I ever not read books? It is only that I read them a bit differently from other men.[24]

As to the enterprise of teaching, Lu's remarks on the self-sufficiency of the mind, on not following in other people's footsteps, and on the simplicity of the task that faces the student could seem, if taken literally, to make systematic or long-term instruction, indeed perhaps even teachers, unnecessary. Lu himself, according to his student Chan Fu-min, claimed to have had no teacher: "I once asked 'Was the Master's learning received from someone?' He said: 'I got it myself, through reading *Mencius*.'" The passage is justly famous. It is perhaps worth pointing out that Lu here locates his own attainment of understanding in an act of *reading*: "getting it oneself" was not inconsistent with approaching "it" through a text. But to imagine, in any case, that Lu thought his own example could easily or often be repeated would again misrepresent his position. "One who studies," said Lu, "must

20. HSCC 35:1b.
21. HSCC 35:28b.
22. HSCC 35:9a.
23. HSCC 34:10a.
24. HSCC 35:11b.

first establish a commitment. Once a commitment is established, he still needs to find an enlightened teacher."[25] Such a teacher, as we have seen, could "reduce the burden" that an incorrect approach to books had placed on the student and show him the proper approach, relaxed and at ease but concentrated on meaning, intensive rather than extensive. He could reveal to the student, by argument and illustration, the reason for the essential simplicity of the task: the constant presence and inward availability of the student's own original mind. Most important, perhaps, the teacher could monitor the student's progress toward his goal and catch him up when he fell into error. In this, Lu could be a stern master. To Liu Yao-fu, a leading student, he wrote:

> In study, to be sure, one does not want to hurry. Wanting to hurry is, to be sure, a great ill for one who studies. But in correcting one's failing and improving oneself one may not be dilatory either. . . . What has delighted me in you is that your will, unwearying, advances and never retreats. Why is it that you are now so dilatory? . . . Being unwearying in advancing is not your failing: your failing lies rather in that what you advance along is not the true Way. . . . When you say that you know your own failings, I do not believe you.[26]

Elsewhere Lu had cautioned that "If one does not cleave to his teacher and friends he will be submerged in the prevailing customs and will be swept into a net, or plunged into an abyss, and will not know how to escape."[27] Evidently Liu was on the verge of this fate. Clearly, just as Liu's *relative* deemphasis of texts and his highly personal approach to reading did not mean an abandonment of book learning, his stress on the inwardness and ready availability of the student's goal did not make outside guidance, correction, and teaching unimportant. There is every evidence that Lu believed instead that they might be required for a very considerable period of time. Many of Lu's students spent long periods of their lives in attendance on him. Lu's own career makes his commitment to the student-teacher relation clear. It is clear as well from his biographical writings: his record of conduct for one brother, Chiu-ling, and his funerary inscription for another, Chiu-kao, dwell at some length and with obvious approval on their activity and achievements as teachers.[28] "For one who studies, not to seek a teacher," wrote Lu, "or, having sought one, to be unable to clear out his mind, unable to yield and listen—this indeed is the failing of one who studies."[29] The teacher-student relation is central to Lu's thought.

---

25. HSCC 34:5b.
26. HSCC 4:5b.
27. HSCC 7:2a. My translation follows Siu-chi Huang, *Lu Hsiang-shan: A Twelfth-Century Chinese Idealist Philosopher* (New Haven: American Oriental Society, 1944), p. 59.
28. HSCC 27:1a–4b, 28:8a–10b.
29. HSCC 1:10a.

I cannot attempt here a thorough examination of Lu's thinking on education. But certain points do, I think, emerge clearly enough even from the little evidence gathered here. If neither book learning nor direct and long-term instruction was as unimportant for Lu as some of his more sloganizing statements might lead one to expect—if, in fact, he encouraged his students to approach books, though in a particular way, and if he saw the role of the teacher as crucial—then there is little obvious reason to see his teachings as a whole as antithetical to either institutionalized education in general or the local academy in particular. Lu's approach to education did stress personal, mind-to-mind, contact and transmission from teacher to pupil, but it is unclear why this approach could not have found expression in local academies. One might indeed argue on practical grounds that, given Lu's undoubted opposition to the proliferation of new commentaries and texts, his teachings could best have been guaranteed transmission if, like Chu Hsi, he had founded a number of academies in his own region and in office and installed trusted disciples as instructors there. Clearly too the disciples who founded academies in the 1230s saw nothing in Lu's philosophy as it had come down to them that made its propagation in an academy inappropriate.

We have direct evidence as well that Lu saw nothing to object to—indeed he found value—in educational institutions of a certain kind. Of only eight commemorative stele inscriptions (*chi*) in Lu's works, three are for the construction or renovation of official county schools; none commemorates an academy. As a group the inscriptions promote a view of study as its own goal, a view not always thought likely to be encouraged by the state-directed and examination-focused education of the official schools; but each honors the achievement of the official responsible for the school's construction or renovation.[30] In his record of conduct for his brother Chiu-ling, Lu devoted special attention to Chiu-ling's achievement in restoring the revenues of the county school of Fu-ch'uan Hsien while in office there.[31] Apparently the idea of a formal institution devoted to a systematic process of education posed, in itself, no special problems for Lu Chiu-yüan.

If Lu's thought on study and teaching does not entail obvious opposition to formal institutions of education and if some direct evidence from his writings implies that at least one such institution—the official school—at times drew his approval, one must look elsewhere, I think, to explain his disinterest in the local academy. To explain a negative—in this case, why a man did *not* promote a particular sort of institution—is a risky and methodologically problematic enterprise. I would not make excessive claims for the argument I will frame below. Lu Chiu-yüan was, in personality, a very different man from Chu Hsi: more impulsive, more spontaneous, perhaps less

30. HSCC 19:2a–3b, 7b–8b, 8b–9b.
31. HSCC 27:3b.

given to cooperative enterprise, and less adept in (or less interested in) achieving a working consensus with men of partly different bent. His personality may have—must have—influenced in some way his approach to institutions. It is possible as well that an attitude of competitiveness with Chu Hsi in some degree discouraged Lu from borrowing models associated with Chu. Finally, although I have argued that nothing in Lu's thought on education would automatically lead him away from an institution like the local academy, it is true as well that little is obvious in that thought that would necessarily lead him toward it. The considerations that one might have expected to interest him in academies were practical—the desire to perpetuate his own thought effectively, to institutionalize it for posterity—more than philosophical. All these factors—personality, competitiveness with Chu Hsi, the absence of strong or obvious "push" factors in his own philosophy[32]—may play some part in a complete explanation of Lu's relative noninvolvement in the academy movement. In the absence of far more extensive material on Lu's life and thinking than now survives, none of them may be excluded. In what follows, however, I seek to identify another factor of a rather different kind. I offer, then, not necessarily an explanation but a piece of one.

To understand fully the meaning that the local academy had for Southern Sung Neo-Confucians—whether for those, like Chu Hsi, who promoted it or for Lu Chiu-yüan who took little interest in it—one must view it as only one of a group of local institutions, all more or less innovative, that spread or were promoted in the new social and political circumstances of Southern Sung. Four of these are of particular importance here because they won the enthusiastic support and promotion of Chu Hsi and, in varying degrees, of other Neo-Confucians of his and later times. These are, along with the local academy, the "community compact" (*hsiang-yüeh*), the community granary (*she-ts'ang*), and the altar honoring men of local renown or Neo-Confucian forefathers (sometimes called the "altar to former worthies," *hsien-hsien tz'u*). It is worth briefly describing each of these before addressing their common character and their place in the social thought of Chu Hsi and other Neo-Confucians.

The community compact, a plan adopted by Chu Hsi from the Northern Sung thinker and official Lü Ta-chün (1031–1082), was the only one of the four institutions addressed here that was not widely put into practice in Chu's own time, though like the others it was influential in later dynasties and in other countries of East Asia. The plan envisioned a voluntary association or "compact" (*yüeh*) among the members of a community, devoted to the maintenance of moral and social order through mutual exhortation and admonition, joint social and ritual action, and organized

---

32. These ideas derive from comments made by Wm. Theodore de Bary, John Chaffee, and Tu Wei-ming on an earlier version of this chapter.

mutual aid. Registers of members were to be maintained and good and bad conduct recorded, called to the attention of members, and publicly praised or blamed. Membership was voluntary, but members were to be expelled in case of repeated offenses against the rules or spirit of the compact. A carefully worked out system of community ritual was to bind the members together and promote a proper recognition of distinctions of age, virtue, and social position.[33] The community granary, like the community compact, was not Chu Hsi's own creation: he borrowed the plan from his friend Wei Shan-chih, who had applied it in Chien-yang Hsien, in Chu Hsi's home prefecture of Chien-chou, in the 1160s. The plan resembled Wang An-shih's "green sprouts" program in its basic operation: the granaries, endowed at the outset with a stock of rice, were to make loans from their stock to farmers at planting time for repayment after the harvest. Where the plan diverged sharply from Wang An-shih was in charging no interest (only a three percent wastage fee)[34] and in being managed, and in many cases founded and endowed, by local gentlemen rather than by the state. The object was, within a framework of voluntary social action, to aid the farmer by meeting his need for credit without oppressive interest charges.[35] The development and spread of altars to local worthies in Southern Sung has not yet been thoroughly explored.[36] The altars differed from the other institutions discussed here in that they were not a medium for voluntary social action by local gentlemen; generally local officials founded them and took the lead in the ceremonies of veneration conducted there. It does seem clear, however, that the founding officials, Chu Hsi and other Neo-Confucian activists prominent among them, hoped to draw local gentlemen into the ceremonies and so use the altars as means to the strengthening of a sense of local community. In my own work on the local elite of Fu-chou, Chiang-hsi, I have found that the altars, which in Northern Sung had been few and

---

33. Chu Hsi, *Hui-an hsien-sheng Chu Wen-kung wen-chi* (Ssu-pu pei-yao ed.) 74:23a–29b. Monika Übelhör has translated Lü Ta-chün's pact as modified and added to by Chu Hsi as a contribution to the International Conference on Chu Hsi, University of Hawaii, July 1982. See also Wada Sei, *Shina chihō jichi* (Tokyo, 1939), pp. 51–52, 119–145, 224–230; and Wm. Theodore de Bary, *The Liberal Tradition in China* (Hong Kong, 1983), pp. 32–34.

34. At least after an initial period, during which 20 percent interest was charged until the original investment in rice stocks had been repaid.

35. The final form of Chu Hsi's plan is found in Chu Hsi, *Hui-an hsien-sheng* 99:5a–22a; for an earlier version, applied in Chien-chou in 1168, see ibid. 77:25a–27b. On the community granary and other Sung granaries, see Sogabe Shizuo, "Sōdai no sansō oyobi sono hoka," in his *Sōdai saikeishi no kenyū* (Tokyo, 1974), pp. 465–494. See also Hymes, *Statesmen and Gentlemen*, pp. 306–315.

36. The topic is broached by Terada Gō in the context of the history of education and the rise of Neo-Confucian educational models in Southern Sung. See Terada, *Sōdai kyōiku shi gaisetsu*, pp. 272–277. A graduate student at Columbia, Ellen Neskar, is currently undertaking research on the problem, and I have benefited greatly from discussions with her.

devoted largely to the memory of local officials—that is, men from outside
Fu-chou who had benefited the locality by their service in office there—in
Southern Sung increased greatly in number and came to be used chiefly to
honor Fu-chou locals themselves, including many who had never held office
and whose prominence and achievements had thus been wholly local.[37] Not
all the founders of such altars were Neo-Confucian thinkers, but when Chu
Hsi and others like him involved themselves they seem to have used the
altars partly, again, to honor natives of the locality but partly also to venerate
Neo-Confucian founders and teachers, such as Chou Tun-i and the Ch'eng
brothers, even in places where they had never lived. The purpose of the altars
may thus have become dual: on the one hand, they celebrated local pride,
promoted a sense of local community, and created a model of the local
gentleman that did not emphasize bureaucratic service; and on the other
they tied local communities together within a larger, Neo-Confucian and
national community united by common veneration of certain leading figures.

These institutions and the local academy, I would argue, shared, apart
from their specific functions, a common purpose in the minds of their
founders, Chu Hsi in particular: this was to give institutional expression and
structure to the local community as something apart from the central state
and its local organs. The case is clearest for the community compact, the
community granary, and the local academy. Each was fundamentally local
in character and function; each was planned as a framework for voluntary
action by local gentlemen (in the case of the community compact, not only
gentlemen), either singly or in concert; and each could be seen as a substitute
or an alternative for a specific state institution of the same or earlier periods.
Thus, the community compact was in its aim a voluntarily based, largely
noncoercive version of the *pao-chia* mutual surveillance organization imposed
(to look at it from the Neo-Confucian point of view) by Wang An-shih on
local communities and surviving in various modified or degenerate forms in
Chu Hsi's own time. The community granary was a transformation of Wang
An-shih's national green sprouts law, long since rescinded but alive in
memory, into a voluntary and community-based welfare institution. The
academy was a direct alternative to the official school, a state institution still
thriving in Southern Sung but deriving ultimately again from the broad,
centralizing, reformist efforts of Northern Sung statesmen like Fan Chung-
yen and Wang An-shih. Chu Hsi and the other promoters of these institutions were thus—among other things—trying to accomplish voluntarily on a
local community basis what Wang An-shih had attempted to do uniformly,
from the center, and through state organs. The altars to local worthies,
again, clearly stand somewhat apart from these three; yet they, too, gave
institutional expression, chiefly in the sphere of ritual, to the local commu-

---

37. Hymes, *Statesmen and Gentlemen*, pp. 263–66.

nity by offering veneration to the memory of the community's leading figures. The altars in some degree distanced this community from the state by honoring men for nonofficial or purely local achievements.

This argument is clearly congruent with and partly influenced by a recent discussion of Chu Hsi's views on popular education by Wm. Theodore de Bary.[38] For de Bary, Chu "sought to incorporate the principle of voluntarism into community structures which might mediate between state power and family interests." I am less certain, however, that one can see Chu's efforts as in part a response to "the steady extension and aggrandizement of state power" in his own time. The memory of an expansionist state—the memory of the failed reforms and the factional excesses of Wang An-shih and of the vigorous centralization and equally vigorous persecutions of the dictator Ts'ai Ching—unquestionably lay behind the community-based voluntarism of Chu Hsi and other Southern Sung Neo-Confucians. But the state that faced them in their own time, far from extending its power and control, had been so weakened by the wars of the Northern Sung/Southern Sung transition and by the enormous burden of maintaining border armies against the Chin that it found itself less and less able to gather revenue and perform the basic function of maintaining order in the localities. It had effectively withdrawn from any serious attempts to influence from the center the welfare of rural communities. I have argued elsewhere that local elite involvement with institutions like the community granary and movement into a wide range of other fields of activity were made possible, and in some instances necessary, by the state's inability or unwillingness to involve itself directly and effectively in the governance of the localities.[39] The state's failures and its partly deliberate withdrawal left a gap into which local gentlemen (and not-so-gentlemen) moved. I would suggest that one may see the community compact, too, as an attempt to fill this gap. Northern Sung reformers had attempted, but failed, to extend the influence of state-sponsored institutions and agencies down to the "bottom," as it were, of society. Neo-Confucian reformers in Southern Sung built their new nonstate institutions in the space left by the failure: the space, to return to de Bary's formulation, "between state power and family interests." Here, in effect, the "local community" was located.

Chu Hsi's explicit concern with this "space," with the notion of a "middle level" between the family and the lowest reaches of the state apparatus, is also shown by his arrangement of ritual material from the *I-li* in his own ritual compilation, the *I-li ching-chuan t'ung-chieh.* Here Chu preserved the traditional sequence of the seventeen sections of the *I-li*, which seem to have been ordered according to the stages of the life-course of the gentleman, but

38. de Bary, *The Liberal Tradition in China*, pp. 32–34.
39. Hymes, *Statesmen and Gentlemen*, pp. 136–76, 196–99.

he introduced a new ordering principle, superimposed on the old, by dividing the sections into six groups. The last two groups, comprising seven sections, were concerned with funerals and sacrifices respectively, thus with rituals that pertain to death and its aftermath; but the first ten sections, concerning rituals between the living, Chu divided into four groups corresponding not to life-stages but to specific levels in the social hierarchy. Between "family rituals" (*chia li*) and "rituals of countries and kingdoms" (*pang-kuo li*)— the latter corresponding to the level of the feudal lords in classical Chou feudalism but to the lowest level of the state, the level of prefectures and counties, in the terms of Chu's own time—Chu placed three sections that he grouped together as "community ritual" (*hsiang li*).[40] In this conception of a separate, middle level of ritual, once again Chu promoted an institutional expression of the local community as something apart from the state (at least as presently constituted) and lying above the family. To this same middle level, it would seem, belonged the community compact, the community granary, and the local academy; and at its boundary with the next level above, local gentlemen and local officials came together to venerate symbols of local community at the altars of former worthies.

The four institutions I have discussed here were of particular importance for Neo-Confucians; but others, in some respects comparable, emerged or spread at about the same period. Charitable estates of various sorts, inspired no doubt by the model of Fan Chung-yen's lineage estate but devoted instead to nonkin groups or purposes, sprang up in considerable numbers, sometimes with the encouragement of officials but often under the management of local gentlemen. A general proliferation of local voluntary organizations is clear in Southern Sung: poetry clubs, philosophical associations, societies of local gentlemen devoted to charity and good works; these may be seen as, in one degree or another, expressions of a new localism characteristic of the period but more specifically of a new urge to found local and voluntary *institutions*. Against this background Chu Hsi's program of community institutions has the look of a systematization and refinement of a tendency more general, though not universal, in his time.

With all of this, not only with the local academy, Lu Chiu-yüan had almost nothing to do. Of the four institutions of particular importance to Chu Hsi, only the community granary seems ever to have commanded Lu's interest; and I will argue that the form his interest took in this case itself reveals his distance from Chu's conceptions. He did not, like either Chu or his intellectual descendant Chen Te-hsiu, promote community granaries while in office elsewhere. I have argued already that Lu was more or less a nonparticipant in the local academy "movement." He seems never to have shown any interest in the community compact scheme, despite a fair famil-

40. This discussion derives from Ueyama Shunpei, "Shushi no 'Karei' to 'Girei keiden tsukai'," *Tōhōgakuhō* 54 (1982):172–256.

iarity with Chu Hsi's activities. In office or out, he never took any initiative in the founding of an altar to former worthies.[41] Nor, in fact, was he ever involved in any of the other sorts of local voluntary associations and institutions so characteristic of Southern Sung and often so deeply interesting to other Neo-Confucians. His disinterest in local academies, then, was only part of a broader disinterest in community institutions of the kind that Chu Hsi enthusiastically promoted: institutions of the "middle level."

Was Lu Chiu-yüan, perhaps, simply not interested in action in society? Again the stress of his philosophical discussions on the processs and nature of self-cultivation, their inward focus, and their rather quietist tone, might lead one to expect so. In fact, however, Lu's own life and his accounts of the lives of others reveal a clear commitment to social action, to the improvement of the world. This is not too surprising: the attention devoted in Lu's surviving works to self-cultivation as process should not distract from the passages, few but crucial, where he attends instead to its goal:

There is of course concrete principle in the universe. What we value in study is becoming able to understand this principle; that is all. If it is understood, concrete action and concrete accomplishments will naturally result.[42]

The affairs in the universe are my own affairs. My own affairs are the affairs of the universe.[43]

It is precisely because of righteousness and public-spiritedness that we Confucianists are engaged in putting the world in order (ching-shih); it is because of their desire for profit and selfishness that the Buddhists withdraw from the world. Even when Confucianists reach to realms of (Heaven) which has neither sound nor smell, (spirit) which is not spatially restricted, and (Change) which has no physical form, they always emphasize putting the world in order.[44]

Lu demonstrated his commitment to social action both in office and in his home district. His record of conduct chronicles his efforts in the last years of his life as administrator of Ching-men prefecture in Hu-nan. From his arrival in the ninth month of 1191 until his death in office in the twelfth month of 1192 Lu organized the construction of a new city wall, with gates, watchtowers, and a moat; rebuilt the prefectural examination hall and other official buildings; established a prefectural hospital; simplified and reformed the

41. He did allow himself to be persuaded to write an inscription for the reconstruction of one such altar, to Wang An-shih, in his home prefecture. But of all the altars built or rebuilt in Fu-chou in Southern Sung, this one least fit the new tendency to use the altars to promote the local community. Wang's altar had been built originally in Northern Sung; he fit an older model of the gentleman deeply involved in government but rather little involved in his own locality's affairs.
42. HSCC 14:1a. My translation slightly modifies that in Chan, Source Book, p. 579.
43. HSCC 22:5a; Chan, Source Book, p. 580.
44. HSCC 2:1b; Chan, Source Book, p. 576.

administration of commercial tax stations within the prefecture so as to lighten the inconvenience and expenses borne by traveling merchants; and abolished a special prohibition, instituted because of Ching-men's position close to the border, on the private circulation of copper cash. He paid special attention to strengthening local military forces by reinforcing the schedule of rewards offered for the capture of runaway troops, instituting archery contests with prizes to sharpen soldiers' skills, and establishing a system of remuneration for the performance of the soldiers' customary labor services so as to improve morale. In spare hours he went to the prefectural school and lectured to the students. Even allowing for the bias of the source, which probably inflates results more than efforts, this is an unusual record of activism for a Southern Sung local official. This activism was not simply ad hoc, spontaneous, and directed toward its own moment but showed a considerable depth and breadth of interest in administrative and institutional reforms of stable and lasting character.[45]

Of equal significance here, however, is Lu's activity while out of office in his own home county. Evidence of this activity is preserved chiefly in a wealth of letters written to local officials mainly during the 1180s and 1190s. Through these letters Lu injected himself directly, or tried to, into the governing of his own community. Through all the letters run three common themes: a localist and basically antifiscalist view of the local official's responsibilities; warnings against the unreliability and the evil practices of government clerks and their powerful local patrons; and attacks on the negligence or malfeasance of local officials. The letters cover a broad range of topics but center chiefly on the economic. In a particularly striking example Lu advises the vice-administrator of Fu-chou to ignore his superiors' concern with the recovery of tax arrears.[46] Elsewhere he writes to urge the elimination of various special levies;[47] to protest plans to sell off various local estates, nominally under state ownership but long the de facto property of their "tenants," to private holders;[48] and to notify officials of impending problems with the Fu-chou rice crop and to ask for reductions in local tax quotas.[49] Occasionally Lu recommends the promotion or punishment of specific officials; in one case he writes to support the confession and plea for leniency of an unnamed felon.[50] It is clear that Lu sees himself as a legitimate participant in decisions that affect his home district and prefecture.

Lu's belief in social action is shown too by his biographical writings, particularly those for two of his brothers, Chiu-kao and Chiu-ling. Chiu-ling's record of conduct includes a lengthy and admiring account of his role

45. HSCC 33:4b–7a.
46. HSCC 7:5b–7a.
47. HSCC 5:6b–7B, 8:1a–2a; 8:2a–3a, 9:2b–3a.
48. HSCC 8:6a–9a.
49. HSCC, passim. in citations above, and 10:2a–b.
50. HSCC 11:4b.
51. HSCC 7:5b–7a.

as a leader of local defense planning in 1175, when tea bandits threatened Fu-chou, and recounts the debates among Lu's family and students over whether such activities were proper for a true gentleman. Chiu-ling's own arguments in favor of his involvement are cited at length and with obvious approval.[52] In the funerary inscription of Chiu-kao, Lu celebrates his brother's role as a local manager of famine relief efforts during 1187 and notes favorably a local official's view that famine relief could only work if run by local gentlemen rather than directly by officials or through clerks.[53] In a third biographical account, a funerary inscription for Lu's neighbor Ko Keng, he praises Ko's own involvement in local defense in early Southern Sung and his sales of grain below market prices during a famine. In these accounts Lu presents a model of the local gentleman as one who not only, like Lu himself, intervenes with local officials for the benefit of his locality but also takes direct action himself for the same goal.

If Lu's lack of interest in the voluntary community institutions promoted by Chu Hsi and others was not founded in a larger disinterest in local social action, what in fact was its foundation? I believe one may find a clue by returning to de Bary's reference to "community structures which might mediate between state power and family interests." As de Bary makes clear and as I have argued, such mediating institutions could serve in fact as alternatives to the downward extension of state power by locating certain functions in the institutionalized community rather than in state organs. But one might also see them as operating in the same way in the other direction by limiting the upward extension of "family interests" or potentially competing with the family for the loyalties of local gentlemen. In this conception, a strong commitment to *either* the central power of the state *or* the primacy of kinship relations or family institutions would make an interest in the creation of new, voluntary institutions at the community level unlikely. In Southern Sung, a strong commitment to centralized state power was rarely expressed except in the upper reaches of the bureaucrary itself; but a principled and intellectually elaborated commitment to a specific kinship grouping, the *chia*, as the primary focus of loyalties was a position articulated in some detail in several Southern Sung works that survive. The most extensive and the most important of these is the *Precepts for Social Life* (*Yüan-shih shih-fan*) of Yüan Ts'ai (fl. 1140–1195).

As Patricia Ebrey has shown in recent work on the *Precepts*,[54] Yüan Ts'ai exhibits a conception of the social world and of a gentleman's responsibilities radically different from the views of Chu Hsi. In the *Precepts*, Yüan Ts'ai upholds the preservation of the *chia* (family sharing a common property) as a

52. HSCC 27:1a–4b.
53. HSCC 28:9a–b.
54. Patricia Ebrey, *Family and Property in Sung China: Yüan Ts'ai's Precepts for Social Life* (Princeton: Princeton University Press, 1984).

central goal; he treats a concern with the accumulation, proper and frugal management, and preservation of property as entirely legitimate, indeed essential for the goal of *chia* survival; and he takes a remarkably pessimistic view of the social world outside the *chia* and the possibilities for effective or beneficent action in that world. On each of these three points Yüan diverged from the usual emphases of Neo-Confucian or classicist thinkers;[55] for the problem at issue here the third point is most important. It is worth quoting Ebrey:

> A negative and often fearful tone pervades much of Yüan Ts'ai's discussion of social relations outside the family. In that sphere it was not the good one could do through local leadership, nor even the good one could gain from appropriate connections, that Yüan Ts'ai emphasized. Rather it was the dangers that one would be wise to avoid. He saw much satisfaction in orderly management of a large and prosperous family, but he did not propose taking the next step in the classical scheme to local leadership. To the contrary, he warned against the dangers of trying to resolve other people's disputes and of standing up to bullies and oppressive officials.[56]

Yüan Ts'ai's example suggests very strongly that a serious commitment to the *chia* as primary institution—what Ebrey has called the *"chia* orientation"*—might imply, or at least complement, a deliberate limiting of commitments and involvements in the larger social world. Lu Chiu-yüan's view of action in that world was far more positive than Yüan Ts'ai's. But I would argue that in Lu Chiu-yüan a Neo-Confucian ethic of social beneficence and involvement grafts onto a set of assumptions about society and the family, mostly not articulated by Lu Chiu-yüan himself, that are largely congruent with the *chia* orientation. In the case of the Lus, commitment to the *chia* manifested itself not in abstention from social activism, as with Yüan Ts'ai, but in a lack of interest in formalizing outside commitments through the promotion of community institutions. Where the *chia* was itself the primary local institution, "mediating" institutions between family and state were superfluous, expensive, and possibly constraining of *chia* action.

What is the evidence for the *chia* orientation in Lu Chiu-yüan? It is largely indirect and comprises three strands: first, the nature of the Lu family itself; second, Lu's treatment of family involvements in his funerary inscriptions for three of his brothers; third, the writings of a fourth brother, Chiu-shao. I will discuss each of these.

Lu Chiu-yüan belonged and took some pride in belonging to an extraordinary family.[57] Founded before the fall of Northern Sung, the household of

55. Patricia Ebrey, "Conceptions of the Family in the Sung Dynasty," *Journal of Asian Studies* 43; no. 2 (February 1984):224–229.

56. Ebrey, *Family and Property*, pp. 153–154.

57. On the Lu family see especially Lu's funerary inscriptions and record of conduct for his brother in HSCC chüan 27 and 28; the materials on the honors received from the court in HSCC 36:34b–36a; and a fascinating discussion by the Southern Sung man Lo Ta-ching in his *Ho-lin yü-lu* (Taipei: K'ai-ming shu-tien, 1967) 5:9–10.

which he and his five elder brothers were members had maintained itself as a continuous unit without dividing its property for five generations by the time of Chiu-yüan's birth; his sons and nephews made the count six generations during his own lifetime. Ultimately, near the end of Southern Sung, the household would be honored by the emperor for maintaining itself and its property undivided for a full ten generations. By Lu Chiu-yüan's time the family already numbered in the hundreds. An internal division of labor was strictly maintained; members were allotted to different management tasks more or less permanently or, in some instances, served in rotation. In Lu's own generation the eldest brother, Chiu-ssu, managed the household as a whole; the next, Chiu-hsü, ran the drug business, the mainstay of the family's income; the third, Chiu-kao, taught in the family school, which was apparently open in part to fee-paying outsiders; the youngest three, Chiu-shao, Chiu-ling, and Chiu-yüan himself, studied for the civil service examinations. Discipline was severe, and the enterprise of the family was treated with the utmost seriousness. Each morning the members gathered to pay their respects to the ancestors at the household shrine and to sing a hymn on their obligations to Heaven.

The Lu household seems to have amounted to a little community in itself. Simply to maintain it as a unit, in the face of the well-known strains to which a Chinese household is subject after the first generation, must have required extraordinary devotion to the group enterprise and the idea of the *chia* as an institution. In size the household surely equaled or exceeded many villages; it maintained its own school, granaries, and shrine, and its members worked variously as teachers, officials, and merchants. An interesting account by a rough contemporary tells of the management of conflict within the household:

> When a junior member did something wrong, the head of the family would assemble all the juniors and upbraid and instruct him. If he did not change, then they would whip him. If he never changed, and they judged (his behavior) intolerable, then he would be reported to the local officials.[58]

To report a family member directly to the local authorities was not an uncontroversial act in Southern Sung. Biographies, legal decisions, and anecdotes reveal that various groups or figures below the state level were often seen as a more natural resort than the local officials when disputes needed resolving or when misbehavior needed correcting. Lineage elders, neighbors, a village as a whole, local *pao-chia* or *pao-wu* units or their chiefs, or a local gentleman with a reputation for wisdom or influence—any of these might be appealed to in deciding disputes or resolving tensions before parties sought recourse in the state judicial system. In fact, this was a major function of Chu Hsi's community compact. If the testimony of the source is correct, however, the Lus recognized, at least for the resolution of disputes, no

58. Lo Ta-ching, *Ho-lin yü-lu*, p. 10.

intermediate level of decision making between family and state. Where a family that was itself virtually a community failed, the state must take over. Here, then, is evidence that a *chia* that absorbed fully enough the energies and loyalties of its members—and it is clear that the Lu household must have done this very fully—might exclude commitment to institutional mechanisms between family and state.

In his funerary inscriptions for his brothers, Lu Chiu-yüan shows explicitly his own commitment to their common *chia*. Ebrey has shown that for Neo-Confucians like Chu Hsi, the advancement or management of the family *as economic unit* was not viewed with particular enthusiasm or indeed even approval: "in epitaphs for men [Chu Hsi] considered it high praise to say they were oblivious to all matters of family economy."[59] The picture was rather different for women, who earned high praise from Chu for their efficient management of household resources; but men, it seems, were to concentrate rather on moral cultivation and on action in the outside world. This contrasts sharply, for Ebrey, with the deliberate stress on economic advancement and management that characterizes the *chia* orientation as found, for example, in Yüan Ts'ai. One might, then, expect an author who shares the *chia* orientation to attend in his biographical writings to his subjects' contributions to their family's wealth. This is precisely what one finds in Lu Chiu-yüan's funerary inscriptions for his brothers Chiu-hsü and Chiu-kao. Lu mentions, in a way quite unusual in Sung funerary inscriptions, his brothers' specific economic contributions to the household. For Chiu-hsü, who managed the family drug business, the discussion is particularly extensive. Lu also stresses in his inscriptions the achievements of ancestors in providing the family with its initial wealth.[60]

In the nature of the Lu household and in Lu's references to the household economy in his funerary inscriptions there are tentative indications of the primacy of the *chia*. But stronger evidence is provided by the surviving works of the fourth of the six brothers, Lu Chiu-shao.[61] There are, of course, methodological uncertainties in using the writings of one brother to evidence the thinking of another; however, contemporaries and later followers of the Lus seem to have regarded the three brothers who achieved particular fame as scholars and teachers—Chiu-yüan, Chiu-ling, and Chiu-shao—as a group, whose teachings, though not the same, largely complemented rather than contradicted one another. The three came to be honored together at a single local altar in late Southern Sung;[62] the later addition of Chiu-yüan's leading local disciple, Fu Tzu-yün, as a fourth figure of veneration at the same altar, suggests an intellectual affiliation rather than mere kinship

59. Ebrey, *Family and Property*, p. 49.
60. HSCC 28:2a–b, 8b.
61. On Lu Chiu-shao see Hymes, *Statesmen and Gentlemen*, pp. 163–164; Ebrey, *Family and Property*, pp. 43–44; Ebrey, "Conceptions of the Family," p. 227.
62. See note 3 above.

behind the grouping. It is well known that Chiu-yüan came to the aid of Chiu-shao in a quarrel with Chu Hsi over the notion of the "Ultimate of Non-being."[63] I have found in Lu Chiu-yüan's works no evidence of disagreement with the ideas from his brother's writings that I will be treating here. And I will try to show specific echoes of Chiu-shao's thinking in the writings and practice of Chiu-yüan.

Lu Chiu-shao was the author of a set of family rules that spelled out in detail the proper organization and management of a household and the role of each member; the work seems in many respects to have been parallel to Yüan Ts'ai's. The rules as a whole have not survived, but something of Chiu-shao's approach may be gathered from passages of his "Daily Notes" (*Jih chi*) preserved in the *Sung Yüan hsüeh-an*. Not unlike Yüan Ts'ai, Chiu-shao stressed economy, frugality, and careful budgeting as means to preserving the family property and so preventing the breakup of the household. Most significant for my purposes here is what Lu says, or implies, about the relation of the household to the outside world.

A passage on budgeting reveals his attitude. He urges that one divide one's after-tax income into ten parts, setting aside three as provision against natural disaster and one for expenditures on sacrifices. The remaining six tenths should be split into twelve, one for each month: each of the twelve parts should be divided further into thirty parts, for the thirty days of the month. The resulting fraction is the highest expenditure allowed for each day. Lu remarks that one need not spend all of each day's share and recommends 70 percent as the proportion to aim at. This will leave a surplus:

> For what is left over, establish separate books, and apply it to summer and winter clothing, repairs to walls and houses, doctors and medicines, entertaining, condolence calls, visits to the sick, and seasonal gifts. If there is still some left over, distribute it among the poor of the neighborhood and the lineage, worthy gentlemen in difficult straits, tenants who are hungry or cold, or passersby without means of support.[64]

Commitments to the outside world are represented here by "entertaining, condolence calls, visits to the sick, and seasonal gifts"—that is, by *li*—and by charity to the needy. Both are here subordinated to the needs of the household: funds are to be allotted to them only if something is left over from expenditures on clothing, repairs, medicine, and so on. And Lu goes further:

> One who has few fields and ample expenses can only take the road of purifying the heart, being frugal and simple, and managing things so as to assure sufficiency of food. As to entertaining visitors, condolence calls, visits to the sick, seasonal gifts, or getting together for eating and drinking: these are not to be considered.[65]

63. Passages from Lu's letters are translated in Chan, *Source Book*, pp. 577–578.
64. Huang Tsung-hsi, *Sung Yüan hsüeh-an* 57:2b–3a.
65. Huang Tsung-hsi, *Sung Yüan hsüeh-an* 57:3a.

Thus *li*—and charity (by implication) all the more—is out of the question for a family whose resources are stretched by other expenses. But Lu steps back from this further on: "I mean only that [where resources are limited] one cannot use one's wealth for *li*."[66] He proposes ways of approaching *li*—coming first to funerals and leaving last, and the like—that will show sincerity and compassion without the expenditure of wealth. Charity, of course, remains out of the question.

In sum, what other Sung men might have seen as obligations to the larger society—charity to lineage men, tenants, and neighbors, for example—are here, on economic grounds, subordinated to the needs of the *chia* itself. This is somewhat akin, although not identical, to Yüan Ts'ai's "negative" approach to social relations outside the family. Two points, however, are particularly important. First, although Lu Chiu-shao applies his caution on the expenditure of wealth only to those whose wealth is limited he leaves it to the household, or its head, to determine when wealth is inadequate; elsewhere he argues that stinginess by those with more than adequate resources risks conflict with those who expect aid and so is to be avoided.[67] This differs sharply from Chu Hsi's community compact plan, which gives to the compact as a whole the power to decide on the contributions by members to their fellows in time of distress. Second, Chiu-shao explicitly encourages approaches to the social world—with reference to *li* specifically but with obvious implications for other spheres of action—that do not divert material resources from the *chia*. Except for the very wealthy, it seems, social action should ideally be cost-free.

This latter approach seems to jibe well with Lu Chiu-yüan's own views as revealed implicitly in biographical writings and elsewhere. I have pointed out examples of beneficent social action celebrated in Chiu-yüan's record of conduct for Chiu-ling and his funerary inscriptions for Lu Chiu-kao and Ko Keng. Upon closer examination only one case—Ko Keng's sale of grain in a famine at less than the market price—seems to have involved the expenditure or sacrifice of private funds. And even in this case the sacrifice may have been more potential than actual: market prices were, of course, at their highest in time of famine; thus, selling below them Ko Keng may have cleared as much as or more than he would have in normal times. All the other examples that Lu Chiu-yüan celebrates in these inscriptions are of essentially managerial tasks, apparently performed without the use of private resources. Lu's own interventions with local officials similarly represent a sort of social action beneficial, if successful, to the larger world yet involving no expenditure of family funds.

The same implicit ideal of cost-free social action seems reflected in Lu Chiu-yüan's single clear involvement with one of Chu Hsi's community

66. Huang Tsung-hsi, *Sung Yüan hsüeh-an* 57:3a.
67. Huang Tsung-hsi, *Sung Yüan hsüeh-an* 57:3a.

institutions. In 1186 the Chiang-hsi Intendant of Ever-Normal Granaries, Chao Ju-ch'ien, tried to recruit Fu-chou locals to found and manage community granaries. Lu Chiu-shao responded, and official funds were disbursed to provide the new granary with its initial stock of grain. Lu Chiu-yüan's role at this stage is unclear; note that the project was not undertaken on either of the Lus' initiative but in response to appeals from a friendly local official and that only a single granary was established, in contrast to the large numbers founded by Chu Hsi and Chen Te-hsiu. In any case, within a year Lu Chiu-yüan began writing to local and regional officials, attempting to secure funds for a "normal-purchase" granary to supplement the community institution.[68] He had become worried that defaults on loans made by the community granary would deplete its stock in a bad year and require the input of new funds—presumably by its managers—if the granary were not to close. This was a recurrent problem with community granaries because of the lack of interest charges. A normal-purchase granary, which bought grain at slightly above market prices when it was cheap and sold it at slightly below market prices when it was dear, not only stabilized grain prices but also cleared a consistent profit. Lu planned to use the surplus funds from the normal-purchase granary to supply the deficits of the community granary. In effect this would convert the pair of them into a single, stable, self-paying institution serving two social welfare functions at once. Lu's experience in this case does not seem to have converted him into an active promoter of either community or normal-purchase granaries on a wider scale: he founded neither while in office in Ching-men soon afterward. But the case does reveal an interest in cost-free or self-funding forms of social action that echoes the approach of Lu Chiu-shao.

That the *chia* was primary for Lu Chiu-shao is clear; I have tried to show that Lu Chiu-yüan's writings and practice show definite parallels to notions found in Lu Chiu-shao in order to support my suggestion that Chiu-yüan shared, at least in some significant measure, his brother's *chia*-orientation. Chiu-yüan, like his brothers, was raised in a household that demanded deep commitment to the common enterprise of the *chia*; he continued to live in that household, when at home in Chin-ch'i, throughout his life. Chiu-yüan's biographical writings celebrate his brothers' economic contributions to the family in a way hardly found in the writings of other Neo-Confucians—least of all Chu Hsi—but highly reminiscent both of Chiu-shao's surviving writings and of Yüan Ts'ai's *Precepts*. The evidence is indirect and sketchy but suggestive.

If indeed Lu Chiu-yüan shared, in some considerable degree, the primary orientation toward the *chia* that I find in both his brother and Yüan Ts'ai, how would this have discouraged involvement with voluntary community institutions along Chu Hsi's lines? I have suggested one small part of the

68. For these letters see HSCC 1:6b–7b, 8:3a–4b, 9:4a–6a.

answer already, in the material constraints placed on outward relations by the commitment to the *chia* as economic unit. Another part may be the constraints on *chia* decision making and flexibility that regular involvement in formal and permanent institutions at the community level might pose: this would be a particular problem, for instance, with the community compact. But I would suggest that, for the Lus at least, the incompatibility may have had broader foundations than these. The Lus, and the men in their own time and after who celebrated their achievement, seem to have had an almost evangelical attitude toward the peculiar organization and the remarkable continuity of their own *chia*. The Lus as a group had their own model of community organization—their family—to offer in place of the various institutions of the middle level promoted by Chu Hsi. The medium for the propagation of the model was Lu Chiu-shao's family rules. In view of the exceptionally strict and detailed organization of their household and the wealth of functions it performed—including, it seems, basic and perhaps more advanced education—I would suggest that the Lus saw the *chia* as, potentially at least, the community institution par excellence. Formal institutions, other than the family and below the established traditional state institutions, may have seemed simply superfluous. For the Lus, then, the *hsiang* was not, as for Chu Hsi, a separate level of society *above* the family but simply the space within which *chia* organizations and their individual members interacted.

The argument, again, is speculative. There can be little doubt, however, that Chu Hsi himself saw excessive emphasis on kinship ties as a possible impediment to the moral reform and institutional revitalization of the local community. For Chu, the family, although the site of the most fundamental moral relationships, could become the focus of selfish interest if not transcended in favor of a larger community and ultimately society at large. However, one is under no obligation, as Ebrey has pointed out, to view the matter in exactly Chu's way. The conflict I have outlined between community and *chia* was not simply between altruistic moral commitment and mere self-interest, much less between ideal and practice. The Lu son who accepted a function allotted to him by the household head that might bear little relation to his personal ambition; the officials who fed their income into the common fund when by dividing the family they could have emerged richer than their brothers; the household head who deferred present enjoyments to maintain a secure property for the next generation and so preserve the institution itself—none of these, surely, was following the dictates of naked self-interest. All were hewing to an ideal, which, of course, they might also sometimes fail to live up to. The issue was not whether self-interest or altruism would win out; it was rather what sort of group, at what level and joined by what sort of ties, was to be the focus of altruism and the transformer of self-interest.

I am not, then, proposing a materialist or otherwise reductionist argument. All men had *chia* of their own; if tensions were inherent or potential in the relations between the *chia* and a wider local community, different men will have resolved or considered them in different ways. Whatever material or social constraints may have influenced the development of the Lu communal household, by the time of Chiu-yüan and his brothers its maintenance was a matter of deliberate choice and considerable effort by its managers. The choice and the effort represented a commitment to one view of how society at the local level should ideally be organized. Two competing ideal principles, I am arguing, shaped the responses of Chu Hsi and the Lus to the problem of how to establish and maintain a moral local order in the special conditions of Southern Sung: a principle of community (*hsiang*) as an ordered social and ritual framework transcending kin yet apart from the state; and, in a rather special form, the principle of kinship. Conflict between the two was potential, not inevitable: Chu's own system, in fact, attempted to join the two by giving the *chia* its proper and essential place below the *hsiang*. But kinship could be treated as a principle capable of organizing a virtual community of its own. When this was done, other principles, and the institutions dedicated to them, could not, perhaps, command equivalent devotion. The urge to order large-scale communities through kinship was by no means unique to the Lus or to the few other families organized as they were; one should not forget that the first roots of the local corporate lineage, an organization transcending the *chia* but transcending it through ties of wider kinship, lie as well in the Sung. In its most highly developed form—the late-Ch'ing lineage familiar in particular from Kwangtung—this organization would come to perform many functions Chu Hsi envisioned for his community institutions but to perform them for a community sharply limited by descent.

Some support for the picture I am drawing here is perhaps to be found in the case of a later family much like the Lus: the Cheng family of Chin-hua during the Yüan and the Ming dynasties. The Chengs have been studied in some detail by John Dardess and more recently by John Langlois: I rely largely on their discussion here.[69] Like the Lus, the Chengs maintained themselves as an undivided household for many generations; like the Lus, they were acclaimed in their own time for their achievement. Because the Cheng family rules survived intact, much more of their organization is known. Several points are of interest here. First, as with the Lus, the Cheng rules prescribed that a member whose offenses against the family had proved incorrigible within the penal framework of the household itself should be turned over directly to the local administrators for punishment;[70] no intermediate level of authority or court of first resort apart from the state was provided for.

69. John Dardess, "The Cheng Communal Family: Social Organization and Neo-Confucianism in Yuan and Early Ming China," *Harvard Journal of Asiatic Studies* 34 (1974): 7–52; John Langlois, "Authority in Family Legislation," in *State and Law in East Asia: Festschrift Karl Bünger*, ed. Dieter Eikemeier and Herbert Franke (Wiesbaden: Harrassowitz, 1981), pp. 272–299.

70. Dardess, "The Cheng Communal Family," p. 21; Langlois, "Authority," p. 286.

Second, the Chengs, who strictly regulated their members' contacts with the outside world,[71] were nonetheless extremely active in that world, as indeed were the Lus, and in particular earned a considerable reputation for charity, not only toward relatives outside their enormous *chia* but also toward nonkinsmen in the wider locality. But their charities, whatever member might pursue them, were subject to the family manager's direct control and approval.[72] The charitable estate established expressly to provide relief outside the *chia* was not, like Chu Hsi's community granary for example, a semipublic institution independent of any single family; rather, it was one Cheng estate among many others, administered and controlled, like the rest, by the family manager.[73] No Cheng, as far as I can discover, ever established any community institution independent of the Cheng household itself.

Finally, Langlois makes a crucial point when he maintains that the Cheng family organization was in many ways functionally equivalent to the *she* 'community' established by the Yuan in 1270 as the fundamental unit in its own attempt at a system (imposed from the top down, to be sure) of community governance: "the larger family, managed by a head, and the community, based upon the natural village or clusters of natural villages, were analogous intermediate stages of government."[74] If one recognizes with Langlois that communal households like those of the Chengs and Lus were indeed a sort of experiment in local *government*, functionally equivalent to and so in effect *alternatives* to the experiments of the state with *she* or *pao-chia*, it will not seem strange that a commitment to them would impede commitment to still other experiments in community organization, the innovative local institutions of Chu Hsi and his followers.

I have moved rather far, it would seem, from education. But if my suggestion has merit—if Lu Chiu-yüan had little interest in the local academy, or indeed in any other community educational institution, not because his notions of education and learning were in themselves antithetical to structure and to institutions but because in some part the local academy was a particular *sort* of institution, for which Lu's primary commitment to the *chia* as community prevented serious commitment—then this examination of Lu's case will have the effect of confirming, by negative example, de Bary's notion that education for Neo-Confucians, particularly but not uniquely for Chu Hsi, found its place and so its significance within a larger conception of the moral transformation of the local community. Lu's disinterest in local academies and other new Neo-Confucian institutions of local community rested in part, I have suggested, on a rather special conception of what exactly the local community should be.

71. Dardess, "The Cheng Communal Family," p. 27.
72. Dardess, "The Cheng Communal Family," pp. 30–32.
73. Dardess, "The Cheng Communal Family," pp. 30–31.
74. Langlois, "Authority," pp. 292–293.

SEVENTEEN

The Institutional Context of Neo-Confucianism: Scholars, Schools, and *Shu-yüan* in Sung-Yüan China

Linda Walton

INTRODUCTION

In the study of Neo-Confucianism, much attention has been focused on the filiation and nature of ideas and relatively little on the specific institutional context in which Neo-Confucianism developed and spread. The origins of the *shu-yüan*, an institution shaped by and designed to propagate Neo-Confucian ideas, can be traced to the T'ang; but, like Neo-Confucianism, the emergence of the *shu-yüan* in its mature form as a semiprivate school or academy was a legacy of the Sung period. Following the decline of the "great" academies of the Northern Sung with the rise of a state-sponsored school system, the next important stage in the history of this institution was the establishment of academies throughout the Southern Sung empire during the late twelfth and the early thirteenth century. The significance of this revival and proliferation of academies during the late Southern Sung and early Yüan periods lay in the central role played by the institution not only in the propagation of Neo-Confucian ideas in the Sung but also in the transmission of Neo-Confucianism through the era of Mongol domination in the Yüan dynasty.

As the major Neo-Confucian educational institution, academies must be understood in terms of the general significance of schools in later Imperial China and culturally specific conceptions of education, as well as Neo-Confucianism. While postulating the essential goodness of human nature and the original equality of human beings, the Mencian tradition emphasized the importance of education in guiding the moral development of the individual. But because, according to the Mencian tradition, man was fundamentally a social creature, education was also identified with the inculcation of values enabling people to function as members of a hierarchically ordered society that reflected a given natural order of the world. Both individual moral development and the internalization of social values were accomplished through not only the study of particular texts under the guidance of teachers who served as moral exemplars but also the learning of customary social practices known as "rites" (*li*). Schools played a key role in both the transmission of textual tradition and the formal training in the practice of rites as the concrete representation of the hierarchical structure in which human relations were framed. Rites performed in schools—such as the *hsiang yin-chiu li* (local libation ceremony), which confirmed the social order through the formal ranking of individuals in a hierarchy determined by age and virtue[1]—both reinforced the concept of hierarchy as a basis for social organization and helped to legitimize the political order because these and other rites held at schools affirmed good government and symbolized the harmony of society under a benevolent and capable sovereign's rule. The significance of schools in later imperial Chinese society thus derived not only from their role in cultural reproduction through the transmission of Confucian tradition but also from their role as institutions of socialization through the performance of rites that confirmed the legitimacy of the sociopolitical order. As educational institutions, academies were similarly characterized by this dual function, and the vicissitudes in their institutional history were directly related to both the changing role of government or official schools and the shifting fortunes of the *Tao-hsüeh* movement.

The role of schools in transmitting the classical literary heritage was enhanced by the increasing importance of the examination system in the Northern Sung, when schools began to function as training institutions for candidates preparing to take the civil service examinations.[2] However, with mounting criticism in the Southern Sung of the examination system and the school system that served it, academies began to be seen by thinkers identified with the *Tao-hsüeh* movement as alternative institutions that could be molded to meet their educational goals and ideals. The revival of academies in the Southern Sung can be closely linked not only to disillusionment with the examination system and state schools but also to the rise of the *Tao-hsüeh* movement. Following the restoration of White Deer Grotto Academy (*Pai-lu-tung Shu-yüan*) by Chu Hsi in the late twelfth century, academies became the institutional base of *Tao-hsüeh* thinkers and provided the means by which their ideas were propagated and eventually accepted. With the adoption of *Tao-hsüeh* as state orthodoxy under Li-tsung in the mid-thirteenth century, academies began to acquire an official role, and by the time of the Mongol conquest academies had spread throughout the Southern Sung empire. In the final stage of this development, the Yüan

---

1. For a brief description of these rites, see John W. Dardess, "Confucianism, Local Reform, and Centralization in Late Yüan Chekiang, 1342–1359," in *Yüan Thought*, ed. Hok-lam Chan and Wm. Theodore de Bary (New York: Columbia University Press, 1982), p. 332. Dardess cites a reference to the rites in Ch'eng Tuan-li's collected works, *Wei-chai chi* (Ssu-ming ts'ung-shu ed. vol. 1, no. 2), 3:4b–5b; hereafter cited SMTS.

2. On the complex relationship between education and the examination system, see Thomas Lee's chapter.

government completed the transformation of academies into official institutions by making them part of the state educational system. Thus, academies served as a principal means by which Chinese cultural tradition was preserved and transmitted during the era of Mongol rule, insuring the content of that tradition would be in large part determined by the interpretations of Chu Hsi and his followers of the *Tao-hsüeh* movement, or Neo-Confucianism.

This chapter will focus on the role of academies in the transmission of Confucian cultural tradition during the Southern Sung and the Yüan periods through a study of scholars, schools, and academies in Ming Prefecture from the Northern Sung through the Yüan. Because academies were directly related to schools as institutions of cultural reproduction and socialization, their significance can best be understood in the context of the changing background of scholarly traditions and educational institutions in local society during this period. Although broad generalizations cannot be supported from evidence obtained through the investigation of only one region, the approach adopted here is premised on the assumption that generalizations can only emerge through the accumulation of information collected from a variety of local studies. Thus, the case study of Ming Prefecture, located in the southeastern coastal core region (Ning-po in modern Chechiang Province), and including Yin (metropolitan), Tz'u-hsi, Ting-hai, Feng-hua, Hsiang-shan, and Ch'ang-kuo counties, is not intended to be representative but to provide a basis for the development and refinement of ideas concerning the relationship between local schools, the development of academies, and the propagation of Neo-Confucianism in Sung-Yüan China (See Map 17.1).

THE CH'ING-LI FIVE MASTERS AND LOCAL SCHOOLS IN
MING PREFECTURE DURING THE NORTHERN SUNG

Although there is a record of a prefectural school (*chou-hsüeh*) first being established in Ming Prefecture during the T'ang, there is little substantive information about it in the Northern Sung, and references concentrate primarily on the Confucian temple complex with which the school was closely connected.[3] However, considerably more information on the county schools (*hsien-hsüeh*) and particularly on the activities of local scholars asso-

---

3. See Chang Chin, comp., *Ch'ien-tao Ssu-ming t'u-ching* [1169] (Sung-Yüan ti-fang-chih ts'ung-shu [SYTFTS] ed.) 9:8a. See also Lo Chün and Fang Wan-li, comps., *Pao-ch'ing Ssu-ming chih* [1227] (SYTFTS ed.) 2:3b–4a. Li Tao, *Hsü Tzu-chih t'ung-chien ch'ang-pien* (Taipei: World Book Company, 1964), has an entry for the second month of *keng-wu* stating that the Ming prefectural school was established with an allocation of five *ch'ing* of land. Although there is no specific reference to this in the local histories, from this and information in the gazetteers, it seems safe to assume that the prefectural school predated the Ch'ing-li reforms and was given imperial support just shortly before the 1044 edict calling for the creation of schools throughout the empire. I am indebted to John Chaffee for this reference and that in note 23 (SHY).

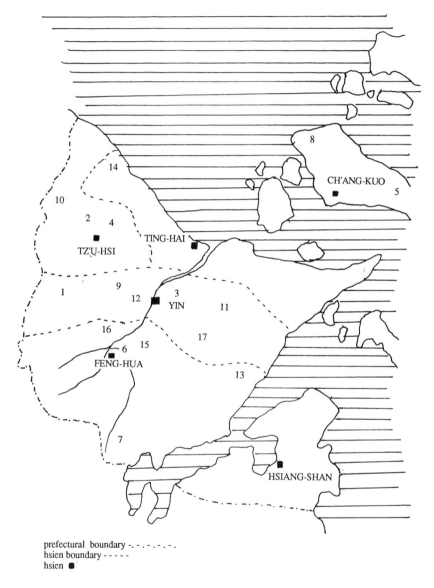

Map 17.1. Ming Prefecture

No.	Academy	Date	Location
1	T'ao-yüan	c.1070	Yin (W 30 *li*)
2	Stone Slope[a]	c.1225–50	Tz'u-hsi[b]
3	Yung-tung	1228–1234	Yin (E 3 *li*)
4	Compassion Lake	1241–1253	Tz'u-hsi (NE 1 *li*)
5	Weng Islet	1241–1253	Ch'ang-kuo
6	Dragon Ford[c]	1260	Feng-hua (E 4 *li*)
7	Teng-ying[d]	1265–1274	Feng-hua (S 60 *li*)
8	Mt. Tai	1273–1274	Ch'ang-kuo
9	Mao Mountain	1298	Yin (W 5 *li*)
10	Tu Islet	1309 [1336]	Tz'u-hsi (NW 30 *li*)
11	East Lake[e]	1327–1330	Yin (E 30 *li*)
12	Lu-chai	1340	Yin (W 1 *li*)
13	Pine Creek[d]	1341–1367	Feng-hua (E 110 *li*)
14	Mt. Tse[f]	1341–1367	Ting-hai (NE 90 *li*)
15	Kuang-p'ing	Yüan	Feng-hua (E 16 *li*)
16	Yin River[d]	Yüan	Feng-hua (?)
17	Original Mind	Yüan	Yin (?)

[a] SYHA 74:16a.
[b] Foothills of Compassion Lake's eastern mountains.
[c] SYHA supplement 76:24a.
[d] *Ning-po fu-chih* 9:472.
[e] SYHA supplement 49:237b.
[f] SYHA 86:2a.

ciated with these schools can be used to shed light on local educational institutions in the Northern Sung.

The concerns of the Ch'ing-li era (1041–1048) reforms to provide education for the people and to meet the practical needs of the state by preparing men for government service through the creation of a network of local schools were reflected in Ming Prefecture in the careers of the "Ch'ing-li Five Masters."[4] Lou Yü, the first member of his lineage to take a *chin-shih* degree (1053), taught at the prefectural school and the Yin county school. Tu Ch'un, a scholar from neighboring Yüeh Prefecture was invited to teach at the Yin and Tz'u-hsi county schools. Local scholar Yang Shih had received an honorary title from Emperor Jen-tsung (r. 1023–1063). And Wang Chih (985–1054) and his nephew Wang Shou (1010–1085) were members of a local lineage that dated its rise to official status from the beginning of the Ch'ing-li era when Shuo took a *chin-shih* in 1041.[5]

Northern Sung statesman Wang An-shih (1021–1086), who served during the early days of his political career as magistrate of Yin in 1047, invited Tu

4. Chang Ch'i-yün, "Sung-tai Ssu-ming-chih hsüeh-feng," in *Sung-shih yen-chiu chi*, vol. 3 (Taipei: Chung-kuo ts'ung-shu wei-yüan-hui, 1966), pp. 50–52.
5. *Pao-ch'ing* 8:8b–13a.

Ch'un to teach at the school there; although Tu at first declined, Wang eventually convinced him of his obligation to teach.[6] Tu Ch'un had been an eremite scholar in Yüeh Prefecture who supported his family through cultivating mulberry trees, fishing, and shepherding. The record of his initial refusal to accept Wang An-shih's invitation to teach at the school in Yin is consistent with the stereotypical portrait of Tu as a penurious scholar devoted to his studies and unconcerned with worldly success and public recognition of his merit. But Wang and others sought to use Tu's talents as a teacher to staff local schools as part of a broad effort by the government to support education at the local level for the recruitment and training of scholar-officials. In 1048 Wang An-shih wrote a commemorative inscription for the school in Tz'u-hsi subprefecture, praising the subprefect for his efforts to promote education in the area, including his invitation to Tu Ch'un to teach at the Tz'u-hsi school.[7] Although there is record of a "Former Sages Hall" (*hsien-sheng tien*) having been established in Tz'u-hsi during the late tenth century, the first evidence of an actual school appears only in 1048, when books were provided and Tu Ch'un was invited to teach there. According to one source, "the flourishing of the two localities' [Yin and Tz'u-hsi] cultural customs" originated with Tu Ch'un, who was known especially for his knowledge of the *Odes* and the *Book of Documents*, as well as for his poetry.[8]

Lou Yü, originally from Feng-hua, was also invited by Wang An-shih to teach at the Yin county school; there he taught for a number of years before becoming preceptor (*chiao-shou*) at the prefectural school, a position he held for more than thirty years.[9] He had been appointed to political office after taking his *chin-shih* degree in 1053 but soon returned home; he ended his career as a teacher and scholar in his native place.

Yang Shih was an eremite scholar who lived in Tz'u-hsi and was known for his study of government. When he traveled to Yüeh Prefecture during Fan Chung-yen's tenure as prefect there, Fan sought him out.[10] Later he became acquainted with both Tu Ch'un and Wang Chih. Although he lived in seclusion for forty years, when a proclamation was issued by Emperor Jen-tsung seeking eremite scholars for recognition, his name came to the attention of the local prefect, who allotted him a stipend. Later he was recommended, received a title, and passed an examination given locally by an official from the Imperial University that entitled him to official status.[11]

---

6. *Pao-ch'ing* 12:3b–4a. Huang Tsung-hsi et al., comps. *Sung Yüan hsüeh-an* (SPPY ed.), 6:3b; hereafter cited SYHA.

7. *Ch'ien-tao* 9:10a–12a.

8. SYHA 6:3b.

9. Ibid., 4b; *Pao-ch'ing* 8:9a.

10. SYHA 6:3a.

11. Wang Ying-lin, *Ssu-ming wen-hsien chi* (SMTS ed.) 1:20a–21a; *Ch'ien-tao* 5:3b.

But Yang declined these rewards and privileges, fitting the stereotype of the eremite scholar who deliberately avoided fame and office.[12] Wang Chih, a friend of Yang and Tu, was active in local political affairs through his discussions with the prefect. But Wang An-shih admonished him also for his reclusive life and for failing to hold office.[13] Wang Chih's nephew, Shuo, was his disciple and held the position of local preceptor for more than thirty years.[14] During the Hsi-ning era (1068–1078), Wang Shuo was recommended for a title by special grace, but he declined and remained a poor eremite scholar throughout his life. After his death in 1085, the place where he taught in T'ao-yüan canton (*hsiang*) became an academy, and he was given the posthumous title of Master T'ao-yüan.[15] T'ao-yüan Academy is the only one known to have existed in Ming Prefecture during the Northern Sung, and the circumstances of its establishment reflect one of the most common origins of academies: reverence paid to a scholar and teacher by making his study or school into an academy where his name and teachings would be preserved. However, no further record of this academy provides information on scholarly or other activities.

From evidence concerning the Ch'ing-li Five Masters and Wang An-shih's activities as Yin magistrate during the Northern Sung, emphasis at the county schools in Yin and Tz'u-hsi appears to have been placed on acquiring local scholars as teachers, perhaps both to recognize their talents and bring them into the service of the state and to use them to train prospective candidates for office. The examples of the Five Masters illustrate this well, with the reluctant scholars being wooed by an ardent official, in this case Wang An-shih, who later proposed the use of schools as a replacement for the examinations. Although one may assume that schools continued to serve as the site for Confucian rites carried out by local officials, judging from the lack of information in the sources concerning the performance of rites at the schools, one may conclude that during the Northern Sung less attention was paid to the traditional rites associated with schools and relatively more attention was devoted to schools as preparatory institutions for the examinations.

The history of schools in other counties of Ming during the eleventh century shows a pattern similar to that of Yin and Tz'u-hsi where the Five Masters were active. Lou Yü's original residence, Feng-hua, had a Confu-

12. SYHA 6:3b.

13. Ibid., 4a. Yüan Chüeh, comp., *Yen-yu Ssu-ming chih* [1314–1320] (SYTFTS ed.) 4:14b.

14. SYHA 6:8a.

15. Ibid. Shen-tsung bequeathed a name tablet for the academy, thus providing official recognition. See references in Ch'üan Tsu-wang, *Chieh-ch'i t'ing chi* (Kuo-hsüeh chi-pen ts'ung-shu ed.), *wai-pien*, 22:953; Li Wei et al., comps., *Ning-po fu chih* (1732; reprint Hong Kong: 1957) 9:440; and *Ta-Ming i-t'ung-chih* (1461 ed.) 46.9a. The latter source claims that Shen-tsung also appointed an official to this academy.

cian temple of T'ang origin that was enlarged to be used as a school in the Ching-yu era (1034–1038) and further expanded by the magistrate in 1066.[16] Hsiang-shan county had a combination school and Confucian temple that had been established in the mid-ninth century, and this was repaired and renewed twice by local magistrates in the mid-eleventh century.[17] A local official in Ting-hai county established a Former Sages Hall in 985 that was restored by the magistrate a decade later, and this apparently served the purpose of a school until the early twelfth century; it was then enlarged and made into a "learning palace" (*hsüeh-kung*) because of the decree implementing the *san-she fa* that made schools the center of recruitment and evaluation of candidates for government office.[18] Ch'ang-kuo county, located on the archipelago off the coast, first established a school only in 1075.[19] The school was abolished at the beginning of the twelfth century, and Ch'ang-kuo's students were sent to a neighboring locality. But in 1116 the magistrate reestablished it, and Ch'ang-kuo's school was the only one in Ming Prefecture to escape destruction with the Chin invasion in 1130, probably due to its location.[20] The local history for the Pao-ch'ing era (1225–1228) records the destruction at this time of schools in Yin, Tz'u-hsi, Feng-hua, Hsiang-shan, and Ting-hai counties.[21]

LOCAL SCHOOLS IN THE TWELFTH CENTURY

The Ming prefectural school was also nearly completely destroyed by the Chin invasion in 1130, and only the Former Sages Hall remained.[22] The school was restored by 1135; and, although the facilities at the school were still inadequate, "the students shouldered their satchels and came, stayed in the ruined dwellings, and the sound of recitation did not cease."[23] After further rebuilding in 1137, there was a central gate with two "fences" (*hsü*) on either side; behind it was the lecture hall, called the "Hall of Clarifying Human Relations" (*ming-lun t'ang*); and the kitchen and bathhouse stood to the east.[24] The Former Sages Hall that remained from the Northern Sung probably stood between the central gate and the lecture hall, and there were

16. *Pao-ch'ing*, 14:5b.
17. Ibid., 21:8a.
18. Ibid., 18:9a.
19. Ibid., 20:5a.
20. Ibid., 20:5b.
21. Ibid., 12:7b, 16:9b, 14:5b, 21:8a, 18:9a.
22. *Ch'ien-tao* 9:5a; *Pao-ch'ing* 2:4a.
23. *Ch'ien-tao* 9:5a–b. *Sung hui-yao chi-kao* (Taipei: Shih-chieh Shu-chü, 1964), *ch'ung-ju*, 2:32b records that because of the numbers of students the post of preceptor (*chiao-shou*) at the Ming prefectural school was specially allowed to be retained even though it had previously been abolished. This suggests an active school, fulfilling essential needs, as indicated in the local history by the speed with which the restoration of the school was accomplished.
24. Ibid., 9:5b.

two corridors (*wu*) with four student dormitories (*chai*) each on the east and west sides of the lecture hall.[25] All the architecture, images, and ritual implements were renewed to imitate the system of the "schools of the feudal lords" (*p'an-kung*); and when it was finished, the students gathered to perform rites and to honor the prefect and the school preceptor.[26] An inscription written to commemorate this, dated the tenth month of 1137, provides some insight into the motives behind the efforts devoted to rebuilding the school:

> The ancients always established schools in their states and in their localities. They were indeed not neglectful, considering them to be the residence of the "superior man" and the source of rites and righteousness. The feudal princes were educated in them and teachers were appointed to assist people from afar. The scholar-officials (*shih-ta-fu*) studied here and at their leisure discussed political affairs. Those who administered the government thereupon examined the advantages and disadvantages of what they said and accordingly reformed their policies. . . .[They] discussed the meritorious ones and raised them up, employing them as officials in the administration of the Son of Heaven. This was the way schools and officialdom at the beginning were joined together.[27]

In 1148–1149 an "Investigate the Ancient Hall" (*chi-ku t'ang*) was established behind the "Hall of Clarifying Human Relations," on the site of the "Nine Classics Hall" (*chiu-ching t'ang*) that had been built to house the bequest of a set of Nine Classics from the imperial government's Directorate of Education during the reign of T'ai-tsung (977–997).[28] The Nine Classics Hall was rebuilt in 1090, and in an inscription commemorating this, dated the eighth month of 1148, Kao K'ang (1097–1153; *chin-shih* 1131), former director of education from Ming, linked the bequest of the Nine Classics with the cultural pacification of the area of Ming Prefecture by T'ai-tsung; and he commemorated the renewal of the hall for storing them as an indication of the prefect's fulfillment of his Confucian duty as custodian of the cultural customs of the area.[29] When the "Investigate the Ancient Hall" was completed in 1149, a set of Classics and histories bequeathed by Emperor Kao-tsung (r. 1127–1162) was stored in the new hall's upper story, which was called the "Imperial Books Pavilion" (*yü-shu ko*).[30]

There was further work on the prefectural school in 1157 and again in 1167, and in the first month of 1169 Prefect Chang Chin led the local scholar-officials in the school rites (*hsü-pai*) held at the prefectural school.[31] An inscription on the land used to support these rites records that it was

25. *Pao-ch'ing* 2:4a.
26. *Ch'ien-tao* 9:6a.
27. Ibid.
28. Ibid., 9:14a.
29. Ibid., 9:12a–14a.
30. Ibid., 9:3a.
31. Ibid., 9:8a–9a.

customary on the first day of each year to honor the "former sages and former teachers" (*hsien-sheng hsien-shih*) and then afterwards to carry out the school rites in the hall of the school.[32] Land had been designated as support for these rites in 1139–1140; but shortly thereafter the land was transferred to support students at the school, and these rites ceased. This situation changed during the administration of Chang Chin, who allotted "officially confiscated land" (*mo-kuan-chih t'ien*) in Yin and Ch'ang-kuo counties to the prefectural school to revive the school rites along with the *chiu-hsing* (libation rites).[33] The inscription records that:

> when they completed the ceremonies, then the customs were transformed for a thousand *li*, and there was none who was not "polished and cleansed." . . . Today the rites are completed in one day and the distinctions between elder and younger, superior and inferior, are illuminated and visible.[34]

This evidence from the twelfth century suggests that support for ritual activities held at the school was more important than subsidizing students.

Precisely what the school rites involved is not clear, but they were concerned with the symbolic affirmation of order and precedence in human relations; along with the libation rites, they were part of the ancient "local libation ceremony" (*hsiang yin-chiu li*). These rites were described in the *I-Li* (Ceremonies and Rites),[35] and carried out locally according to the following description:

> Formerly it was customary on the first day of the year or the last day of winter for the prefect to lead the local scholar-officials in sacrifices to the former sages and former teachers; and afterwards they assembled in the worship hall where old and young were in order [of precedence], ascending and descending [the stairs of the chamber] were ceremonial, and the primary and secondary guests were numbered [according to rank]. They imitated the ancient local libation ceremony.[36]

The veneration of "former sages and teachers" was one principal function of schools as ritual centers that sanctified tradition and its transmitters. The performance of such rites provided an opportunity for the local scholar-officials to confirm publicly their role as cultural leaders and to reaffirm the order of society that placed them in a position of superiority. These rites also formed a ceremonial renewal of the bonds that linked the scholar-officials to the state as local representatives of Confucian social order and moral exemplars in their native area, as the Son of Heaven was for the empire in his

32. Ibid., 9:9a.
33. Ibid., 9:9b.
34. Ibid.
35. For a translation of the *I-Li*'s description of these rites, see John Steele, trans., *The I-Li or Book of Etiquette and Ceremonial* (1917; reprint, Taipei: Ch'eng-wen, 1968), chap. 4.
36. *Pao-ch'ing* 2:16b.

ritual and symbolic role as guardian and human manifestation of cosmic order.

The prefectural school was restored again in 1170, and in 1186 further financial support was allocated to the school by the prefectural government.[37] Representatives of the local elite, Wang Ta-yu (1120–1200; *chin-shih* 1145) and Shih Mi-ta (*chin-shih* 1169), son of Chief Councilor Shih Hao (1106–1194; *chin-shih* 1145), led other members of the elite in underwriting labor and materials for the restoration of the school.[38] The library (Imperial Books Pavilion), the halls, and the adjoining corridors, as well as the central gate, were all repaired, and a new student chamber was erected.[39] Two years later, in 1188, the student chambers were rebuilt, and a new one was established that subsequently became a primary school (*hsiao-hsüeh*).[40]

The revival of county schools in Ming Prefecture after the devastation of the Chin invasion in 1130 followed the same general pattern of rebuilding and development as the prefectural school, and these schools followed the same basic structural form as the prefectural school, with only minor local variations.[41] The central hall for rites, the "Hall of Great Completion," and a lecture hall, the "Hall of Clarifying Human Relations," were supplemented by student chambers arranged symmetrically along corridors on the east and west sides of the lecture halls. There were gates and often a pond, modeled on the *p'an-kung*.

In contrast to the Northern Sung, the sources indicate that the early Southern Sung was a transitional period from support of schools as officially sponsored and subsidized institutions where local scholars lectured and taught students who were primarily potential examination candidates, to a renewed emphasis on schools as not only teaching institutions but also ritual centers devoted to the veneration of sages and scholars. The structure of the school complex, with the rites hall at the very core, attests to this in a concrete way. The emphasis on rites apparent in the sources, however, does not mean that teaching was no longer a basic function of the schools but that rites played a more prominent role than they had during the Northern Sung, when the general pattern was for Confucian temples to become schools. It could almost be said that this pattern was reversed during the Southern Sung, although schools retained their teaching function, too, just as Northern Sung schools continued rites associated with Confucian temples. Efforts to renovate both the prefectural and county schools were officially sponsored,

37. Ibid., 2:4b.
38. For biographical information on these persons, see Ch'ang Pi-te et al., comps, *Sung-jen chuan-chi tsu-liao so-yin* (Taipei: Ting-wen shu-chü, 1974–1976) 1:714, 490; hereafter cited SBM.
39. *Pao-ch'ing* 2:4b.
40. Ibid.
41. For information on these individual county schools, see *Pao-ch'ing* 12:7b, 14:5b–6a, 16:9a–b, 18:9a, 20:5b, 21:8a.

but there is also evidence of private support by local patrons such as Wang Ta-yu and Shih Mi-ta, who provided support for the renovation of the prefectural school in 1186.⁴²

THE CH'UN-HSI FOUR MASTERS OF SSU-MING AND
INTELLECTUAL TRENDS IN THE LATE TWELFTH CENTURY

The renovation of the Ming prefectural school in 1186–1188 coincided with the end of the Ch'un-hsi era (1174–1189), associated locally with the activities of the "Four Masters of Ssu-ming" (a literary name for the area of Ming Prefecture): Yang Chien (1141–1226); Yüan Hsieh (1144–1224); Shen Huan (1139–1191); and Shu Lin (1136–1199).⁴³ The Ch'un-hsi Four Masters were the twelfth-century counterparts of the Ch'ing-li Five Masters, and both their scholarly lives and political careers reflect the considerable political, social, and intellectual changes of more than a century in Ming Prefecture from the mid-Northern to the mid-Southern Sung.

The Ch'ing-li Five Masters were identified with the Northern Sung Ch'ing-li era educational reforms, which were designed in part to create a comprehensive system of state schools throughout the empire to facilitate preparation for the examinations and provide the institutional means for exhorting the populace to follow Confucian norms of behavior. By the Ch'un-hsi era of the Four Masters in the mid-Southern Sung, political, social, and intellectual circumstances had changed dramatically: the northern half of the empire had been absorbed by the Chin state (1115–1234); new families from south of the Yangtze River were beginning to dominate Southern Sung society and imperial politics; the examination system was coming under attack as a vehicle for opportunists to achieve status and power; and Chu Hsi, a contemporary of the Four Masters, was actively promoting ideas that were to become the foundation for Neo-Confucian orthodoxy in late Imperial China.

Although the Four Masters have been considered the major disciples of Lu Chiu-yüan (1139–1193), the chief philosophical opponent of Chu Hsi, their ideas reflect the eclectic intellectual tradition characteristic of their time rather than rigid adherence to a specific doctrine. The intellectual tradition associated with the region of Ssu-ming during the Southern Sung can most accurately be described as one that was influenced by a variety of philosophical schools of the time, including not only the ideas of Chu Hsi and Lu Chiu-yüan but also those of Lü Tsu-ch'ien (1137–1181) from neighboring Chin-hua. The broad spectrum of intellectual influences on the Four Masters and their political careers set them apart clearly from the Ch'ing-li Five

42. Ibid., 14:6a, 2:4b.
43. SBM 4:3142–3144, 3:1859–1860, 1:681, 4:3058–3059.

Masters, who pursued their scholarly careers in seclusion and independence, rejecting both office holding and public recognition of their talents.

Unlike the Ch'ing-li Five Masters, only one of whom took a *chin-shih* degree and held office (Lou Yü), all of the Ch'un-hsi Four Masters both took *chin-shih* degrees and held important offices in the imperial government. Although undoubtedly due in large part to the shift of political power to the Southeast following the loss of the North, their prominent political careers as well as their intellectual and scholarly orientation distinguished the Ch'un-hsi Four Masters from their Northern Sung predecessors. All four studied at the Imperial University around 1165, approximately twenty years after its reestablishment in the Southern Sung during the reign of Kao-tsung under the direction of Kao K'ang from Ming.[44] All four took *chin-shih* degrees: Yang Chien and Shen Huan in 1167, Shu Lin in 1172, and Yüan Hsieh in 1181; and all but Shu Lin held office in imperial educational institutions at the capital.[45]

The origin of scholarly traditions in Ming during the Sung period was attributed to the Ch'ing-li Five Masters, and the transmission of their names to posterity was due to recognition of their contributions as local teachers in the newly established prefectural and county schools of the era. The reputation of the Ch'un-hsi Four Masters, however, was a product both of their scholarly position as the major disciples of Lu Chiu-yüan, begun when they studied under his elder brother, Lu Chiu-ling (1132–1180),[46] at the Imperial University, and of their local scholarly activities during the Ch'un-hsi era. Yang Chien was Lu Chiu-yüan's principal disciple, and the Four Masters were regarded by posterity as the primary transmitters of Lu Chiu-yüan's thought;[47] but the variety of contemporary intellectual influences on the Four Masters is apparent in their broad network of affiliations with other prominent philosophers of the time.

Shu Lin followed the teachings of Chu Hsi and Lü Tsu-ch'ien when the two philosophers were lecturing together in Chin-hua, although he, too, later became a disciple of Lu Chiu-yüan.[48] Shen Huan's father had been a follower of the Ch'eng brothers, and his younger brother, Ping, a disciple of Lu

44. Chang Ch'i-yün, p. 52.

45. Yang Chien was appointed professor of the Directorate of Education (*Kuo-tzu po-shih*) from 1190 to 1194 and librarian of the Imperial Library (*mi-shu lang*) in the beginning of the Chia-ting era (1208–1224). Yüan Hsieh was appointed administrator of the Imperial University (*T'ai-hsüeh cheng*) and director of education (*Kuo-tzu chi-chiu*) before becoming executive of the Ministry of Rites (*Li-pu shih-lang*), the government agency for administering the examinations. Shen Huan was appointed intendant of the Imperial University (*T'ai-hsüeh lu-shih*), and only Shu Lin remained in relatively lowly posts during his political career. For this information, see individual references in SBM.

46. SBM 3:2664.

47. Chang Ch'i-yün, p. 53. See also Shimada Kenji, "Yō Shikō [Yang Tz'u-hu]," *Tōyōshi kenkyū* 24 no. 4 (1966):123–141.

48. Chang Ch'i-yün, p. 53.

Chiu-yüan.[49] When former Chief Councilor Shih Hao retired to his home at the close of his political career around 1180, he became a patron of the Shen brothers.[50] Hao built a residence for them on Bamboo Islet, in the south part of Yin's West (Moon) Lake, where they taught students, including the sons and younger brothers of Shih Hao.[51] The Shen brothers were joined there by Lü Tsu-chien (d. 1196), Lü Tsu-ch'ien's younger brother, who took up office as granary intendant in Ming Prefecture in 1182, following mourning for his brother's death. Lü Tsu-chien held this post for six years, and during his tenure in office he often traveled by boat to the island from his official duties in the prefectural capital to see the Shen brothers, who lived on the island.[52] Shen Huan had studied with the Lü brothers in Chin-hua around 1177, and this relationship continued with Lü Tsu-chien's frequent visits to Bamboo Islet in 1181–1187. Ch'ing scholar Ch'üan Tsu-wang (1705–1755) went so far as to say that the "learning of the Shen clan can truly be considered one with Ming-chao [mountain in Chin-hua where Lü Tsu-ch'ien lectured], but there are few in the world who know it."[53] Ch'üan wrote this in an inscription on Bamboo Islet Three Masters Academy, but, because there are no contemporary references to this *shu-yüan*, it is likely that Ch'üan simply called the association of these three scholars an "academy."[54]

Shih Hao had recommended Chu Hsi to be prefect of Nan-k'ang, and later, when he was intendent of the Evernormal Granary, Tea, and Salt for Che-tung (1181–1182), Chu Hsi traveled to Ming where he visited Shen Huan at the residence provided by Shih Hao.[55] Shih Hao had also recommended both Yang Chien and Yüan Hsieh, as well as Lu Chiu-yüan.[56] During the period of Shih Hao's retirement in the latter part of the Ch'un-hsi era, Yang Chien, Shen Huan, and Yüan Hsieh were teaching at home in Ming Prefecture: Yang Chien at Jade Islet in the north part of Yin's West Lake and Shen Huan at Bamboo Islet, both under the patronage of the Shih family; and Yüan Hsieh at the *ching-she* of the Lou family, descendants of Lou Yü, one of the Ch'ing-li Five Masters.[57]

49. Shen Huan, *Ting-ch'uan i-shu* (SMTS ed.), supplement 2:24b.
50. *Pao-ch'ing* 9:25a.
51. Shen Huan, supplement 2:23a.
52. Ibid., 2:23b–24a.
53. Ibid., 2:24b.
54. Ibid., 2:23b–25a. See also note 57 below.
55. Chang Ch'i-yün, p. 53.
56. *Sung-shih hsin-pien* (Taipei: Commercial Press, 1974) 141: "lieh-chuan" 83, p. 25.
57. SYHA 51:952. Ch'üan Tsu-wang, *Chieh-ch'i t'ing-chi* (SPTK: *ch'u-pien* ed.), chüan 16 includes inscriptions on Bamboo Islet Three Masters Academy (Shen Huan's), Jade Islet Yang Wen-yüan Academy (Yang Chien's), and Ch'eng-nan Academy (the former family school of Yüan Hsieh). Although Ch'üan states that the last was founded in the Sung along with the others but its records were not transmitted, no contemporary records refer to any of these as academies; it is reasonable to assume in all three cases that during the Sung these were really lecturing places in the form of family schools, subsidized by the Shih family for Yang Chien and

Writing during the eighteenth century, Ch'üan Tsu-wang emphasized the diversity of thought that characterized the Four Masters and defended their ideas against charges of Ch'an Buddhist influence that had traditionally been leveled at them, particularly at Yang Chien.[58] He pointed out the breadth of their learning, arguing that schools of thought must be distinguished by emphasis on different things; for example, this separated Chu Hsi from Lu Chiu-yüan. But it was not true, according to Ch'üan, that the Four Masters, as followers of Lu Chiu-yüan, rejected the Classics and histories. He cited the fact that Yang Chien and the others wrote on the Classics; and the Shen brothers, in particular, investigated history, reflecting influence from the Chin-hua school of Lü Tsu-ch'ien. As Ch'üan concluded: "Those who took various paths, but returned to the same place, simply sought the sages and that is all."[59]

In their scholarly lives and professional careers, the Ch'un-hsi Four Masters reflected the prevalent intellectual and political atmosphere of the late twelfth and early thirteenth centuries. With the exception of Shu Lin, all attained national prominence through the offices they held in the imperial government, and both Yang Chien and Yüan Hsieh were demoted in connection with the 1195 "False Learning" (*wei-hsüeh*) prohibition directed against Chu Hsi and his followers of the *Tao-hsüeh* movement.[60] Although neither Shen Huan nor Shu Lin lived beyond the end of the twelfth century, both Yang Chien and Yüan Hsieh survived to be reinstated in high office after the "False Learning" Prohibition was rescinded in 1202.

Following the deaths of Yang Chien and Yüan Hsieh in the 1220s, the Four Masters posthumously joined their Ch'ing-li predecessors as objects of veneration in rites honoring them at the Ming Prefectural School. Although their careers differed greatly, both the Ch'ing-li Five Masters and the Ch'un-hsi Four Masters were revered in the late Southern Sung, along with officials who had served in the area, as local figures to be honored together with philosophers designated by the imperial government. Unlike earlier references to the "local libation rites" and other rites performed at the school in the twelfth century, these rites focused on specific individuals who had a direct relationship with the area: those who had held office there, or native scholars who had attained recognition over time, such as the Ch'ing-li Five Masters, or were known by their contemporaries for both scholarly and

---

Shen Huan and by the Lou family for Yüan Hsieh. As suggested in the text, Ch'üan probably referred to them as academies even though they had not really been established as such in the Sung. Thus, in an effort to maintain some consistency, I do not include them among the academies in Ming Prefecture established during the Sung and Yüan. See also note 97 below.

58. Shu Lin, *Shu Wen-ching-kung lei-kao* (SMTS ed.), supplement *hsia* 21a–22a.

59. Ibid., 23b.

60. For a study of the "False Learning" Prohibition, see Conrad Schirokauer, "Neo-Confucians Under Attack: The Condemnation of *Wei-hsüeh*," in *Crisis and Prosperity in Sung China*, John Haeger ed. (Tucson: University of Arizona Press, 1975).

political achievements, such as the Ch'un-hsi Four Masters. The attention paid to specific local figures in rites held at the school may well reflect a developing sense of local elite identity. And, by the latter part of the thirteenth century, the expression of local consciousness seen in these rites was increasingly represented by the academy movement, as academies were established by disciples of scholars to revere them.

LOCAL SCHOOLS AND ACADEMIES IN MING PREFECTURE DURING THE LATE SOUTHERN SUNG

The Ming prefectural school and county schools in Yin, Tz'u-hsi, Feng-hua, Ting-hai, Hsiang-shan, and Ch'ang-kuo were renovated and received both official and private support during the latter half of the Southern Sung. In the early thirteenth century, according to the local history for the Pao-ch'ing era (1225–1228), the Ming prefectural school held "first [place] among the best [schools] of the various eastern prefectures."[61] This local history further records a list of "predecessors" (*hsien-chin*) for whom shrines were set up at the school in the early part of the thirteenth century. The list included the Ch'ing-li Five Masters, who "by their learning of righteous principle [*i-li*] caused the cultural customs to flourish," as well as prominent individuals from the area who had held office in the central government's educational hierarchy during the Northern and Southern Sung and local prefects who had supported the school.[62]

The local history also lists the school's collection of sacrificial vessels and ceremonial garments that was acquired in the early thirteenth century.[63] The extensive inventory of sacrificial vessels and implements as well as the designation of "predecessors," who either were from the area, like the Ch'ing-li Five Masters, or served in office in the area, indicate the important role of the school as a center of ritual and ceremony for the prefecture and illustrate the significance of ritual in education.

Rites performed to venerate past masters and teachers had two dimensions. First, the individuals for whom sacrificial images were erected represented a basic Confucian pedagogical ideal: the teacher-student relationship as one of master-disciple, in which the master taught by moral example. The transmission of knowledge was direct, personal, subjective, and immediate. Through ritual reverence of "predecessors," homage was paid to them as models of a cultural ideal, and this enhanced textual instruction necessary for both social reproduction and cultural preservation. Second, these rituals concerned the relationship between figures symbolic of the area and its particular interests and the affirmation of the area's link to the center

61. *Pao-ch'ing* 2:5a.
62. Ibid.
63. Ibid., 2:6b–7a.

through veneration of figures designated by the central government because of their significance outside the local area.

During the Chia-hsi period (1237–1240), there was an imperial edict declaring Chou Tun-i, Chang Tsai, the Ch'eng brothers, and Chu Hsi "former sages," and these men were added to the roster of those venerated in the local school.[64] In 1245 the prefect sacrificed to Chang Shih, Lü Tsu-ch'ien, and Lu Chiu-yüan on the left of the Hall of Clarifying Human Relations; and on the right of this hall, sacrifices were held for those local men who had "attained the traditions of the three masters [Chang, Lü, and Lu]": Yang Chien, Yüan Hsieh, Shen Huan, and Shu Lin.[65] The "former worthies" venerated at the school, from the Ch'ing-li Five Masters through the Ch'un-hsi Four Masters, including local prefects and prominent philosophers, served as models for the elite to encourage their emulation of the ideal gentleman scholar. In turn, the elite served as models to the whole population, fulfilling classical ideals of education and government through moral example.

The Ming prefectural school in the Southern Sung, however, was more than a center of ritual. In addition to the extensive inventory of sacrificial vessels and ceremonial garments, the school housed an impressive collection of books and printing blocks in the Imperial Books Pavilion that included several thousand volumes of Classics, histories, miscellaneous writings, and collected works.[66] The prosperity of the prefectural school reflected in its library is further attested to in records of the mid-thirteenth century. The school section in the local history for the K'ai-ch'ing period (1259–1260) states that, among prefectural schools, Chang in Fu-chien was ranked first because of the richness of its financial provisions, and Ming was ranked second because of the splendor of its buildings.[67] Ming's finances, however, were far from spare. The regular school finances listed in detail in the previous gazetteer show a variety of resources allocated to the prefectural school, including specific allocations made for the support of school rites.[68]

The performance of rituals honoring "former worthies" was not limited to local schools. Around the time of his death in 1226, "local gentlemen" in Tz'u-hsi county sacrificed to Yang Chien, known as Master Tz'u-hu (Compassion Lake), at his former residence on the shores of Compassion Lake.[69] A prefectural official moved the sacrificial place to an islet in the middle of the lake during the Chia-hsi period (1237–1240), and in 1271 Prefect Liu Fu (1217–1276) moved the sacrifices from that location to a retreat (ching-she) built on the shores of the lake to the east of the T'ien-t'ai sect P'u-chi

64. Ibid., 2:5b.
65. Ibid.; SBM 5:4213–4214.
66. Pao-ch'ing 2:7a–11a.
67. Mei Ying-fa and Liu Hsi, comps., K'ai-ch'ing Ssu-ming hsü-chih [1259] (SYTFTS ed.) 1:6a.
68. Pao-ch'ing 2:12a–18b.
69. Yen-yu 14:30a.

Temple.[70] In the next year, he appropriated "officially confiscated land" in Ting-hai county to support it.[71] Liu Fu had been master of the hall (*chai*) at the Imperial University where Yang Chien studied, and there Liu Fu had become acquainted with his ideas. When Liu became prefect of Ming, he memorialized to the Court of honor Yang Chien by establishing an academy.

Wen Chi-weng (*chin-shih* 1253),[72] a former student of Yang Chien, wrote an inscription commemorating the founding of Compassion Lake Academy, dated 1273, in which he praised his teacher's doctrine of "mind" and criticized the scholar-officials' prevalent attitude toward learning:

> The *Changes* explains "mind." The *History Classic* transmits "mind." The *Rites* orders "mind." The *Music Classic* regulates "mind." The *Odes* gives sound to "mind." The *Spring and Autumn* [Annals] censures [the iniquities of] "mind" [*chu-hsin*]. Therefore, that whereby the emperor is emperor, the king is king, and that whereby the sages and worthies are sages and worthies, how can this be learned apart from "mind"? . . . The scholar-officials as youths study empty confusion and deception. They do not know what kind of thing "mind" is. They spew blood and breath vying for a meritorious name. They determine their fate by grasping at riches and wealth, destroying their spiritual faculty and thereby losing the "empty mind" [*ling*]. It is always [so].
>
> The volumes stored in the mountain number in the thousands, the scrolls stored on the shelves number in the tens of thousands. Hands ceaselessly unroll them, and mouths ceaselessly repeat them, taking this to be learning. In other words, they only thereby fish for the sound of praise to achieve profit and salary. They lubricate the lips, decorate the documents, and nothing more. The learning that goes in the ears and comes out the mouth, they consider to be true; and, on the contrary, they consider the doctrine of "mind" to be false, even to the point of faulting the Master's [Yang Chien's] learning as "Ch'an learning."[73]

This inscription was composed by Wen Chi-weng, written out by prominent politician, Ch'en I-chung (*chin-shih* 1262; chief councilor, 1275) and presented by Ming prefect Ch'en Ts'un (*chin-shih* 1247–1252).[74] Wen reached the office of assisting civil councilor of state; thus, clearly this academy was not only officially supported by Liu Fu's allotment of land but also recognized by men who were in the very top ranks of government. Wen's criticism of the scholar-officials reflects an attitude similar to that critical of official schools as primarily means to success in the examinations and appointments to office. This is coupled with Wen's defense of Yang Chien's doctrine of "mind" in response to attacks on Yang and his disciples as proponents of

70. SBM 5:3908. Huang Jun-yü, comp., *Ning-po fu chien-yao chih* (SMTS ed.), 5:4b.

71. *Yen-yu* 14:30a.

72. SBM 1:41.

73. *Yen-yu* 14:30b–32b. For the translation of *chu-hsin* see Morohashi Tetsuji, *Dai Kan-wa jiten* (Tokyo: Taishūkan, 1955–1960)10:465.

74. SBM 3:2586, 2435, *Yen-yu* 14:32b.

Ch'an Buddhist enlightenment and thereby suspect of unorthodox influences. Another academy was established in Ming Prefecture during the administration of Liu Fu. This was Mt. Tai Academy in Ch'ang-kuo, in the Chou-shan archipelago off the coast of Ming. Local scholar Wei Chü, a follower of Yang Chien and Yüan Hsieh, and others requested the establishment of a place for "impoverished scholars" at the ruins of a distillery on Mt. Tai.[75] Liu Fu complied with this request and contributed the old distillery foundation as well as additional financial aid.[76] Another local scholar, also a follower of Yang Chien and Yüan Hsieh, was made teacher at the academy.[77] In 1273 the Ch'ang-kuo magistrate wrote an inscription on Mt. Tai Academy, citing the essays by Chu Hsi on Stone Drum, Lü Tsu-ch'ien on White Deer Hollow, and Chang Shih on Yüeh-lu Academy as precedents[78] and distinguishing the academy movement from Taoist eremitism:

> Yüan-hui [Chu Hsi] was a classicist [*ju*]. When he used learning to manage his locality and to perfect his disciples, it was not like the hermits and eremites who seclude themselves in the mountains and valleys, clothing themselves in air and [living on] fungus in order to imitate the prevalent customs of the Taoists.[79]

Praising the academy and its students, the inscription continued:

> If they emulate the followers of Confucius and Mencius, if they [at least] are able to imitate the rules of Stone Drum, White Deer, Yüeh-lu, and Wu-i, even if they are not yet able to be like Confucius and Mencius, [the] Ch'eng [brothers], and Chou [Tun-i], are they not able to be compared with Chu [Hsi], Chang [Shih], Lü [Tsu-ch'ien], and Han [Yü]? Even if they are not able to be like Chu, Chang, Lü, and Han, are they not able to be compared with Hsü, Wei, Chu, and Hsü [local scholars who founded the academy]? . . . Honoring the former sages in the present day is the intention of establishing academies.[80]

The primary purpose of academies is clearly stated here. It has been shown that the ritual function of schools was important in the practice of various local rites and ceremonies affirming the harmony and order of society under the authority of the elite and officials of the state, as well as in the form of veneration of "former worthies." Similarly, as suggested in this inscription, academies were established to pay reverence to a master and his teachings, to venerate "former sages." *Shu-yüan*, then, could be regarded as "temples" of

75. SBM 5:2439, SYHA 74:1414.
76. *Yen-yu* 14:28a. Feng Fu-ching et al., comps. *Ta-te Ch'ang-kuo-chou t'u-chih* [1297–1307] (SYTFTS ed.), 2:13a–b.
77. SBM 4:3592, 3:2155.
78. *Yen-yu* 14:25b.
79. Ibid., 14:25b–26a.
80. Ibid., 14:26b–27a, SBM 1:565.

Neo-Confucianism, dedicated by disciples to the transmission and preservation of their masters' teachings.

Huang Chen (1213–1280),[81] a prominent official and scholar from the area, also wrote an inscription on Mt. Tai Academy, dated 1275:

> Even though scholars desire to shoulder their book satchels and go to the prefectural and county schools, they cannot. . . . In ancient times five hundred households made a *tang* and each *tang* had a local school [*hsiang*]. Today Mt. Tai has perhaps 3,000 households and yet, contrary to ancient times, it is not even as good as one *tang* [i.e., it has not even one official school]. Because of this, in 1271 Wei Chü and others petitioned the Prefect Liu Fu to obtain the abandoned distillery foundation to build Mt. Tai Academy in order to sacrifice to former sages and to study their teachings.[82]

In citing the lack of a local school as a reason for the establishment of Mt. Tai Academy, Huang made clear the educational function as well as the ritual function of the academy, and he stated succinctly the purpose of the academy "to sacrifice to former sages and to study their teachings."

He also discussed the philosophical orientation of Mt. Tai Academy:

> Now, what is orthodox learning? . . . Yang-tzu's egotism and Mo-tzu's universal love were not orthodox. Mencius explained it and returned to the orthodox. Lao-tzu's pure seclusion and the Buddhists' individual extinction were not orthodox. Master Han [Yü] explained it and returned to the orthodox. Those who in discussing emptiness transgress the heights, and those who in striving for profit transgress the depths, are not orthodox. Master Chou [Tun-i] and [the] Ch'eng [brothers] explained it and returned to the orthodox. For every heterodox doctrine that rose up, there was always an orthodox doctrine to save posterity. . . .
>
> Regarding the Six Classics as footnotes, regarding filial piety and brotherliness as branched and separate, regarding investigation and learning as a heterodox doctrine—these are the theories that the former sages never had but that we have today. Master Wen-kung was produced in the midst of this and he rejected and explained it. . . . Mt. Tai's explication of the learning of Wen-kung is orthodox, indeed! Those in the world who assault the learning of Wen-kung are numerous . . . [but his followers] . . . diligently work to cause the orthodox doctrines to flourish and the heterodox doctrines to disperse.[83]

Huang Chen has presented here a strong argument in support of the doctrines of Chu Hsi. Without directly naming Lu Chiu-yüan, he has implicitly criticized his school of thought, including Lu's local followers. "Regarding the Six Classics as footnotes" is a reference to a famous quote from Lu Chiu-yüan that is supposed to typify his disdain for the accumulated

81. SBM 4:2870.
82. *Yen-yu* 14:27b.
83. Ibid., 14:27b–29a.

textual tradition.[84] It is apparent that Huang was attacking the intuitive rationalism of Lu and his followers. He suggested that these ideas represented a new heterodoxy similar to that of Yang Chu, Mo-tzu, the Buddhists, and the Taoists and that Chu Hsi, in the tradition of orthodox thinkers associated with the transmission of the Way (tao-t'ung), like Mencius, Han Yü, and the early Northern Sung philosophers Chou Tun-i and Ch'eng I, had successfully countered this heterodoxy of the Lu school to "return to orthodoxy." It is significant that even in Ming Prefecture, where the influence of Lu's followers was strongest, the emphasis on Chu Hsi's thought can be observed already before the fall of the Sung.[85]

Two other academies were established in Ming Prefecture in the early and mid-thirteenth century. During the Shao-ting period (1228–1233) Cheng Ch'ing-chih (1176–1251), protégé of Shih Mi-yüan who became chief councilor at Shih Mi-yüan's death in 1233, built a sacrificial hall in Yin county to honor his former teacher Lou Fang (chin-shih 1193).[86] There was land to support it, and the "local libation rites" were held there.[87] This later became known as Yung-tung Academy, referring to its location east of the Yung River that flowed from the prefectural capital out to the sea. In the Ch'un-yu period (1241–1252), emperor Li-tsung bequeathed the name 'Weng Islet" in his own calligraphy to a newly established academy at the site of the former residence in Ch'ang-kuo of Ying Su, who took his degree in the same year as Lou Fang (1193) and who was a local colleague of his.[88] His son, Ying Hsü (chin-shih 1223), assisting civil councilor of state under Li-tsung, was also a student of Lou Fang.[89] According to the local history, the sons and brothers of the Ying family were educated in it, and thus Weng Islet Academy initially was a family school.[90]

Other academies originated as family schools. T'ao-yüan Academy from the Northern Sung was originally the family school of Wang Shuo. It was subsequently abandoned during the twelfth century and later reestablished

---

84. Carsun Chang, The Development of Neo-Confucian Thought, vol. 1 (London: Vision Press, 1958), p. 288. Huang Siu-chi, Lu Hsiang-shan: A Twelfth-Century Idealist Philosopher (New Haven: American Oriental Society, 1944), p. 16.

85. Shih Meng-ch'ing (1247–1306), a grandnephew of Shih Mi-yüan, can be regarded as the local founder of Chu Hsi's thought in Ming; Chang Ch'i-yün, p. 60; SBM 1:489. Scholars of the Shih lineage had previously been followers of Yang Chien and Yü Hsieh, but Shih Meng-ch'ing took up the tradition of one of Chu Hsi's major disciples; Chang Ch'i-yün, p. 60. Shih Meng-ch'ing's most famous disciples were another set of Ch'eng brothers, Ch'eng Tuan-li (1272–1348) and Ch'eng Tuan-hsüeh (chin-shih 1321) from Yin (Chang Ch'i-yün 1966, p. 60; SYHA 87:3a).

86. SBM 5:3721.

87. Wang Yüan-kung, comp., Chih-cheng Ssu-ming hsü-chih [1341–1367] (SYTFTS ed) 8:12b.

88. Ta-te 2:10a–b, SBM 5:4092.

89. SBM 5:4083, 3721–3722.

90. Ta-te 2:10b.

within the Yin county seat by descendants of Wang Shuo, probably during the thirteenth century.[91] Kuang-p'ing Academy in Feng-hua, the former private school of the Shu family, was named after the honorific title of one of the Four Masters, Shu Lin (Master Kuang-p'ing).[92] Wang Ying-lin (1223–1296) from Yin wrote an inscription for the academy, dated the fourth month of 1275, in which he described Shu Mi's establishment cf the school in the same year.[93] Shu Mi (*chin-shih* 1244) was Shu Lin's grandson, and after serving as teacher at the Hsiang-shan county school he retired to his family home in Feng-hua where he established the Kuang-p'ing family school, called Kuang-p'ing *Shu-shu* by Wang Ying-lin.[94] This became an academy in the Yüan period, and Shu Mi's grandson held the post of headmaster (*shan-chang*) at the academy sometime during the last two decades of the thirteenth century.[95] Wang Ying-lin's description of the intellectual atmosphere at the school reveals an eclecticism that included Lu Chiu-yüan and Chu Hsi as well as Chang Shih and Lü Tsu-ch'ien.[96]

As indicated by these examples from Ming Prefecture, the term *shu-yüan* was applied to a wide variety of institutions during the Southern Sung.[97] Compassion Lake Academy originated as a sacrificial temple for the philosopher Yang Chien, and Mt. Tai Academy was established as a center for scholars in an isolated area of Ming Prefecture. Although the first teacher at the academy was a follower of Yang Chien and Yüan Hsieh, Mt. Tai Academy was modeled on the academy movement associated with Chu Hsi, and it is clear from Huang Chen's inscription that the ideological orientation was toward Chu Hsi's thought. Yung-tung Academy was founded as a sacrificial temple to the scholar and teacher, Lou Fang. Weng Islet Academy was founded at the residence of Ying Su, a colleague of Lou Fang, and it acquired the character of a family or clan school for Ying's descendants,

91. *Ning-po fu chih,* 9:440.

92. Shu Lin, *Shu wen-ching-kung lei-kao,* supplement 20a.

93. Wang Ying-lin, *Ssu-ming wen-hsien chi* 1:17a, SBM 1:369–370.

94. Wang Ying-lin, *Ssu-ming wen-hsien chi* 1:17a. Wang Tz'u-ts'ai and Feng Yün-hao, comps., *Sung-Yüan hsüeh-an pu-i* (SMTS ed) 76:23b. Hereafter cited as SYHA: supp.

95. *Ning-po fu chih* 9:472. SYHA: supp. 76:23b [addendum].

96. SYHA: supp. Wang Ying-lin, *Ssu-ming wen-hsien chi* 1:16b.

97. SYHA: supp. 76:24a. Sun Yen-min, *Sung-tai shu-yüan chih-tu-chih yen-chiu* (Taipei: Kuo-li cheng-chih ta-hsüeh, 1963), pp. 46–48, list half a dozen more academies founded in Ming prefecture during the Sung. Two of these I believe are mistakenly attributed to Ming Prefecture's Ting-hai county from a Ch'ing source because Ting-hai included more territory during the Ch'ing than during the Sung. Although I have not been able to check Sun's Ch'ing sources, I have found no references at all to the remaining academies in Sung, Yüan, or Ming sources, and this leads me to question their authenticity for the Sung. There is a strong tendency for later sources to name as academies places that were almost certainly not known as academies in the Sung and some that perhaps never were, for example, the study places of scholars venerated in later times but whose studies were never formally made into academies. Following the same criteria discussed in note 64 above, I have not included these academies in my list for the Sung and Yüan.

including his son, Ying Hsü, who had been a student of Lou Fang. Both T'ao-yüan Academy, the only one founded in Ming during the Northern Sung, and Kuang-p'ing Academy were also family or clan schools. In the latter case, the actual naming of the school as an academy did not occur until the Yüan, and one must look to the early Yüan period for the full development of the academy in Ming Prefecture and the standardization of the institution by the central government.

SCHOLARS, SCHOOLS, AND SHU-YÜAN IN MING PREFECTURE DURING THE YÜAN

Yüan records of local schools and academies founded in Ming Prefecture during the Southern Sung show a high degree of continuity between the fall of the Sung and the beginning of Mongol rule. As a result of destruction connected with the establishment of Mongol control in the area, only the outer gate of the Ming prefectural school remained in 1282.[98] But by 1292, when the Yüan government ordered local schools established, prefectural officials and the local elite had already cooperated in successful efforts to rebuild the school.[99] Wang Ying-lin wrote an inscription for this restoration of the school at the end of the thirteenth century in which he referred to the Ch'ing-li Five Masters and Ch'un-hsi Four Masters as transmitters of orthodox learning and linked them to the pedagogical ideals symbolized by the school:

> The Ch'ing-li elders set the standards and their successors, the great classicists of the Ch'un-hsi period, explained and clarified orthodox learning. The sages and worthies—these were the models. Moral nature—this was what was revered. When young, there was "sprinkling and sweeping," facing and answering [the elementary forms of education]; when grown, there was the investigation of things and the extension of knowledge [ko-wu chih-chih]. It was thoroughly absorbed and completely obtained. Every year in the first month of spring, the officials gathered in order, lined up straight like teeth. The teachings of the ancient school officials and the rites of the ancient local administrators were transmitted and bequeathed as moral customs and perpetuated without decay.[100]

According to Wang's inscription, education at the school included the inculcation of social values through the emulation of models and the following of set behavior patterns, as well as the "investigation of things." He also

98. *Yen-yu* 13:2b.
99. Ibid. During the Yüan, in addition to the Confucian school (*ju-hsüeh*), chiefly functioned as the agency through which official recruitment was carried out. There were also prefectural medical schools, as well as a "Yin-yang Professional Bureau" (*yin-yang chiao-shou ssu*), the duties of which included calendar-making, mathematics, sorcery (*wu-shu*), and ritual (literally, "copper urns"). See *Yen-yu* 14:21b–22a.
100. Ibid., 14:9b–10a.

referred to the rites held at the school by local authorities for the purpose of exhorting the populace to follow "moral customs."

In another inscription for the restoration of the Confucian temple at the school, Wang stated, "I have heared that the *Analects* begin with the 'superior man' and end with the 'superior man.' What the student studies is the 'superior man.'"[101] The model of the "superior man" was the object of study at the school, reinforced by veneration of the prototypical "superior man," Confucius, and his latter-day transmitters at the school, and pedagogical emphasis clearly was placed on master-disciple transmission of learning.[102] The Former Worthies' Sacrificial Hall (*hsien-hsien tz'u-t'ang*), established with the further renovation of the school in 1309, was a visible expression of the importance attached to the recognition of models to be followed and imitated. In addition to the Ch'ing-li Five Masters, this hall was dedicated to important local figures such as Lin Pao (1079–1149) and Wang Ta-yu, as well as a series of prefects who had served the area.[103] By the end of the first decade of the fourteenth century, in addition to the Former Worthies' Sacrificial Hall, the library ("Revering Classics Pavilion" [*ts'un-ching ko*]), the lecture hall ("Hall of Clarifying Human Relations"), and the Confucian temple ("Hall of Great Completion") had all been reestablished.[104] The school was restored again in both 1326 and 1338.[105] Following the latter renewal, Hanlin Academician Ch'en Lu[106] wrote an inscription commemorating it, dated ninth day of the seventh month of 1345:

> Our Emperor Shih-tsu [Khubilai Khan, r. 1260–1294] unified the four seas and the canopy of Heaven in order that the Way of Confucius could have a foundation to prosper and transform. . . . The Way of Confucius is the means by which Yao, Shun, Yü, T'ang, Wen, and Wu perfected the Empire. Confucius thus used it to perfect the myriad generations. This principle [*li*] is complete in the heart of man and is expressed in the relations between ruler and minister, father and son, older and younger brothers, husband and wife, and between friends. This teaching is laid out in the Six Records [Six Classics] and explicated in the local schools. It is carried out in the temples and court of the state and in the homes and courtyards of the localities. When men know investigating and studying, the Way of Confucius is clear. When the Way of Confucius is clear, then [the halcyon days of] Yao and Shun and the Three

101. Ibid., 14:8b.
102. See Hayashi Tomoharu, "Chūgoku shoin ni okeru kyōikuhō no shūkyōteki teiryū," in *Chūsei Ajia kyōikushi kenkyū*, ed. Taga Akigorō (Tokyo: Kokushokan, 1980), p. 109, for a discussion of the "question and answer" pedagogy in the *Analects* and later. Hayashi claims that Chu Hsi and his followers continued it, eventually forming the core of China's educational method.
103. *Yen-yu* 13:2b; SBM 2:1344.
104. *Yen-yu* 13:2a–b.
105. *Chih-cheng* 7:2a.
106. Kinugawa Tsuyoshi, comp., *Sō-Gen gakuan, Sō-Gen gakuan hō-i: jimmei jigō betsumei sakuin* (Kyoto: Research Institute for Humanistic Studies, 1974), p. 171.

Dynasties will not exist [only] in [the time of] Yao, Shun, Yü, T'ang, Wen, and Wu, but in the generations of the present [as well]. Those who rule the Empire are unable to cause all men to follow the Way. Therefore, school officials have been created to teach them.[107]

For Ch'en Lu, schools were a means to achieve unity with the sage traditions transmitted from the past, and it was the responsibility of school officials to help bring about harmony in the social order through instruction in the schools on the good government and society of antiquity. As a spokesman for the Yüan government, Ch'en Lu was making sycophantic claims for the cultural beneficence of his Mongol lords; but, as a Chinese official, he was acting in accord with his duty and conscience in presenting his lords as protectors of the "faith" and in emphasizing the transmission of the orthodox 'Way' from Confucius to the school officials of his own day.

For the most part, the development of county schools in Ming followed the pattern of the prefectural school, although during the Yüan administrative changes increased the importance of certain former county schools. Ming Prefecture (*chou*) had been raised to Ch'ing-yüan Prefecture (*fu*) in 1195, but it continued to be referred to as Ssu-ming or simply Ming. Ch'ang-kuo county (*hsien*) was raised to a prefecture (*chou*) by the Yüan in 1280, and Feng-hua county also became a prefecture in 1295.[108] Thus, the former county schools in these two areas became more important during the Yüan, and both new prefectures were the sites of medical schools, as was Tz'u-hsi county.[109] Support for both prefectural and county schools came largely from land income.

Official schools continued to exist under the Yüan, but their function had changed significantly from the Sung. During the Northern and early Southern Sung official schools had been linked to the examination system, but gradually the almost exclusive concentration on training for the examinations in these schools was seen to be contrary to educational ideals as defined in the classical tradition. By the late Southern Sung, there was a return to the traditional emphasis on schools as transmitters of values necessary to maintain social order: the sacrificial halls attached to the schools and the rites performed at the schools once again became important. In part, this was related to the reassertion of Confucian tradition through Chu Hsi's emphasis on rites and social institutions to bring order and harmony to the local community and to reaffirm the principles of moral education. Local scholars as models of morality and virtue were a central part of this moral education, achieved through a pedagogy that emphasized the master-disciple transmission of learning by combining textual study under teachers with sacrifices to

---

107. *Chih-cheng* 7:2b–3a.
108. *Ta-te* 2:9a.
109. *Yen-yu* 14:19b, 17a, 21a.

former sages and worthies.[110] It was especially important that local scholars were designated as "former worthies" so that the local elite were provided a direct link to the schools. During the Yüan, emphasis on schools as instruments of social control intensified, and they were used to transmit Neo-Confucian ideas as orthodox tradition inherited from the past, as well as to reinforce a view of the Mongols as enlightened rulers dedicated to the preservation of Chinese cultural tradition.

These aspects of official schools as they developed in the late Southern Sung and early Yüan can be seen in local academies as well. Academies focused on individual scholars or groups of scholars, and although lectures, discussion, and study took place there, the academy was primarily an institution designed to honor a scholar and preserve his memory and was usually established either by disciples or descendants. In the latter case, the academy was somewhat similar to an ancestral temple, and this and other differing characteristics of the origins of academies make it difficult to define the term precisely until the Yüan government attempted to standardize the institution. An imperial edict of 1291 concerning the funding of public schools and academies, the appointment of personnel, and the sequence of promotion presented the government view of academies as official institutions.[111] The growing institutionalization of academies as a result of these efforts can be seen in their development in Ming Prefecture from the late thirteenth through the fourteenth centuries.

Following the establishment of Compassion Lake Academy by Liu Fu near the end of the Southern Sung, the next important date in the history of this academy came in the early Yüan period (1285) when "Buddhist priests from P'u-chi Temple . . . usurped its land, burned its sacrificial images, and slandered all its students to the officials."[112] Two years later, Yüan officials took over the remaining foundation of Yang Chien's former dwelling, presumably ousting the Buddhists from it.[113] The academy was reestablished there, and a sacrificial hall to Yang Chien was built within the county seat. In the third month of 1292, Wang Ying-lin wrote an inscription on the rebuilding of the academy. He began by citing the various kinds of local schools that had existed in antiquity and developed his argument to place academies in that context:

> [The ancient schools and private tutoring] . . . were the means to unify the Way and virtue and to clarify principle and righteousness. In the establishment

---

110. See Hayashi, "Chūgoku shoin ni okeru kyōikuhō no shūkyoteki teiryū," pp. 106, 202, for the role of sacrifices in *shu-yüan*.

111. *Yüan shih* 81:2032–2033, cited in Lao Yan-shuan, "Southern Chinese Scholars and Educational Institutions in Early Yüan: Some Preliminary Remarks," in *China Under Mongol Rule*, ed. John Langlois (Princeton: Princeton University Press, 1980), p. 111.

112. *Yen-yu* 14:30a.

113. Ibid.

of academies the intention is similar to that of antiquity. Sui-yang and White
Deer are praised as being first, in accordance with their being the places where
Chou [Tun-i], [the] Ch'eng [brothers], Chu [Hsi], and Lü [Tsu-ch'ien]
carried out [their] teaching.[114]

Wang went on to praise Yang Chien and Compassion Lake Academy,
lamenting its decline because of the Buddhists. It is significant that Wang,
not noted as a follower of either Lu Chiu-yüan or Chu Hsi, emphasized Yang
Chien's role in the "School of the Way" (*tao-hsüeh*) movement and his
dismissal in connection with the "False Learning" Prohibition.[115] Wang
continued:

> It has been said that the classicist obtains the people by the Way and the
> teacher obtains the people by virtue. The teacher speaks of virtue and does not
> speak of the Way. He himself is simply the Way. . . . Only the Master [Yang
> Chien] lacked preconceptions and yet naturally obtained it. Modest and
> reverent, stern and respectful, what was not proper, he did not do. In speaking
> of human nature, he always referred to Yao and Shun. In discussing good
> government, he always referred to the Three Dynasties. . . . The learning of the
> Master is the learning of Wen-an [Lu Chiu-yüan] Wen-an lectured on the
> *Analects* at White Deer. . . . Those who listened were excited and their hearts
> were moved. . . . Chu Wen-kung [Hsi] also declared that what Master Lu said
> concentrated on "revering moral nature."[116]

Here Wang has attempted to weave together the ideas of Yang Chien and Lu
Chiu-yüan with those of Chu Hsi to show that they were fundamentally
similar and that, superficial differences aside, they were both talking about
the same principles. Not the resolution of narrow philosophical disputes but
the transmission of the Neo-Confucian synthesis of the inherited tradition
was critical in the Yüan, and the mission of academies such as Compassion
Lake correspondingly took on greater significance. From the perspective of
the need for cultural preservation, philosophical differences between individual thinkers were relatively unimportant.

By the eighth month of 1292, the same year the prefectural school was
restored, the rebuilding of the academy was completed.[117] At the front was
the rites hall (*ch'ung-li tien*), in the middle, the sacrificial hall (*yen-tz'u t'ing*),
and, in back, the lecture hall (*p'i-chiang t'ang*), with two corridors and four
student chambers. There were images for all the sages and teachers, a place
to store books, and an altar for the God of Earth (*hou-t'u*), as well as kitchen
and bath buildings.[118] The rebuilt academy was similar in form to the
prefectural school, and its restoration by Yüan officials reflected government

114. Ibid., 14:33b.
115. See note 60.
116. *Yen-yu* 14:34b–35a.
117. Ibid., 14:36a–b.
118. Ibid.

policy encouraging academies as supplementary institutions of local education.[119] The local history records that sixty-one Confucian scholarly families (*ju-hu*) were associated with the academy, and it was supported by land and tax grain allotments.[120] Compassion Lake Academy was restored again in 1319 and continued to flourish throughout the Yüan.[121]

Mt. Tai Academy in Ch'ang-kuo was reestablished around the same time as Compassion Lake Academy. In 1293–1294, salt market officials bought two "frames" (*chien*) of people's dwellings and moved the academy to the market (*shih*) "so that the name of the academy would be perpetuated."[122] A headmaster (*shan-chang*) was appointed, but, according to the local history for the late Yüan, there was no means of support for it at the time.[123] In 1336, a local official revived the academy, and it was allotted "rich mudlands" to support its "sacrificial affairs.[124] The *Sung-Yüan hsüeh-an* states that schools were needed in the area because of the coastal people's lack of civilized habits.[125] Following the rebuilding of the academy in 1293–1294, there were altogether only three rooms, but with the revival of the academy in the mid-fourteenth century, the buildings included gate towers, a three-"frame" lecture hall, and a three-"frame" ritual hall.[126] There was also at this time a collection of ritual implements similar to those held by the prefectural school.[127] Near the end of the Yüan, Tz'u-hsi magistrate Ch'en Lin (1312–1368) contended with salt pirate and rebel Fang Kuo-chen and was forced to retire to Mt. Tai, where he "styled himself 'foot-hasty,' leaned on a staff, donned a Taoist cap and robes, made a garden, and supported himself by planting and herding."[128] He restored Mt. Tai Academy, lectured to students, and carried out the "local libation rites" there.[129]

By the early Yüan, Weng Islet Academy in Ch'ang-kuo had fallen into a state of decline and lacked a means of support.[130] Furthermore, according to an inscription on the academy by a prefectural official, scholars were attached to the prefectural schools (in Ch'ang-kuo, which was a prefecture at that time), and teaching and learning were completely absent from the academy.[131] Ying Hsiang-sun, a descendant of Ying Hsü, who had founded

119. Hayashi, "Chūgoku shoin ni okeru kyōikuhō no shūkyoteki teiryū, p. 7.

120. *Yen-yu.* 14:37b–38a. The *ju-hu* were Confucian scholarly families, registered as a separate group. See Morohashi, *Dai Kan-wa jiten* 1:951–952.

121. *Chih-cheng* 8:9a.

122. *Ta-te* 2:13a–b.

123. *Chih-cheng* 8:7b.

124. Ibid.

125. SYHA: 3:21b [addendum].

126. *Ta-te* 2:13b.

127. *Chih-cheng* 8:8a.

128. SYHA 93:8b; Dardess, "Confucianism," pp. 342–352.

129. SYHA 93:8b.

130. *Ta-te* 2:10b.

131. Ibid., 2:11a.

the academy, observed the ruins of Weng Islet Academy and decided to restore it.[132] In 1295–1296 he led his relatives to allot property to the academy for the support of teaching and was appointed headmaster at the academy, which was thus transformed from a clan school into a prefectural academy with official status.[133] At this time the academy consisted of a rites hall, a gate, and student chambers.[134] In addition, Ying Hsiang-sun established a separate sacrificial hall for Chu Hsi.[135] The inscription presents the usual description of the various local schools of antiquity and then continues:

> There was no foot of land where they did not raise up a school, nor was there a single person who did not receive education. . . . How is it like the prefectures and localities of later generations, which whether 100 or 1000 *li*, have only one school? In the beginning of the Sung there were the four academies, which were also established on the initiative of the locality. They were not produced from the urging of the authorities. . . . Today we reestablish the academy to continue this. . . . The establishment of this academy was to revere the learning of Hui-an [Chu Hsi]. . . . Today his writings are completely preserved. From the elite [*kung ch'ing-ta-fu*] above to the sons of the poor below, there is no family that does not transmit them and no person who does not recite them.[136]

A typhoon destroyed Weng Islet Academy in 1307, and in 1320 the rites hall and the main gate were rebuilt.[137] Further additions were made in 1336–1338, including a sacrificial hall for Ying Hsü and Ying Su.[138] In 1340 the academy was renewed and Ying Kui-weng from T'ian-t'ai (neighboring T'ai Prefecture), a descendant of Ying Hsü, wrote an inscription for it in which he attacked the "heterodoxies" of Taoism and Buddhism and praised the academy as a bastion of orthodoxy in a hostile environment:

> The Taoists and Buddhists seek so-called purity and individual extinction. . . . As for the Way of Yao, Shun, Yü, T'ang, Wen, Wu, the Duke of Chou, Confucius, or the learning of the Six Classics, in general [they] have not heard of it. Weng Islet is situated at the mouth of the Great Sea. Weng Islet is what the various coastal barbarians look to and listen to. It causes followers of "others" to reject thoughts of revering and performing rites for Taoism and Buddhism and to revere the Way of Confucius. It extends their seeking to hear the chants of purity and individual extinction to a search for the learning of the Six Records [Classics]. Thus, the establishment of the academy here truly aids the sacred teaching, and the moral transformation of this holy dynasty can also be broadened, indeed! How can it not be recorded! Mencius said: "Whoever is

132. SBM 5:4096.
133. SYHA supplement 73:52a.
134. *Yen-yu* 14:24b.
135. *Chih-cheng* 8:5b.
136. *Ta-te* 2:11a–12b.
137. *Chih-cheng* 8:5b.
138. Ibid.

able to oppose Yang and Mo is a disciple of the sages." It can also be said of those who aid academies.[139]

According to the prefectural official's inscription, Weng Islet Academy followed the standards of Chu Hsi's White Deer Grotto, and, according to another inscription, Mt. Tai Academy "imitated the complete standards of Stone Drum, White Deer, Yüeh-lu, and Wu-i."[140] Chu Hsi was revered as a sage whose theories successfully countered the prevalent heterodoxies of Buddhism and Taoism, and the location of both Mt. Tai and Weng Islet academies made them particularly significant for the protection of coastal inhabitants who were distant from the centers of culture and thus dangerously prey to such ideas.

Closer to the center of the prefecture, Mao Mountain Academy was established in the eastern part of Yin county in 1298 at the request of Chao Shou to honor Chu Hsi because his grandfather, Chao Shan-tai (1128–1188), had been a follower of Chu Hsi.[141] A sacrificial hall was set up, one ch'ing of land was provided for support, and a headmaster was appointed to administer the academy.[142] Mao Mountain Academy was completed in 1303, and in spring 1307 the record of its establishment was committed to stone in an inscription by Yüan Chüeh (1266–1327); this descendant of the same lineage as Yüan Hsieh, one of the Ch'un-hsi Four Masters, related the intellectual orientation of the academy to the dominance of Chu Hsi's thought throughout the southeastern part of the empire:

> The regions of Wu, Shu, Min, and Yüeh all revere only Chu Wen-kung as teacher. Emperor Shih-tsu unified the seas and canopy of Heaven. He established the School of the Elders' Sons (wei-tzu hsüeh), selecting Wen-kung's interpretations for the school system.[143]

As an important official of the Yüan government, Yüan Chüeh used phrases similar to those used later by Ch'en Lu in his inscription on the prefectural school regarding the good intentions of the Mongol rulers in conquering the empire to preserve its culture. Yüan Chüeh concluded his inscription by praising the establishment and completion of the academy and stated that "it is because of this that the learning of Wen-kung does not decline."[144]

In this statement by Yüan Chüeh and in other explicit statements concerning the organization of academies in Ming Prefecture on the basis of Chu Hsi's rules for White Deer Grotto Academy, the essential connection between the institution and the spread of Chu Hsi's thought is apparent.

139. *Ibid.*, 8:6a.
140. *Ta-te* 2:10b; *Yen-yu* 14:26b–27a.
141. SBM 4:3576; *Yen-yu* 14:22a.
142. *Yen-yu* 14:22a.
143. Ibid., 14:22b.
144. Ibid., 14:23a.

Regardless of the specific intellectual orientation of founders of academies in Ming during the reign of Li-tsung or later during the Southern Sung, with the reestablishment of many of these academies during the last two decades of the thirteenth century, both the structural organization and the intellectual orientation of the academies were linked to Chu Hsi, through the rules he constructed for academies as an institutional setting for the practice of Neo-Confucian ideas. Although some academies were dedicated to followers of Lu Chiu-yüan and his thought, Chu Hsi's emphasis on an institutional setting aided the propagation of his ideas. An institutional framework was ideally suited to Chu's thought and related well to the ideas themselves. It would seem to have been less appropriate for the approach of Lu Chiu-yüan and his followers, with their emphasis on individual, intuitive perception of the Way.

In 1309 T'ung Chin established a "charitable school" (*i-hsüeh*) in Tz'u-hsi and allotted five *ch'ing* of land for its support.[145] T'ung Chin was the grandson of T'ung Chu-i (*chin-shih* 1223), a follower of Yang Chien, and professor at the Imperial University under Li-tsung.[146] T'ung Chu-i had retired from his political career to an islet in Tu Lake (Tz'u-hsi county) where he gathered disciples and was known as Master Tu Islet.[147] This was the site of the school founded by his grandson that became known as Tu Islet Academy. T'ung Chin's son, T'ung Kui, increased the allotment of land for the school, and in 1336 the official name of Tu Islet Academy was given to the school.[148] Huang Chen's son, Huang Shu-ying (1273–1327), who held office as an educational official in Fu-chien, also lectured at Tu Islet Academy.[149] He had been taught by his father and was thus a follower of his father's interpretation of Chu Hsi's thought.[150] Although Tu Islet Academy was founded originally by the T'ung family, adherents of Yang Chien's thought, shortly after the academy's official recognition a Yüan educational official and proponent of Chu Hsi's thought, Huang Shu-ying, came to lecture there. However, other disciples of Master Tu Islet also continued to be active at the academy, and thus a plurality of philosophies was represented here. In his inscription on this academy, Ch'üan Tsu-wang stated that "of the many academies established at this time in the area, Tu Islet was the most flourishing."[151] In the mid-fourteenth century, the land owned by the academy included more than four *ch'ing* of arable land, the buildings were extensive, and there was a large collection of ritual implements as well as a

145. Kinugawa, *So-Gen gakuan, So-Gen gakuan ho-i*, p. 194; *Chih-cheng* 8:9b.
146. SBM 4:2784.
147. SYHA 14:17a.
148. *Chih-cheng* 8:9b–10a.
149. Umehara Kaoru and Kinugawa Tsuyoshi, comps., *Ryō-Kin-Gen denki sakuin* (Kyoto: Institute for Humanistic Studies, 1972), 2263; hereafter cited as Umehara. SYHA 86:13b.
150. Chang Ch'i-yün, p. 60.
151. SYHA 74:17b.

substantial library.[152] There was a sacrificial hall for Yang Chien and a local masters' sacrificial hall dedicated to T'ung Chu-i, his sons, T'ung Chung, and T'ung Hung, Huang Chen, and others.[153] Ch'üan Tsu-wang pointed out that although Huang Chen originally studied together with T'ung Chu-i, he eventually diverged from him intellectually.[154] However, Ch'üan continued, because Huang's disciples emphasized practice rather than theory, this distinction between Huang Chen's thought and the followers of Yang Chien was never clarified. Thus, Huang Chen was also venerated at Tu Islet Academy.[155]

The peak of official academy development in Ming Prefecture was the request in 1340 for the establishment of an academy to honor Hsü Heng (1209–1281), the famous director of education at the early Yüan court.[156] Ch'en Jen (1269–1348) from T'ai Prefecture was responsible for this request for Lu-chai (Hsü Heng's honorific) Academy, and, according to the local history for the late Yüan, it was located within the Yin city wall.[157] Director of Education Hsü Heng played a key role in the adoption of Chu Hsi's ideas by the Mongol rulers in educational policies carried out during the early years of the dynasty.[158] The establishment of a *shu-yüan* honoring Hsü Heng in Ming Prefecture during the latter part of the Yüan symbolizes both the role of academies in the transmission of Neo-Confucianism through the Yüan and the adoption of the academy by the Mongol rulers as an official institution.

CONCLUSION

In a discussion of the rise of Neo-Confucian orthodoxy in Yüan China, Wm. Theodore de Bary has suggested that, because there was no established church to define and protect Confucianism apart from the authority of the

152. *Chih-cheng* 8:10b.
153. Ibid.; Kinugawa, *Sō-Gen gakuan, Sō-Gen gakuan hō-i*, pp. 194, 278.
154. SYHA 86:2a.
155. Ibid.
156. Umehara, #1903. *Chih-cheng* 8:12b. Although Neo-Confucianism had been officially espoused by the Mongol rulers in North China with the establishment of T'ai-chi Academy in 1238 at Yen-ching, Hsü Heng was instrumental in the adoption of Chu Hsi's thought at the Mongol court. In 1261 he became director of education briefly, and five years later he presented to Mongol Emperor Shih-tsu a tract; in "Five Items of Contemporary Affairs" he outlined his plans for using Chinese law to govern Chinese territory, including a plan for emphasizing agriculture and schools. After holding high offices in the Mongol government, he was responsible for the reestablishment of the *Kuo-tzu hsüeh* under Shih-tsu, and in 1271 he was reappointed director of education. See Abe Takeo, "Gendai chishikijin to kakyō," in Abe Takeo, *Gendaishi no kenkyū* (Tokyo: Sobunsha, 1972), pp. 30–36.
157. *Ning-po fu chih* 9:441.
158. Abe, "Gendai chishikijin to kakyō," p. 36. See also Wm. Theodore de Bary, *Neo-Confucian Orthodoxy and the Learning of the Mind-and-Heart* (New York: Columbia University Press, 1981), pp. 1–66.

state, schools, especially academies, had to carry the burden of transmitting orthodox tradition and stand as an alternative locus of authority to the state.[159] From classical antiquity, however, schools had been assigned a major role in the ordering of society by the state as institutions of both cultural reproduction and socialization through the transmission of textual tradition and the performance of sociopolitical rites, and thus a certain ambiguity existed in the relationship between schools and state authority. If the educational history of Ming Prefecture is not necessarily representative, it nonetheless illuminates some aspects of this relationship with regard to political and ideological interaction between the state as a centralized political structure and local educational institutions as reflections of local interests and potential alternative sources of ideological authority.

When the reclusive scholars later known as the Ch'ing-li Five Masters were brought into the service of the state as teachers in local schools during the Northern Sung, their scholarly talents were solicited to train potential office-holders who would also serve the state as administrators in the centralized bureaucracy. This link established in the Northern Sung between center and region with the growth of local schools was enhanced in the Southern Sung when the Ch'un-hsi Four Masters, who had held important posts in the central bureaucracy, were venerated at the prefectural school along with other officials and scholars, including the philosophical fathers of Neo-Confucianism. By the mid-thirteenth century, *Tao-hsüeh*, the School of the Way, had achieved acceptance and approval by the state; and those who had been associated with it, including two of the Four Masters who had been purged along with Chu Hsi in 1195, were honored by the state in the local school. During the reign of Li-tsung (1225–1264), the academy movement identified with Chu Hsi was also in full swing, and many academies, such as Weng Islet in Ming Prefecture, were formally recognized by Li-tsung and supported with allotments of land by local officials. Although the academy movement began in opposition to state-supported schools as an institutional alternative for scholars whose ideas were viewed unfavorably by the state, approximately half a century after the death of Chu Hsi, not only were his ideas regarded as orthodox, but also the primary institutional means used to propagate the School of the Way, academies, were given official recognition.

The longevity of Confucianism was due in the part to its flexibility in absorbing and adapting contending ideas and claiming them as its own; the strength of the state lay in its ability to coopt the talents of scholars in its service and to transform private institutions into official ones, simultaneously deflecting either latent or overt opposition and turning it into support through formal recognition. This was not difficult, considering that the realms of public and private could not effectively be separated and that the entire Confucian tradition, however interpreted, was predicated on the

159. de Bary, *Neo-Confucian Orthodoxy*, p. 2.

individual's obligation to serve society. At least since the Han, society was represented by the bureaucratic state, and whenever possible, even during the rule of conquerors like the Mongols, service to the state was regarded as the chief responsibility in the fulfillment of Confucian ideals.

In an important sense, schools extended the state, and, although private schools such as academies in the Southern Sung could survive in an atmosphere of either state neglect or tolerance, they could only thrive as they did in the late Southern Sung and early Yüan with state approval and recognition. The political crises faced by the state in the late Southern Sung made it imperative to consolidate support, both ideological and political. Given the success of the *Tao-hsüeh* movement, including the role played by its followers in the government after the rescinding of the *wei-hsüeh* prohibition, there was really no alternative to recognizing the School of the Way as state orthodoxy and conferring ideological authority on its followers as interpreters of and spokesmen for the "True Way."

With the establishment of Mongol rule, the Yüan government in turn coopted the academy movement in its own service as academies became part of the Confucian school system. Yüan rulers, inheriting and continuing in many respects basic elements of the Confucian state, considered the promotion of schools and education as a primary task and, following policies advocated by Chinese advisers to the Mongol court, regarded Neo-Confucianism as the orthodox tradition. Thus, the tendency for the Confucian state to absorb challenges to its ideological authority was continued and even strengthened under Mongol rule. The state ultimately defined what was ideologically acceptable, even though scholars like Chu Hsi could challenge the state with new interpretations and over time influence it to change the definition of orthodoxy, as the proponents of *Tao-hsüeh* were able to do.

Crucial to the success of the *Tao-hsüeh* movement, however, was the role of academies as revived by Chu Hsi in the late twelfth century. Although initially conceived by him as an institutional alternative to state schools, by the Yüan most academies had, in fact, become part of the state school system and even during the Sung it is difficult to make a sharp distinction between schools and academies with regard to their institutional character. Both local schools and academies might be seen as representing different points along an institutional continuum, linked through not only their teachings, but also their ritual function. Northern Sung schools would be placed at one end, reflecting their concentration on training for the examinations, and academies at the other, reflecting their focus on the veneration of scholars. Southern Sung schools would be placed somewhere in the middle; they shared the function of Northern Sung schools in preparing candidates for the examinations and were similar to academies in attention devoted to veneration of local scholars and officials and officials through rites performed at the schools. From evidence in Ming Prefecture alone, one can see that academies themselves exhibited a broad range of characteristics that might be presented along a similar continuum, where one end is represented by academies such as Mt. Tai, which was close to being a prefectural school, and where the other end is represented by Compassion Lake Academy, which began as a sacrificial temple to Yang Chien. Family or clan schools, including the *i-hsüeh* or "charitable schools," such as Tu Islet Academy, belong to yet another category that might be placed in the middle because it was established as a school initially to honor an ancestor of the founders.

A distinction could be drawn between local schools and academies in the late Southern Sung with regard to their differing roles in the relationship between center and locality. Prefectural or county schools, directly linked to the state, were largely products of official sponsorship and support; but academies initially were the result of local efforts, even if on the part of local officials such as Liu Fu, and they reflected local interests, ideas, and personalities. The establishment of academies in late Southern Sung Ming Prefecture can thus be viewed in part as an indication of the growth of a localized identity among elite families there, and most were either founded to honor a local scholar, such as Yang Chien at Compassion Lake, or similar in some way to family or lineage institutions, such as Weng Islet, the Ying family school, or Kuang-p'ing Academy, the family school of Shu Lin. Some academies combined these characteristics: Mao Mountain Academy was founded to revere Chu Hsi by Chao Shou, who wished to honor his grandfather, a follower of Chu Hsi; and Original Mind Academy was established by the Ch'üan lineage, antecedents of Ch'üan Tsu-wang, to transmit the learning of Yang Chien.[160] A follower of Yang Chien also established Mt. Tai Academy, although it eventually venerated Chu Hsi's thought. Mt. Tai Academy was most like a prefectural or county school in the motives that led to its establishment, and its shift to the ideas of Chu Hsi during the Yüan is a clear reflection of a general pattern by which Neo-Confucianism as defined in the works of Chu Hsi came to dominate educational institutions, both schools and academies.

However, evidence concerning academies in Ming Prefecture suggests that the widely accepted view of a sharp division between the Chu and Lu schools may well be a product of Ming and Ch'ing times and does not accurately reflect the circumstances of the late Southern Sung and early Yüan periods. It is conceivable that the absence of a sharp demarcation between the two schools in the sources for this period is a result of the dominance of Chu Hsi's followers in the thirteenth century, whereby contending ideas were simply submerged or blended together with their own. Whether the drawing of such a demarcation in later periods thus reveals a genuine philosophical split that had been blurred or is the result of Ming and Ch'ing writers' distortions of Lu's ideas, and hence those of his principal disciple, Yang Chien—perhaps in order to trace the filiation of concepts that

160. SYHA 74:30a.

led to Wang Yang-ming—is a question that I can only raise here. Records of academies in Ming Prefecture reveal that both Chu Hsi and Yang Chien were honored there, although by the late Yüan there are both indications of a shift to Chu Hsi's ideas, as at Mt. Tai Academy, and suggestions of what later developed into the standard view of Yang Chien's ideas as "tainted" with Ch'an Buddhism.

Clearly whatever the dimensions of the dispute between the Chu and Lu schools, Chu Hsi's emphasis on the need for an institutional setting for the propagation of his ideas ultimately strengthened the prospects for adherents of his thought to triumph; and, even though Yang Chien continued to be revered during the Yüan in an academy dedicated to him, Compassion Lake, he was a native son of the area and important in that respect apart from any objective evaluation of his significance as a philosopher. Chu Hsi was identified with the academy movement, and his prototypical White Deer Grotto was used as a model for academies established in Ming Prefecture and elsewhere throughout China during the thirteenth and the fourteenth century. The success of the *Tao-hsüeh* movement was in large part attributable to the success of these academies.

EIGHTEEN

Mandarins as Legal Experts: Professional Learning in Sung China

Brian McKnight

In *The Aims of Education* Alfred North Whitehead speaks of education as "the acquisition of the art of the utilization of knowledge."[1] Whitehead speaks to the desires of teachers, but in the real world teachers know that what is called education always has a multiplicity of goals. It serves to socialize the young, to entertain in the old, to pass on skills and knowledge that will be rewarding in the workaday world, and to "inculcate the art of using knowledge." In traditional China as in today's world the motives and goals of education were thoroughly mixed. Both participants in education and its supporters had multiple aims.

Not only did different people have different aims in education, but also individuals approached education with mixed goals. Young men who pored over the Classics were often seeking a sense of themselves and their place in a larger tradition; they were also usually preparing for the state examinations and hoping to enjoy all the economic and social benefits attached to membership in the civil service. Neo-Confucian teachers might see the improvement of the self and the search for sagehood as the most worthy ends of education, but they had to face the ambitions of young and old. The most important institutional supporter of education, the government, encouraged different kinds of education in a variety of ways for a variety of reasons. First, through its use of the civil service examination system, the government encouraged families to invest in a process that indoctrinated young men in a set of beliefs acceptable to the state. The civil service system aimed to certify that graduates were dyed with the Confucian equivalent of redness. But the state was also seeking experts. In the People's Republic the balance to be struck between redness and expertness has been problematical. For the authorities

1. Alfred North Whitehead, *The Aims of Education* (London: Williams and Norgate, 1932), p. 6.

in Sung China the problem was perhaps simpler: the Confucian analog of redness came first. If a young man aimed for a career in the influential levels of the civil service, he had first to pass through an examination system designed to certify the acceptability of his values. Having been assured of his acceptability, the state could then safely encourage him to develop his expert skills for the use of the government. We have abundant evidences of the vitality of Confucian education in the Sung; it is important to recognize that education which might be non-Confucian, or only indirectly and peripherally Confucian, also flourished during this era.

The officials of traditional China are often pictured as self-conscious amateurs, dilettantes, and gentlemen of cultivated tastes who disdained technical expertise as beneath them. Unquestionably many officials believed in, and some government policies encouraged, this amateur ideal vision of the bureaucrat. The traditional state was dominated by humanistically educated generalists. And yet at times, most notably during the Sung dynasty (960–1279), many literati were remarkably well informed on specialized subjects. This more favorable climate for the cultivation of expertise is no doubt reflected in the adoption by the Sung government of policies designed to promote the development of specialized skills among officials. The Sung government encouraged something very like professional education among its bureaucrats.

The presence of specialized career patterns among Sung fiscal officials has already been studied in some detail; less well known is the set of policies that encouraged the development of legal expertise among bureaucrats.[2] In order to raise the level of legal learning among judicial and administrative personnel Sung authorities deliberately provided the opportunity, means, and motivation for cultivating a knowledge of the law. They adopted policies and procedures designed to encourage study of the law among prospective officials, evaluate the level of expertise among active officials, and certify the skills of those seeking some government posts. As a result during much of the Sung it would have been difficult for an official to secure and hold an appointment and advance in reasonable time, without having the expertise needed to find pertinent legal rules and the knowledge needed to understand them.

The laws these men needed to know were of two basic sorts—prescriptive administrative laws specifying procedures and practices and proscriptive penal laws specifying forbidden acts. The administrative laws were of three types: specifications (*shih*) largely established formats for official correspondence or specified the physical characteristics of ritual objects; regulations (*ko*) dealt with matters of quantity or level such as official salaries or numbers of personnel; and ordinances (*ling*), the broadest category, included general administrative rules. Texts of these three did not indicate the penalties for

2. For expertise among fiscal officials see Robert Hartwell, "Financial Expertise, Examinations, and the Formulation of Economic Policy in the Northern Sung," *Journal of Asian Studies* 30 (1971):281–314.

infraction. These penalties were set by a few general rules, were very light, and could be converted into administrative sanctions. The penal laws, statutes (*lü*), were compiled as the *Sung Penal Code* (*Sung hsing t'ung*) in 963. These statutes proscribed certain behavior and indicated the punishments for transgressions. They usually took the form: "If you commit act A, you are liable for penalty B."[3]

Laws of these various sorts were originally established and could be amended by issuing an imperial edict or indicating imperial approval of a memorial. Thus, the body of rules applicable at any given time included not only legal compilations, such as the *Penal Code*, but also any pertinent later edicts or approved memorials. These later amending rulings might, in terms of content, correspond to any of the four law types described above.

Fortunately for officials, an extensive knowledge of regulations and specifications was not important for career success. No doubt officials did become familiar with many such rules in the course of their work, but their knowledge of them was not tested in any of the government's systems of assessing bureaucrats' legal expertise. Infractions against them entailed only trivial penalties.

Ordinances were more important because an understanding of general official procedures was essential to effective official action. For this reason some of the Sung system's testing for legal knowledge included questions on the ordinance. Still, the punishment for breaking an ordinances was relatively light, and most testing systems did not touch the ordinances.

Lacking familiarity with administrative laws might cause an official some inconvenience; failing to understand the penal laws could seriously hinder his career. Improper application of these laws might result in heavy penalties not convertible to administrative sanctions. Furthermore, all the Sung devices for testing legal expertise focused most heavily on these penal laws.[4]

During the early years of the dynasty the task facing officials who wanted to learn the penal laws was not overly difficult. The *Penal Code*'s five hundred odd rules, not too numerous to be easily used, were explained carefully in the accompanying commentary and arranged in a manner that made locating pertinent rules relatively easy. However, the Sung was a prolific producer of new rules. One Japanese scholar compiled a list of 180 compilations and recompilations of laws during the Sung; his list is far from complete.[5]

3. On the types of Sung laws see Brian E. Mcknight, "From Statute to Precedent: The Evolution of the Sung System of Laws," in *Law and the State in Traditional East Asia*, (ed.) Brian E. Mcknight (Honolulu: Asian Studies At Hawaii, 1985), vol. 1.

4. The punishment for breaking specifications was very light, only forty blows of the light rod. Penalties for infractions against regulations are not clear, but because violation of the even broader ordinances entailed relatively minor penalties one may presume that violations of regulations were lightly punished.

5. Asai Torao, *Shina hōsei shi* (Tokyo: Hakubunkan, 1904). See also Yang Hung-lieh, *Chung-kuo fa-lü fa-t'a shih* (Taipei: Commercial Press, 1967), and Sogabe Shizuo, "Sōdai no hōten rei," *Tōhoku daigaku bungakubu kenkyū nempō* 15 (1965):1-48.

Sung leaders made repeated attempts to prune the collections, but they could only slow down, not reverse, the trend. Although many, perhaps most, edicts in these collections were administrative, there were many new penal laws with which officials had to be familiar. One example will give some idea of the problem. Early in the eleventh century, outside the *Penal Code*, 46 laws called for registered exile (*p'ei*) as a penalty. By the middle of the century this had risen to more than 70. A little more than a century later 570 items were current. Amidst this welter of rules there were some contradictory stipulations; thus, an official faced not only the greater difficulty of locating the relevant items but also the task of judging which one should be cited.[6]

This growing burden may have been one factor in the tendency in the later Northern Sung to cite case precedents rather than laws in making judgments. The precedents used were decisions by the judicial review organs at the capital handed down in the form of edicts deciding particular cases; this development further complicated the job of learning the laws.[7]

The task of learning the law became increasingly burdensome as the decades passed, but it was not insuperable. Although enormous numbers of edicts were issued, most were not relevant to the systems of legal testing established by the authorities. Also, recompilations served periodically to reduce the total number of laws. Finally, the *Penal Code* remained a key text in the systems of testing, even though it became less and less important in the actual judging of cases.

But even if a Sung mandarin was not prevented from attaining a familiarity with the current laws by their sheer numbers, would he have had the motivation and opportunity to do so? The answer clearly is that opportunities did exist, both before and after a man joined the civil service. Two small but interesting groups, ex-clerks and graduates with degrees in law (*ming-fa*), may be presumed to have had considerable legal expertise before joining the civil service.

The recruitment of officials from the ranks of clerks was a regular Sung personnel practice. The capital offices had established annual quotas for nominations of senior clerks to civil service ranks; the *Sung Standard History* lists some thirty-six agencies with the right to recommend such advancement. And at times local administrators were also asked for nominations. However, they presupposed very long service. The requirements varied from seven to as many as nineteen "selections" (*hsüan*)—a term that seems to indicate an annual review. Moreover, it seems possible that these reviews were not cumulative but refer to reviews occurring after the clerk had begun serving in the upper levels of the subbureaucracy. One entry even indicates that a total of thirty years service was necessary before recommendation.

6. Anon., *Sung shih ch'uan-wen hsü tzu-chih t'ung-chien* (Taipei: Wen Hai Publishing Co., 1969), p. 2169; hereafter cited SSCW.

7. McKnight, "Statute to Precedent." See also Miyazaki Ichisada, "So-Gen jidai no hōsei to saiban kiko" *Tōhōgakuhō* (Kyoto) 24 (1954):120–122.

The quotas are unclear, but it is apparent that the number of men recruited in this fashion was small.[8] Nonetheless these men brought a unique element into the civil service. They had spent decades of their adult working lives handling documents, the bulk of which were legal materials. Indeed, at times regular bureaucrats bemoaned the technical legal expertise of the clerks, an expertise that permitted them to obstruct government policy for their own ends.

At least from the Hsi-ning period (1068–1076) clerical personnel seeking entrance to the civil service were allowed to take examinations on case judgments. This system was abolished in 1088, but beginning in 1091 the clerks in many central government offices were allowed to take the tests according to the old system. The tests, given every three years, seem to have resembled the tests given potential judicial officials.[9] Such tests are not mentioned in Southern Sung sources, but it is known that in that period examinations on law were given to those seeking places as *clerks* in the central judicial offices.[10]

Once taken into the civil service these ex-clerks might be given posts of considerable responsibility, even if they were fated to remain low in the ranks. Many key posts in the central judicial review units, for example, were staffed by ex-clerks during the opening decades of the dynasty, and later ex-clerks served in other low-ranking but functionally important posts in central offices.[11]

Possibly the state was concerned to evaluate the legal expertise of clerks because such men would be appointed to positions calling for application of the details of the law, rather than broad policy making. The same concern may also have influenced requirements, apparently enforced during much of the Sung, that other men entering the civil service in "irregular" ways (not through the examinations) be tested on law. Officials qualifying for office because of the "protection" (*yin*) of highly placed relatives apparently were tested on law. Similar tests were at times given to irregular (*she*) officials in some regions, and legal tests seem to have been open to supplementary officials (*pu-kuan*) who wished to regularize their status.[12]

---

8. For materials on inducting clerks into the civil service see T'o T'o et al., *Sung shih* (Taipei: Yee Wen Publishing Co., 1965) 169:17b–20a; hereafter cited SS.

9. Li Tao, *Hsü tzu-chih t'ung-chien ch'ang-pien* (Taipei: Shih-chieh shu-chü, 1954) 413:5b, 468:14a, 495:4a; hereafter cited HCP. On the general question of clerks entering the civil service see Miyazaki Ichisada, "An-seki no ri-shi goitsu saku," *Ajia-shi kenkyū* (Kyoto: Kyōto daigaku tōyōshi kenkyū kai, 1957), vol. 1, esp. pp. 353–357.

10. Hsü Sung, ed., *Sung hui-yao chi-kao* (Taipei: Shih-chieh shu-chü, 1965) chih-kuan 15:21a, 25a; hereafter cited SHY.

11. Ma Tuan-lin, *Wen-hsien t'ung-k'ao* (Kuo-hsüeh chi-pen ts'ung-shu ed.) 166:1445; hereafter cited WHTK. SHY, chih-kuan 15:34a–b. For another view of Sung clerks, see James T. C. Liu, "The Sung Views on the Control of Government Clerks," *Journal of the Economic and Social History of the Orient* 10, nos. 2–3 (1967):317–344.

12. HCP 111:3b, 122:11b, 145:9b, 155:15a, 218:4a; SSCW, p. 1385; Hsieh Shen-fu, *Ch'ing-yüan t'iao-fa shih-lei* (Tokyo: Koten kenkyū kai, 1968), p. 211; hereafter cited TFSL.

Graduates with the degree in law also brought to the civil service a knowledge, bookish rather than practical, of legal materials. First mentioned during the early years of the T'ang (A.D. 646) the field in law (*ming-fa*) remained a part of the state examination system through the T'ang, Five Dynasties, and early Sung. In 979 it was decreed that "because what is dealt with in the books for the examination in law is not broad in content this field shall be abolished," but in 985 the field was reestablished and functioned with only minor changes until the major reform of education under Wang An-shih in the 1070s.[13]

The examination procedures for the field of law were identical with those of other fields. Candidates, selected in the autumn, assembled in the winter at the Ministry of Rites, and were tested in the spring. The examination was designed to evaluate knowledge of the statutes and the ordinances. Candidates might be required to answer memory questions, given a few words from a passage they would have to complete it correctly. Or they might be asked to write discursively on the general meanings of a number of passages from the laws. During the first century of the Sung the mix of these two sorts of questions was changed on several occasions, indicating a continuing dissatisfaction with the effectiveness of the tests; in the perennial struggle the advocates of memory tests stressed the objectivity of their questions and the advocates of essays pointed to the need to discover a candidate's ability to analyze and express himself.[14]

The most interesting Sung innovation in the field was the introduction, apparently in 985, of a session on the Classics. In 1005 the number of sessions for the field was increased from six to seven: the first two sessions were to be on the statutes; session three was on the ordinances; sessions four and five were on the minor Classics; session six was again on the ordinances; and the last session was on the statutes.[15]

The authorities saw to it that the means of preparing for the examinations were made available. In 1026 an official in the Directorate's of Education (*kuo-tzu chien*) noted that, of the miscellaneous examination fields, only that for law lacked a definitive edition of the required materials. As a result of his memorial six members of the Directorate staff were ordered to act as collating

13. For the T'ang examinations, see Ou-yang Hsiu, *Hsin T'ang shu* (SPPY ed.) 44:1a; Robert des Rotours, *Le Traité des Examens*, (Paris: E. Leroux, 1932) 1:453–455; *T'ang liu tien* (SKCSCP 6th coll.) 21:14a–15a; Kao Ming-shih, "T'ang-tai te kuan-hsüeh hsing-cheng," *Ta-lu tsa-chih* 37 no. 11 (1968): 52; Teng Ssu-yü, *Chung-kuo k'ao-shih chih-tu shih* (Taipei: Student Book Co., 1967), p. 77. For the Five Dynasties, see Wang P'u, *Wu-tai hui-yao* (Shanghai: Shanghai ku-chi ch'u-pan she, 1978), 23:285–286. For the early Sung, see HCP 20:19a, 26:2a; P'eng Pai-ch'uan, *T'ai-p'ing chih-chi t'ung-lei ch'ien-chi* (SKCSCP, 5th coll.) 28:6a Wang Ying-lin, *Yu hai* (1866 woodblock ed.) 116:12a–13a; hereafter cited YH.

14. SHY, hsüan-chu 3:28b; SHY, chung-ju 4:6b–7a, 7a; HCP 47:10b, 61:18b, 217:4a; WHTK 30:283.

15. P'eng Pai-ch'uan, *T'ai-p'ing chih-chi t'ung-lei ch'ien-chi*, 28:6a; YH 116:12a–b; HCP 61:18b 26:2a–b.

investigators, and two other high officials were appointed as final editors to prepare an authorized version of the *Penal Code* for student use. Three years later this group submitted their revised *Penal Code*, with an added guide to pronunciation of difficult characters, and a commentary.[16] The state also made available to at least some groups of students copies of the state legal collections, and at times permitted the Directorate of Education to print legal materials privately for sale to those studying the law.[17]

During the first century of the Sung the numbers of men graduating in the field of law remained small. The classes of 968 and 977 are probably typical. In 968 there were twenty-six graduates with the degree in letters (*chin-shih*), ninety-six others in miscellaneous fields, and only five in law. And in 977 there were fourteen law degress out of nearly two hundred degrees in the miscellaneous fields. This situation remained true, as suggested by the class in 1009: twenty-six degrees in letters and only forty-eight in all other miscellaneous fields, including law.[18]

Unfortunately very little is known about the men tested in law. Supposedly the field was popular with supplementary officials (*pu-kuan*), who perhaps saw it as a good means of regularizing their position in the government.[19] Graduates presumably served either in low-level local posts, or in the central offices that dealt with the laws. For example, one graduate in 1070 was immediately appointed to a post in the Bureau for the Compilation of Edicts as an editor.[20] Most, however, were probably treated according to the general Sung policy of appointing new men to local posts.

That this policy may have been followed in dealing with law graduates is suggested by a memorial from 1001 in which an official complained that on the local level men skilled in the reading and interpretation of the laws were being used for police work while others unskilled in dealing with legal materials were doing judicial work. He asked that men for the key prefectual judicial posts of police inspector (*ssu-fa ts'an-chün*) and judicial inspector (*ssu-li ts'an-chün*) be chosen from among graduates in the field of law.[21]

The field of law continued for more than a century to draw into the civil service a small number of men whose primary training was in the use of legal materials. Then, in 1071, in a key reform of the statesman Wang An-shih, the examination field in Classics and the miscellaneous fields including the old degree in law were abolished, leaving only the degree in letters. When those

---

16. YH 66:28a–b; SHY, ch'ung-ju 4:6b–7a; Hsü Dau-lin, *Chung-kuo fa-chih shih lun-lüeh* (Taipei: Cheng chung shu-chü, 1961), pp. 63–64.

17. The use of other collections of laws by students in the school is noted in SHY, ch'ung-ju 3:96. See also SHY, hsuan-chü 14:1b–2a. The publication for sale of legal materials had been authorized prior to 1099. See SHY, chih-kuan 28:14b.

18. HCP 71:25a; WHTK 30:156; YH 116:10b.

19. WHTK 31:293.

20. HCP 217:4a.

21. HCP 47:106.

who had been preparing for the miscellaneous fields and Classics complained bitterly, a "New Field in Law" (*hsin-k'o ming-fa*) was established to provide them with an alternative to the degree in letters.

Candidates in this new field were tested in accordance with the rules governing the examination of civil servants for positions in the central judicial organs; that is, they were examined on case judgments that required them to deliver correct sentences for actual cases drawn from the files and on the general meanings of the laws.[22]

Problems arose almost immediately. People who did not meet the criteria for participation in the new field sought to take the tests, and men who had taken and passed the new law field in the spring went on in the fall to take the voluntary examination for potential judicial functionaries given to those already in the civil service. Because the New Field in Law was modeled on this voluntary testing system, these recent graduates were able to benefit doubly from their preparation. Their legal expertise not only gained them entrance to the ranks of potential civil servants but also shortly there after gained them accelerated advancement and desirable placement.

Critics asked with understandable bitterness why graduates in law should receive such double good fortune. In response to the recommendations of these critics it was ordered that when men did attempt this double testing only those in the top rank were to receive appointments as judicial officials. The others might be spared the test, given all degree holders applying for initial appointments, but should receive no further benefits.[23]

The new degree was by no means easy to achieve. At the autumn examinations in the circuits 20 percent of the candidates are said to have qualified for further testing at the capital. Of this group only 10 percent survived the capital tests, an overall success rate of 2 percent. However, the degree holders were given preference to those with degrees in letters for some jobs. With this sort of career opportunity open to them men flocked to the new field. In 1076 there were 39 graduates; in 1079 there were 146 graduates, discounting the men who were tested under the easier rules of the facilitated examinations. A class of this size would have provided approximately 11 percent of the total number of new officials needed to maintain the civil service at its existing size.[24]

In the early Sung the candidates in the field of law had been tested on the Classics, but during the first few years of the New Field in Law all the sessions dealt with the law. When the reform party fell from power after the death of the emperor Shen-tsung (r. 1068–1086), the opponents of Wang An-shih began to dismember his new policies. The New Field in Law was

22. HCP 220:1a–2a; SHY, hsüan-chü 14:1a.

23. HCP 281:8a; SHY, hsüan-chü 14:1a–b.

24. WHTK 32:303; SHY, hsüan-chü 14:1b. On the numbers of civil servants, see E. A. Kracke, Jr., *Civil Service in Early Sung China* (Cambridge: Harvard University Press, 1953), p. 59.

attacked because it had no test on the Classics. In 1086 the conservative Liu Chih remarked that:

Of late the system for candidates for the degree in law tests them on the general ideas of the Statutes, on administrative Ordinances, and on the *Penal Code*, as well as on the judgment of cases. This is called the New Field in Law. The Ministry of Personnel fills future vacancies among law officials (*ssu-fa yüan*) by noting in order those who have passed, placing [these graduates] ahead of those who have a degree in letters. . . . In the past the degree in law was a field of low prestige, but the candidates were always tested in the Classics. Even if they did not truly understand their meaning, still they could chant several of them. This embodied the intent of the former kings. Now in this new degree this test on the Classics has been abolished, and they concentrate entirely on the books of law. Also, many more men are being brought in than in the past. . . . I ask that in the field of law a question be added on the basic meanings of the Analects and the Classic of Filial Piety, and that the quota of graduates be halved.[25]

Liu Chih had his way in part. According to the new rules of 1087, beginning with the examinations of 1090, candidates for the degree in law were to be tested on three passages calling for case judgments, five passages concerned with the general meaning of the *Penal Code*, two passages on the general meaning of the *Analects*, and one on the *Classic of Filial Piety*. In the following year the requirements for some candidates were again altered so that the degree became largely a test on Classics, with a lesser emphasis on the meaning of the *Penal Code*.[26]

Liu's original criticisms had been seconded by his colleague Ssu-ma Kuang, who memorialized that candidates for the degree in law were to be tested on the minor Classics; however,

The Statutes, Ordinances, Edicts, and Specifications (*lü-ling-ch'ih-shih*) are still matters that must of necessity be dealt with by active officials. Why then the need to set up a field in law so as to cause scholars to become familiar with them? What passes beyond rites and righteousness comes into the law, so those who are scholars, as a result of their familiarity with the Way, will conform to the legal. But to daily intone books on penal servitude, exile, strangulation, and beheading, and the practicing of investigative matters is not good for scholars.[27]

Ssu-ma Kuang's objections bear emphasizing. He does not argue that a knowledge of laws is unimportant, but that its importance is pervasive, something necessary to all active officials. To set up a separate field in law is

25. HCP 368:11a–b; WHTK 31:295; SHY, hsüan-chü 3:49a, 14:2a. See also Ch'en Chün, *Huang-ch'ao pien-nien kang-mu pei-yao* (Taipei: Ch'eng Wen Publishing Co., 1966), p. 1020; hereafter cited KMPY.

26. HCP 407:5a–b; SHY, hsüan-chü 14:2a–b.

27. Chao Ju-yü, *Chu ch'en tsou-i* (Taipei: Wen Hai Publishing Co., 1970), p. 2807; HCP 371:5a; WHTK 167:1449, 31:295.

thus doubly unfortunate. First, it distracts the authorities from an appreciation of the universal need for a knowledge of law. Second, it overlooks the fact that the true aim is justice rather than legalistic behavior, and justice can be achieved only on the basis of a firm grasp of fundamental values such as those embodied in the Way.

Ssu-ma Kuang's arguments were not merely rhetorical. Some months later he again indicated that he viewed a knowledge of the law as important. In discussing the ten categories of men who deserved annual recommendations he lists as his eighth group those who are learned concerning trials and the ferreting out of the facts and as his tenth category those learned in the law and able to decide properly. He is writing not about the qualifications for entering official life but about judging the quality of those already serving the government, men who in his view would already have learned the law in the course of their duties.[28]

The final step in scaling down the New Field in Law in the Northern Sung came in 1102 when the degree seems to have been abolished. It was revived in the late 1120s when there were vacancies in the legal offices, although few men competed in it until the 1140s. In 1141, "in the various circuits they began to examine men [in law]. In the Autumn test they qualified one man in five, and at the [ensuing] departmental examinations they took one man in seven. In all cases these men were not concurrently [examined on] Classics."[29]

Several years later the quota for passing was increased. In order to pass the candidates had to perform satisfactorily in a test on making judgments, and they had to display a complete grasp of the *Penal Code*, as demonstrated in essays on the general meanings of a number of passages. There is some indication that the field was quite popular. And then, having devised this system, the authorities reversed their policies and in 1146 abolished the degree in law. For almost two centuries tests in law had provided one path for entry into the civil service; during the last century of the Sung this field was no longer used, but legal tests continued to be given to some officials already in the government.[30]

Another device for encouraging potential officials to study the law was the requirement that candidates in other examination fields be tested on some legal materials. Such tests existed from the early years of the dynasty. In 979 for example, in ordering changes in some miscellaneous examination fields, a decree noted that the candidates were "still to study the laws (*fa-ling*)" and

28. HCP 382:3b–4a.
29. SHY, hsüan-chü 14:4a; SSCW, p. 1561; WHTK 32:303; SS 157:17b. Li Hsin-ch'uan, *Chien-yen i-lai hsi-nien yao-lu* (Peking: Chung-hua shu-chü, 1956), p. 266; hereafter cited HNYL. Li Hsin-ch'uan, *Chien-yen i-lai ch'ao-yeh tsa-chi* (Taipei: Wen Hai Publishing Co., 1967) 13:14a; hereafter cited CYTC. SSCW, p. 1606 suggests the possibility that there may have been a large number of graduates in 1145.
30. SHY, hsüan-chü; HNYL 154:2494; SS 157:18a.

that those with a degree in letters or in one of the miscellaneous fields, on the day when they were questioned in audience, were "all to be questioned on the meanings of the statutes and commentaries." In 983 this oral quiz was supplemented by a requirement that candidates for the degrees in letters or in miscellaneous fields be asked ten questions on the meaning of the laws. Candidates for degrees in letters were freed from this written test in the following year, but it seems possible that those in other fields continued to be tested on the law.[31]

The requirement that letters candidates be tested on the law was revived during the reign of Shen-tsung. In 1073 it was ordered that all such candidates, except the top three, were to be quizzed on the general meanings of the statutes and ordinances and judgment of cases. This prompted an official to protest that if the top men were excused all would consider the test demeaning; as a result after 1075 all candidates were examined. Some sources suggest that this mandatory test on law was abolished in 1079, but there are also reports that such a requirement was revived in 1081, abolished in 1086, and then reinstituted in 1102. Unfortunately, there is no evidence concerning such added law tests during the Southern Sung (1126–1279).[32]

The Sung also continued the old tradition of appointing professors in law (*lü po-shih*) who acted both as legal advisers to the government and as teachers of students. Professors in law had first been appointed under the emperor Ming of the Wei dynasty (220–265) in the first quarter of the third century. Many later dynasties, from the Chin (265–420) to the Sung, followed this precedent. During this period the numbers of such professors varied, from one to eight, as did their ranks, but they all seem to have fulfilled similar functions—to advise on difficult legal cases, aid in the compilation of *Codes*, and train law students (*lü-po shih-yüan* or *lü-sheng*).

The use of professors in law as formal teachers seems to date from the Northern and the Southern dynasties period (420–589). Most students were from humble backgrounds, although an occasional student came from the nobility. In an attempt to raise the prestige of legal studies an official of the Southern Ch'i (479–502) even suggested that students, selected from the royal family and from the families of high-ranking officials, be taught more formally by preceptors in law (*lü-hsüeh chiao-shou*) under the auspices of the Directorate of Education.[33]

All of his proposals were ignored at the time, but two centuries later, in the first year of the T'ang (618), a Directorate of Education was established

31. HCP 26:2b says that the test for the degree in letters, the degree in Classics, and "other lower (degrees)" was dropped two years later, in 985. SS 155:5b seems to imply that the test on laws continued for the miscellaneous fields. See also SHY hsüan-chü 3:4b–5a.

32. SS 155:17b; HCP 243:11b, 246:8b, 266:8a, 298:11b; WHTK 31:294; SHY, hsüan-chü 2:11a, 11b, 3:49b; KMPY pp. 932, 1213.

33. Ch'en Shou, *San kuo chih* (SPPY ed.) 21:106; Hsiao Tzu-chien, *Nan Ch'i shu* (Peking: Chung-hua shu-chü, 1972) 48:837–838.

with a School of Law (*lü-hsüeh*) as one of its six units. Although on two occasions the School of Law was disestablished for brief periods, for most of the rest of the T'ang it continued to function. The faculty consisted of one professor of law ranked at the lower eighth grade (in the nine grade system), one teaching assistant (*chu-chiao*) ranked in the upper ninth grade, and two school guardians (*tien-hsüeh*).

The students, whose numbers varied from fifty in 618 to twenty in 662 to thirty in 807, were chosen from the sons of commoner families or the families of officials of the eighth or ninth ranks, to study a six-year curriculum. These young men, between eighteen and twenty-five years of age, studied the T'ang statutes (*lü*), the ordinances (*ling*), the edicts that modified other sorts of rules (*ko*), and the by-laws applying general rules to local situations (*shih*). They are said to have studied the laws of earlier dynasties and were also encouraged to study the Classics.

The students were subjected to periodic examinations, including an annual oral examinations that consisted of ten questions. A student who could not answer half of these questions was a failure. If he failed in three successive years, he would be expelled from the school.[34]

The Sung, like the T'ang, appointed professors in law from the early years of the dynasty and continued the T'ang innovation of an examination field in law, but there is no indication that a School of Law was established during the dynasty's first decades. A school was in operation during the minor reform period of the 1040s, but the founding of the School of Law as an important part of the state university system dates from the early months of 1073.[35]

The new school was placed administratively under the Directorate of Education, which was ordered to establish the rules governing the testing and ranking procedures. Four instructors (*chiao-shou*) were appointed, and an initial sum of 15,000 strings of cash was granted, the interest from which was to be used to help support students. If they performed satisfactorily, the students, drawn from among active officials or degree candidates (*chü-jen*), were to be given rations, necessities, and housing. At first the school was housed in the Hall of Imperial Assembly (*ch'ao-chi yüan*), but the Directorate of Construction (*chiang-tso chien*) was ordered to construct suitable facilities.[36]

The Directorate of Education submitted its recommended rules a few months later, suggesting that students in the School of Law in general follow the practices of the Imperial University (*t'ai-hsüeh*). On entering the school prospective students had to present family certificates (*chia-chuang*). In

34. See note 12.
35. For evidence suggesting the existence of a school of law in the 1040s, see SHY, ch'ung-ju 1:29a–b. For the founding of the school under Shen-tsung, see SHY, chung-ju 3:7a; HCP 244:2a; SS 15:9a; KMPY, p. 867.
36. SHY, ch'ung-ju 3:7a; HCP 244:2a.

addition, those who were merely degree candidates rather than active officials had to secure two officials to guarantee their good character. They then had to take an examination on their readings skills, administered jointly by the instructors and by staff supervisors (*chien-chu p'an kuan*) from the Directorate of Education. Those who did best were accepted as students, provided with food, other necessities, and dormitory housing. They also received medical care from the students at the Imperial Medical School.[37]

The lives of students in the dormitories were controlled with some care. Each living unit chose one member to serve as dormitory head (*chai-chang*). Students were given single days off on the first days of the Winter Solstice, the New Year, and the Cold Food Festival. But, except for such holidays, the degree candidates who were students were expected to return to their living quarters at the sound of the evening drum. Active officials who were studying in the school could leave the premises for the night.[38]

Students had to concentrate either on the reading of the law or on the judging of the cases. Their proficiency was tested twice each month. In the public examination (*kung-shih*) those who had chosen to specialize in judging cases (*tuan-an*) were examined on one passage that involved decisions on five to seven items of sentencing. The aim was to arrive at the legally correct sentence given the specific situation in question. Those specializing in reading the laws were tested on five legal passages. They were expected to be able to describe the general meanings of the materials they had read. In the closed examination (*ssu-shih*) the judgment specialists were tested on one case involving three to five questions of sentencing and the law specialists on two passages. Elaborate rules governed the evaluation procedures, and fines were established as sanctions against cheating.[39]

Students in the school were able to study not only the *Sung Penal Code* but also the newly compiled decrees of the Hsi-ning period. Moreover, when they found the decrees difficult to understand they could submit them to the High Court of Justice (*ta-li ssu*) and the Bureau of Judicial Investigation (*shen-hsing yüan*) for clarification.[40]

For most of its history the School of Law had two professors of law on its faculty; between 1088 and 1095 there was only one. These men were ranked, as in the T'ang, in the lower eighth grade. A school director (*hsüeh-cheng*) and a recorder (*hsüeh-lu*) were appointed, both from the upper ninth grade. It is not clear whether the four preceptors were appointed in addition to the above men or were serving concurrently.[41]

The low rank of these men does not adequately reflect their prestige.

37. SHY, ch'ung-ju 3:7b–9a; SS 164:7b.
38. SHY, ch'ung-ju 3:7b, 9a–b; SS 157:7a–b.
39. HCP 244:2a; SHY, ch'ung-ju 3:7b–9a; SS 157:7a–b.
40. SHY, ch'ung-ju 3:9b.
41. SHY, chih-kuan 28:5b, 6b; SHY, ch'ung-ju 3:10a; HCP 244:2a; WHTK 167:1449; SS 157:7a–b, 162:2a; Sun Feng-chi, *Chih kuan fen chi* (SPPY ed.) 21:16a.

Academic personnel tended to placed far down in the official hierarchy. Nonetheless jobs in academic units commanded considerable respect. Among other advantages their incumbents might hope for relatively rapid advancement. After as little as five years a member of the staff of the School of Law might hope to be promoted from the class of executory personnel (the lower eighth and the ninth grade) to the select group of administrative personnel (grades one through upper eighth).[42]

The duties of school personnel were not onerous, but they were required to present lectures daily and at times concurrently served in school administrative slots. In addition, they acted jointly with the staff supervisors from the Directorate of Education in administering the student examinations.[43]

During the heyday of legal studies under Shen-tsung the school functioned well, and for some time students in the Imperial University were encouraged to participate in its classes, but with the decline of imperial interest during the reign of Che-tsung (r. 1086–1100) and Hui-tsung (r. 1101–1126) the morale among both students and faculty fell sharply. In 1112 an official complained that the faculty[44]

> merely play around every day, and do not attend classes or exams or practices. In improper dress they roam the city for amusement. At dawn without even bothering to report they go out. At dusk they wait by the gate and then return, making a mockery of the gate registry clerk. A warning is needed for subordinate officials to fulfill their pedagogical responsibilities. Decree: From now on the law instructors and school director are to abide by the regulations (*ko*) governing the officials of the High Court of Justice (*ta-li-ssu*). Except for the instructors they are not to be allowed to use precedents granting them grace.

The school continued in active operation at least until the end of the Northern Sung, but very little is known about it during the Southern Sung. There is one indication that it may have continued at least a nominal existence. In 1143 a government bureau charged with making recompilations of current laws submitted a collection on the government schools, with the School in Law among those listed. Because the purpose of recompiling laws was in part to permit the deletion of laws no longer effective, this suggests that the school in some form continued to exist.[45]

The various policies and institutions described above served for the most part to bring into the government men with a working or a literary knowledge of the law. Also a variety of policies was designed to encourage

42. SHY, ch'ung-ju 3:10a.
43. SHY, ch'ung-ju 3:7b–9a, 10a; SHY, chih-kuan 28:6a.
44. SHY, ch'ung-ju 3:10b–11a; SS 156:17b.
45. For the continued existence of the school to the end of the Northern Sung see SHY, ch'ung-ju 3:11a; SHY, chih-kuan 28:22b. For evidence suggesting that it may have continued if only nominally in the Southern Sung see SSCW, p. 1586. We also know that Erudites in Law continued to be appointed. See SS 168:2b.

cultivation of legal knowledge by active officials and to certify the expertise of men destined for certain posts. On the most mundane level Sung personnel placement policies promoted a study of law, by placing men new to the service in initial positions that required regular reading of legal materials.[46]

In structure the personnel of the nine-grade Sung civil service formed a sharply tapering pyramid. The great majority of officials were classified in the lower eighth or the ninth grades, the executory class; only a small proportion of officials fell in the upper, policy-making administrative class that occupied the first through the upper eighth grades.

Many men in the executory class had entered the civil service by being promoted from the clerical group, by transfer from the military hierarchy, or through the "protection" privilege that allowed high-ranking officials to secure low civil service ranks for protégés, usually younger relatives. Such men probably formed a majority in the Sung civil service, but their numbesr did not give them much power. Because of their less esteemed methods of entering the service they were almost certainly doomed to spend their entire careers in executory class positions. These positions, low in the protocol hierarchy, were for the most part in local administration.

Graduates of the civil service examinations also began their careers as members of the executory class serving in local administration. The officials on the highest levels of the government were overwhelmingly examination graduates and in particular holders of the degree in letters, but almost all such men had begun their careers by serving in a succession of low level posts in the counties or, for a handful of truly outstanding graduates in letters, in the prefectures. Although the pattern was not rigidly fixed, the general practice was to appoint most new graduates to positions as county registrars (*chu-pu*) or sheriffs (*hsien-wei*). Such men advanced through a sequence of posts that might include such offices as assistant magistrate (*hsien-ch'eng*), or prefectural police inspectors (*ssu-li ts'an-chün*), but almost always they would include one or more terms as a magistrate (*hsien-ling*) or county administrator (*chih-hsien*).

In some later dynasties the men administering local units were assisted by private secretaries who were experts in finance or law, but in the Sung the private secretary system had not yet appeared. As Ssu-ma Kuang remarked, to perform their duties properly such officials needed to cultivate a knowledge of the laws. Any man ambitious for a successful career and desiring a good record as a local official would have reason to develop a modicum of legal expertise.

The government, however, did not always trust to the voluntary commitment of officials. At times, and in particular early in the dynasty when there was concern about the quality of officials inherited from earlier dynasties, the authorities instituted compulsory testing on the law for men already in office.

46. Kracke, *Civil Service*, p. 87.

In 986, as a check on the competence of local personnel, it was decreed that prefects, prefectural vice administrators (*t'ung-pan*), civil aides (*mu-chih kuan*), and other prefectural and county personnel on the expiration of their terms in office were to go to the capital where they would be tested on legal texts. Those who did poorly were to be given demerits and fines according to the degree of their ignorance. The decree states:

> Punishments are the measures of the state and its devices of control. If severity and lenience are not lost then the wind and rain of the four seasons will not be confused. Administrative rank officials, as well as civil aides and other officials in the prefectures and counties must from now on study the laws.[47]

It is not clear how long this policy was followed but Wang Yung (fl. 1190) in his *Bequeathed Plans for Tranquility in the Sung (Sung-ch'ao yen-i i mou lu)* says that in his day the policy was longer enforced.[48] However, one note suggests that circuit judicial intendants may have been tested on occasion and that prefectural instructors were tested on law during the reign of Shen-tsung. Furthermore, during the Southern Sung the policy of testing the legal knowledge of some low-level local officials was revived (in 1178). The Board of Personnel was ordered to examine certain candidates for county sheriff, county administrator, or garrison service agents (*chien-chen*) on the reading of the statutes. Furthermore, there are indications that some executory class personnel, in applying for their initial appointments, were tested on their legal expertise.[49]

Compulsory testing, which might include questions on law, might also be required of military officers who wished to transfer to the civil service. Under the rules recorded in the early thirteenth century *Classified Laws of the Ch'ing-yüan Period (Ch'ing-yüan t'iao-fa shih-lei)*,

> Military officials who are being examined for transfer into the civil hierarchy (are to be tested on) one Classic from among the *Book of Changes*, the *Poetry*, the *Book of History*, the *Rites of Chou*, or the *Book of Rites*, together with the *Analects* and the *Mencius*. Those who wish to do so may be tested on poetry or rhymeprose or, according to the rules governing legal officials, may be tested on judgments or cases and the general principles of the code.[50]

This rule implies that such testing was voluntary, but other materials imply that it was required, at least during the Northern Sung. Such testing of legal expertise began at least as early as the 1030s. The early notices refer simply to the reading of statutes, but a decree of 1077 specified that candidates be

---

47. SHY, hsüan-chu 13:11a–b.
48. Wang Yung, *Sung-ch'ao yen-i i mou lu* (Pai-pu ts'ung-shu chi-ch'eng ed.) 3:5b–6a. See also WHTK 166:1444.
49. SS 10:9a; SHY, chih-kuan 48:79a, 88b–89a; HCP 155:15a; YH 116:13a.
50. TFSL, p. 214.

MANDARINS AS LEGAL EXPERTS

tested on the general meaning of ten passages from the statutes and the ordinances. The requirements were revised in 1090 when an approved memorial specified that military officials being tested on the meaning of the *Penal Code* were to sit for only a single session covering five passages. Standards for grading were to follow the laws of the Yüan-feng period (1078–1086).[51]

The authorities tested actual and potential local officials because they were understandably concerned that those who handled police or judicial matters might be unfamiliar with the law; they were even more concerned to verify the legal expertise of members to the central government judicial offices. During the opening decades of the dynasty many lower level personnel in these offices were clerical workers, but as early as 988–990 there was a suggestion that clerks be replaced by civil service officials. The key device for selecting such officials was to be a mandatory evaluation of their legal expertise. Qualified candidates might either themselves petition to take the examinations or be recommended by others. Success could lead to desirable jobs at the capital and the possibility of accelerated advancement.[52]

A decree of 989 ordered that all administrative class officials knowledgeable in the law might submit petitions to be tested. If they passed, they would be given posts in the Ministry of Justice or the High Court. Satisfactory service for a mere three years would be followed by promotion. Similar tests were given to men, including executory class officials, who were candidates for slots in other central judicial organs.[53]

The character of the tests involved is described in a report by Chief Minister Chang Chi-hsien; in 999 he remarked that in the past when the Bureau of Judicial Investigation (*shen-hsing yüan*) was selecting deliberating officials (*hsiang-i kuan*) the Ministry of Justice merely questioned them on the general meanings of two passages of case judgments. Chen-tsung (r. 998–1022) suggested that those who had recommended unqualified men for these tests should be punished, but in practice the most important change was a great increase in the number of passages required in the compulsory examinations.[54]

The procedures involved were further elaborated during the eleventh century. There were many minor changes, often only briefly described in the sources, in a system made more complex because it aimed at selecting officials from different levels of the bureaucracy to fill a variety of posts. This complexity precludes any simple description of the system; nonetheless, certain general features are clear.

51. HCP 446:14a, 282:17a, 109:6a, 156:7b.
52. SHY, hsüan-chü 13:11b; SHY, chih-kuan 15:32a; HCP 30:20a.
53. SHY, hsüan-chü 13:11b; SHY, chih-kuan 15:32a; HCP 30:20a.
54. SHY, chih-kuan 15:32a–b; Ch'iu Han-p'ing, *Li-tai hsing-fa chih* (Taipei: Commercial Press, 1965), p. 386.

Qualifications for candidacy were defined more exactly as time passed. Generally speaking to be a candidate an official had to have served in the government long enough to have acquired a number of annual merit ratings (*k'ao*) and to have been in a post at least one term of three years (*jen*). In some instances candidates were not eligible if they had not already served in certain local administrative or judicial posts. They would also be ineligible if they had been convicted of certain crimes. Often their dossiers had to include general recommendations from superiors, and at times they needed recommendations from superiors in certain specified posts such as circuit judicial intendant. Most were considered qualified to participate because a superior had specifically recommended that they be tested, although men with outstanding records might take part even without such a recommendation. The tests, most often described as tests for members of the executory class, seem to have been aimed particularly at low-level local officials; they were also open in some cases to men with administrative class rank and might be taken even by those currently serving in central judicial posts who wished to accelerate their promotions.[55]

Procedures were also fixed more exactly as time passed. Eventually most tests were given at fixed dates, usually once or twice a year. Those wishing to participate were bound by rules specifying how long they could be excused from their current posts. The tests themselves seem often to have been given in stages, where satisfactory performance in one stage permitted participation in the later stages. Initially there were problems because information concerning the question was leaked by clerical personnel, but eventually the cases to be used were selected by civil service officials who used elaborate safeguards to maintain secrecy, and the administration of the examinations was under the joint control of members of the Censorate, the Ministry of Justice, and the High Court.[56]

Standards for success and the rewards entailed were also specified in detail. Not only were there rules on the number of questions that had to be answered correctly but also rules indicating just what "correctly" meant, what constituted a fully satisfactory answers, what a "rough" understanding. Rewards varied with the quality of the answers and also according to the rank of the candidate.

The authorities wished both to encourage legal studies and to improve the quality of judicial personnel. One method of trying to accomplish these two goals was to shorten the path of official advancement for those men who excelled in the examinations, while allowing those who were marginal to take further tests. The authorities also reserved the prestigious judicial appoint-

---

55. SHY, chih-kuan 15:32a, see especially pp. 39a–40a; HCP 110:2a.
56. SHY, hsüan-chü 13:12b, 13a; SHY, chih-kuan 15:37b–38a, 35b, 24:11b–12a; HCP 408:15a.

ments for the top men in the examination but rewarded others who did less well by giving them other sorts of bureaucratic rewards. A typical decree specifying rewards, issued in 1077, ordered that those passing the examination in the top grade be appointed as legal officials (*fa-kuan*), those in the second grade be granted two advancements in seniority (*hsün liang tz'u*), those in the third grade one advancement in seniority, those in the fourth grade ministerial recommendation for a commission (*t'ang-ch'u*), and those in the fifth grade exemption from the usual test given men seeking new official appointments.[57]

The details of the testing varied, but one example from 1020 may give a general picture of the process. In that year the three central judicial organs—the Bureau of Judicial Investigation, the Ministry of Justice, and the High Court—submitted a joint report in which they recommended that local officials who were qualified to take the tests for appointment as scrutinizing officials or judicial examiners (*fa-chih kuan*)

> first must go the Bureau of Judicial Investigation for a test on five passages of the general meaning of the statutes. Those who understand three, if they are applying for posts as judgment officials (*tuan-kuan*) should then again be tested on case judgments using one medium or small case. Those whose selection of decrees and use of language is appropriate, if their examination matches the original decree giving judgment, may be reported for appointment. If in their understanding of the statutes they only grasp two or more and in their judgment of the case they do not conform exactly with the original judgment in terms of the punishment ordered, but in their citation of rules they are concise, and in the case particulars they do display some understanding of the differences of degree, then they should be sent from the Bureau of Judicial Investigation for testing on twenty passages of cases. The officials for deciding affairs (*p'an-shih kuan*) are to be made responsible for guaranteeing them, writing out whether they are acceptable or not, and reporting this in memorials. Those (seeking posts as) judicial examiners (*fa-chih kuan*) who, in addition to their first test on general meanings, show understanding in their judgment of the medium or small case, even if their use of the laws is not wholly in conformity with the original case judgment document but does indicate their familiarity with the law, may all in accordance with the precedent be reported on and sent to the High Court for testing on cases.[58]

As in other areas of the legal system there were many changes in these testing policies during the reign of Shen-tsung. Most seem to have been rather minor modifications in rules that were to remain basically as they had been until the end of the Northern Sung. There were, however, two changes of significance. First, in 1074, active local officials were forbidden to take the

---

57. HCP 282:1b. For an example of defining a "rough understanding," see SHY, chih-kuan 15:39a–40a.

58. SHY, chih-kuan 15:37a–b.

tests. If this rule were followed the number of those eligible to compete for central judicial posts would have been sharply reduced. Unfortunately there seems to be no further information on this policy. Second, in 1086, it was ordered that judicial investigators of the High Court of Justice (*ta-li p'ing-shih*) or higher not be tested. This office was ranked high eighth, the lowest grade of the administrative class of officials. Presumably, if this policy was enforced the legal tests were thereafter open only to executory class personnel.[59]

Examinations in law were held during the whole of the Southern Sung period (1126–1279). As initially established in 1133 they were aimed at men already in the civil service who were seeking accelerated advancement. Candidates were questioned on hypothetical cases. Those who succeeded were ranked in grades and given appropriate bureaucratic advancements. Other evidence suggests that candidates were also questioned on statutes and on case judgments.[60]

Because the New Degree in Law was a virtual copy of these examinations it is hardly surprising that Sung writers continually confuse the two sorts of tests. Indeed, it is possible that in practice the New Degree in Law during the Southern Sung consisted of these examinations in law, when they were being taken by candidates qualified in the local examinations of the regular civil service examination system rather than by men already members of the civil service.

After the mid-twelfth century it does not appear that men could initially enter the civil service in this way, but tests on law continue to be given to men already having official status. As under the Northern Sung these tests seem to have been given to volunteers seeking accelerated promotion or improved civil service status, candidates for certain judicial positions, and at times apparently to all executory class personnel seeking new appointments.[61] Such tests were a pervasive part of official life throughout the period.

For the whole of the Sung dynasty a number of interrelated devices were designed to encourage legal learning among officials and potential officials. Knowing that these devices existed cannot, of course, show their effectiveness. It does suggest that the stereotype of traditional Chinese officials and regimes as being chary of the law needs to be qualified. True, a dislike of legal studies did exist in the Sung. The Northern Sung official Liu K'ai (947–1000) chided a relative for seeking a degree in law. The degree in law

59. SHY, chih-kuan 15:7a, 42b, 24:5a, 19a–b, 5b, 15:9b, 10a–b, 24:8b, 9b; SHY, hsüan-chü 13:13a; SHY, ch'ung-ju 3:7b; KMPY, p. 816; HCP 7:38a, 215:8a, 233:18b, 242:14a–b, 255:7b, 253:12b, 252:21b, 12506:4a, 282:1b, 287:16a, 289:13a, 15a, 291:6a, 312:18a, 304:12b, 14a, 377:18a.

60. WHTK 32:202; CYTC 13:13b; SHY, chih-kuan 24:16b; SS 157:17b–18a.

61. SHY, hsüan-chü 14:4a; CYTC 13:14a; SS 157:20a; TFSL, pp. 60–62, 211, 212; SSCW pp. 1133 1611, 2239, 2336, 2374, 2391, 2409, 2449.

was for "lowly clerks," an easy way out that could not lead to a high position. And Chao Meng-chien (b. 1199) said that the reading of laws was shameful.[62] But in their times these views were probably in the minority. Ssu-ma Kuang was perhaps a better model of the views of contemporaries. A study of the law, without the ideological training gained from imbibing the Classics, was improper. But, having revealed his commitment to cultural values by passing the examinations on the Classics, an official had of necessity to go on to learn the laws. A knowledge of them was universally necessary among civil servants.

Common sense would suggest that Ssu-ma Kuang is at least partly correct. Functioning officials must have developed at least a passing familiarity with the law; the continuing existence and use of the devices for encouraging legal study among officials indicates that a considerable number developed a degree of expertise in legal matters.

An interest in the law and its importance to officials is also suggested by a variety of other evidence. During the Sung a number of books appeared aimed specifically at helping active officials with the practical aspects of the law. Extant works such as the *Tso-i tzu-chen* provide helpful models for the writing of proper official contracts for local workers,[63] and from the late Southern Sung a special guide to forensic medicine and its associated legal rulings was compiled for the use of local officials.[64] Furthermore, extant Sung bibliographies list more than one hundred other works, now lost, that dealt with various aspects of legal practice. The vast majority of these were collections of legal rules, with titles such as the *Stipulations and Specifications for the Storehouses of the Various Offices in the Capital* (*Tsai-ching chu-ssu k'u-wu t'iao'-shih*) or the *Compiled Edicts of the Ch'ing-li Era* (*Ch'ing-li pien-chih*). However, there were also works like the *Important Precedents of Penal Law* (*Hsing-fa yao-li*), *On Determining Criminal Judgments* (*Che-yu li-ch'eng*), *Important Points Concerning the Five Punishments* (*Wu-hsing tsuan-yao lu*), or the *Mirror for Statutes and Ordinances* (*Lü-ling shou-chien*).[65]

The interest in matters of law even extended beyond this group of those professionally involved. In a justly famous passage in his *Meng-ch'i pi-t'an*, Shen Kua remarks that:

> traditionally the people of Chiang-hsi love to litigate. There is a book called the *Teng Ssu-hsien*, which contains all forms of litigation documents. First, they teach the use of insulting language. If they cannot get their way with insulting language then they use deceit and fraud to succeed. If deceit and fraud do not

62. Liu K'ai, *Ho-tung hsien-sheng chi* (SPTK ed.) 7:10a; Chao Meng-chien, *I chai wen-pien* (SKSCP ed.) 1:23a.

63. Li Yüan-pi, *Tso-i tzu chen* (SPTK ed.).

64. Sung Tz'u, *Hsi yüan lu* (Tai-nan ko ts'ung-shu ed.). See also Brian E. McKnight, trans., *The Washing Away of Wrongs* (Ann Arbor: University of Michigan Center for Chinese Studies, 1983), Science, Medicine, and Technology in East Asia series, vol. 1.

65. Liu Chao-yu, *Sung shih i-wen chih shin pu i-chi k'ao* (Taipei: Published by the author, 1973).

work, then they seek his crimes so as to plunder him. Ssu-hsien is the name of a man. Men transmitted his method, and then gave his name to this book. In the village schools they often use it to teach the students.[66]

The Sung government, ever sensitive to threats to its prerogatives, attempted to ban the circulation of this and other legal texts among private individuals but without complete success. The *Sui-ch'u t'ang shu mu*, the catalog of a Sung private library, lists thirty works under the category of legal writings. These include not only the T'ang Code and the Sung *Penal Code* but also many other collections of government laws, the famous Five Dynasties case book, *Che-yü kuei-chien*, and a work on forensic medicine.[67] The *Chun-chai t'u-shu chih*, a private catalog dated 1151, lists a dozen works on law, including the Sung *Penal Code*, several sets of collected edicts, and the tenth-century casebook *I-yü chi*.[68] The largest catalog of a Sung private library, the *Chih-chai shu-lu chieh-ti*, lists fifteen legal works of Sung times, all collections of various sorts of laws. Some were quite large. The *Essentials of the Village Service System (I-fa t'so-yao)*, which covered only the period from 1147 to 1198, was 189 chapters long.[69]

Families not only owned such books, they used them. The late Southern Sung official Lou Yüeh, bewailing the legal suits used by families to avoid unwanted fiscal burdens complains that the suits are "based on rules and cite precedents which cannot be ignored."[70]

Simplified guides to the law, like the *Ssu-yen tsa-tzu*, and Fu Lin's *Hsing-t'ung fu*, a rhymed guide to the Sung *Penal Code*, also circulated during the Southern Sung. Circulation of the so-called casebooks, like the tenth-century *I-yü chi* by Ho Ning (898–955) and his son Ho Meng (951–995), the *Che-yü kuei-chien* of Cheng K'o, and the twelfth-century *T'ang-yin pi-shih* of Kuei Wan-yung, was not confined to officials.

Finally, fiction with a heavy legal element probably originated in this era. Although specialists in the field hesitate to assign Sung dates to any extant short stories, we do know from the Southern Sung work *Tu-ch'eng chi-sheng* that the category *kung-an* later used for detective fiction, already was in use to cover a category of storyteller's material.[71]

The Northern Sung, and especially the reign of Shen-tsung, marks the high point in the government's concern that officials learn the law. In the late Northern Sung, and even more during the Southern Sung, there was less emphasis on legal expertise, but even in this later period there was still

66. Shen Kua, *Meng ch-i pi-t'an* (SPTK ed.) 25:7a.
67. Yu Mou, *Sui ch'u t'ang shu-mu* (TSCC ed.).
68. Ch'ao Kung-wu, *Chun-chai t'u shu chih* (SPTK san pien ed.).
69. Ch'en Chen-sun, *Chih-chai shu-lu chieh-ti* (Kuang-hsu woodblock ed.).
70. Lou Yüeh, *Kung kuei chi* (Wu-ying tien chu chen pen ch'uan shu ed.) 26:4b.
71. Patrick Hanan, *The Chinese Short Story* (Cambridge: Harvard University Press, 1973), pp. 170–171.

concern that government officials have some knowledge of the laws. The attitudes of later dynasties, insofar as they slighted legal training, seem a world apart from an era when Ssu-ma Kuang, a staunch defender of the Classics and of the gentleman ideal, could say that a knowledge of the laws was absolutely necessary for all active officials.

This attitude of Ssu-ma Kuang probably was common among thoughtful active officials, but what of the Neo-Confucians, whose goals transcended effective service to the state? Clearly, to men representing some strands of Neo-Confucian thought, epitomized by the followers of Lu Chiu-yüan, the study of law not only would be irrelevant but actively pernicious. If the Classics themselves were mere footnotes, what could possibly justify spending time on the study of materials as mundane as the rules of law?

The problem was different for Chu Hsi and his school. Chu Hsi himself was active as both a judicial official and a commentator on judicial cases. Obviously he had learned something about the law. However, in his writings he does not say much about how and when the law should be learned. That such learning could be a legitimate if very subordinate part of education can clearly be deduced from his more general views. First, we must keep in mind Chu Hsi's stress on the value of the *Great Learning* and particularly his interest in the passage "The investigation of things consists in the extension of knowledge." According to the commentary

> If we wish to extend our knowledge to the utmost we must investigate the principles of all things with which we come into contact. For the mind and spirit of man are formed to know, and the things of the world all contain principles. So long as principles are not exhausted, knowledge is not yet complete.[72]

In the writings of Chu Hsi and his followers it is made abundantly clear that book learning plays a considerable part in this process of learning. An observer at the Goose Lake conference distinguishes the approaches to learning of Chu Hsi and Lu Chiu-yüan by saying,

> At the Goose Lake Temple meeting, when discussions finally turned to the method of instruction, [Chu] Yüan-hui's idea was to require the student to begin by reading and studying extensively and then to focus his attention on what is essential. On the other hand, however, the two Lus [Hsiang-shan and Chiu-ling] were of the opinion that the recovery of the original mind must precede extensive study.[73]

As Chu Hsi himself said, "There is no other way to investigate principle to

72. James Legge, trans., *The Confucian Classics* (Hong Kong: Hong Kong University Press, 1960) 1:365.

73. From a letter of Chu Heng-tao cited in Yü Ying-shih, "Morality and Knowledge in Chu Hsi's Philosophical System" (paper presented at the International Conference on Chu Hsi, Honolulu, 1982), p. 55.

the utmost than to pay attention to everything in our daily reading of books and handling of affairs."[74]

The writings to be read first were the Four Books and the Classics, followed by the histories, but Chu Hsi also clearly believed in the relevance and importance of other kinds of writings for promoting moral growth and development. In the words of Professor Kao Ming,

> Chu was a man with keen interest in social rules, believing that social unrest was caused by the decay of moral virtues in society which was in turn attributable to the failure to assign sufficient authority to rules of social life. Thus, he had repeatedly asked the government to promulgate books of propriety as well as to revise and add to those already available.[75]

Books on law, like books on propriety, could never play a large role in the proper education of a serious scholar, but like books on propriety they could be read without harm and with possible usefulness because they embodied Confucian beliefs. With the increasing Confucianization of the content of the law that occurred after Han times, any doubts Confucians might have had about the propriety of being concerned with the law were much reduced. In reading the law, students were in effect reading about the ways in which Chinese values, many of them championed by Confucians, were to be applied in maintaining the desired social order. Reading law, then, was harmful only insofar as it might preclude studying other more important texts.

Will Rogers remarked that all of us are ignorant; we are simply ignorant about different things. The areas about which we can afford to be and remain ignorant depend on the goals toward which we move. In the Sung, any man who wished to become an active official could not fail to study the content of the law; but any man who wished to become a worthy person could not fail to put first overcoming his ignorance about himself through the proper study of the Confucian texts.

---

74. Wing-tsit Chan, *A Sourcebook for Chinese Philosophy* (Princeton: Princeton University Press, 1963), pp. 610–611.

75. Kao Ming, "The Discipline of Propriety' of Chu Hsi," in *Chu Hsi and Neo-Confucianism*, (ed.) Wing-tsit Chan (Honolulu: University of Hawaii Press, 1986), p. 313.

CONTRIBUTORS

Bettine Birge did her undergraduate work at Princeton and received her M.A. in Chinese studies from Cambridge University. Now a doctoral candidate at Columbia, she is doing research on Sung history at the Institute of Humanistic Studies of Kyoto University on a grant from the Social Science Research Council.

Peter K. Bol, assistant professor of Chinese history at Harvard University, was educated at the University of Leiden and Princeton University (Ph.D. 1982), after which he was a member of the Society of Fellows in the humanities at Columbia. His main research interest is the intellectual history of the literati in Sung China.

John W. Chaffee received his B.A. from Swarthmore College and his M.A. and Ph.D. from the University of Chicago. Since 1980 he has been teaching at the State University of New York in Binghamton, where he is associate professor of history and director of the East Asian Studies Program. He is the author of *The Thorny Gates of Learning in Sung China: A Social History of Examinations* (1985) and is the editor of the *Bulletin of Sung-Yuan Studies.*

Wing-tsit Chan is Anna R. D. Gillespie Professor of Philosophy Emeritus at Chatham College and professor emeritus of Chinese philosophy and culture at Dartmouth College. His numerous works on Chinese philosophy include *A Source Book in Chinese Philosophy* (1963), a translation of Chu Hsi's *Reflections on Things at Hand* (1967), and *Chu Hsi and Neo-Confucianism* (1986).

Ron-Guey Chu received his Ph.D. in Chinese history and thought from Columbia University in 1988. His dissertation is entitled "Chen Te-hsiu and the *Classic on governance*: the Coming of Age of Neo-Confucian Statecraft." Presently he is working on Hsieh Liang-tso and tenth-century Neo-Confucian thought.

Wm. Theodore de Bary is John Mitchell Mason Professor of the University at Columbia University, where he has also served as vice-president and provost. His most recent works are *Neo-Confucian Orthodoxy and the Learning of the Mind-and-Heart* (1981), the *Liberal Tradition in China* (1983), and *East Asian Civilizations: A Dialogue in Five Stages* (1988).

Patricia Ebrey is professor in East Asian Studies and history at the University of Illinois at Urbana-Champaign. Her books include *The Aristocratic Families of Early Imperial China: A Case Study of the Po-ling Ts'in Family* (1978), *Chinese Civilization and Society: A Sourcebook* (1981), *Family and Property in Sung China: Yuan Ts'ai's Precepts for Social Life* (1984), and *Kinship Organization in*

Late Imperial China, 1000–1940, the last coedited with James L. Watson. She is currently engaged in research on marriage and funerals in the Sung period.

Robert Hymes was educated at Columbia College and the University of Pennsylvania (Ph.D. 1979). He is now associate professor of Chinese history at Columbia. His *Statesmen and Gentlemen: The Elite of Fu-Chun, Chiang-hsi, in Northern and Southern Sung* (1986) received the 1988 Joseph Levenson Prize of the Association of Asian Studies.

M. Theresa Kelleher did her graduate work at Columbia (Ph.D. 1982). She is currently assistant professor of religion at Manhattanville College. She has written a study of the fifteenth-century Ming thinker Wu Yü-pi, "Personal Reflections on the Pursuit of Sagehood: The Life and Journal (Jih-lu) of Wu Yu-pi (1392–1469)."

Thomas H. C. Lee received his doctorate from Yale and is now senior lecturer in the Department of History at the Chinese University of Hong Kong as well as director of the International Studies Program there. He specializes in Sung history and has published *Government Education and Examinations in Sung China* (1985).

Brian McKnight, professor of history at the University of Hawaii, is a specialist in Chinese legal institutions. He is the author of several books including *Village and Bureaucracy in Southern Sung China* (1971) and *The Quality of Mercy: Amnesties and Traditional Chinese Justice* (1981) and is currently completing a study of law enforcement in traditional China.

Tu Wei-ming, professor of history and chairman of the Department of East Asian Languages and Cultures at Harvard University, is the author of *Neo-Confucianism in Action: Wang Yang-ming's Youth* (1976) and *Confucian Thought: Selfhood as Creative Transformation* (1985) as well as numerous articles on Chinese thought.

Monica Übelhör (Ph.D., Hamburg University, 1968) has recently been appointed professor of Chinese at Marburg University. Her special research interest is in the history of Sung and Ming thought and in social and governmental institutions on the local level.

Linda Walton, associate professor of history at Portland State University, received her Ph.D. at the University of Pennsylvania (1978). She is the author of a study on "Education, Social Change, and Neo-Confucianism in Sung-Yuan China: Academies and the Local Elite in Ming-chou (Ningpo)."

Pei-yi Wu teaches Chinese at Queens College, City University of New York, and Columbia University. He is the author of *The Confucian's Progress: Autobiographical Writings in China*.

Chün-fang Yü is associate professor of religion at Rutgers University and specializes in the history of Chinese Buddhism since the T'ang dynasty. She was educated at Tunghai University and Columbia University (Ph.D. 1973). Her publications include *The Renewal of Buddhism in China: Chu-hung and the Late Ming Synthesis* (1981) and a chapter on Ming Buddhism for the *Cambridge History of China*, Vol. 8. She is currently writing a book on the cult of Kuan-yin in China.

Eric Zürcher is professor of East Asian history in the Sinologisch Instituut, University of Leiden. His main interest is in the historical encounter with foreign cultures, and especially religions, in China. He is the author of *The Buddhist Conquest of China* and coeditor of the sinological journal *T'oung Pao*.

GLOSSARY

a-she-li	阿闍梨
Ajia shi kenkyū	アジア史研究
An Lu-shan	安祿山
Araki Toshikazu	荒木敏一
Banzan Zenshū	蕃山全書
Bosatsukai	菩薩戒
Busshō Kaisetsu Daijiten	佛書解説大辭典
chai	齋
chai chang	齋長
ch'ai-i fa	差役法
ch'ai-i kung-shih	差役公事
Chan Fu-min	詹阜民
Chan-liao Chi-hung	澹寮紀洪
Ch'an	禪
Ch'an-lin pao-hsün	禪林寶訓
Ch'an-lin pao-hsün chiang-chi	禪林寶訓講記
Ch'an-lin pao-hsün ho-chu	禪林寶訓合註
Ch'an-lin pao-hsün shun-chu	禪林寶訓順註
Ch'an-lin seng-pao chuan	禪林僧寶傳
Ch'an-men kuei-shih	禪門規式
Ch'an-ti t'i-yen	禪的體驗
Ch'an-tsung ti chiao-yü ssu-hsiang yü shih-shih	禪宗的教育思想與實施
Ch'an-tsung ts'ung-lin chih-tu yü Chung-kuo she-hui	禪宗叢林制度與中國社會
Ch'an-wen hsiu-cheng chih-yao	禪問修証指要
ch'an-yeh	產業
Ch'an-yüan ch'ing-kuei	禪苑清規
Chang	漳
Chang	張
chang-che	長者
Chang Chi-hsien	張齊賢
Chang Chih-kung	張志公
Chang Chih-po	張智白

Chang Chin	張津
Chang-chou	漳州
Chang-chou fu-chih	漳州府志
Chang Fu-ying	張富盈
Chang Hsia	張洽
Chang I	張繹
Chang I-chien	張易簡
Chang Kuo-ch'uan	張國佺
chang-lao	長老
Chang Lei	張耒
Chang Pang-wei	張邦煒
Chang P'eng-nien	張彭年
Chang Po-hsing	張伯行
Chang-p'u	漳浦
Chang Shih	張栻
Chang-shih yüan-t'ing chi	張氏園亭記
Chang-shui Tzu-hsüan	長水子璿
Chang Tsai	張載
Chang Tsai chi	張載集
Chang Tun	章惇
Chang Tzu ch'üan-shu	張子全書
Chang Wen-chia	張文嘉
Chang Yang-ch'ing	張揚卿
Chang Yen-hsien	張彥先
Chang Yen-pao	張延寶
Ch'ang-chou hsien che i-shu	常州先哲遺書
Ch'ang-chou I-hsing hsien hsüeh chi	常州宜興縣學記
Ch'ang-kuo	昌國
Ch'ang Pi-te	昌彼得
Ch'ang-sha	長沙
Ch'ang-shui	長水
Ch'ang-t'ai	長泰
Chao-chou Ts'ung-nien	趙州從諗
Chao chü-jen ju shu-yüan chuang	招舉人入書院狀
Chao Hsiung	趙雄
Chao Ju-ch'ien	趙汝謙
Chao Ju-yü	趙汝愚

Chao K'uang-yin	趙匡胤
Chao Meng-chien	趙孟堅
Chao Shan-tai	趙善待
Chao Shou	趙壽
Chao Tzu-ming	趙子明
ch'ao-chi yüan	朝集院
Ch'ao-jan t'ai chi	超然台記
Che-chiang	浙江
Che-tung	浙東
Chen-ch'eng	貞乘
Chen-ch'ing Ke-wen	眞淨克文
Chen-chün	眞峻
Chen-hui	眞慧
chen-liu	枕流
Chen Te-hsiu	眞德秀
Chen-tsung	眞宗
Ch'en	陳
Ch'en Chen-sun	陳振孫
Ch'en Chia	陳賈
Ch'en Ch'un	陳淳
Ch'en Hsiang	陳襄
Ch'en Hsien-chang	陳獻章
Ch'en Hsün	陳塤
Ch'en I-chung	陳宜中
Ch'en Jen	陳仁
Ch'en Kuan	陳瓘
Ch'en Liang	陳亮
Ch'en Lin	陳麟
Ch'en Lü	陳旅
Ch'en Mi	陳宓
Ch'en Pai-sha	陳白沙
Ch'en P'ing	陳平
Ch'en Jung-chieh (Wing-tsit Chan)	陳榮捷
Ch'en Shih	陳宧
Ch'en Shih-chih	陳士直
Ch'en shu	陳書
Ch'en T'ai-ch'u	陳太初

Ch'en Tsu-yung	陳祖永
Ch'en Ts'ui	陳倅
Ch'en Ts'un	陳存
Ch'en Tung-yüan	陳東原
Ch'en Yüan-hui	陳元暉
cheng	正
Cheng	鄭
Cheng Ch'in-jen	鄭欽仁
cheng-ching	正靜
Cheng Ch'ing-chih	鄭清之
Cheng Chü-chung	鄭居中
Cheng-ho	政和
Cheng-ho wu-li hsin-i	鄭和五禮新儀
cheng hsüeh	正學
Cheng-i	正義
Cheng I-chih	鄭一之
Cheng-i t'ang ch'üan-shu	正誼堂全書
Cheng-meng	正蒙
Cheng-tao ko	証道歌
Ch'eng	程
Ch'eng-chai chi	誠齋集
Ch'eng Chü-fu	程鉅夫
Ch'eng chün Cheng-ssu mu-piao	程君正思墓表
Ch'eng Hao	程顥
Ch'eng Hsün	程洵
Ch'eng I	程頤
[Ch'eng] I-ch'uan I chuan	程伊川易傳
Ch'eng-ming	誠明
Ch'eng-shih chia-shu tu-shu fen-nien jih-ch'eng	程氏家塾讀書分年日程
Ch'eng Tuan-hsüeh	程端學
Ch'eng Tuan-li	程端禮
Ch'eng Tuan-meng	程端蒙
Ch'eng Tung erh hsien-sheng hsüeh-tse	程董二先生學則
chi (sacrifice)	祭
chi (record)	記
chi (stele inscriptions)	記

Chi An	汲黯
Chi-chiu	急救
Chi-chiu p'ien	急就篇
chi-feng	機鋒
chi-i	吉儀
Chi K'ang-tzu	季康子
chi-ku	稽古
chi-ku t'ang	稽古堂
Chi Tuan-ming Su kung wen	祭端明蘇公文
chi-yüan	機緣
Chi-yün	集韻
ch'i	氣
Ch'i-an	齊安
ch'i-chang	耆長
Ch'i-chou chiao-shou t'ing chi	蘄州教授廳記
ch'i so i jan	其所以然
ch'i so tang jan	其所當然
Ch'i-sung	契嵩
Ch'i T'ung-wen	戚同文
Ch'i tz'u Pai-lu-tung Shu-yüan ch'ih-e	乞賜白鹿洞書院勅額
chia	家
chia-chuang	家狀
Chia fan	家範
Chia-hsi	嘉熙
chia-hsün	家訓
chia-i	家儀
Chia-li, chia-li	家禮
Chia-li i-chieh	家禮儀節
chia miao	家廟
chia-shu	家塾
Chia-t'ai p'u-teng lu	嘉泰普燈錄
Chia-ting	嘉定
chia-yen	嘉言
Chia-yen hsing-kung pien-tien tsou-cha erh	甲寅行宮便殿奏劄二
chiang	講
Chiang-chang i-feng: ssu-jen chiang-hsüeh ti ch'uan-t'ung	絳帳遺風：私人講學的傳統

Chiang Chih	江贄
Chiang-chou	江州
Chiang-hsi	江西
chiang-hsüeh	講學
Chiang-kung	姜肱
Chiang-nan	江南
Chiang-nan-tung	江南東
Chiangsu	江蘇
Chiang-t'ang ts'e-wen	講堂策問
Chiang-tso chien	將作監
Ch'iang-lu	羌廬
chiao	教
chiao-hua	教化
chiao-shou	教授
Chiao-yü shih tzu-liao	教育史資料
Ch'iao Chi	喬吉
chieh-shih	揭示
Chieh-tzu t'ung-lu	戒子通錄
Ch'ieh-yün	切韻
chien (offerings)	簡
chien (room)	間
chien (among, in)	間
Chien-an hsien	建安縣
Chien-ch'ang (hsien)	建昌（縣）
Chien-ch'ang chün chin-shih t'i ming chi	建昌軍進士題名記
chien-chen	監鎮
chien-chih	儉質
Chien-chou	建州
chien-chu p'an-kuan	監主判官
Chien-chung Ching-kuo hsü teng-lu	建中靖國續燈錄
Chien-fu Wu-pen	薦福悟本
Chien-k'ang fu-hsüeh Ming-tao hsien-sheng tz'u chi	建康府學明道先生祠記
Chien-nan shih-kao	劍南詩稿
Chien-yang (hsien)	建陽（縣）
Chien-yang hsien-chih	建陽縣志
Chien-yen i-lai Ch'ao-yeh tsa-chi	建炎以來朝野雜記

ch'ien	乾
Ch'ien-chou hsüeh chi	虔州學記
Ch'ien Mu	錢穆
Ch'ien Shih	錢時
Ch'ien-tao Ssu-ming t'u-ching	乾道四明圖經
ch'ien tsang-ching mu	欠藏經目
Ch'ien-tzu wen	千字文
Ch'ien Tzu-yen	錢子言
Ch'ien Wen-shih	錢聞詩
chih (paper)	紙
chih (will)	志
chih (annals)	誌
chih (straight)	直
chih (to know)	知
chih-cheng	執政
Chih-chai shu-lu chieh-t'i	直齋書錄解題
Chih-cheng Ssu-ming hsü-chih	至正四明續志
chih-chia	治家
chih-chih	致知
chih-fen	職分
chih-hsien	知縣
chih i lun	致一論
chih-kuan	職官
Chih-p'an	志磐
Chih-sheng wen-hsüan wang	至聖文宣王
chih-shih chai	治事齋
Chih-shun	智舜
Chih-yüeh lu	指月錄
ch'ih	敕
Ch'ih-ts'ai shih-mo chiao	喫菜事魔教
Chikusa Masa'aki	竺沙雅章
Chin	金
Chin-ch'i hsien	金溪縣
Chin Ch'ü-wei	金去偽
Chin Chung-shu	金中樞
Chin-hsi	金谿
Chin Hsiang Kung	晉襄公
Chin-hua	金華

chin hung fan piao	進洪範表
Chin-kang ching	金剛經
Chin kuang-ming ssu	金光明寺
Chin kuang-ming ssu hsieh ching jen-ming	金光明寺寫經人名
Chin-ling ts'ung-shu	金陵叢書
Chin-men	金門
chin-shih	進士
Chin-shih ts'ui-pien	金石萃編
Chin shu	晉書
Chin-ssu lu	近思錄
Chin-ssu lu chi-chu	近思錄集註
chin-te	進德
Chin-Yüan tsa-chü	金元雜劇
ch'in (affection)	親
ch'in (diligent)	勤
Ch'in-chou	秦州
Ch'in Kuei	秦檜
Ch'in shih huang-ti lun	秦始皇帝論
ching (classic)	經
ching (to revere)	敬
ching (quiet)	靜
Ching-ai	靜藹
Ching-chao	京兆
Ching-chia ting-pen Sui-an Hsü-shih ts'ung-shu hsü-pien	景嘉定本隨盦徐氏叢書續編
ching-chieh	經界
Ching-chien chih t'ang	敬簡之堂
Ching-hsüan	靖玄
Ching-hsüeh li-k'u	經學理窟
Ching-hsüeh li-shih	經學歷史
ching-hsüeh po-shih	經學博士
Ching-hu	荊湖
Ching-hu-nan	荊湖南
Ching-hu-pei	荊湖北
ching-i	經義
ching-i chai	經義齋
Ching-men	荊門

ching-ming hsing-hsiu	經明行修
Ching-shan	淨善
ching-she	精舍
ching-shen	敬身
ching-shih (classics & history)	經史
ching-shih (world ordering)	經世
Ching-te ch'uan-teng lu	景德傳燈錄
Ching-t'u ssu	淨土寺
ching-yen chiang-i	經筵講義
Ching-yu	景祐
ch'ing	頃
Ch'ing	清
Ch'ing-chü	清居
ch'ing-kuei	清規
Ch'ing-li	慶歷
ch'ing-ta-fu	卿大夫
Ch'ing-tai k'o-chü chih-tu yen-chiu	清代科舉制度研究
Ch'ing-tai k'o-chü k'ao-shih shu-lu	清代科舉考試述錄
ch'ing yin-yüan	請因緣
Ch'ing-yüan	慶元
Ch'ing-yüan t'iao-fa shih-lei	慶元條法事類
chiu-ching t'ang	九經堂
Chiu-fa tang	舊法黨
chiu-hsing	酒行
Ch'iu Chun	邱溶
Ch'iu Yung	丘雍
Ch'iung-chou hsüeh chi	瓊州學記
Chou	周
Chou Fang	周方
Chou Feng-shu	周奉叔
Chou Fu	周覆
Chou Heng-chung	周亨仲
Chou Hsing-ssu	周興嗣
chou-hsüeh	州學
Chou I	周頤
Chou-i cheng-i	周易正義
Chou li	周禮

Chou-li i hsü	周禮義序
Chou Mo	周謨
Chou Pi-ta	周必大
Chou-shan	舟山
Chou Shao	周韶
Chou Shen-kuei	周神歸
Chou Te-chih	周得之
Chou Tun-i	周敦頤
Chou Tzu ch'üan-shu	周子全書
chu	主
Chu	朱
Chu Chia-yüan	朱家源
chu-chiao	助教
chu-ch'ih chih tao	住持之道
Chu Fo-nien	竺佛念
chu-hou hui-wen	柱後惠文
Chu Hsi	朱熹
Chu Hsi yü Chin-men	朱熹與金門
Chu-hsüeh lun-chi	朱學論集
Chu-ko Liang	諸葛亮
Chu-ko Liang lun	諸葛亮論
Chu-lin Ching-she	竹林精舍
chu mu	諸母
chu-p'i	竹篦
Chu Pien	朱弁
chu-pu	主簿
chu-se jen	諸色人
Chu Tzu Chia-li	朱子家禮
Chu Tzu hsin hsüeh-an	朱子新學案
Chu Tzu men-jen	朱子門人
Chu Tzu nien-p'u	朱子年譜
Chu Tzu nien-p'u k'ao-i	朱子年譜考異
Chu Tzu shih-chi	朱子實紀
Chu Tzu ta-ch'üan	朱子大全
Chu Tzu tzu-ch'eng	朱子自稱
Chu Tzu wen-chi	朱子文集
Chu Tzu wen-chi ta-ch'üan lei-p'ien	朱子文集大全類編
Chu Tzu yü-lei	朱子語類

Chu Tzu yü-lei ta-ch'üan 朱子語類大全

Chu Wen Kung 朱文公

Chu Wen-kung wen-chi 朱文公文集

Chu-yen Shih-kuei 竹奄士珪

Chu Yü 朱玉

chü (raise) 舉

Chü-chia pi-yung shih-lei ch'üan-chi 居家必用事類全集

chü-jen 舉人

ch'u chia 出家

Ch'u san tsang chi chi 出三藏記集

Ch'u-shih piao 出師表

ch'u ts'ai 取材

Ch'ü li 曲禮

Ch'ü-wei chiu-wen 曲洧舊聞

ch'ü wu 驅烏

Ch'ü Yüan 屈原

chüan (chapter) 卷

Ch'uan-hsi lu 傳習錄

Ch'uan-t'ung yü-wen chiao-yü
  ch'u-t'an 傳統語文教育初探

Ch'üan Chin-sun 全晉孫

Ch'üan-fu 全付

Ch'üan Ju-mei 全汝梅

ch'üan-nung wen 勸農文

Ch'üan T'ang-wen 全唐文

ch'üan-t'i ta-yung 全體大用

Ch'üan Tsu-wang 全祖望

ch'üan-yü wen 勸諭文

chuang 莊

Chuang Tzu 莊子

Chüeh-an 覺岸

ch'üeh-ching mu 缺經目

Chūgoku hōsei shi kenkyū 中國法制史研究

Chūgoku shisō ni okeru risō to genjitsu 中國思想に於ける理想と現實

chün-ch'en 君臣

ch'un 淳

Ch'un-ch'iu 春秋

Ch'un-ch'iu Tso-chuan cheng-i 春秋左傳正義

Ch'un-hsi	淳熙
Ch'un-yu	淳祐
chung	重
Chung-ching mu-lu	眾經目錄
Chung-feng Ming-pen	中峯明本
chung hsiao lien ch'ih	忠孝廉恥
Chung-hua	中華
Chung-kuo ch'an tsu-shih chuan	中國禪祖師傳
Chung-kuo chiao-yü shih	中國教育史
Chung-kuo fa-chih shih lun-chi	中國法制史論集
Chung-kuo fo-chiao shih lun-chi	中國佛教史論集
Chung-kuo k'ao-shih chih-tu shih	中國考試制度史
Chung-kuo ku fang-chih k'ao	中國古方志考
Chung-kuo ku-tai chiao-yü shih	中國古代教育史
Chung-kuo ku-tai ti shu-yüan chih-tu	中國古代的書院制度
Chung-kuo li-shih nien-chien	中國歷史年鑑
Chung-kuo shu-yüan chih-tu	中國書院制度
Chung-kuo tzu-hsüeh ming-chu chi-ch'eng	中國子學名著集成
Chung-lu	仲履
chung-shih	中世
Chung-suan-shih lun-ts'ung	中算史論叢
Chung-t'iao shan	中條山
Chung-tsung	中宗
Chung-yung chang-chü	中庸章句
Chung-yung lun	中庸論
Ch'ung-an	崇安
Ch'ung jen Wan Huang chiao-k'an pen	崇仁萬璜校刊本
Ch'ung-ju	崇儒
ch'ung-li tien	崇禮殿
Ch'ung-wen tsung-mu	崇文總目
Ch'ung-yu	沖佑
Chūsei zenshū shi no kenkyū	中世禪宗史の研究
Daigaku Chūyō	大學中庸
Daikanwa jiten	大漢和辭典
Dōchū	道中

E-chou chou-hsüeh chi ku ko chi	鄂州州學稽古閣記
Erh-Ch'eng chi	二程集
Erh-Ch'eng ch'üan-chi	二程全集
Erh-Ch'eng ch'üan-shu	二程全書
Erh-Ch'eng i-shu	二程遺書
Erh-lao-t'ang tsa-chih	二老堂雜志
Erh-ya	爾雅
fa	法
fa-chia	法家
fa-chih	法制
fa-chih kuan	法制官
Fa-ching	法經
fa-kuan	法官
Fa-lang	法朗
Fa-lin	法琳
fa-ling	法令
Fa-min	法敏
fa-t'ang	法堂
fa-t'ung sha-mi	法同沙彌
Fa-yün Fa-hsiu	法雲法秀
Fan Chung-yen	范仲淹
Fan Ch'ung	范沖
fan-i	犯義
Fan t'ai-shih chi	范太史集
Fan Tsu-yü	范祖禹
Fan-wang ching	梵綱經
Fan Wen-cheng kung chi	范文正公集
Fan Yeh	范曄
Fang Hao	方豪
Fang Kuo-chen	方國珍
Fang Mo	方謨
fang ssu-lo	紡絲羅
Fang Wan-li	方萬里
Fei Han-ying	費漢英
fei li	非禮
fen	分

Fen-yang Shan-chao	汾陽善昭
Feng-ch'üan yün-ho	風泉雲壑
Feng-hsiang	鳳翔
Feng-hua	奉化
Feng I	馮椅
feng-shui	風水
Feng Tao	馮道
Feng Yün-hao	馮雲濠
Fo-chien Hui-chin	佛鑑慧勤
Fo-chih Tuan-yü	佛智端裕
Fo i-chiao ching	佛遺教經
Fo-tsu li-tai t'ung-tsai	佛祖歷代通載
Fo-tsu t'ung-chi	佛祖統記
Fo-yin Liao-yüan	佛印了元
fu (poetry)	賦
fu (prefecture)	府
fu (blessing)	福
Fu-chang	傅章
fu ch'i hsing	復其性
Fu-chien	福建
Fu-chou	撫州
Fu-chou cheng-i hsüeh-yüan	福州正宜學院
Fu-ch'uan hsien	富川縣
fu fu chih pieh	夫婦之別
Fu Hsi	伏羲
Fu Hsü	符絃
Fu Meng-ch'üan	傅夢泉
Fu Pi	富弼
Fu-shan Fa-yüan	浮山法遠
fu-tzu hsien yü Yao Shun	夫子賢於堯舜
Fu Tzu-yün	傅子雲
Fu Yüeh	傅說
Fukanzazengi	普勸坐禪儀
Gendai no jugaku kyōiku	元代の儒學教育
Godai shi jō no gunbatsu shihonka	五代史上の軍閥資本家
Gotō Shunzui	後藤俊瑞

hai	亥
Han Ch'i	韓琦
Han Ching-ti	漢景帝
Han-ch'üan Ching-she	寒泉精舍
Han-hsüeh chi-k'an	漢學季刊
Han-men chui-hsüeh	韓門綴學
Han shu	漢書
Han Yü	韓愈
Han-yü yin-yün hsüeh	漢語音韻學
Hang-chou	杭州
hang-lao	行老
Hao-han ti hsüeh-hai	浩瀚的學海
Heng-chou	衡州
Heng-chou Shih-ku Shu-yüan chi	衡州石皷書院記
Heng-shan	衡山
ho	喝
Ho-hsi-t'ai	赫曦台
Ho-lin yü-lu	鶴林玉露
ho-mu	和睦
Ho-nan Ch'eng-shih wai-shu	河南程氏外書
Ho-nan Shao-shih wen-chien lu	河南邵氏聞見錄
ho-shang	和尚
Ho-pei	河北
Hokusō kajo no okeru kanshyun no tekitei	北宋科舉の於ける寒暖の櫂第
Hou-Han shu	後漢書
hou-t'u	后土
Hsi-ning	熙寧
Hsi-ning tzu shuo	熙寧字說
Hsi-shan hsien-sheng Chen Wen-kung wen-chi	西山先生眞文公文集
hsi-yeh	習業
Hsia-t'ang Hui-yüan	瞎堂慧遠
hsiang (community)	鄉
hsiang (school)	庠
Hsiang An-shih	項安世
Hsiang-hsi Ching-she	湘西精舍
hsiang-hsü	庠序

hsiang-hsüeh	鄉學
Hsiang-i	鄉儀
hsiang-i kuan	詳議官
hsiang-li	鄉禮
Hsiang-shan	象山
Hsiang-shan ch'üan-chi	象山全集
Hsiang-shan Shu-yüan	象山書院
hsiang-shih	鄉試
Hsiang-shih chia-shuo	項氏家說
Hsiang-yen Chih-hsien	香巖智詵
hsiang-yin-chiu	鄉飲酒
hsiang yin-chiu li	鄉飲酒禮
hsiang-yüeh	鄉約
hsiao	校
hsiao-ai	孝愛
Hsiao ching	孝經
Hsiao-ching k'an-wu	孝經刊誤
Hsiao-hsüeh, hsiao-hsüeh	小學
Hsiao-hsüeh chi-chieh	小學集解
Hsiao-hsüeh chi-chu	小學集註
hsiao-hsüeh chiao-shou	小學教授
Hsiao-hsüeh ta-i	小學大義
Hsiao I	蕭懿
Hsiao-shan Lai-shih chia-p'u	蕭山來氏家譜
Hsiao-shun shih-shih	孝順事實
hsiao t'ieh-tzu	小貼子
hsiao-ts'an	小參
hsiao tsung	小宗
Hsiao-tsung	孝宗
hsiao-tzu	小子
Hsiao-yüeh Kung-hui	曉月公暉
Hsieh	契
hsien (county)	縣
hsien-ch'eng	縣丞
hsien-chin	先進
hsien-chü	仙居
hsien erh yu fa	儉而有法
hsien-hsien tz'u	先賢祠

hsien-hsien tz'u-t'ang	先賢祠堂
hsien-hsüeh	縣學
hsien-ling	縣令
hsien-sheng hsien-shih	先聖先士
hsien-sheng tien	先聖殿
hsien wang chih chiao	先王之教
hsien-wei	縣尉
hsin	信
Hsin-chou	信州
Hsin-chou Ch'ien-shan hsien hsüeh chi	信州鉛山縣學記
Hsin-chou chou-hsüeh ta-ch'eng tien chi	信州州學大成殿記
hsin-hsüeh	心學
hsin-k'o ming-fa	新科明法
Hsin-k'o tseng-pu Wen-kung chia-li ch'üan t'u	新刻增補文公家禮全圖
hsin-min	新民
Hsin-pien shih-wen lei-yao ch'i-cha ch'ing-ch'ien	新編事文類要啓箚青錢
Hsin-pien shih-wen lei-chü han-mo ta-ch'üan	新編事文類聚翰墨大全
hsin-shu	心術
Hsin T'ang shu	新唐書
Hsin-wen Yün-fen	心聞雲賁
Hsin Wu-tai shih	新五代史
Hsin-ya hsüeh-pao	新亞學報
hsin-yang	信仰
hsing-che	行者
hsing-ch'i	形氣
hsing-chih	性質
hsing ch'ing	性情
hsing-chuang	行狀
hsing-fen	性分
Hsing kung pien-tien tsou-cha erh	行宮便殿奏箚二
Hsing-li ching-i	性理精義
Hsing-li ta-ch'üan	性理大全
Hsing-li ta-ch'üan shu	性理大全書
Hsing-li tzu-hsün	性理字訓
hsing ming	性命

Hsing Ping	邢昺
hsing shuo	性說
hsing-tao	行道
hsing-t'ung sha-mi	形同沙彌
Hsing-tzu (hsien)	星子（縣）
hsiu-chi	修己
hsiu-chi chih-jen	修己治人
hsiu-ch'ih	修持
hsiu-shen	修身
hsiu-tao	修道
hsiu-ts'ai	秀才
Hsiung Chao	熊兆
Hsiung Ho	熊禾
hsiung-i	凶儀
Hsiung Jen-chan	熊仁瞻
hsü	序
Hsü	徐
Hsü Chin-hua ts'ung-shu	續金華叢書
Hsü Fu	許浮
Hsü Heng	許衡
hsü-hsin	虛心
Hsü Kao-seng chuan	續高僧傳
Hsü Kuan-hsing	徐貫行
hsü-pai	序拜
Hsü Shang	徐商
Hsü Sheng	許升
Hsü Sung	徐松
Hsü Tao-lin	徐道鄰
Hsü tzu-chih t'ung-chien	續資治通鑑
Hsü tzu-chih t'ung-chien ch'ang-pien	續資治通鑑長編
Hsü Tzu-ch'un	許子春
hsüan	選
Hsüan	宣
Hsüan-ch'ang	玄暢
Hsüan-ching	玄景
Hsüan-chüeh	玄覺
Hsüan-tsang	玄奘
Hsüan-tsung	宣宗

Hsüan-yen	玄儼
Hsüan-yüeh	玄約
hsüeh	學
hsüeh-cheng	學正
Hsüeh-chin t'ao-yüan	學津討源
hsüeh-hsiao chih cheng	學校之政
hsüeh-hsiao chih she	學校之設
Hsüeh-hsiao kung-chü ssu-i	學校貢舉私議
hsüeh-kuei	學規
Hsüeh-kuei lei-pien	學規類編
hsüeh-kung	學宮
hsüeh-ling	學令
hsüeh-lu	學律
hsüeh-sheng yüan-sou	學生淵藪
hsüeh-(shih-)lang	學〔士，var. 仕〕郎
Hsüeh t'ang wen P'an Pin-lao	雪堂問潘邠老
Hsüeh-t'ang tao-hsing	雪堂道行
Hsüeh-tou Ch'ung-hsien	雪竇重顯
hsüeh-tse	學則
Hsüeh-yen Tsu-ch'in	雪巖祖欽
hsün-chien	巡檢
hsün-liang tz'u	循兩資
Hsün-meng hsin-shu	訓蒙新書
Hsün t'ung-hsing	訓童行
Hsün t'ung-hsing ko	訓童行歌
Hsün Tzu	荀子
hsün-wei	巡尉
Hu An-kuo	胡安國
Hu-chou	湖州
Hu-ch'iu	虎丘
Hu Chü-jen	胡居仁
Hu Hung	胡宏
Hu-nan	湖南
Hu-nan ch'üan-sheng chang-ku pei-k'ao	湖南全省掌故備攷
Hu Wen-k'ai	胡文楷
Hu Yüan	胡瑗
Hu Yüan-li	胡元禮

Hu Yung	胡泳
hua	化
Hua-hsüeh yüeh-k'an	華學月刊
Hua-yen P'u-tzu	華嚴普孜
Huai-hai	懷海
Huan-chu-an ch'ing-kuei	幻住庵清規
Huan-hsi Ching-she	環溪精舍
Huan-t'ang Shou-jen	佝堂守仁
Huang-chou An-kuo ssu chi	黃州安國寺記
Huang Chen	黃震
Huang Hao	黃灝
Huang Jun-yü	黃潤玉
Huang Kan	黃榦
Huang-lung Hui-nan	黃龍慧南
Huang Po-chia	黃白家
Huang Shang	黃裳
Huang Shang-po	黃商伯
Huang Shu-ying	黃叔英
Huang Sung chung-hsing liang-ch'ao sheng-cheng	皇宋中興兩朝聖政
Huang Tsung-hsi	黃宗羲
hui	慧
Hui-an	晦庵
Hui-an hsien-sheng Chu wen-kung wen-chi	晦庵先生朱文公文集
Hui-an hsien-sheng fei su yin	晦庵先生非素隱
Hui-ch'eng	慧乘
Hui-chiao	慧皎
Hui-chou Wu-yüan hsien-hsüeh tsang shu ko chi	徽州婺源縣學藏書閣記
Hui-chün	慧顗
Hui-heng	慧晒
Hui-hung chüeh-fan	慧洪覺範
Hui-k'uan	慧寬
Hui-li	慧立
Hui-ming	慧明
Hui-pin	慧斌

Hui-shan ssu	惠山寺
Hui-shan ssu chia-shan chi	惠山寺家山記
Hui-t'ang Tsu-hsin	晦堂祖心
Hui-tsung	徽宗
Hui-yen	慧嚴
hui-yüeh	會約
Hung-chih Cheng-chüeh	宏智正覺
Hung Mai	洪邁
Hung Wen-fu	洪文撫
Huo-yen Shih-t'i	或庵師體
i (suspect)	疑
i (righteousness)	義
I-chiao ching	遺教經
i-chieh	義解
I-chien chih	夷堅志
I ching	易經
I-ching	義淨
i-ch'ing	疑情
I-ch'uan chi	伊川集
I-ch'uan hsien-sheng nien-p'u	伊川先生年譜
i-fu	衣服
i-fu chieh-fu	義夫節婦
i-hsüeh	義學
i-hsüeh sha-men	義學沙門
i-hsüeh yüan	義學院
i-li	義禮
I li	儀禮
I-li ching-chuan t'ung-chieh	儀禮經傳通解
i li chü	議禮局
I-Lo yüan-yüan lu	伊洛淵源錄
I-pai erh-shih wen	一百二十問
I-shu	遺書
i tao-te	一道德
I Yin	伊尹
Imaeda Aishin	合枝愛眞
Ishida Hajime	石日筆

jang	讓
Jao-chou	饒州
Jao Kan	饒幹
Jao Lu	饒魯
jen (humanity)	仁
jen (responsibility)	任
jen-che an jen	仁者安仁
Jen-chih	仁智
Jen-t'ien yen-mu	人天眼目
Jen-tsung	仁宗
Jih-chi	日記
jih yü shuo	日喩說
Jih-yung suan-fa	日用算法
jou	柔
ju	儒
Ju-chung hsü-chih	入眾須知
Ju-chung jih-yung ch'ing-kuei	入眾日用清規
ju-hsüeh	儒學
ju-hsüeh tz'u-ti	入學次第
ju-hu	儒戶
Ju-jen	儒人
ju-lai ch'an	如來禪
ju-shih	入室
ju-tsang	入藏
Ju tsang lu	入藏錄
Jui-yen Ku-yüan	瑞巖谷源
K'ai-ch'ing Ssu-ming hsü-chih	開慶四明續志
K'ai-feng	開封
K'ai meng yao hsün	開蒙要訓
K'ai-ming shu-tien	開明書店
K'ai-pao t'ung-li	開寶通禮
K'ai-yüan li	開元禮
K'ai-yüan shih-chiao lu	開元釋教錄
Kan Pao	干寶
Kan-su ta-hsüeh hsüeh-pao	甘肅大學學報
Kan-t'ang Wen-chun	湛堂文準
k'an-ching t'ang	看經堂

k'an-ching-tsang	看經藏
k'an-tu chuang	看讀床
kang	綱
K'ang-chai chi	康齋集
K'ang-hsi	康熙
Kao Ch'ing-tzu	高清子
Kao K'ang	高閌
Kao Ming-shih	高明士
Kao-seng chuan	高僧傳
Kao-tsung	高宗
Kao Tzu	告子
Kao Tzu Kao	高子皐
Kao-yen Shan-wu	高菴善悟
k'ao	考
k'ao-shih ching-i	考試經義
K'ao-t'ing	考亭
K'ao-t'ing Shu-t'ang	考亭書堂
Kawahara Yoshirō	河原由郎
Keigen jōhō jirui to Sōdai no shuppanhō	慶元條法事類と宋代の出版法
Kinsei Chūgoku sōzoku no kenkyū	近世中國宗族の研究
Kinsei kanseki sōkan	近世漢籍叢刊
ko	格
ko chung ti-i	格中第一
Ko Keng	葛賡
Ko Sheng-chung	葛勝仲
ko-wu	格物
ko-wu chih-chih	格物至知
k'o	科
k'o-chi fu-li	克己復禮
K'o-chu: Sui, T'ang chih Ming, Ch'ing ti k'ao-shih chih-tu	科學：隋唐至明清的考試制度
Ku-chin t'u-shu chi-ch'eng	古今圖書集成
Ku Hsien-ch'eng	顧憲成
Ku-ling	古靈
Ku-shan	古山
Ku Tuan-wen Kung i-shu	顧端文公遺書
ku wen	古文

Kuan Chung	管仲
kuan-hsüeh	官學
kuan-hu	官戶
kuan-k'o	館客
kuan shih	官師
kuan-t'ung	貫通
Kuan Tzu	管子
Kuan-yin ts'ung-ming chou	觀音聰明咒
k'uan-hui	寬惠
kuang	広
Kuang-hsin hsien	廣信縣
Kuang-hui Yüan-lien	廣慧元璉
Kuang-i	光儀
Kuang-nan-tung	廣南東
Kuang-p'ing	廣平
Kuang-wen shu-chü	廣文書局
Kuang-yün	廣韻
K'uang-shan	匡山
kuei	規
Kuei-ch'i hsien	貴溪縣
Kuei-shan chi	龜山集
Kuei-shan ching-tse	溈山警策
Kuei-shan Ling-yu	溈山靈祐
kuei-ssu	癸巳
Kuei-ssu ts'un-kao	癸巳存稿
Kuei-t'ien lu	歸田錄
Kuei Wan-jung	桂萬榮
Kumazawa Banzan	熊泥蕃山
K'un-hsüeh chi-wen	困學紀聞
kung (impartial)	公
kung (reverence)	恭
Kung-an Ch'an	公案禪
kung-fu	公服
Kung-k'uei chi	攻媿集
kung-kuo ko	功過格
kung-shih	公試
K'ung-tzu Hsiang T'o	孔子項陀
Kuo-an Shih-yüan	廓庵師遠

Kuo Chih	郭植
Kuo feng	國風
Kuo-li T'ai-wan ta-hsüeh wen-shih-che hsüeh-pao	國立台灣大學文史哲學報
Kuo T'ai	郭泰
Kuo-tzu chi-chiu	國子祭酒
Kuo-tzu chien	國子監
Kuo-tzu hsüeh	國子學
Kuo-tzu po-shih	國子博士
Kuo Yao-ling	郭堯齡
Kwangtung	廣東
Lan-t'ien hsien-chih	藍田縣志
Lan-yen Tao-shu	懶菴道樞
Lan-yen Ting-hsü	懶菴鼎需
Lang-ya Hui-chüeh	瑯琊惠覺
Lang-yeh	瑯琊
Lao-hsüeh an pi-chi	老學庵筆記
Lao Lai Tzu	老萊子
Lao Tzu	老子
Le-tan Yin-ch'ien	泐潭印乾
Leng-yen chou	楞嚴咒
li (principle)	理
li (ritual)	禮
li (official)	吏
li (unit of distance)	里
Li	李
Li Ch'ang	李常
Li Chen	李貞
Li chi	禮記
Li chi cheng-i	禮記正義
Li chi hsün-tsuan	禮記訓纂
li-chiao	立教
Li Chih	李隲
Li Ching	李景
Li Ch'ing-chao	李清照
Li Chün	李濬
Li Chung	李重

Li Ch'ung	李沖
Li Fan	李燔
Li Han	李瀚
Li Hsin-ch'uan	李心傳
Li Hui	李輝
Li Hung-ch'i (Thomas Hong Chi Lee)	李弘祺
Li Kuei-ch'en	黎貴臣
Li-kuo ti hung-kuei	立國的宏規
Li Lin-fu	李林甫
Li Ling	李陵
Li-ling	醴陵
Li Lüeh	禮略
Li lun	禮論
Li Min-ch'iu	李敏求
Li-niang	麗娘
Li Po	李渤
Li Po (poet)	李白
li-pu shih-lang	禮部侍郎
Li-sao	離騷
li-shen	立身
Li Shen	李紳
Li Shen-tzu	李深子
Li-sheng-men	禮聖門
Li-sheng tien	禮聖殿
li-su	禮俗
Li T'ai-po p'i-p'ei chin-ch'ien chi	李太白匹配金錢記
Li Tao	李燾
Li Ting	李定
Li-tsung	理宗
Li Tung-yang	李東陽
Li T'ung	李侗
Li Wei	李衞
Li Yen	李儼
Li yüeh lun	禮樂論
Liang-che	兩浙
Liang-che-tung	兩浙東
liang chieh kung-te shih	兩街功德使

Liang Keng-yao	梁庚堯
liang-shan	涼衫
lieh-chuan	列傳
Lieh-nü chuan	列女傳
Lien-ching	聯經
Lien-teng hui-yao	聯燈會要
Lin-an	臨安
Lin-chien lu	林間錄
Lin Ch'ing-chang	林慶彰
Lin-ch'uan hsien-sheng wen-chi	臨川先生文集
Lin Pao	林保
Lin Yu-yü	林幼玉
Lin Yung-chung	林用中
ling (command)	令
ling (guide, control)	領
Ling-yin Te-ching	靈隱德經
Ling-yüan Wei-ch'ing	靈源惟清
Liu	劉
Liu Cheng	留正
Liu Chih	劉摯
Liu Chih-fu	劉智夫
Liu Chin	劉瑾
Liu Ch'ing-chih	劉清之
Liu Chung-ying	柳仲郢
liu fa ti-tzu	留髮弟子
Liu Fu	劉黻
Liu Hsi	劉錫
liu-hsiang	六相
Liu Hsiang	劉向
Liu Huan	劉煥
Liu I	劉彝
Liu-i chü-shih chi hsü	六一居士集敍
Liu K'ai	柳開
Liu K'uan	劉寬
Liu Kuang-tsu	劉光祖
Liu Pen	劉賁
Liu P'ing-shu	劉平叔
Liu-shih Chia-hsün	柳氏家訓

Liu Shu	劉恕
Liu Tsai	劉宰
Liu Tzu-chien	劉子健
Liu Yao-fu	劉堯夫
Liu Yin	劉因
Liu Ying-li	劉應李
Liu Yüeh	劉岳
Lo	樂
Lo Chün	羅濬
Lo Ta-ching	羅大經
Lo Ts'ung-yen	羅從彥
Lo Yü-chang chi	羅豫章集
Lou Fang	樓昉
Lou Yu	樓郁
Lou Yüeh	樓鑰
Lu	陸
Lu-chai	陸齋
Lu Chiu-hsü	陸九欵
Lu Chiu-kao	陸九皋
Lu Chiu-ling	陸九齡
Lu Chiu-shao	陸九韶
Lu Chiu-ssu	陸九思
Lu Chiu-yüan	陸九淵
Lu Chü-ching	陸居敬
Lu Fa-yen	陸法言
Lu Fang-weng ch'üan-chi	陸放翁全集
Lu Hsiang-shan	陸象山
Lu-shan	廬山
Lu-shan Pai-lu-tung Shu-yüan yen-ko k'ao	廬山白鹿洞書院沿革考
Lu Ssu-ch'eng	陸思誠
Lu Tien	陸佃
Lu T'ien-yu	陸天祐
Lu Yu	陸游
lü	律
lü-hsüeh chiao-shou	律學教授
Lü I-chien	呂夷簡
Lü K'un	呂坤

lü-ling-ch'ih-shih	律令勅試
Lü Pen-chung	呂本中
Lü Po-kung	呂伯恭
lü-po shih	律博士
lü-po shih-yüan	律博士員
lü-sheng	律生
Lü-shih chia-li	呂氏家禮
Lü-shih hsiang-yüeh	呂氏鄉約
Lü Ssu-hsing	呂嗣興
Lü Ta-chün	呂大鈞
Lü Ta-chung	呂大忠
Lü Ta-fang	呂大防
Lü Ta-lin	呂大臨
Lü Tsu-chien	呂祖儉
Lü Tsu-ch'ien	呂祖謙
Lü Wei-fu	呂渭夫
Lü Yen	呂炎
Luan-ch'eng chi	欒城集
Lüeh-lun Sung-tai ti-fang kuan-hsüeh yü ssu-hsüeh ti hsiao-chang lun	略論宋代地方官學與私學的消長論
Lun Sung-tai shu-yüan chih-tu chih fa-chan chi ch'i ying-hsiang	論宋代書院制度之發展及其影響
Lung-hsi	龍溪
Lung-ya Chih-ts'ai	龍牙智才
Lung-yen	龍巖
ma-chen	罵陳
Ma Jen-shou	馬仁壽
Ma Tuan-lin	馬端臨
Ma Yüan	馬援
Ma Yung-lung	馬永隆
Makino Shuji	牧野修二
Makino Tatsumi	牧野巽
Man-t'ang chi	漫塘集
Mao	鄑
Mao Li-jui	毛禮銳
Mao-shan	茅山

Mao shih	毛詩
Matsumoto Koichi	松本浩一
mei-shih	媒氏
Mei Ying-fa	梅應發
Meitoku shuppansha	明德出版社
men-k'o	門客
Meng-ch'iu	蒙求
Meng Hsien-ch'eng	孟憲承
Meng K'o lun	孟軻論
Meng-ku hsüeh	蒙古學
Meng-liang lu	夢梁錄
Meng-shan te-i	蒙山德異
meng-shih	蒙士
Meng Yüan-lao	孟元老
mi-shu lang	秘書郎
Mi-yin An-min	密印安民
miao	廟
Michihata Ryōshū	道端良秀
Mien-chai chi	勉齋集
Mien-chou	綿州
Mien-yang	綿陽
min (people)	民
min (intelligent)	敏
Min	閩
Min-tuo tsa-chih	民鐸雜誌
ming (engrave)	銘
Ming-chao	明邵
Ming chi-li	明集禮
Ming-chiao	明教
ming-ching	明經
Ming-chou	明州
ming-fa	明法
ming-lun	明倫
ming-lun t'ang, Ming-lun-t'ang	明倫堂
ming shih	命士
Ming-tao	明道
Ming-tao hsien-sheng wen-chi	明道先生文集
Ming-tao wen-chi	明道文集

ming-t'i shih-yung	明體適用
ming-t'i ta-yung	明體大用
Miyazaki Ichisada	宮崎市定
mo-chao ch'an	默照禪
Mo-chiao	魔教
mo-kuan chih t'ien	沒官之田
Mo-ni chiao	摩尼教
Mo Ti	墨翟
mo-tsung	魔宗
Mo-tzu	墨子
Morohashi Tetsuji	諸橋轍次
mou	畝
mu	穆
Mu chai chi	牧齋記
mu-chih kuan	幕職官
mu chih ming	墓誌銘
mu-yu	幕友
Naba Toshisada	那波利貞
Naikaku bunko kanseki bunrui mokuroku	內閣文庫漢籍分類目錄
Nan-chien chou Yu-ch'i hsien hsüeh chi	南劍州尤溪縣學記
Nan hsing ch'ien chi hsü	南行前集敘
Nan-hsüan wen-chi	南軒文集
Nan-k'ang (chün)	南康（軍）
Nan-k'ang chün feng-shih-t'an chi	南康軍風師壇記
Nan-k'ang fu-chih	南康府志
Nan-Sung ti nung-ts'un ching-chi	南宋的農村經濟
Nan Sung Yüan Ming ch'an-lin seng-pao chuan	南宋元明禪林僧寶傳
nei	內
nei-chu	內助
nei-jen	內人
nei-tse	內則
Neng-kai-chai man-lu	能改齋漫錄
nei-p'ien	內篇
Ni shang tien cha-tzu	擬上殿箚子

nien (remember)	念
nien (choose)	拈
nien-ku	拈古
nien-p'u	年譜
nien-sung	念誦
Niida Noboru	仁井田陞
Ning-po	寧波
Ning-po fu chien-yao chih	寧波府簡要志
Ning-po fu chih	寧波府志
Niu-yün	牛雲
Nü-chieh	女戒
nü-shih	女師
nü-tao	女道
Ogawa Kan'ichi	小川貫弌
Okada Takehiko	岡田武彦
Ou-yang Hsiu	歐陽修
Ou-yang Wen-chung kung chi	歐陽文忠公集
Pa	巴
Pa Ching-hsi wai chi	跋荊溪外集
Pa Chün-mo fei pai	跋君漠飛白
pa-hsing	八行
Pa Ssu-ma Wen-kung pu-ch'in ming hou	跋司馬溫公布衾銘後
pa t'iao-mu	八條目
Pai-chang ch'ing kuei	百丈清規
Pai-chang kuei-sheng sung	百丈規繩頌
Pai-chia hsing	百家姓
Pai-fa ming-men lu	百法明門錄
Pai-hu t'ung-te lun	白虎通德論
Pai-lu Shu-yüan chih	白鹿書院志
Pai-lu-tung	白鹿洞
Pai-lu-tung Shu-yüan	白鹿洞書院
Pai-lu-tung Shu-yüan chi	白鹿洞書院記
Pai-lu-tung shu-yüan chieh-shih	白鹿洞書院揭示
Pai-lu-tung shu-yüan chih	白鹿洞書院志

Pai-lu shu-t'ang ts'e wen	白鹿書堂策問
Pai-yün Shou-tuan	白雲守端
p'ai	牌
Pan Chao	班照
Pan Ku	班固
p'an-kung	泮宮
p'an-shih kuan	判事官
pang (proclamations)	榜
pang (blows)	棒
pang-kuo li	邦國禮
pao	保
pao-chia	保甲
Pao-ching san-mei	寶鏡三昧
Pao-ching sung	寶鏡頌
Pao-ch'ing Ssu-ming chih	寶慶四明志
Pao Hsien	包咸
pao-wu	保伍
Pao Yang	包揚
Pei-hsi hsien-sheng ch'üan-chi	北溪先生全集
Pei-hsi ta-ch'üan chi	北溪大全集
pei-jo	卑弱
Pei-Sung k'o-chü chih-tu yen-chiu	北宋科舉制度研究
Pei-Sung tsu-tien kuan-hsi ti fa-chan chi ch'i ying-hsiang	北宋租佃關係的發展及其影响
pei-tzu	背子
p'ei	配
p'ei-chung	陪衆
P'ei Hsiu	裴秀
Pen-chüeh	本覺
pen-hsin	本心
P'eng Fang	彭方
P'eng Hsün	彭尋
P'eng Li	彭蠡
P'eng-li	彭蠡
P'eng Shih-ch'ang	彭世昌
Pi-kan	比干
Pi-shu lu-hua	避暑錄話
Pi Yüan	畢沅

p'i-chiang t'ang	闢講堂
P'i Hsi-jui	皮錫瑞
Piao-chih chi	表制集
pieh-chi	別集
Pieh-feng Pao-yin	別峯寶卯
pien-wen	變文
pien-yün	篇韻
pin-i	賓儀
p'in kuan	品官
Po-i	伯夷
po hsüeh	博學
pu an	不安
Pu ch'an-lin seng-pao chuan	補禪林僧寶傳
pu-hsiao	不肖
pu-kuan	補官
Pu-k'ung	不空
pu li wen-tzu	不立文字
pu-shu ch'i-hui	簿書期會
P'u-chi	普濟
P'u-hua	普化
P'u-ming	普明
p'u-sa chieh	菩薩戒
Rekishi ni okeru minshū to bunka	歷史に於ける民衆と文化
san-chang	三章
San-chieh ssu	三界寺
San-chieh ssu li-nien hsin hsieh tsang-ching mu-lu	三界寺歷年新寫藏經目錄
san-hsüan san-yao	三玄三要
san-kang	三綱
san kang-ling	三綱領
san-kuan	三關
San-shan Lai ch'an-shih wu-chia tsung-chih tsuan-yao	三山來禪師五家宗旨纂要
san-she fa	三舍法
san sheng jen	三聖人

san-ts'ung	三從
San-tzu ching	三字經
San-tzu hsün	三字訓
Satō Issai	佐藤一齋
Seng-chao	僧照
Seng-ch'ing	僧清
Seng-feng	僧風
Seng-min	僧旻
Seng-pao cheng hsü chuan	僧寶正續傳
Seng-shih lüeh	僧史略
seng-t'ang	僧堂
Seng-t'ang chi	僧堂記
Seng-yu	僧祐
Seng-yüan	僧瑗
Sha-mi shih chieh-fa ping wei-i	沙彌十戒法並威儀
Sha-mi shih chieh i-tse ching	沙彌十戒儀則經
Sha-mi wei-i ching	沙彌威儀經
sha-t'ai	沙汰
shan-chang	山長
Shan-fu	善伏
shan-hsing	善行
shan-lin	山林
shan-lin chih shih	山林之士
shan nan-tzu shan nü-jen	善男子善女人
Shan-tung	山東
Shan-yin	山陰
Shang-hu i-shu	上湖遺書
Shang jen shu	上人書
shang-shih	上世
shang-shu-sheng	尚書省
shang-t'ang	上堂
Shang Tseng ch'eng-hsiang shu	上曾承相書
Shang Yen-liu	商衍鎏
shao-chang	少長
shao-che	少者
Shao-chou chou-hsüeh Lien-hsi hsien-sheng tz'u chi	韶州州學濂溪先生祠記

Shao-hsi	紹熙
Shao-hsing	紹興
Shao Po-wen	邵博溫
Shao-ting	紹定
shao-yu	少幼
Shao Yung	邵雍
she	攝
she	社
she-hsüeh	社學
she-ts'ang	社倉
Shen Chi-tsu	沈繼祖
Shen-chieh	神楷
Shen-ch'ing	神清
shen-hsing yüan	審刑院
Shen hsiu Pai-lu-tung Shu-yüan chuang	申修白鹿洞書院狀
Shen Huan	沈煥
shen-i	深衣
Shen Ping	沈柄
shen-t'ou	神頭
Shen-ts'ou	神湊
Shen-tsung	神宗
Shen-yung	神邕
sheng jen chih tao	聖人之道
Sheng Lang-hsi	盛朗西
sheng-tso	陞座
Sheng-yen	聖嚴
Sheng-yin	聖印
shih (literati)	士
shih (poetry)	詩
shih (real)	實
shih (market)	市
shih (pattern)	式
shih-ch'eng	師承
Shih chi	史記
shih-chia	世家
Shih-chieh shu-chü	世界書局
Shih-ching tu-seng	試經度僧

Shih-ch'uang Fa-kung	石窗法恭
shih-chün	士君
shih-feng	士風
Shih Hao	史浩
shih-hsüan	十玄
shih-hsüeh (history)	史學
shih-hsüeh (practical learning)	實學
Shih hun li	士昏禮
Shih K'ang-nien	施康年
shih-k'o	十科
Shih-lin i-shu	石林遺書
Shih-lin kuang-chi	事林廣記
Shih Meng-ch'ing	史蒙卿
Shih Mi-ta	史彌大
shih-min	士民
Shih-niu t'u-sung	十牛圖頌
Shih-san ching chu-shu	十三經注疏
Shih-san shih-ssu shih-chi Chung-kuo min-chien shu-hsüeh	十三十四世紀中國民間數學
shih-shen kuo-hai	十身果海
shih shih	適士
Shih-shih chi-ku lu	釋氏稽古錄
Shih-shih t'ung-chien	釋氏通鑑
Shih-shih yao lan	釋氏要覽
shih-ta-fu	士大夫
Shih-tsu	世祖
shih ts'ung kuan	侍從官
Shina hōsei shi kenkyū	支那法制史研究
Shina chihō jichi	支那地方自治
Shina mibunhōshi	支那身分法史
Shōgaku	小學
Shōgaku shoto inkatsu sanyō	小學書圖斂括算用
shou (transmit)	授
shou (longevity)	壽
Shou chieh p'in	授戒品
Shou-shen Sheng-nien	首山省念
shu (multitude)	庶
shu (virtuous)	淑

shu (school)	塾
Shu	蜀
Shu-ch'i	叔齊
Shu Hung Fan chuan hou	書洪範傳後
Shu-i	書儀
shu-jen	庶人
Shu-kuei Ching-she	叔圭精舍
Shu Lin	舒璘
Shu Liu-i chü-shih chuan hou	書六一居士傳後
shu-lou	書樓
Shu Mi	舒泌
shu-sheng	書生
shu-shih	庶士
Shu-shu	書塾
shu-t'ang	書堂
Shu wen-ching kung lei-kao	舒文靖公類稿
Shu Wu Tao-tzu hua hou	書吳道字畫後
shu-yüan	書院
Shui-hsin chi	水心集
Shumon deshi shiji nenko	朱門弟子師事年考
Shun	舜
shun	順
Shun-tien	舜典
Shuo-lüeh	說略
Shuo-wen	說文
Shuo-wen chieh-tzu	說文解字
Shushi	朱熹
Shushigaku taikei	朱熹學大系
Shushi no chichi to shi	朱子の父と師
Shushi no "Karei" to "Girei Keiten chūkai"	朱熹の「家禮」と「儀禮經傳注解」
Sōdai Bukkyōshi no kenkyū	宋代佛教史の研究
Sōdai kakyo seido kenkyū	宋代科學制度研究
Sōdai kyōiku shi gaisetsu	宋代教育史概說
Sōdai no sanso oyobi sono ta	宋代の三倉及びその他
Sōdai Saikeishi no Kenkyū	宋代財經史の研究
Sōdai shakai keizai shi kenkyū	宋代社會經濟史研究
Sogabe Shizuo	曾我部靜雄

Sōkaiyō to Sōdai no shuppanhō	宋會要と宋代の出版法
Sorei, sarei ni miru Sōdai shūkyōshi no ichi keikō	葬禮祭禮にみる宋代の宗教史一傾向
Sou shen chi	搜神記
ssu	私
Ssu	巳
ssu chao-yung	四照用
Ssu-ch'ao wen-chien lu	四朝聞見錄
ssu-fa ts'an-chün	司法參軍
ssu-fa yüan	司法院
Ssu-fen lü	四分律
Ssu-fen lü hsing-shih ch'ao tzu-ch'ih chi	四分律行事鈔資持記
ssu-hsüeh	私學
Ssu-k'u	四庫
Ssu-k'u ch'üan-shu chen-pen	四庫全書珍本
Ssu-k'u shan-pen ts'ung-shu	四庫善本叢書
ssu-li ts'an-chün	司理參軍
ssu liao-chien	四料簡
Ssu-ma Ch'ien	司馬遷
Ssu-ma Hao	司馬昊
Ssu-ma Kuang	司馬光
Ssu-ma shih shu-i	司馬氏書儀
Ssu-ma Wen-cheng kung ch'uan-chia chi	司馬文正公傳家集
Ssu-ma Yen-i	司馬延義
Ssu-men hsüeh	四門學
Ssu-ming	四明
Ssu-ming ts'ung-shu	四明叢書
Ssu-ming wen-hsien chi	四明文獻集
ssu pin-chu	四賓主
Ssu-pu pei-yao	四部備要
Ssu-pu ts'ung-k'an	四部叢刊
ssu-shih	私試
Ssu-shu chi-chu	四書集註
Ssu t'ang chi	思堂記
ssu-yeh	肄業
su	俗

Su Ch'e	蘇轍
Su Hsün	蘇洵
su-li	俗禮
Su Ping	蘇炳
Su Shih	蘇軾
Su-shih hsiang-i	蘇氏鄉儀
Su-tsung	肅宗
Su Tung-p'o	蘇東坡
Su Wu	蕭武
su-yü	俗語
Sui-chou	遂州
Sui-ning	遂寧
Sui-yang	睢陽
Sun Ch'üan	孫權
Sun Fu	孫復
Sun Hsieh	孫奭
Sun Kuo-tung	孫國棟
Sun Mien	孫勉
Sun Ts'e	孫策
sung	誦
Sung	宋
Sung-ch'ao ti fa-lü k'ao-shih	宋朝的法律考試
Sung-ch'ao ti kuan-hu	宋朝的官戶
Sung-ch'ao yen-i i-mou lu	宋朝燕翼詒謀錄
Sung Hsi	宋晞
Sung hsing-t'ung	宋刑統
Sung hui-yao chi-kao	宋會要輯稿
Sung hui-yao chi-pen	宋會要輯本
Sung jen hsü	送人序
Sung-jen chuan-chi tz'u-liao suo-yin	宋人傳記資料索引
Sung-jen i-shih hui-pien	宋人逸事會編
Sung Kao-seng chuan	宋高僧傳
sung-ku	頌古
Sung, Liao, Chin she-hui ching-chi shih lun-chi	宋遼金社會經濟史論集
Sung Min-ch'iu	宋敏求
Sung shih	宋史
Sung-shih yen-chiu chi	宋史研究集

Sung-shih yen-chiu lun-ts'ung	宋史研究論叢
Sung-shih yen-chiu lun-wen chi	宋史研究論文集
Sung ta-chao-ling chi	宋大詔令集
Sung-tai chiao-yü san-lun	宋代教育散論
Sung-tai fo-chiao tui she-hui chi wen-hua chih kung-hsien	宋代佛教對社會及文化之貢獻
Sung-tai kuei-hsiu i-wen k'ao-lüeh	宋代閨秀藝文考略
Sung-tai ssu-chia ts'ang-shu k'ao-lüeh	宋代私家藏書考略
Sung-tai t'ai-hsüeh yü t'ai-hsüeh-sheng	宋代太學與太學生
Sung-tai tu-tieh k'ao	宋代度牒考
Sung-yang	嵩陽
Sung Yüan hsüeh-an	宋元學案
Sung Yüan hsüeh-an pu-i	宋元學案補遺
Sung Yüan ti-fang-chih ts'ung-shu	宋元地方志叢書
Ta Chang Chia-wen shu	答張嘉文書
Ta Chang Wen-ch'ien shu	答張文潛書
Ta Chang Yüan-te	答張元德
ta-ch'eng tien	大成殿
Ta Ch'eng Yün-fu shu	答程允夫書
Ta-chou	達州
Ta-chüeh Huai-lien	大覺懷璉
ta-fa	大法
ta-fu	大夫
Ta Fu Pin-lao chien	答傅彬老簡
Ta Han Ch'iu-jen shu	答韓求仁書
Ta Hsieh Min-shih shu	答謝民師書
Ta-hsüeh	大學
Ta-hsüeh chang-chü	大學章句
Ta-hsüeh chang-chü hsü	大學章句序
Ta-hsüeh huo-wen	大學或問
Ta-hui P'u-chüeh Ch'an-shih nien-p'u	大慧普覺禪師年譜
Ta-hui Sung-kao	大慧宋杲
Ta-i	大義
ta-jen	大人
Ta jen lun	大人論
Ta-li	大曆
ta-li p'ing-shih	大理評事

ta-li ssu	大理寺
Ta-lu tsa-chih	大陸雜誌
Ta Lü Po-kung	答呂伯恭
Ta Ming hui-tien	大明會典
Ta Ming seng-pao chuan	大明僧寶傳
Ta-pei chou	大悲咒
ta-ssu t'u	大司徒
Ta Sun Chang-ch'ien shu	答孫長倩書
Ta Tai li chi	大戴禮記
Ta T'ang K'ai-yüan li	大唐開元禮
Ta-te Ch'ang-kuo-chou t'u-chih	大德昌國州圖志
ta-te	大德
Ta Tseng Tzu-ku	答曾子固
Ta Tzu-en ssu san-tsang fa-shih chuan	大慈恩寺三藏法師傳
Ta Wang shang-shu	答汪尚書
Ta Wu Hsiao-tsung	答吳孝宗
Ta-yüan Tsun-p'u	大圓遵璞
Ta-yün ching	大雲經
Taga Akigoro	多賀秋五郎
Tai	岱
Tai Hsien	戴銑
Tai K'an	戴侃
Tai-tsung	代宗
T'ai	台
T'ai-ch'ang yin-ko li	太常因革禮
T'ai-chi	太極
T'ai Chia	太甲
t'ai-chiao	胎敎
T'ai hsi i shou	太息一首
T'ai-hsüeh	太學
T'ai-hsüeh cheng	太學正
T'ai-hsüeh lu-shih	太學錄士
T'ai-jen	太任
T'ai-kung chia-chiao	太公家敎
T'ai-p'ing chou hsin hsüeh chi	太平州新學記
T'ai-tsu	太祖
T'ai-tsung	太宗
Taishō shinshū daizōkyō	大正新修大藏經

Takao Giken	高雄義堅
tan	石
Tan-yang chi	澹陽集
T'an-chou	潭州
T'an Fu	檀敷
T'an-tsang	曇藏
Tanaka Kenji	田中謙二
tang	黨
T'ang (dynasty)	唐
t'ang-chang	堂長
T'ang chih-yen	唐摭言
t'ang-ch'u	堂除
T'ang Chung-yu	唐仲友
T'ang hu fa sha-men Fa-lin pieh-chuan	唐護法沙門法琳別傳
T'ang-jen hsi yeh shan-lin ssu-yüan chih feng-shang	唐人習業山林寺院之風尚
T'ang liu-tien	唐六典
T'ang-shih yen-chiu lun-ts'ung	唐史研究論叢
T'ang Sung chih chi she-hui men-ti chih hsiao-jung	唐宋之際社會門第之消融
T'ang-tai ssu-hsüeh ti fa-chan	唐代私學的發展
T'ang-tai tung-ya chiao-yü ch'üan ti hsing-ch'eng	唐代東亞教育圈的形成
tao	道
Tao-ch'eng	道成
tao-fu	道服
Tao-hsüan	道宣
tao-hsüeh, Tao-hsüeh	道學
Tao-hsüeh hsing-fei	道學興廢
Tao-hung	道洪
Tao-p'ei	道丕
Tao-piao	道標
tao-t'ung, Tao-t'ung	道統
Tao-wu	道悟
Tao-yüan	道圓
T'ao	陶
T'ao Ch'ien	陶潛
T'ao K'an	陶侃

T'ao-shan chi	陶山集
T'ao-yüan	桃源
te hsing	德行
Te-shan Tzu-chüan	德山子涓
Tei Meidō shōkō: jiseki, shinpō, gakkō kyōiku	程明道小考：治績，新法，學校，教育
tenarai-sei	手習い生
Teng Kuang-ming	鄧廣銘
teng-lu	燈錄
Teng Ssu-yü	鄧嗣禹
Teng T'ao	鄧絢
Teng-ying	登瀛
T'eng Lin	滕璘
Terada Gō	寺田剛
ti-che	敵者
ti-kuan	地官
ti-tzu	弟子
t'i	提
T'i Hui-shan ssu shih hsü	題惠山寺詩序
t'i-tz'u	題辭
tiao-hua	釣話
t'ieh ju-i	鐵如意
tien-chung chiang-chün	殿中將軍
tien-hsüeh	典學
t'ien chih tao	天之道
T'ien-i I-huai	天衣義懷
T'ien-sheng kuang-teng lu	天聖廣燈錄
T'ien-t'ai (sect)	天台
T'ien-t'ai (county)	天台
ting	丁
Ting Ch'uan-ching	丁傳靖
Ting-ch'uan i-shu	定川遺書
ting-hai	丁亥
Ting-hai	定海
T'ing-lao	廷老
t'ing ts'ung	聽聰
Tō shoki irai no Chōan no kudokushi	唐初期以来の長安の功徳使
Tō shōhon Zōsho kō	唐抄本雜抄考

T'o T'o	脫脫
Tōdai bukkyōshi no kenkyū	唐代佛教史の研究
Tōdai kyōiku shi no kenkyū	唐代教育史の研究
Tōdai shakai bunka shi kenkyū	唐代社會文化史研究
Tōhōgaku	東方學
Tōhōgakuhō	東方學報
Takikawa Masajiro	瀧川政次郎
Tonkō butsuji no gakushirō	敦煌佛寺の學士郎
Tonkō shutsudo "sha" bunsho no kenkyū	敦煌出土「社」文書の研究
Tsa-ch'ao	雜抄
Tsa hsüeh pien	雜學辨
Tsa-tzu	雜字
tsai chia p'u-sa	在家菩薩
Tsai ta Kung Shen-fu Lun-yū Meng-tzu shu	再答龔深父論語孟子書
Ts'ai Ch'en	蔡沉
Ts'ai Ching	蔡京
Ts'ai Nien-ch'eng	蔡念誠
Ts'ai-shih chiu-ju shu	蔡氏九儒書
Ts'ai Tsung-yen	蔡宗兗
Ts'ai Yüan-ting	蔡元定
Tsan-ning	贊寧
tsang-chu	藏主
Ts'ang-chou Ching-she	滄洲精舍
Ts'ang-chou ching-she pien	滄洲精舍辨
Ts'ang-chou ping-sou	滄洲病叟
tsao-shan	皂衫
Ts'ao Chien	曹建
Ts'ao Li-chih	曹立之
Ts'ao-tung kuang-lu	曹洞廣錄
Ts'ao Yen-ch'un	曹彥純
Ts'ao Yen-yüeh	曹彥約
Tse	澤
ts'e	策
Ts'e-fu yüan-kuei	册府元龜
Ts'e lüeh ti ssu	策略第四
Tseng Chih-hsü	曾致虛

Tseng-jen	增忍
Tseng Kung	曾鞏
Tseng-pu Su Tung-p'o nien-p'u hui-cheng	增補蘇東坡年譜會證
Tseng-sun Lü-shih hsiang-yüeh	增損呂氏鄉約
Tseng Tzu	曾子
Tso-Ch'an i	坐禪儀
Tso chuan	左傳
tso kung-fu	做工夫
tso-wu	作務
tso-yu-ming	座右銘
Tsou Shou-i	鄒守益
tsu-shih ch'an	祖師禪
Tsu-yüan	祖源
Tsukamoto Zenryū	塚本善隆
tsui shang-cheng ch'an	最上乘禪
tsun-che	尊者
Ts'un-ssu ch'ing-kuei	村寺清規
ts'un-ching ko	尊經閣
Ts'un-ts'ui hsüeh-she	存萃學舍
tsung	宗
Tsung-mi	宗密
Tsung-tse	宗賾
tsung-tzu	宗子
Ts'ung-jung lu	從容錄
ts'ung-lin	叢林
Ts'ung-lin chiao-ting ch'ing-kuei tsung-yao	叢林校訂清規總要
Ts'ung-shu chi-ch'eng	叢書集成
Tu	杜
Tu-ch'ang	都昌
Tu Ch'un	杜醇
tu-hsing chih	篤行之
Tu liang Ch'en ch'ien-i i mo	讀兩陳諫議遺墨
tu-shu	讀書
tu-shu fa	讀書法
tu-shu-jen	讀書人
tu-shu kung-ch'eng	讀書工程

Tu Su-shih chi nien	讀蘇氏紀年
Tu-t'ing	都亭
Tu-tsung	度宗
Tu Yen	杜衍
Tu Yu-sui	杜友遂
tuan-an	斷案
Tuan-chiao Miao-lun	斷枝妙倫
tuan-kuan	斷官
t'u-ching	圖經
T'u-shu kuan hsüeh chi-k'an	圖書館學集刊
tuan	端
Tuan Wei	段維
Tun-weng	遯翁
t'un-t'ien	屯田
Tung-ching meng-hua lu	東京夢華錄
Tung Chu	董銖
tung-chu	洞主
Tung Chung-shu	董仲舒
Tung Kao	董誥
Tung-lai chi	東萊集
Tung-lai po-i	東萊博議
Tung-lin	東林
Tung-lin hui-yüeh	東林會約
Tung-shan shui shang hsing	東山水上行
Tung Shu. *See* Tung Chu	
T'ung-an	同安
T'ung-an hsien-yü hsüeh-che	同安縣諭學者
T'ung-chien kang-mu	通鑑綱目
T'ung Chin	童金
T'ung Chü-i	童居易
T'ung Chung	童鐘
t'ung-hsing	童行
T'ung hsüeh i shou pieh Tzu-ku	同學一首別子固
T'ung Hung	童鋐
T'ung Kuei	童桂
t'ung-lun	通諭
T'ung-meng hsün	童蒙訓
t'ung-pan	通判

T'ung tien	通典
t'ung-tzu	童子
T'ung-wen	同文
tzu (character)	字
tz'u (ordered)	次
Tzu-chih t'ung-chien	資治通鑑
Tzu-lin pao-hsün	緇林寶訓
Tzu p'ing wen	自評文
Tzu-shu	字書
Tzu-shuo	字說
Tzu Ssu lun	子思論
tz'u-ti	次第
tzu-wu men	自悟門
tz'u (poetry)	詞
tz'u (sacrificial hall)	祠
Tz'u-hsi	慈溪
Tz'u-hsi hsien hsüeh chi	慈溪縣學記
Tz'u-hu	慈湖
Tz'u-hu hsien-sheng i-shu	慈湖先生遺書
Tz'u-ming	慈明
tz'u-pan	祠版
tz'u-t'ang	祠堂
Ueyama Shunpei	上山春平
Uno Seiichi	宇野精一
Wada Sei	和田清
wai-p'ien	外篇
wan	婉
Wan Jen-chieh	萬人傑
Wan-ku ssu	萬固寺
wan wan	婉娩
Wan-yen Tao-yen	萬菴道顔
Wang An-shih	王安石
Wang Ch'ang	王昶
Wang Ch'ao	王朝
Wang Chi	汪紀
Wang Chieh-fu	王介甫
Wang Chien-ch'iu	王建秋

Wang Ch'ien-chung	王謙仲
Wang Chih	王致
Wang Ch'in-jo	王欽若
Wang Chung-chieh	王仲傑
Wang Fan-chih	王梵志
Wang Fen	汪汾
Wang Hsien-ch'ien	王先謙
Wang Huai	王淮
Wang Juan	王阮
Wang Lang-yin	王蘭蔭
Wang Li	王力
Wang Mou-hung (also Mao-hung)	王懋竑
Wang Pao-chen	王保珍
Wang Shih-han	汪師韓
Wang Shou-jen	王守仁
Wang Shuo	王說
Wang Ta-yu	汪大祐
Wang Te-chao	王德昭
Wang Tseng-yü	王曾瑜
Wang Tzu-ts'ai	王梓材
Wang Yang-ming	王陽明
Wang Yao-ch'en	王堯臣
Wang Ying-ch'en	汪應辰
Wang Ying-lin	王應麟
Wang Yüan	王沅
Wang Yung	王梌
wei chi	爲己
Wei chih	魏志
Wei Chu	魏絜
wei hsüeh (not yet studied)	未學
wei-hsüeh (study)	爲學
wei-hsüeh (spurious learning)	僞學
wei-i	威儀
wei jen	爲人
Wei-nan wen-chi	渭南文集
Wei Shan-chih	魏掞之
wei shih che	爲士者
wen, Wen (culture)	文
Wen (prefecture)	溫

Wen-an	文安
wen-chi	文集
Wen Chi-weng	文及翁
Wen-chung	文忠
Wen-hsi	文喜
Wen-hsien t'ung-k'ao	文獻通考
Wen-hsüan	文選
wen hsüeh	文學
Wen-kung	文公
Wen-kung chia-fan	文公家範
Wen-kuo Wen-cheng kung wen-chi	溫國文正公文集
wen-ming	問名
Wen-tsung	文宗
wen-tzu ch'an	文字禪
wen-tzu chih hsüeh	文字之學
Wen wang	文王
wen yang sheng	問養生
Wen Yen-po	文彥博
Weng	翁
Weng T'ung-wen	翁同文
wu	廡
Wu (surname)	吳
Wu (King, military)	武
Wu Ch'eng	吳澄
Wu-ch'ien-men	午乾門
Wu chih	吳志
Wu-chou	婺州
Wu-chün Shih-fan	無準師範
Wu-fu-li	五夫里
Wu-hsi	無錫
Wu-hsien tz'u	五賢祠
Wu Hsüan	吳鉉
Wu-i	武夷
Wu-i Ching-she	武夷精舍
Wu-i-shan min-chien ch'uan-shuo	武夷山民間傳說
Wu-lao	五老
Wu-li	五禮
Wu-men Hui-k'ai	無門慧開

wu-shu	巫術
Wu-tai ti chiao-yü	五代的教育
Wu Tao Tzu	吳道子
Wu-teng	五燈
Wu-teng hui-yüan	五燈會元
Wu Tseng	吳曾
Wu-tsu Fa-yen	五祖法演
wu-tsung kang-yao	五宗綱要
Wu Tzu-mu	吳自牧
wu-wei p'ien-cheng	五位偏正
Wu Wen-ch'eng kung ch'üan-chi	吳文成公全集
Wu Yü-pi	吳與弼
Wu-yüan hsien	婺源縣
Wu yüeh	五嶽
Yakuchu Zen'on shingi	譯注禪苑清規
Yamazaki Ansai	山崎闇齋
Yang Chien	楊簡
Yang Chin-hsin	楊金鑫
Yang Chu	楊朱
Yang Hui	楊輝
Yang Jih-hsin	楊日新
Yang-ming ch'üan-shu	陽明全書
Yang Mo	楊墨
Yang Po-ch'i	楊伯起
Yang Shen-ch'u	楊愼初
Yang Shih	楊適
Yang Ta-fa	楊大法
Yang Wan-li	楊萬里
Yang Wei	楊瑋
Yang Yu-chih	楊友直
Yao	堯
Yeh Hung-li	葉鴻麗
Yeh Kung-hui	葉公回
Yeh Meng-te	葉夢得
Yeh Meng-ting	葉夢鼎
Yeh Shao-weng	葉紹翁
Yeh Shih	葉適

Yeh Yung-ch'ing	葉永卿
yen	言
Yen-chou	袞州
Yen-chung	彥忠
yen erh yu fa	嚴而有法
Yen-ho-tien tsou-shih	延和殿奏事
Yen Hui	顏回
Yen Keng-wang	嚴耕望
Yen kuan ta pei ko chi	鹽官大悲閣記
Yen-ling chiang-i	嚴陵講義
Yen-nan Shu-yüan	燕南書院
Yen-shan chi	演山集
Yen-shih chia-hsün	顏氏家訓
yen-t'a	驗他
Yen-tsung	彥宗
Yen ts'ung	彥悰
Yen Tzu	顏子
Yen-tzu fu	燕子賦
yen-tz'u t'ing	嚴祠庭
Yen-yu Ssu-ming chih	延祐四明志
yin	蔭
Yin	鄞
Yin-shua shu tui-yü shu-chi ch'eng-pen ti ying-hsing	印刷術對於書籍成本的影响
yin-ssu	飲食
yin-tz'u	淫祠
yin-yang chiao-shou ssu	陰陽教授司
yin-yüan	因緣
Ying Hsiang-sun	應翔孫
Ying Hsü	應㒇
Ying Kuei-weng	應桂翁
Ying Su	應俫
ying-t'ang	影堂
Ying-t'ien	應天
Ying-t'ien fu	應天府
Yu	由
yu-che	幼者
Yu Chien-shan chi	游薦山集

yu-chih	幼稈
yu-chü wu-chü, ju t'eng i-shu	有句無句，如藤依樹
yu-fang	遊方
Yu-p'o-sai chieh ching	優婆塞戒經
Yu yü hsüeh-che	又諭學者
Yü	禹
Yü Ch'eng-hsiang cha-tzu	與丞相箚子
Yü Cheng-hsieh	俞正燮
Yü Chieh	余潔
Yü-hai	玉海
Yü-ch'iu Chü-ching	愚丘居靜
Yü Jui Kuo-ch'i	與芮國器
Yü-lei	語類
Yü Li chiao-shou shu	與李敎授書
Yü Lü Po-kung lun shu-yüan chi shu	與呂伯恭論書院記書
Yü-lu	語錄
Yü-shan chiang i	玉山講議
Yü shang-shu cha-tzu	與尚書箚子
yü-shu ko, Yü-shu-ko	御書閣
Yü Shu-lin	余書麟
Yü Sung-chieh	余宋傑
Yü Ting Yüan-chen shu	與丁元珍書
Yü Tsu Tse-chih shu	與祖擇之書
Yü Tung-lai lun Pai-lu shu-yüan chi	與東萊論白鹿書院記
Yü Yü	余隅
Yüan	元
Yüan-chao	元照
Yüan Chen	袁震
Yüan-chen	圓震
Yüan Chüeh	遠桷
Yüan-chüeh ching ta shu ch'ao	圓覺經大疏抄
Yüan-feng	元豐
Yüan Fu	袁甫
Yüan Hsieh	遠燮
yüan hsing	原性
Yüan shih	元史
Yüan-shih shih-fan	袁氏世範
Yüan Ts'ai	袁采

Yüan T'ung-li	袁同禮
Yüan-t'ung Tao-min	圓通道旻
yüan-wai	員外
Yüan-wu K'o-ch'in	圓悟克勤
yüeh	約
Yüeh(1)	粵
Yüeh(2)	越
Yüeh-lu	嶽麓
Yüeh-lu chih	嶽麓志
Yüeh-lu Shu-yüan t'ung-hsün	嶽麓書院通訊
Yün-chü Tao-ying	雲居道膺
Yün-feng Wen-yüeh	雲峯文悅
Yung-an ssu	永安寺
Yung-chia Hsüan-chüeh	永嘉玄覺
Yung Hsiao-ching	詠孝經
Yung-lo ta-tien	永樂大典
Yung-tung	甬東
Zenrin shōkisen	禪林象器箋
Zoku-zōkyō	續藏經

INDEX

academies, 8, 10–11, 50, 67, 107, 112–13, 135, 136, 158, 187, 210–11, 221, 256, 261, 358, 388, 389–413, 414–31, 432–35, 440, 441, 444, 456, 457–61, 472–92; Neo-Confucian, 202, 216–17, 389–413, 415, 431, 458–59, 489–93. See also *ching-she; Shu-yüan*
Accounts of the Yüeh-lu Academy. See *Yüeh-lu chih*
"Admonitions of Kuei-shan" (*Kuei-shan ching-tse*), 98
affairs of government. See *cheng-shih*
Aims of Education, 493
altars to former worthies. See *hsien-hsien tz'u*
"Amended Community Compact of Mr. Lü." See *Tseng-sun Lü-shih hsiang-yüeh*
An Lu-shan, 3, 33
Analects (*Lun-yü*), viii, 8, 46, 49, 81, 90, 92, 98, 123, 139, 140, 143, 156, 179, 186, 189, 192, 207, 233, 237, 318, 354, 355, 363, 397, 399–400, 401, 413, 480, 508
ancestral shrines (*chia-miao*), 288, 292, 301–2
Ancient Record of Master Yün-men. See *Ku Yün-men lu*
archery ceremony, 386
aristocratic families, 25, 109, 129
Arithmetic for Daily Use. See *Jih-yung suan fa*
Articles for Learning. See *Articles of the White Deer Grotto Academy*
Articles of the White Deer Grotto Academy (*Pai-lu-tung Shu-yüan chieh-shih*), 136, 199, 202–4, 208, 211, 214, 264, 334, 396–99, 407, 408, 410, 412, 423, 434, 486
artisans, 308, 309
Awakening of Faith, 81, 82

Bequeathed Plans for Tranquility in the Sung (*Sung-ch'ao yen-i chih-mou lu*), 508
Biographies of Monastic Treasures of the Ch'an Forest. See *Ch'an-lin seng-pao chuan*
Biographies of Women (*Lieh-nü chuan*), 338, 348, 354, 356
Birge, Bettine, 12

Blue Cliff Record. See *Pi-yen lu*
Bol, Peter, 6, 7
Book of Changes (*I-ching*), 90, 98, 176–77, 181, 183, 207, 329, 354, 371, 397, 474, 508
Book of Etiquette and Ritual. See *I-li*
Book of Filial Piety. See *Classic of Filial Piety*
Book of History (*Shu-ching;* also cited as *Documents*), 48, 90, 168, 176, 207, 270, 350, 437, 462, 474, 508
Book of Mencius, 90, 142, 144, 147, 207, 226, 232, 237, 355, 364, 397, 399, 400, 401, 403, 413, 437, 508
Book of Ritual. See *Li-chi*
Book of Songs (*Shih-ching;* also of *Odes* or *Poetry*), 47, 168, 207, 234, 318, 350, 462, 508
books, prices of, 107, 129
Buddha, 169, 170, 263
Buddha Hall, 72, 83, 96
Buddhism, 2, 3, 4–6, 7, 11, 13, 86, 150, 162, 188–89, 193, 218–20, 227, 243, 248, 250, 254, 256–59, 267–68, 280–85, 304–5, 317, 334, 354–55, 357–59, 366, 389, 392, 393, 394, 395, 402, 412, 418–19, 422–23, 429, 477, 482–83; 385–86. *See also* Ch'an Buddhism
Buddhist clergy. See *saṅgha*
Buddhist education, 19–104, 105–6, 116, 135, 317
Buddhist establishment. See *saṅgha*
Buddhist laity, 20–21, 39–50, 267–68, 357–59; lay organizations, 381–82
Buddhist monasteries, 29–30, 32, 35–36, 39, 44, 46–50, 52, 54, 58, 72, 74, 78, 81–83, 91, 93, 98, 105, 116, 365, 399; Ch'an (Doctrine) monasteries, 71, 82; landholding of, 259; Lü (Discipline) monasteries, 71, 81–82
Buddhist monks. See *saṅgha*
Buddhist retreats. See *vih ra*
Buddhist scriptures (*sutras*), 26–27, 34–35, 51–55, 66, 71, 79–88, 98, 263, 267, 347, 349, 354–55, 357
Bureau of Judicial Investigation (*shen-hsing yüan*), 505, 509, 511
Burma, 56

Compositor: Interactive Composition Corporation
Text: 10/12 Baskerville
Display: Baskerville
Printer: Braun-Brumfield, Inc.
Binder: Braun-Brumfield, Inc.